THE CRISIS O

From the years leading up to the First World War to the aftermath of the Second, Europe experienced an era of genocide. As well as the Holocaust, this period also witnessed the Armenian genocide in 1915, mass killings in Bolshevik and Stalinist Russia, and a host of further ethnic cleansings in Anatolia, the Balkans, and Eastern Europe. *The Crisis of Genocide* seeks to integrate these genocidal events into a single, coherent history.

Over two volumes, Mark Levene demonstrates how the relationship between geography, nation, and power came to play a key role in the emergence of genocide in a collapsed or collapsing European imperial zone—the Rimlands—and how the continuing geopolitical contest for control of these Eastern European or near-European regions destabilised relationships between diverse and multifaceted ethnic communities who traditionally had lived side by side. An emergent pattern of toxicity can also be seen in the struggles for regional dominance as pursued by post-imperial states, nation-states, and would-be states.

Volume I: Devastation covers the period from 1912 to 1938. It is divided into two parts, the first associated with the prelude to, actuality of, and aftermath of the Great War and imperial collapse, the second the period of provisional 'New Europe' reformulation as well as post-imperial Stalinist, Nazi—and Kemalist—consolidation up to 1938. Levene also explores the crystallization of truly toxic anti-Jewish hostilities, the implication being that the immediate origins of the Jewish genocides in the Second World War are to be found in the First.

Mark Levene is Reader in Comparative History at the University of Southampton, and in the Parkes Centre for Jewish/non-Jewish Relations. His writing ranges from Jewish history to genocide and anthropogenic climate change, including, most recently *History at the End of the World? History, Climate Change and the Possibility of Closure* (co-edited with Rob Johnson and Penny Roberts, 2010). He is founder of Rescue! History, and co-founder of the Crisis Forum. The two volumes of *Crisis of Genocide* continue a multi-volume project—begun with *The Meaning of Genocide* and *The Rise of the West and the Coming of Genocide* (2005)—to chart the history of genocide in the age of the nation-state.

Devastation

The European Rimlands 1912–1938

MARK LEVENE

OXFORD

UNIVERSITY PRESS

Great Clarendon Street, Oxford, OX2 6DP,
United Kingdom

Oxford University Press is a department of the University of Oxford.
It furthers the University's objective of excellence in research, scholarship,
and education by publishing worldwide. Oxford is a registered trade mark of
Oxford University Press in the UK and in certain other countries

First published 2013
First published in paperback 2016

Published in the United States of America by Oxford University Press
198 Madison Avenue, New York, NY 10016, United States of America

British Library Cataloguing in Publication Data
Data available

Library of Congress Cataloging in Publication Data
Data available

ISBN 978–0–19–968303–1 (Hbk.)
ISBN 978–0–19–879169–0 (Pbk.)

For Jeannie

'This empire's had it. As soon as the emperor says goodnight, we'll break up into a hundred pieces...All the peoples will set up their own dirty little statelets...I tell you gentlemen, unless we start shooting, it's all up. In our lifetime, I tell you.'

Joseph Roth, *The Radetsky March*

.

Contents

PART TWO: INTERREGNUM BETWEEN GREAT WARS

List of Maps

Preface

GENOCIDE IN THE AGE OF THE NATION STATE: CONTINUING THE QUEST

The Crisis of Genocide continues an ongoing project of historical synthesis, the aim of which is to understand the phenomenon of genocide as an aspect of modern world-historical development. Two previous volumes, *The Meaning of Genocide* and *The Rise of the West and the Coming of Genocide*, were published in 2005, running under the generic title *Genocide in the Age of the Nation State*.[1] These works were built on the premise that to properly comprehend genocide in its totality one has to approach it not only both transnationally and diachronically, but also in relation to a much broader historical landscape of political, economic, social, and cultural interactions. As such, these studies implicitly go against the grain of a research field often described as comparative genocide studies; not because the latter approach lacks purchase but rather because, inadvertently or otherwise, it conveys the notion that genocides occur in situations radically outside, or at least at the margins of, 'normative' existence. The whole thrust—and burden—of this project, by contrast, lies in the argument that the significance of the phenomenon is precisely on account of it being integral to a 'mainstream' historical trajectory of development towards a single, global, political economy composed of nation states. Or, to put the matter bluntly, the phenomenon is not aberrant but systemic.

The Rise of the West, which took us to 1914 and the outbreak of the First World War, traversed more than 600 years of history and, with the actions of the avant-garde West as its primary focus, covered an increasingly global—imperial—range. *The Crisis of Genocide* quite intentionally telescopes its chronology to little over a forty-year period and focuses on a geographical arena in which there was a persistent accumulation and concentration of genocidal violence. We call this arena the European rimlands. This will sound unfamiliar to most readers, and so a full explanation follows in the Introduction. But to put the issue of nomenclature aside for one moment and simply state that what we are considering has the Holocaust at its latter end, and the Armenian genocide (the *Aghet*) near its beginning, should be enough for most readers to gauge that the temporal aspect relates to a series of sustained, exterminatory assaults on whole communal groups rather distinct from anything we would otherwise associate with military conflict, including total war. More pointedly, these *genocides* did not happen at some distant corner of a Western gaze but close to, or within, Europe. At the outset of this study, thus, it is important to affirm that the emphasis on a European or

---

[1] Mark Levene, *Genocide in the Age of the Nation State*, vol. 1: *The Meaning of Genocide*; vol. 2: *The Rise of the West and the Coming of Genocide* (London and New York: I.B. Tauris, 2005).

near-European range is not the consequence of some implicit Westernocentrism on the author's part, but because this is where a critical sequence of communal mass murders, at this time, took place. The very fact, indeed, that we can perceive a pattern of exterminatory violence would seem to demand that we give both sequence and pattern—the Holocaust included—our closest attention.

That last remark in itself will excite some comment from scholars and opinion formers who argue that the Jewish case is so large and exceptional that it must be separated from the run of other genocides and be treated accordingly as sui generis. There is, too, another argument that has entered the field in response to recent studies which *have* attempted to situate and contextualize the Holocaust within a bigger picture of mass murder and ethnic cleansing.[2] The argument, exemplified by Omer Bartov, urges that the proper path of genocide studies should be towards greater concentration on the voices of the victims and less on 'the generalised overview of events'.[3] The latter point also implies that the big exogenous factors need to make way for more attention to the local, intimate, and endogenous. This author certainly has no issue with scholars pursuing this route, nor better integrating the victims' stories into the wider historical picture. Saul Friedländer, the historian who began by wanting to resist the historicization of the Holocaust, through his landmark two-volume history of it, has demonstrated just how well this can be done.[4] But Friedländer's history *is* a history of the Holocaust while Bartov's proposed method, whether or not it seeks to embrace other genocides, still begs a historical question, particularly germane to this study, which will not go away: why is there an approximate coincidence between the Holocaust (or for that matter the *Aghet*) and so many *other* genocidal events? And if the close timing and spacing of these *multiple* events matters, how does that change our understanding of the world we have inherited? Indeed, what might it tell us about where we are heading?

Clearly, I am sounding a more distinctly personal note here. But then, sometimes this helps the reader to know something of where the writer is 'coming from' and what—behind any attempted goal of objective detachment—subjectively impels her/him.[5] So let me try and offer the very briefest of explanations. These genocide volumes fall in the interstices of an adult life in which issues of peace and the environment have loomed large. In the early 1980s, it was the imminent threat of total human obliteration through nuclear war which was uppermost in my mind, shared as it was by millions of others. In more recent years, a growing awareness of

---

[2] Donald Bloxham, *The Final Solution: A Genocide* (Oxford: Oxford University Press, 2009)); Mark Mazower, *Hitler's Empire: Nazi Rule in Occupied Europe* (London: Penguin, 2009); Timothy Snyder, *Bloodlands: Europe between Hitler and Stalin* (London: The Bodley Head, 2010), for notable examples.

[3] Omer Bartov, 'Genocide and the Holocaust: What Are We Arguing About?', in Uffa Jensen, Habbo Knoch, Daniel Morat, and Miriam Rürüp, eds., *Gewalt und Gesellschaft: Klassiker modernen Denkens neu gelesen* (Göttingen: Wallstein Verlag, 2011), 381–93.

[4] Saul Friedländer, *Nazi Germany and the Jews: The Years of Persecution, 1933–1939* (New York: Harper-Collins, 1997); Saul Friedländer, *The Years of Extermination: Nazi Germany and the Jews, 1939–1945* (New York: HarperCollins, 2007).

[5] See Christopher Powell, *Barbaric Civilisation: A Critical Sociology of Genocide* (Montreal and Kingston: McGill-Queen's University Press, 2011), ch. 1, 'A Critical Sociology of Genocide', for a critique of the supposedly 'objective' researcher.

anthropogenic climate change has led me to conclude that humanity—albeit by related if more complex and tortuous routes—is still set on the *same* self-oblitera-tive course. Being a subscriber to such bleak forecasts inevitably carries corollaries on a subjective level. One has been immersion at various stages, over the last thirty and more years, in campaigns and initiatives which have sought to confront or resist the dread verdict. Another more cerebral tack has involved efforts to better understand why humanity is where it is. As someone who has always carried a historical kink within them, that, almost inevitably, has involved reading back into the past to find the source or sources of the complaint. As a Jew, the possibilities of group obliteration were practically built into my cultural DNA. But the historical kink always carried an irritant voice which seemed to want to know from a quite early age not only the facts of *similar* incidents but, as I became better versed, why there was so much apparent historical synchronicity involved. Could it be that, taken together, these multiple acts of extreme violence represented a subset of some larger and wider human trajectory leading towards general disaster? The implica-tion is ruled out of court in any standard Western narrative, on the grounds that the dominant (hegemonic) political and social order is fundamentally benign. And, one striking thing about the incidents related in *The Crisis of Genocide* is that (bar-ring massacres—not genocide—committed by German troops in two world wars) none of these took place in the West, nor were committed by Western polities. Instead, the majority of the *genocidal* violence reviewed in these two volumes was perpetrated at one remove from Western soil, and in societies which, though pass-ingly familiar to Westerners, were also, to varying degrees, quite different.

Reaching out to other disciplines, most obviously geography, has helped frame the 'where' of the 1912–53 sequence. And geology, too, has provided a vulcano-logical metaphor to more fully delineate its zonal range—yet also fluidity. But not only does this not explain the 'why' of genocide in this place, at this point in time; it doesn't really enlighten the reader as to what such genocides in the past have to do with the 'us' of the contemporary world or, for that matter, how this relates back to my *other* peace and environmental concerns. However, as I was completing *The Crisis of Genocide*, I was struck by a current story in the British press which seemed to offer a further interesting, if alarming, metaphor. The story is of an encroaching ecological disaster, involving a fungally carried disease which is causing the dieback of ash trees, a major component of British woodlands. There appears to be no cure. The backstory, however, suggests that the fate of the ash is far from novel. A whole range of tree diseases caused by diverse pathogens have been devastating British woodlands for generations. Dutch elm disease, for instance, began to spread to Britain from the Continent in the 1920s; perhaps rather significantly, it has been suggested, as a direct consequence of the churning up and ravaging of woodland in the trench-warfare-ridden Picardy of the Great War.[6] Once in Britain the disease proved ineradicable, though what eventually did for the British elms was a further virulent strain that also came in from abroad and which, in a few short years in the 1970s,

---

[6] According to plant pathologist Professor Clive Brasier, in 'Dutch Elm Disease and Ash Dieback', *The Long View*, BBC Radio 4, broadcast 27 November 2012.

wiped out almost the entire remaining population. The point about the ash, the elm, the horse chestnut, and the oak, all of which were, or are, threatened by a range of diseases, is that their individual crises are not just some unfortunate coincidence. The spread of tree infections in epidemic form is a consequence of a much wider and profound destabilization, involving, above all, a *global* trade in saplings and the organic material (soil) which comes with that. Once out there, the bacteria, fungal spores, or insect carriers, do the rest. In terms of local perturbation this translates into a potential to devastate arboreal and hence wider biodiversity in woodlands, and turn what is left into increasingly monotonal plantations, or worse, to borrow a term from the Nazi eastern empire, 'dead zones'.

The spread of tree diseases might act as a metaphor for this study in that it offers a very 'unnatural' tale of processes and patterns of destruction which do not happen stochastically, or purely by chance, but as a consequence of chartable trajectories whose source is macro, even while the devastating consequences are felt most keenly at the micro-level. Of course the obvious riposte is that while woodland trees may organically interact, we do not tend to think of them as cognisant actors in their own right. To imply thus that the peoples of the rimlands, like our trees, were simply victims of some extraneous 'disease' would hardly seem sufficient, let alone plausible, to develop an argument about *genocide*. Yet it is an implication of this project writ large that a considerable proportion of those who led, followed, or were drawn into extreme violence of this kind were, in some profound sense, 'dis-eased'. By which I mean that they were radically unhinged from their traditional moorings, saw themselves increasingly as victims of forces beyond their control, the result of which was various manifestations of psycho-cultural disturbance which were often exhibited in emotions of hurt, rage, envy, fear, even phobic and delusional anxieties.

Granted, this is not the sort of terminology with which most empirical historians feel comfortable. Thus the proposal that collective psychopathology is a key vector of this particular historical phenomenon will depend to a considerable degree on yet-to-be-fully-undertaken interdisciplinary research, before it is likely to become standard academic currency. In the meantime, to sparingly deploy terms such as schizophrenia, in the *informal* sense of experiencing or maintaining contradictory attitudes and emotions, does not seem to me to be inappropriate to this work, especially where it feeds into another condition, cognitive dissonance, which, in particular instances, is especially relevant to our discussion. Nor do I eschew use of the term paranoia, again at least in the informal sense of repeated intense feelings of persecution being visited upon the person, or his/her group, society, or state.[7]

---

[7] There is a dearth of studies which interconnect the psycho-cultural and the historical–social in cases of mass violence. Roger D. Petersen, *Understanding Ethnic Violence: Fear, Hatred and Resentment in Twentieth-Century Eastern Europe* (Cambridge and New York: Cambridge University Press, 2002) is one valuable study, though it does not pursue the argument into the realms of the phobic and delusional. By contrast, Jeffrey Herf, *The Jewish Enemy: Nazi Propaganda during World War II and the Holocaust* (Cambridge, MA: Harvard University Press, 2006), arguably goes too far the other way, with a repetitive usage of the terminology of paranoia. See A. Dirk Moses, 'Paranoia and Partisanship: Genocide Studies, Holocaust Historiography and the "Apocalyptic Conjuncture"', *The History Journal*, 54:2 (2011), 553–83, for critical commentary.

To be sure, implying that these tendencies, latent as they may have been, were radically amplified and accelerated towards a thoroughly toxic condition as a direct or indirect result of destabilizing, exogenous influences, carries its own problems and challenges. For one, it would seem to diminish the personal or, for that matter, collective responsibility of those who committed the resulting mass murders. Or, indeed, offer the feeble excuse that those who did so were not in their right mind. The vast majority of *génocidaires* in our period, or any other, were neither psychopaths nor clinically insane.[8] Which makes the way so many of them bought into projective fantasies of retribution and reckoning all the more perplexing. Equally noteworthy is the manner in which some leading, particularly medically trained perpetrators—I am thinking here especially of Ottoman Committee of Union and Progress (CUP) and Nazi examples—often used very precise language to describe and justify their actions as matters of inoculating the social organism, or body politic, against infection. So these actors, at least, had a very strong and, in their own way, entirely coherent sense that there was something fundamentally wrong with their societies. A question to my mind is, did they *choose* to interpret this condition in terms of a socio- or biopolitical threat from *within* the social organism (communal groups), or was this failure to see the wood for the trees an aspect of some intrinsic human blocking-off mechanism, which determined that they could not cope with, or, indeed, could not even *see* the broader environmental aetiology of their collective illness?

The question in itself strays into territory far beyond what purports to be a short preface. Two comments will have to suffice. Firstly, it is clear that in the context of the rimlands' sequence of genocides the sort of traditional restraints most obviously provided by organized religion, which—to pursue the tree analogy—might have come into play to prevent the social organism responding to the infection through a virulent assault on its own diverse parts, were largely if not entirely cancelled out—or directly co-opted—by the countervailing toxic forces. Secondly, many genocide scholars would dismiss the need for exogenous factors to be part of the equation at all. Instead, they would argue that the explanation for why polities and societies commit genocide is usually a matter of homespun ideology. In other words, genocide is committed within, or by, polities whose regimes are already radically predisposed towards hostile intent against specific ethnic or other communal groups. If this standard proposition is correct then it would make the bunching of genocides between 1912 and 1953 either nothing more than coincidence, or a case of an all-purpose ideology infecting a range of states simultaneously. But in arguing, as I will do, that the framework of genocide is altogether more systemic, am I myself in danger of reading the phenomenon into an incidence of events where the nomenclature is not deserved? I ask the question in part because among the many important books published on mass exterminatory violence since I began writing *The Crisis of Genocide* some seven years ago, two stand out for their eschewal of the term genocide.

---

[8] See the essays in Leonard S. Newman and Ralph Erber, eds., *Understanding Genocide: The Social Psychology of the Holocaust* (New York and Oxford: Oxford University Press, 2002), Part 1, 'Becoming a Perpetrator'.

The first, by Christian Gerlach, asserts his opposition in the very title, *Extremely Violent Societies*, which he ventures is a more appropriate and empirical describer of a range of mass violence in the twentieth century. Gerlach cites multiple elements which he argues cannot be encompassed under the rubric of genocide. These include the participation of diverse social groups in acts of mass violence in addition to, or separate from, agencies of the state; often various group targets as opposed to one single one (e.g. Nazis versus Jews); and a range of types of not necessarily murderous assault, including profiteering and asset-stripping which, he says, are often understated in the genocide literature. Gerlach's case studies, including the destruction of the Armenians, develop further his proposition that crises of state and society leading to mass violence can be pervasive rather than purely episodic, while profound socio-economic pressures—which impact especially on traditional, agriculturally based societies as they are forcibly integrated into a broader, including world, economy—are key to the 'bulk of modern mass violence'.[9] What to my mind is strange about this otherwise very acute and astringent presentation, however, is that Gerlach, in spite of himself, seems to be making a perfectly sound case for a *complex* picture of genocide, even if alongside other related forms of mass violence. All that is in fact missing from the argument is a clear acknowledgement that what he is actually describing are the extremely violent fundamentals not of *some* societies but of an emerging world system.

The second book, Timothy Snyder's much discussed and generally much lauded *Bloodlands*, is actually considerably more relevant to this study in that it covers some of the same geographical and chronological range. More precisely Snyder's geography is that of the 'Lands Between' (for which see the Introduction herein) and chronology that of the period 1933 to 1945, in which the Hitler and Stalin states between them were responsible for the deaths of some fourteen million people over and beyond those directly killed in Second World War military engagement, in, and for, the region.[10] The fact that Snyder treats this historical–geographical range in its totality, rather than by way of a standard German- or Soviet-centred approach, in itself offers illumination as to how the two histories of mass murder were closely intermeshed and entangled. To be sure, my own 'rimlands' terminology is not nearly as compelling or bitingly macabre as that of the 'bloodlands'. Yet unlike in his earlier *Reconstruction of Nations*,[11] in which the actual peoples of the 'Lands Between' are presented as dynamic, flesh-and-blood actors in their own right, including, in some cases, as protagonists for, or perpetrators of, mass murder and ethnic cleansing, Snyder in *Bloodlands* reduces their role largely to that of victims (though not necessarily passive victims) of Hitler or Stalin. The physical and human geography of the region, too, mostly comes across as an almost incidental backdrop. Snyder's view of it as a killing zone is certainly both panoramic and grimly detailed, but what the presentation essentially

---

[9] Christian Gerlach, *Extremely Violent Societies: Mass Violence in the Twentieth-Century World* (Cambridge and New York: Cambridge University Press, 2010), especially 'Introduction', and 'Conclusions'.

[10] Snyder, *Bloodlands*.

[11] Timothy Snyder, *The Reconstruction of Nations: Poland, Ukraine, Lithuania, Belarus, 1569–1999* (New York and London: Yale University Press, 2003).

suggests is that of lands desired by two great, powerful, rival regimes rather than imbued with any significance of their own.[12] To get to grips with that reality we would have to unravel the story back at least to the collapse of empires in 1918, which, in turn, would make the interplay of political and social forces a whole lot more complex. Is then Snyder's avoidance of the term genocide in a study which, among other things, examines the Holocaust, the Ukrainian *Holodomor*, and a range of mass deportations, a further example of a shying away from complexity or, as he himself proposes, because using the term might give rise to 'controversies'? Certainly, his specific reasons are different from those of Gerlach. Snyder claims that to use the term genocide for events other than the Holocaust would be misread by societies and states with a vested interest in either advancing or refuting the comparison. He also argues that the 1948 UN Convention on Genocide (UNC) definition, especially with regard to the notion of 'intent to destroy', carries limitations which would deny acceptance of some examples of mass killing as genocide.[13]

Of course, Snyder is correct on that latter score. Even for those who circumvent the UNC as a useful interpretative tool (as I do), definitional issues remain part of the bugbear of working within the field. An overarching theory of genocide, despite some powerful recent stabs at it, remains elusive.[14] None of this, however, provides good reason for assuming the term lacks serviceability. The fact is that when Raphael Lemkin coined 'genocide' in the early 1940s, he opened up a range of possibilities for how a *particular* form of sustained mass violence, which could not be directly embraced under the heading of 'war', might be interpreted and understood.[15] The proof of that lies in the manner in which scholars in many very diverse disciplines have run with it, each usually recognizing that they cannot fully do so without cross-reference to insights from other disciplines. For good measure I am adding here a thumbnail proposition for a human ecology of genocide, not least because it might assist in more broadly framing how destabilizing tendencies at the macro-system level have local outcomes.

Genocide is the consequence of a very particular 'dis-ease' of humanity but not one, I venture, built into the human condition. In its modern pathology it is a consequence of drives for the attainment and consolidation of socio-political power as channelled through projects of development, integration, and consolidation aimed at transcending the limiting factors imposed by the wider conditions associated with the emergence of a single, world political economy. Part of what makes genocide so compelling yet problematic is why failure to achieve those goals, usually associated with monumental crises of state and society, is taken out, relieved, or, indeed, *put to advantage* through sustained murderous assault on perceived groups within, at the

---

[12] Snyder, *Bloodlands*, xviii: 'The bloodlands are no political territory, real or imagined, they are *simply* where Europe's most murderous regimes did their most murderous work' (my emphasis).
[13] Snyder, *Bloodlands*, 412–13.
[14] Powell, *Barbaric Civilisation*, is particularly thought-provoking, if only for his eminently succinct if equally discussable conceptualization of genocide as 'an identity-difference relation of violent obliteration' (127).
[15] Raphael Lemkin, *Axis Rule in Occupied Europe* (Washington, DC: Carnegie Endowment for International Peace, 1944).

margins of, or beyond state boundaries. One can certainly read a tangible economic calculus in many if not *all* occasions of genocide: most obviously associated with the asset-stripping of the communal group or groups' wealth and lands for the benefit of regime, state, and/or wider society. But one can hardly avoid the fact that the will to genocide is also symptomatic of acute psycho-cultural disturbance. A holistically inclined human ecology might offer one method by which to better understand the relational threads between a state or society's perception of one or more communal groups as toxic threats to its wellbeing and integrity, as well as the toxicity built into contemporary systemic pressures on exactly those same states and societies.[16] That said, such an ecological method for comprehending genocide in the round would be entirely anchorless without historical context. To my mind, history, above all, is a case of joining up the dots between events and then trying to fill in the processes and patterns which give coherence to the whole. That can never be complete, not least because history is itself contingent. And, hence, complex. All the more reason why making *some* sense of it is imperative if we are to understand where genocide fits into, *and* helps explain, why we are where we are. The crisis of genocide between 1912 and 1953 was fundamentally a crisis of the semi-periphery, but one whose lethal devastation was enacted at the European interface between that semi-periphery and a metropolitan core. In other words, in the rimlands.

*

Readers who feel distaste, or horror, at the very hint of historical meta-narrative will be relieved at this juncture of any need to venture further. That said, if for no other reason than an organizational one they may have good grounds for raising the alarm! Trying to mesh together a vast array of information into some kind of big yet coherent picture has not been an easy task—not least as it has been done mostly at second hand. Without the growing corpus of archivally based studies of the very diverse but discrete elements which make up this attempted synthesis, *The Crisis of Genocide* would have been much the poorer. The very fact that ongoing scholarship on the Holocaust is now accompanied by an increasingly wide and sophisticated range of works on other genocides in our somewhat broader chronological range—the *Aghet* and aspects of Soviet mass violence in particular—is both evidence of the opening of critical archives—in the post-Soviet case amounting to a small revolution—and a tribute to the researchers who are developing their respective fields. Indeed, one of the ironies involved in writing a book such as this comes from the very proliferation of relevant monographs and articles. Trying to keep abreast of all of them, even when limited to Western languages only, has been a little like what used to be referred to as painting the Forth Bridge. Having taken several years to reach the far end it would then be time to start the process all over again. By that stricture, this book could never have been written at all. To be sure, with that comes regret, especially with regard to many recently published—yet

---

[16] Lewis Williams, Rose Roberts, and Alastair Macintosh, eds., *Radical Human Ecology: Intercultural and Indigenous Approaches* (Farnham and Burlington, VT: Ashgate, 2012), here nominated for inspiration.

unread—studies which might have enriched *The Crisis of Genocide*, or perhaps, even changed its direction in subtle and not so subtle ways.

Paradoxically, the dilemma of not reading all the books is offset by another, in which one reads as much as one can on a particular subject, only to be presented with quite different statements of fact and/or wildly different interpretations of what those facts mean. How does any student operating from secondary sources discern what is polemic or apologia and what genuinely illuminates our understanding of historical events? How much more fraught and difficult does the effort become when one realizes that the fractious disagreements between some of the relevant scholars themselves are more often than not a product of what is most at stake for them—an interest to present their own, usually national, community or collectivity in the best possible, least genocidal, light. It would be nice to say that steering through these issues is a matter of adopting a detached, judicious, common-sense approach. But such care, in itself, does not necessarily lead to getting it right. What is 'right' when it comes to allegations of vast numbers of people murdered, supposedly for who they are, on the one hand, and denial that any such thing took place, or at least not in that way or at the hands of those accused, on the other? Readers be warned: entering into this arena can sometimes feel like entering a minefield. And, one might add, with some remaining no-go areas—for which the shorthand might read 'forgotten genocides'—which nobody much seems to want to research, or discuss.

And yet I have clearly failed to provide a fully adequate response to my own query. Even more lamely, I suspect that answering the question as to how one goes about sifting out the bias, the exaggeration, the special pleading, and multiple other pitfalls which must accompany such a journey, would require the writing of a very different essay, even book. In the interim, all I can say is that having a 'method' for discerning what is good, sound, and purposeful in the genocide literature, and evaluating what might be deemed 'dodgy', extraneous, or wilfully misleading, cannot be wholly scientific. To say that what one is left with as one's final guide is little more than intuition, will hardly satisfy all, or any, of my disciplinary colleagues. So why, in spite of this confession, have I persisted on this perilous course? The answer, in part, is sheer cussedness. That, combined with a dogged commitment to the notion that there is some point in trying to consider this wretched landscape *as a whole*. For any mistakes, failings, or key omissions, I necessarily take full responsibility. Meanwhile, I would like heartily to thank all those who, through their generosity of spirit or simply kind words of support, have buoyed me up, nourished the exercise, and kept me going thus far. They include Lynne Viola, Taner Akçam, Tony Barta, Norman Naimark, Mike Joseph, Damien Short, Tim Cole, Welat Zeydanlioglu, Metin Sönmez, Mehmet Ratip, Peter Morgan, Adrian Gallagher, the inestimable Colin Richmond, Jeff Benvenuto, Angela Debnath, Philip Spencer, Soner Çağaptay, Alexander Prusin, Mark Biondich, Cathie Carmichael, Dave Patrick, Adam Jones, Tony Kushner, Sarah Pearce, Anton Weiss-Wendt, Matthew Kott, Tove Eriksen, Joyce Apsel, Rikke Juel Madsen, Jon Egeris Karstoft, Sheila Christie, Elissavet Stagoni, Matthew Frank, Panikos Panayi, Paul Salmons, Emma O'Brien, David Cesarani, Jürgen Zimmerer, Nigel Eltringham, Wendy Lower, Uğur Ümit Üngör, Herb Hirsch, Paul Bartrop, Sam Totten, Harry Hagopian, Ara Sarafian, Raz Segal, Nafeez

Ahmed, Helga Lees, Joan Tumblety, Mark Cornwall, Matt Kelly, Neil Gregor, Jane McDermid, Tony Campbell and family, Penny Roberts, and Sarah Richardson. Special thanks go to Jenny Ivory for her persistent, grass-roots encouragement. And to all my undergraduate students over the years who have willingly engaged with this unlovely subject, not least Rory Grant and Mark Chadwick, who not only 'got' the argument but were able to run with it.

Though writing this book has mostly been to plough a rather long and lonely furrow I could have not arrived at its necessary end without some very critical support. I would like to thank the Leverhulme Foundation for a Research Fellowship in 2004–5, which enabled me to get started in the first place. More recently, my thanks go to the Humanities Faculty at the University of Southampton, and more especially to Mark Everist, for providing the 'extra time' with which to bring things to completion. Even then, like all the best-laid plans of mice and men (to pursue the agricultural allusion), this project got itself radically unstuck quite close to the final furlong. My further sincere thanks thus go to Lester Crook and Jo Godfrey for all their support, plus valiant efforts to keep things on course, and to both Avril Mujis and John Oldfield for sound advice and encouragement. More particularly, my special and heartfelt thanks go to Christopher Wheeler at OUP who, if I may resort to the colloquial, played an absolute blinder to bring things back from the brink. In addition to his immense effort, wisdom, and acuity he has also brought a wider team at OUP to my assistance. I would particularly like to thank Cathryn Steele and Emma Barber not just for their professionalism but also for being kind, considerate, and great to work with. The same goes for Elizabeth Stone, who has done a truly superb job on the copy-editing, Francis Eaves for proofreading, and Geraldine Begley for the index. Similar earnest thanks, too, go to the truly wonderful Jennifer Craig-Norton without whose help it is doubtful that a coherent rendition of endnotes and bibliography could *ever* have been accomplished.

Returning to the academic side of things, my gratitude also goes to two anonymous readers who provided extremely valuable support, in the first case through a very encouraging but nevertheless incisive summary of the manuscript, and in the second through a finely detailed critique of some of the early chapters which has, it is to be hoped, enhanced the final outcome. For the long haul though, I would particularly like to salute my good colleagues, Dirk Moses and Donald Bloxham. I esteem these two scholars' work immensely. In turn, they have always been on hand for me and this project. In its final stages both have not only gone to the trouble of reading great sections of this hardly lightweight tome but have offered genuinely constructive advice and correction. In short, I have been very fortunate to have had the benefit of their professional acumen, moral support—and friendship.

Friendship, indeed, and family are what keeps a project such as this sustainable. My good fortune extends to the support of a stable and loving family and a broader community of good folk, not least where I live. As for the environment in which that community is set, for all the encroaching degradation, it continues to nourish and provide solace.

ML

Kineton, Warwickshire
December 2012

A Brief Note on Languages and Transliteration

This study's geographical focus is on regions of once great ethnic and linguistic complexity. Across many languages, this author has thus opted for names as commonly cited in standard works. While the aim is to be consistent, it is not to render, for example, Polish or Czech names as if they were Russian, or, for that matter, English. Readers should be able to spot the differences soon enough. Place names, however, are that much more problematic in the sense that what, for example, in 1914 might have been referred to by the politically dominant group as Lemberg, by 1919 had become Lwów, and then again, by 1945, Lviv. Our response has been to use the most appropriate name at any given time, at least with reference to the linguistic group which named the place as such. But sometimes we offer a second name in brackets, especially where at that given time, another group (referred to in the text at that point) had its own alternative appellation for the place in question. There is also an issue of nomenclature where a group's self-designation is not the same as that used often pejoratively by others. The obvious example here is 'gypsy', which we use when we are referring to the negative appellation by those outside the community, while opting for 'Roma' as our standard ascription. The general point is that if some of this may read ambiguously, it is because ambiguity was built into the historical predicament in question.

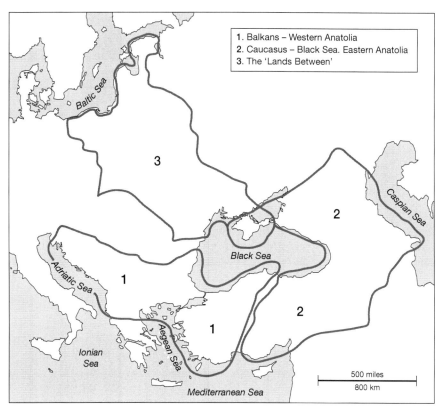

1. Balkans – Western Anatolia
2. Caucasus – Black Sea. Eastern Anatolia
3. The 'Lands Between'

Baltic Sea

3

Caspian Sea

2

Black Sea

Adriatic Sea

1

2

1

Aegean Sea

Ionian
Sea

500 miles
800 km

Mediterranean Sea

Map 1. The European Rimlands

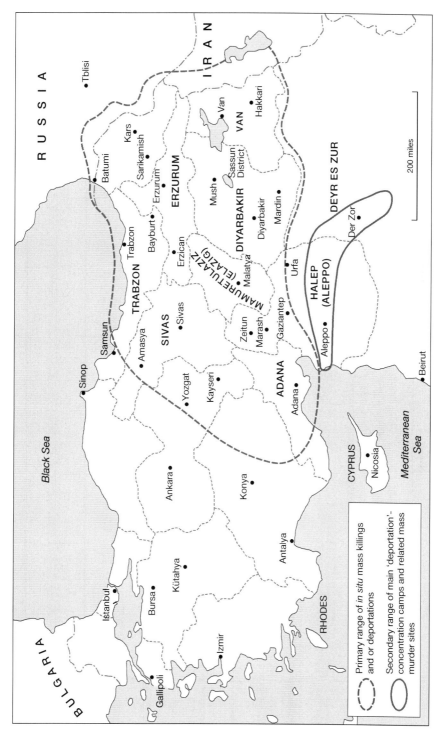

Map 2. Armenian and Syriac Killing Zones, 1915–16

RUSSIA

IRAN

Tblisi

Van

VAN

Hakkari

Kars

Sarikamish

Batumi

ERZURUM

Erzurum

Mush

Sassun
District

DIYARBAKIR

DEYR ES ZUR

200 miles

Bayburt

Erzican

Diyarbakir

Mardin

Der Zor

Trabzon

Trabzon

MAMURETULAZIZ
(ELAZIG)

Malatya

Urfa

HALEP
(ALEPPO)

Samsun

SIVAS

Sivas

Zeitun

Marash

Gaziantep

Aleppo

Amasya

Beirut

Sinop

Black Sea

Yozgat

Kayseri

ADANA

Adana

CYPRUS

Mediterranean
Sea

Ankara

Konya

Nicosia

BULGARIA

İstanbul

Bursa

Kütahya

Antalya

RHODES

İzmir

Gallipoli

Primary range of *in situ* mass killings
and or deportations

Secondary range of main 'deportation'-
concentration camps and related mass
murder sites

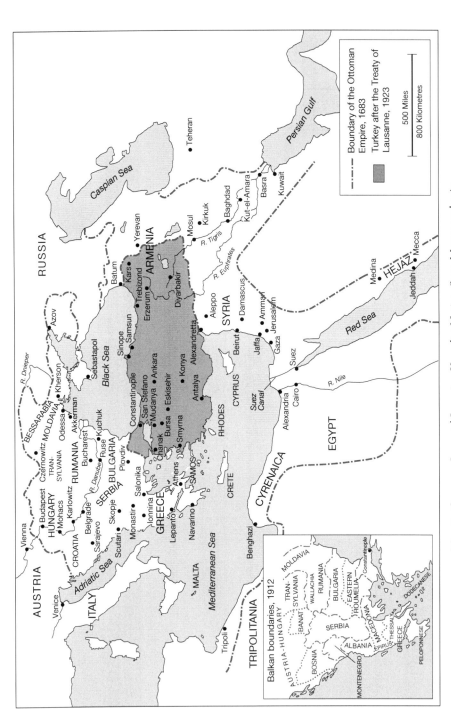

Map 3. Ottoman Imperial Legacies, Kemalist Nation-State Metamorphosis

Legend:
- ─·─· Boundary of the Ottoman Empire, 1683
- Turkey after the Treaty of Lausanne, 1923

500 Miles
800 Kilometres

AUSTRIA
RUSSIA
HUNGARY
Vienna
Budapest
Mohacs
Karlowitz
CROATIA
Venice
ITALY
Belgrade
Sarajevo
Scutari
SERBIA
Skopje
Monastir
Adriatic Sea
MALTA
Lepanto
Navarino
Athens
GREECE
Ioannina
Salonika
BULGARIA
Ploydiv
Ruse
Bucharest
RUMANIA
TRAN-SYLVANIA
MOLDAVIA
BESSARABIA
Czernowitz
R. Dnieper
R. Danube
Kuchuk
Akkerman
Odessa
Kherson
Azov
Sebastapol
Black Sea
Constantinople
San Stefano
Chanak
Bursa
Smyrna
Mudanya
Ankara
Eskisehir
SAMOS
CRETE
RHODES
CYPRUS
Sinope
Samsun
Trebizond
Erzerum
Kars
Batum
Yerevan
ARMENIA
Diyarbakir
Konya
Antalya
Alexandretta
Mediterranean Sea
TRIPOLITANIA
CYRENAICA
Benghazi
Tripoli
EGYPT
Alexandria
Cairo
R. Nile
Suez
Suez Canal
Gaza
Jaffa
Jerusalem
Beirut
Amman
Damascus
Aleppo
SYRIA
Mosul
R. Tigris
R. Euphrates
Kirkuk
Baghdad
Kut-el-Amara
Basra
Kuwait
Persian Gulf
Caspian Sea
Teheran
Red Sea
Medina
Mecca
Jeddah
HEJAZ

Balkan boundaries, 1912
AUSTRIA-HUNGARY
TRAN-SYLVANIA
MOLDAVIA
WALLACHIA
RUMANIA
BANAT
SERBIA
BOSNIA
MONTENEGRO
ALBANIA
MACEDONIA
BULGARIA
EASTERN ROUMELIA
Constantinople
EPIRUS
THESSALY
GREECE
PELOPONNESE
DODECANESE

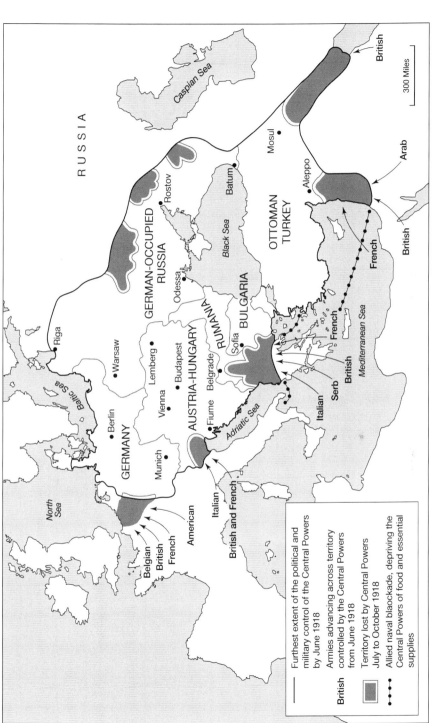

Map 4. The European 'World' Empires at their Twilight and under Western Allied Attack, 1918

Map 5. The 'New Europe', 1923–38

Introduction: The Structural Underpinnings of European Genocide, 1912–1953

Who rules eastern Europe, commands the Heartland;
Who rules the Heartland, commands the World-Island;
Who rules the World-Island, commands the World.[1]

Professor Toynbee has, for both Turk and Greek, sympathy rather than blame. Both are the victims, he would say, of our Western civilisation.[2]

To begin a study on the history of genocide in its most virulent phase with these two rather opaque statements must appear a little odd. They belong to two near-contemporary British academics who, at the height of their powers before the Second World War, exerted a marked influence not only in their respective fields but well beyond, amongst policymakers, opinion formers, and the educated public alike. The first comes from Sir Halford Mackinder (1861–1947), an eminent geographer with a great historical sweep (and much else besides). His insights into how relationships between physical and human geography can determine the bases for political power have provided a critical foundation stone for the study of geopolitics. This last term has been appropriated by German Nazi sympathizers to the extent that it continues, perhaps fairly, to have a rather suspect quality, compared, for instance, with the more insipid-sounding 'international relations', of which it is a fundamental part.[3]

The second relates to a review cited in one of the books, *The Western Question in Greece and Turkey*, by another great polymath, Arnold J. Toynbee (1889–1975).[4] A historian of humanity's entire civilizational—and hence geographical—sweep, most cogently developed in his multi-volume *A Study of History*, Toynbee is nowadays often less remembered, or even valued, by historians for this work than for his compilation of a British government-sponsored report adumbrating and analysing the atrocities committed by Ottoman Turks against Armenians in eastern Anatolia in 1915.[5] Paradoxically, *The Western Question*, written just a few years later in the wake of further atrocities, this time in western Anatolia, is a barely veiled, even coruscating attack on Western, and more specifically British, responsibility for these latter events, not least, in the broadest sense, through the introduction into the region of 'the Western political idea of nationality'.[6]

The question might be posed, however, as to why one would need to intrude a discussion on the relationship between geography and power, or, arguably cross-related to that, of the transmission belt by which societies beyond the West got *their* national bug, when one could take a much more straightforward and direct route towards explaining genocide in our period. After all, *The Rise of the West*, our previous related study, more or less concluded with those disastrous assassin's bullets at Sarajevo, at the end of June 1914: in other words, at the moment in which Europeans leapt into the vortex of what at the time was called the Great War. Few historians today would dispute this event's being the essential catalyst for a whole sequence of further European—and global—catastrophes, including that truly epoch-making act of genocide we commonly know as the Holocaust. This historian is no different. He would affirm that the Great War primed the violence which, within a generation, was to lead to an even more devastating second global war and, with it, to the attempted mass murder of the entirety of European Jewry. 'No Hitler, no Holocaust' is the well-rehearsed maxim. But without the First World War, no Hitler either. At least, not in any conceivable position of power. We have at first sight, thus, a clear cause and effect for at least the main trajectory of our phenomenon. And one or more shorthands, too, for its culminating outcome.

Today we often use the term Holocaust, or even more tersely, Auschwitz, in recognition of some terrible, dark potentiality which exists in our contemporary world; our (albeit primarily Western) imaginations transfixed by the extraordinary scale—and effort—of what we have imbibed as a systematically focused, ordered, even routinized killing machine. Moreover, unless one is entirely contrary, or just plain perverse, there can be no dispute as to the significance of the process of European Jewish extermination, at least, again, for contemporary Western culture. Accepted and confirmed in both popular perception and state-led commemoration as not just a crossroads and paradigm but a warning for our times, it is hardly surprising if so many, including serious essayists and philosophers, have been tempted 'to reformulate the Jewish question as the question of humanity or society at large'.[7]

The problem here, however, is that we would already seem to be shifting explanation for genocide away from relationships between time, space—and war—towards some other entirely sui generis factor. If the Holocaust is 'phenomenonologically unique',[8] an event so exceptional in the way that millions of Jews were slated for annihilation, whatever their national citizenship, then there can be no case to answer. Even if the proposition itself would seem to rest on a rather all-embracing assumption that the Holocaust was a *single coherent event*. But even for a moment putting that issue to one side and accepting the totality of the outcome, how should we treat other examples of exact or near synchronicity, where, while the scope or scale of the exterminatory undertaking was not as large, there is evidence of some similitude? Does it follow, for instance, in the case of the Roma *Porrajmos*, that their fate is essentially a codicil to a main Jewish narrative? Or, by another route, that the overwhelming nature of Jewish mass murder determines that it is *the* key to a broader landscape of genocide? Or, alternatively, as implied in the previous paragraph, as its metaphor? Is this good history? Or a mistaken premise? Does, for instance, what happened to the Armenians in 1915–16 *need* the comparison of the Holocaust to be validated as genocide?

We posed these questions, in some shape or form, in *The Meaning of Genocide*. But they are particularly pertinent to this study because so many genocidal events, over and beyond what I would be the first to dub the 'ultimate genocide', are also crowded into a quite definite time frame and, equally importantly, a series of mostly quite definable geographical spaces. Which must lead this author again to at least ponder why, contra 'the Holocaust', there is relatively little scholarship devoted to, or, beyond that, broader awareness of, some of these other instances. At one end, the range of repeated people deportations, some more total than others, carried out in Stalin's Russia, for example, have impinged more fully on historical consciousness. At the other, events such as the mutual exterminations committed by Ukrainians and Poles, in Volhynia and eastern Galicia, during the latter part or at the end of the Second World War, or, for that matter, the Turkish military 'pacification' (as they termed it) of the Dersim district in eastern Anatolia in 1937–8, are so obscure to general view as to be practically unknown, except to the relevant area experts. Such distinctions inevitably mean that while many people in the West can often reel off names of the main *German* architects and organizers of the Holocaust, none of their counterparts in Stalin's Russia, Ittihadist or Kemalist Turkey, or other European and Near Eastern perpetrator regimes are likely to have any purchase.

Does this limiting of our cognitive map of genocide matter? The answer ultimately depends on whether we are content with a partial, or even arguably skewed, view, or a much fuller spectrum. This author would argue that understanding the nature and causation of genocide fundamentally depends on the latter. Paradoxically, this might also enable a fuller understanding of the specifics of the Holocaust, not least in the way in which it would give due weight to the state and societal violence done to Jews by non-Germans, or for that matter, by both Germans and non-Germans to other non-Jewish European peoples. The result may be to complicate the picture of 'the Holocaust', as well as making it less utterly Germanocentric. However, it may also ultimately explain why the destruction of the Jews cannot be understood quite so simply as a stand-alone event. On the contrary, what it should confirm is that it is part and parcel, albeit in its most crystalline form, of a specific phase of European toxicity, the highest, most lethal dosages of which were limited to particular, if repeated, moments—mostly, though not exclusively, in the context of wider war—and across *particular*, if also shifting, zones.

This is the point at which Mackinder and Toynbee's geographical and historical insights may assist us in our fundamental thesis. Mackinder's turn-of-the-twentieth-century prognostications about Eastern Europe as the pivot for some form of struggle between the Great Powers—further developed during the Paris Peace Conference in 1919—were predicated on the assumption that the land areas of the globe were already effectively staked out and accessible to the political and military interference of those self-same powers.[9] Mackinder's anxieties about who would ultimately attain Eastern Europe—he had in mind especially Germany and Russia, either alone, or in combination—might ultimately have been impelled by what this would mean for a traditionally maritime-based British Empire. Nevertheless, his further key point was that, once achieved, such a controlling position in this region could enable access, with the assistance of modern communications (most obviously the railway), to a potentially resource-rich Eurasian land mass from which a bid for global hegemony could then conceivably be launched.

Mackinder's hypothesis has nothing to do with genocide per se. But it does throw into relief the probability that once loosened from its traditional political anchor, as indeed was the case from 1918 in the whole zone of the Eastern European 'Lands Between' (longer still, if we include the Balkans), the regions' peoples—and more particularly allegedly 'suspect' peoples—could become especially vulnerable to the consequences of any such inter-power struggle. Towards the end of *The Rise of the West* we proposed how such a situation arose in the pre-1914 period along a particular East–West seam, or, arguably, tectonic plate of instability. Stretching from Central Asia to the Balkans as a result of the indirect pressures exerted by the advancing global powers on the remaining traditional, land-based 'continental' empires, we argued how genocidal events were one consequence. This potential did not entirely go away along this seam thereafter, any more than it did in some of the territories which the advancing Western imperialisms had conquered or were still to conquer elsewhere in Asia or Africa. Incidences of serious 'native' resistance or insurrection continued to be dealt with in these zones by lethal force though, post-1919, with aeroplanes strongly to the fore as the main method of delivery.[10] But if this is a reminder of what, in previous *Genocide in the Age of the Nation State* volumes, we described as War Type Two, or Three, spilling over into the possibility, if not always actuality, of genocide, what Mackinder's more immediate geopolitical dimension points to is a correlation between a new series of stress points and fault lines developing as a consequence of an entirely more metropolitan, European crisis from around 1912, and a new, intensified phase of genocidal violence. In fact, these fault lines were not entirely new, in the sense that one of them, re-emerging through both eastern Anatolia and the contiguous Caucasus, was actually a restatement of part of the Central Asian fault evident from the pre-war period. Another, in the Balkans, as we will see, represented a further restatement but was, in a sense, not entirely contiguous with its more eastern cousin.

For our purposes, one key consideration about this post-1912 series of emergent or reconstituted fractures is the degree to which their inherent destabilizing effects on the human geography of these regions was either mitigated or neutralized by some countervailing force. A normative response would be to propose that an antidote did exist, at least in principle, in the shape of the Western Allies; their 1918 victory enabling them to nurture a liberal post-war order in the 'New Europe' and Near East. But then there is the problem of the Toynbee riposte, one which would suggest that that solution was equally part of the problem. Toynbee's negativity on the matter is shocking if one starts from an assumption that Westernization is essentially benign. Or, put in more Mackinder-style geopolitical terms, that without the Allies radiating their post-Versailles power to the east, there would have been nothing to stop either Bolshevik—later Stalinist—Russia, or a re-emergent, revanchist Germany (Nazism for short) filling the political vacuum, as indeed both eventually attempted to do. From this perspective, the responsibility for any ensuing genocide would lie entirely with these two monstrosities, Western responsibility, if at all, lying only in a failure to be resolute and properly plug, then cement, a too provisional eastern dyke.

However, Toynbee's blast was written in 1923, that is, several years before either the worst Stalinist atrocities, or the Holocaust. Yet the historian had just personally witnessed something of the mass atrocities committed by both Greeks and Turks which, he was very careful, nevertheless, *not* to delineate as something endemic to these societies. Instead, said Toynbee, the outcome ought to be seen as the culmination of 'a prolonged epidemic...from the time when they lost their indigenous civilisations until they became acclimatised to the intrusive influence of the West'.[11] In other words, even where the *génocidaires* in western Anatolia were not being directly abetted by Western polities, it was the Western idea of nationalism which Toynbee was holding most to blame for the murderous consequences. And, indeed, if this argument is correct, then it might equally be applied to the entire imperial shatter zone of violence which opened up from the Black Sea to the Baltic in this period; even, arguably, without either the ideological extremism or territorial revisionism of Germany or Russia as a necessary concomitant cause.

In short, seeking explanation for the totality of the genocide landscape, at least in its primary European and near-European setting between 1912 and 1953, requires acceptance of multi-causal factors. One of these undoubtedly was an underbelly of unresolved long-term but very specific European heterogeneity aversion towards the Jews. If their extermination was ultimately dependent on a hegemony-driven Nazi engine, this also however carried in its train an assorted pan-European crew whose collective head of steam was triggered, then amplified, by the general 1914 crisis. But this alone is clearly insufficient to understand the repeated extermination, or, beneath that, mass ethnic cleansings of *other* European and Near Eastern populations before, during, and after the Holocaust. Where Mackinder and Toynbee assist is in pointing to two highly unstable elements, whose synchronous protrusion also at, or in the wake of, the Balkan Wars/Great War watershed, add further grist to our genocidal mill. The one, imperial reformation (and, of course, with it, ideological reformulation), with a view to a much more focused and totalized renewal of the pre-1914 global struggle; the other—paradoxically—the West's sponsored alternative, in the form of a phalanx of nation states designed to keep both Russia and Germany at bay. It is the intersection of all three elements: the anti-Semitic drive, restated empire, *and* nation state, which provide the essential cornerstones of our analysis. In which case one has to ask: *where* do they intersect? To which the answer is: in the rimlands.

RIMLANDS

This is not the first study to identify particular Eastern European or near-European regions as the sites of a genocidal-type exterminatory violence. Quite recently, Timothy Snyder has made the case for 'a zone of death', embracing 'today's Ukraine,

Belarus, Poland, western Russia and the eastern Baltic coast'. However, his chronological range is limited essentially to 1933–45, with his 'Bloodlands' in question those European countries caught 'between Hitler and Stalin'.[12] From a different perspective, one which foregrounds cases of ethnic cleansing, both Norman Naimark and Benjamin Lieberman have delineated a landscape of violence which is broader than Snyder's and more closely akin to our own. In each case the chronological range extends beyond the Cold War to the 1990s. While Naimark is strong on the historical connections between his five case studies, Lieberman evinces a richer and more audacious sense of the links between history and geography.[13] That aside, Snyder's emphasis on post-imperial violence, on the one hand, and Naimark and Lieberman's on nationalist violence, on the other, when taken together bring us closer to the equation we are seeking. Thus it is perhaps significant that the study which brings us closest to it still comes from Terry Martin, an authority on Soviet *nationality* policy. In his important 1998 article 'The Origins of Soviet Ethnic Cleansing', Martin seeks to place the Soviet (hence 'revisionist'– imperialist) sequence of ethnic cleansing within a broader historical–geographical nexus. He identifies the period 1912 to 1953, that is, until the death of Stalin, as the relevant time frame, while spatially delineating an L-shaped swathe of territory 'extending southwards from Leningrad through the Balkans, and then eastward across southern Ukraine and Turkey into the Caucasus region'. Martin calls this area the 'Eurasian borderlands'.[14]

My own chronological delineation of genocide in this period dovetails with Martin's for ethnic cleansing. While one might argue that *most* of the Soviet deportations were completed by 1949, the ongoing potential for more, not least those projected for Soviet Jewry very close to Stalin's death, makes Martin's case for a 1953 end of sequence a sound one. Nor do I have any disagreement with Martin's basic geographical frame of reference, bar two caveats. The first is of a general nature and relates to terminology. 'Eurasian borderlands' offers a perspective essentially from a Russocentric viewpoint. I have opted in its place for European 'rimlands'. 'Rimlands' is a less familiar term than 'borderlands' and it may take readers time to digest and assimilate it. However, there is a particular reason for this nomenclature. One could consider the European rim as an area on the edge of what Mackinder might have viewed as 'genuine' Europe (i.e. its western and central parts) and through which powerful actors (those who 'rule' and 'command') would have to pass to subjugate and control an Asian 'heartland'. In itself there is something dark and sinister about the implication, most particularly for those living in the regions in question. However, a world-systems conceptualization may offer greater insight as to the relationships at stake. By the fin de siècle a core of modern, industrialized 'Western' states, through their political, economic, and military muscle were making of the once very powerful and 'normative' 'eastern' world empires, within or close to Europe, weaker neighbours. In Wallersteinian terms, this paradigm shift made of the first group a metropolitan core of power, and the latter a semi-periphery,[15] but, crucially, with the regions at the outer western or southern edges of that semi-periphery most vulnerable to metropolitan impacts and influences (for which amongst other things read, with Toynbee, 'nationalism').

What is thus presented in this study as a crisis of the semi-periphery as a consequence of more general Great Power conflict, had its main locus in the regions which bore the full brunt of the breakdown, that is, precisely on the European semi-periphery's exposed rim.

My second caveat is simply one of attempting to more closely demarcate discrete areas within Martin's 'L-shaped swathe'. Putting aside the fact that there are some incidences of genocide—not least, as we will see, in tsarist Central Asia during the First World War—which are outside of Martin's geographical framework (in turn suggesting the continuance of imperial–colonial issues from the pre-1912 period), let me offer a threefold delineation:

1. The Balkans: from a northern line at Trieste running east towards the river Drava contiguous with Hungary, embracing thereby the entirety of the peninsula: Croatia, Bosnia, Serbia, Albania, Macedonia, and Thrace—with the exception of pre-1912 Greece—but leapfrogging both Aegean and Dardanelles to include western Anatolia and its adjacent islands.[16]

2. A Caucasus–Black Sea–eastern Anatolia zone, running approximately from a northern boundary of the sea of Azov in the west to Astrakhan in the east, thereby incorporating the whole North Caucasus and Transcaucasian ranges between the Black and Caspian seas, though in its southern part broadening out to embrace the eastern Anatolian plateau at least as far as Trabzon in the west, Mosul in the south.[17]

3. 'The Lands Between',[18] that is, a giant sliver of territory running from the Baltic southwards, to include Belorussia and right-bank Ukraine in the east, and as far as the Crimea in the south, while in its western reaches embracing the lands of historic Poland, with an approximate north-west, south-east line running from Silesia through the Carpathians and sub-Carpathian ranges towards an intersection with the Danube at its deltaic point of entry into the Black Sea.

Are such proposed zones of genocide clear-cut? No. There is clearly some inexactitude, some fuzziness, even some spillover into adjacent regions. 'The Lands Between', for instance, include the great swathe of once Polish eastern borders known as the *kresy*. Yet this zone cannot be limited to the *kresy* alone. On the other hand, the historic Czech lands and much of sub-Carpathian Hungary are not directly included in it, but at various *moments* in our narrative would almost appear as if they were. Perhaps, rather than being able to confirm a distinct boundary around our zones, what we should visualize for each is a central, 'hot' core, with cooler, outer layers, which at critical moments seem to be drawn by the core's heat. The geological reference, by way of a volcanic metaphor, just as elsewhere by reference to tectonic plates and fault lines, is quite intentional. Some of the 'hot' area should also be imagined as at junctures between the zones. This may lead to some geographical confusion. Should we understand, for instance, a subregion such as the Banat as in the Balkans, or, given its proximity to the 'Lands Between', as belonging to that latter zone? By the same token, does the Crimea—a clear hot spot point of intersection between the 'Lands Between' and the Caucasus–Black Sea–eastern Anatolia zone—belong more to one than the other? Or should it actually be treated as distinct in its own right?

What is most relevant here is not discussion of the geographical niceties per se but the interaction between the geography and the history, insofar as it points to a crystallization of our genocidal potential. Certainly, the fact that underlying much of the southern area under consideration (that is, in all three zones) was a longue durée of Ottoman occupation and rule, which, in more recent times, buckled or collapsed under pressure especially from Russian or Austrian interlopers, is germane; just as in the northern region it was a once dominant Polish–Lithuanian commonwealth which succumbed to Austrian, Russian, or German partition. Nevertheless, the real key to what eventually transpired after 1912—the opening up of a series of giant territorial fissures—is not a matter of imperial supersession alone. Having one master replace another in these regions was not in itself historically abnormal. What arguably was more so was the ongoing proximity of other contending powers—in other words, the persistence of geopolitics—combined with the fact that none of the new imperial masters was able to stabilize the situation by proper absorption or integration of the territories in question into their historic cores. As such, these regions continued in a somewhat contradictory fashion to be contested yet marginal, in so doing reinforcing their status not simply as border territories but as *on the rim*.

Paradoxically, this situation, while politically unstable, was, for the peoples living there, quite tolerable on a year by year basis, provided no serious exogenous factors intervened or, alternatively, welled up. Part of this 'welling up' was the emergence of national or proto-national movements, sometimes from within, sometimes from adjacent areas. That these sorts of elements together could produce intense danger to rimland communities is perhaps best exemplified, pre-1912, by the trajectory which led to the Armenian massacres of 1894–6:[19] in years, that is, which were not marked by general war. As we will venture to expound later in this Introduction and, more fully, in Chapter 4, the further paradox is that all these rimlands had certain characteristics which—against standard assumptions—made inter-communal coexistence quite plausible.[20] Ultimately, then, it was the violence of exogenous interference—in the form, primarily, of localized and then more general war from 1912—which tore up the political, the societal, and the economic fabric of this *entire* territorial range, converting it, instead, into a series of shatter zones. It was this political vacuum that our two major groupings of modern political animal, one post-imperial, the other national, strove to fill, and in which they attempted to impose new forms of *dirigiste* order. That their efforts perpetuated, even exacerbated, the crisis of the rimlands, says much about the toxicity of their respective projects. But then again, perhaps it says something too about the extraordinary, now almost entirely extinguished human geography of the rimlands themselves.

*

To speak of a commonality in these regions, when what best exemplifies them is a multifaceted ethnographic diversity, would seem to be a contradiction in terms. Yet if we were to gaze upon a quintessential rimland—eastern Galicia, for instance, or for that matter eastern Anatolia before, that is, their near-contemporary parox-ysms—what immediately strikes one is the degree to which their human composi-tion completely and utterly defied the developmental imperatives of the modern state. It is not only, thus, that the populations of these regions were intrinsically poly-ethnic but as if these same populations had an inbuilt aversion to *any* form of pigeonholing. At the outbreak of the First World War, the British writer Arthur Ransome, travelling close to the front line in eastern Galicia, thus observed:

> The peasants working on the land were very unwilling to identify themselves as belong-ing to *any* of the warring nations. Again and again, on asking a peasant to what nation-ality he belonged: Russian, Little-Russian, or Polish, I heard the reply 'Orthodox', and when the men were pressed to say what actual race he belonged I heard him answer safely: 'We are local'.[21]

Ransome's observations were not in isolation. Time and time again, they have been corroborated in other sources, many of which repeat the general verdict well into the interwar period.[22] But then one has to ask what the cause was of this localism and why it often not simply bewildered but seriously irritated outsiders. An answer to the first of these questions might be found in the economic geography of the rimlands. By modern standards, each of these regions was 'backward'; that is, their relationship to metropolitan centres, and thereby to a larger emerging global marketplace, was tenuous or weak.[23] At the turn of the twentieth century, thus, the rimlands were almost in their entirety rural backwaters, with both poor internal and external com-munications; in which peasants (or even nomads) not townspeople were the norm; where the economy was still largely self-sufficient, and hence marginal to transforma-tive state agendas, even where those states were themselves, in Wallersteinian terms, semi-peripheral. This did not mean that there was no change. A *normative* history of these regions might emphasize the arrival of railways, the opening up of cash-crop agriculture, demographic change—and consequent stress—and top-down state plans aimed at integration into 'imperial' or national society. Under communism or nation-statism after the Great War watershed, this would certainly be the envisioned, if to varying degrees enacted, trajectory.

Yet the obverse side of the coin shows people throughout this period repeatedly resisting conformity to any such preordained script. Just a few years after Ransome, Ernst Zechlin, a leading official of General Ludendorff's wartime administration of the Ober Ost, an area still within 'the Lands Between' but to the north of eastern Galicia, embracing much of present Belarus and the Baltic, wrote:

> Objectively determining conditions of nationality comes up against the greatest diffi-culties… It is indeed often difficult to decide whether someone is a 'Lithuanian', or a 'Pole', or 'White Russian', or 'Great Russian'. There are 'Lithuanians' who speak no word of Lithuanian, and vice-versa there are committed 'Poles' in a religious or other tradition, who speak only Lithuanian. Often members of one family count themselves to different nationalities. The low level of education of the population worsens the chaos even further and opens the door to national agitation of every kind.[24]

The administrator's exasperation is almost palpable. But what it equally might sug-gest is that the very elements which gave to each of these regions 'its unique character as a land of syntheses, anachronistic survivals, and local adaptations',[25] and which to lovers of difference and inter-communality might be grounds for celebration, were the self-same elements that confounded all streamlining modernist projects aimed at 'reimagining and reorganising the political space'.[26] Above all, it was in the obduracy of the people themselves as regards fitting into any single, preferably monocultural, categorization as labelled and 'knowable groups'[27] which has led Pierre Bourdieu correctly to note how these realms increasingly became 'perceived, experienced and *criticised* as specifically multi-ethnic' rather than as what they were, namely, 'polyethnic, polyreligious and polylinguistic'.[28]

None of this requires us to suspend our own critical faculties by assuming that pre-1912 life in the rimlands was kind, gentle, or untouched by violence. Scarcity, poverty, and increasing population pressures begat persistent struggles over land, leading often to banditry, localized insurgency, and, in some areas, chronic insecurity and instability.[29] In specific parts of the Balkans, the North Caucasus, or eastern Anatolia, for instance, the endemic nature of this violence had been the case sometimes for decades, if not centuries. Even in 1913, in the Hazakh (present-day Idil) district in eastern Anatolia, Kurdish and Yezidi tribes were still busily resolving their inter-communal disputes with murderous *razzias* against one another— disputes which often pulled in local Syriacs and Armenians of different communal hues—where the destruction of villages and accompanying atrocities were frequent consequences.[30] Equally, however, such power struggles almost always cut across ethnic and religious boundaries, rather than lining up groups behind some national or other political banner. That hardly made tribal warfare nicer than what came thereafter. What it might suggest, however, is that the impact of national or post-imperial conflict in and on the rimlands was not only altogether of a different scope and scale, but had conscious aims which, by seeking the elimination of difference within the 'multi-ethnic' context of the rimlands, could not be anything but ultimately exterminatory.

Of course, this goes against the grain of a conventional wisdom, which argues that much of the rimlands' propensity to violence in contemporary times has come essentially from within, or, alternatively, from some *other* long-lasting residue of extraneous nastiness. The upsurge of a murderous inter-communal conflict in the Balkans in the early 1990s, for instance, had even highly informed individuals such as the late George Kennan expostulating that the cause was a background of 'Turkish domination thrusting into the south-eastern reaches of the European continent a salient of non-European civilisation'. This, in turn, accounted for an 'undue predominance among the Balkan peoples of these particular qualities', by which he presumably meant the preservation of certain 'non-European characteristics'.[31] The equation is a very neat one, not least as Kennan was writing an introduction to a republished version of the Carnegie report on the Balkan Wars of 1912–13, thereby reinforcing a message in exact contradiction to that of Toynbee in 1923. Kennan's conclusions, however, with their implicitly essentialist indictment of the barbaric qualities of benighted peoples, have been of little surprise to Maria Todorova who, more recently still, has conducted a grand survey of the Western literature on the Balkans. Her findings point to a representation in which the Balkan male, in particular, is nearly always 'uncivilised, crude, cruel and, without exception, dishevelled'.[32]

The key question then is, who is right: those of the ilk of Kennan who see the 'Europeanization', 'Westernization', or 'modernization' of the rimlands, most obviously via some nation-state model in the liberal Western image, as the route to the civilizing and quieting of the violent tendencies inherent in these regions; or those like Toynbee or Todorova, albeit approaching the issue from very different perspectives, who see in 'the ultimate Europeanisation of the Balkans',[33] or for that matter, the Caucasus, or the Carpathians, the clue to the violence done in the twentieth century *to* these regions.

What one surely cannot escape is the geographical density within the rimlands of cases of genocide;[34] this combined with the telescoping of the majority of such instances into a quite confined time frame, albeit with a specific recrudescence most particularly in the Balkans and Transcaucasia at the end of the Cold War. Nor can we avoid the fact that when groups were targeted for ethnic cleansing, or even slated for extermination, it was rarely in complete isolation. Certainly, the Jewish case appears at first sight to be the exception—except that even what began with them could, simultaneously or later, engulf Roma, while in specific regions like eastern Galicia and Volhynia, the seismic shift of Jewish destruction seems to have acted as a catalyst for a series of exterminatory conflicts, which have sometimes been described as a 'war of all against all'.[35] If this is true for this zone, it is equally so for our other two zones. In Ustasha-controlled Croatia and Bosnia-Herzegovina in 1941, for instance, Jewish and Roma destruction was paralleled by exterminatory assaults on Serb communities, which, in turn, triggered a series of other 'wars of all against all' throughout the breadth of the dismantled Yugoslav state. A world war earlier, the Ottoman assault on the Armenians also carried with it an effort to extirpate the Nestorians, as well as other Syriac communities. And, even then, this does not end the litany. We can extend it by degrees backwards across the Aegean to the genocidal or near-genocidal assaults by Ottomans and their Christian state adversaries on 'enemy' populations, especially in the Second Balkan War of 1913. And we can do the same forwards to a further 'war of all against all' in eastern Anatolia in the aftermath of the 1915–16 genocide, in which Armenians and other Christian *indigènes* were often as much perpetrators as they were victims of Muslim Turks, Kurds, and others.

Our argument rests on an appreciation of this bigger picture, and, hence, the impact primarily of 'out' onto the 'within' as the way by which explanation for these repeat catastrophes can be found. This is not to suggest that internal factors were lacking. In spite of the observations of Ransome and Zechlin, nationalism in the rimlands clearly did not develop entirely ex nihilo, even where it did evolve by imitation and outside example. If, moreover, one can discern a contempt for the rimlands and their mosaic of peoples from outsiders with designs, or simply a modernistic distaste for what could not be put into neat and tidy order, there were also plenty of native sons, egged on by their own social, communal, or perceived ethnic resentments, who held similarly negative attitudes. Stalin, Hitler, Talât—indeed a whole bevy of Committee of Union and Progress (CUP) men, not to mention

Kemal—were all products, or near-products of the rimlands. So, too, of course, was Raphael Lemkin, a Jewish son of the Białystok region, founder of the study of genocide and himself clearly taken with the idea of nations. Except that, as Dirk Moses has pointed out, 'Growing up in the multinational world of east-central Europe, his [Lemkin's] cultural imagination was irreducibly particular'.[36]

Why was it, then, that between 1912 and 1953 the voices of those who held views like Lemkin's—in other words, not just for ethnic and religious diversity but for the right of all communities to have an untrammelled existence and unfettered future—were not only completely drowned out but so decisively, irrevocably, murderously, trampled on by the likes of the Hitlers, the Stalins, and the Talâts? Our answer may, in part, have something to do with the very personalities involved. Except that, perhaps, it is not quite so easy to say, 'no Stalin: no Gulag', or 'no Talât: no *Aghet*', as it is to repeat the Hitler/Holocaust dictum. In truth, the states which all of these upstarts came to lead were also impelled by *other* forces, whose first source was the turn in the global contest from *c.*1912 but whose geographical pivot, as Mackinder implied, was none other than the European rimlands. That each of these states thereafter made their revisionist bids for power, primarily through quite specific efforts at imprinting their mark on these regions, even where their intended horizon was somewhere else, brings us a little closer to our necessary focus.

However, the contest for the rimlands was not about these would-be contenders alone. If Germany in 1918 attempted to 'balkanize' the east,[37] just as the Great Powers in consort in Berlin had carved out of the Balkans a series of little nation states forty years earlier, the ensuing catastrophe of genocide also had its origins in the efforts by the victorious Western allies to support or endorse further nation building in all three zones. Told, and sold to their publics by the respective national elites of each, as a case of self-willed ethnogenesis, international recognition, and hence normalization of these new or reformulated polities as modern nation states, the development was actually dependent upon, and in turn required, a significant degree of political, fiscal, and economic support from the new post-1919 liberal order. Henceforth, in place of poly-ethnicity, the rimlands would now be home to national 'majorities' and other so-called 'minorities'. And, necessarily, to state-led projects of homogenization. In short, exposure to the potentiality of genocide for rimland peoples would be two-pronged: from a post-imperial revisionism against the international system, or from a nation-statism *supported* by that system and which in practice (if not in principle) offered little or no sanctuary against nationalism's relentless logic.

STRENGTHS AND WEAKNESSES OF THIS APPROACH

That still, of course, begs the question: 'what about the Holocaust?' Surely, by narrowing our geographical scope to a given frame of reference, we are cutting out from consideration the full dimension of this catastrophe. Let me emphasize in response, that on the score of the Holocaust the landscape *is* bigger and broader, in spite of the fact that the rimlands, more particularly 'The Lands Between', played both an inordinately large and uncannily persistent part in the unfolding and making of the European Jewish genocide, or as will be argued here, *genocides*. But to pursue the devil's advocacy, if one is conceding here that our historical–geographical nexus is not the totality of the story, why not also concede that there might be some other more cogent and coherent narrative approach to the whole genocide picture in the first half of the twentieth century? After all, while, to date, we may still lack a broad analysis of the phenomenon *tout ensemble*, no such argument can be used for the specific cases committed by the Nazis, the Bolshevik-cum-Stalinists, or, to a lesser extent the CUP. Why attempt to reinvent the wheel (why indeed expend further energy) when there is already abundant information and analysis available?

In briefly noting some of the standard elements on that wheel, our aim is neither, on the one hand, to restate their arguments ad nauseam—or, for that matter, their key exponents—nor, on the other, to put a spoke in them. Each has a legitimacy and value in its own right, just as do other less favoured approaches which put their focus, for instance, on medical or cultural modes of inquiry. They, too, may not be particularly pertinent to this very politically centred study, but our understanding of the bigger picture would undoubtedly be the less without their insights.[38] The fundamental issue we have set for ourselves, however, *is* the bigger picture of genocide, thus posing the question of the degree to which some of the more powerful explanatory frameworks currently available are adequate or sufficient to the task. To a considerable extent we have already been over this ground in *The Meaning of Genocide*. In revisiting Nazism, totalitarianism, modernity—the latter as it merges into analysis of nationalism—our question is simple: to what extent can each offer an explanation for the broad incidence of rimlands genocide, 1912–53?

Nazism is so familiar it hardly needs spelling out. Descriptive, in the first instance, of an extraordinary German 'regime change' around the movement and political party led by Adolf Hitler, and hence hardly conceivable except as 'Hitlerism', its key problem for our purposes is that it can only tell us everything about genocide in this period if we block from view the incidences, synchronous or not, which were *not* committed by the Nazis. Of course, we could extend Nazism's primacy as begetter of genocide, with its overt racist ideology and practice, ultranationalism, and cult of violence, by reference to other European regimes which chose to emulate it. The Szálasi regime in Hungary in autumn 1944; the Iron Guard at least in joint power in Rumania from late 1940 through to the very beginning of 1941; above all, the Ustasha puppet regime in Croatia, from spring 1941 to spring 1945: all might superficially fall into this category. There is only one small problem. While all three countries were involved in genocide against Jews and others in the course of the Second World War, only in the Ustasha case was the main thrust of these actions committed by notably Nazi acolytes. Even then the record suggests that they were scarcely obedient ones, constantly exasperating Berlin by the unruliness of their behaviour.[39] As for the Iron Guard, for all their extraordinary violence and visceral hatred of Jews, they were not perpetrators of the mass exterminations committed by Rumanian military and police in late 1941 because, as a political force, their leadership had already itself been eliminated by the Antonescu regime. At the other end of the Second World War, the Szálasi regime was responsible for killing large numbers of Hungarian Jews in the autumn and winter of 1944. However, this was only *after* the main thrust of Hungarian Jewish deportations to Auschwitz had already been organized and undertaken by Budapest administrators in association with German 'Final Solution' counterparts, technically under the aegis of the extreme authoritarian but *not* Nazi regime of Admiral Horthy.

One might, of course, argue that these discrepancies are minor points of pedantry. Certainly, all three countries were imbued with either radically fascistic if not Nazi ideas, regardless of the exact nature of changing administrations. But then this reference to wider ideological inclinations can only compound our conundrum here. Outside of Hitler's Germany, the military and diplomatic *apparat* of the one genuinely long-standing and authentic European fascist regime to which other aspirants might have looked, namely Mussolini's Italy, while indubitably responsible for major colonial bloodbaths in north and north-east Africa in the course of the 1930s, in its own European adventures between 1939 and 1943 moved by degrees towards *protecting* Jews, Roma, Serbs, and sometimes, though not always, other peoples under its control.[40] Conversely, other satellite regimes which showed some propensity to cooperate with at least elements of the 'Final Solution': Pétainist France, Tisoist Slovakia, and again, for all its supposed Nazi-style credentials, Pavelić's Croatia—seem to have been as strongly motivated in this direction by a political Catholicism in the most reactionary sense of the term, and, thus, by an ideological tendency which entirely preceded, where it was not in direct conflict with, Nazism.

None of this diminishes in any sense the significance of the fact that the main driver of European Jewish destruction was Nazism and that this had its own particular anti-Semitic animus variously described, in terms of its racism or of its redemptive or simply eliminationist ingredients.[41] Yet the fact that extermination itself was largely played out not in the German heartlands but rather in the 'Lands Between' to the east, involving often self-willed non-German actors, already suggests a matrix of complicities over and beyond the Hitlerite. Add to this the ambiguous failure of European 'bystander' neutral states, Allied belligerents, or, for that matter, the Vatican, to put any serious brake (at least until very late in the process) on this most complete and successful act of a collective group extermination in history, and it begins to look less like the responsibility of Nazism *alone* and more like a genuinely pan-European project.

This, at least, might suggest grounds for some wider theory of genocide, if only as it pertains to the European region and its hinterlands, and particularly if we were to take into account all other instances of non-Jewish genocide. Paradoxically, the nearest we have traditionally tended to get to such a broader theorization actually only embraces two of our genocide states, Nazi Germany and communist, more specifically Stalinist, Russia. But again, given the scope and scale of the latter's actions against various real or imagined communities on a par with or even exceeding those of the Nazis—the high degree of synchronicity; plus notable similarities in the exterminatory roles of their 'inner state' specialist forces, the NKVD and SS respectively—is not the case for the 'totalitarian state' as prime focus for genocide—regardless of Stalinism and Nazism's radically divergent ideologies—a perfectly valid one?

Hannah Arendt's pioneering work on totalitarianism from the 1950s did not set out to explain genocide as such and, moreover, became notably unfashionable as the Cold War waned.[42] However, her approach has become increasingly pertinent to contemporary genocide scholars, through two sets of discourses. The first relates to her view of totalitarianism emerging out of *broader* European state politics associated particularly with the fin-de-siècle urge to imperialism and the extreme violence which went with it. Interestingly, while Arendt did not single out Wilhelmine Germany or late Romanov Russia as prime culprits in this aspect of her approach—not least given that her subject matter was largely Africa, where tsarist imperialism played no part—recent genocide scholarship in this vein has tended to focus on the links between pre-1914 German practice in Africa and Nazi *Ostforschung* agendas in the Ukraine, Poland, and elsewhere; or again, in the case of Russian specialists, the continuities rather than caesura between tsarist colonialism, particularly in the Caucasus, as well as in the western rimlands up to and beyond the First World War, and subsequent Stalinist exterminatory trajectories.[43]

The second discourse revolves around another post-Cold War re-evaluation of the totalitarian thesis, most particularly in countries such as France, where the intellectual force of doctrinaire leftist Marxism strongly diluted tendencies towards acknowledging either the scale of communist mass murder, or the possibility that these might be comparable with an ultra-rightist Nazism. What Arendt forcefully proposed and others more recently have pursued is the degree to which both these regimes were not only founded on untrammelled violence, but the way they justified it as being in order to strive for utopian goals. As Alain Besançon has put it, what ties these two regimes 'most closely together is that they ascribed to themselves the right, and even the duty, to kill, and that both did it using methods that resembled each other, and on a scale unknown before in history'.[44] 'The essence of totalitarianism', confirms Pierre Hassner,

> lies in the complete rejection of all barriers and all restraints that politics, civilisation, morality, religion, natural feelings and compassion, and universal ideas of fraternity have constructed in order to moderate, repress, or sublimate the human potential for individual and collective violence.[45]

To significantly follow this route would not be so much to find linkage with previous tsarist or Wilhelmine regimes or indeed anything in a recent European past. On the contrary, as Krzysztof Pomian has put it, reinforcing Hassner's drift, totalitarian states operate by repudiating 'all legal, customary, religious or moral controls from the past', abolishing in the process any distinction between public and private spheres, in order 'to submit the totality of personal, family and collective life to the surveillance of their administrative political and police organs'.[46]

The most immediate value in these two sets of discourses for our rimlands-focused study is the recognition, firstly, that the USSR, like Nazi Germany is a, if not the, major European perpetrator of mass murder in our time frame and, secondly, that the relationships between the pre-1918 Russian and German empires, and what took their places, is essential to charting any broader genocidal trajectory. That would still leave open the fraught debate as to whether Bolshevism or Stalinism involved *exterminatory* assaults on specific communal or ethnic groupings (the subject of Soviet 'genocide' being a major facet of this study's discussions), while it also crucially leaves in abeyance why the primary (though not exclusive) arena of this type of killing was either in the rimlands, or was done to rimland peoples. Just as, one might add, was the case where other state regimes not generally labelled as 'totalitarian' were the perpetrators. As Benjamin Lieberman has put it, 'While control over a powerful government provides a means for ethnic cleansing'—he could equally mean genocide—'it does not provide a motive'. Nor, as he also astutely notes, do the enormity of Stalinist or Nazi killings provide a template for other more 'typical examples'.[47]

Granted, the manner in which both Nazi and Stalinist regimes 'set out to transform and overcome history',[48] and thus, taken together, most particularly through their direct rivalry and entanglement, shaped twentieth-century, certainly twentieth-century European history, could be read as proof of their exceptionality. But could it be that while the persistence, scope, and scale of the mass murders they perpetrated is indisputable, their causation is not so much at variance with a broader landscape of genocidal killing, but rather evidence that these regimes were the most far-reaching, most radicalized, and extreme examples of a more *general* pattern? Both Nazism and Bolshevik communism were, of course, more clear-cut, ultra-ideologicized entities than anything comparable in the 1912–53 European frame; the very specific and closely proximate bastard offspring, if one likes, of the First World War and all its woes. And, as Omer Bartov has iterated, it was these two things, modern war and totalitarianism, which led to humanity being perceived 'as a mass of matter to be moulded, controlled, moved, purged, and annihilated'.[49] But Bartov himself has equally posited that 'the project of remaking humanity and defining identity', with all its destructive urges, 'has been at the *core* of this [twentieth] century'.[50] In which case totalitarianism per se, even if we were to accept in toto the nightmare portrayal of it as offered by Arendt and others with regard to Stalin's Russia or Hitler's Germany, is insufficient to our task.

For instance, if moulding and remaking the identities of human beings into something other than what they previously were is the issue, then we could find multitudinous examples *across* our rimlands' arena. A single example will suffice. In autumn 1916, immediately *after* the great year-long wave of killings of Armenians in Anatolia by the CUP—a regime, incidentally, generally considered of a 'hard' authoritarian, but not totalitarian, type—the CUP began forcibly deporting large numbers of Kurdish tribes from Diyarbekir province, further west to central Anatolia. The aim was to 'remake' them not only from nomads into settled agriculturalists but from Kurds into Turks. As one perspicacious, on-the-spot German observer noted at the time, what the Young Turks were trying to do was create a unitary homogeneous nation state on the *European model*, forcing all the Christian 'nations' within the empire to become both Muslims and Turks or be killed, and all the non-Turkish Muslim ones—Kurds, Persians, Arabs, and others—to similarly Turkify, if not voluntarily, then by coercion.[51]

Zygmunt Bauman, picking up on categories created by the anthropologist Claude Lévi-Strauss, would describe this modern societal route to dealing with alterity as *anthropophagic*: namely, 'annihilating the strangers by *devouring* them and then metabolically transforming them into a tissue indistinguishable from one's own'.[52] How it was that Muslim Kurds could come to be 'strangers' at all, when they had always been an *integral* part of a poly-ethnic Ottoman society is disturbing enough in itself. But putting these specifics aside, Bauman's point is of a generalizing kind. The modern drive to assimilation, that is, 'making the different similar; smothering of cultural and linguistic distinctions; forbidding all traditions and loyalties except those meant to feed the conformity of the new and all-embracing order; promoting and enforcing one and only one measure of conformity'[53]—suggests not something aberrant, but rather something essentially normative to the modern world.

Even so, Bauman's proposition still sounds like it has an inbuilt tension: as if what he is actually describing *is* the exceptionalism of the Nazi or Soviet model rather than a condition which would explain at least the possibility of particular forms of violence directed by a variety of *different* states in an Eastern European and Near Eastern range; not necessarily against each and every unassimilated ethnic or communal body in their midst (at least not necessarily to the same degree) but certainly, in some cases, in very particular instances, with a lethal, concentrated, exterminatory force. The Soviet Union's ultra-modernist but, more importantly, inherently anti-nationalist credentials would seem to preclude the possibility of bridging this dichotomy by means of a nationalist explanation. Unless, of course, one takes the drives to Soviet homogenization *tout court* as essentially statist-driven, regardless of whether they were formulated in overtly nationalizing categories or not. The alternative proposition would be to concede that the sociological reordering of society that the Soviet Union propounded was not nearly as colour-blind as it claimed to be but impelled (certainly not all at once but through a process) by its own underlying *ethnic* conception, however convoluted, of what constituted the ideal *Homo sovieticus*.

Picking up on aspects of recent scholarship, Eric Weitz has notably, if controversially, integrated Lenin and Stalins' Russia into a broader comparative study of genocide in which he has argued that the key driving force towards socially engineered (and totalitarian) utopias has been none other than the categories of race and nation.[54] Weitz's study is quite unusual in attempting to forge a Soviet/non-Soviet linkage. That said, the national bug is there too, in other recent works—notably that of Michael Mann. A key focus in Mann's study is nationalizing Eastern European polities, in which to greater or lesser degrees the competing, or sometimes complementary, behaviour of state elites and demotic grass-roots elements amplifies ethnic hatreds against non-majoritarian peoples.[55] The key question for this work, however, is not whether these various studies are, or are not, full of insight: they are; but the degree to which the 'isms' they consider, or alternatively the internal, domestic structures of different social and political formations they describe, can get us to the heart not of what these states *are* but what, in exceptional conditions, they *do*. It was a basic premise of the *Genocide in the Age of the Nation State* volumes that our phenomenon is a product of acute societal and more obviously state crisis, which may itself reflect, on the one hand, the cultural mores and phobic, psychological projections onto particular communal groups of their dominant, hegemonic counterparts; on the other, an emergent if highly dysfunctional international *system* of nation states, whose origins lay in the rise of the West. Striving for cultural homogenization, contra a habitus of human diversity, with all its potential for structural violence, is indicative in itself of something seriously, systemically, wrong. Yet this condition was firmly rooted in not an Eastern but a Western conception of the body politic. In this sense, as we argued in *The Rise of the West*, the distinction between some benign Anglo-Saxon or French civic model of the nation state and a more overtly ethnicized German or Eastern European version, can be seriously overstated.

Yet, in the period 1912–53 it was clearly not Western states who were the primary proponents of a coercive, assimilative reordering of society. They had, by various methods, *already* done it. Nor were they the primary protagonists of what Bauman describes as a further *anthropoemic* strategy through which society deals with the perceived outsider by '*vomiting* the strangers, banishing them from the limits of the orderly world and barring them from all communication from those inside'.[56] That said, one would have to add the caveat that there were, into this period, Western variations on the theme, as particularly practised with regard to the residues of already often catastrophically genocided indigenous peoples, in 'off-the-map', out-of-way places, at the margins of the new Neo-European 'civilizations'.[57] For our rimlands, however, this second homogenizing strategy had become so commonplace, for the best part of a generation, as to be treated as practically normative.

Of course, it was not continuous but was rather enacted at moments of unusual crisis or opportunity. Even so it begs the question of the degree to which this ' "cleansing"—expelling the strangers beyond the frontier of the managed and manageable territory'[58]—was itself 'genocide'. To a considerable extent, we will be proposing in this study that it almost always *was* genocide—forced removal by its very nature, usually under conditions of already intense and extreme conflict, precipitating repeated atrocity and massacre, arbitrary or otherwise, where it was not a way-station to a quite conscious and willed process of people-liquidation. This would certainly chime in with another of our contentions about the nature of genocide, namely, that far from being an absolute category it has to be seen on a spectrum of possibilities. Whether such complete physical destruction lies on this spectrum in between assimilating and vomiting the 'outsider', or rather at some extreme end, perhaps is a moot point. As is the degree to which genocide requires some premeditated, intentional policy to deserve that name, as opposed to the possibility that it might also sometimes, even commonly, arise by default, or a series of defaults, in response to a shifting set of contingent circumstances.

Part of the problem with theories of genocide is that the issue of the 'other' is usually conceived in cool abstraction; that is, if we may return to our earlier vulcanological metaphor, in a solidified state, often empathetically divorced from the sequence of hot, viscous, pyro-elasticity, or to put it more prosaically, a highly unstable situation, in which a latent dynamic of violence—a genocidal process—is converted into the actuality of *genocide* itself.[59] The latency similarly covers up one other critical problem: why it is that some ethnic or communal groups *end up* being assimilated, others vomited, and others annihilated. Explaining a group's fate purely through an ideological prism—totalitarian, modern, national—could still leave us grasping at why. Why during and after the conquests of the Balkan Wars, for instance, dominant Serbian political elites remained wedded to the notion that Macedonian Muslims were potentially assimilable while Muslim (or Christian) Albanians were 'logical candidates for deportation or murder'.[60] Or why, for that matter, turning it on its head, some Croats looked on Serbs in a similar vein to that in which some of their Serb counterparts looked on them.

The explanation might, superficially, seem to lie with the degree of 'threat' that a group presented, or at least seemed to present, to the body politic. Keeping one's head down, or being passed over for another target, might tell us why demographically small rimland groups such as Vlachs, Laz, or Kashubians, in communal terms at least, avoided extermination—though this would hardly seem to work for the Lemko of the Polish–Ukrainian borderland, who, despite offering no threat whatsoever, were, in 1947, the victims of an exterminatory-style ethnic cleansing by a communist-led Poland. Does luck thus come into the equation: being in the wrong place at the wrong time or, perhaps more pungently put, changed, even contingent, geopolitical circumstances? That might give us our answer for why Volksdeutsche, by turn potentially powerful or extremely vulnerable, across a swathe of our geographical range throughout our period, suffered the most murderous ethnic cleansing at the end of the Second World War. By the same token, it might just tell us something of why Armenians represented part of a geopolitical equation in 1915. That said, how one might quantify in this regard would be altogether more problematic, to say nothing of why, unlike the Volksdeutsche, the Armenians were given the collective coup de grâce.

But if the inference is that we are already close to the edge of a 'realist' radar screen, would not the Nazi drive to exterminate the Jews take us completely off it? And even more so for the Roma, a ubiquitous but non-national people, whether travelling or sedentary, whose 'atemporal value-pattern',[61] or in other words whose relationship to the world around them, put them so at odds with the European norm (with which, incidentally, the vast majority of Jews, as historical self-identifiers par excellence, would have felt perfectly at home), that any attempt at a politically grounded explanation for the Nazi assault upon them would be nonsensical. Looking at this picture as a whole, are we left, at best, with what Mann has spoken of as a 'patterned mess',[62] or worse, a whole jumble of 'facts and ideas that cannot be crammed in pre-existing schemata'?[63] The simple answer to this is affirmative. There is no *straightforward*, neat and tidy, monocausal explanation for either specific cases of genocide or the overall picture. At least, not one founded on some purely 'scientific' examination of the phenomenon's aetiology. Germany's 'vomiting out' or destruction of its own Jews, to say nothing of those of the rest of the continent, removed a particularly able and dynamic section of the European population, which, in the context of a second great global war, it could ill-afford not to have on side, however paradoxically that may read. By the same token, a Soviet Union that entered into that same conflict without its 'kulaks', without its leading military and political cadres, without large swathes of the many other communities it had pulverized and decimated, was immeasurably the poorer and weaker.

For this writer, what all this points to, however, is not that there is absolutely no causative rhyme or reason to these killings, only that it is a *complex* one. If we are prepared to engage with that complexity—and, not least, with the inherent contradiction between rational, planned acts of systematic people-destruction and 'mad' precipitative lashings out by a society overwhelmed by its own sense of fear and insecurity—both of which operate regularly in tandem in cases of genocide—then we may, in turn, also be able to discern the larger patterns involved. If the Nazi extermination of European Jews involved a centripetal pulling *in* of peoples from as far away to the west as Norway, or the Channel Islands, to its designated killing fields in the rimlands, there was also, immediately before, and immediately thereafter, a centrifugal pushing *out* by the Soviets of large swathes of rimland peoples, even further to the east, to Kazakhstan and beyond. This hardly makes the two sequences 'symmetric'—there was no equivalent of Treblinka in Kazakhstan— any more than it explains, in itself, why Russian Central Asia, part of our highly unstable nineteenth-century fault line, continued in its own right to be a site of potential genocide well into the twentieth century.

None of these developments could have been 'scientifically' predicted. On the other hand, just as with hindsight we can discern how an actual volcanic eruption is contingent on latent geophysical or other environmental factors and conditions coming together in a particular concatenation to produce a chain reaction, so in human terms particular matrices of time, space, and agency can also be seen to produce their own fissile outcomes. Mackinder, in the early 1900s, could not have known the role railway lines were to play across the Eurasian land mass in shipping cargoes of unwanted human 'cattle' backwards and forwards to their literal termini, but had already foreseen the centrality of railways in linking the Russian 'pivot area' with Germany via the rimlands.[64] In the final phase of our genocide sequence, not only were swathes of rimland peoples being expelled east by the Soviets, but a Volksdeutsche community amounting to millions was eructed west, again largely by cattle truck, by other rimland peoples themselves. Destinations, as outcomes, were different—the monstrous centrality of Auschwitz, quite literally as epicentre of this traffic flow, not in dispute. Perhaps all this sounds rather reminiscent of Tolstoy's verdict on the Napoleonic Wars as a great mass of people locked into movement 'from west to east and from east to west'.[65] But equally could one not see in this rimlands-centred landscape an entire continent and its hinterlands working through a set of competing states, a series of dystopian developmental trajectories, sometimes by design, more often by fortune or consequent disaster, to a point of societal 'completion' where the 'need' for genocide, at least for the time being, had been exhausted?

This is not to presume that it was *only* here in the European rimlands that geno-cide was enacted in this period. The crisis of a globalized imperialism, prevalent at the fin de siècle, may have been largely in abeyance for the short durée through to the post-1945 era of decolonization. But it had its continuing resonances in our period, not least in the great Japanese surge into east and south-east Asia and beyond, from Manchurian beginnings in 1931: a series of extraordinarily brutal assaults, whose accompanying atrocities necessarily invite consideration as to whether the term, for at least some of them, is genocide.[66] Elsewhere, a cluster of overtly racist massacres in the Caribbean and Central America, one in Cuba in 1912, a second in El Salvador in 1932, a final one in the border regions of the Dominican republic with Haiti in 1937, all further have in common the role of the military, acting in support of state plantocracies in the extirpation of real or per-ceived threats from poor, marginalized, black, indigenous, or 'outsider' communi-ties, plus the fact that the systematic scope and scale of the killings have, in various studies, been described as genocidal.[67] Some of these events will need to be revis-ited in the context of the more global landscape under examination in a further study.

Nor do they exhaust the litany of suspects—and victims. As we have implied, closer to Europe late Italian imperialism involved one rather clear-cut case of exter-minatory practice, in 1930–31, in Mussolini's attempt to quash Sanusi resistance in Cyrenaica—not to mention a spasm of mass atrocities in 1935–6 as he sought to conquer and then subdue Abyssinia.[68] Fascist Italy, of course, also collaborated with Nazi Germany to back Franco's military insurrection against Republican Spain, thus turning a large part of this far western peninsula of Europe between 1936 and 1939 into an arena of quite extraordinary violence and atrocity. If the executions and massacres, even where against specific national communities, nota-bly the Basques and Catalans, are rarely considered as genocide,[69] the human con-sequences necessarily impinge upon and intersect with the catastrophes further east. Tens of thousands of Spanish ex-Republican soldiers and refugees, for instance, ended up in French holding camps after Franco's victory, before many then per-ished alongside Jews and others in Mauthausen, Buchenwald, Dachau, and other Nazi concentration camps.[70]

The fact that Spaniards from another war ended up in Nazi camps, just as some Jews fleeing Europe ended up in Chinese cities such as Harbin and Shanghai under Japanese rule, may suggest how inappropriate it is to set geographical parameters to a study such as this, let alone some metanarrative-style frame of reference, when we have already gone to some length to propose that ideological prisms, even that of Nazism, cannot in themselves provide comprehensive explanation for the broader occurrence of genocide. The European and near-European genocides in our time frame clearly were not all the same in terms of scope, scale, or immediate causation. But we propose that a connecting pattern is, nevertheless, chartable. It may lack succinct shorthand. It certainly has to operate on the basis of an overall picture of the phenomenon's occurrence, which is larger, broader, and denser than that found in many more traditional interpretations. Whether the resulting inter-pretation is itself convincing can only be for the reader to judge.

SETTING OUR *OWN* AGENDA

The period 1912–53 involves intersections of political history and human geography, a key *by-product* of which was a series of genocides, enacted primarily, though not exclusively, in the European rimlands. One needs to emphasize the usage here of by-product. Far from being singular, these genocides were the outcomes of a systemic crisis—other, more widely spread, symptoms of which included one particular case of global epidemiological near-collapse; regional famines; mass social, economic, as well as literal physical dislocation across several continents; and radical regime changes, in part through revolution; but, above all, repeated recourse by the leading and more minor powers to war, initially centred on Europe but otherwise global in its dimensions and impact. Indeed, war is so obviously the driving force of the crisis of genocide and, at the same time, so closely associated with the majority of its incidents, that it would seem logical to treat the latter as a subset of the former.

In *The Meaning of Genocide*, we proposed that genocide *is* a form of warfare. However, we also went on to argue that it did not fit neatly into the categories of war we described as Types One to Three (each of which, in the period 1912–53, reached its own heights of paroxysm), not least because the targeting for extermination of largely or wholly passive, non-state communities would seem to defy rational calculus. Thus, the aerial bombardments of, notably, Hamburg, Dresden, Tokyo, Nagasaki, and Hiroshima may have been misconceived, even perverse, elements in Allied strategies for winning the Second World War, but they could at least be described as based on rational, realist assumptions about 'the enemy' *society* and its military threat.[71] By contrast, Auschwitz represents the culmination of thought processes that seem to confer collective resources and attributes on a dispersed if ubiquitous community, and which have no relationship to reality. In a nutshell, this is why 'the Holocaust' appears not simply as the most overwhelming but the most perplexing example of people-extermination. And hence one, if it needs repeating, which would appear to be most symptomatic of a perpetrator projective mindset gone completely mad.

Even so, as Donald Bloxham proposes, 'Understanding perpetrator and perpetration is *the* essential element to understanding genocide. Other "lessons" are ancillary'.[72] In other words, even actions/decisions that seem to the outside lay observer to be demented or deranged nevertheless require of the genocide scholar the ability to empathize with the perpetrator's own perception that what he or she is doing is based on a perfectly conscious, rational, and, indeed, justifiable defence of his/her state or society. If the Holocaust were entirely sui generis we might have grounds for dispensing with these ground rules. Instead, because there is so much genocide in our relatively short time frame—and most of that in a relatively confined geographical arena—we have no choice but to probe further the geopolitical, as well more domestically political and socio-economic, conditions and context within which a panoply of separate state actors chose to respond, amongst other actions, in this way.

The obvious starting point for this exploration would be with the great caesura: the abyss which was the First World War—as it itself emerged out of the uncontainable Balkan catastrophe of the previous two years. Sarajevo 1914 to Berlin 1945 would thus provide not only the template for at least the European dimensions of global war, but at least the approximate dimensions upon which genocide might appear as a form of codicil to the main text. Moments of particular significance would follow from this lead. The date of 9 November 1918, for instance, was not only the date upon which the German pursuit of Great War victory was effectively terminated through the threat of revolution at home, but one which Nazis would look back upon as the seminal moment of betrayal, above all, *Jewish* betrayal, which 'never again' would be allowed to happen.[73] Yet there is a conundrum here. Golo Mann attests that German anti-Semitic passions were much more intense and violent in the months and years immediately after this Wilhelmine collapse than in either 1930–33, as the Nazis fought for and achieved power, or even 1933–1945, when their anti-Semitism metamorphosed from idea into exterminatory practice.[74] In other words, if Golo Mann is correct, we might expect a full-scale German genocide to have taken place much earlier than it did. Or, to put it another way, while its subsequent enactment may equally suggest that only under the cover of a new global conflict was extermination on the grand scale operable, the tortuous trajectory by which Nazi Germany arrived there may not be founded simply on following the broader contours of the two world wars but might actually imply that genocide has *autonomous* causative factors of its own.

There is, moreover, an alternative approach by which we might understand its accelerating potential *after* 1918, though paradoxically—even counter-intuitively—this might begin less by emphasizing the caesura of 1912–14, and more the elements of *continuity* with the imperial hegemonies of our 'core' geographical arena which pre-dated these catastrophes. This would neither be to dispute the collapse of all three, indeed four—Ottoman, Romanov, Wilhelmine, and Habsburg—imperial powers, a critical consequence of which was the potential fragmentation—the shatter-zone effect—on the rimlands; nor to disavow that the new political actors who most forcefully—and successfully—sought to fill that vacuum were all, in key respects, radically different from their predecessors.

Neither Nazi Germany, nor Bolshevik-cum-Stalinist Russia, nor CUP or Kemalist Turkey, claimed to be a political entity in a historic 'world-empire' sense. Indeed, the credentials of each were founded on an implicit, if not overt, overturning of ancien régime conventions—politically, culturally, and socially. In the case of Bolshevik Russia, the revolutionary implications went much further still. The new regime uniquely sought to create not only a genuinely egalitarian *economic* system against the dominant norms, as well as the obvious hegemony of capitalism, but defiantly in opposition to nationalism as the founding, or justifying, principle for the existence of what, from 1924, was the Union of Soviet Socialist Republics (USSR). However, for all its ideological distinctiveness and consciously transformative agenda, the strangest thing about Soviet Russia, once the dust had settled, was the degree to which it sought to ensure its ongoing grip on all the territorial domains of *imperial* Russia, and its markedly similar geostrategic goals and anxieties. At first sight that might make the contrast with Kemalist—though not CUP—Turkey rather marked, given that the former could not possibly stake a serious claim to the territories of the Ottoman Empire irrevocably lost to it by late 1918. Even so, the Kemalists claimed to be the authentic purveyors of that part of the Ottoman entity which really mattered: its Turkishness, and, along with that, its genuinely core *Turkic* domains. As for the Hitlerite revolution, the Nazis effectively claimed the territorial inheritance of not one but two Germanies: the Germany of the Prussian, state-created Wilhelmine Reich, which had been radically shorn at Versailles of much of its own eastern rimland, and, arguably more potently still, that of Habsburg Austria, which, through the dual monarchy of Austria–Hungary, had provided the primary *German* glacis to the east.

We might at this point go off at some critical tangents about the cunning vagaries of history. The way for instance that what, for German nationalists, had been left incomplete in 1866–7, through the Austrian *Ausgleich*, was only bridged through its Anschluss and hence absorption into a *single* Germany in 1938, at the behest of (from an earlier perspective) the wholly unlikely figure of Adolf Hitler. Equally, though the USSR never publicly described itself as heir to the notion of Moscow as the Third Rome (harping back to some medieval fantasy of a unique imperial mission to the world) the sense that through itself the moment of some *Russian* sacred destiny had arrived was never far below the surface. The tendency was particularly palpable during the Second World War.[75] Indeed, with the Nazis wallowing in the glories of the Holy Roman Empire, or the Kemalists conjuring up a past—replete in their educational curricula—with none other than the Turks as the mythic purveyors of *all* civilization,[76] the sense that all of these revolutionary regimes continued to be obsessed—and entrapped—as had their reactionary predecessors, in their 'weak–strong' state straitjacket, that is, in the context of a *Western*-dominated international system, is all too evident. Only a different book could do justice to this entire subject and, as already stated in *The Meaning of Genocide*, being a 'weak–strong' state, just as being an 'old–new' state, while usually significant in the making of a genocidal mentality, would be entirely insufficient to explain genocide itself.[77]

Yet equally insufficient would be an explanation which emphasized the ideological newness of Nazi racialism, the Soviet striving for a universal, classless society, or a CUP-cum-Kemalist dream of a national community inhabited only by Turks, to the exclusion of the wider and deeper geopolitical realities which produced these regimes in the first place.[78] Their lethality lies not in their revolutionary, ideological credos, or, alternatively, in their retreading of older state-bound, geopolitical imperatives, but rather in a particular combination and configuration of *both*. Indeed, what is most striking about these regimes, insofar as this study is concerned, is the degree to which each, while following notably different routes to the achievement of its goals, sought to radically reformulate the basic nature of their pre-1914 domestic social organisms in order to meet international system realities which they—like, in more muted form, their predecessors—had felt themselves to be fundamentally hostile to and pushing against.

Two critical factors are important to note here. Firstly, prior to the 1912–22 watershed, the intolerable nature, real or simply perceived, of the power discrepancy between the 'old' system in which the world empires still played a role, and the emerging Western-dominated *international* political economy, had been masked by a set of increasingly fragile bilateral or multilateral 'Great Power' arrangements, which prevented a direct military confrontation. When this finally, irretrievably broke down post-Sarajevo, the fact that one of the old empires, Russia, was on the side of the Western Allies continued, initially, to belie what was actually crystalliz-ing through the development and final outcome of the war. With the breakdown and collapse of all four imperial entities, in the final year of its paroxysm, however, the key question thus posed was not simply what sort of domestic regimes—that is, covering all or part of the imperial domains—would replace them. Rather, it was to what degree these regimes would be able to integrate into the now victori-ous, ostensibly affirmed, Western-led international order; or whether they would instead seek to repudiate this order either through autarkic, political–economic isolation, direct military confrontation, or both.

That each of the post-1914 imperial successor regimes that we associate with genocide was also intensely politically revisionist in the face of the new system can-not thus be somehow divorced from the fact and act of genocide. Nor, and this is our second point, can one but note the brevity of the 'liberal' phases in each of the post-imperial states: in other words, domestic attempts at alignment to the norms and values of the dominant West. Indeed, this brevity can only confirm the under-lying bedrock of a historic imperial counterpoint to the West. Henceforth, the counterpoint would be more coherently reformulated and overtly ideologized by succeeding Kemalist, Stalinist, and Hitlerite regimes, each intent on overturning the 1918 verdict. Only under the extreme exigencies of the Balkan War crisis, in the winter of 1912–13, again in the wake of Great Power defeat, was Itilaf—the 'liberal' but essentially weak Ottoman grouping opposed to both the CUP and Kemal—in power and, in the latter case, entirely dependent on close Allied super-vision and military support, as it faced up to the ultimately more powerful Kemal-ist challenge. Russia's liberal phase lasted a matter of months, from the first revolution in early 1917 to its overturning by the Bolsheviks at its end. Weimar Germany enjoyed the most successful of the efforts at liberal reorientation, though this too was not enduring. When it came crashing down in 1933, its defeat was absolute. Not until the Western Allies, in consort, paradoxically, with Stalinist Russia, had completely pulverized and then occupied the Nazi state by direct mili-tary means was a further attempt at liberalizing the country conceivable again, in the first instance under Allied supervision, and then only in that part of Germany under Western occupation.

In the interim, it is no coincidence that the Nazi bid not only to challenge the entirety of the Western international system but to take on militarily its most pow-erful, Soviet rival marks also the key point of no return for its Jewish policy. War geared towards imperial expansion or, failing that, covert occupation without direct military confrontation, represented the most direct and obvious route by which the imperial successor states drove down the road towards both repudiation of and potential confrontation with the West *and* genocide. It happened in 1915–16 as the transitional CUP regime strove not only to claw back former Ottoman power but launch its own *Drang nach Osten* into the Caucasus. The Armenians were the project's first collective casualty. And, as the Red Army took Soviet power back into and beyond former Romanov domains in 1940–41, and again from 1944, Polish, Ukrainian, Baltic, and other rimland peoples paid a similar penalty.

However, the geopolitical linkage between a revisionist-orientated expansionism, including resort to war and the potentiality or actuality of genocide, does not represent the totality of routes by which 'system' defiance can result in exterminatory consequences. A litany of mass killings in the USSR, as 'Socialism in One Country' took root, bear witness to the possibility of genocide as a result of imperial successor states' efforts to remould, refashion, and 'sculpt' the body politic in 'peacetime' circumstances too.[79] Whether peace is an appropriate term to describe Russia in this phase of its most tumultuous and devastating *internal* upheaval is debatable. Under each of these genocide-linked regimes, nevertheless, a pre-1939 social engineering, with exterminatory implications or acts, was pursued as part of conscious efforts to make society and state 'stronger'—however misplaced the reasoning—and thus better equipped for confrontation with the regime's external enemies.

Turkey, it is true, represents a complication of the pattern. Having both militarily defied the terms of the 1920 Allies-dictated peace and violently eructed or extirpated most of its indigenous Greek as well as what remained of its Armenian populations (in the wake of the aborted, Allied-sponsored Greek state invasion of Anatolia) Kemal not only came to terms with the West but began reorganizing the post-Ottoman state on lines entirely compatible with Wilsonian terms of reference. Operating in consonance with the Polish dictator Piłsudski's dictum 'It is the state that makes the nation, not the nation that makes the state',[80] Kemal and his successors proceeded to re-inaugurate the CUP's programme of Turkification across the entirety of the country. In practice, especially in eastern Anatolia, this amounted not simply to internal colonialism and colonization but to repeated punitive campaigns against recalcitrant Kurdish communities, culminating, in 1938, in the Dersim genocide.

Kemal's methods must therefore give us pause to consider whether it was only post-imperial revisionists *opposed* to the West who committed genocide. Certainly, as the later Atatürk, Kemal was lionized by Western politicians and other opinion formers for his modernizing and Westernizing programme—the success of this public relations exercise usually extending to either justifying or, more usually, airbrushing out of existence altogether, any of the atrocities which linked his aims or methods back to the CUP. Closer to the knuckle, however, is the degree to which what he set out to do represented a harder, more forcefully authoritarian version of what was not simply, in Bauman's terms, a general principle of modernity, but something that the Western Allies actively sought to endorse and encourage in the context of the post-1918 'New Europe' and its hinterlands.

By implication, this is a very serious charge. It is one which would suggest that the Allies themselves—in contradistinction to their own liberal value system—were, if not intent on, then at the least complicit in the extermination of communities who, for whatever reason, were considered beyond the redemptive embrace of the new or enlarged nation states to which they had given their imprimatur at Versailles. The counter-evidence from the Paris Peace Conference, in the form of the Allied-initiated Minorities Treaties, might imply otherwise: that far from seeking annihilatory solutions, the Allies actually sought to provide safeguards for the estimated one in four people—some 25 to 30 million souls—who now fell into the 'minority' category in the new states.[81] Yet if this was the case, one has to ask why the sane and accomplished C. A. Macartney, for many years League of Nations secretary with day-to-day interwar oversight of these very matters, long anticipated Bauman's analysis by noting that only three resolutions were considered available to the 'problem' of difference within the 'New Europe'. The first was revision of frontiers to minimize the numbers of difficult minorities within the state. The second was emigration, or population exchange. The third was physical slaughter. There was a fourth option: namely, changes in sovereign constitutions away from the nation-state form, as he himself favoured.[82] Significantly, only this idea, Macartney noted, was completely off the international agenda.

This does not in itself add up to a verdict of *direct* Allied culpability for genocide. What instead it points to are key moments of crisis or opportunity when the West, in defence of its post-1919 settlement, was prepared to jettison its safeguards, even where these involved situations which were potentially genocidal or actually crossed that Rubicon. The first occasion, critically, was in the lead-up to the Treaty of Lausanne with Kemal, in 1923, when a massive sequence of mutual killings and counter-killings by Greeks and Turks (as described by, amongst others, Toynbee) were effectively rewritten by the Allied signatories as if they were an element of an orderly, humanitarian, and League of Nations-supervised exchange of populations. Such an exchange did take place *after* the treaty. However, by airbrushing out of the narrative the exterminatory violence which had preceded it, the West, at the very least, signalled its reactive acquiescence in the notion of sovereign states eructing those they deemed to be difficult or suspect populations—by whatever means. The West's critical let-out clause was one of refusing to acknowledge those means. In 1923, Western responsibility, by the way—given the United States' effective interwar withdrawal from political engagement in European affairs—meant that of Britain, and, to lesser extents, France and Italy. The second instance was twenty-two years later at Yalta. Here the Lausanne principle was again applied, this time proactively, and to the entirety of the 'Lands Between'. On this occasion the protagonists were not only the British prime minister, Winston Churchill, but also the US president, Franklin D. Roosevelt—alongside Stalin. Certainly, the expulsion of Germans and other peoples in this sequence falls into a category of misery and violence which was less than 'optimal' when compared with the Holocaust. Not everybody was killed; indeed, the majority of those evicted survived. However, vast numbers also suffered violent death not only en route, through deprivation and the extremities of flight, but sometimes also through atrocity and massacre.

Tellingly, by this time the West had abandoned all commitment to the Minorities Treaties—which confirms that a critical task of this two-part study involves charting two dialectically interacting and sometimes colliding patterns of extreme violence. One was overtly post-imperial and revisionist. But the second, nation-statist, one was, in key respects, the product of a Western Allied determination to create effective counterweights and rimland buffers to a revanchist Germany, residual Ottomania, and Bolshevik Russia.

To be sure, this does not provide the sum total of the *potential* trajectories of genocide in the rimlands or beyond. Not least when one acknowledges that the Allies' attempt to found a 'New Europe' out of the rimlands' shell was predicated, on the one hand, on notions of developmental state-building towards national economies, and, on the other, on these economies being tied in—most tangibly through fiscal regulation and control—to a Western liberal world order which was itself intrinsically fragile. When the system's *economic* crisis came in 1929, in the form of the Wall Street Crash, 'New Europe' dependency on US loans was fully exposed.[83] But with the drying up of the money markets and consequent abandonment by Western banks, not to say lack of British political leadership in particular, the rimland nation states had no choice but to seek salvation beyond the international laissez-faire framework. That, as a further consequence, societal rage and despair should have been taken out on Jews—given all we know about an historical European hostility towards them—should not particularly surprise. A pre-1914 Ottoman state and society in conditions of almost apocalyptic crisis had its scapegoat in Armenians. The parallels are acute. In both instances, blame was laid on distinct subcultures whose members were perceived as 'outsiders'. More tellingly, in both instances, one of the key charges against them was association and ties with extraneous powers, primarily the West, held responsible both for the crisis in the first place and for the nation's straitjacketed impotence to defend or heal itself.

In the rimland Balkans and the 'Lands Between', it was thus not just a state such as post-Trianon Hungary, nursing its already manifold grievances from defeat and dismemberment, where 1930s anti-Semitism was endemic. Practically all these states and societies, whether nominally in the Allied camp or not, succumbed to the already latent infection. Not in their entirety, of course, but especially among the nationally conscious middle classes. And it is a paradox that in their search for answers to their economic plight, their statist national elites increasingly turned to the one country whose pronouncements on the Jewish question were unequivocally and openly saturated with lethal animus. There is a further paradox here. One of the reasons the pattern of rimlands' realignment was to Nazi Germany rather than to Soviet Russia—the other obvious economic and political alternative to the seemingly redundant Western model—was precisely that the latter was itself perceived as ridden with Judaeo-communism. Or, to put it more pungently, that at the centre of some alleged international Jewish conspiracy was none other than the Kremlin. The fact that by the mid-1930s Stalin was busily eviscerating from the Soviet body politic that essential element of the revolution which had been not only ethnically Jewish but consciously internationalist cut no ice with purveyors and followers of this conspiracy-laden world view.

Perhaps this may give some hint as to how embedded a projective Judaeophobia had become by the onset of the Second World War. It had become a facet not simply of the domestic but of the *geopolitical* calculations of rimland leaderships—whether openly fascistic or not—even where such calculations were entirely distant from, or confabulated in, almost wilful disregard of actual economic and political realities. Perhaps, too, it gives some indication, in the vortex of war and genocide most forcefully initiated from the moment of the Nazi-led invasion of the USSR, as to why the exterminatory anti-Jewish drive took on multifaceted forms, including some which were, at the very least, quasi-autonomous of German control. We use the term Holocaust throughout this study, given its common usage, but this does not imply unquestioning deference to some monolithic or streamlined explication of it, either in its rimlands' implementation or as it developed elsewhere in Nazi-dominated Europe. Indeed, on occasion we will refer to 'the Holocaust' to underscore how and where the complexity of events requires a more circumspect and variegated exploration of the processes and patterns involved.

Of course, there can be no debate that the dominating and driving force in Jewish destruction during this second global war was Nazi. Or that where genocide extended to other peoples, even where this was committed not by the Nazis themselves but, as we shall expound, by other state or putative-state parties, the overall context in which this occurred was the German bid for hegemony by way of their rimlands' drive into the 'heartland' of Mackinder's aphorism. But there is a final paradox here. The deportations and genocides which the Nazis set in motion paved the way for a range of *final* rimland reckonings—most keenly against the Volksdeutsche—in which the protagonists were either the now victorious Soviets, their immediate Eastern European acolytes (the Titoist partisans to the fore), or authentic state nationalists acting not only with Soviet approbation but with that of the West. At the end of the day, nation-state 'New Europe', initiated originally under Western aegis in 1919, was, in 1945, re-established and reaffirmed in a now more concretized and homogenized form by a Soviet–Western accord underwritten by its own version of exterminatory violence. Of course, for the Western Allies the accord did not constitute a convivial arrangement. It involved fractious disputes over the territorial boundaries of states, which now literally had to make way for a Stalinist ingestion of the overwhelming proportion of what had been the 'Lands Between' into the USSR, itself signalling the emerging fissures of the East–West confrontation of the Cold War. Even so, what on a macro-level had been a contest for direct or indirect political control of the rimlands and, on another, had developed as one for the heart and soul of its peoples, was now more or less resolved by the expurgation of those rimlands' very existence. This effectively represents the end of this study and the beginning of a further one, in which genuinely bipolar confrontation also reset the mechanisms for genocide—not unlike in the pre-1914 period—towards a much more overtly, extra-European struggle for a 'Third World' *periphery*.

*

That study, however, must await another day. Here, our immediate task is to enable the reader to navigate with relative ease through these two hefty volumes. Those familiar with *Genocide in the Age of the Nation State* will know that this author's method is discursive and, periodically, chronologically loops back on itself as appropriate to the argument and development of themes. Sometimes this means discussions of synchronous events, especially where comparison and parallels are in order.

But, where appropriate, this may also involve a diachronic reading, including episodes outside or beyond this specific study's chronological parameters. Necessarily, the Jewish theme weaves in and out of our presentation, on occasions even in chapters or sections where it is not the main point of discussion. One would not expect otherwise for a study of the period 1912–53, where in key respects it is the Jewish aspect which provides the truly transnational thread. But, by the same token, that would imply reference to Jewish–Gentile relationships embedded in the deeper history of a troubled continent, which may throw light on ultimate genocidal outcomes. That in itself is a problematic statement as it implies latent historical tendencies, which may only lead to the actuality of exterminatory violence in very specific conditions. It was a key premise of *Genocide in the Age of the Nation State* that one can only understand genocide through considering a much broader range of genocidal processes, *most* of which may *not* lead, or at least not immediately, to genocide itself. Clearly, there was something about the time and place of our study which determined that whatever underlying genocidal potential there was *could* explode into actuality. But this again assumes foregone conclusions. Inbuilt into any study of our phenomenon there has to be consideration of factors which might restrain that actuality or perhaps, at some stage, halt killings already in progress. This study engages in those considerations. Equally, however, it does not necessarily take the distinction between mass killings which we normally view as non-genocidal and those that are as a given. At stake is not so much the locations of instances of mass violence on a spectrum or scale of genocide, but rather the possibility of more fully interpreting the relationships between what we term genocide, and that broader range, in order that we might more clearly understand how our phenomenon is not aberrant from but actually *feeds* contemporary historical development.

Having thus set the ground rules let us very briefly outline the main component parts of Volume One of *The Crisis of Genocide*, a similar brief survey of Volume Two following at its outset. Volume One divides into two parts, the first associated with the prelude to, actuality of, and aftermath of the Great War and imperial collapse, and the second with the period of provisional 'New Europe' reformulation as well as post-imperial Stalinist, Nazi, and Kemalist consolidation up to 1938. We begin proceedings in Part One with a chapter on the impact of the Great War in terms of its widest national, geopolitical, and psycho-cultural ramifications. A range of near-genocidal events in the rimlands and beyond are examined. But we also highlight the crystallization of truly toxic anti-Jewish hostilities, the implication being that the immediate origins of the Jewish *genocides* in the Second World War are to be found in the First. In the second chapter, we turn to *the* case of Great War genocide, committed by the Ottoman CUP against its Armenian population in 1915–16. Here again, we treat an earlier episode, the ethnic violence of the Balkan Wars of 1912–13, as a key prelude to the Armenian catastrophe, as we also look sideways at the fate of Syriac communities alongside that of the Armenians themselves. A key overall aim in the study is to understand the linkage between the stress upon and collapse of imperial states and what that meant for particular communities. If the Armenian tragedy is the example par excellence, what happened to a whole host of mostly rimland societies in the wake not just of Ottoman but also Austrian and

Russian demise from 1918 to 1922 is a considerable portion of the third and final chapter of Part One.

Out of the shatter zones of imperial disintegration, however, were already emerging new, reformulated polities, of both a post-imperialist and a nationalist kind, many of which perpetrated genocidal violence as they attempted (successfully or unsuccessfully) to consolidate their rule. However, the opening chapter of Part Two draws back initially from this violence per se to ask: could it have been different, could the advent of a more general 'peace' have been accompanied by alternative ways of thinking and practising inter-communal coexistence? We look at some experimental efforts, not least those associated with Soviet *korenizatsiia* (indigenization) as potentially hopeful signs. In the upshot, however, we are forced to conclude that the outlook for what had become communal 'minorities' in the rimlands' arena was a decidedly bleak one. If a key indicator of just how nasty state responses could be to recalcitrant *ethnies* is presented by way of Turkish and Iraqi military operations against the Kurds and 'Assyrians', what distinguishes the regimes which were responsible for these actions from Soviet Russia and Nazi Germany is that they had come to some form of political arrangement with the liberal hegemonic system. The latter two, by contrast, stood foursquare against that system, as against each other. Our penultimate chapter in Part Two considers the profound implications that fact carried for people in the USSR. What began as an assault on the whole of society's peasant base, as the drive for a military-focused industrialization got under way, transmuted into a series of more targeted campaigns—'terror through famine' wiping out swathes of Ukrainians and Kazakhs in particular—before, again, leading to much more focused attacks on rimlands' communities at the highpoint of Stalin's 'Great Terror'. The Nazi anti-system between 1933 and 1938, which is the subject of the final chapter of this first volume, produced nothing initially comparable in the scale of its violence. And so long as it remained relatively weak internationally its shrill denunciations of its relatively small Jewish population were held in partial check. Even so, the regime's drive for racial purity strongly suggests where, unchecked, it was heading. And not just as regards its Jews. As Germany girded its loins for war it became clear that Roma, too, stood entirely outside its universe of obligation; as did large numbers of ordinary Germans whom Nazism deemed 'unworthy of life'. That said, it was the way Hitler's aggressive, expansionist, geopolitical agenda intermeshed with his projective accusations against a supposed *world* Jewish enemy which most clearly signalled who were his prime target. At the point reached by the end of Volume One, not only is all rimlands' Europe at the edge of the Nazi abyss, but the events of *Kristallnacht* are as raw an indicator as any of how a radicalized state might emotionally prepare for future genocide.

*

Should we congratulate ourselves at this point on having offered a tidy exposition of our first volume's contents? Perhaps not. Putting aside the questions of whether the results of rimlands' devastation—whether that accomplished by 1938 or in the years that followed—could ever be described as 'tidy', this is certainly as good a moment as any for author and readers alike to take a deep breath and remind ourselves that for all the grand discussion of geopolitics, elite actors, and the rest, it was, nevertheless, *people* who were the perpetrators, *people* who were their victims. So, just in order to bring us back to something of the visceral, gut-wrenching reality of it all, here is a single, short episode, in the process of the rounding up of Hungarian Jews en route to Auschwitz, as described without embellishment by a clear-eyed observer, Jenö Lévai:

> On May 22 [1944] the ghetto of the city of Munkás (Mukachevo) was also emptied and most of Munkás' 12,000 Jews were driven on the route from the ghetto to the brickyard, by guards using whips, machine-guns, and rifle butts. There they were compelled to lay down their baggage and undress—men, women and children alike. Stark naked, they were then ordered to move back a few steps, and the women who were called in specially, together with Gestapo men, policemen, and gendarmes went through their baggage and clothing, even opening stitches to discover whether the Jews had hidden anything. Those who did not undress or step back fast enough were beaten. Most of the people were bleeding and stood silently, naked and numbed. The searchers, however, were all the more loud. The clothes were then returned, the personal documents were torn, and everybody became a non-person. They were then driven by night-sticks and rifle butts to get dressed. The crush of the desperate crowd and the frenzied confusion were terrible. Here, 90 persons were crowded into a freight car: obviously there were too few cars and too many Jews! The cars were then chained and padlocked. Each got a bucket full of water and an empty one for the excrements. The train, however, was left standing in the station during the hot May day and was allowed to leave only on the following days. By that time many became mad and even more died, since the Jewish hospital patients were also included. The doors were not opened on the day of departure. The corpses were removed three days later at Csap, where also the mad were clubbed or shot.[84]

This little vignette is not offered because, on the one hand, the perpetrators were German and Hungarians, on the other, their victims Jewish. It could apply to any group of people. Nor does it represent the worst, most gratuitous episode of violence we could find. Nor even one where the implications of perpetrator venality are particularly shocking: we will find regular, repeated occasions when people, rich and poor, men and women alike, took the opportunity afforded to them to steal from other people so diminished, humiliated, and degraded that they were entirely unable to stand up for themselves, their families, or others around them.

All this episode reveals is an aspect of the human condition. But it is, of course, only an aspect, and, as we have suggested, one specifically *afforded* by other conditions and circumstances, in turn created by human beings. If we want to understand the 'why' of genocide we have no choice but to try and understand those human-made conditions. To do so, we must turn again to the long-term, latent crisis of Europe's powerful and would-be powerful, but nearly always highly dysfunctional, elite actors. They were to be found in Berlin and Vienna certainly. But also in Petrograd, London, Paris, Constantinople, and Belgrade. The ones who 'went to war to determine who would control Europe and the world',[85] and in so doing precipitated a prolonged and seemingly uncontrollable spasm of self-mutilation, which, at the bottom rung, crystallized hopes, hatreds, and longings for transcendence in their most paranoid and obsessive forms.

PART ONE

GREAT WAR AND REVOLUTION

1

The Great War: Site of Genocide or Signpost to its Future Enactment?

SETTING THE SCENE

My Russian opinion is that all Jews should be wiped off the face of the Russian empire and that's the end of it.[1]

> Mr N., Russian reserve soldier (respondent to Maxim Gorky's 1915 questionnaire on the 'Jewish problem').

I should welcome the formation of a National Council of Righteous Retribution—a National Vendetta, pledged to exterminate every German-born man...in Britain—and to deport every German-born woman and child...I would put in the field an army of Zulus and Basutos and other native and half-civilised tribes—and let them run amok in the enemy's ranks. I would give them all the asphyxiating gas they wanted. I would allow no prisoners to be taken, on either land or sea, and I would do a lot of other things.[2]

> Horatio Bottomley, *John Bull*, 15 May 1915

A pervasive knowledge of the *Second* World War, its catastrophic scale, millions of casualties, and brutality—particularly, in the latter case, linked to the role of the Nazis—is nowadays also commonly linked in the popular mind to its genocidal dimensions, above all to the European-wide extermination of the Jews. But what of the First World War—the Great War—which preceded it? Everybody, historians included, acknowledges that the second great conflagration was inextricably linked to, and could not have taken place without, the first. But if that is so, two questions immediately present themselves for this study. First, to what extent were the genocidal outcomes of Second World War the consequence of, or even, in some sense, programmed or synchronized by the events of First? Second, to what extent were the genocidal events in the 1939–45 conflict prefigured in its 1914–18 predecessor?

A simple answer presents itself. The genocide of the First World War was that visited on the Armenians in 1915–16. As such, this provides not only a Great War parallel with, but potential template for, what the Nazis were to do to even greater effect in 'the Holocaust'. Vahakn Dadrian, in particular, has devoted himself in voluminous publications to making the comparison and, indeed, establishing the connectedness between these two events.[3] Moreover, with the *Aghet*, the Armenian extermination, regularly presented and accepted without demur—even amongst scholars—as the first genocide of the twentieth century, the argument that it should be understood as both precursor and prototype of others which were to follow might appear equally plausible.[4] Certainly, while we find this symbolic or actual status historically unsatisfactory, this major case of genocide undoubtedly deserves critical analysis, which we seek to offer in Chapter 2. We do so, however, by consciously eschewing focus on its Holocaust linkage or affinities. Instead, we favour placing it in a more historically synchronous context associated with a broader Ottoman catastrophe, and with its own immediate precursors, in the form of mass communal killings perpetrated during the Balkan Wars of 1912–13. This in no way detracts from it as a seminal event of the 1914–18 conflict. On the contrary, and in line with a major theme of this book, the *Aghet* is evidence of an emerging rimlands shatter zone whose full dimensions were realized only through that war. Yet, with origins also inherited from pre-1914, not least with the collapse of Ottoman rule in its western—Balkan—zone, there are elements to the Armenian and related killings which cannot be circumscribed by reference to the Great War *alone*.

What, by contrast, interests us in this chapter is the broader pan-European issues and consequences thrown up by the Great War itself; or, to put it slightly differently, the degree to which the war provides evidence of genocidal violence during its course—over and beyond Armenia—while at the same time storing up neuroses and frustrations which might help explain the even greater explosion of genocide a world war later. Perhaps, unsurprisingly, there is considerable evidence in the affirmative on both counts. However, because there are various elements and components to consider here, these need to be broken down, with some minimal cursory explanation, in each instance.

First of all, we treat the theme of total war itself, which has often been taken as, in some sense, causal to the enactment of the Holocaust. We find this not entirely sufficient but put the issue on hold until later in the chapter, while we explore a second theme, more closely tied up with the fate of the multi-ethnic rimlands: namely, the behaviour of the historic imperial powers at war, as they struggled with the intrusion of nationalism into their domestic and geopolitical calculations. Following on from this, our third section considers an actual (non-Ottoman) crisis of empire as a direct consequence of potential military defeat, which, while it produced extreme violence and expulsion in the 'Lands Between', did not carry through to a mass extermination of the Armenian kind. This in itself poses questions as to the nature of political brakes upon, as well as of accelerators to, genocidal violence.

A further, fourth, consideration thus regards regions *beyond* the rimlands; more exactly, specific colonial environs where genocide, or at least extreme and sustained exterminatory violence, *did* take place as a by-product of the Great War. In itself, this begs the question of whether it is the perception of peoples as 'colonized' which provides the key to assaults *à outrance* upon them, and if so, whether it is such perceptions, imported back to a Europe *integrale*, which might account for

the withdrawal or even repudiation of restraints on violence against whole communities. There is a sequence of German atrocities in Western Europe at the very
outset of the war, against primarily Belgian and some northern French border-
landers, with regard to which this connection might be worthy of further attention.

However, in our brief examination of these events, in our fifth section, we are as
much concerned with the relationship between the contingent nature of this initial
war campaign, set against illusory expectations of what it was supposed to deliver,
than anything specifically 'colonial'. The outcome was a particularly virulent form
of phobic projection which, we will argue, provides a signpost to arguably the most
significant and lasting legacy of the war *tout ensemble*: the psychic harm done by its
European survivors to *themselves*. The Great War historian John Morrow has put
the case succinctly but sharply: 'Prior to August 1914 Europeans had presumed to
control the world; they were now to learn that they could not control themselves'.[5]
Our sixth and final section takes up this argument, to consider the relationship
between a pervasive unwillingness, especially evident among national and state
elites, to face up to the mass murder and destruction they had caused, and the
psychological necessity, as a result, to find one or more scapegoats. That a resulting
fixation on Europe's Jews emerged, given all we know about the Continent's inner
demons, should not really surprise. But its ability in the context of the war to come
to political centre ground at moments of extreme crisis—and for *all* the main
belligerents—surely should. The consequences of this First World War subtext, if
they did not directly create, certainly crystallized a stored potency of Judaeophobic
obsession, the transmission belt of which provides direct linkage and causation to
what would happen almost a quarter of a century later.

TOTAL WAR

An ostensibly logical place to begin any examination of either the actuality or
latent potentiality of genocide in our period is by treating it as symptomatic of the
broader landscape of unrelenting and unprecedented carnage which was the Great
War. Its more than four years' duration consumed human beings, primarily men
in the trenches of both combat and attrition, in an almost perpetual meat grinder
of quite extraordinary proportions. States were forced to operate not only on the
merciless elimination of the male citizens or subjects put into the field by their
opponents,[6] but to accept the expendability of their own mostly young men in the
process—and all as if this were somehow the norm. As Jay Winter has been at pains
to emphasize, the result was a mass slaughter that 'passed a threshold beyond previous experience'.[7] Of an estimated 65 million men inducted into the belligerent
armies, at least 8.5 million were killed and another 21 million wounded, but with
many of the further 8 million listed as missing or as prisoners of war (POWs) also
immediate or eventual fatalities.[8] And this, of course, does not take account of the
brutalization, trauma, and very often premature death of survivors. Put in terms of
specific states, the immensity of the toll is both appalling yet also, at the same time,
revealing. For instance, if one in eight British servicemen was killed, and one in

six French and Germans, for Rumanians, Turks, and Bulgarians the chances of dying were roughly one in four, while for Serbs—37 per cent of whom perished—the odds were even slimmer.[9]

Such figures ought in themselves to give us some indication of where the most intense—and most barbaric—fighting took place. Western attention, understandably, tends to be focused on the fronts at which their own young men were combatants, most particularly the Western Front. However, while the undoubted horror of trench warfare is the constant theme of such accounts, a common myopia as to what was happening in other theatres, most particularly in the rimland Balkans, Anatolia, and Caucasus, as well as on the larger Eastern Front, can have the effect of distorting our understanding of the *nature* of the Great War elsewhere. The leading British military historian John Keegan, for example, characterizes it—with the single exception of what happened in Ottoman Armenia—as devoid of genocide, and leading to 'no systematic displacement of populations, no deliberate starvation, no expropriation, little massacre or atrocity'. 'It was', he purports, 'despite the efforts of state propaganda machines to prove otherwise, and the cruelties of the battlefield apart, a curiously civilised war'.[10] Even blame for the Armenian episode is consciously shifted from the war to its being a consequence of Ottoman imperial policy.

Keegan's interpretation certainly stands in stark contrast to that of others, such as Winter, who have placed the Armenian genocide firmly within the context of total war. Winter argues that the 1914 conflict not only inaugurated but 'provided the space in which genocidal crimes could and did take place'.[11] Yet that still, in a sense, leaves something of a pervading conundrum. How does this macro-violence writ large explain the way military violence took hold on the rimland war fronts to—contra Keegan—increasingly engulf non-combatants? And if there is a further linkage between this violence and the targeting of specific communities for annihilation a world war later—as in the case of the Jews—what is the connecting thread?

Neither Keegan nor Winter can take us fully towards this goal. Even putting aside the more vicious turn of war in the east, in the context of the fight between Germany and the Western allies, the restraining firewall erected on the basis of the pre-war Hague Conventions, specifically to prevent conflict between the Great Powers moving beyond 'civilized' bounds, was rapidly swept aside in order to provide the edge for one or other side to *win*.[12] Perhaps significantly it was Germany, on so many occasions, that crossed the Rubicon first. It initiated the use of poison gas, the flame-thrower, aerial bombing of cities, and unrestricted submarine warfare. The sinking of the Cunard liner RMS *Lusitania*, with over a thousand passengers and crew, in early May 1915, represented a particular watershed, not least for the then neutral USA, whose loss in the attack of over a hundred citizens was treated as a moral violation of the first order. But if this would seem to suggest a nexus between a willingness to wage a more thorough and systematized warfare by land, sea, and air—in the process, as Winter argues, blurring the distinction between combatants and non-combatants—and the ability through industrialized methods, advances in military technology, and organization of resources to sustain it, it is debatable that this explains specific instances of genocide, Armenian or otherwise.

Paradoxically, Winter's reading of connections is made more cogent by reference to some of the cultural and societal side effects of total war that he enumerates, notably the mobilization of the popular imagination in its support, not to say the cultivation of hatreds within or without the body politic. Even here, however, we need to be a little cautious. Students of the origins of fascism and Nazism, in particular, and the emergence of the cults of violence so prevalent in interwar Europe more generally, have assiduously mined the relationship of these to the front-line experience in writings such as Ernst Jünger's 1922 best-selling novel *Storm of Steel*.[13] Jünger's idealized, even erotic aesthetic of violence undoubtedly tells us a great deal about *some* veteran, masculine self-images as heroic, hard, 'new' men, purified and transformed by their individual baptisms of fire. It also tells us about their sense of some intimate affinity with all those other trench warriors who had undergone this same devastating metamorphosis—or indeed those too young to fight who sought to emulate them. What it does *not* quite tell us, however, is where, or towards whom, the violence—in their heads, or in actuality—was directed. Fantasies of race war were, of course, already a common feature of the fin de siècle but this hardly explains why German, but not just German, animus should have been particularly directed at Jews, who, albeit it in smaller numbers, were also numbered as comrades-in-arms, amongst the front-fighters. Perhaps, behind the *experience* of war, we need to turn to the *circumstances* from which it emerged—and then took on its seemingly inexorable momentum—to get a firmer grip on what exactly, in the imaginations of so many of those who lived through it, was irredeemably sullied.

*

The most peculiar, and perhaps frighteningly schizophrenic, aspect of the European political scene in 1914 was the searing tension between its huge potential for, and military build-up towards, internecine war between its two distinct Great Power blocs—the 'Two Germanies' of the Central Powers, on the one hand, and the French, Russian, and British Allies, on the other—and the insistence of its leading policymakers and opinion formers that this could and would not happen. It was not that Europe did not 'do' war: its very drive to world dominance had been predicated on nothing less. But this involved the Great Powers individually, or, very occasionally—as in the case of the 1900 suppression of the Chinese Boxer rebellion—acting in consort to subjugate or, if necessary eliminate, insolent 'black', 'red', 'yellow', or other 'lesser' peoples *beyond* the bounds of a 'civilized' Europe, itself at peace. As Sigmund Freud acerbically put it, the 'great world-dominating nations of white race' were meant to find other ways 'of settling misunderstandings and conflicts of interest' amongst themselves.[14]

Moreover, time-honoured Westphalian checks and balances existed to prevent exactly such a catastrophe. The diplomats and statesmen who had endorsed the 1815 Treaty of Vienna had quite consciously sought to build a durable peace founded on the concept of the balance of power, and their successors too, for the most part, had been remarkably successful in managing a rapidly changing Europe, including the formation of new, sovereign nation-states, without recourse to *general* war. Of course, this had been far from the whole picture. Post-1815 Europe had been punctuated by a series of crises—1848, 1854–6, 1859, 1864, 1866, 1870, again in 1877–8—but the ensuing wars had been either localized or contained. The more recent Great Power quarrels, again over imperial spoils or the territorial proceeds of the most recent Ottoman retreat, had been equally neutralized. For many eminent commentators, such as the British journalist and pacifist Norman Angell, the fact that Europe had emerged as the industrial and financial centre of the world, whose very existence was predicated on a peaceful yet interdependent economic exchange, ensured that war made *no sense* whatsoever.[15]

The problem was that the likes of Angell and others completely underestimated the geopolitical frustrations and resentments within the European system. As we have already seen, in *The Rise of the West*, these were particularly prevalent in leading elements of a German state and society which saw the Second Reich as permanently hemmed in and blocked off from its rightful position of hegemony within Europe and the world. What Hans Mommsen has referred to as the 'topos of inevitable war' led German military strategists, most famously Graf von Schlieffen, to plan for daring campaigns for Cannae-style obliteration of the Reich's European military opponents, academics of the ilk of Treitschke to embrace the drive to war as 'God-given', and a plethora of other critical actors in the Kaiser's court, chancellery, and elsewhere, to incessantly invoke zero-sum forecasts in which Germany would either win through or perish.[16] This may tell us much about the nature of the German neurosis; the problem, however, is that it was to a greater or lesser extent shared by all the other main European players. As Hew Strachan has put it, 'By July 1914, each power conscious in a self-absorbed way of its own potential weaknesses, felt it was on its mettle, that its status as a great power would be forfeit if it failed to act'.[17] Without, then, the endemic nature of the neurosis and the assumption that went with it that the only way to resolve what was perceived as the broader international stalemate was through military-driven breakout, it is highly doubtful, after the post-Sarajevo diplomatic breakdown, that the belligerents would have mobilized for war with the speed and precision which they did.

If this is simply to rehearse a familiar story, it is with the second stage of the crisis that we get closer to what Ron Aronson would refer to as a 'rupture with reality',[18] and hence to its relevance for us. Having committed themselves to this catastrophic course, against the grain not only of their own public pronouncements but of rational deduction, the Great Power leaders—and those elements of their populations with heavy emotional investment in the national cause—then had to convince themselves that it would all come right and hence be justified through the war being won in some rapid, outright fashion. Germany's Schlieffen plan represents the most notorious of these imagined knockout-blow scenarios: the French armies being enveloped and destroyed by a flanking movement through neutral Belgium, enabling Germany to then turn its full weight against a supposedly not yet fully mobilized Russian opponent on its Eastern Front. Yet the generals and politicians of all sides were fancifully contending in July 1914—perhaps not surprisingly given what was at stake—that their armies would soon be in their enemies' capitals and the war over by Christmas.

All the best empirical evidence then available would have told them otherwise. Back in 1898, the thoroughly independent Polish Jewish banker and savant, Ivan

Bloch, had published a six-volume masterpiece, *The Future of War*, which, with uncanny accuracy, had detailed how the military doctrine of the offensive would be rapidly neutralized in practice by the reality of modern battlefield technology—heavy weaponry, enhanced armoury, barbed wire, devastating firepower including machine guns, and the rest—leading not only to instant, massive losses, but the mutation of the offensive into a long-term defensive quagmire, without military rhyme or reason. Bloch's clear message to the Powers was perfectly simple: do not go there, it will amount to civilizational suicide. And his prescience was borne out in the high summer and early autumn of 1914, in the initial great battles of the war that we have all but forgotten: Charleroi, the Marne, Tannenberg and the Masurian lakes, the first battle of Langemarck, and that on Cer mountain on the Serbian front, with human losses so immense that a sickened Europe should surely have stopped the madness then and there.[19]

But, of course, that is exactly what did not happen. Having staked everything on the knockout blow, and then failed, the German High Command was neither going to capitulate to the Allies nor call for a referendum back home. With emergency powers in place to suffocate dissent, and with the generals effectively in control to determine the organization of the domestic economy for war, Germany was set on a course for a fight to the finish, and hence to an instrumentalization of military state violence which could only be ratcheted up, degree by degree, until victory was achieved. Or, alternatively, as their own prophets of doom had prognosticated, until a *Götterdämmerung*-like downfall. With the gauntlet thus thrown and atrocities, as in Belgium, already committed, it is of no surprise that the political adversaries of the 'Two Germanies' could only respond in kind. The Great Powers thus became locked into a conflict which demanded not simply more and more resources poured into it—we forget at our peril the great swathes not just of human beings but of livestock, horses, dogs, and all manner of creatures requisitioned in the cause of war, not to say all the forests and fields sequestered and smashed up in the process—but more and more slaughter of all, in a continuous paroxysm.

The point though is this. We can quantify what happened—the military campaigns, the death tolls, the capital and resources which went up in smoke, and the political shifts as the 'lily-livered' politicians of peacetime, not to say the generals with less than absolute killer instincts, gave way to the most hard-headed, military-minded, and chauvinistically aggressive politicians, or even—as effectively happened in Germany from 1916—to an authoritarian military junta. What is much less easy to observe or calculate is the impact on the psychological balance of individuals, collectivities, and self-professed nations; that is, on human beings caught up in this maelstrom yet required to *believe* that this war had *purpose*.

An alternative possibility, that there might have been a broad repudiation or resistance to the mendacity, had been effectively suffocated through the failure of the international trade union and socialist movement—the one obvious trans-European force—to put a spoke, as supposedly existed, on paper, into the initial statist mobilization plans. The assassin's bullet which killed the great French socialist leader, Jean Jaurès, at a peace rally on 1 August 1914, laid to rest any remaining hopes on the matter.[20] This is doubly significant because we know now that enthusiasm for the war at its outset was not nearly as prevalent amongst ordinary people as has been traditionally assumed by reference to the photographs of euphoric, nationally minded crowds which have been imprinted on our memories.[21] There was, of course, another genuinely supranational movement throughout Europe in the form of the organized church, which had arguably even more public sway and power to confront the lie. But, even more than with the socialists, any residual element of the churches' solidarity across state borders, let alone of their respective abilities to speak truth to power, was rapidly 'forfeit to national priorities'.[22] Instead, Christianity in each country was rapidly and single-mindedly mobilized to fight for the national cause, as if God's Christ were an Englishman, a German, a Serbian, or whoever. More than any other institution, indeed, the churches played a critical, self-propelled role throughout the war by representing the struggle not only as a just cause but as a holy crusade. Thereby, they instilled into the notion of sacrifice a sense of transcendent meaningfulness and purposeful redemption, the psychic harm of which was literally immeasurable.[23]

With even Europe's dominant religion in abject thrall to the triumphant god of nationally sacralized war—with all its resonances of Jacobinism—each combatant state sought to position itself as if it had some absolute authority to undertake every means towards achievement of the ultimate goal. By the autumn of 1916, the German generals were even planning for it in terms of what they called *Material-schlacht*: a gigantic struggle of attrition in which every fit and able person would play his or her part and every 'useless' one, including old men and women, pregnant mothers, and small children, would be outside the state's duty of care—even if this meant a slow starvation to death.[24] For national elites—and the multitudes of followers who had imbibed what Strachan has aptly termed a 'vocabulary of absolutes',[25] all this could be justified by the higher cause. There was just one small problem with this attempted rationalization of the utterly irrational: the yawning gap between the illusory aspiration and the realities of unending violence. With 'national' Europe thus in a state of denial as to either the causes of the war or its outcomes, and hence blocked off from understanding, let alone attending to, the pervasive sickness *within*, the need for displacement onto some other culprit or culprits, even from the earliest days of the war's unmaking, became an urgent quest.

EMPIRES AND THEIR RIMLAND PEOPLES

But the question was displacement onto whom exactly? In the avowed nation states of the avant-garde West, the already well-trodden process by which Auvergnais peasants were taught to think of themselves as Frenchmen, Welsh-speaking hill farmers embraced Britishness, or, for a late arrival in the war, the peoples of the *Mezzogiorno* declared their allegiance to Italy, created a rather solid notion—even if it was actually built on a series of fantasies—of national cohesion and unity. That in itself should have calmed any societal fears in these countries that the advent of war would see 'enemies within' sprouting up out of every orifice and crevice. As we will see by reference to that which at the time liked to call itself Great Britain, in the absence of any real fifth columnists—outside of the island of Ireland—you could always invent them. That aside, even the national fantasy offered safeguards not obviously available to the imperial contestants to the east.

All the belligerents, of course, were at one in trying to dampen down social conflicts and urge their populations to support a *union sacrée* or a *Burgfrieden*, for the war's duration. But Austria–Hungary famously entered into it having to issue mobilization orders in eleven languages.[26] In the old days, the fact that an empire's reservoir of peasant conscripts came from diverse ethnic backgrounds mattered not a jot. All that did matter was that it had sufficient production and supply of ordnance, food, and other war materiel for its armies' needs, plus a modicum of organizational efficiency to get these items to the right places and at the right time to see the thing through, while hopefully coming out of it, if not necessarily victorious, then at least not territorially diminished. As for the peasant conscripts, they simply took their orders, did their duty, and died, were crippled, or survived unblemished, by the grace of God and the emperor.

It was not the Great War per se which wrecked this simple equation, but rather the years of previous peace when the concept of nationalism—that is, as derived from the principle and practice of it in the West—had been gnawing away at the imperial Romanov, Habsburg, Ottoman and, slightly more tangentially, Hohenzollern edifices. The ongoing problem for each, necessarily, had been what to do about it. You could try and ignore or alternatively pulverize it, by turns the preferred Russian methods. You could concede to it—decidedly Austrian. Arguably, you could even attempt to co-opt it by declaring everybody a member of the same imperial nation and, if you were very clever, thereby make it invisible—Ottoman sophistry, at least for a time. Certainly *state* nationalism was also a ploy toyed with by the Russians, with usually coercive formulas in mind, and so, too, the Austrians, through more Byzantine politicking (though nearly always tinged with elements of retreat and regret). While the preservation of general peace, however, kept the door largely shut on the problem, at least in so far as it presented the sort of danger likely to threaten the integrity of the state, the war blew it wide open. Or at least that is how many of the empires' military strategists saw it.

It all came down in the end to statistics. Or, more accurately, the way these self-same strategists had been busily imbibing or interpreting them. Social cataloguing of populations, of course, was a standard project identifying a state as modern. With the publication for instance, in eighty-nine volumes no less, of the first all-Russian census in 1897, the Romanov Empire not only stated its adherence to a sociologized modus operandi considered as normative in the dominant West, but, in the process, found out a great deal about the composition of its peoples, province by province.[27] Or at least imagined that it had done so. As with all sociological investigation the conclusions arrived at were highly dependent on the approach utilized. And by delineating people by language, one critical result was to add grist to the mill of all those Russian bureaucrats and military men increasingly obsessed by what has been referred to as a 'geography of unreliability'.[28] In other words, their conclusion was that there were elements, or, more exactly, ethnic *populations* in one's domains, who, by dint of the language they spoke, particularly when set against other social or religious information, one should treat as either reliable, suspect, or, at worst, downright pernicious. As a St Petersburg military school text-book for 1909, in somewhat tortuous language, put it:

> The further we move from the central Russian core to the peripheries, the population density decreases and its ethnic composition becomes more and more diverse, and the percentage of the Russian element in it decreases...It is evident that such a composi-tion of the population in the peripheries is impossible to consider advantageous in a political or military sense. Without even speaking of cases of military conflicts on the territory of these peripheries [the composition of the population] is unfavourable even in peacetime.[29]

What, of course, this underscored was that the views of military academicians on the subject were ultimately neither the product of statistics, nor even of the way they had been formulated. They were simply evidence of deep underlying fears about the non-Russian peoples of the empire, especially those who amounted to substantial and often majority populations in the most geopolitically sensitive regions of the western and Caucasian rimlands. This is not to make light of these fears. The key, formative, and long-lasting experience for most serving Russian officers throughout the nineteenth century had been associated with the pacifica-tion of Central Asia and the Caucasus. The fact that only genocidal violence ulti-mately broke much of the mountain peoples' resistance in the latter case offered small comfort against the possibility of more general rimland insurrection break-ing out, especially in the context of a Great Power conflict where the state's scarce resources would inevitably be directed elsewhere. Moreover, the strong national components of the failed 1905 revolution, not to mention some of the accompa-nying inter-ethnic violence particularly, at that juncture, in Transcaucasia—to be considered in later chapters—suggested that the upholders of the imperial status quo arguably had a point: if rimland nationalism really did take off under the cover of more general war, the whole empire could fall apart. After all, this is exactly what did happen to Austria–Hungary in 1918, and arguably would have happened in equal measure in Russia at the same time, if it had not been for the stronger, coun-tervailing if contradictory counterpoints of the Red revolution and White counter-revolution.

Yet back in 1914, before the repeated exertion of war had torn apart the sinews of the remaining world empires from both within and without, the military strate-gists' presentiments as to the specifically nationalist threat to the jugular still presents us with something of a paradox. Putting aside the question of whether the causation of Chechen, Avar, and Circassian resistance—among others—to tsarist rule can be described as nationalist at all, when their inspiration was so clearly derived from the militant Islamic revivalism of the Naqshbandi order,[30] there is little evidence that national consciousness was a significant motivating factor for the vast majority of peoples inhabiting the western 'Lands Between' rimlands either. In the main peasants, and hence lacking the time, education, or inclination to be galvanized by such ethereal concerns, the very concept of having an identity rooted in anything other one's local habitus, or, beyond that, religion, was—as we have already suggested in our Introduction—the preserve of landed elites or towns-folk; that is, those who had food in their bellies and the money and leisure to buy or read books and newspapers.

What is thus significant about the new military science being taught in army academies across Europe—as it became diffused or borrowed, largely from Prussian army manuals and curricula—is the way it overrode facts on the ground in favour of grand abstractions. People became populations, and communities components of broader demographic aggregates, either to serve statist ends, or fulfil statist phobias. In the Russian case, indeed, before 1914, this amounted to plotting ratios of Russian or ostensibly 'reliable' Slavic populations against others—especially in the western rimlands: Jews, Germans, and Poles—with the assurance of security and safety in any given region only being derived where the favoured component exceeded 50 per cent.[31]

And so we enter into the world of national assets. How do you determine who is a Russian and who is not? The answer is that it depends primarily on what you take as your marker of difference. In the original public outing of the national assets terminology, involving a German scholar's 1905 efforts to unpick who was Czech and who German in the Bohemian province of Austria–Hungary where the two populations were intermixed, the marker was again language. But underlying this ostensibly innocent exercise was an entirely more politically charged consideration regarding national entitlements. If the demographic weight of one 'national community' in certain areas turned out to be greater than the other across the region as a whole, then issues of state resource allocation followed. If, moreover, this really was about national groups, then the issue became not simply one of proportional representation in the civil service or parliament, or even relevant language provision in schools—it implicitly carried with it discussions about territorial space, and even 'ethnographic' boundaries.[32]

This did not necessarily have to work against the imperial interest. In the Hungarian part of the dual monarchy, for instance, the 1910 census, by using language as the criterion of nationality, enabled large number of Jewish Magyar speakers to be classed as 'Hungarians', in so doing conveniently pushing the Hungarian percentage of the total population into the hegemonic position.[33] Did this still make any difference to peasant populations who cared for ethnic identity not a jot? Actually, the answer could now become 'yes' if that meant that their children were having to go to school and be inducted in a language foreign to them. And this indeed is exactly what fin-de-siècle Hungarian state planners were requiring for their Romanian, Croat, Slovak, and other subject populations, possibly as much to nip these potential national dangers in the bud as to hubristically proclaim the superiority of the Magyar over less 'civilized' Danubian neighbours. The only problem was that in such conscious state mobilization of the national idea, even upping the ante in the process through a programme of enforced national homogenization, the dangers of actually instigating counter-nationalisms from below (and beyond) threatened to blur the distinction between imagined asset-seekers and asset-seekers with real constituencies behind them.

How potentially fraught and divisive this could become, even before the Great War provided added acceleration, is illustrated by an Ottoman example, to be further pursued in Chapter 2. In what of the Balkans remained still under Ottoman control, the pre-1908 Hamidian regime might have wished to develop a comprehensive programme of school-centred Ottomanization, not unlike that of their Magyar counterparts. However, the weakness of its position in this Macedonian region meant the best it could hope for was to continue to hold the ring between competing claims of different national contenders, most particularly by playing off a major Bulgarian bid to control an emerging school network by actively supporting alternative Serb and Greek schools.[34] Clearly, this *Kulturkampf* in the making was the sum of several parts, not just top-down imperial diktat but indigenous, as well as sideways-on, national provocations. And what made the situation more flammable still was the way the language question was manipulated and massaged by the key contending parties to arrive at entirely contradictory accounts of their supposed constituencies' respective demographic weights.

Thus, for instance, while a Serb analysis in 1899 found there to be over 2 million Serb speakers in Macedonia compared with less than 58,000 Bulgars, a Bulgarian one, a year later, not only reversed the findings by claiming there to be 1,200,000 of their own kind compared with a mere 700 Serbs, but completely lost the other 921,000 souls also presumably living in these three vilayets, including substantial numbers of people who we may assume were Greeks or Vlachs. Other partisan surveys, over the next few years, produced equally extraordinary results.[35] Clearly, what people actually spoke as their native lingo, or identified as in religious terms—whether as Orthodox, Exarchist, Patriarchist, or other—had become quite immaterial to the advocates of the 'nation'. But, equally, the latters' efforts expended in demonstrating that the phonetics, or morphology, of such and such a dialect spoken by mountain villagers in the upper valleys above Üsküb or Monastir 'proved' that these people really did belong to one ethnic group and not some other, did have profound consequences. These lay not only in the way young peasant Macedonians began imbibing a sense of national consciousness through what they learned about their own alleged history and language in the schools, or in counter efforts by the CUP, after 1909, to attempt to clamp down on them.[36] They also came in the wider circulation of the idea throughout Europe that there *were* genuine ethnographic boundaries out there in the Balkans and the other rimlands, and that these were founded on sound scientific evidence.

Just as the imperial military statisticians had staked out their rendition of the relationship between ethnicity and geography through their sociologizing analyses, dutifully copied into their manuals, so the would-be nation-builders simply created their own by producing a lavish volume in Leipzig or Vienna, replete with maps delineating their claim to a region, or the accession of another to an already existing Piedmont-like mini-state. It was the maps, above all, with their bright colours denoting this or that geographical zone belonging to this or that 'nation', which arguably made all the difference. Alongside this was the fact that the production of these volumes in Central Europe gave to them a supposed scientific imprimatur, not to say a wider, educated market. And where inconvenient facts got in the way, like the existence of a people who were not of your own, you simply blanked them out, or reinvented them as *indigènes* who were really yours but through some misfortune of history had mistakenly forgotten the truth about themselves.

The so-called Arnauts of the Macedonian and, more particularly, Kosovo region, according to Serb ethnographers, were a case in point. We might otherwise know them as Albanians. Nevertheless, Belgrade was so taken with the notion of them as Albanianized Serbs that it paid for the requisite Vienna-printed German translation in 1889, despite it being rubbished by one genuine German Balkan expert as 'a mass of crude lies'.[37] When later, in the First Balkan War, the 'Arnauts' clearly hadn't got the message but chose instead to defy Serbian annexation, Belgrade duly recast them in a 1913 memorandum to the Great Powers as 'invaders', which conveniently dovetailed with the further assertion that as they lacked 'the moral right of a more civilised people'[38] (in other words, the Serbs), it was the latter who should inherit territory which was rightfully theirs anyway.

The toxicity of the situation in the rimlands, as the Great War approached, was thus not a symptom solely of the *mentalité* or behaviour of imperialists as against that of nationalists. Rather it was that of a dialectical relationship, or more accurately a several-sided one, between the old imperial masters as they strove to hold on to their border regions, and one or more up-and-coming contenders who sought to wrest these same regions for their own imagined national communities. In that, though, lies the critical distinction. In the context of 1914, 1915, or 1916, it was less the nature of the thinking that was radically different between them—both imperialists and nationalists alike increasingly treating rimlands' populations as ethnic quantities to be aggregated or disaggregated at will—but the ability to translate this into their mobilization or, alternatively, terrorization. On this score, so long as the empires were standing, it was clearly the imperialists who had the whip hand.

A recent work by Gabriel Liulevicius on the Ober Ost—the Baltic region and hinterlands designated by German army chief Ludendorff as such and as a military fiefdom distinct from the rest of the imperial armies' 1915 Russian borderland conquests—illustrates this well. Replete with notions of war land, war geography, and of a geopolitics of movement in which 'races and spaces' were key, it is clear from Liulevicius' account that the military occupation was seen as prelude to a radical peacetime reorganization of this *Ostraum*, which would lead, on the one hand, to the excision of unwanted and 'unreliable' population elements, and, on the other, to a programme of rapid German settlement, which would thereby radically advance Germany's colonial reach into this formerly Russian 'space'. Clearly, there were already genocidal implications here. A comprehensive ethnographic and occupational screening of the base population of three million was designed to remove from it those perceived as dirty, primitive, and vermin-ridden: their fate, to be dumped in an ultimately conquered Russia. By the same token, suitably deloused, the region was to be sealed off both from Germany proper, at least for the time being, and from unwanted refugees from elsewhere.[39] In short, the degree to which the Ludendorff agenda anticipated Nazi plans for the entirety of western Russia a generation later is both uncanny and striking. Moreover, the fact that the Ober Ost was a 'special' zone of occupation under strict martial jurisdiction, a micro-system if one likes of what might be applied at a later stage to a larger grid, meant that the German Eastern Command were well positioned to put its transformative goals into practice by whatever means it chose. The means included extreme violence.[40]

That said, and with due reference to the draconian nature of the military control system, not to say its key immediate purpose of cutting down vast swathes of the region's timber reserves for war use, with consequent hyper-exploitative labour service requirements on the population—unsurprisingly, with often calamitous results[41]—the Ober Ost does not stand out as a notably violent place. At least, not by more general Great War, Eastern Front standards. Could this be because, para-doxically, once taken by the Germans the situation in the region was largely stabi-lized, that is, until quite late on in the war? Elsewhere in the 'Lands Between' this was very far from being the case—Galicia and the Bukovina, in particular, being overrun by one side or the other with nightmarish regularity. Bukovina's capital, Czernowitz, for instance, changed hands no less than fifteen times in the course of 1914–17.[42] In themselves, these are very much archetypal conditions in which hyped-up yet also exhausted soldiery of advancing and, more particularly, retreat-ing armies take out their fear and frustration on quite possibly hostile, or at the least antipathetic, civilian populations, either in spite of, or even with the tacit or active assistance of, at the very least, low-level officers. Random violence, rape, looting, pyromania, and more serious atrocity, are, alas, the signature of such pro-longed degenerate warfare, whatever the historical framework—not least where it leads to no clear military result.

However, the fluidity of the Eastern Front, particularly as the crisis of war deep-ened, also carried with it more high-level considerations. A critical one was the degree to which the possibility of military breakthrough, in other words of the overturning of the overall military stalemate, might be facilitated by fifth columns or even open insurgency from communal populations willing to collaborate against their own imperial masters.

The inference should not in itself shock. All the major protagonists in the war sought to identify collaborators of this kind, and all the more desperately as the possibility of outright military victory receded. The British, for instance, from 1915 looked to the possibility of an Arab revolt against the Ottomans; the Ottomans to awakening Turkic and Muslim opposition to the tsars both in the Russian Caucasus and beyond. The Russians, in turn, placed largely illusory hopes on the Ruthenes or, further afield, the Czechs joining in some grand pan-Slavic crusade against Austro-Teutonic enslavement. Significantly, Austrians and Germans had similar notions about the Ruthenes, otherwise known as Ukrainians, turning the tables on Petrograd. Everybody, from every side, sought to entice and cajole the subject Poles, caught between the three empires of

Russia, Austria, and Germany.[43] In a critical sense, all this was evidence of the degree to which the idea of the nation had captured, or if under duress haunted, the wartime imagination of imperial elites. Certainly, by the middle of the war, Congresses of Oppressed Nationalities taking place in neutral venues such as Lausanne were attracting attention from the belligerents in ways which hardly would have been conceivable before this time. German Chancellor Bethmann-Hollweg, in a Reichstag speech in April 1916, even seemed to be offering German support for the self-determination of one such grouping when he referred to a 'League of Russia's Foreign Peoples'.[44]

Of all this 'mobilisation of ethnicity',[45] or more exactly in this case of sub-imperial ethnicities on the opposite side to one's own, two things need to be said. Firstly, while it certainly encouraged self-styled national leaders to assume that they had importance and could be listened to by imperial statesmen—eventually leading, especially later in the war, to some emerging relationships, even unwritten alliances (however tortuous, convoluted, temporary, and opportunistic these may have been) between themselves and their Great Power patrons—any actual tangible results of these efforts, in terms of undermining the ability of the enemy to continue to wage war, were patchy where they were not downright futile.[46] Certainly, again at various stages in the conflict, there were some notable attempts to create military units out of captured POWs, or diasporic volunteers. One thinks of the Polish, Czech, and even Zionist-orientated Jewish legions created by the Entente, and, obversely, a Georgian legion mostly sponsored by the Germans, and a Polish one, mostly by the Austrians; each of these with varying degrees of military efficacy.[47] Yet critically, with some caveats about the Ottoman situation, there were no mass *grass-roots* insurrections of this kind—except, of course, in the fevered imaginings of military intelligence officers attempting to covertly foment them on behalf of their respective imperial staffs.

Secondly, it is exactly in this gap between belligerent aspirations and the reality of communal quiescence that the potential lay for paranoid projection against subject rimland populations; on the part, that is, of imperial state and society. By seeking to encourage revolt, sabotage, or even plain dissent among ethnic communities who were the subjects of enemy powers, the Great War adversaries were not simply implicating such communities in their own devious stratagems but encouraging them, whether through passive non-action or even active betrayal, to behave treasonably. Rather, in an already highly charged situation, it was as if they were offering on a plate to enemy state and dominant demos just cause to vent their wrath against these communities.

There is, however, one small problem with this line of reasoning. It presumes the necessity for some intentional subversion on the part of one Great Power protagonist against another to precipitate the latter's accusation against one or more of its own subordinate *ethnies*. What makes Russia notably interesting yet frightening in the context of the Great War is the fact that it needed no such provocation. Rather it anticipated that, at the very least, key elements of its subject populations would seek to sabotage its war effort.

THE MILITARY AS DRIVERS OF COMMUNAL
ONSLAUGHT? THE RUSSIAN GREAT RETREAT

In the event of war, 'out of the fifty million non-Russian subjects which Russia possesses, thirty million would render espionage service to the attackers, and would start a civil war inside the country'.[48] So predicted the distinctly out-of-favour Russian elder statesmen, Count Witte, in an interview with a German newspaper correspondent in March 1913. Whether Witte was, or was not, trying to send a signal to Berlin regarding why Russia would not be going to war with Germany anytime soon, is immaterial to our discussion.[49] What matters is that his assessment would seem to corroborate the gathering and—since the failed empire-wide revolution of 1905—notably heightened sense among Russia's ruling elite that its 'minority' subjects were not to be trusted. Witte's arch-rival and first minister successor, Peter Stolypin, for instance, having convened the ominously sounding 'Special Commission for the Formulation of Measures towards Counteracting the Tatar–Muslim Influence in the Volga Region' in 1910, duly received its report, which insisted that behind an ostensibly innocent Tatar educational programme, a carefully organized pan-Islamic and pan-Turkic programme was being prepared.[50]

At the outset of actual war, however, it was not Volga Muslims who bore the brunt of tsarist paranoia but those inhabiting the Kars and Ardahan provinces contiguous with the Ottoman borders. The Porte reported that Russian Cossack troops had busily massacred entire Muslim communities, to the tune of thousands, in the Chorokhi valley and beyond, after being liberated, in spring 1915, from an initial Ottoman incursion.[51] Yet this was arguably no more than a prelude to a more systematic plan, put on the table to the Russian Council of Ministers by Caucasus viceroy, Count Vorontsov-Dashkov: to strip *all* Muslims from the border region of their Russian citizenship and then deport them beyond the Urals on the grounds of their collective 'collaboration' with the enemy. Interestingly, and portentously for the future, the ministers did not protest this plan in principle. Instead, the Justice and Foreign ministries warned that if the government proceeded with the project Russia was likely to be inundated with possibly millions of expelled non-Muslim Turkish subjects in a more than tit-for-tat retribution at the war's end. It was this consideration which led the ministers to draw back from the brink.[52] Even so, on his own initiative, Vorontsov-Dashkov was not deflected from arresting many thousands of Adzhars—Georgian-speaking Muslims of Russian citizenship—as well as many Ottoman-subject Laz, caught at the war's outset on the wrong side of this historically porous border. Crimean Tatars who had moved back and forth between Romanov and Ottoman territories also found themselves caught up in this dragnet. Certainly, no mass killing of those who were Russian subjects, now designated as *byvshie liudi* (former people), took place. Nevertheless, their deportation by train transports to provinces in the interior, where they were greeted with the anathema of regional governors, who refused to have these alleged pan-Turkic security risks deposited on their terrain, was ominous. By now ill-treated and racked with typhoid, at least 5,000 of the deportees ended up incarcerated on the uninhabited Nargen Island in the Caspian, before eventual intercession by

Georgian Duma members and others allowed the survivors their return—in 1917.[53]

In fact in winter of 1914–15, several thousand Adzhar guerrillas—acting in support of the initial ill-fated Ottoman Third Army thrust led by Enver Pasha—at least gave some credence, in this case, to tsarist fears,[54] just as, vice versa, the involvement of Ottoman Armenians in volunteer units operating on the Russian side in this campaign fed CUP obsession with a general Armenian sabotage effort. If the CUP response, in the summer and autumn of 1915, vastly surpassed anything the Russians, or indeed anybody else, could dream up against their own alleged fifth columnists, in the earlier months of the year it remained, if anything, level pegging. The only irony was that the Russian regime anxieties were focused not so much on what was happening on their south-western Ottoman front as along the vast, and indeed vastly more critical, military theatre in the 'Lands Between'.

*

If the really quite moderate and progressive—at least in Russian terms—Witte was a convinced believer in the malevolence of Russia's 'other' peoples, it should hardly be surprising if at the outset of war the Russian military view on the matter was close to histrionic. It goes without saying, of course, that the military apparatuses of the warring Great Powers represented both the bottom line in the integrity, preservation, and survival of their respective polities, with usually right-wing, if not downright reactionary, views and prejudices to match. In other words, these command structures, especially through their intelligence bureaux, had particularly sensitive, if arguably entirely overwrought antennae focused on lurking dangers from potential spies, sabotage, and political, industrial, or communal action perceived as spiking their respective war efforts. Even putting aside the cultural predispositions of the Russian military as upholders of a brittle, brutally autocratic yet unstable regime to the degree that, excluding the Ottomans, it was usually considered the scandal of the European ménage, it would logically follow that, of necessity, the Russian military would be on high alert.

Yet clearly the military's *collective* cultural predispositions and prejudices did greatly influence matters. And not least, given that the balance of domestic power shifted even more ominously towards that of Stavka, the Army High Command, at the war's outset. Under the nominal headship of the tsar's uncle, the Grand Duke Nikolai Nikolaevich, but actually under the strategic direction of Chief of Staff N. N. Ianushkevich, Stavka had sweeping powers, under regulations—the *Polozhenie*—promulgated in line with the July 1914 mobilization orders. These effectively transferred the entirety of Russia's rimlands, and—as the war front ebbed and flowed—territories both Russian and non-Russian beyond, from the authority of the tsar-appointed and extremely reactionary Council of Ministers, to Stavka.[55] Tensions associated with this duality of power would become highly significant as the near-debacle of 1915 unfolded. But even before that point, Stavka ascendancy suggested that the fate of borderland communities was now very much in its hands, not least because that fate had become so closely intertwined with the professional competency of the generals themselves.

Reeling from the initial disasters at Tannenberg and the Masurian lakes, fought largely on Prussian soil, Stavka was actually able almost immediately to regain the initiative by a successful offensive that took Austrian eastern Galicia: in other words, extending Russian rule, albeit briefly, into an archetypal rimlands region peopled with folk we would now delineate as mostly Poles or Ukrainians (but then Ruthenes) but also with significant, ubiquitous communities of, amongst others, Germans and Jews. Witte, in 1913, had cited Poles and Finns as the most likely insurrectionary elements in Russia's ethnographic mosaic. In Galicia and across the frontiers into Russia *integrale*, it followed that many suspected Polish political, religious, and cultural leaders were vulnerable to military arrest and deportation into the Russian interior. But then, so were members of the Ruthenian elite, even though, given the less 'advanced' state of Ukrainian nationalism, they were fewer in number.[56]

One prominent figure, however, was the Lemberg (Lwów)-based metropolitan Andrii Sheptyts'kyi, who will reappear as a noteworthy figure in Volume Two, with regard to a further world war. Here, his removal from the leadership of the Uniate (Greek Catholic) church—that is, of a historic religious community increasingly associated in the twentieth century with Ukrainian nationalism—dovetailed with some immediate efforts of the occupying regime in Galicia to carry through a programme of Russification. These plans included the enforced conversion to Orthodoxy of swathes of Sheptyts'kyi's flock,[57] a practice we will find repeatedly utilized by different putative or actual state-builders and extenders throughout the further ebb and flow of violent encounters in the rimlands. Lemkin would have had no doubt what in his own terms this amounted to: a facet of 'genocide' aimed at undermining 'the essential foundations of the life of national groups'.[58] In 1914 much of this Russification project ostensibly came under the cover of a rapidly appointed civilian governor. However, Ianushkevich remained a dominating force in what amounted to a crude softening-up programme, the ultimate aim of which was to 'reunite' (his words) the lost Slavs of the Habsburg province with their authentic Russian brethren.[59]

Yet this episode also gives a clue as to why Stavka's search for 'enemies' was not firmly, or at least not coherently, directed at Poles and Ukrainians. They were, if not actual, then potential 'friends'; the ones most like 'ourselves', to be induced and cajoled and, if absolutely necessary, bludgeoned into some Russian-led pan-Slavic brotherhood. For all the inconsistency and sometimes violence which thus accompanied Russian invasion and retreat, Stavka's already inbuilt preconceptions acted as a block against assaulting majority populations. Consequently, it made the contrast with their readiness to accuse and violate German and Jewish minorities all the more striking.

*

Of the two, military and more general state actions against Germans might appear at first sight to involve a semblance of logic. After all, there were a lot of German and indeed Austro-Hungarian citizens living within the empire, and it was plausible that some of these might be fired up by the sort of rhetoric emanating from the Pan-German League, not to say the actual military planning of German High Command (OHL), which may have surmised that German agricultural colonies, such as those in the Volhynia borderlands, might act as some sort of glacis for a military assault against the Russian heartlands. Moreover, given the way the major Russian cities, certainly early on in the war, were in thrall to both war hysteria and spy mania it made sense to take precautions.[60]

One cannot beat about the bush though with regard to the fact that the measures adopted were, as with those against Ottoman subjects, comprehensively brutal. At the very outset of hostilities, the main department of the General Staff issued orders to commanders of military districts to make *all* German or Austro-Hungarian subjects domiciled in Russia prisoners of war (POWs) without respect to age, sex, or, for that matter, nationality. Consequently, Austrian Polish and Czech speakers found themselves arrested alongside Austrian Germans.[61] A more frenetic aspect of this picture was in the way General Bonch-Bruevich, the head of the Petrograd Military District, was given sweeping powers by the Grand Duke to pursue spies *throughout* the empire.[62] This, of course, threatened almost anyone and, as we will see, with a man with the antipathies of a Bonch-Bruevich in the driving seat, ensured that Jews could be equally if not more often designated as the prey. But this hardly offered consolation for German nationals. With all rights under international agreements and conventions voided in September 1914 by state decree, thus negating any hope of redress through the civil courts, up to 330,000 were deported to camps or exile across the Volga, mostly to Siberia.[63] The Volhynian cohort suffered particularly disastrously. Of some 50,000 transported to distant *gubernii* beyond the Urals in 1915, the majority are believed to have perished.[64] Nor, once set on this path, did Stavka propose anything but ratcheting up the deportation programme further—'cleansing' ever larger areas of the Polish *kresy* or the Baltic coastline of these supposedly dangerous 'aliens' through late 1914, and into early 1915. Perhaps though, it is significant that while 'military necessity' was always implicit justification for such measures, the orders were increasingly restated (almost as if to reassure Stavka itself), as being 'countermeasures': that is, a legitimate response to alleged German and Austrian atrocities, with the further implication that anything less would cause popular outrage.[65]

Does this tell us something about the mercilessness of war, underlying instrumental policies of the military and state, or something more psychologically projective as Stavka sought to cover itself for its increasing failures? Certainly, the growing onslaught on 'Germans' seemed to apply not only to those who were subjects of the 'Two Germanies' living in Russia but, as in occupied eastern Galicia, members of the German-speaking community there, who instantly became 'unreliables' subject to harassment, or possible deportation—not to mention all the Germans living in Russia itself. There were, after all, an estimated 1,621,000 of the latter in 1914, the majority of whom had lived in the country for generations and thus were not, in any technical sense, foreign at all.[66] Moreover, the historical relationship of the tsarist state to these people, until recent times, had been benign. Indeed, Germans had been specifically invited by successive tsars to settle in the empire—often with definite privileges of autonomy, plus military and tax exemptions in their favour—either as peasants, to create compact, self-governing communities as, notably, under Catherine the Great in the then unconsolidated steppe lands of the Volga, or to fulfil a wide range of service functions. Germans, in fact, provided the very backbone of the regime as administrators, policemen, foreign diplomats, and, of course, professional military men. It was through these occupational roles, alongside those of university teachers, merchants, and specialist artisans, that necessarily very diverse groups and strata of Germans contributed directly and massively to Russia's long-term, state-led drive for modernization. Of course, in the absence of a sufficiently strong base among native Russians to fulfil these roles, other ethno-religious groups, including Poles and Jews, might willingly have done so. Which is why it is ironic that, as late as the 1880s, tens of thousands of German farmers were still being encouraged as immigrants to rimland areas such as Volhynia, not least to bolster state efforts to block out property and land purchases by these much less desired competitors.[67]

Is there a case then for saying that the war provided an opportunity for an overtly nationalizing Russian agenda, the aim of which was to consciously overturn a form of alleged 'foreign' dependency, and to which the military consciously, or unconsciously, were prepared to play handmaiden? A tendency to represent groups such as Germans—alongside Poles, Finns, and Jews—as privileged yet parasitic nationalities giving to society and state 'a non-Russian character' had certainly been a facet of a growing right-wing critique of the tsarist malaise since the 1860s.[68] In the context of war, ultra-nationalist groups like 'The Society for Russia' ('Za Rossiiyu'), pressed for a complete package of German expulsion to Siberia.[69] The demand was mirrored in more demotic fashion in a vicious anti-German Moscow pogrom in May 1915, in which popular clamour for expulsion was taken up by the appointed city head, who expressed regret that the 'outsiders' could not all be fitted into a concentration camp on a Volga island.[70] Such sentiments would seem to chime in too with the urgings of the clearly statistically minded Bonch-Bruevich on Ianushkevich, in 1915, in favour of an 'exact registration of all deported *enemy* subjects, in order to liquidate without a trace this entire alien element at the end of the war'.[71] In some ways even more disturbing because actually implemented—and with heavy forebodings of NKVD operations a world war to come—was the manner in which, in June 1916, the much lionized General Brusilov, in the immediate wake of a major and indeed temporarily successful campaign to retake Volhynia from the Central Powers, chose to devote his energies to deporting some 13,000 German colonists, who had previously been spared that fate by dint of the earlier German advance into the region. Eric Lohr describes how 'in minute detail' Brusilov plotted 'every step of the operation'.[72] Both tsarist generals would later serve as advisers to the Red Army.

The 'chilling efficiency and striving for totality that had become part of mass deportation practices'[73] might indeed suggest that, far from these deportations being a wartime exigency undertaken by the military arm of state without reference to long-term political or economic considerations, they were on the contrary carried out with exactly these goals in view. Evidence to this effect would certainly seem to be on hand not only in the February 1915 law which allowed for the expropriation of 'colonist' deportees' landholdings in the entirety of a 100- to a 150-kilometre rimland strip and their permanent transfer to the state, the proceeds of expropriation being channelled through a peasant bank, but also in a series of further, albeit convoluted, liquidation enactments over the next two years, by which increasing numbers of ethnic Germans (that is, including Russian-born or naturalized ones, though exempting the seriously large group of German Baltic landholders) found themselves compelled to sell for a song and then vacate land, property, or other capital holdings.[74] The fact, moreover, that these liquidation laws were eventually extended to the entirety of the empire would certainly suggest a notion of some final reckoning. It is true that persistent rumours that the tsar signed a general anti-German deportation decree lack evidence.[75] On the other hand, there was a 1916 directive to expel the Volga communities the following spring, while premier Alexander Kerensky's post-revolution stay of execution was only firmly rescinded by the Bolsheviks.[76]

Perhaps, then, it should be no surprise that when, in late spring 1915, the struggle on the Eastern Front began to turn decisively against the Russians with a major Austro-German breakout from Gorlice in Galicia combining with the Ludendorff offensive towards Kurland in the Baltic north, ethnic Germans would bear the significant brunt of Russian military frustration and ire. As the Central Powers' advance moreover threatened to develop into a pincer movement enveloping the main bulk of Russian forces, a general retreat ensued, before a new front line was finally stabilized at the end of the summer. In the intervening months, practically the whole of the 'Lands Between' under Russian sovereignty, including Congress Poland, the Baltic region, and a further vast swathe of territory—not least Podolia and Volhynia—were lost to Stavka control, as was previously conquered eastern Galicia.[77] And, in the wake of the retreat, practically everywhere that German communities remained there were military hostage-taking, the burning of villages, shootings, and forced evacuations. Yet, paradoxically, it was not Germans who became the prime, or only, target of the army's wrath. It was the Jews.

*

'It was Germany who declared war but the Jews who chose Germany as an instrument of their designs'.[78] So declared the right-wing Russian newspaper *Zemshchina* during the 1915 crisis. That this wartime motif had its roots in the most deep-seated elite anti-Semitic animus would hardly be a revelation to any student of Russian Jewish history. And though something of this needs to be drawn out further, at least insofar as it can throw light on the extremities to which, in conditions of total war, this psychosis led—to be pursued in our final section of this chapter 'Blaming the Jews'—what primarily concerns us at this juncture is the way it converted into the specificity of a military response that was 'clearly an outgrowth and a product of the policies of the Army High Command'.[79] In other words, the protagonists were given the resources, not to say a monopoly of violence, at the Stavka's behest, with the real potential not just for sporadic acts of violence but for a systematic, even exterminatory onslaught against the Jewish communities of the rimlands.

Rimlands, one should add, which were, in 1914, Jewish heartlands. It was exactly here, in the 'Lands Between'—certainly to a degree in regions such as the Austrian Bukovina and Galicia, as well as Rumania, but, above all, in the territories where Romanov writ ran—that the majority of north European, historically Yiddish-speaking (that is, Ashkenazi) Jews resided in a great spread of either urban centres or otherwise predominantly or even exclusively Jewish townlets (*shtetlach*). Religiously and culturally distinct and indeed occupationally so, too, from the ethnographically diverse, mostly peasant but also mostly non-Russian populations amongst whom they dwelt, and notwithstanding a 2.5 million-strong mass migration to Western Europe, North America, and other Neo-Europes from the 1880s to the outbreak of war (as economic and political conditions in the so-called Jewish Pale of Settlement deteriorated), the Ashkenazi subjects of Tsar Nicholas II continued to be the demographic powerhouse of a much broader Jewish diaspora, even while its overall composition remained much more varied and complex.[80] In short, a tsarist military attack on the Pale would tear at the very guts of *all* Jewish life and culture.

One additional point of information before returning to this critical matter: Germans and Jews in Russia were clearly, in some respects, comparable. They were historically diasporic, both actually drawn from Germanic backgrounds (Yiddish, after all, was a Judaeo-German dialect whose speakers were originally exiles or fugitives from extreme crusader-linked violence in the medieval Rhineland). They were often (though in the German case not exclusively) dependent for existence in their *new* contexts on their provision of middlemen services, or, as Yuri Slezkine would aptly put it, on their role as Mercurians, that is, 'service nomads' to peasant and land-based Apollonians.[81] Finally, in 1914 terms, they were two extremely valuable (though not homogeneous) communities with increasingly modernizing attitudes in the mainstream European mould, plus organizational and technical skills to match. In other words, with attributes which an unreformed tsarism, in the context of a totalized military–industrial, life-and-death struggle against much better equipped and more capable adversaries, could ill afford to ignore, let alone persecute and punish. The parallels with Greeks and Armenians in the Ottoman Empire are obvious. This hardly, incidentally, required Germans and Jews to have a consonance of interests, or to like each other. They generally did not; any more than Greek and Armenian competitors. The key Jewish–German difference that matters here, however, is that tsarism inherited the former from the Polish partitions of the 1790s: it was to the medieval Polish crown and nobility that Jewry owed its historic allegiance. Tsarism, by contrast, never managed to reconcile itself to Jews, and despite various, always abortive, efforts throughout the nineteenth century to find ways of assimilating or forcibly absorbing them into Russian society, ultimately it was unable to move beyond an entirely negative, distrustful, discriminatory, and, above all, holding-at-arm's-length approach to what it saw as potential Jewish contamination and 'takeover'. The territorial expression of this negativity was none other than the Pale of Settlement: the means by which the vast majority of Jews were kept tightly circumscribed within the rimlands and away from Russia's heartlands.

Is our question regarding the Stavka's anti-German actions also, then, applicable here? Did Ianushkevich and his senior colleagues see the war as an opportunity, given the extraordinary powers now vested in them—especially in the rimlands war zones—to offer a military solution to the 'Jewish question', perhaps even under the right circumstances bringing it to an abrupt foreclosure? Or was what transpired in

1915 much more an on-the-hoof reaction to the circumstances of retreat, defeat, and chaos? It should be emphasized that there is no evidence of an exterminatory blueprint. But then, as we have repeatedly argued in *Genocide in the Age of the Nation State*, this is not in itself necessary for genocide to occur. What, arguably, is needed is some indication as to the mindset of the core organizing perpetrators—to the effect that they nurse embedded grievances and antipathies towards a communal population sufficient to the articulation or imagining of their destruction— merging with contingent circumstances or possibilities which might make the actual implementation of such a notion, or notions, operable. In these terms, what matters is charting not simply the explosion of violence at the moment of crisis from April 1915, but what led up to it in the first phase of the war. And with this in view, we can perhaps discern intentions and actions on the part of Stavka which we might broadly compartmentalize into three types.

The first we might label 'anticipatory and practised'. Right at the outset of the war at least 100,000 Jews were forcibly removed by the military from rural areas to the rear of the front, on grounds of their potential *collective* danger as spies and saboteurs. The number may have doubled or trebled by the winter of 1914–15.[82] These displaced people found themselves as internal refugees dependent on limited charity and welfare resources in Warsaw and other big towns, especially in Poland, precipitating a major food and public health crisis. That this sweeping expulsion should have been applied at all is in itself somewhat bewildering, given that in spite of the tranche of discriminations and disqualifications which applied to Jews as a lesser form of Russian subject, their able men were still required to fulfil military service. In fact, leading communal spokesmen responded to the July 1914 call to arms with unequivocal enthusiasm, while evidence of general, loyal participation is confirmed in the estimated half-a-million serving Jews (that is, one-tenth of the Russian Jewish population) between 1914 and 1917.[83] Certainly, there were some crude, inflammatory, and quite inept attempts by the German and Austrian High Commands, either through direct proclamations, or operating through a German Jewish organized (and crassly named) Committee for the Liberation of Russian Jewry, to foment Jewish insurrection.[84] But while we do not have to take Jewish elite proclamations of loyalty and patriotism as the absolute truth about grass-roots Russian Jewish views and responses to a persecuting regime, neither do we have to assume that the quiescence of the majority of Jewish non-combatants is proof that they were really all eagerly awaiting a German victory.

The minds of Ianushkevich and the generals were of course already made up, whatever evidence was put before them.[85] The Jews were guilty, and where they could not be bottled up in a town the only other 'defensive' precaution to be taken was to deport (alongside other suspect peoples) the allegedly most hostile and unreliable amongst them to the east—an unfortunately time-consuming procedure which also drew on scarce military transport and personnel—or to take hostages in situ in order to scotch in advance the anticipated acts of espionage or sabotage. With the Grand Duke's proclamation in late November 1914 emphasizing the point by openly describing the Jews as Russia's most resolute of enemies, and with the further authorization to execute Jewish hostages 'in cases of necessity', the scene was set not only for this to become a standard operating procedure but also for a self-reinforcing process of accusation against Jews on almost any count where the war effort was not going well. Whether in the military, the Red Cross, or against civilians far from the front, a fabulous concoction of anti-Jewish charges ensued, ranging from signalling to the enemy from windmills, spreading venereal disease in the army through unclean prostitutes, disrupting the flow of internal military communications traffic while also communicating with the enemy through underground telephones, to hiding German soldiers in their potato cellars.[86]

Can we discern in Stavka's order a developing effort of legitimization in preparation for a wholesale military assault on rimland Jewry? A second type of Army High Command behaviour might suggest such an instrumentalizing way of thinking, though a more appropriate label for this case might read 'anticipatory but *lacking* implementation'. In eastern Galicia, for instance, in the spring of 1915, General D. Shcherbachev, the commander of the Eleventh Army, proposed to Count Bobrinsky, Russia's acting civil governor in the occupied province, that all the Galician Jews should be collected in a giant dumping ground along the Rumanian frontier where, consciously denied sustenance, they would be forced to cross en masse into, at that time, neutral Rumania. Shcherbachev calculated that this would upset the Rumanians to such a degree that they in turn would expel the lot to Austria, of which, of course, the Galician Jews were citizens.[87]

Two things are immediately arresting about Shcherbachev's version of some 'final solution' to the Galician Jewish problem. The first is that it was not, in Stavka terms, outlandish. Indeed, in February the Grand Duke had tightened up his own already draconian anti-Jewish orders by proposing the expulsion across the lines to the enemy side of all Jews, 'regardless of age or sex', in regions of military activity.[88] If this had a definite sense of the impractical about it and hence was also *not* acted upon, the reason for the failure of the Shcherbachev scheme again appears to have had nothing to do with questions of morality. Military and civil authorities, after all, were at one in wanting Jews expunged from the Galician economy and social life. Rather, Bobrinsky's doubts related to how the Rumanians might react (the Allies after all were attempting to coax Bucharest onto the side of the Entente), and he also warned that such action might trigger large-scale Jewish retaliation.[89] All of which elements lend to this forgotten moment of the Great War an uncanny resemblance to how a Heydrich, or, for that matter, an Antonescu, might have thought through their own similar stratagems. With, of course, one singular difference: impractical or not, dogged by the projective fantasy of a Jewish ability to strike back or not, *they* would have striven for implementation.

Ironically, back in 1914 or 1915, Galician and Bukovinan Jewry had a habit of not waiting for the worst the Russians might do. Where they could, they fled westwards to the point where, by late 1915, there were 157,630 registered Jewish refugees in Austria proper.[90] Their flight was with good cause. From the very start, Russian military advance—or retreat—was accompanied by human rights violations and brutalities by mounted Cossacks or other Russian soldiery which, while widespread, also seem to have been perpetrated particularly against Jews. That this should have been the case has a certain familiar ring about it, without necessarily implicating Stavka. Anti-Jewish pogroms, after all, had been an intermittent yet repeated feature of pre-1914 'peacetime' life in the Russian rimlands for more than a generation, and while recent revisionist history has drawn back from assumptions of tsarist state complicity in most, or all, of these incidents, that they clearly involved grass-roots, demotic participation is not in dispute.[91] The same is true of many of the pogroms which beset Galicia in the wake of the Russian invasion, very often ordinary peasants joining in as soldiers looted, raped, and extorted their way across defenceless communities.[92]

However, as the late John Klier has emphasized,[93] the military pogroms of 1914 and 1915 were entirely different from their pre-war communal counterparts, not only in terms of nature, scale, and ultimate devastation but in terms of responsibility, too. Military discipline, imposed according to the book by officers, should have acted as a firm block against transgressions committed by ordinary soldiery. As it was, it was exactly the command structure which not only enabled but arguably encouraged and fostered such transgressions to take place. Our third and final type of military thought process and follow-though action would suggest, however, that while the green light to military anti-Jewish violence was grounded in pre-existing views of Jews, these were both reinforced and radically exaggerated by the circumstances of war itself: the relevant signpost here, perhaps, reading 'anticipated but contingent'.

An early but ominous indication of how these elements were prone to congeal is documented in what happened in the eastern Galician capital, Lemberg, in late September 1914. With the offices of the Russian occupying military administration hardly set up, an apparently unanticipated disturbance involving gunfire led to a day and night rampage through the city centre by Cossacks and other units. However, the army search for the alleged firer, or firers, quickly alighted on the substantial Jewish quarter, the consequent looting and destruction of property (aided and abetted by some non-Jewish Lembergers) being accompanied by indiscriminate shooting of residents 'regardless of age or sex', both on the pavements and as homes were broken into and raided. Between twenty and fifty Jews were killed, and over one hundred injured.[94]

Nevertheless, what mattered for Stavka was not the loss of civilian life, or the potential bad press this would bring in neutral countries such as the USA, but what was allegedly proven by the incident: namely, that the Lemberg Jews had been responsible for the trouble from first to last. Critical to this charge was the story that it had been a young Jewish *woman* who had fired the first shots from a window at Russian troops. Not only was this narrative of the hidden Jew with a firearm—in other words, the Jew as cowardly villain—destined to become a regular justifying motif for anti-Jewish violence in the eastern borderlands in subsequent years;[95] but doubly so, in accord with the gendered implication it contained, the Jewish female was cast as a wholly unnatural transgressor against the dictates of her own sex. Just as with the women of the Vendée in the face of French Republican virtue, back in 1793–4,[96] so here now, the women, as much as the men, of Jewish race had supposedly displayed their true diabolical colours.

Except, of course, it was entirely fabrication. The subsequent civil administration investigation found no evidence of either any single Jewish malefactor acting alone or of a more grandiosely planned but abortive Jewish uprising, as had been insinuated by the local Russian military commander, before the story was taken up and magnified by a local pro-Russian newspaper. Did the investigation's rebuttal of Jewish conspiracy cut any ice, however, with Ianushkevich? Not a bit of it. Overriding Bobrinsky's civil authority, the chief of staff instigated further reprisals, including hundreds of arrests of the more prominent members of the community, not only for what had already happened but for what, in Ianushkevich's clearly overwrought imagination, the Jews would do if they were not stopped in their tracks.[97]

And so the Stavka case against rimland Jewry was signed, sealed, and delivered. Though possibly, ironically, with more than a helping hand from the military administration itself, even perhaps with the assistance of the tsarist secret political police, the Okhrana: Jewish witnesses alleged that they had instigated the whole train of events in the first place.[98] This itself is non-proven, and, for all its inference that the Lemberg pogrom may not have come out of the blue after all, should not unduly detain us. What matters more is the Lemberg feedback effect on the conduct of Russian soldiery more generally. Having been presented with an official version in which Jews—Russian, Galician, whatever—were deemed malevolent and dangerous (which may have simply confirmed what many Russians in uniform believed anyway), the idea that they might henceforth take out their frustrations on Jewish communities in their path with impunity, perhaps even feeling themselves to be acting with the full affirmation of the High Command, becomes less implausible.

*

In these terms, the forcible evacuations and/or deportations of anything between half a million and 1 million Russian Jews[99]—as the Great Retreat gathered pace in the high spring and early summer 1915—has a certain air of wretched predictability about it. In two days at the height of the process, on 30 April and 3 May, for instance, an estimated 190,000 Jewish inhabitants, mostly in Kovno (Kaunas) province but also from neighbouring districts, including Kurland, were ejected with only twenty-four or possibly thirty-six hours to clear out.[100] These measures were mostly directed and carried out by relatively low-level officers, police chiefs, and gendarmerie, and sometimes, perhaps more significantly, political counter-intelligence personnel.[101] However, the process was clearly inaugurated and monitored by Stavka from the Baltic in the north, to Volhynia and Podolia in the south, on the basis of the single collective charge 'of spying, signalling, and in other ways helping the enemy'.[102] The consequence, of course, was a mounting range of anti-Jewish violence committed by Cossacks and other soldiers in the line of retreat, as duly compiled and, in the case of the neutral USA, published, by Western Jewish organizations.[103]

Indeed, it is with the retreat in full swing that we might begin to discern similarities with events almost simultaneously unfolding in Ottoman Anatolia. With hindsight, we know that what happened to the Armenian communities there proved to be entirely more exceptional and catastrophic: they suffered genocide, the Russian Jews did not. Yet both Russian Jews and Ottoman Armenians, in the lead-up to their respective deportations in the spring and summer of 1915, found themselves in remarkably similar peril. A majority of their populations were not simply caught up in, or in the immediate rear of, an intensifying war zone where the 'enemy' was strongly on the offensive (paradoxically, while Russian armies were in retreat on the Eastern Front, they were advancing on the Caucasus one) but were openly charged in both cases with being accomplices of that enemy. Thus, each community was in imminent danger—if nothing else—of being overwhelmed in a wave of retributive fury administered not just by the polity or military but by local populations, too. Understanding of the divergence between the fate of the two communities can only be developed by fuller examination of the Armenian case, which will follow in Chapter 2. Yet if the similarity between the circumstances is so close, it still rather begs the question: how it was that in the Jewish case genocide was averted? Was it ultimately that Russian animus was less intense, less 'organized' or systematized into a programme of extermination? Or does this in itself carry with it too many assumptions about some predetermined CUP genocidal intent with regard to the Armenians?

A mitigating factor which might at first sight appear relevant in the case of Russian Great Retreat, is that Jews did not suffer its consequences alone. Stavka orders, as the military retreat got underway, were for 'scorched earth', that is, at least initially, for wholesale evacuations of subject populations in the path of the advancing Austrian and German armies, plus the firing or destruction of not just military but all civilian machinery, plants, villages, crops, and beasts which could not be removed further east. The complete chaos that ensued proved the Ianushkevich strategy to be entirely self-defeating: the refugee flood impeded military movement, clogging up and overwhelming hastily improvised relief stations, and led to a general epidemiological breakdown, the most immediate consequence of which was a cholera epidemic with consequent fatalities on an enormous scale.[104] Similarly, included in a total estimate of over 7.4 million Russian subjects displaced by the war by 1917—a very hefty proportion as a result of the events of 1915—the Jewish deportations may appear less exceptional.[105] But then, if one looks more closely at the Anatolian situation in 1915 and 1916, here, too, there were general mass evacuations or flights of population—not just of Armenians— with similarly disastrous results in terms of famine and disease and consequent soaring mortality.[106]

What, however, cannot to be lost sight of in either the Russian or Ottoman cases, is the way specific communities were targeted for exemplary punishment, deportation, or worse. Certainly, because the whole military conduct of the operation was manic, frenetic, and bungled this could mean that Lithuanian farmers who were Lutheran could be as easily taken out of their homes and strung up or shot, on the grounds that they were Germans, as those who *really* were ethnic Germans.[107] Clearly, the latter were one group who were required to pay the price for Russian military failure. But so, too, were the Jews, and arguably even more so. Prince Scherbatov, the newly appointed head of a revamped Council of Ministers, itself a consequence of the military disaster, asserted in closed session in September 1915: 'Ianushkevich wants to make the Jews responsible for all our reverses. The policy is successful and the pogroms are becoming more frequent. I suspect Ianushkevich wants to use the Jews as an alibi'.[108]

That Stavka were indeed prepared to go to inordinate lengths to dissemble their own culpability for defeat by playing the Jewish card is amply demonstrated by the Kuzhi affair. At the height of the Great Retreat, on 11 May, Stavka announced that they had found specific evidence of Jewish collaboration with the enemy in the village of Kuzhi, in Kovno province. Here it was alleged the fifth columnists had hidden German troops who had then ambushed a Russian infantry regiment. The fact that a thorough investigation by Duma deputies, Kerensky and N. M. Friedman, found that all the Kuzhi Jews had been evacuated a day before the supposed incident had taken place seems no more to have deterred Stavka from their course of action than the exposing of the Lemberg travesty.[109] On the contrary, not only were the Kuzhi allegations widely disseminated throughout the empire's press but a specially convened Stavka meeting, on 23 June, expressly sought to agree 'measures for the cleansing of several places on the northern and southwestern fronts by our troops'.[110]

Again, what is intriguing if bewildering in these examples is the way, on the one hand, long-term political aspirations to irrevocably disgorge as many Jews and other unreliable elements as possible from the rimland zone—even to the detriment of pressing military priorities—jostled, on the other, with a wholly less governable range of desires and passions to incriminate the Jews for just about everything which had gone wrong. That this was so, even after Ianushkevich had been relieved of his overall command and removed to the Caucasus front, is illustrated by the manner in which his successor, General Alekseev, continued to stoutly defend the rights of army commanders to hostage-take or deport Jews from regions of troop deployment, albeit no longer with mass deportation in view. It is equally apparent, in late 1915, in General Brusilov's retrospective endorsement as commander on the South-Western Front, of the *specifically* Jewish deportations earlier that year.[111]

Nor is there any obvious evidence to suggest that Petrograd's political elite did anything but share Stavka's idée fixe. As we will see further in 'Blaming the Jews', high officials of state, even in the new, supposedly more liberal Scherbatov administration, were equally obsessed with Jewry's collective malevolence towards the Russian state, though, at least as disturbingly, as much with a reputed international, especially financial aspect in mind, as on account of mere domestic sabotage. Even so, Jewish guilt as regards espionage was so clearly entrenched in Petrograd that its veracity was practically unquestioned by Allied officials, military attachés, or other observers. British ambassador Sir George Buchanan, for instance, in spring 1915, wrote to his own Foreign Office, 'There cannot be the slightest doubt that a very large number of Jews have been in German pay and have acted as spies during the campaigns in Poland. Nearly every Russian officer who returns from the front has stories to tell on the subject'.[112]

Which, finally, must return us to our leading question: if the accusation levelled here was, in effect, the same as that equally made by the CUP against the Armenians, how do we account for the absence of exterminatory follow-through in the Jewish case? After all, Alexander Prusin, one of the most astute interpreters of the Russian events, accepts that anti-Semitism reached its fullest expression in the 'angst-ridden psychological atmosphere of World War One'.[113] However, he argues it was the lack of 'an ideological doctrine of extermination' on the part of the Russian military combined with an equal lack of unity 'between military and civil structures' that saved the day.[114] But even this may be to assume too much about the necessity for ideological foundations in order for genocide to take place. Or, indeed, about the support of what was actually a quite febrile civilian arm of an autocratic state in the face of—for the duration of the war at least—its praetorian overlords.

This author would instead propose that a genocidal potentiality was actually high, most specifically in the late spring of 1915, when Stavka began losing control of the deportations it had set in train. In turn, the local civil authorities were equally overwhelmed by the sheer weight of the refugee flow—whether complicit or not with Stavka's anti-Jewish animus (many provincial officials were themselves from military or ultra-nationalist backgrounds and clearly in sympathy with Stavka's venom).[115] Simultaneously, the imperial government appeared monumentally paralysed as the yawning crevice opened up between official tsarist policy, dating back to the time of the Polish partitions, and the new reality on the ground. The Pale of Settlement, after all, had been specifically inaugurated to keep Jews out of the Russian heartlands. Now Stavka, in its anti-Jewish drive, was moving them exactly in that direction.

The crisis began to focus in May on a critical number of communication hubs to which refugees were being sent. Kiev, still within the geographical area of the Pale, but technically outside it, stands out as the key. Boxcar upon boxcar of rail freight carrying thousands upon thousands of exhausted, dehydrated, and increasingly ill Jews were arriving there before being shunted into railway sidings.[116] As with Aleppo, the centre point of the Armenian deportations, neither officialdom nor voluntary charitable groups were able to cope with the sheer weight of humanity (Jewish and non-Jewish) needing to be fed, housed, and sustained. In terms of high politics, moreover, the time for decision-making was reaching a crunch. Should the Jews be moved on much further east, even to Siberia and Turkestan—as some of them, on the diktat of local officials, already had been—with the consequent threat of spiralling fatalities; or should they be sent back from whence they came?[117] Except that, logistically, given the overburdening of an already weak and disabled communications infrastructure, not to mention the chaos associated with the retreat, this was now impossible.

Here, we genuinely do have grounds not only for Armenian but for some Holocaust comparison. Historians charting the crystallization of the 'Final Solution' of all European Jewry have noted the significance, in the early winter of 1941, of key rimland cities, notably Riga, Kovno, and Minsk, to which thousands of German Jews were, without prior warning or preparation, deported by railcar, and in which Nazi SS and other 'men on the spot' found themselves thereby presented with an acute dilemma. With already burgeoning numbers of indigenous Jews incarcerated in these towns' ghettos, and food stocks critically low and prioritized for the Wehrmacht, the immediate failure of Operation Barbarossa underscored the fact that there was nowhere further east to which to send any of this human 'cargo'. Thus, with nowhere to which to return it, these officials were faced with what amounted to a human logjam, the functionalist historians' view on which is that resolution was found by the *expedient* of its literal liquidation.[118]

Such an expedient, of course, did *not* materialize in 1915. But perhaps because it did not we should not easily assume that this was a foregone conclusion. Certainly, unlike all but the most rare examples under the Nazis, there *were* tsarist officials who held out against military deportations in the first place.[119] However, comparable individuals can also be found among Ottoman officialdom, without in any way demonstrating their intrinsic ability to prevent genocide. In short, the brakes on the military deportations carrying forward into something far worse came not as a result of strenuous opposition from the administration as such. There was such civil opposition, but this came in the form of protests from Russian parliamentarians, writers, and other intellectuals, many of whom may also have been aware of a growing media campaign in the USA where the scope and scale of the deportations and accompanying atrocities were being vigorously reported and condemned.[120] Rather, it was the almost paranoid sense of Russia being under pressure not only from the outside world but more exactly, through the conduit of viva voce Allied representations, *from 'international' Jewry itself* which, more than anything, finally goaded the Council of Ministers into a circumscribed but crucial act of damage limitation.

The minutes of the emergency Council meetings of the 4 and 6 August are acutely revealing on this score. The voice of the finance minister P. L. Bark, the key tsarist official mandated at this juncture to travel to the West to secure loans, more specifically US bank loans, so that the Russian war effort might be kept afloat, is a particularly insistent one. Bark cited repeatedly not only the power of leading Western Jewish financiers upon whom the fate of Russia now supposedly depended, but the way elite non-Jewish actors, such as the British war minister, Lord Kitchener, were being inveigled into the Jewish defence by insisting to the tsarist minister how the 'amelioration of the lot of Jews in Russia' was essential for the ultimate success of the Allied war effort. Other officials could only lament the situation: 'The knife is at the throat and there is nothing to be done', intoned agriculture minister Alexander Krivoshein, while Scherbatov could only add, 'We are helpless for the money is in Jewish hands'.[121]

The extraordinary degree to which this late government of the Romanov dynasty, on this and other occasions, felt they were being lent upon directly or indirectly by the Jews themselves—with a requirement to make concessions or suffer disastrous consequences—thus presents us with a twist of events in stark contrast to the near-synchronous *Aghet*. Whereas in the latter case Armenian treason, not least on the charge—however confabulated—of acting in circumstances of war as the proxies, agents, spies, and saboteurs of other powers, provided the ultimate sanction for genocide, in the Russian Jewish case in 1915 a similar course of state action, founded on *exactly* the same run of charges, appeared to be trumped by resources of such magnitude and power held by the accused group itself as effectively to give it immunity from its self-evident criminality. Or so the Council of Ministers seemed to believe. In short, if there were in the ministers' minds inhibitions and scruples about following the Stavka's lead, which impelled them to put a brake on its deportations, and, arguably of much more critical consequence still, prevent the possibility of a 'functional' cul-de-sac by allowing refugee Jews, albeit temporarily, to reside in towns beyond the Pale, these were not primarily motivated or propelled by moral rectitude, let alone humanitarian concern. On the contrary, what the ministers conceived this all to be about—as the records of their minutes amply demonstrate—was a straightforward quid pro quo: the rich Western Jews give their money—credit—to allow Russia to continue fighting the war, while leaning on their brethren inside the country to stop revolutionary propaganda within the army: in return the army's iron fist, at the least for the time being, is gloved.[122]

Pragmatic politics, albeit based on a premise utterly false, not to say crude in the extreme, had prevented enactment of the greatest threat to the Jews in the context of the First World War. This was, however, far from the end of the matter, and as we will see, the notion of international Jewish power would come to haunt the actions of other, more decisive players in the conflict, with immediate and much more long-lasting consequences. For the Russian military, as their army and country crumpled in the complete collapse of 1917, 'Jewish' treason' was neither forgotten nor forgiven, but rather stored for a denouement which would not be long in coming. The irony was that while considerable Western attention was focusing on exactly these dangers to the Russian Jews in the rimlands, something more overtly genocidal was on the point of exploding in the Romanov Empire. It just happened to be, then, as now, off almost everybody in the West's cognitive map.

COLONIAL REVOLT AND RETRIBUTION

In the summer of 1916 anti-tsarist disturbances throughout wide swathes of Russian Turkestan turned into something wholly more explosive in the high eastern plateau steppe lands around Semirechye: the land of the seven rivers. Indeed, the rebellion here proved to be of such seismic proportions that Joshua Sanborn has described it 'as the beginning of the civil wars that would both destroy and then reconstitute the Russian imperial *ecumene*'.[123] At the same time, a revolt many thousands of miles away, in the Upper Volta region of French West Africa, initially mounted in late 1915, had itself taken on such a scale as to precipitate, in the words of its governor-general, 'a repression effort without precedent in the history of the French Soudan'.[124] As with Turkestan, so too, in this instance, the long-term consequences of the Volta–Bani War would prove to be profound, not least by shifting the whole balance of colonial activity in West Africa from an east–west to a north–south axis, thereby drawing in the labour potential of the interior towards an entirely dirigiste economic development on the coast.[125]

What matters more immediately to this discussion, however, is the extreme efforts to which Russian and French authorities went to extirpate these revolts. Mahir Saul and Patrick Royer, who have uncovered much of the largely unwritten and, certainly in the English-speaking literature, largely unknown history of the

Upper Volta insurrection, have insisted that its violent suppression was far in excess of what the Germans had done a decade earlier against the Maji Maji insurrection-ists in Tanganyika, or for that matter against the Herero and Nama in South-West Africa.[126] Actually, no figures exist for the communal fatalities from the Volta–Bani War, over and above the estimated 30,000 killed in pitched battles. What we do know, from the testimony of Governor-General Joost van Vollenhoven, is that a calculated military policy of scorched earth throughout the region—to produce famine conditions—resulted in a mass refugee flight of the population to neigh-bouring areas, in some parts reducing the population by at least half and with the further consequence that 'one of the richest regions of the colony' was transformed into a desert.[127] The devastation of the Semirechye region was equally bad, if not worse. Here the effects of scorched earth led to the flight of perhaps as many as 200,000 Kazakh, Dungan, and Kirghiz pastoralists into Chinese eastern Turke-stan—Sinkiang—the native population collapse in some specific *uezd*s such as Przhevalsk and Jarkent reaching over 70 per cent.[128] Our knowledge of overall fatalities is certainly hazy, the distinction being between those directly killed—es-timates of 100,000 often being cited—and a much higher figure of half a million (as, for instance, stated by Toynbee some years later), possibly extrapolating sketch estimates of displaced nomads who died from starvation and exposure in the deso-late, open steppes on both sides of the Russo-Chinese border.[129]

Whatever the exact degree of communal catastrophe—and, in these cases, we are never likely to know precise figures—what is clear is that even in the midst of the much broader global conflagration, we have here two instances which seem to represent a continuation of the intense pre-1914 phase of colonial genocide, com-mitted by both declining and advancing empires, as previously described in *The Rise of the West*. Whether we should specify them as optimal or suboptimal exam-ples could certainly be a question for academic debate. What is immediately strik-ing, however, particularly when put alongside the convulsions in the imperial rimlands of the Great War, is the degree to which these events have remained so outside the mainstream historical discussion zone as to be practically invisible. All the more so when it is evident that, say compared with the Russian military's assault on the Jews, no civil brakes seem to have been applied to the actions in Semirechye or Upper Volta. Of course, to argue therefore that the violence engen-dered in these instances was either more gratuitous, more systematic, or more far-reaching than that meted out to Jews or Germans in Kovno or the Kurland, presumes that one can somehow differentiate between points on some imaginary Richter scale of pain or suffering. In Russia, Jewish male leaders were held as hos-tages; in Upper Volta, ordinary women and children. Perhaps that already tells us something about similarities, but also critical differences. As does the fact that in all these cases the enactment of scorched earth was a facet of response, but again with the critical distinction that in the rimland scenario it was a reactive and wholly counterproductive one, without specific discrimination against any particular community, while in the case of Upper Volta and Semirechye it seems to have been developed with a quite conscious intent to destroy the life-support systems of the rebels for good.

A Lemkinian definition of genocide associated with the destruction of the essential foundations of life would seem to be much more overtly applicable here than in the case, say, of the Galician Uniates referred to in 'The military as drivers of communal onslaught?' section in this chapter; even where, in these colonial cases, repeat massacre was not *always* part of the operating procedure. Thus, in Upper Volta, while the machine-gunning of defeated villagers may only have been *recorded* on a limited number of occasions—the column under the command of Col. Molard, one of three in the main anti-rebel campaign, being the chief offender[130]—the poisoning of wells, destroying of crops, and driving off of livestock were all standard. So was the wiping of entire villages off the map, if not through their initial destruction by military assault involving high explosive melinite shells, then through much more systematic razing, house by house. We can discern, too, a very similar pattern in the pacification of Semirechye, again with villages obliterated, livestock slaughtered, irrigation channels consciously destroyed, and fodder crops burnt or left to rot, all with the deliberate purpose of radically curtailing all and every effort at post-conflict recuperation.[131] Moreover, we know that Russian settlers here, armed by the military and actively supported by conscript troops and reservists—clearly again with the green light from the authorities—went on the rampage against the indigenous inhabitants of the steppe. A Duma investigation by the ubiquitous Kerensky tersely concluded that the steppe inhabitants had been exterminated 'by the tens of thousands in an organized and systematic way'.[132]

How then we do account for these extreme, no-holds-barred responses? We could at this point revisit the long discussion in *The Rise of the West* about the wellsprings of colonial genocide. Except in a sense we have no need. There, we proposed that racist attitudes, or, at the very least, forms of cultural contempt in which colonized peoples were held by the majority of European settlers or colonial enforcers—if not always by military or civil administrators—always carried in their wake a huge, if essentially latent, potential for violence. At crisis points too, these attitudes could translate into acquiescence in annihilation on the part of metropolitan constituencies. In 1923, Toynbee, looking back on the events of 1916—at a juncture when, at the behest of the British government, he was finishing his report on the Ottoman destruction of the Armenians—lamented that 'while people in England were raking up the Ottoman Turks' nomadic ancestry in order to account for their murder of 600,000 Armenians' neither the tsar's government nor 'the great public in the West' seemed to care a fig about an almost equivalent number of nomads extirpated in Central Asia.[133] Tellingly, Toynbee was bringing attention to how, in such Eurocentric not to say solipsistic constructions of the human family, only certain sorts of people could be cast as victims. The others, however wretched their condition, were always villains.

Yet racism alone, we previously proposed, even in combination with commercial and economic drives, or, for that matter, settlement programmes 'swamping' and wrecking native habitus, were rarely in themselves sufficient explanations for extermination. Certainly, we can point to the salience of these further ingredients in the case of Central Asia in a way which does not apply to the sub-Saharan reaches of French West Africa. The post-conquest incorporation of Turkestan into the

Russian Empire in the 1860s and 1870s had only begun to be genuinely realized at the fin de siècle, through development plans—in which none other than Witte, then finance minister, was the main driver—to radically transform and connect this remote and inaccessible region through cotton production supported by railway lines to bring the product both to Russian heartlands and overseas markets. If cotton was 'the colonial pot of gold',[134] and the Fergana valley the projected epicentre for this take-off, Semirechye, further to the east, was earmarked as a zone for speedy and extensive Russian agricultural settlement. This, incidentally, was an agenda very much on the US model for opening up its own continental interior and, like it, presupposed that the native pastoralists would be tightly sedentarized in order for the settlers to parcel up the vast majority of the 'space' into fenced-off 'plots'.

Almost inbuilt into this programme was thus a recipe for inter-communal conflict not least given that by 1914, out of some half-million Russian migrants who had flooded into Turkestan—nearly all in the previous decade—three in five had headed for the Seven Rivers region. Ranged against them were some one million native peoples in danger of displacement, or worse, and with no guarantees that a recently formed government Resettlement Commission, headed by Krivoshein, would do right by them, any more than in the USA a Federal Bureau of Indian Affairs had done in relation to *its* natives.[135] Perhaps not surprisingly, contingency plans for trouble had been drawn up in 1910 by the then military governor of Turkestan, Aleksei Kuropatkin. These plans included both the arming of settlers and taking of hostages,[136] of course, the assumption being that the trouble would come from the natives, not the settlers.

If this would strongly suggest that the contours for violence in 1916 Central Asia were, in key respects, structurally predetermined, it does not however mean that an outcome of genocide or something not far removed from it was predictable, let alone inevitable—any more than in Upper Volta where the colonial settlement aspect was, in any case, not relevant. Rather, as with so many genocide scenarios, we need to turn both to the unanticipated factors and, at the same time, to a further element of the equation much less accessible to rational evaluation. On both counts, the context of the European Great War itself is fundamental, as it infected and ultimately destabilized the norms of existence even in these distant colonial peripheries.

*

By late 1915, as the constant provisioning of total war and, with it, the necessary manpower reserves to either fight or service it began to strain metropolitan capabilities to the limit, the belligerent powers increasingly sought to milk colonial resources. This included the potential mobilization of active males, if not for the front then certainly for labour battalions; or, put more bluntly, for purposes of hyper-exploitation, often far, even continents apart, from home. For colonial administrations this also carried with it a level of risk, not least as compulsory military service was often specifically excluded from the terms of colonial subject status. Even with absorption into the empire the nomad peoples of Central Asia, for instance, specifically remained *inorodtsy*, that is, a second class of 'foreign', and as implicitly conceived more primitive, set of tribal communities, but also with legal exemption from any form of military call-up.[137] In the villages in the *cercle de Dédougou* from which the revolt in Upper Volta spread, as more generally in Turkestan, and as elsewhere (for instance, in the rapidly quelled insurrection in British Nyasaland in 1915),[138] it was none other than this entirely unprecedented conscription which was the initial spark to resistance. This was just as it had been in the Vendée: that other paradigmatic encounter between a militarized state in danger and a compact community unwilling to bow to its emergency diktat.

One can, of course, make too much of French-revolutionary parallels. What happened in Kirghizia, as in Upper Volta, had, after all, resonances of pan-native struggles at the height of the US conquest of the trans-Mississippi region, as too of, for instance, the great anti-colonial rebellions in German East and South-West Africa at the turn of the twentieth century. But then these insurrectionary wars—as with the Vendée—had quasi-messianic features. Here, however, we enter into territory where it is as much colonialist perceptions of a politico-religious threat, as the threat itself, which really matters. The spectre of the Vendée was associated in Jacobin minds with an ultra-Catholic crusade against them. What exercised the fevered imaginations of Allied ministers and officials about some of their less than enthusiastic or loyal imperial subject peoples, by contrast, was a call for Islamic holy war against them. This nightmare scenario seemed to duly materialize in November 1914, when, on Turkey's entry into the war on the side of the Central Powers, and with undoubted encouragement from the Germans, the Caliphate's Sheikh-ul-Islam, in the presence of the Sultan, enjoined Muslims worldwide—all 270 million of them—to participate in a jihad against the infidel Allies.[139]

In fact the fatwas were to prove a notable damp squib. No major uprisings anywhere in British, French, or Russian domains can be specifically linked to the Caliphate's call to arms. Allied fears of some pan-Islamic movement sweeping all before it remained, however, very real. British efforts to get up an Arab revolt have been directly linked to Cairo Office anxieties to counter the alleged danger of some fanatical anti-British Islamic upsurge.[140] As we have already seen, Russian worries of some sort of civilizational clash, embracing all the Muslim peoples under Russian suzerainty from the Caucasus through to Turkestan, seemed to be realized in the Central Asian revolt. In West Africa, the French hardly waited for the portents, instead themselves fabricating a story of marabout conspiracy and of a Mahdi waiting in the wings, almost as if to confirm their own chimerical fantasies.[141]

Perhaps the Allies had reason to be scared. But not on the count of Islam. Both the revolts in what are today part of northern Burkina and southern Mali, on the one hand, and the Tian Shan mountain steppes on the other, arguably represented the very last spasm of that quite extraordinary sequence of intense native resistance to the late imperial carve-up of the globe, which was largely completed by the early years of the twentieth century. Looked at with hindsight, the protagonists in these codas from the Great War had no more chance of success than their forebears. Daniel Brower, for instance, describes the Semirechye revolt's goal to drive the colonialists and settlers completely out as 'wildly quixotic'.[142] Yet, however incoherently formulated, what cannot be denied is that both sets of revolts caught the French and

Russians off balance, as it were, at a time when the very future of their own autonomous metropolitan existences was in jeopardy. The Muqrani revolt in Algeria in
1871, at the time of apparent French collapse during the Franco-Prussian War, had
had something of the same quality—and murderous results.[143] Emanating in the
first instance, of course, from the insurrectionists.

In the Semirechye revolt, for example, especially in the Pishpek and Przhevalsk
uezdy, Kirghiz and Dungan nomads slaughtered all settlers, farmers and their families, that they could lay their hands on—an estimated 3,000 meeting this fate.[144]
General Fol'dbaum, the military governor of the region, also accused the insurgents of perpetrating all manner of sexual mutilations and tortures of victims prior
to their deaths.[145] Romanticizing the insurrectionists in the light of such evidence
would be grotesque. And the fury of the settlers' response might equally be understood in terms of retribution exacted. Of which there was plenty. In spite of the
ostensible appeals of Kuropatkin, recalled as military supremo for the region, to
avoid 'unnecessary' and 'harmful' cruelty, there was both lynch law from settlers
and unequivocal orders from Kuropatkin's immediate subordinate, Fol'dbaum, 'to
drive the Kirghiz into the mountains and to destroy them there'.[146]

So, was the nature of colonial response a case of mass, unbounded reprisal, a
more calculated policy, or something else again? In favour of the calculated theory,
efforts by Kuropatkin, after the expunging of the revolt, to devise a master plan for
separating out the problem 'elements' of the population—in other words, the remnants of the crushed indigenous peoples—both hark back to the social engineering
propounded in pre-war tsarist military manuals yet also point forwards to full-
blown Stalinist implementation. Indeed, the territory designated for the some
200,000 surviving Kazakhs and Kirghiz, who were to be ejected from the good
lands around the Chu valley and the Issyk-Kul basin, was none other than the bar-
ren Naryn plateau: a notorious dumping ground for undesirables from all over
Stalinist Russia. Kuropatkin's proposition, back in autumn 1916, was that the confiscated lands would be turned over to five new Cossack *stanitsy*. He thereby confirmed not only the intent to create an ethnographically contiguous Russian zone,
but also, through this specific form of militarized settlement—in fact backed up by
tight border controls—a framework in which the expelled and by this time entirely
destitute indigenous population would remain locked out and virtually locked up
in their own more or less valueless, ethnic *uezd*, presumably until such time as they
would wither away through lingering starvation. Paradoxically, the plan submitted
in detail to the tsar the following February itself fell victim to the revolutionary
moment, and then, after the Bolshevik seizure of power, an apparent overturning
in favour of the *indigènes*.[147]

But behind the abortive blueprint how much was the actual atrocity of the prior
killing phase an outcome of retributive fury, pure and simple? Or was some deeper
anxiety at work; some embedded aporia about the very nature of Russian empire
and state, which the insurrectionists had too openly exposed? Pure desire for vengeance should of itself never be discounted or marginalized as possible motive. It is
surely significant that an unknown number of Kirghiz and Kazakhs were massacred in the autumn and winter of 1916 by eastern Kalmyks, as these peoples fled

into Chinese Sinkiang—it generally being agreed that the Kalmyks were exacting their own retribution for what had been catastrophically visited on them by Kirghiz and Kazakhs during their own flight from the Russian steppes back in 1771.[148]

The virulence of the mainstream Russian reaction against the1916 insurrection, however, might also have its own deep historical roots, perhaps even some unsettling sense that these rebelling Muslim nomads—diverse descendants indeed of the Golden Horde who, in centuries past had ruled over Muscovy and Rus—were seeking to overthrow a contemporary normative order in favour of what once was. Fanciful, perhaps, but a subject to which we have no choice but to return when examining some of Stalin's more choice assaults on Muslim 'nations'. Equally, what the French seemed to have found so difficult to acknowledge in the case of the Upper Volta revolt was not simply the complete repudiation of the invincibility of their colonial mandate, but that it should have come from an extensive, indeed pan-regional, federation of autonomous village-based, non-centralized peoples, whose social, cultural, and cross-ethnic complexity embodied a multitude of elastic linguistic groupings and religious affiliations that, by European—more specifically Parisian—criteria, was too fragmented, disorganized, and politically anarchic to be able to mount anything quite so heavy-duty as a coordinated military strategy against the *entirety* of French colonial rule in West Africa.[149] It was much simpler to fall back on the almost comforting notion of Islamic conspiracy—that is, ignoring the heterogeneous nature of the insurrection's protagonists—while, of course, at the same time, obliterating their communities under a barrage of ordnance.

That the French carried out this campaign under conditions of almost complete media blackout is hardly surprising,[150] not least given that at the same time thousands of other black West Africans were being sent to die on the Verdun front, partly in order to staunch the flow of exclusively white man's blood in the killing zones.[151] But then supposing the news had leaked out to the USA or other neutral countries: would there have been Western champions willing to protest on behalf of the Bwa, the Bobo, the Marka, the Minyaka, the Samogo, or Gurunsi-speaking peoples? Or complain at how Senegalese *tirailleurs* were being sent not just to be killed on the Western Front, but to kill fellow Africans much closer to home? The people of Upper Volta paid the price, as did those in Semirechye, in large part precisely because there were no foreign advocates, no diplomatic entreaties, no intelligentsia to protest at genocide against disobedient peoples on the periphery of empires.

But that still begs a question. Was the gap between the outcome in Central Asia and that in the Russian rimlands because the former was colonial, the latter not? In which case, under what circumstances, if any, might this unrestrained form of colonial warfare have been imported *into* Europe? Or again, is it this assumption itself which is misinformed, or at least inexact? Eastern Anatolia, where the Armenian genocide began, was neither Europe proper, nor colony. Could it be that it was the circumstances of total war itself between 1914 and 1918 which engendered tendencies, at some moments and in some places, towards a notable amplification of latent hostile feelings against some groups in, or beyond, the dominant social matrix? And could it equally have been the case that these tendencies, especially of course at the moments of extreme wartime crisis, produced quite irrational fears of the danger emanating from such groups? Could it even have been that these fears, in turn, had the capacity to fuel explosions of violence—whether emanating from dominant community or, even more lethally, from military formations—almost regardless of whether the context was colonial or metropolitan?

COLLECTIVE PARANOIA IN ACTION: BELGIUM 1914

It practically goes without saying that the war acted as a dramatic radicalizer of pre-war societal neuroses. They operated on all sorts of levels. One notable one was sexual. As men across the Continent (and beyond) were inducted into military service, both need and opportunity increased prostitution, and, with it, exponential rises in venereal disease. The phenomenon, in turn, increasingly invited accusations—especially from opinion formers claiming to represent 'respectable' society—against 'loose' women who were deemed to be sapping national morale. In France, these charges took on a decidedly racist tone, when it was suggested that French women were consorting with black soldiers and workers.[152] In Britain, where colonial enlistees were less visible, the charges became part of an altogether more sinister if bizarre narrative. A secret German-backed cabal, 'the Hidden Hand', was said to be undermining the very ability of the country effectively to pursue the war not only through female prostitution and bondage rackets but through high-level vice rings, whose 'Hunnish erotomania', including homosexuality, had so enthralled and entrapped leading figures of government and City alike that it was causing a creeping paralysis from the top down.[153] By the latter years of the war—though such stories continued to have their primary source in the right-wing yellow press—far from being the preserve of scurrilous rabble-rousers and marginal conspiracy theorists they had become almost standard, quotidian fare in Britons' cultural diet.

The consequence was a welter of public finger-pointing statements and declarations. In March 1917, for instance, the newly founded Women's Imperial Defence Council passed a resolution demanding a Royal Commission to investigate 'that treacherous influence in our midst known as the Unseen Hand'.[154] The implication was that it was not simply sexual propriety which was at stake but that an entirely more fiendish plot aimed at the wholesale collapse of the British war effort from 'within' was afoot. The key accusers' question thus became: *who* was behind it? To which, as we will see, answers nearly always had a very specifically 'Jewish' leitmotif. What the accusations in themselves equally imply is the ability, at the very least, for large sections of a population to surrender itself to 'collective self-suggestion'. Or, put more precisely, to surrender to a situation where underlying assumptions and mentalities are allowed to take sway to such an extent as to be *seen* as 'substantive historical phenomena, with a capacity to shape actions and events'.[155]

Indeed, under such circumstances what is most terrifying is the degree to which such delusions take on a life of their own, or, to put it another way, ensure that what is believed to be the situation is acted upon—if not always by the apparatus of state then certainly by self-styled vigilantes, regardless of the empirical evidence for or against. As an example, there was actually no single known instance on British soil of sabotage—(with the exception of an increasingly rebellious post-'Easter Rising' Ireland) during the entirety of the war.[156] Yet repeated waves of popular violence against an estimated 60,000 German inhabitants during it, included, in the middle weeks of May 1915—according to Panikos Panayi—the worst, most widespread communal riots in Britain's entire history.[157]

One might argue these events were not linked to fears of sabotage per se but rather were popular explosions of anger at critical junctures when the war took a turn for the worse; usually when the German military were seen to be upping the ante. The May riots themselves came in Britain, as in Russia, in the immediate wake of the sinking of *Lusitania*, and the first gas attacks at Ypres, as well as the Russian Great Retreat. While they were certainly fanned by the inflammatory rhetoric of the likes of *John Bull*'s Horatio Bottomley, cited at the outset of this chapter, their fundamental causation could hardly be deemed delusional. Equally, however, one might argue that incitements and riots alike were symptomatic of an increasingly pervasive climate in which people sensed their own normal assumed control on life and destiny was rapidly being overturned, to be replaced instead by often acute uncertainty and anxiety about sudden, unexpected death, from sea, air, or land attack. To attempt to chart the gamut of psychological reactions to these fears would take us into a territory very different from the main thrust of this study. However, the actual roller-coaster of events leading towards war and its actual outbreak in the summer of 1914 is highly indicative of how panic, even hysteria, could result.

Britain was hardly alone in being gripped by what was called 'spy fever'. Indeed, elements, primarily urban elements, of all the belligerent societies seem to have been caught up in the search for agents and spy rings working for the enemy, leading in turn to denunciations, occasional lynchings, but also state police action, involving the mass round-up and incarcerations of alleged suspects.[158] In Britain panic was certainly fuelled and amplified by a whole genre of novels whose repeated motif was the Trojan horse, which would soften up the country ready for German invasion. In 1915, 40,000 copies of *When William Came, German Spies in London*, by the popular writer Saki, sold out in the first week of its publication.[159]

What is most relevant here though, in this early wartime rendition of the 'stab-in-the-back' theme, is the essential invisibility of the alleged villains. To make them visible—to 'out' them—inevitably involved, in the absence of any other evidence, recourse to already embedded xenophobic fears and prejudices. Thus, even in the still neutral United States, where the dangers of invasion or 'takeover' were even less plausible than in Britain, a growing anti-German and 'paranoid atmosphere' in 1915 and 1916 led to an increase in mob violence and murder not only against Germans but against a spectrum of other racial and social 'undesirables', including black migrants to cities, and incoming Puerto Rican and Mexican labourers, as well as pacifists, anarchists, and socialists.[160]

In this we can perhaps discern how the heightened climate of war offered both cover and pretext for the exercise of a untrammelled populist racism *and* instrumental opportunities for governments to increase surveillance and censorship of their own populations under the guise of fighting espionage and flagging morale.[161] Thus though the USA was far removed from the fighting, its entry into war paved the way for a Sedition Act, an Alien Act, and an Espionage Act, not to mention the initial formation, under J. Edgar Hoover, of what was to become the Federal Bureau of Investigation; each of these, in its own right, a measure of consciously targeted repression. Meanwhile in Australia, Prime Minister William Morris Hughes equally utilized the war, not simply to initiate a root-and-branch expunging of domiciled Germans in order to expropriate their businesses and property, but to declare an openly racist agenda to keep the continent 'clean' of yellow men and other so-called Asiatics.[162] By contrast, German military behaviour towards 'enemy' civilian populations, in the early stages of the attempt to execute the Schlieffen plan, would seem to throw us back into a much more confused and chaotic world of mental shadows, unadulterated hysteria, and mass delusional self-suggestion.

*

The German atrocities in Belgium and northern France in August and early September 1914 have been fully analysed and documented in a major, mould-breaking study by John Horne and Alan Kramer.[163] Their analysis came after many decades in which claims of repeated military massacres perpetrated by German units were discounted, or completely repudiated, as wartime propaganda. Indeed, some earlier dismissals of witness evidence, such as that by Arthur Ponsonby, in a 1928 study, went so far as to argue that survivor testimony of these events was compromised by the nature of a wartime climate 'where bias, passion and so-called patriotism disturb the emotions'.[164] Putting aside the whole issue of a methodology whereby the victim's evidence is discounted as unreliable, the great paradox here is that at the core of understanding of what happened was certainly mostly to do with a disturbance of the emotions—but, first and foremost, on the part of German perpetrators. This is important for us, not so much for the light it throws on what actually happened in this war zone at this particular moment, but rather for how it connects with other critical themes in this chapter: war psychosis, the nature of 'rationalized' responses to communal (Type Three) resistance against the hegemonic state—as exemplified in the colonial wartime revolts—and, above all, the transmission belts by which alleged, but actually entirely imagined, charges of subversion against state military power could be translated into long-standing and exponentially self-reinforcing myths of collective *conspiracy*.

The events in Belgium provide a microcosm of this larger picture. The German high summer campaign was designed to knock out not neutral Belgium but belligerent France. It was thus predicated on the assumption that there would be no military resistance from the Belgians, who were expected and indeed required to acquiesce in the passage of more than a million German armed men through the breadth of their territory, in order for the latter to strike at the French from their exposed flank. In practice, Belgian military defence of its internationally recognized sovereignty, most specifically through its key fortifications at Liège, held up a necessarily rigid German timetable, the upshot being that, in very large part, it critically changed the course of the war.

The *psychological* impact on the German army can be discerned in two critical respects. The first began with sheer shock for conscript soldiers and officers who had assumed that their advance through Belgium would be trouble-free. Instead they found themselves thrown into unexpected and repeatedly intense fire-fights, from which they began to take mounting casualties. The initial panic, however, gave way with great rapidity to a form of almost consensual fantasy explanation for what was happening. According to this, the troops were being shot at not by authorized combatants but *franc-tireurs*—a terminology itself borrowed from the previous Franco-Prussian War of 1870–1—meaning armed civilians who not only had no business whatsoever on the battlefield but who were purported to fire on the troops from secret hideouts, often behind the front lines. We have already seen something of this sort of confabulated trope from the Lemberg affair, suggesting further that it was hardly exclusive to German soldiery. However, the specifically *Frontsoldaten* narrative also escalated and metamorphosed into something yet more sinister. Comrades were not only being killed. They were also being mutilated, by women and young girls, at the behest of Belgian Catholic priests. This charge not only seemed to reek of colonial-style inferences as to the naked cunning of treacherous and vicious natives who could stoop to such savagery, but the gendered aspect also carried with it resonances of the Vendée where, at the heart of what the Jacobins saw as an illegitimate people's war against a sanctioned and normative monopoly of violence, was a supposedly diabolical nexus between a 'fanatic' priesthood and its equally crazed female congregants.[165] The fact that in the Vendée, as in Belgium, the narrative was entirely 'imagined' by the state apparatus of violence can only reinforce the degree to which what followed involved a projective rupture with reality.

The immediate consequence in 1914 was a series of orders from the highest echelons of the German command, requiring officers on the ground to take collective exemplary punishment measures against villages and villagers close to where the alleged offences had occurred. As early as 9 August—only five days into the campaign—General von Bülow, commander of Second Army, both countenanced hostage-taking and village-burning as the appropriate response, and publicly warned the Belgians of this intention. By 25 August, however, the Prussian minister of War, Falkenhayn, had issued a much more far-reaching decree, declaring that anyone found resisting German authority who was not a combatant under Article 1 of the Hague Convention would be summarily dealt with 'regardless of age and sex'.[166] As Article 1 referred to uniformed combatants this was, as Horne and Kramer have correctly noted, not simply 'tantamount to an invitation to liquidate civilian resisters on the spot' but actually implied a carte blanche mandate for the military execution of *any* suspects without trial.

The results of this type of authoritative command were somewhat predictable. It involved a series of massacres in towns and villages in the immediate rear of advancing German forces, culminating in the worst single atrocity of its kind, at Dinant, on 23 August. Here, 674 people, including large numbers of women and children, were lined up and shot. Two days later the razing of Louvain by fire, including the destruction of its ancient Catholic university library, excited even more outrage in the Allied and neutral press, with the death toll from the mass executions later put at 248.[167]

Of course, Horne and Kramer's overall estimate of 6,500 civilians killed (not to speak of the thousands more deported),[168] put against the massive casualty figures of the Great War, represent a drop in the ocean. Moreover, the perpetration of these outrages would seem to fall short of a verdict of genocide, as the German military drive to take retribution on the Belgian civilian population for the 'invisibility' of its country's defenders rapidly fell away as German troops came to engage directly with the French army, mostly, though not exclusively, on French soil. Indeed, the massacres remained notably localized: confined to areas where non-combatants were unlucky enough to find themselves caught up in a very intense, if rapidly shifting, battle zone.

Nevertheless, as an indicator of how preconceived ideas charged with emotional and historical significance can be translated in extremis into a fixed explanatory narrative from which violent, even genocidal, action can either result or, at some later moment, act as justification, the Belgian case has profound implications. Horne and Kramer in their assessment draw on the 1916 work of the Belgian sociologist Ferdinand van Langenhove, who was the first to make the connection between the atrocities and what he described as a series of 'myth cycles',[169] as well as the great French historian Marc Bloch, who drew on Langenhove's findings for his own study of culturally reinforced belief systems and mentalities. Reviewing these earlier studies, what the later historians have done is connect the notion of myth cycles or, as they have preferred to describe it, 'myth complex', both backwards to embedded aspects of German political culture and forwards to a post-event official narrative in which, in place of the original panic and inexplicability, clarity and, with it, 'a sense of control' were restored to 'the believer'.[170]

This does not furnish us with a case of a 'perpetrators' "never again" syndrome' which we introduced in *The Meaning of Genocide*, and which, in conclusion to this chapter, we will infer is central to how the myth of international Jewish conspiracy—as it crystallized at the end of the First World War—was transmitted with genocidal consequence to the Second.[171] However, the Belgian case study does suggest a second longer-term element of psychological displacement, which does help illuminate the nature of the syndrome. Critical to this particular case, as Horne and Kramer show, is the long-standing aversion, amounting to obsession, on the part of the German, more exactly Prussian, political-cum-military establishment to the notion of the politicized citizen. The very primacy of the army within the Prussian state and of that army's focus on hierarchy, draconian discipline, and an ultra-regimented conception of warfare were thus closely intermeshed with the authoritarianism of a polity whose pervasive incubus, especially after 1871, was of its ordinary people wresting democratic control.[172] Implicit in this nightmare of the elite, however, was not only the spectre of revolution; it also carried with it a virtually phobic antipathy to the notion of *Volkskrieg*: war prosecuted by the people, for the people. A specifically Nazi manifestation of this trope can be seen in their horror of Russian Bolshevism as a military apparatus—for which, of course, 'the Jews' were held responsible. Yet what the Belgians had supposedly engineered in 1914 against German power was yet another version of this illegitimate, demotic form of warfare.

Thus, the orders that emanated from German High Command in August 1914 did not come out of nowhere, but rather were elaborations upon an 1899 Imperial Ordinance, which had already set out the relevant procedures for the execution of extraordinary military criminal justice.[173] In this sense, the German military were instinctively responding to their own worst imaginings. However, in their reading of resistance in Belgium as a case of communal insurgency there was something else: a classic case of deflecting blame not only away from those entirely responsible for it—namely, themselves—but also *onto* an entirely demonic enemy whose explicit purpose was to wreck the Kaiser's rightful drive for destiny. For true believers, such as Rudolf Eucken, one of Germany's leading philosophers of the day, the denial of that destiny was *impossible* as it 'would signify the collapse of mankind'.[174] If so, while what the Belgians purportedly did in 1914 was not the mortal 'stab in the back' of 1918, it was not that far short—or that less culpable. And the fact that the blow had been delivered by an illegitimate and Catholic nation not only confirmed to the Lutheran-dominated Wilhelmine state that there was no case to answer as regarded the charge of atrocity—Germany's own investigation, compiled in the White Book of 1915, vindicated its military absolutely—but also quickly reinforced for both officer class and subalterns, German elite and populace alike, what they had already fully imbibed from voluminous wide-ranging publications on the matter: it was they who were the 'victims'.[175]

BLAMING THE JEWS

'With "great Jewry" against us, there is no possible chance of getting the thing through—it means optimism in Berlin, dumps in London, unease in Paris'.[176] So wrote Sir Mark Sykes, in March 1916. The 'thing' he is referring to is none other than the war, while the further inference that the Jews hold the key to it would appear to be so fantastic as to invite ridicule. Diasporic Jewry may have been notably ubiquitous but as a community it was not governed by any single political or even religious authority, had no equivalent of a Pope, no territory, no national resources, and no administrative or military agency as such in the wider world. Its European numbers, estimated at nearly 8.7 million in 1900, were citizens or, as in the case of its Russian cohort, subjects of their respective states and were expected, accordingly, to fulfil their patriotic duties, including on the battlefield. That, in demographic terms, the Russian element constituted 5.2 million of the total, most of these being domiciled in our critical rimlands, *is* highly significant.[177]

However, Sykes, in addressing himself personally and privately to Sir Arthur Nicolson, the permanent under-secretary at the British Foreign Office, was not at this juncture focusing on them particularly, nor indeed was any part of his official brief at this moment to do with 'Jews' at all. On the contrary, at the time of writing Sykes was in Petrograd, to negotiate a secret arrangement which, in the event of Allied victory, would divide the Ottoman Empire into French, British, and Russian zones of control. The letter of our diplomatic troubleshooter is thus all the more remarkable in the degree to which it is a confession—and a slightly embarrassed one at that, coming from an otherwise entirely self-confident aristocrat—that he had hit upon the answer to something even more important than the future shape of a British-dominated Middle East: 'I am afraid this sounds rather odd and fantastic but when we bump into a thing which is atmospheric, international, cosmopolitan, subconscious and unwritten, nay often unspoken, it is not possible to work and think on *ordinary* lines'.[178]

In other words, what Sykes was attempting to articulate was the notion that if the Jews could be *collectively won over*, they would bring to the Allies an entirely *extraordinary* not to say supranational set of attributes which would assure them victory. Eighteen months later the fruits of these initial musings would be realized in the Balfour Declaration, the British public commitment to the creation of a Jewish National Home in Palestine, the chief handmaiden of which would be none other than Sykes himself. At the time this historic event was cause for much—though not universal—Jewish acclamation, as it continues to be to the present day. Yet this rendition of the Declaration as essentially philosemitic, and hence benign, blocks us from recognizing Sykes' proclivities both to see 'Jews in everything' and to ascribe to them, against all the evidence, not only a corporate but supremely powerful will. More critically, it poses the question as to whether we are dealing with the overworked imagination of a single, albeit politically significant, individual in isolation, or whether a more pervasive mindset both in Britain and abroad is rather revealed.[179]

In support of the latter thesis Léon Poliakov has argued that fin-de-siècle political, academic, and ecclesiastical elites across the Continent, not to mention high society and especially court circles, were thoroughly obsessed with Jews in a way 'unknown to their great-grandchildren or buried in the depths of their unconsciousness'.[180] Indeed, if Poliakov is correct it is a relatively short step from casting Jews as a collective, supranational entity essentially outside the national mainstream to believing them to be operating according to their own monolithic rules and ends, whether these are, or are not, in accord with the goals of Gentile polities and culture. The implications of such *political* lines of thinking had already been clearly visible, in the Russian case, for more than a generation. While the state-cum-societal crisis precipitated by the assassination of Tsar Alexander II in 1881, for instance, is embedded in Jewish memory as the occasion of the first traumatic wave of pogroms, spread particularly, though not exclusively, across south-western *gubernii* of the Pale, at a state level the disturbances exemplified the degree to which the Jews were not only themselves to blame for popular antipathy but also were that essential heart of 'alien forces' who were seeking to take over the country lock, stock, and barrel. At a juncture when the discrepancy between Third Rome-informed notions of Russia's special salvationist role in the world and the threat of a falling behind, even falling in thrall to the industrialized and increasingly powerful West was becoming quite glaring, it is not that surprising that reactionary tsarist officialdom opposed to Russia's modernization on Western lines—as supported and informed by an equally rabid, right-wing press—should resort to an analysis of the situation in terms of Jewish manipulation, above all, of the money markets.[181]

Bar a handful of Jewish bankers and entrepreneurs who were involved in capitalizing Russia's infrastructural development (at the behest of those like Witte who saw their value) the fact that the vast majority of Russian Jews were themselves slipping into immiseration and worse seems to have been lost on policymakers in the Interior Ministry intent on deepening the 'temporary' framework of the post-1881 May Laws. These were designed to squeeze the Jews out of the rural economy while at the same time preventing their legal access to the towns and metropolises beyond the designated Pale. The point, however, is that by the time of the next major crisis of Russian state in 1904–5—a near-fatal revolution, itself precipitated by crushing military defeat by the Japanese in the clash over Pacific spoils—the projective accusation against the Jews had metamorphosed into an entirely more potent narrative of *international* Jewish conspiracy whose alleged aim was the subversion of Christian civilization *tout ensemble*. The Okhrana fabrication of what came to be known as the *Protocols of the Elders of Zion*—the classic rendition of the plot theme—may actually have begun life in the late 1890s as a rather crude weapon against Witte: evidence in itself of the degree to which the regime was suffering from one of its perennial bouts of paranoia in the face of modernity.[182] In fact, the *Protocols* story of a carefully constructed Jewish plan to take over the world by fomenting diabolical ideas, such as liberalism and democracy, actually had little popular impact in its early published outings beyond the secret police vaults. Nevertheless, some of its key motifs surface in a memorandum put to the tsar by his foreign minister, Count Lamsdorff, in early 1906, the main thrust of which was to propose that the only antidote to the clear and present Jewish-led, European-wide revolutionary danger was the formation of an equally formidable Christian alliance between the Papacy, the Kaiser's Protestant Germany, and Holy Mother Russia.[183]

That such a proposal, even in extremis, could come from the highest level of Russia's policymaking apparatus is bizarre enough. That it was treated with all due seriousness, moreover, is evident in the way Tsar Nicholas responded by requesting that negotiations for the alliance be entered into immediately. We know that by this juncture he had thoroughly imbibed the anti-Semitic rationale for the 1905 pogroms, writing to his mother that they were the *narod*'s natural reaction 'to the insolence and audacity of the revolutionaries...because nine-tenths of them are Yids'.[184] But in the Lamsdorff proposal we have something more than simply an ancien régime interpreting the world and operating according to the tenets of its own peculiarly closed and myopic cultural bubble. At a critical point in his exposition Lamsdorff proposed that 'the coincidence of several phenomena' in the revolutionary sequence 'could hardly be accidental'. He went on to state that the critical strike wave broke at exactly the moment when the government was attempting to bring about a large foreign loan without the participation of the Rothschilds. The inference of this explication pointed to more than simply a nexus of interests between 'Jewish' revolutionaries and 'Jewish' bankers: the scuppering of the loan and the consequent hurried sale of securities allegedly led to 'new profits for the Jewish capitalists and bankers'.[185] Indeed, the real power of the Jews was inferred through an analysis of the 'timing'. If the Jewish bankers knew in advance about the importance of the loan and so wanted to wreck it, all they needed to do, according to

Lamsdorff, was look into their crystal ball and so mobilize the most effective elements on the spot to create the necessary disturbances, which, of course, they duly marshalled through the offices of their revolutionary Russian Jewish 'brethren'.

The suggestion is breathtaking. Prefiguring Sykes' unreasoned reasonings a decade later, it is not simply that 'great Jewry' were operating according to an ethnic solidarity which entirely transcended distinctions between socialists and capitalists, but further, that this carried with it a potential threat to the rest of humankind through powers which were not only omnipresent but also omniscient. Indeed, 'the Jews', in this world view, do not simply have the ability to know what is going to happen before it happens, but to control and manipulate this foreknowledge for their own nefarious ends. Hence, for both Lamsdorff and Sykes the only way of neutralizing the danger was either to appease it, that is, bring it onside—preferably in the widest geopolitical terms—or alternatively, rally together as potent an international countermovement as one could possibly muster in order to prepare for some final Manichaean-style showdown.

The obvious empirical response to these psychotic imaginings is to question whether political actions were consequent upon them. Lamsdorff's proposal, after all, was dropped with his fall from power in the spring of 1906, while Sykes' utterances, in isolation, do not prove a direct causal relationship with the Balfour Declaration. One might alternatively argue that while an anti-Jewish animus *is* self-evident in the behaviour of tsarist state and military in the context of the Great War, the emphasis which this regime placed on both the power of, and danger from, its Jewish population only goes to demonstrate its exceptionality when set against the European norm.

*

Technically, the major difference between Russia and the rest of Europe, Austria-Hungary included, was the emancipated status of the Jews in the latter. In the decades prior to the Great War, Jews across the Continent had had to weather varying degrees of antipathy from their non-Jewish neighbours, with the French Dreyfus affair, at the fin de siècle, arguably the most acute and destabilizing challenge to what has become known as the liberal ideology of emancipation.[186] For Western and Central European Jewish elites this ideology was predicated on the assumption that Jews were to be considered and treated in every legal respect as identical to non-Jews, their distinction being no different from that of other *religious* groups. In other words, under the aegis of the modern nation state, a line had been drawn under the historical exceptionality of the Jewish condition in favour of a complete social, cultural, and political integration, which thereby made of them simply another component of civil society.

That this assimilative process proved to be not quite as smooth as its liberalizing protagonists, Jewish or non-Jewish, had anticipated, is evident in the growing wave of anti-Semitic diatribes emanating from the late 1870s onwards. True, they were hardly all of a piece. Accusations of continued Jewish difference, excited particularly by mass Jewish refugee flows from Russia, vied with often equally vitriolic denunciations of Jewish economic, social, and educational mobility, not only thereby denying non-Jews their birthright and livelihood but, equally, making the alleged interlopers 'invisible' in Gentile space. As in Russia, anger was also notably directed at Jewish plutocrats who were ostensibly taking over the European stock exchanges by stealth and running them in their own interest.

On one level this was all really quite odd. In Western and Central Europe, even with the significant influx, pre-1914, of migrants from the destabilized Pale, communal numbers were, demographically speaking, insignificant, save in some notable metropolitan quarters where the *Ostjuden* congregated. But in a sense this simply underscores the degree to which a Jewish profile in society, however small, could excite passions, regardless of the observable facts. Fin-de-siècle conspiracy theories—just as in Russia—did the rounds, and there were attempts too at the creation of overtly anti-Semitic political platforms, parties, and movements, especially in France, Germany, and German Austria, each of which propounded that the woes of society all emanated from the Jewish menace. Dark clouds were also evident in the way Rumania overtly flouted international efforts at the 1878 Congress of Berlin to require it—as a condition of its newly recognized sovereignty—to enact Jewish citizen rights. Even in laissez-faire Britain, a major player in such foreign policy initiatives, a domestic Aliens Act in 1905 sought to put brakes on Jewish immigration into the country.[187]

Yet for all the obvious amplification of anti-Semitic discourses, including an increasingly racialized construction of the 'Jew' in the arts and medical science alike,[188] what is equally striking about the pre-1914 period is the degree to which the attacks not only remained primarily rhetorical but were held in clear political check. This is not to deny a background noise of street violence, especially where immigrant Jews lived cheek by jowl with other, often newly urbanized but equally impoverished social and ethnic communities. However, these did not translate, even under overtly anti-Semitic city regimes such as Vienna's, into endemic pogrom-style attacks. Nor were the German anti-Semitic parties able to make any serious inroads among voters. On the contrary, in elections to the Reichstag in 1912, their previously upward-bound trajectory practically collapsed to a mere 0.86 per cent of the vote and the loss of all but three of their seventeen seats.[189] At the outbreak of the Great War the radical Zionist critique, which saw in the whole liberal proposition of Jewish engagement with European society and values not simply a false consciousness but a lethal cul-de-sac, remained non-proven.

Which thus begs the question, does the Great War really represent the critical watershed: the moment from which the European Jewish position can be clearly charted as on a downhill slide to a Holocaust terminus? To assume such inevitability, or at least predictability, goes strongly against the grain of our overall thinking. Nevertheless, it also operates on the premise that there were critical tipping points both in political terms and, equally, in those socio-cultural manifestations wherein latent anti-Jewish animus took on both a new and, in some ways, entirely reshaped vibrancy—and virulence. We have already proposed why the war, to a critical degree, provided this essential framework. With no obvious way out from what the belligerent powers in 1914 had set in train, their policymaking and opinion-forming elites resorted increasingly to our 'vocabulary of absolutes' to justify the war's untrammelled pursuit.[190] Psychological retreat from its demands thus became impossible. Displacing guilt onto something or somebody else, to fill an otherwise searing void of despair, consequently had its own inherent logic.

Historically, in times of crisis and beyond, Jews had always fulfilled this unsolicited role. Christian anti-Semitism was bound up with a narrative of alleged collective Jewish culpability for the death of a suitably de-Judaicized yet equally deified Christ. In the medieval period this took on a particularly visceral aspect with the Western Latin fixation on the mutilation of Jesus at his crucifixion. Jews thus were associated with malice against the most sacred body of all and, by extension, with the same towards the body politic of Christ, whether by stealth or by direct assault on the individual and collective personality of Christian society. By further extension, Jews were the cause of illness and disease, filth and contamination—a catastrophe such as the Black Death only confirming Gentile convictions of this inherent truth.[191]

Of course, in a post-emancipation, and, in a critical sense, secular, if not necessarily dechristianized Europe, these sorts of anxieties should have had considerably less purchase. A spate of ritual murder accusations in Russia and Eastern Europe at the fin de siècle—classically reconfiguring in the process earlier European obsessions with blood sacrifice onto the very population which sought to distance itself from immersion in this (to Jews) God-given source of life—might thus be passed off as a residue of peasant atavism. The future Czech president, Tomáš Masaryk, a much acknowledged defender of the Jews from one of these blood libels, for instance, remembered as a child imbibing the same accusation from his mother. Yet this liberal and very 'modern' figure, later in life, found himself 'involuntarily inspecting the hands of Jews whom he met to see if they contained tell-tale traces of blood'.[192] That such fears were barely beneath the surface is equally evident in the way that in 1916, after its direct assault on Jews had been stymied, Stavka went to enormous lengths to exclude Jewish doctors and medical orderlies from all contact with its soldiers directly or via the Red Cross.[193] Even in avant-garde Britain, the Jewish threat to health could take on an eerie resonance of earlier times. Just a few days before the outbreak of war, for instance, *The Times* ran a report from the medical officer for Stepney, an area of high Jewish concentration in London's East End, claiming that these immigrants were contracting tuberculosis at a high and increasing rate but that their coughing and expectorating 'quantities of sputum laden with tubercule bacilli' was not replicated in Jewish deaths. It was Gentiles who caught the disease from the Jews and died: the clear implication being that a disease-ridden and infectious Jewish population was set, nevertheless, to become dominant in the quarter.[194]

If Jews were so easily associated with bodily disease and its contamination it was only a short step to portraying them as carriers too of mental paralysis and political subversion. While good Christian men were marching off to war, as one popular German writer put it, 'willed by God of the deepest miracle of life, the death of Christ',[195] Jews were—it was implied—not simply profaning against the sacredness and heroism of this godly sacrifice but quite literally putting the knife in, to destroy—and crucify—it.[196]

We have already noted in the British popular press insinuations that behind the wartime rise in venereal disease were underworld Jewish syndicates operating what was euphemistically called the 'white slave trade'. The charge, pre-1914, was hardly uncommon. What made it potent in the wartime context was its claim that Jews were fulfilling some preconceived plan to literally emasculate the nation's fighting capacity at its very fount. Fed naturally by the yellow press, popular rumours of a Jewish affront to the nation's manhood were embellished with a veritable chorus of stories, across all belligerent states by the middle years of war, in which Jews were accused not simply of shirking war service and profiteering to boot by their avoidance of it, but infecting others with their feminized degeneracy.[197] Charges of cowardice, under the cover of neurasthenia (shellshock)—itself contradictory given that this rather suggested Jews *were* fighting—had a specifically Russian elaboration in the claim that those Jews who were wearing uniform were mostly behind the lines in roles such as army telephonists, Red Cross orderlies, and the like, which they abused in order to directly sabotage the war effort or to disseminate political propaganda to honest Russian soldiers.[198] The infamous *Judenzählung*, or 'Jew count', of October 1916, organized by the German War Ministry to determine exactly how many Jews were serving in the Kaiser's armed forces, may have been, in Omer Bartov's words, 'an almost foolproof way to direct the people's growing anger and resentment away from the political and military leadership onto "a numerically almost irrelevant minority"'.[199] However, it was also arguably a cynical state response to a wider unease that Jews were somehow a force, or even *the* force, which was causing communal demoralization and, in doing so, ungluing the sinews of national cohesion.

Exactly *how* widespread and deep-rooted this wartime angst about Jews really was is certainly much less easy to quantify.[200] What is much clearer is its particular prevalence amongst those who either claimed to speak for the nation, or even who were at its helm. Moreover, there is a metamorphosis in the substance of this anti-Jewish thinking in the course of the conflict which is critical to our discussion here. In Britain, for instance, at the outset of war, self-styled patriots of the ilk of Leopold Maxse of the *National Review* were hard at work arguing that there was a 'Potsdam party' operating from within the very corridors of power and attempting to wreck the British war effort by any means available.[201] Central to this idée fixe was, as Henry Wickham Steed, the leading *Times* journalist tersely put it, 'the pro-German and pan-German tendencies of Jewish finance'.[202] That this was the real threat to Britain was also reflected in some extraordinary missives from Britain's then Washington ambassador, Sir Cecil Spring-Rice. Writing to British foreign secretary Sir Edward Grey in November 1914, he warned that 'openly pro-German' Jewish bankers in the USA were 'toiling in a solid phalanx to compass our destruction'.[203] These themes of Jewish power were certainly, at the time, given even greater airing in the more rabidly xenophobic press but, again, with the underlying argument that collective Jewish treason lay in its *alliance* with, if not necessarily subservience to, the Germans.

By 1917, however, something entirely more sinister seemed to have intruded into the Jewish leitmotif. One senior official from Britain's War Cabinet secretariat wrote in April, 'In Russia it appears that the Jews are taking the extreme line, probably in the hope of splitting Russia into fragments'.[204] The inference that 'the Jews' had become decoupled from the German interest and were now acting as an autonomous force certainly did not take off or congeal into a definite myth complex all of a piece. British reception of the notion of Bolsheviks and Bolshevism, for instance, was dependent on newspaper correspondents such as Robert Wilton of *The Times* and Victor Marsden of the *Morning Post*, both of whom repeatedly warned in the autumn of 1917 that, backed by Jewish capital and the supposed takeover of the press, Russia was on the point of falling under the jackboot of pacifist yet revolutionary Jews. Nevertheless, Lenin and crew were, as a *Times* editorial put it after the Bolshevik coup in late November, 'adventurers of German-Jewish blood and in German pay, whose sole object is to exploit the ignorant masses in the interests of their employers in Berlin'.[205]

Certainly, both Wilton and Marsden were instrumental in developing the specificity and singularity of the 'revolutionary Jew' theme. Wilton did so, after the murder of the tsar and his family in July 1918, by charging Jewish Bolsheviks not only with a deicidal Christian martyrdom but with supposedly putting up a statue in Moscow dedicated to Judas Iscariot. Meanwhile Marsden, in the summer of 1920, initiated an eighteen-part serialization of the *Protocols* story in the *Morning Post*, and its first full British publication that autumn under the title, *The Cause of World Unrest*.[206] The two dates are significant, representing the high-water marks of the international Jewish conspiracy scare as the war neared its cataclysmic end, only to be succeeded by revolutionary chaos, or—as in Britain and its colonies—the threat of it. By this juncture, with the Bolsheviks still very much in power in Petrograd and with their destabilizing energy felt across Europe, it almost seemed as if the traditional establishment had succumbed en masse to hysteria. 'We may be shot at any moment', Lady Cromer told an incredulous Virginia Woolf, who, on further enquiry as to who would be doing the shooting, was told, 'Oh, the Jews, the Russian Jews'.[207]

Perhaps the fact that this incident, from February 1919, was also at the height of the great post-war influenza pandemic may suggest—under conditions of acute stress and uncertainty—the degree to which even the ruling elements in society could be swept up by quite delusional self-suggestion. Like the flu, Bolshevism was no respecter of national or international boundaries: so it had to be, as many leading British figures including Lloyd George and Churchill intoned, a form of mental and moral disease. That the very nature of Bolshevism as *Jewish* was by this point a given at least offered a straightforward explanation as to the threat involved: that of both political infection *and* actual bodily harm. That there was clearly a programme to this end, moreover, was famously put forward by no less a figure than Churchill, in February 1920:

> From the days of Spartacus-Weishaupt to those of Karl Marx, and down to Trotsky (Russia), Béla Kun (Hungary), Rosa Luxemburg (Germany), and Emma Goldman (United States), this world-wide revolutionary conspiracy for the overthrow of civilisation and for the reconstitution of society on the basis of arrested development, of envious malevolence, and impossible equality, has been steadily growing...It has been the mainspring of every subversive movement during the Nineteenth Century; and now, at last, this band of extraordinary personalities from the underworlds of the great cities of Europe and America have gripped the Russian people by the hair of their heads and have become practically the undisputed masters of the enormous empire.[208]

Churchill, himself certainly had no doubt that the 'extraordinary personalities' in question were defined by their Jewishness. Just as Jews had created a 'benevolent' Christianity, so now 'atheistical', 'international' Jews were creating 'another system of morals and philosophy' but this time of a wholly 'malevolent' kind. Churchill also intruded a further, gendered element into this tale of the 'divine and the diabolical' with the claim that major players in the Bolshevik terror developed to combat the counter-revolution included Jewesses.[209] A series of reports from British officers serving with the White armies in Russia, and published under parliamentary auspices in 1919, went even further. The Bolsheviks, they asserted, had nationally mobilized all women between sixteen and fifty to serve their sexual needs, and where women in several towns had refused to comply they had been flogged.[210]

With such supposedly unimpeachable *British* government and military sources confirming that the conspirators were prepared to smash all and every moral boundary to achieve their perfidious ends it should be of little surprise to learn that other, less guarded opinion formers had arrived at their own even more far-reaching conclusions. In Britain, by late 1918, the argument that the war itself had been none other than a Jewish plot aimed at world takeover was being stated openly and categorically, with a significant receptive audience. The anonymously written *England under the Heel of the Jew*, published shortly before the armistice, proposed that it was not even the Kaiser who had been to blame for the war, but international Jewish financial 'Shylock-racy', by which the Germans had, in effect, been duped.[211] Behind it all, argued another ultra-nationalist, Ellis Powell, was 'the unseen hand': 'he' who had determined the sinking of the *Lusitania*, the torpedoing of Lord Kitchener's boat, HMS *Hampshire*, zeppelin attacks, and Irish rebellion. Indeed, all the woes of the war could be laid at the door of this 'Arch-Contriver', this force 'omnipotent, but invisible; all-pervasive, but intangible; ubiquitous as the ambient air but just as impervious to assault or capture'.[212]

And so we seem to be back with a fetid imagining not just à la Sykes but one which saw itself as struggling against a literally Satanic enemy: operating in the dark shadows, rather than out in the open, and through the most devious and fiendish of stratagems. Is this, then, projection gone completely mad? And even were this the case what, one might ask, had this got to do with *genocide*? If significant elements of the British society and state in 1918 were in thrall to such phobias why did they not initiate some massive pogrom against the Jews? There were some quite nasty *demotic* anti-Jewish riots in Leeds and London in the spring and summer 1917 but then, two years later—at the height of the Jew 'scare'—it was blacks and Chinese who, in a number of British cities, bore the brunt of popular wrath.[213] Xenophobia was rampant, and nobody, not even the famously German-sounding Saxe-Coburg-Gotha royal family, before they changed their name to innocuous 'Windsor', was immune. The wartime linkage in the popular mind between 'German' and 'Jew' certainly did not help.[214] Elite Anglo-Jewish fears that that linkage might spill over into even more violent anti-Jewish demonstrations, not to mention the sort of state legislation that had already been visited on the German population of wartime Britain, were certainly palpable.[215] But by the end of the war it was the Jewish–Bolshevik connection that was uppermost in their minds. In April 1919, a group of Jewish grandees went out of their way to write a notably craven letter to *The Times*, disassociating themselves from 'foreign' Jews who, despite having 'sought and found refuge in England', nevertheless might have embraced 'Russian' Bolshevik ideals.[216]

Was this an inadvertent indication, after all, that there was something, at the very least, in the Jewish–Bolshevik accusation? By noting that the motif was as prevalent in end-of-war Britain as it was in Central Europe or Russia we can at least confirm its ubiquitous, pan-European nature. But this still does not provide a connection between a *mentalité collective* and mass murder. Nor does it tell us why it was Germany, not Britain, which was the prime engine to follow through. For all the violent rhetoric, even overt hostility, of British politicians and rabble-rousers in the aftermath of war towards actual Jews, domiciled or foreign, Britain's primary state role in relation to anti-Jewish exterminatory violence committed on the Continent, either at this post-war juncture or a world war on, was, at worst, as a passive, sometimes consciously negligent bystander and, at best, as an active defender and rescuer. The last part of this section, and hence chapter, thus concentrates on how, in the final critical phase of the war from spring 1917 onwards, the convoluted relationship between reality and entirely misconceived, confabulated, and fundamentally phobic perceptions about Jews led to disastrous state actions and recriminations. This was particularly the case in what were to be defeated states, most obviously Germany—with the consequence of creating a latent store of terrible legacies for the years to come.

*

'Half the lies are true', goes a Hibernicism about Ireland's colonial relationship with Britain.[217] By the same token, had Sykes, Wilton, and all the other conspiracy theorists cottoned on to something about a minority Jewish relationship to dominant mainstream Western culture, which, however distorted, contained some intrinsic grain of truth? It is a paradox that in the absence of serious, principled Christian, or even mainstream Labour opposition to the war, critical pockets of dissent—especially, though not exclusively, from radicalized socialist groupings—often contained many prominent voices from Jewish backgrounds. In the face of the 1917 German turn towards rule by the generals, for instance, it is notable that cautious extra-parliamentary opposition came from the Jewish-owned *Frankfurter Zeitung* and *Berliner Tageblatt*, which supported the ultimately abortive left-centrist efforts in the Reichstag for a negotiated peace. Meanwhile, overt opposition to the conflict had already coalesced the previous year around Rosa Luxemburg's USPD, which had broken away from the socialist SPD for their continued adherence to the war effort.[218] For conspiracists, Luxemburg was the quintessential Jewish internationalist saboteur. But she was far from an isolated figure. At the time of the high revolutionary moment in Germany, in December 1918, the ultra-nationalist *Der Bayerischer Wald* offered both this roll-call and lament:

> Among the people's representatives and other leading men in Berlin we find the names of Cohn, Bernstein, Haase, Oppenheimer, Rosenfeld, Herzfeld, Simon, Landsberg,

etc. Among the radical Independents and Spartacists Liebknecht, Levi, and Rosa Luxemburg play the leading role. The foreign policy of the member states is conducted in Bavaria by Eisner, in Württemberg by Heymann, in Saxony by Lipinski, in German Austria by Bauer… Who are the true victors over Germany? The French, the English, the Americans? No! No one rules so absolutely in the German 'Free States' as Jewry.[219]

How this could be reconciled with the *British* conspiracist argument that the Jews were all working in the pay of the Kaiser (putting aside the fact that some of these named names were not of Jewish origin) is another matter; though perhaps by the war's end there was no need for further justification, as the notion that Bolshevik revolutionaries were simply operating to a *single* Jewish interest had become practically common fare amongst out-and-out conspiracists. And not just amongst them. Sir Eyre Crowe, a senior British Foreign Office official, in August 1919, commenting on a request from the Zionist leader Chaim Weizmann to mount an investigation into anti-Jewish atrocities in the Ukraine, for instance, acidly noted, 'It is to be remembered that what may appear to Dr Weizmann to be outrages against Jews may, in the eyes of the Ukrainians be retaliation against the horrors committed by the Bolsheviks who are organised and directed by the Jews'.[220]

Crowe was at least half correct. The original Bolshevik Central Committee, in power in Petrograd from the time of the coup in November 1917, included a substantial number of 'Jewish' figures. Indeed, Trotsky, Zinoviev, Kamenev, Sverdlov, Joffe, Uritsky, and Radek all became quite familiar names outside Russia on account of their Jewish antecedents, rather than anything else.[221] Trotsky, of course, as key theoretician and protagonist, alongside Lenin, in the Bolshevik seizure of power, was in a class of his own. With responsibility for negotiating terms with the Germans at Brest-Litovsk, in order to take Russia out of the war, and thereafter as the figure who effectively rescued the regime from defeat at counter-revolutionary hands, through the creation of the Red Army, Trotsky has aptly been described as 'the greatest Jew since Jesus Christ'.[222] Other Bolshevik leaders, including Lenin, were often assumed to be Jewish, or Judaicized, a deft way of implying that they had been 'taken over' by the dominant—and demonic—force. Moreover, if statistically those of Jewish origin were significant in the Bolshevik revolution, one might argue that in the short-lived Béla Kun-led Soviet experiment in Hungary in 1919 their preponderance in the commissariats was even more obvious and visible.[223] All of which might further suggest that at stake was not a question of denying a relationship between Jews, Marxism, and revolution—as those British Jewish grandees in 1919 were so keen to do—but judiciously understanding, analysing, and explaining it.

Many excellent academic studies have, of course, done just this. These have carefully demonstrated, often in quite close social anthropological terms, the degree to which these revolutionary activists, supporters, and sympathizers represented a quite distinct subculture in the modern Jewish experience but one, nevertheless, which was largely marginal to either normative Jewish or mainstream non-Jewish worlds.[224] For one thing, practically all the revolutionary figures of the Luxemburg, Trotsky, and Kun ilk were utterly vociferous in their repudiation of their own Jewishness—indeed, for those of this way of thinking religious or ethnic particularity of any sort was little short of anathema.[225] Famously described by Isaac Deutscher as 'non-Jewish Jews', or by George Mosse as 'Jews beyond Judaism', what makes the liminal backgrounds and milieux of these intellectual activists so interesting is exactly the manner in which they provided them with a sufficient distance from which to observe and dissect the nature of state, economy, and society around them to such devastating effect. It may have been these qualities and attributes that enabled many of these people to be so visible in the ranks of those who were to stand out resolutely against the war. And perhaps it is in this that we come close to an essential paradox of the situation, picked up by the *marxisant* Deutscher himself: namely, that these difficult, extraordinary, and certainly devoutly anti-Jewish thinkers were, in their searing and often frighteningly undaunted commitment to ideals of peace, equality, and social justice, 'very Jewish indeed'.[226]

There is just one problem. The reading is entirely selective. Even amongst the Russian Jewish revolutionaries, the vast majority were not Bolsheviks but Mensheviks, Bundists, anarchists, and social revolutionaries. The majority of these, especially amongst the Menshevik and Bundist groupings, were for the continuation of the war as pursued by the Provisional Government, which, having taken the reins of power in the wake of the February Revolution, had gone on to emancipate Russia's Jews. The point is underscored by the fact that Jewish revolutionaries were involved in key attempts, in August 1918, to assassinate Bolshevik leaders, including Uritsky and Lenin. The first attempt was successful, the latter not—but it led to murderous Bolshevik retribution against these individuals' wider party networks.[227] Kerensky, who had been the last and most important of the Provisional Government premiers, was also of the opinion that '99 per cent of the Russian Jews were *against* the Bolsheviks', which—even if an exaggeration—would be more closely in line with the support, or at the least acquiescence, which *most* Jews, in all belligerent countries, gave to their respective governments.[228]

If this however underlines the degree to which those who employed what we might call a crude analysis—from which to derive linkage between the anti-war Bolsheviks in Russia and some more all-embracing international Jewish conspiracy—had got it woefully wrong, the key point is that in the delusional atmosphere of 1917, or 1918, even thoroughly educated and learned people in high office were not much interested in the fine empirical details. There is evidence to suggest that British policymakers, for example, wilfully ignored intelligence pointing out the complexity of the Jewish situation in Russia prior to the Bolshevik takeover, in order to pursue what they had already determined to be the *inherent* truth of the matter.[229]

On a 'realist' level, of course, one might fairly assume that identifying and naming one's enemy is half the battle in finding an effective response to the threat. But in identifying the enemy on this occasion as a monolithic and seamless Jewish collectivity what actually was taking place was an unconscious or subconscious form of release from what none of the belligerents elites dared look in the face or take responsibility for themselves: the criminal perpetuation of a war that was going nowhere, had become beyond resolution, yet was steadily dragging Europe into the abyss. Certainly, in turning to ancient myth for absolution in this way, believers were indirectly confirming the degree to which they saw themselves as powerless and lost. Historic Christian anti-Semitism, after all, was not just about loathing of Jews. It had a very real counterpoint in fear. The Jews, in the mythic narrative, were the providers of the Christ—the Godhead—yet at the same time the God-killers: the people who, by some extraordinary act of trickery and manipulation, had at a critical moment defied and destroyed the Christ, and thereby changed the course of world history. The great paradox of this for Christians was that the world as they knew it began with the Jews yet could not end without them.[230]

Translated into the circumstances of 1917, what we actually see is the unconscious recrudescence of this unusual psycho-cultural formation as a fissile factor in 'last resort' political calculations. What is equally extraordinary is that to the fore of this tendency were the two major European political actors with sufficient will still to be seeking a way out of the military impasse towards clear blue water and, hence, victory: the Germans and the British. In both cases too, their focus hinged on the fate of Russia, the acknowledged weak link in the Allied camp. We have already noted how tsarist calculations themselves at the time of the Great Retreat revolved around quite bizarre notions that, if 'Jewish' money in the West could be placated by the regime showing willingness to halt the Stavka deportations, the banking houses—and with them 'Jewish' influence—might be brought to Russia's defence. Up to 1916 the propaganda competition for the Jewish interest had largely revolved around Jews in the neutral USA, and more particularly those very rich Jews who supposedly controlled its purse strings. But with the USA in the war as of April 1917—yet Russia in serious danger of removing itself from it—the supposed role of the rimland-centred Jewish revolutionary masses now very dramatically came centre stage.

If only the 'true' force among them, proposed Sykes, could be captured and assisted, this would surely result in 'powerful and impalpable benevolence deflecting hostile forces, calming excitement and transmuting various Pacifist tendencies of thought into friendly political elements'.[231] No wonder Sykes was excited. He believed he had found an antidote to the destructive Jewish tendency, one which, as Churchill also posited in his famous 1920 article, if properly utilized could be brought to harmonize with British imperial interests, not least in the Middle East. For Sykes, as for Churchill and many other policymakers, it is interesting how taming and domesticating the diabolical in 'the Jew' implied backing Zionism. Palestinocentric Jewish nationalism made of the Jews a national entity—like *other* people: visible, normative, and part of a general human development which reflected and reaffirmed the West's own avant-garde trajectory. National Jews were *good* Jews,[232] another powerful motive for publicly supporting Zionist aims as a route by which Trotsky and company, even at this late hour, in late 1917 or early 1918, might yet be deflected from their dread withdrawal of Russia from the war.[233]

It is, of course, not so much the counter-intuitive but rather entirely anomalous nature of this equation which has caused many historians of the Balfour Declaration to steer in some altogether more plausible direction.[234] To assert that at the climacteric of the war the nation many still considered as the most powerful on earth made a gamble on its outcome based first on 'Jewish' support, and then, by contrast, on some atavistic terror of this particular communal group's alleged possession of knowledge of the world unbeknown to the rest of humankind, yet which it could manipulate it in its *own* conspiratorial interest, makes no sense whatsoever. Yet, even more paradoxically, what the British were doing through the Sykes stratagem of attempting to ride the tiger not only clearly resonated with, but in a critical manner simultaneously enmeshed with, opposing calculations at the highest levels of the German war effort.

A half a year prior to the Declaration, the Kaiser's inner circle took a highly secret but utterly momentous decision to expedite Lenin and his entourage, plus a welter of other Russian political émigrés, in sealed trains from exile in Switzerland and elsewhere through Germany to the ultimate destination of Petrograd's Finland station. The purpose was to intrude this overtly anti-war element into an already chaotic revolutionary Russian scene, in order to sufficiently destabilize the situation there as to prise Russia completely out of the war. In turn, so the reasoning went, this would allow Germany the critical opportunity to finally concentrate its maximum military weight on the Western Front and thus, at the second attempt, deliver the crushing blow which would bring to the Kaiser's armies the victory denied to them in the autumn of 1914.[235]

Just as the Balfour Declaration was predicated on a fear of exactly this outcome, so the German high-risk subterfuge was directed at rapidly advancing its realization before the full impact of US entry into the war might once again scupper Wilhelmine prospects. The convergence of the strategies came in early November 1917, when the German-supported 'Jewish' revolutionaries took power, and the British, in equally misconceived terms, sought to parry them with their *own* 'benign' Zionistic counter-force. One might protest, of course, that the German decision to covertly back Lenin and his crew was in no direct sense on a par with Britain's public support for a national Jewish goal. But then the Germans were doing the very thing the British proponents of the Declaration were themselves consciously attempting to prevent: giving wing to entirely supranational forces, allegedly known and recognized for their intrinsic destabilizing and anti-civiliza-tional characteristics. The mere statistics supposedly spoke for themselves: 17 out of the 29 revolutionaries in Lenin's train were Jews, as were at least 99 (or 62.3 per cent) of the 159 radicals overall who returned to Russia in this way.[236] And capping it all was the éminence grise of the operation: Alexander Helphand ('Parvus'), the Russian Jew who by turns was international financier and international revolution-ary, not to say a key reformulator of Marx's theory of permanent revolution, as taken up and developed by Trotsky.[237]

In a garbled form, Wilton had picked up on Parvus, and then reformulated him as the quintessential Jewish archetype, when he alleged, in 1920, that the Bolshe-viks were funded by 'X': a German Jewish mastermind banker operating from Petrograd.[238] That there can be no doubt that the actual German collaborators in the Parvus scheme saw themselves as attempting to 'control' demonic Jewish forces—albeit in order ultimately to defeat them—is evident, moreover, from the Kaiser's fulminations against the Bolsheviks when things started, from the German standpoint, to go radically sour. At the time of Brest-Litovsk, when the whole exercise in forcing peace on Russia should have been being celebrated in Berlin as evidence of the success of their strategy, the Kaiser was instead darkly warning that the Russian people 'are at the mercy of the revenge of the Jews, who are allied with all the Jews of the world'. Never one to keep his vulgar views to himself, he insisted to the important Crown Council meeting at Bad Homburg in mid-February 1918 that the only suitable rejoinder was to beat them to death, or encircle and then shoot them down as if on 'a tiger hunt'.[239]

Why such vitriol? In significant part because, far from capitulating to German terms at Brest-Litovsk, as required at this critical juncture in the war, Trotsky was busily playing games with his German negotiators, and day by day thereby making final German victory all the harder to grasp.[240] But in even greater part, one might argue, it was a function—three months on from their seizing of power in Petrograd—of the Bolsheviks still being *there*. This had not been part of the German intended script, any more than it had been part of the obverse British emergency game plan. Could it be that both great belligerent powers had been duped? That 'the Jews' from different directions had not simply bitten the hands which had fed them but had manipulated the entire situation into play: the destruction of the European old order and with it all its social and economic conventions, not to mention a value system founded on Christianity? In other words, phase one of their project had been propelled by general war; phase two would involve the old order's replacement by something entirely alien of which they, of course, would make themselves the permanent masters.

One observer of the situation in Petrograd in the winter of 1917–18, who predicted this denouement, was Walther von Kaiserlingk, the German Admiralty's chief of staff. His reports home described the new regime as an 'insanity in power' run by Jews, in the interests of Jews, and, as such, representing a mortal threat not just to Germany but to the entire civilized world.[241] The tenor of such reports fed not only the Kaiser's vituperations but much broader elite fears of what we might now call 'blowback'. We associate the term today more exactly with outcomes emanating from US covert operations in 1980s Afghanistan that went radically wrong. Seeking to incite not only indigenous but broader pan-Islamic sentiment against Soviet occupation in the country, as a conduit by which to confront the Kremlin's power more generally, the CIA arming of *mujahidin* from across the Muslim world—including from its Arab heartlands—in the longer run actually sowed the seeds out of which jihadist animus was turned against the West and led thus to the so-called 'war on terror' of the contemporary era.[242]

It is rather significant how *this* conflict is so often portrayed, promulgated, and perpetuated in today's media as a one-dimensional 'civilizational' struggle between Christians and Muslims. Indeed, this may give some insight into both the nature and wellspring of the equivalent crude analyses of 1918.[243] Except that, in the first place, the situation was very much more obviously highly charged and hence open to rampant suggestion than today's, while the almost constant equating of Bolshevik menace with Jewish plot made all the more plausible and persuasive deeply embedded European anxieties about *Jewish* trickery and entrapment.

The years 1918 and 1919 were certainly years in which *British* official disap-
pointment about the fate of Russia—against the background of the failed Zionist
stratagem—mixed with a now fully blown animus against 'Jewish Bolshevism' to
produce some extremely worrying signposts to the future. Confidential Foreign
Office memoranda, nearly all repeating the conviction that Jews in Eastern Europe
were the enemies of the Allies and intent on stirring up trouble, were mirrored in
US missives of a notably similar hue.[244] In conversation with Balfour at the time of
the Paris Peace Conference in 1919, President Wilson's confidante, Colonel House,
was hardly coy in offering a scheme for dealing with the Russian Bolsheviks: 'I suggested putting them, or the best of them, in Palestine and holding them responsible for the orderly behaviour of the Jews throughout the world. Balfour thought
the plan had possibilities'.[245] Or so House claimed. The *Protocols* had certainly also
arrived on Balfour's desk by this time, one conduit being none other than US naval
intelligence, though we are not aware of his reaction—positive or negative—
towards it.[246]

Nevertheless, in the critical months in which the war moved towards its final
resolution we can discern a key divergence between Allied and Central Power
responses to the conspiracy narrative. The peace at Brest-Litovsk came too late for
the Germans. The transfer of Eastern Front troops to the Western Front and the
great spring offensive which followed, despite initial success, failed to realize the
necessary breakthrough. From the summer onwards it was the German High
Command, not the Allies, who had to grapple with the prospect of looming defeat.
With the other Central Powers approaching military and political collapse, and
with no remaining expectation on the basis of which it might yet pull its chestnuts
from the fire, it was in Germany that the blame game could be given full rein.

In July, Lieutenant-Colonel Max Bauer sent his analysis of the situation to the
Crown Prince, who duly forwarded copies to the Kaiser and Ludendorff. Bauer was
no ordinary officer, but chief of operations at Army High Command. In fact, Bauer
was much more than this. He was head of OHL's Section II, with responsibility for
industrial and technological innovations to meet the demands of the army at the
front. He was a leading protagonist of the theory of total war, including the complete subordination of the economy to its military imperatives. And he was a cham-
pion of a Bonapartist-style dictatorship, with Ludendorff as its de facto head. In
short, Bauer, arguably more than any other OHL officer, represented the extreme
authoritarian, ultra-nationalist direction in which, up to the summer of 1918, the
Wilhelmine state had been travelling.[247] Bauer now saw the writing on the wall. But
the problem was not the army, the monarchy, nor the state itself: it was instead a
multi-headed hydra made up of liberalism, parliament, social democracy, the press,
and capital. It was this threat from within which was not only denying the Reich its
glorious victory but actually setting out to destroy it. And who was spearheading the
threat? The Jews.[248] Privately, Bauer gave full vent to his feelings on the matter:

> A terrible rage has broken out everywhere against the Jews and justly so. When one is
> in Berlin and goes through the economic offices or along the Taunentzienstrasse, one
> can easily believe that one is in Jerusalem. On the front on the other hand one hardly

ever sees a Jew. Almost every thinking person is outraged at the modest contribution made by Jews but nothing can be done. To get at the Jews, that is, capital, which has both press and parliament in its hand, is impossible.[249]

The story of the Jewish chicanery and perfidy, not least through its alleged abnegation of wartime responsibilities and hence sacrifice at the front, spread far and wide, especially among the officer class. And not just in Germany. Admiral Miklós Horthy, the future dictator of Hungary, a world war later would recall to one Adolf Hitler how, in his country, 'when every decent man was at the front, the Jews had organised revolution and established Bolshevism'.[250] In Germany itself a young staff officer, Ludwig Beck—though future architect of Hitler's army otherwise best remembered as one of his regime's major resisters—wrote in a private letter at the end of November 1918, 'At the most difficult moment in the war we were attacked in the back by the revolution, which I now do not doubt for an instant had been prepared long before'.[251]

In Britain, as we have counter-intuitively proposed, with its elites and subordinates in many respects equally in thrall to the conspiracy myth, at least there had been no defeat and no revolution. The Armistice on 11 November may have been pyrrhic but the victory which went with it meant that the king stayed on his throne, the integrity of the state was confirmed, society, though severely battered, had survived. Somewhere solace could be found and the inner demons assuaged.

There could be no such consolation for German elites or those followers for whom the nation, the Kaiser, and his war meant all. With its Prussian-informed and hence notably authoritarian, buttoned-up, and anti-democratic traditions, defeat for the 1871 Reich followed by popular revolution on the very streets of its main capital and leading provincial cities, represented just about the worst thing imaginable. As Jonathan Steinberg has succinctly put it, the war—and, one might add, its apotheosis—'drove Germany mad'.[252]

And in that mental state—for those in high office and military command who had been criminally culpable of the war and its perpetuation, or for the mere cogs in the wheel who had imbibed the story, the symbols, the rhetoric, and the lies as if they were God-given truths—there could be only one possible psychological escape from all this: that of utter denial. For these people—not all Germans, of course—retreat into myth was absolute. It was not us, it was *them*. Already in exile in the Netherlands, having been forced to flee as Armistice terms were being prepared, the Kaiser, in early December 1918, gave full vent to his spleen in a private letter to his confidante, Field Marshal von Mackensen:

> The deepest vilest disgrace which any people in all of history has ever suffered, the German people has brought upon itself... urged on and seduced by the hateful tribe of Juda who enjoyed rights as guests among them. That was its thanks! May not Germans ever forget it and not rest until these parasites have been crushed and exterminated: this poisonous fungus on the German oak.[253]

As for Adolf Hitler, preparing his notes for an early speech in his political career in February 1920, entitled 'The Jew is to blame', the army corporal jotted down the gist of his argument:

Peace treaty and Jewish question—
The instigators of the war
The instigators of the German defeat
The instigators of the revolution
The instigators of the armistice
The instigators of the Peace Treaty are the same
as the instigators of the Russian Bolshevism
Western and Eastern Jews.
Germany's fate is the fate of Western culture.
Our task
The destruction of Jewish
Capital and its religion: Bolshevism.[254]

If nothing else, Hitler in his head was imagining a future reckoning. Yet in the course of the Great War a major reckoning had already taken place: not with the Jews, but with the Armenians.

2

Armenian Genocide: Ottoman Catastrophes

SETTING THE SCENE

You must understand that we are now fighting for our lives at the Dardanelles and that we are sacrificing thousands of men. While we are engaged in such a struggle as this, we cannot permit people in our own country to attack us in the back. We have got to prevent this no matter what means we have to resort to.[1]

Enver Pasha, utterance, as reported by US ambassador Henry Morgenthau, 1915

The extermination of the Armenians and confiscation of their property and land flowed from decisions made by the Central Committee of Union and Progress. Bahaeddin Shakir organised battalions of butchers in the area under the jurisdiction of the Third Army and coordinated all the crimes committed in this region. The state was complicit in these crimes. No government official, no judge, no gendarme ever stepped in to protect the populations subject to these atrocities.[2]

Prosecutor's statement before the State Commission to Investigate Criminal Acts, drawing on deposition of General Vehib Pasha, January 1920

For all the horrors perpetrated on and off the battlefields of the Great War, what happened from the late spring of 1915 through 1916 in Ottoman eastern Anatolia and the Tigris–Euphrates desert belt to the immediate south takes us into a realm of violence more extreme, sustained, and systematically implemented than any comparable act against a communal population until the extermination of European Jewry a world war later.

In recent years there has been both an increasingly wide-ranging and rigorous analysis of, and critical scholarly efforts towards overcoming, the polarization of positions which have bedevilled contemporary Turkish and Armenian understandings of these events.[3] That said, the potential flowering of this debate remains overshadowed by Turkey's ongoing refusal to accept that its predecessor imperial state, as led by the CUP, was *primarily* responsible for the violence, or that this amounted to a clear and unequivocal case of genocide. Our historical agenda obviates direct engagement in this political controversy, not least since the weight and veracity of the empirical evidence so clearly points to one conclusion only. Nor, actually, is our interest to pursue a blow-by-blow case study of the genocide qua genocide when an increasing number of historical monographs—especially those developing the contours of the violence in particular Ottoman provinces—are beginning to provide both a more detailed yet also necessarily more nuanced sense of the processes, causative factors, and circumstances involved. Our concern is much more to place this episode of extreme violence within its broader historical context.

That in itself, however, carries its own challenges. If the Armenian genocide turns out to be part of a *pattern* of violence, which can be correlated to a discrete geographical and chronological range, its singularity, within implicit and sometimes quite explicit hierarchies of genocide valorization, may itself be jeopardized. The *Aghet* was certainly not the first genocide of the twentieth century. Nor was it *simply* the genocide before 'the Holocaust', hence demanding a line of enquiry which demonstrates only that exclusive relationship. In terms of synchronicity, 1915 is also remembered by other Ottoman Christian, more especially Syriac-speaking communities, as *Sayfo*: 'the year of the sword'. They, too, were struck down by the CUP, or at least provincial actors operating under their aegis, in largely the same eastern Anatolian range as the Armenians. In terms of diachronicity, however, these events should be seen as a Richter-scale-type high point in a long sequence of Ottoman rimlands violence. These stretch back to and, indeed, beyond the *sökümü*—the great unweaving of the 1870s—in which the main body of victims, either in terms of those killed or radically displaced, were Balkan or Caucasian Muslims. They also stretch forward, at least into the 1920s and 1930s, with another remarkable high point between 1919 and 1923 (to be discussed in Chapter 3) when—especially in western Anatolia, Thrace, and around the Black Sea—other ethnic populations such as Muslim Turks and, even more so, Christian Ottoman Greeks, found themselves murderously cleansed and turned into strangers from their place of long-term habitus. In the space between these two particular peaks many Kurdish communities—among others—also suffered an inordinate degree of state-organized mass violence. Indeed, in the decade from 1912–13 to 1922–23, as core imperial territories were lost to, or alternatively reclaimed for, the new Kemalist-inspired Turkish nation state, somewhere along the east–west axis of the central, *historic* Ottoman belt—from the slopes of Ararat to the banks of the Drina one could be fairly certain of finding a case of genocidal or sub-genocidal violence.

This chapter's purpose then is *not* to diminish the extraordinary status of the *Aghet*; nor to simply place it as another item on a list of predicted and all-too predictable atrocities. For all the many factors which, with hindsight, historians might marshal to bring us to do so, the fusion of forced collective displacement *and* direct physical annihilation is nevertheless what, in Donald Bloxham's words, 'renders the Armenian experience really peculiar'.[4] Which actually only further underscores our task of trying to understand it *historically*, assessing the deeper structural issues alongside, and sometimes against, those of a shifting, contingent, and often entirely unexpected nature.

Nevertheless, it is a premise of this work that we can only really do this within the broadest Ottoman as well as international—hence *systemic*—parameters. Some of the *preconditions* of the *Aghet* have already been laid out in *The Rise of the West*, not to say moments when its actualization appeared to be prefigured. The 1894–6 massacres, though suboptimal in nature compared with the 1915–16 sequence, also mostly took place in the historic Armenian heartlands of eastern Anatolia. Paradoxically, there is considerably more evidence for these earlier events of Armenian revolutionary elites attempting to instrumentalize and even fan the violence in order to elicit European Great Power intervention on their behalf at a time when an embattled Ottomania was already suffering severe destabilization through European interference. A good case could thus be made for arguing that, despite radical regime change, Turco-Armenian animosities in 1915 sprang from the bitter memories of almost a generation earlier. This would also chime with the concept of a 'perpetrators' "never again" syndrome', which we have extensively employed to suggest how stored legacies of some previous, critical—and, in the minds of the later *génocidaires*—grievous experience, for which the 'victim' group was collectively held responsible, took on a latent purchase at a further moment of extreme political crisis.

The key problem with this argument is the assumption that there was only a single Ottoman state-communal dynamic in operation, and, by implication, only two avowedly *national* groups—Turks and Armenians—involved. Certainly, we could avail ourselves of a restricted teleology of this kind, leading from Turkish violence in the 1890s, through 1909, the year of the Armenian massacres in Adana, and from there to 1915, which again, if we were read it retrospectively, might be found to provide the necessary toxic ingredients for which we were looking. Except that if Adana is the way-station, we then have the small problem of the CUP and Dashnaksutiun being, at the time, *allies*.

If, however, we were to add into the picture the other pre-1915 conflicts that beset the self-styled defenders of Ottoman integrity, we might more persuasively register the general background noise against which a hardening of CUP ethnic policy can be gauged. The key crisis at its heart was the Balkan Wars of 1912–13, where the Armenian role or presence was a fairly minimal element in the equation. Again, by beginning here, we run the further risk of treating the mass violence of these events as either a prequel to, or adjunct of, the *Aghet*, rather than as a series of communal catastrophes in its own right. Indeed, if, as we will argue, CUP attention in the immediate aftermath of the wars was fully engaged by the loss of these *European* heartlands and the consequent defence of contiguous territories along the Aegean coastline and in Thrace, it would also seem to foreground Greeks, rather than Armenians, as the existential enemy par excellence.

The conundrum might be answered in part in our next section, 'Turkish new thinking'. This considers something of the evolution—and radicalization—of CUP state, territorial, and ethnic policy as it struggled before, during, and after the Balkan disasters to reconceptualize the Ottoman entity as ethnically single rather than as a diverse multiplicity of peoples—and in which loyalty to the state became much more closely interwoven with questions of supposed ethnic reliability. Given the renewed focus on the eastern Anatolian rimlands as, on the one hand, critical to the territorial preservation of the empire (at a juncture, moreover, when Russian designs on this weak point were being restated with unadulterated menace) and, on the other, and almost in complete contradiction, as the potential springboard for a conceived 'Turkic' advance into a once Ottoman, now Russian-controlled, Caucasus, the sort of obsessive anxieties about Armenians exemplified by the utterance of a leading protagonist at the outset of this chapter may seem less surprising.

But that, in turn, poses questions about the Armenians themselves. Or, to be more exact, their political elites. One of the things which recognition (contested or otherwise) of genocide does to 'victim' groups—the received terminology itself is problematic—is repeatedly reflect them through a one-dimensional prism that inherently flattens any opportunity to see their own political aspirations (or lack of them) in the round. If, instead, we could treat Armenian elites as on a par with, say, those of Bulgarians or Albanians (or, for that matter, Poles or Czechs), we might then be better placed to get to grips with their *own* often virulent, rancorous, not to say provocative, agendas and actions.

That said, section four, 'The struggle in the east', while essentially about the pre-1914 Turco-Armenian contest for eastern Anatolia, also seeks to remind us of the complexity of the situation, on account of the many *other* potential national or proto-national players—not least Kurds—involved. Again, the degree to which we are dealing with those claiming to speak on behalf of these communities, rather than the communities themselves, is a particularly moot point. And there is the further irony, too—critical to our overall discussion—that of all these many group-ings, the CUP, even as it shifted away from a conception of an Ottoman state of nationalities to one controlled and streamlined by one ruling Turkish *millet*, looked to Dashnaksutiun as, in some ways, a kindred, progressive partner. Raymond Kévorkian, right at the outset of his magnum opus, indeed acknowledges 'the trou-bling resemblance'.[5] This insight further begs the question as to whether genocide was the result of some irreconcilable tension between two *peoples* or, rather, a ter-rible falling out between two nationalizing elites over the nature and method by which compromise and coexistence *might* be achieved.

Perhaps one clue to failure on this score lies in the external pressures on the empire, which were building up—pressure-cooker like—to a peak by 1914, not to say driving the CUP to ever more extreme courses of action. The very fact that Enver and company took the Porte into the Great War—as it happened, on the side of Germany—might give the impression of an altogether suicidal regime intent on causing as much havoc as it possibly could to all those around, even as it succumbed in its final death throes. Or should we, instead, be viewing these actors as a group of vigorous, albeit utterly ruthless, new leaders, set on giving the lie to Great Power wisdom of a generation (or several) to the effect that Ottomania was finished? Section five, 'War as catalyst' thus considers the degree to which the com-ing of the Great War was not only the breaking point that pitchforked the CUP into the assault on the Armenians, but was itself terrifyingly indicative of a wilful Turkish defiance and repudiation of the writ of interfering foreigners.

Yet it is very far from clear that even at this late juncture the entire destruction of a people was pre-planned or, hence, inevitable. In a sense, what we have here is an important test case of how a genocide, or genocides—given the largely simulta-neous destruction of the Syriacs—'happens', which may also undermine some conventional assumptions as to the nature of the phenomenon. We turn, briefly, to the fraught subject of state decision-making for genocide in section six, 'A decision for genocide?', while, in the following closely linked section, 'The contours of mass murder', we try to consider both the morphology of the annihilation process and what that might, or might not, tell us about Ottoman rimlands society, as well as imperial administrative structure and organization at its twilight.

In conclusion, we offer some brief commentary on the events of 1915–16, in a broader Ottoman and comparative context. We look at this, in the first instance, as an indicator of the shattering of a complex, plural, non-essentialist rimland society under the exigencies of geopolitics and war; and, in the second, as evidence of a concerted effort by a single-minded, authoritarian elite to economically and politically build a nation state over the body of communal groups deemed surplus to requirement or inimical to the vision of a more streamlined, coherent, content, and *grateful* future body politic.

GENOCIDES BEFORE *THE* GENOCIDE? WAR IN THE BALKANS, 1912–13

'*Dhen einai anthropoi*' (They are not human beings). With such words, according to the Carnegie-sponsored international commission on the causes and conduct of the Balkan Wars, Greek soldiery repeatedly justified their atrocities against Bulgarians in the summer of 1913. To exemplify the relationship between word and deed, the compilers of the report reproduced a poster entitled *Bulgarophagos* ('Bulgar eater'), in which a Greek combatant is biting into the face of his still-alive Bulgarian opponent. Another reproduced illustration shows Greek troops bearing down on fleeing Bulgarians with, in the foreground, a Greek *evzone* gouging out the eyes of one of them. As a Greek officer ineptly explained to a member of the commission, 'When you have to deal with barbarians, you must behave like a barbarian yourself'.[6]

It was the behaviour of the erstwhile brothers-in-arms of the original Balkan League—Serbs, Montenegrins, Greeks, and Bulgarians—which really shocked readers of such reports in the world's metropolitan press. The 'liberation' of Macedonia from the Muslim Turks, after all, was not just allowable, it was a subject for decent Christian celebration. Balkan *andartes*, *komitadji*, or *çetes* were viewed in the West as plucky freedom fighters in some Byronic tradition, whose only goal was the freeing of *their* Macedonian hearths, womenfolk, and children from rampaging hordes of *bashi-bazouks*. The point had been firmly fixed in Western minds for the best part of two generations, certainly as far as back as 1876 when Gladstone, Britain's great political moralist as well as leader of the Liberal Party, had blasted atrocities committed against Bulgarian villages as proof positive that the Turks were that one 'great anti-human specimen of humanity'.[7] Overlooking the fact that Muslim villages had suffered the same, if not worse, fate from their Christian neighbours, the succeeding struggle for Macedonia had been more recently popularized by writers such as H. N. Brailsford as one for peasant freedom against a barbarous Asiatic yoke.[8]

Now, beyond the Balkans, urbane Western audiences were having to absorb the Carnegie verdict of a population whose members 'had mutually slaughtered' each other,[9] indeed a conflict in which every side had committed its share of repeat atrocities across the entirety of the war zone. Or, as one bewildered Greek enlistee more bluntly put it, 'The things that are now occurring have not happened since the days of Jesus Christ . . . We have gone back to eating each other'.[10] The Carnegie commissioners sought in part to explain the 'fratricidal' elements of the Greek–Bulgarian violence by describing it as the consequence of a 'race hatred' whose roots went back to 'the dawn of history'; though elsewhere they also conceded that behind the immediate fighting appeared to be a 'megalomania of the national ideal'.[11] Others, like the British diplomatic commentator Lucien Wolf, could only fulminate at 'a game of shameless grab in which all national rights have been cruelly and cynically trampled in the dust'.[12]

If Western commentary thus appeared to shift from almost narcissistic hurt to something closer to outrage that Balkan peoples were behaving outside the parameters of how they themselves imagined they would conduct a civilized war, some of those nearer to the scene were a good deal more discerning of what was actually at stake. Dimitrije Tucović, the dissident leader of the Serbian Social Democrats, and himself an unwilling participant in Belgrade's army, for instance, proposed that what the Serb 'capitalists' were doing through their own 'colonial' murders was seeking to join 'the capitalist company of the English, the Dutch, the French, the Germans, the Italians and the Russians'.[13] The language might read crudely but Tucović was surely correct in pointing to the way the instigators of the war were simply emulating Great Power fin-de-siècle carve-ups, scrambles, and pushings at open doors—albeit in their own backyard and to a much more frenetic schedule: that is, while the opportunity lasted. Of course, they were also ultimately prepared to do so by walking all over each other. However, what seemed to irk Western policymakers and opinion formers was not so much this: after all, Triple Entente and Alliance diplomats were involved in an almost constant round of Machiavellian intrigues to win over one or more of the new Balkan states to *their* side, regardless of the regional consequences. Nor, in fact, was it the naked aggression committed at the expense of a sovereign Ottoman Empire, let alone large swathes of its population, Christian or otherwise. No, what seriously irritated the Great Powers was their inability to *manage*, let alone determine the outcome of, the actions of these upstarts.[14]

With this broader European realization we may come closer to recognizing the paradigmatic nature of the wars and, with it, the key to their singular violence. At the heart of the 1912–13 atrocities was not the untutored, lawless proclivities of Balkan folk per se, nor some innate, peculiarly Balkan inability to master their own violent impulses. If this were the case then the finger of blame would have to be more firmly pointed at the aptly named Internal Macedonian Revolutionary Organization (IMRO), which claimed to speak for all Macedonian peoples in demanding not just their liberation but genuine independence from Ottoman rule. IMRO, however, was neither directly party to the Balkan alliance nor, having been decimated in the previous decade of grass-roots insurgency and Ottoman counter-insurgency, able to play an effective autonomous role in the ensuing conflict.[15] But where IMRO failed, the real instigators of the onslaught on residual Balkan Ottomania utterly succeeded: the state political and military elites who led the charge, asserting their sovereign independence and right to action in the most powerful and direct challenge to Great Power authority—and, of course, hypocrisy—imaginable. They went to war without Russian, Austrian, or anybody else's say-so, each with an agenda predicated on massive territorial expansion and 'long-range demographic goals'.[16]

What, however, did this mean in practice? On one level it was founded on a notably cynical restatement of the classic national principle. In other words, large chunks of the newly liberated 'incomer' populations—regardless of local linguistic habituation or religious sensibilities—would be assimilated, socialized, and 'streamlined' to the practice of the already 'core' group of citizens/subjects of the state, with, or without, the 'incomers' assent.

A handful of examples from the war period itself should suffice as illustration. In the contested Greco-Bulgarian zone in western Thrace, around Sérres and Kukuch, leading members of Exarchist Slavophone congregations were intimidated by Greek soldiers' words, 'If you want to be free, be Greeks'.[17] The implication concerning the required linguistic and religious direction of travel for their flocks was all too transparent. In another bitterly contested area—in the heart of Macedonia, around Veles, Üsküb, and down to Monastir and Ohrid, in which again the Bulgarians had lost out, this time to the Serbs—the same basic principle was applied, but here with the religious leadership of the Exarchist community finding themselves 'invited' to declare for Serbian Orthodoxy en masse.[18] Other, perhaps more surprising, examples, also followed this pattern. In the Rhodope Mountains thousands of Bulgarian-speaking Muslims—Pomaks—found themselves inducted into the Bulgarian Exarchist Church in mass ceremonies. The compulsory rite of passage was the biting of a pork sausage: hence a conscious slap in the face of Islamic culinary prohibition.[19] Similar antics occurred in much of the area around Peć, in Kosovo, which had come under Montenegrin occupation. Here, too, thousands of Albanian Catholics and Muslims, townspeople and villagers, were rapidly turned into Orthodox congregants.[20]

Clearly religion played a crucial role as handmaiden in all these examples of 'nationalization'. One might even argue that the two went hand in hand. Thus, one striking aspect of the episodes from all over this 1912–13 zone of violence is the way the apparatus of transformation was administered through specially created commissions usually controlled by prefects, police officers, or other officials of the state, but with priests repeatedly acting as a legitimizing authority. But such transformation rarely included the enthusiastic embrace of those inducted into the body politic. On the contrary, we have already seen the overweening contempt of Greeks for Bulgarians, as if they were some lesser race, while Tucović's comment on the new Serb regime in Kosovo and north-central Macedonia would today be restated as one of 'internal colonialism'. Here, while the in situ population became overnight, administratively speaking, 'Serbs', they were allowed neither the constitutional rights nor the municipal self-government of their now fellow citizens in the old provinces—instead finding themselves under military administration and governed by a set of extraordinarily draconian emergency regulations.[21] In Kosovo the situation under both Serb and Montenegrin occupation was arguably even worse, with 'systematic hostility and hatred on a scale that the region had never seen before'.[22]

The question might even arise: are we in Lemkinian terms (if not those of this author) looking at a series of prima facie cases of genocide? That the process of forced assimilation was designed to pulverize communities into submission and so disintegrate their previous group identities and loyalties is underscored by the degree of violence, including torture and outright murder (especially of teachers and priests)—as fully testified in the Carnegie report—employed against all potential foci of resistance. Looked at through the mindset of the conquerors, what is disconcertingly obvious is the degree to which any grace for those earmarked for assimilation was founded on the negative premise that these poor benighted distant cousins were really primordial Serbs, Greeks, or Bulgarians who through some historical misfortune or wrong turn had come adrift from their authentic selves. Hence, this view arguably provided grounds for some longer-term if entirely dubious *mission civilisatrice*. In the interim, the best one could say in its favour was that its identification of sections of the subordinated population as *less* dangerous from a security standpoint saved them from a worse fate.

The assertion of the national interest in the Balkans through aggressive war thus came—with notable resonances of the pre-1914 Russian military manual—at the price of treating practically the entire population of Macedonia as unreliable. This, in turn, logically determined instrumental policies ranging from compulsory incorporation at one end to outright liquidation (presumably of those deemed *most* dangerous or in the way of the state's developmental programme) at the other. In those quarters where it registers as significant, the violence of these first twentieth-century Balkan Wars is, after all, best remembered in terms of what was done not to those who were allowed to stay but rather to those who were massacred or forced to flee at the point of the bayonet.

Of the latter, anybody considered in ethnic or communal terms loyal to the old Ottoman regime was an obvious target. Estimates of numbers of Muslim *muhajirun* forced into flight range widely. The Carnegie report has a figure of 200,000.[23] This is definitely an underestimate. At least 240,000 fled through the critical choke point of Salonika alone to the relative safety of Asiatic shores.[24] Salonika, however, was only one of several *muhajir* escape routes from the war zone. That said, whether those ethnically cleansed had any control over their own fate is doubtful, as each of the military commands of the Balkan allies strove to cleanse their zones of 'Turks' even if it meant dumping expellees in the zones of their fraternal neighbours.[25]

What is not in doubt is the scale of the forced evacuation. Justin McCarthy, an expert on the demography of late Ottomania, extrapolates from 1911 census figures a total Balkan Wars' loss of 1,445,179 people from the Macedonian region, or, put another way, 62 per cent of its then total population of over 2,315,000. McCarthy's inference is that most of this loss was Muslim, including his estimate of 632,000 *deaths*, or 27 per cent of the region's inhabitants.[26] McCarthy's figures appear very high, in terms both of a historic Muslim preponderance, and of mortality as a direct or indirect result of the fighting or ethnic cleansing. Yet more localized, contemporary reports would suggest that the general thrust of his thesis—if not necessarily the accompanying figures—is accurate. In the vilayet of Monastir, for example, where Muslims constituted 40 per cent of the population, agents of the British Macedonian Relief Fund estimated that 80 per cent of *their* villages had been set on fire and destroyed.[27] Multiple eyewitness accounts throughout the region, moreover, confirm that the process of removal was nearly always accompanied by massacres. While the particularities of these atrocities certainly read as utterly shocking in themselves, taken together they do not suggest randomness—the actions *simply* of local armed bands, thugs, pyromaniacs, or neighbours settling scores—but rather something more akin to a standard operating procedure.

Thus, in one notably well-recorded example, that of Strumnista, close to where both Serbian and Bulgarian troops were operating in the first war, 590 men and boys—having been identified as Muslims in a sham court martial—at the behest of the Serbian commander were then marched into an abattoir and bayoneted to death. Similar sites of execution—schools, prisons, *konak*, quarries—were recorded by the Carnegie commissioners across the entirety of the war zone. In each the story was very similar. If the actual killing was often subcontracted to self-appointed *çetes*—irregulars operating beyond the bounds of military regulation—the commission for murder came from authorized state military actors, whether Serbian, Greek, Montenegrin, or Bulgarian. All were responsible for atrocities in their own zones, all were seeking the same goal: to soften up the local population by killing those most capable of resistance, setting fire to homes and mosques, terrorizing those who had not yet picked up their bags and fled, and using the pretext of military reprisal as an instrument for the much more thoroughgoing goal of ethnic cleansing. The parallels with the Balkan Wars of the 1990s, with their own repeat incidence of terrorization by paramilitaries, the killing of men à la Srebrenica, and the mass rape of women, is too close to need further spelling out. The result, moreover, as one British observer put it, was the sense of an entire population on the move 'fleeing southwards'.[28] Significantly, too, this mass movement included groups who, in ethnic terms, could conceivably have been treated as potential cases for coercive assimilation. The wilful eruction of Macedonian Citaks and Torbeses, that is, small endogamous communities of Slavophone Muslims, by the Serbs[29]—contra the experience of Pomaks under the Bulgarians—would thus seem to confirm Tucović's verdict that all parties were operating to an agenda to remove from the face of the earth any 'enemy with whom they otherwise would have to deal in the future'.[30]

Indeed, when the allies in June 1913 seriously fell out over the territorial spoils and Bulgarians found themselves pitted against the rest of the League, as well as Turks and Rumanians, the 'enemy' population could as easily be Christian. Thus, the Greek defeat of the Bulgarian army in Thrace was rapidly followed by the systematic Greek devastation of every Bulgarian village around Kukuch 'to a distance of about one hundred miles'. The total number destroyed in this way, the Carnegie commissioners estimated, was 160. Kukuch itself was fired and looted, with more than seventy of its inhabitants, mostly old women and children who had not already fled, being slaughtered in its taking by Greek cavalry.[31] Meanwhile in early August, Strumnista, already the scene of the massacre of so many of its Turkish inhabitants in the first war, now became a cause célèbre in a different way as the

Greeks, unable to wrest control of the town under the terms of the newly signed peace agreement, quite systematically set about its conflagration, in order to deny it to the Bulgarians. Those deemed Greeks within it were encouraged by the Hellenic king, no less, to evacuate.[32] Elsewhere in Thrace large numbers of Grecomans did so regardless; terror tactics, at the behest of Sofia, thought the Carnegie commissioners, were responsible for the flight of 100,000 of their number from Ottoman territories taken by the Bulgarians in 1912–13.[33]

Against the grain of ethnographic realities on the ground, each party to the carve-up thus seemed intent on guaranteeing the security of their gain through displacement, replacement, consolidation, and, above all, imagined homogenization of populations. Only one community as a compact body avoided this fate in 1913. The survival in situ of the mostly Sephardi Jews of Salonika is certainly paradoxical. The port was definitively conquered by the Greeks despite the Bulgarian presence at the onset of the second war. And as a community, albeit a very multifaceted one known for its absolute loyalty to the Porte, its majority, up to 90,000-strong, Jewish population should surely have been deported across the Aegean to Ottoman Asia Minor, just as the city's much smaller number of Bulgarians were ejected in the direction of Sofia-controlled eastern Thrace. The perception that a financially powerful and well-connected Jewry with the ear of governments in metropolitan capitals might lead to a challenge to the territorial adjustments of the wars, and hence to Balkan state developmental agendas if anything seriously untoward befell the Salonika community, significantly proved one step too far for even the Greeks to contemplate.[34]

*

So far, this survey of the violence perpetrated in the Balkan Wars might be read as an adjunct to the main matter of genocide. Ethnic cleansing aggravated repeatedly by instances, if not sequences, of diverse atrocity, including communal massacre, is clearly evident. But this has not led us to suggest a case, or cases, of systematic extermination of any Balkan communal population. Significantly, too, the onus of blame for the violence *so far* has been put not on Turks—who would appear to be primarily its recipients and victims—but on provocatively and aggressively anti-Ottoman agendas promulgated by ex-Ottoman, Balkan successor states. In considering two further Balkan War episodes, however, where the term genocide—in specific geographical locales—might well apply, we also might come closer to reminding ourselves of the connection between these wars, the broader crisis of the empire, and what was to follow in Ottoman Anatolia thereafter.

In the first instance, we return geographically to the north-western theatre of war, to territories of what today we would understand as ex-Yugoslav Kosovo: the northern parts of the independent republic of Macedonia and the Ottoman administrative Sanjak of Novi Pazar—then sandwiched between Serbia and Montenegro but which ceased to exist after its 1912 occupation by these countries. In this arena Serb and Montenegrin advance meant the takeover of lands with either significant or majority Albanian populations. According to the intrepid and often highly astute turn-of-the-century English traveller in the Balkans, Edith Durham, Serbian nationalists would dearly have liked nothing other than expulsion of the lot of them in order to recreate what they saw as an historic, medieval, greater Serbian Empire peopled (entirely against the grain of historical truth) by Serbs.[35] Durham's observation is an important reminder of the degree to which the Balkan states' drive to war in 1912 was fuelled by confabulated obsessions with the past, which were, in critical part, compensations for relative latecomer status in the European nation-state ménage. Specifically, in the Serb case, this centred on an entirely mythologized rendition of the 1389 Battle of Kosovo against the Ottoman Turks. This was where a Serb army, with a prince at its head, had supposedly laid down life and independent existence as a sacrifice in defence of Christian civilization.[36] National resurrection was now predicated on the notion that liberation of the sacred site and its region was a moral act which demanded that those who were, all these generations on, implicated in, or tainted by, the Turkish calamity would have to leave or perish.

Albanians were at the very heart of this animus. Contemporary Serb behaviour to them, however, oscillated wildly between the notion that, as 'Arnauts', they were really just some lesser, more feral version of themselves who, given the steadying hand of Belgrade, might be upgraded into decent, civilized human beings—shades here of Elizabethan self-congratulatory attitudes to the 'wild' Irish—and actual practice, for instance during the previous major bout of expansionist warfare at Ottoman expense, in 1878, when Serbia had consciously expunged tens of thousands of mostly Albanian Muslims from the Toplica and Kosanica districts.[37] Mutual hatred certainly became more firmly embedded after these events, not least as Albanians still in Ottoman Kosovo and the Sanjak repaid the Serbs in kind between 1878 and 1912 by 'encouraging' an estimated 150,000 of them to pack their bags and leave for Serbia.[38] The fact that in these territories Albanian chieftain-led clans also had the upper hand as historically loyal defenders of the Ottoman body politic could only have intensified a growing Serb tension between their own supposed superiority and the Albanians' apparently more privileged position within the imperial system.

There was something else, too. Albanians were also in this period developing a distinctive national consciousness. But at its core were notions of kinship which seemed to cut breezily across what for Serbs were all important religious, even linguistic, markers. Thus, though the majority of Albanians were Sunni, it was also quite acceptable to be Catholic, Orthodox, or perhaps even from some deviant Shiite or crypto-Christian background.[39] Indeed, there were instances, such as in the Luma district of the far north-western reaches of Macedonia, where whole communities during the eighteenth century had gradually gone over from being Christian and Slavic-speaking to Muslim and Albanian-speaking.[40] The Arnaut thesis clearly had something in it. But its recent history clearly demonstrated that assimilation could work in the direction opposite to that which, according to Serb nationalists, it was meant to. Moreover, a growing mainstream Serb political conviction that Albanian nationalism was treacherous and dangerous seemed to have its worst fears realized when, of all things, the Albanians revolted against CUP rule, first in 1910, then more successfully in the spring of 1912: ultimately achieving, later that year, their own declaration of independence.

The key irony of these events was that it was precisely Albanian fears—growing since the 1870s—that neither the historic Porte nor, more recently, the CUP, could guarantee their security and integrity *within* the empire which had galvanized their own bid for sovereignty. This, in turn, had been a critical factor in speeding up Balkan League preparations to take further advantage of Ottoman weakness. In the Serbian case, this was doubly urgent, however, because of the now clear and present danger that a nascent, vigorous but of course in their view entirely illegitimate Albanian movement—with its own aims to unite all its kith and kin within a greater *Shqiperia*—would cancel out the greater part of the Serbian mission to the world, or put more brutally, Serb covetousness of an Adriatic coastline, all of Kosovo, and most, if not all, of north-central Macedonia.

It is in this context that the very high level of Serb atrocity visited on Albanians in 1912–13 should be examined and understood. While other belligerents also mercilessly attacked Albanians—some two hundred villages, for instance, in the south were burnt down by the Greek army[41]—the Serbs, perfectly aware that the *Shqiptar* were too large, entrenched, and also, critically, martial a population to simply shift, resorted instead to a different method to resolve at least *some* of the problem: they *killed*. One acute observer—operating under his given name of Lev Bronstein—when filing a report for the Ukrainian paper *Kievskaya Mysl* noted that the Serbs, in order 'to correct data in the ethnographical statistics not quite favourable to them, are engaged quite simply in the systematic extermination of the Muslim population'.[42] Trotsky firmly ruled out of court the Serb official version, which proposed that atrocities had been isolated and, where they had occurred, were the work not of regular units but overzealous *Chetniks*, or just plain criminals. Mainstream commentators—in addition, that is, to Tucović, and including Brailsford, Durham, and the Austrian social democrat Leo Freundlich—came to similar conclusions; Freundlich's evidence being compiled in a 1913 collection suitably entitled *Albaniens Golgotha*.[43] The evidence, indeed, was all too abundant. There were major military massacres of Albanian men throughout Kosovo: at Gjilan, Gjakova, Ferizaj in the Peć region, and, above all, in the major centres of Prizren and Prishtina, bringing total deaths in the region to around 25,000 by early 1913.[44]

But this was not the peak of Serb anti-Albanian violence. That did not come until late September 1913, that is, more than a month after the Treaty of Bucharest had brought official hostilities between the former League members to an ostensible end. Its immediate cause was an Albanian revolt against Serbian control in the Luma district, down to and including the town of Dibra. Luma, as we have already noted, was identified in the Belgrade world view with historic treachery, as an area that had repudiated its intrinsic Serbianness and instead 'gone Albanian'. But combined with this—not unlike famous Armenian thorns in the side of Ottomania such as the Sassun region, or that of the so-called Armenian Montenegro, Zeitun—Luma was known as a particularly, indeed famously, independently minded component of the Malësi: the highland zone of the central Balkans. It was from Luma that serious Albanian resistance against CUP tax impositions had kicked off in 1910, causing, in turn, sufficient concern in Belgrade for it to authorize Serb *çetes* in the area to *support* the CUP's quelling of the insurrection.[45]

If Luma, in an existential sense, spelt danger to the Serbs' colonial project in Macedonia in 1913, its immediate threat was also a matter of its geographical location. At the end of the two wars, Albania as an entity, despite massive depredations from its League neighbours, had managed to defend its neutrality and—albeit largely thanks to Austrian backing—had survived on the international map. In national terms, however, large chunks of the Albanian people were now stranded on the wrong side of the border, in Macedonia and Kosovo, which were primarily under Serbian rule. Luma happened to be keenly poised in this new reality, not only because it was literally beyond the Black Drin, Albania's eastern fluvial frontier, but because it also was at the furthest western edge of territories which had been claimed by the *Bulgarians*.

When Serbian units entered in force into Luma, in mid-September 1913, terrorizing the population, killing local tribal chieftains, removing the highlanders' cattle, and setting fire to villages, something more than simply the usual opportunity to pillage, loot, and rape may have been behind their orders. Here was occasion to stamp Serbian control on the district and to make it utterly clear to its population, Albanian and Bulgarian alike, that dissent, foreign intrigues, and opposition of any sort were not going to be tolerated and would be met, henceforth, with an iron fist. Whatever the intent the operation badly misfired, a general grass-roots insurrection ensuing. What then followed, though localized, closely follows the pattern of the genocidal, imperial small wars of fin-de-siècle Africa and elsewhere. Violent uprising was met by the full force of the Serbian army, with scorched earth, systematic butchery, and outrages which extended beyond adult men to women, children, and the old. The massacres included barricading communities in their homes or mosques and setting fire to or shelling them.[46] As one Serbian soldier reported in a letter to a friend, reprinted in the socialist paper *Radnitchke Novine*:

> ...Luma no longer exists. There is nothing but corpses, dust and ashes. There are villages of 100, 150, 200 houses, where there is no longer a single man, literally *not one*. We collect them in bodies of forty to fifty, and then we pierce them with bayonets to the last man. Pillage is going on everywhere.[47]

Radnitchke Novine's report concluded by noting that this was not the worst the soldier had seen but the rest of his account was too horrible to publish. Information on these events, beyond such reports, is sketchy. We have no obvious figures for how many people were killed in the insurrection—though we do know that some 25,000 Albanians fled western Macedonia and Kosovo in its wake.[48] Too out of the way, or insufficiently significant in itself, to be remembered, except as part of the broader swathe of atrocity of the Balkan Wars, this event—a localized genocide within a much larger, extraordinarily brutalized landscape—has been largely lost to history's gaze.

Yet Luma was not alone. A second comparable event also took place two months prior to the Serb assault, specifically in the south-east Thracian districts of Malgara, Rodosto, and Airobol, close to the Sea of Marmara and the Gallipoli peninsula. The morphology of killing here has noted similarities to that visited on Luma. For instance, what happened at the village of Mavro in early July 1913, where 300 men were ordered out of their homes and fields and collectively fusilladed, was, according to the Carnegie report, not an isolated event but consciously enacted throughout this region. The report cited forty-five other villages where 'men, women and children were separated, and all killed without exception'.[49] Systematic rape, implied but not dwelt upon in the Luma episode, was specifically reported by the Carnegie commissioners in relation to these atrocities. The Carnegie report again could not specify the exact Malgara and hinterland death toll, though out of a population of 15,960 people, their assessment was that all those targeted had either been 'killed or burned in the houses or scattered among the mountains'.[50]

There was, however, one sense in which this sequence was different not only from that of Luma but also from the general thrust of the Balkan conflict. Its prime perpetrators were clearly and unequivocally Turks. The episode was part of a late CUP bid to take advantage of the intra-League struggle and recapture a smidgeon of the European territories lost specifically to the Bulgarians in the First Balkan War. Its target was Bulgarian-speaking villages, including, in some instances, Pomak settlements that had recently been forcibly converted to the Exarchist rite. Greek *andartes* also participated in these massacres, in a not very novel case of a traditional enemy allying itself pragmatically with the devil in order to get at a more immediate demon—the Bulgarians—and in the full expectation that in the long run it would be the Greeks themselves who would be the 'rightful' recipients of this remaining corner of Thrace. On the Turkish side there were *bashi-bazouks*, who were fully engaged in the killing. But, as in Luma, it was regular army units, or those under direct military command, who were at the forefront of operations. As befitted an empire of many peoples, these included Arab and Kurdish cavalry; in effect, Cossack rampage, Ottoman style.[51] Also, more ominously, there were forces specially created by the CUP for 'dirty' roles such as the *Teşkilat-ı Mahsusa*, who were also reported to have had a hand in this little, off-the-map genocide.[52]

CUP NEW THINKING

A Turkish parliamentary deputy in 1918 claimed that 'we learnt deportations from our neighbours'.[53] The following year the Greeks, deporting Turks from areas of Asia Minor they had just occupied, claimed they were simply following a technique they had learnt from their Turkish opponents.[54] Who was right? Was everybody to blame and hence no one? Or can we put down all these atrocities to a transmission belt of revenge killings, the first cause of which has been lost in the mists of time?

Ever since the Turks had begun losing territory to embryonic Balkan statelets in the early nineteenth century (to say nothing of from Austrians and, more particularly, Russians), they had been seeing *their* people having to flee for their lives, humiliated, broken, and with terror in their eyes.[55] But hitting back was nothing new either. Nor something Ottoman leaders, whatever their hue, *ever* flinched from. Midhat Pasha, the very model of an Ottoman reforming vizier—best known, even lionized, in the West as a progressive intent on dragging a hopelessly auto-cratic and 'Asiatic' regime into the light of a British- or French-style parliamentary democracy—was, at the very same time (in the mid-1870s) referred to in the Bal-kans as the 'Bulgar executioner' for the scale of retributive punishment he had exacted on insurrectionary villages.[56] Such episodes were, from the Ottoman stand-point, not simply justifiable tit for tat. Bulgarians and the like were meant to be subject peoples, *dhimmi*, whose protected position as non-Muslims in the Otto-man Islamic firmament was guaranteed by the state on the strict condition that they behaved themselves according to the rules of their subordinate, passive, and pacific status. For these *gavûr* (infidels) to rise up and tear away at the imperial fabric was thus not just a transgression against the *pax Ottomana*; it was utter blas-phemy against the very notion of *Dar al-Islam*.[57]

The violence of 1912, as done to Muslim Ottomans by these upstart nations, undoubtedly caused a new peak of panic—and outrage—at the Porte and beyond. The Bulgarians again seemed to be at the cutting edge of the anti-Turkish violence, not least because they were the ones who had engaged Ottoman forces full-frontally in the Thracian theatre. News that as many as 30,000 Turkish POWs had been simply left to starve to death on a river island near Adrianople (Edirne), during the winter months of the first war, was piled upon reports that Bulgarian troops and *komitadjis* were engaging in a programme, in the rich tobacco-growing zone around Cavalla, of systematic de-Turkification, village by village.[58] As the Bulgarian army, moreover, closed in on Constantinople's own last-ditch defence lines at Çatalca, *muhajirun* fleeing across them brought more immediate and vivid eyewitness accounts of terrible atrocities, conflagrations, and stories of how former neigh-bours, encouraged by the authorities or not, had taken to looting and pillaging their homes at will. The evidence of these catastrophes was all too abundant in Constantinople itself. By early 1913 the great city on the Bosphorus was simply overflowing with refugees. Where they could not find refuge in the great mosques, they camped out in cemeteries, or on any open spaces. Fears of a cholera epidemic were rife. To add insult to injury, Great Power warships had been given sullen leave by the Porte to land and deploy troops in the city to protect its *Christian* population.[59]

With this as backdrop we might consider what the Turks did at Malgara as an example of purely reactive, retributive, Balkan-style massacre, or, if we prefer a more universal reading, what human collectivities do when they seek to be avenged on those whom they perceive as having fallen upon them like thieves in the night and who, in return, deserve no mercy. However, another arguably even more sober-ing reading is possible. This would address the physical liquidation of the district's Bulgarians as a quite conscious, even premeditated effort to underpin the return of Ottoman sovereignty in the area—in this particularly sensitive corner of eastern Thrace, close to the Dardanelles—through the removal of a population deemed as a likely Trojan horse in the event of any future foreign invasion. Significantly, some Christian villages that had protected Muslim neighbours were untouched in the atrocities which ensued. But other communal inhabitants, notably Armenians, seem to have been particularly targeted for violence, and worse.[60]

Were the Turks in Malgara doing anything essentially different from their Balkan adversaries? In a sense, no. All of them were of the same mind in their respective drives to ensure that only 'loyal' people would be allowed to inhabit their territories. And, where this involved recourse to exterminatory violence, calculated reasoning did not itself require passionless slaughter among any of them. What was different about the Turks at Malgara was neither some distinct modus operandi, nor a cultural disposition which somehow made their killing more grotesque or vicious than that of their opponents. Rather, it was in the way it signalled the implementation of an emerging CUP policy which was prepared to carry through the quest for all-empire population security, if necessary by the most drastic and extreme means.

Early evidence of this intended course can be found in the post-Balkan War Turkish–Bulgarian peace agreement, a protocol of which confirmed that a fifteen-kilometre Thracian border strip would be underpinned by an 'exchange' of respective populations. As most Turks and Bulgarians had already fled the zone or been massacred, the agreement was clearly academic. However, soon afterwards, Eleftherios Venizelos, the aggressively dynamic Greek prime minister, and an architect of the Balkan League, entered into negotiations with the Porte for a similar, but in this case, *voluntary* exchange of Greek-speakers in Ottoman Thrace and the Aydin vilayet along the Aegean, in return for the remaining Muslims in now Greek Macedonia and the Epirus.[61] Here then, we see examples where sovereign Balkan polities were clearly prepared to enter into pragmatic bilateral negotiations in which both acknowledged the existence of respective 'problem' populations who might more readily 'fit' in the other's state and, in the latter case, operating on what amounted to a precautionary principle. Or, put more bluntly, remove the problem now, in order to avoid extermination later. Not only was this a foretaste of standard 'New Europe' policies towards so-called 'minorities' in the post-Great War period; it rather suggested that the leadership of pre-Great War Ottomania was already *thinking* as if it were inhabiting a nation state.

The suggestion carries with it multiple caveats, as we examine further later in this section. What matters here, however, is that Enver (minister of war from January 1914) did not wait for an agreement with Athens but instead began a full-scale, unilateral, but also significantly covert implementation of compulsory evictions of Greeks in the Aegean area. On a Richter-type scale, what transpired here was less total or violent than what would happen to the Armenians, or, for that matter, Greeks, in the following years. And in some sense we can again see an element of pure revenge at work: an occasion to assault *Rumlar* Greeks because of what had been done by *other* Greeks to Turks in Rumelia during the recent wars. Unable to defend themselves, these communities could find CUP spleen vented against them with complete impunity. But passionate and nasty as the campaign was intended to be, its motivation was also calculated. The *Teşkilat-ı Mahsusa*—the Special Organization—was again employed to spearhead the campaign. Their method: straightforward intimidation, laced with murder and looting. They worked in association with provincial governors and with the assistance of locally organized *çetes*, whose remit was to systematically clear whole towns and districts in order, as Enver tersely put it, 'to separate the loyal ones from the traitors'.[62]

That the latter meant Christians is clear from the speed with which Greek Phocea, Ceshme, and Bergama became almost entirely ghost towns; in the case of Ceshme, its 40,000 people fled in conditions of mass panic and disorder in the space of two chaotic weeks, in May 1914. By October, between 150,000 and 200,000 Greeks from the Aegean coast had gone in this way, mostly across the narrow sea to the de facto Greek-controlled islands of Mitylene and Chios.[63]

Rational, obsessive, or both, the ethnic cleansing of the Aegean Greeks can be considered to be part and parcel of a heightened state-security psychosis stretching back to the moment of CUP takeover in 1908; yet with the added paradox that the existential threat, and with it the danger of imminent imperial dissolution, was perfectly real. The possibility of direct military action striking at the Porte's heart had already been amply demonstrated when, in spring 1912, Italian warships had bombarded or torpedoed the Dardanelles forts as part of Rome's bid to wrest Tripolitania from the empire—just as, more famously, the British and French would take similar action two years later, in their attempt to force the straits.[64] In this siege-mentality-driven state of perpetual emergency, one critical security question for the regime was whether the economically powerful and demographically more than 2 million-strong Greek community in Asia Minor was to be trusted as loyal, or to be treated as simply yet another Trojan horse. The notion of *Megali Idea*, of a Greek–Byzantine-style state on both sides of the Aegean was, by this time, part of a common Greek political currency. By the same token, the long struggle for Cretan *enosis*—unity—with Athens had been finally set in stone through the latter's Balkan War victory.

CUP anger at what was thus seen as Hellenic machinations had already taken on very full public expression in a blanket anti-Greek economic boycott and, with it, a sort of ongoing cold war between itself and its primary Christian *millet*.[65] In spring 1914, it seemed quite possible that this cold war might metamorphose into an actual Third Balkan War, fought exclusively between Greek and Ottoman states.[66] Military and geopolitical considerations on both sides acted to dampen this outcome, at least until 1916. That there was no *general* Ottoman assault on its *Rumlar* Greeks, as there was on its Armenians, up to this point owes much to CUP concerns not to provoke Athens into siding with the Entente.[67] It is notable that once that Great War threshold had been crossed, however, CUP anti-Greek violence began to escalate exactly in the direction already visited on the Armenians. The Greek Pontic community of the Black Sea region, previously off-limits from the massacres and deportations suffered by their Armenian neighbours, were particular casualties of this disastrous turn of events.[68]

Which is perhaps another way of saying that, looked at logically, there was no obvious reason why it should have been Armenians in the *east* who became the first and primary victims of CUP mass murder, when the Greeks in the *west* presented themselves as the *more* obvious and immediate target for Turkish national animus. Back in the terrible months of 1913 and 1914 when the regime was struggling to find shelter in Constantinople for the hundreds of thousands of Muslim refugees from Macedonia and Thrace—reflected, in turn, in the creation of a special (re)-settlement directorate[69]—we know that revenge for the loss of hearth, homeland,

mosque, and orchard, was the repeated motif on the lips of Enver and other prominent Ittihadists.[70] And it was hardly surprising. The CUP leadership, with a few
notable exceptions, was drawn from *Rumeli*: from Macedonia, Albania, and Thrace,
the sons—or very occasionally daughters—of Edirne, Monastir, and, above all,
Salonika. Indeed, practically every one of them, born there or not, had some political or social connection with the now Greek-annexed port city.[71]

*

However, while it is easy enough to read CUP motivations for violence against
particular groups through the prism of revenge, this is not sufficient to take us to
the heart of the matter. What we are actually more broadly dealing with here is a
process of Turkish national identity formation founded on thoroughly schizophrenic qualities. After all, leading CUP cadres already identified themselves as
members of a ruling Turkish–Muslim nation within the empire—theirs by right
and might—not to mention with the capability and resources to strike out *always*
victoriously on the interstate battlefield. Thus, despite all the disasters of recent
years and decades, those who identified themselves in these terms had gone to war
in 1912 in full expectation that they would give the Balkan *gavûr* a good trounc-
ing. In itself this was not unusual. Consider the Great Powers as they blithely
railroaded their way to mutual mass murder in July and early August 1914. Shrill
calls that Ottomans would march 'to the Danube' and so regain all the lands lost
to the infidel in the last two centuries were quite of a piece with French or German
calls 'to Berlin', or 'to Paris'.[72] The difference was that the Ottoman fantasy was so
out of kilter with reality as to produce nothing less than absolute trauma, absolute
bitterness, hurt, and, above all, humiliation when the actual result sank in. The
very nadir of imperial fortunes, to add insult to injury, had not even come at the
hands of a *great* nation, but, in Ottoman minds, at those of the most miserable and
inferior of former subject peoples. Worse still, it actually brought those for whom
the empire *really* mattered face to face with the possibility of its complete
extinction.

  In other words, here was a stratum of society which not only traditionally took
it for granted that its state was strong but believed this to be so because of an
ingrained and inculcated sense of cultural and religious superiority. Yet, at the same
time, this elite group was having to face up not just to the state's acute weakness,
but to something more akin to its complete powerlessness on the world stage. This
searing new reality was exemplified during the worst moments of the Balkan Wars,
when none among the Great Powers, including those who had come to its apparent rescue in 1878, seemed prepared to lift even a finger in its defence. Its supposedly staunchest defender, Britain, politely told the Porte, when faced with the loss
of Edirne in 1912, to simply accept the League's terms, just as collectively, with the
French and Russians, it had done two years earlier, when Italian demands on Ottoman Libya had been at full tilt.[73] Western commentators had been predicting the
Turkish demise for decades. Lord Salisbury, the leading late nineteenth-century
British statesman, had said as far back as 1878 that 'setting the Turkish Government back on its legs again as a genuine, reliable power' was an impossiblity.[74] Such

diplomats' talk, of what they more politely called 'the Eastern question', was regularly interspersed with references to the 'sick man of Europe': an image of Ottomania which suggested a body politic not just ephemerally ill but rotten to the core.

According to Taner Akçam, the CUP and the other groupings we loosely describe as the 'Young Turks' had, to a great degree, imbibed exactly this European verdict.[75] One might go further and suggest that their negative self-assessment had the added potential to combine with a strain of Islamic fatalism which posited that Ottomania was bound to fall (as had other past, great Muslim empires) as its *asabiyya* (its group cohesion)—so evident in the unravelling of ties between its diverse Muslim, to say nothing of its non-Muslim, peoples—began to disintegrate.[76] As a consequence, these Young Turks found themselves caught in an absolute contradiction between a 'sacred' world—as they understood it was meant to be—and a 'profane' one on the verge of oblivion.

But what made this situation truly toxic was the fact that these were the exact conditions in which the CUP sense of self, of national identity, and, above all, of national mission arose. In short, the CUP profile closely mirrors the sort of psycho-cultural pathologies and obsessions which we have elsewhere identified as key preconditions for genocide: not least the subjective insistence on the regaining of power in an international context as set against the objective reality of weakness.[77] Indeed, there is no better illustration of the refusal of the CUP 'hardmen' to bow to what otherwise seemed inevitable than the famous *Bab-ı Âli baskını* 'raid' on the Sublime Porte. When Enver, Talât, Cemal—the future CUP triumvirate—and threescore of their supporters shot their way into the palace and declared a little revolution on 23 January 1913, their justification was none other than the need to halt the official government's acceptance of Great Power peace terms, including the loss of Edirne. At this moment internal power was in their hands of their rival: consciously oppositional Young Turk grouping Hürriyet ve Itilaf Fırkası (Freedom and Coalition Party). Itlilaf's stance on the future direction of state and society pointed, in their minds, to the need for *realistic* concessions to the *others*—the non-Turkish peoples remaining within the empire—as well as to keeping the Great Powers sweet.[78] The raid on the Sublime Porte thus marked a critical parting of the ways in response to the question on all patriots' lips: 'how to save the empire'. By acting as they had done the CUP leaders restated who they were and what they stood for—just as they had done at the time of their first dramatic entry onto the state scene in 1908. Against the grain of received wisdom they were the 'no surrender' Turks: the ones who were not going to make concessions to anybody inside or outside the empire. Instead they would be its salvation.

The gargantuan question was how? The simple but perhaps rather too simplistic historical answer would seem to be, by enunciating a policy of 'Turkey for the Turks'. In other words contra Itlilaf's decentralizing and federalist approach geared towards appeasing the nationalist tendencies of non-Turkish peoples still within the empire, the CUP stuck out firmly for a *single* nationalizing route, founded on either absorbing or obliterating all separatist tendencies in favour of a Turkic *Gleichschaltung*. The only problem with this argument is that it is built on hindsight: that is, on the assumption that the CUP clearly knew where it was going against the grain of a social organism and territorial range which remained firmly Ottoman.

This is not to suggest the CUP were not groping towards something radically new; indeed, that *is* what we are proposing. Yet there remains quite intense academic debate as to when, or even the degree to which, it ever consciously intended to overthrow Ottomanism in toto as its guiding principle for *imperial* rule.[79]

While that debate has to be for the specialists, it is also an issue rather too seminal to the matter of the CUP assault on Armenians and other non-Turkish peoples to be entirely avoided here. Not until Mustafa Kemal Pasha (the later Atatürk) in 1924, was there a clearly articulated secular nation state of Turkey, the first of its kind in the Muslim world. By contrast, to be considered as a progressive throughout the later years of Ottoman rule usually meant eschewing the notion of Turk altogether—with its entirely negative and derisory images of ignoramus, or peasant—in favour of self-definition as an Ottoman.[80] And until certainly the 1890s, the apparatus of the Porte had been notably non-discriminatory in its employment of non-Turks, including non-Muslims. This did not make it any less autocratic. But then the most liberal Ottomans were those simply trying to push it towards a more inclusive, civic, and parliamentary version of itself, not the opposite. These included, back in 1889, the very original *Ottoman* Committee of Union and Progress, a small grouping of students at the Royal Medical Academy at Constantinople—the Tibbiye—drawn from Kurdish, Albanian, and Circassian backgrounds but, in the first instance, without a Turk among them.[81] Ottomanism thus represented an overriding principle that all within the state, Christians and non-Christians alike, should be treated equally, and that the guarantee of that 'citizenship' principle would reside in a European-style parliament and constitution. What, of course, is significant is that by the time of the CUP coup in 1908—whose ostensible goal had been to restore exactly that constitution, as denied by Abdülhamid back in 1876—not only had much water passed under the bridge but an entirely reformulated CUP was itself responding accordingly.

While internal opposition to the regime had largely come during the 1890s and early 1900s from an often privileged, very disparate set of intellectuals and aristocrats able to sit out Hamidian repression in Cairo or Paris, the dominant cadres of the new CUP were military officers, with practical, often brutalized experience of what was happening to the empire, particularly through counter-insurgency service in Macedonia.[82] It was no accident that the centre of clandestine CUP activity post-1905 was Salonika. Or that despite their commitment to the regime's overthrow, these secret society oppositionists were, to a critical degree, establishment careerists drawn from the elite, Tanzimat-founded metropolitan military academies, the Tibbiye, and, more especially, the Harbiye—the senior School of Military Science.[83] In an important sense this already locates them within an Ottoman milieu—the ultimate aim of which was to equip an emerging 'ruling nation' meritocracy with a sufficiency of Western science and know-how in order to stem the European neocolonial tide and reassert imperial independence. Their training thus predisposed them, as Feroz Ahmad has put it, to being 'empire men', though one must add relatively junior ones, whose required role was to serve, not control, the Porte, let alone replace it.[84] This would have been even more the case with the non-military figures within the CUP, the archetype of whom was none other than Talât, the Macedonian postmaster of possibly Bulgarian Roma origin, who would rise, still only in his early forties, to be both future minister of interior and later vizier—as well as chief architect of the Armenian genocide.

Yet if, as Ahmad argues, these Ittihadists were socially conservative and from really very modest, even ethnically diverse rimlands backgrounds, reinforcing their innate uncertainty and disquiet about taking the reins of absolute power themselves, we can also see how the exigencies of perpetual crisis drove on their salvationist mission to an ever more extreme determination. The CUP thus may not have set out with any given nationalizing blueprint; nor set themselves up to be either, on the one hand, revolutionary Jacobin ideologues, or, on the other, men on horseback—Kornilov-style—riding to the Porte's rescue. We may discern a lack of real coherence in their policy development, just as, by the same token, we may find their resort to violence against Itilaf and others symptomatic of an increasingly paranoid rule and lack of actual control. Yet at one and the same time we might also recognize in the CUP the very prototype of military or military-bureaucratic regimes in the post-1945 Third World, who, having taking power by force in response to some real or perceived threat to the integrity of state, then committed themselves to courses of action—however radical and ruthless—geared towards confirming that they were indeed providers to the people and saviours of the nation.

But who were the people, or the nation? At bottom we still have here the Khaldunian conundrum: how to maintain political and societal group cohesion in the face of inevitable entropy. The obvious colour-blind revitalizer was Islam. But the Hamidian regime, for all its efforts to reaffirm this formula, had failed to stop the rot. So too had Ottomanism. As for Turkism, for very obvious reasons this was, at the very least, problematic, if only because Turks, however you defined them, were an absolute minority within the empire.[85] Nor had nationalism ever been part of the raison d'être of the Porte. The concept of the ruling nation might have been implicit. However, not unlike the wisdom of ruling circles in the Russian Empire, the official version sought to promote the inclusive, cosmopolitan nature of the beast, not least as a counterbalance to any destabilizing forces from within or without.

Certainly, by the 1900s, there was a groundswell of nationalism at work among the empire's Turkish literate, educated, professional elites.[86] In some small part, the process had been state sponsored, not least in the Porte's late nineteenth-century efforts to standardize Turkish-language teaching throughout the school system as well as in military and other academies.[87] It was a paradox, of course, that the work of European lexicographers had been a goad to these policies just as, in turn, more forthright European orientalists were the first to promote the notion of a Turanian race—rather than Greeks or Persians—as forerunners of European civilization.[88] Critically, however, it was the way such ideas were picked up by those who were at odds with the Hamidian regime, even in some sense radically beyond it, which is generally acknowledged as key to the spread of nationalist thinking among self-styled Young Turks and their fellow travellers.

It was refugee Turks from the Russian Empire such as the Baku Azeri Hüseyinzade Ali, or, more prominently, the Kazani Tatar Yusuf Akçura, who began to gain a constituency for their pan-Turkic creed in the mid-1900s. It is not difficult to see why. Their promotion of a fabled history of Turkic peoples who had spread from an authentic Central Asian homeland and who, as a peace-loving and tolerant nation had been the progenitors of a great, racially pure Turkish *civilization*, could not but offer a form of psychological compensation to all those who had imbibed those European images of self as vile, murderous, barbarians. Not surprisingly, the nascent metropolitan Turkish-language press enthused about this feel-good message. Suitably entitled, nationally-orientated papers such as *Ikdam* (Effort) and the CUP's own *Tanin* (Echo) provided something of a cultural bedrock for this Turkist movement. However, its real political take-off significantly came with the impact of the Italian aggression and Balkan Wars. It was against this harsh backdrop that a range of societies emerged to try and coordinate a nation-wide inculcation of Turkifying ideas. The societies, which eventually coalesced as *Türk Ocağı* (Turkish Hearth), had their corollary in the largely Akçura-founded journal *Türk Yurdu* ('Turkish Homeland'),[89] as well as *Türk Gücü* (the Association for the Promotion of Turkish Strength), which promoted adolescent paramilitary training in defence of the fatherland.[90] Turkish words themselves suddenly took on new positive meanings. For instance, *halk*, formerly 'peasant', now denoted the authentic Turkish 'people'. Even more portentously *kavim* was intended to signify membership of the Turkish 'race'.[91]

While we can obviously recognize components here of a modern nationalist discourse which emanated out beyond the capital to provincial centres, and, with it, a more unpleasant, increasingly racialized rhetoric of the nation replete with borrowings from European pseudo-science, this in itself does not confirm a successful CUP diffusion of ideas into the wider 'Turkish' population, let alone a programme of action. There was undoubtedly a vogue for the notion of a pan-Turan state: a vast state that would link up all the Turkish-speaking peoples both within and beyond the Ottoman Empire, even into the far reaches of Central Asia. Enver, as we will see, with his eye on the main chance of recovering the Caucasus territories lost to the Russians in 1878, was a particular enthusiast for this very ungrounded idea. But, for the main attempt to genuinely work theory into practice we need briefly to turn instead to Ziya Gökalp, chief theoretician of the CUP and, perhaps more importantly, a member from 1911 to 1918 of its central committee.

The clue to Gökalp's own obsessive embrace of *Türklük*—Turkishness—may classically reside in the fact that though from a middle-ranking, state-serving, administrative background, he was, nevertheless, half-Kurdish and, hailing from Diyabekir, was apparently embarrassed in more refined Salonika and Constantinople circles by his eastern Anatolian accent.[92] Be that as it may, what matters about Gökalp are not his not particularly original observations about nationalism, even if we can see, in his efforts to promote a distinctively primordial notion of nation, a motif which would be later regurgitated in different contexts worldwide, time and time again. Rather, it is his recasting of the Khaldunian problem in more European, sociologized, indeed more specifically Durkheimian, terms. What thus was at stake for Gökalp was the gel which would hold the empire together and enable it to participate as an entirely *independent* polity within a dynamic, European-led international system. To do so, he argued, was a matter of historical necessity, which in turn meant embracing to the full Europe's material achievements and scientific methods.[93] But this could not be achieved on the basis of a plural Ottoman society. On the contrary, that was exactly the inertial, if not fatal, drag on the creation of a *milli iktisat*—a truly national economy. Indeed, it was the 'ethnic traders'—the Greek, Armenian, and Jewish middlemen—who were denying to the state its opportunity to create its own *autonomous* national bourgeoisie.[94]

Thus, we get to the heart of Gökalp's analysis, which is fundamentally about how latecomer states, faced with neocolonial terms of engagement with the modern world, might reshuffle the cards in their own favour and so develop their own unfettered and necessarily rapid catch-up with the avant-garde West. And so *be saved*. The point for Gökalp though, is that this can *only* be achieved through the social cohesion of national culture. This, in his view, did not necessarily mean a complete elimination of Islam, which was too bound up with *Türklük*. Nevertheless, his implication is clear: it would have to be divested of all its legal and economic power, effectively subordinating, or if one prefers 'streamlining', it to state modernizing and, hence, secular imperatives. As for the 'Greeks, Armenians and Jews who lived in Turkey...they would remain a foreign body in the national Turkish state', a problem which could only be rectified by their forcible Turkification or removal.[95]

What part, or perhaps how much, of Gökalp's reading can be taken to be indicative of the new CUP thinking? The most important marker the theoretician actually set down was the empire's rejection of the West. There would be no truck with its laissez-faire economics, nor indeed with its prescription for political change founded on an all-embracing notion of citizenship represented through parliamentary democracy. These were the factors which had weakened Ottomania, indeed, turned its majority peoples into victims. Yet at the same time, such rejection was clearly much more ambiguous. Like Germany, an obvious role model, Turkey would claw its way *back* into the internationally powerful set of states by a state-sponsored, Listian-style, economic dirigisme. And it was not the notion of a constitutionally based parliament as such which was the problem; CUP credentials rested, in part, precisely on its restitution. Rather, it was the way parliament was perceived to give to non-Turks the pretext for their own separatist ambitions, in particular those from the subordinate non-Muslim *millets* who, in the Gökalpian analysis, had benefited from the neocolonialist prescription at Turkish expense. The position was closely reflected in the CUP's own revolutionary slogan: not 'Liberty, Equality, and Fraternity', but 'Liberty, Equality, and *Justice*'.

Gökalp's vision of union and progress thus offers a good indication, at least in general terms, of what the CUP in power sought to attempt. They would bring justice—for which also read 'order'—from the top down and, where necessary, by diktat. There would be no unequal deals with foreign powers, no Europeanization for its own sake, no concessions to some concept of a hybrid nationality which might otherwise enable non-Turks to coexist within an Ottoman firmament. These were all trademarks of Itilaf, meaning—to stalwart CUP supporters—*weakness*.

Above all, there would be no concessions to the *others*, the other, non-Turkish, nationalities.

*

Indications that the CUP intended to come down heavily on the non-Turkish nationalities can be traced to the August 1909 Law of Associations, which prohibited bodies 'which serve the goals of disturbing the political integrity and sovereignty of the Ottoman state'.[96] Ostensibly, the law's aim was to uphold and preserve the union of Ottoman peoples at a time of emergency: the CUP's initial 1908 'revolution' having almost come unstuck through a very nearly successful 'counter-revolution' the following spring, involving a range of opponent groups. Strangely, this challenge had actually been mounted from Ottoman enemies close to the seat of power, pro-sultan or otherwise, not from the non-Turkish parties. Yet it was these national groups who interpreted the law as an attack on their very existence, just as ongoing CUP efforts to bring compulsory Turkish-language teaching into schools throughout the empire were read as the thin end of a much nastier Turkifying wedge.[97]

More alarming reports came from the CUP's annual Congress, much of it held behind closed doors, in Salonika the following year. Already, an apparently heated pre-Congress meeting in Monastir, addressed by Talât a few months earlier, provided evidence, according to the Porte's British ambassador Sir Gerard Lowther, that 'the Committee had given up any idea of Ottomanising all the non-Turkish elements... To them (the CUP) Ottoman evidently means... pounding the non-Turkish elements in a Turkish mortar'.[98] Given the obsessive secrecy of CUP decision-making—much in line with the conspiratorial nature of all Balkan and Anatolian parties—foreign governments resorted to infiltrating such meetings with their agents. French and Austrian sources, however, confirmed the veracity of the British report, the French Salonika consul reporting that the CUP, having given up on the cohabitation of communal groups in *both* Macedonia *and* Anatolia, now favoured military methods to resolve the problem. The only issue at stake apparently was whether the most efficacious route was one of 'expulsion' or 'massacre' of the Christians.[99]

Vahakn Dadrian has taken this information, and evidence of similar discussions at the 1910 Congress, as the origins of a CUP genocidal blueprint directed at the Armenians.[100] While this may be a tendentious and unsubstantiated reading, what is certainly significant is that the Congress seems to have laid the groundwork for a striking and utterly radical empire-wide programme of mass social engineering. The programme, consistent with the broader genocidal preconditions of state rimland thinking of this period, was, in the first instance, predicated on a CUP anxiety about the *general* unreliability of large swathes of the Ottoman population. Before the advent of full CUP rule, British sources thought there to be some 6 to 8 million Turks in the empire compared with 25 to 30 million non-Turks. However, another leading exponent of the idea of a Turkish national economy, the Salonika Jew Moise Cohen, suitably self-identified by his taken Turkish name, Tekinalp, proposed instead that *only* one-tenth of the Ottoman population was of the right stuff.[101] Worse, none of these other peoples could be trusted. Greeks and Armenians were the most dangerous, not to say economically problematic. However, other populations, compact or scattered, numerically large or small—Syriacs of diverse churches, Albanians, Kurds, Arabs, Alevis, Yezidis, Jews, Druzes, Shi'ites; Muslims or non-Muslim alike—were *all* in some way tainted, or, even more tellingly, in the CUP's own words, 'susceptible to negative foreign influences'.[102]

What thus begins to emerge from the 1910 Congress and subsequent ones held in Salonika or Constantinople in the immediately following years, was a plan not of wholesale extermination of all these peoples—a seeming impossibility—but a policy which would compulsorily shift great numbers of them hundreds of kilometres from their place of domicile to entirely new and strange locales within the empire. Thereby stranded, the dispersed 'incomers' would have no choice but integrate into their immediate society *as Turks*. Alternatively, one could conceive of the programme as a way of punishing and emasculating the most recalcitrant groups by sending them not just far away from home but to harsh, inhospitable environments where their chances of eking out a living were slim.

To be sure, one could make a case for continuity in Ottoman resettlement practice dating back centuries. It was part and parcel of the Porte's long-term strategic thinking. Moreover, decades before the advent of the CUP, having to deal with external pressures from the Great Powers impacted on Hamidian thinking on how, most effectively, supposedly recalcitrant people might be replaced in strategic locations with those considered more loyal.[103] It was also ironic that the notion of a national homogenization of the Ottoman Anatolian heartlands through some form of radical surgery had actually first been articulated by the *German* polemicist Siegfried Lichtenstädter, operating under the quaint Turkish pseudonym of Dr Mehemet Emin Effendi. Lichtenstädter's *Die Zukunft der Türkei*, published in 1898, proposed that there was no future for a multi-ethnic Ottomania and, given that it would have to be replaced by a Turkish national entity whose territorial range was indeed Anatolia, the vast majority of its Christians there would have to 'disappear'. Lichtenstädter got round the violent inference in this proposal, however, by suggesting what, in his view, was an entirely logical way by which this could be accomplished. There would be a twofold emigration—an 'exchange of population'—in which Anatolian Christians would take the homes and possessions of Balkan Muslims, thereby foreclosing the outstanding territorial issue of a redundant Ottomania in Europe—and the Balkan Muslims, vice versa.[104] The only problem was that this neat and supposedly prophetically foresighted proposition was a far cry from how things actually transpired, not to mention certain gaping holes in its theorization. Who, for instance, among the Balkan nation-states would take the displaced Armenians, Syriacs, or, for that matter, Jews?

There is no evidence that Lichtenstädter's proposals had any direct bearing on the CUP's demographic politics. Yet equally, with the culmination of the Balkan Wars, the Ittihadists, as we have seen, were perfectly willing to entertain the notion of mass population transfers with Greeks and Bulgarians. Moreover, by this time their *own* proto-national population scheme was beginning to move towards practical implementation. It was in every way as grandiose as Lichtenstädter's plan but with a primary focus on internal rather than external migration, and involving a much wider range of population groups. It also demanded huge government resources—including revenues—at a time when these were stretched to the absolute limit. An early pilot scheme appears to have been agreed at the 1910 Salonika Congress. Its main mover was not Gökalp, however, but the veteran CUP Salonika activist Dr Nâzim, better known as another seminal actor in the Armenian genocide. Nâzim was able to gain official funding for a large-scale resettlement project for *muhajirun* from the Russian and Persian border region to an area around the key eastern Anatolian centre of Erzurum as well as to designated parts of the Balkans.[105] On one level, this was nothing particularly novel, given that Muslims as well as Armenians had been *voluntarily* migrating—though sometimes at the end of a gun barrel—in opposite directions every time another Russian invasion of the region flared, since the first major incursion in the 1820s.[106]

What made the Nâzim scheme—as it evolved into its full-blown conception during the Great War—so utterly new, not to say breathtaking, was its sheer audacity. The CUP was in effect saying that in response to a state of siege it was entitled, according to its own criteria, to compulsorily and forcibly move any part of the Ottoman population to anywhere in the empire that it chose. The scheme's legitimization, moreover, was twofold: on the one hand, it was necessary as the *only* prophylactic to the empire's inherent pluralistic disease; on the other, it was good because it was modern, progressive, and founded on (supposedly) scientifically based evidence. Eventually, in the context of war, this could mean that 'concentrations of non-Turkish population that had accumulated at strategic points' could be 'liquidated'[107] as security risks, even if the term 'liquidation' meant being forcibly moved, not killed. Yet what became known as the 5–10 per cent rule was a fundamental aspect of the original design. The notion of Armenian communities, for instance, being resettled in territories to the south of their main eastern Anatolian range—in the torrid Jazirah of present-day Iraq or Syria, where, broken up into small groups, they would never constitute more than 5 to 10 per cent of the total population in their new locations, and so be more easily inducted into 'good', even Turkish, behaviour—can be traced back to pre-war CUP deliberations.[108] In 1916, as some one million Kurds fled, of their own volition, the eastern Anatolian war zone, the CUP equally took advantage of this situation to move them into designated resettlement areas in central and western Anatolia and, where possible, handed over their native hearths—and those of their Armenian neighbours—to Bosnian, Albanian, and Thracians *muhajirun*, or other reputedly loyal groups: indigenous Turks or already previously resettled Circassians or Laz. These latter two communal bodies, with their known martial abilities, were deemed especially valuable as settlers around key points of security sensitivity such as main towns and railways, including as far south as Arab Mecca and Medina.[109] By contrast, desert Arabs, a significant element of the Ottoman population—although treated by elite Turks with a mixture of racist contempt, ridicule, and distrust[110]—were earmarked for removal from south to north. However, no group, whatever its claimed reliability, would have any say in the matter. It would all be determined from on high, as the CUP envisaged major ethnographic surveys, maps, and the preparation of statistical data down to the most localized detail to facilitate their Herculean task.

The great paradox is that if all this sounded like hubris in action, the Balkan catastrophe of 1912–13 not only confirmed an element of this analysis—at least from a nation-building standpoint—but seemed to make its concretization halfway plausible. After all, by losing its richest European provinces and, with them, their fractious and antagonistic Christian populations, the possibility of a leaner yet more coherent Turkish redoubt in Anatolia was itself advanced. With possibly as many as 7 million *muhajirun* having migrated into the region between 1856 and 1914, moreover, the demographic weight of its Christian population was proportionately diminished, possibly from as much as one-third of the total to around one-quarter.[111] The *muhajirun*, the argument went, were ripe for Turkification. It was an opportune moment for Gökalp, in March 1913, to publicly enunciate his famous 'Principles of Turkism'. In this, he declared Ottomanism and Islam insufficient to meet either the challenges from the other threatening *millet*s or the needs of modernization. Only Turkism could do that. As for the Turks who '*had lived unaware* within the Ottoman state', only by way of a Turkifying path could they be saved.[112] It was as if CUP was coming out from behind the shadows to finally don its true colours. Soon after, new laws were introduced increasing government control over all resettlement matters, vesting the army with comprehensive powers to carry these policies out, and initiating the body which, as the Directorate for Settlement of Immigrants and Tribes (IAMM), would, during the Great War, actually attempt to implement the party's grand population strategy.[113]

If this was intended as the CUP path to the strengthening of the empire qua 'Turkey', it was also, paradoxically, bound to act as a self-fulfilling prophecy of the deceit and treachery of its nationalizing groups. Revolts in the Druze Hauran, in the Yemen, above all in supposedly loyal Albania, were already ample indications that notions of Turkish solidarity elicited not the slightest sympathy from the empire's other Muslims. As for CUP dreams of pan-Turan ventures beyond the bounds of the redoubt, the fact that only the tiniest fraction of ethnic 'Turkish' peasant or tribal communities in Anatolia itself had any inkling, let alone understanding, of what the CUP were on about, surely only underscores the very narrow, even fantastical, realm the ideologues inhabited.

Yet the world of the CUP movers was anything but rarefied. Their radicalized vision of the future was developed against a rapidly moving backdrop of both internal struggle and foreign policy intrigue, in which the stakes were enormous. Paranoid it certainly made them, but their creation of a Committee of National Defence after the *Bab-ı Âli baskını* was not simply a result of that. In June Itilaf attempted one last bloody throw of the dice to take power again. The coup's failure finally gave the CUP the pretext it needed to 'seize the reins of power and eliminate the opposition once and for all'.[114] For Turkish patriots, perhaps, it was just as well: rumours were rife that behind the coup were the Russians.[115]

THE STRUGGLE IN THE EAST

Of course, what is particular noteworthy about this narrative so far is, if not the absence, then at least marginality of the Armenians within it. Almost as if it were avoiding the fundamental question: why of all the groups in the Ottoman empire was it the Armenians who suffered a full-blown genocide? Returning the Armenians to centre stage, however, is closely bound up with the CUP's sense of external, potentially mortal threat to the empire, a threat in which, of all the interfering states, it was Russia that always figured as the most immediate and menacing.

The direct linkage between Russian danger and the Armenian question came with a St Petersburg *démarche* in late 1912, resurrecting an earlier shelved, so-called Reform Plan for a decentralized administration of eastern Anatolia—or, more precisely, the six so-called Armenian vilayets and the adjacent Black Sea one of Trabzon—under international supervision.[116] Indeed, it was less a case of returning and more one of catapulting the Armenians back into the limelight, and arguably at exactly the wrong time. The Russian calculation, for one thing, was rather too transparent. St Petersburg had been behind the original efforts to create a Balkan League in what they hoped would be a covertly Russian-controlled and managed anti-*Austrian* alliance. Instead, when Serbs and Bulgarians went their own way and struck out, with their new Greek friends, against Ottoman Macedonia, the Russians were left high and dry. Proposing that a huge chunk of Anatolia be brought into the Great Powers' Ottoman deliberations, at the height of the Balkan War crisis, was not just a case of shrewd timing by St Petersburg—as everyone else's attention was firmly fixed on another corner of the receding Ottoman map;[117] it was Russia's explicit reminder that the fate of the empire would be determined by its great contenders, not the little ones. Above all, of course, by itself.

Russia was also being adroit by claiming to be coming to the defence of the Armenians when conditions in the six vilayets were clearly on a markedly downward turn. Curiously, St Petersburg had been notably reticent when it came to supporting the earlier, overtly humanitarian, clearly pro-Armenian reform package as largely sponsored by the British in 1895.[118] But at that juncture, Treaty of Berlin rules still essentially prevailed: the official Great Power line being to preserve the empire, not destroy it. In 1913, by contrast, all the private diplomatic talk was not of 'if' but 'when' it would break up; the consequences of which Lowther, for one, reported to British foreign secretary Grey, would include its Russian neighbour wresting a sphere of influence for itself in north-east Anatolia.[119] A decade before the Berlin arrangement, the then Russian foreign minister, Gorchakov, had infamously remarked that the solution for the region could only either be 'autonomie ou anatomie'.[120] Now with Entente backing for the Reform Plan—even in the watered-down version the CUP was finally prevailed upon to accept in February 1914—it looked like the former was going to be essentially a prequel to the latter. Or more exactly, a pretext for a wholesale carve-up of remaining Ottomania.[121] Which, in the context of the Great War, is exactly what the Entente proceeded—through the secret March 1916 Sykes–Picot–Sazonov Agreement—towards.

St Petersburg—now Petrograd's—direct Great War military intervention across the border onto Ottoman soil also rather suggests that true Romanov intentions towards the region were not motivated by altruism, let alone the long-term interests of Armenians. True, the limited Russian—in fact ad hoc—advance towards the besieged Armenian community in Van, in May 1915, saved it from certain CUP annihilation, though thousands of Armenian refugees from here and elsewhere in the region were to die in the subsequent Russian retreat.[122] More to the point, however, even under the exigencies of total war General Iudenich, the Caucasus Front commander, drew up extensive plans for a far-reaching resettlement of some of the more fertile valleys of the east Anatolian plateau, in which either Armenians murdered (by the Turks) or Kurds consciously expelled (by the Russians) were earmarked for replacement by more 'loyal' and 'reliable' people from across the border. Iudenich seems to have had Cossacks from the Don and Kuban particularly in mind, groups which, as we will see in Chapter 3, 'The First Crisis of the Rimlands', were notable as both protagonists and victims of massacre and ethnic cleansing in revolutionary and post-revolutionary Russia.[123] On a much more limited scale, a pilot scheme was attempted in the Kars area using more local and available Ossetians, Circassians, and Lezgins—some of these, of course, Muslims— and, surprisingly, as late as January 1918.[124] None of this suggests Russian benevolence towards Armenians, let alone Armenian national aspirations. On the contrary, Armenian survivors of the genocide who attempted to return home—now under Russian occupation—later in the war, found their only option was to lease their *own* land from a military administration operating in accordance with a decree which had declared such land official state property in February 1916. This was none other than an anticipation of the arrival of those demobilized Cossacks at the war's end. Indeed, one of Iudenich's subordinate commanders, Prince Gadzhemukov, openly extolled what the CUP had done the previous year, reminding his superior that they 'have left us an Armenia without Armenians which is far better for Russia'.[125]

Gadzhemukov's views represented a definite anti-Armenian strain in Stavka and more general Russian state thought. And they dovetail with ultimately successful efforts in the summer of 1916 to have the Armenian volunteer *druzhiny*, fighting under Russian auspices, closed down.[126] In these circumstances, it almost beggars belief that there were Armenian nationalists prepared to look to Russia as their potential saviour. But this carries too much hindsight with it as it avoids consideration of Armenian nationalizing imperatives through their *own* prism. This is in no sense to assume Armenian political elites were monolithic and streamlined in their aspirations and ambitions—any more than were the Turks or, for that matter, any other national political tendency—across time and space. In fact, there were major ideological differences and tensions between the *once* leading Hnchaks (the Social Democratic Hnchakian Party), and the now dominant Dashnaks (the Armenian Revolutionary Federation), as there were within these two major Armenian political parties themselves. The Dashnaks were for autonomy, the Hnchaks for independence. Political rivalry went deeper, not least given that each party had constituencies in both Russian-controlled eastern and Ottoman-controlled western Armenia. That said, the fact that both revolutionary elites aspired to unite all Armenians in one national territory suggested that, for all the differences within the Armenian revolutionary movement, there were at least some historically grounded common points of departure.[127]

Another one of these was the very assumption that having had their case internationalized at Berlin in 1878, they had been denied the fruits of that success. The towering figure of the period, Archbishop Khrimian, himself the Armenian representative at the conference, had famously charged that the difference between the Bulgarians, Serbs, and Montenegrins, on the one hand, and the Armenians on the other, when presented with Berlin's dish of liberty, was that the first had put down their 'iron spoons', while the Armenians had only 'paper spoons'.[128] Khrimian, before that moment, was already revered in national circles as the great revitalizer of Armenian consciousness in the very place where it really mattered: the heartlands of the six vilayets.[129] His efforts were a vivid reminder that a modern Armenian cultural efflorescence—the *Zartonk*—was already at least a generation if not more in advance of other potential national movements, the Turks included, that might yet seek to galvanize their avowed constituencies on the plateau.

Yet built into this avant-garde Armenian self-awareness was a double paradox. The movement itself had emanated primarily from *outside* the main concentration of Armenians on the plateau or its immediate hinterlands, either in Ottoman metropolitan centres, across the border in Russia—notably in Tiflis (Tbilisi), or, for that matter, in the growing Armenian diaspora overseas. It was here amongst the rising, Western-orientated, occupationally trade-focused, self-consciously modern bourgeoisie that the notion of a self-governing Armenian community was most fervently imagined and in turn projected *back*—not least by those like Khrimian himself—onto eastern Anatolia and neighbouring Cilicia. Central to such narratives was a retelling of *medieval* Armenian history in which great warrior dynasties were revitalized, the continuity of (albeit martyred) Armenian nationhood emphasized, and Armenia's place as a great cradle of Christian civilization rapturously celebrated.[130] The problem was that while these ideas certainly infiltrated Armenian consciousness in the heartlands, it was primarily in urban centres among a growing and certainly increasingly vocalized, Western missionary school-educated middle class. The same does not seem to have been true of *most* Armenians: the peasantry.[131]

The slow pace of pre-1914 peasant integration into the Armenian nationalizing fold matters because it highlights the second element of our paradox: the underlying *weakness* of the Armenian cause. If Ottoman Armenian peasants encountered Hnchaks or Dashnaks it was more than likely as communal outsiders coming in to demand financial exactions to support some revolutionary struggle which the peasants understood little, and cared for even less.[132] Or, worse, to inveigle them into possibly political or criminal activity which, if found out, would certainly invite the state's individual or collective punishment and wrath against the *raya*: the most searing recent memory of which was the massacres which had swept the Armenian vilayets in 1894 and 1895. Underlying all this, however, was the conundrum for all nationalists—not just Armenians—here as in all the other European and near-European rimlands: how to impose an essentialized coherence and categorized order on a region whose basic ethnographic realities militated against any such design.

It was not just that eastern Anatolia was *the* classic plural arena, with literally dozens of identifiably distinct ethnic and religious communities. More to the point, the social and cultural interactions between these groups cut directly across any supposed national boundaries. This does not mean there were not traditional, strictly enforced ethno-religious boundaries, the transgression of which was quite likely, in itself, to lead to inter-group violence. Nor, indeed, does it mean the social and economic position of the majority of Armenians was fundamentally the same as that of other groups. On the plateau a largely semi-enserfed Armenian peasantry in hock to Kurdish feudal *agha*s or suffering more unpredictable encroachment from tribal Kurds—who increasingly quartered their flocks without compensation on peasant land—found their position worsening through an increasing range of additional taxes, tributes, and entirely arbitrary exactions which were, in themselves, a form of structural violence and part of the immediate backdrop to the outbreak of inter-communal bloodshed in the 1890s.[133] Those underlying factors had not gone away by 1914. Indeed, from an Armenian national perspective they were part and parcel of a deteriorating overall situation.

The specific focus of that alarm was demographic. If the region until recently had been notably underpopulated, the ebb in a series of cholera and other epidemics from the mid-nineteenth century, and a net migration into the region, combined to create a 50 per cent population rise by the turn of century.[134] But not to Armenian advantage. Many of the incomers were Kurds from further south or east, some in the process of sedentarization, others not. But there were also significant numbers of *muhajirun*, Tatars, Chechens, above all, Çerkez—Circassians—many of whom may have been consciously directed to the plateau by the authorities, thereby putting a further squeeze on the Armenians.[135] Either way, a growing competition for land resources was becoming apparent.[136] In addition, a quite conscious post-1878 administrative redrawing of provincial boundaries—replacing a small number of eyalets in the east with a larger number of vilayets—represented a quite blatant example of gerrymandering designed to 'disappear' the ongoing preponderance of Armenians, especially in Van, Bitlis, and, to some extent, Erzurum, within apparent Muslim majorities.[137]

It is significant, therefore, that state–communal battle was joined in 1912–14; in other words, at the moment not just of general Ottoman crisis but particularly of renewed international interest in this region as to the numerical strength of its respective ethno-religious groups. The instrument, as in all such 'national asset' exercises, was the census. However, as we have seen in the section 'Genocides before *the* genocide' with regard to the Balkans, where diverse parties with a vested interest in the result offered their own competing versions, the data on offer could also radically differ. Thus, the first of these Ottoman censuses was published not by the government but by the Armenian Patriarchate, with the claim that *its* community in the six vilayets was one million-strong and amounted to 39 per cent of the total population. Interestingly, it split Turks and Kurds, as two separate ethnic entities, but still managed to suggest that even combined their numbers were only very slightly larger than that of the Armenians.[138] With over 2 million Armenians in the empire overall—according to this census—its wider implication was perfectly clear: with net Armenian migration from other provinces into the six vilayets, Armenians there could and would constitute a majority. Not surprisingly, therefore, the subsequent Ottoman census almost completely reversed this verdict. In part it did so by presenting all the Muslim elements of the regional population as a compact bloc, and hence as unquestionably dominant. But it also indirectly poured scorn on the Patriarchate figures by suggesting the Armenian population of the region was no more than 600,000: a mere 17 per cent of its total.[139]

What was at stake here was less the figures themselves, or even some creative accounting being employed on either side, but rather their semiotics. The censuses, after all, were not just produced for domestic consumption but as signals to the Great Powers: in the Porte's case to stonewall their interference in sovereign Ottoman territory; in the Armenian nationalists' case, to encourage it. Logically, for the latter, it made little or no sense to remain silent if the empire was on the cusp of dissolution anyway. And if it was the Russians who were making all the running on the future of the region the Armenians saw as *theirs*, it surely behoved them to be ahead of the game. Particularly so if further, more cautious Great Power interpretation of *both* sets of statistics was to confirm that Armenian primacy on the plateau was far from conclusive. With the Reform Plan, even in its diluted form, proposing that only the sedentary population be enfranchised; with the mostly Kurdish Hamidiye regiments—which in the 1890s had wrought so much destruction on Armenian communities—disbanded; with and the *muhajirun* expelled, it was hardly surprising if enthusiastic Armenian support came not only from across the Russian border, in the person of the Catholicos—apostolic Armenians' spiritual leader no less—but from Armenian delegates to the Ottoman National Assembly.[140] By contrast, the CUP saw Armenian support for the scheme as nothing short of perfidy, the effect of which, according to the *Tanin*, would be to fragment the remaining empire into a decentralized confederation of Arab, Greek, and, of course, Armenian parts—the very thing the CUP was striving to prevent. More pointedly, Armenians' support for the scheme proved what the CUP had suspected all along: they were willing tools of Russian designs.[141] It was the definitive parting of the ways. Or was it?

*

If we would appear to have found at least one causative factor for the 1915 genocide, a slightly more careful examination of elite Turco-Armenian relations within the broader political–ethnic context of pre-Great War eastern Anatolia, however, might be grounds for being less precipitate. It is well to remember that from the time of Battle of Chaldiran, in 1514, when the Ottomans had wrested the plateau from their major Persian Safavid adversary, until the time of the nineteenth-century Russian invasions, the region had been relatively calm and, in terms of intercommunal relations, relatively peaceful. What destabilized that situation then, as it had previously, was eastern Anatolia's geostrategic significance. To contest or defend these borderlands required serious military power. During the centuries of peace the Ottoman state had effectively subcontracted this role to Kurdish chieftains, the result being a series of semi-autonomous dominions under which the diverse communities got by and generally got on. The Russian menace, however, especially from the 1820s onwards, led to efforts on the part of the Porte to claw back firmer control of the region. It brought in its wake varying degrees of communal tension, some—as we saw with regard to the Nestorians, in *The Rise of the West*—of a really serious nature but without an unequivocal Ottoman subordination of Kurdish power itself. Instead, the latter tended to become more localized and fragmentary, its leaders and followers increasingly looking to alternative sources of authority, notably from Sufi Naqshbandi *shaikhs*.[142]

It was in this fluid political context that socio-economic relations between the two most demographically significant communities on the plateau, Armenians and Kurds, began dangerously to falter. The problem was heightened by the fact that the former, or rather a substantial elite element thereof, were increasingly seeing themselves—and behaving accordingly—in national terms. This is not to dismiss the Kurds: far from it. However, the complex, and indeed increasingly fractured nature of Kurdish traditional society—under late Ottoman and, equally, Persian rule—proved to be a critical factor in the consequent slow pace of modern Kurdish identity formation. Its pre-Great War origins can be traced to the tiny exile groups who founded the journal *Kurdistan* and to the early post-1908 metropolitan clubs—such as the *Hiva-ya Kürd Jamiyati* (Kurdish Hope Society) and the *Kürd Teavün ve Terakki Cemiyeti* (Society for Mutual Aid and Progress). Actually these groupings were not exclusively metropolitan, the *Teavün* in particular drawing support in Bitlis and Diyarbekir.[143] But strictly speaking these tendencies only underscore the groups' initial remoteness from Kurdish realities on the plateau. In turn, this lack of Kurdish national penetration had a marked bearing on Armenian–Turkish relationships as the empire shifted from Hamidian autocracy to a new CUP-led interpretation of communal rights and responsibilities.

Indeed, what this situation particularly suggests is that in the circumstances of a potential triangular struggle for power on the plateau—in which no single element was dominant—it made sense for the CUP and Dashnaksutiun to come together in a *common* cause. On one level, this may sound not simply counter-intuitive but absurd. Turkish elite opinion was as full of prejudice, if not outright animus, towards Armenians as were great swathes of urban Europeans towards Jews. The Armenians' minority, metropolitan, allegedly comprador profile, and hence their *perceived* status (à la Slezkine) as Mercurians in a sea of Apollonians—regardless of the fact that the majority were peasants, artisans, or migrant workers—practically ensured it. Talât, for one, in his memoirs was full of accusations against them as exploitative moneymakers, busily sucking the country dry at its expense, not to say, in its hour of need, seeking to carve out their own state from the Ottoman patrimony. His verdict: 'History has not known such ingratitude'.[144]

Yet Talât also had many Armenian political friends, not just in the CUP but among the Dashnaks. This was the other side of the coin. The two groupings in 1908 had much in common. Both were progressive, modernizing parties, committed to radical change. They both may have been nominally less than secular but they implicitly stood for the dynamic development of society against the dictates of hierarchy, privilege, or religious authority, whether that of *ulema* or *ecclesia*. It is quite true that these similarities only went so far. In practice, the much less *socially* progressive CUP was perfectly ready to co-opt *ulema* and notables into its ranks. On the other hand, just like the Dashnaks, it also drew most of its cadres from young men and women of the Western-educated but middle tiers of Ottoman society. At the time of the CUP's initial seizure of power the Dashnaks were clearly the more advanced and powerful on this score, with an avowed membership of 165,000.[145] All the more reason for the CUP to emulate and learn from the organizational experience, methods, and contacts of their Armenian revolutionary comrades. Indeed, there was already a history of cooperation not only between these two parties but between the various Armenian groupings and other Ottoman oppositionists going back at least to the turn of the century, and with the former often assumed to have provided the initiative and direction to the general anti-Hamidian campaign. Moreover, many of the leading CUP cadres, Talât and Nâzim included, had personal reasons for being grateful to their Dashnak friends, many of whom sheltered them during the attempted 1909 Hamidian counter-coup.[146]

One might at this point mention the slight impediment of their respective political positions. But even putting aside the fact that both CUP and Dashnaks were pragmatists whose party platform could change according to the situation around them, their ambitions were not *necessarily* irreconcilable. On paper at least, the CUP remained committed to the notion of *Ittihad-ı Ansar*, a union of Ottoman peoples who would resolve their differences through a parliamentary, constitutional framework. Similarly, the Dashnaks, up to 1917, were for autonomy, not for a sovereign, independent Armenia. Moreover, with the most overt assault on Armenian life in the early 1900s taking place in Russian Armenia, with a tsarist attempt to seize control of Armenian church-run schools and seminaries which were believed to be a breeding ground for Dashnak mobilization—followed, in turn, by a major grass-roots pogrom in Baku's Armenian quarter[147]—an accommodation with progressive forces on Ottoman territory began to look increasingly attractive. The Dashnak Congress, in 1907, in explicitly calling for democratic federalism as the political route to this goal was still in keeping with the CUP's principled position. The CUP repaid the compliment, once in power, by extending, under the cover of their consulates, especially in Persia, money, weapons, and legal protection to anti-Russian Dashnaks. The more overtly insurrectionist Hnchaks, not to be outdone, also opted for a similar pro-Ottoman posture two years later, voting not for political independence but for a socialist-orientated cultural autonomy *within* a united Ottoman body politic.[148]

What followed in August 1909 was an agreement at the most senior executive levels of both the CUP and the Turkish Section of Dashnaksutiun to work together through a joint high-level committee and 'above and beyond formal contact and parliamentary negotiations'. The agreement involved an attempt to forge a common platform, especially with regard to restraints on development in the east. It assumed that tackling head-on the problem of land reform would require dealing, on the one hand, with entrenched feudalism, on the other with the range of arbitrary—and hence extralegal—exactions sapping 'settled' life on the plateau. In other words, while it posited the problem as one of the rich taking from the poor, it also implicitly represented an acknowledgement by the CUP of the Dashnak analysis that it was the Kurds and *muhajirun* who needed sorting out, not the Armenians.[149]

What is perhaps even more significant is that the agreement came *after* the searing crisis in state–communal relations which—looked at objectively—might have been expected to wreck any chance of a political modus vivendi for good. The Adana massacres in April 1909 involved a major subaltern assault on Armenians, which, in the latter stages, also involved loyal Rumeliot troops who had been sent to the Cilician province by the CUP to put down the disturbances. The origins of the violence remain much disputed. Like many such events the massacres may have actually begun not as a premeditated act but as one or more local communal incidents or disputes, which quickly snowballed into something entirely more serious.[150] A more sociological analysis might also focus on Adana as a classic testing ground of modernity, where port facilities, or an emerging market-orientated agricultural sector in the surrounding countryside, were attracting a growing influx of often seasonal workers from different ethnic groups, including *muhajirun*.[151] Armenians who were already long established as part of the business community and as skilled artisans, plus a new stratum of modernizing farmers, may have been one obvious target for the outlet of animosity in what, for many incomers, was an alien, challenging, and certainly cut-throat competitive environment. From this perspective, too, one can make an obvious comparison with the violence between Azeris and Armenians which had swept Baku four years earlier.[152]

Equally significant, however, is the fact that in both these cases the killing took hold during a moment of hiatus in state power: the Baku massacres in the midst of the failed 1905 Russian Revolution; the Cilician Vespers, as it became known, in the period when the loose oppositionist coalition attempted to overturn the CUP 'revolution' of 1908. It was precisely in these conditions of acute political uncertainty that rumours rapidly spread that behind the Cilician massacres were conspiratorial forces. The British were certainly sufficiently alarmed for Grey to veto intervention on the grounds that Armenian protagonists had consciously provoked the violence to garner Great Power involvement.[153] Uncorroborated Western reports that there may have been local Armenian plotting towards somehow wresting from the political chaos an internationally backed Armenian Cilician statelet—à la Lebanon—contrast with post-event investigations, which suggest that the CUP's failure to act decisively to put down the disturbances was because it was party itself to their instigation.[154] What matters here is not the proof—one way or the other—as to who ultimately should shoulder the blame for up to 25,000 mostly Armenian deaths, plus the estimated 200 villages ravaged.[155] Especially so when it is also clearly evident that grass-roots anti-Armenian antipathies were quite sufficient in themselves to lead to unbridled atrocity in town and countryside alike. What would instead appear to have greater significance, in the face of this ominous turn of events, is that CUP and Dashnaks were still apparently able to pick up the pieces and cobble together a joint Turkish–Armenian way out of disaster.

Except that this did not materialize. The official Adana commission of enquiry exonerated the state, while, more importantly, according to the Dashnaks, the CUP began dragging its heels on the joint commission whose remit was to report on the social problems in the east. The 1909 agreement had also stipulated the creation of regional and district committees with membership from both groups working together for the constitution and against reactionary forces and anti-Armenian prejudice. These committees, too, failed to materialize. By 1912 one of the Dashnaks' leading supporters of the agreement was openly stating, in the party newspaper *Azatamart*, that while they had kept their side of their bargain, supporting the CUP without qualification, it had become more interested in cosying up to landowners, *mullah*s, and Kurdish chieftains, involving them in their clubs, and co-opting them as members of parliament.[156]

Warning signs that the CUP was not going to get to grips with fundamental structural problems on the plateau actually pre-dated the 1912 crisis surge. Part of that surge, however, involved a new bout of Kurdish rebellions, with the very real danger that secession on the plateau would come from this source, not from the Armenians. Behind the crescendo of insurrections, culminating in what appeared to be the most coordinated of them—in the Bitlis area in the spring of 1914—it was also evident that the Russians were heavily involved.[157] It was further evident that the Russian interest was purely Machiavellian; truculent Kurdish tribes were seen as malleable to bribery and incitement and then disposable when the Russians had no further use for them. Theirs was also a value which made them ostensibly less complicated than the Armenians, with their underlying claim to humanitarian justice. Turned on its head, and viewed from the CUP perspective, it was exactly this Kurdish fissile quality—combined with many Kurds' underlying antagonism to a regime seen as undercutting their power, undermining *sharia* law, not to mention appearing to be too much in love with equal rights for Christians—which made sense of why the CUP had looked to the Armenians as a possible regional counterweight in the first place. The problem was that the Armenians could only be cemented in their loyalty to the cause through the implementation of social reform and the backing of a liberal constitution, with its plural, federalist implications. And so, paradoxically, as soon as trouble reared its head in the form of Kurdish insurrection, the implicit triangular struggle on the plateau, at least in the short term, could *only* be resolved, for a regime whose bottom line was the preservation of state, by placating the Kurds. Which, increasingly, through financial subsidies and making some of them senators and deputies, the CUP very purposefully did.[158]

CUP abandonment of the Armenians was neither open nor total. Nor was there any formal repudiation on the other side. Indeed, as late as the Bitlis revolt, Dashnak cadres were both authorized by the CUP to arm themselves against Kurdish attack and, in notable instances, supported Ottoman regular troops in battles with the insurgents.[159] Yet, from an Armenian nationalist perspective, the lack of manoeuvre for their own position from *within* the Ottoman construct was becoming all too evident. Was it really possible under such circumstances to ignore the appeals made by the Catholicos in Etchmiadzin to Russia's Caucasus viceroy, Count Vorontsov-Dashkov, at the outset of the European conflict—anticipating that now would be the occasion for Russia to unite eastern and western Armenia as an autonomous single province? Or the message Vorontsov-Dashkov, three months later, would convey from the tsar informing Armenians of a 'brilliant future'?[160] Implicit in these announcements was the hardly veiled quid pro quo that Russia would expect unconditional Armenian support. But if that were not forthcoming how could Armenians—in the summer of 1914, at the very moment when the two European inspectors, from Norway and the Netherlands, were due to take up their posts to supervise the international Reform Plan—hope to achieve anything at all? The Dashnak cadres who gathered together in August at Erzurum for their annual Congress must have been painfully aware that this could well be one final opportunity to wrest clear advantage for a national entity.

Yet again, while there is evidence of quite heated debates at the Congress, there is none of any mass Dashnak acclamation for the Russians. Certainly, there were those who decided now *was* the moment. There were Armenians, too, in uniform in the Ottoman Third Army, who went with the flow and joined some of the veteran Dashnak guerrilla leaders who, grouping them together in scratch units, crossed to the Russian side. Estimates of Ottoman Armenian volunteers of this kind number between five and eight thousand. An Armenian National Bureau in Russian-controlled Tiflis also began busily recruiting from further afield. Yet while the haemorrhage is significant, it was only a fraction of the 200,000 Armenian men who remained in Ottoman uniform.[161] Indeed, what happened at this moment was entirely consistent with the picture across the rimlands, with small groups of ideologized men of military age seeing the war as a great opportunity for the making of the nation—Czech, Polish, Ukrainian, 'Yugoslav', or, for that matter, Arab or Jewish Zionist—and preparing to take enormous personal and collective risks in order to fight for it on the *other* side.[162] Yet the vast majority, for whatever reason, did not do this; they stayed put in the uniform of their given state, even where that meant fighting and dying *against* the national cause.

If, thus, in the summer of 1914 we can see a chasm opening up between 'Armenians' and 'Turks', and recognize that part and parcel of this emerging scenario was a betrayal by some of the former of Ottomania, it still does not in itself add up to the reason for a whole community to be earmarked for destruction. But then ascription of blanket guilt does not of itself require detailed corroboration, for those who are already convinced of its veracity. Another Oriental Christian community, after all, was already firmly in the sights of the CUP as supposedly proven kite runners of the Russian game: the Nestorians.

WAR AS CATALYST

We last came across Nestorians in more detail in *The Rise of the West*, not least when the run-in between their majority Hakkâri community and the Kurdish Emirate of Botan, in the 1840s, led to a great wave of anti-Nestorian killing. By that time that community was getting used to the ascription given them by British and American missionaries as latter-day 'Assyrians'.[163] The killings were the first critical warning sign in eastern Anatolia of the extreme violence to come. But they were also a symptom of a more general Ottoman destabilization as a consequence of foreign interference—of which the Assyrian attribution was one small if significant irritant symptom. Assessment of how much the Hakkâri community recovered from the

1840s catastrophe by the time of the Great War is outside the scope of this study. Russian estimates put the total number of Ottoman Nestorians in this period at 135,000, though Nestorians were actually only one of the several distinct communities of *Suryoyo*—Syriac-speaking Christians—straddling the Persian–Ottoman frontier belt and found in northern Mesopotamia.[164] If estimates of total numbers suggest a Syriac population in excess of 600,000, what made the possibly 75,000-strong Hakkâri element unique was its compact territorial, if tribally based, cohesion around Kohanes, the main seat of the Nestorians' religious leader, the Mar Shamun. In effect, XXI Benyamin, the reigning titular holder in 1914, was also head of a confederated tribal *ashiret*, a quasi-political configuration which, even putting aside other considerations, was a complete anomaly according to the CUP's modernizing and centralizing projections. What worked in the Hakkâri community's favour was its remarkable isolation and mountainous remoteness: a situation which, in less stressful times, might have enabled it to soldier on in obscurity in the middle of what amounted—by cosmopolitan standards—to nowhere.[165] The trouble, in 1914, was that that middle of nowhere also happened to be contiguous with the Ottoman–Persian border.

This frontier zone's heightened importance was a simple but brutal consequence of geopolitics. In 1907, after a century of facing each other off in Central Asia—the so-called 'Great Game'—Russia and Britain had come to an 'amicable' arrangement, the chief consequence of which was that Whitehall lined up behind the Winter Palace and the Quai d'Orsay against a Wilhelmstrasse-dominated Triple Alliance. A further consequence was that the supposedly independent, once great Persian Empire found itself, without so much as a by-your-leave, divided up into northern and southern—respectively Russian and British—spheres of influence. Not quite a 'scramble for Africa' scenario but a clear enough forewarning to the CUP—if one were needed—of Ottomania's likely fate, too, if its own international visage continued to broadcast weakness. More immediately, and concretely, what it also meant was that Russian frontage onto Ottoman eastern Anatolia was now extended several hundreds of kilometres south, albeit along a topographically challenging frontier. Russia, actually, at the outbreak of war, lacked either the intention or the capability to launch a major invasion here, as its forces were already heavily committed in the Carpathians and Baltic: hence the paradox that the Russian arming of Nestorian and other Christian communities on the Persian side of the border—in the Urmia region—was primarily in the expectation of *their* exposure to Ottoman attack. And with it came the double paradox that, in this poorly connected back-of-beyond region and in lieu of good intelligence, rampant rumour fed back to the CUP the story that it was not the Urmia Nestorians alone who were threatening *them* but their near cousins in Hakkâri.

That the Mar Shamun might be a willing stalking horse for a full-scale Russian invasion was founded on a recent history of well-received Russian overtures to Kochanes. In the nineteenth century it had been French Catholic, then Anglican or American evangelical blandishments to the Hakkâri community—offering material assistance in return for a nominal changing of its religious spots—which had helped fuel the neighbouring Kurdish explosion of violence against it. More contemporaneously, the special spiritual mission of the Russian Orthodox church in Urmia had raised the stakes even higher: the possibilities of religious protection clearly being penetrated by more overt political calculations.[166] In June 1914 an Ottoman Nestorian delegation covertly approached the Russian vice-consul in Urmia with an appeal for 35,000 rifles with 300 rounds apiece.[167] As leader of an armed proto-nation, XXI Benyamin was clearly playing according to the highest, not to say reckless, stakes. Perhaps inbuilt into his calculation was the recognition that a full-steam-ahead CUP-led Ottomania literally had no place for a religio-tribal presence such as that of Hakkâri. If, on the other hand, the empire was to fall apart it made sense to get firm Russian guarantees now.

Russian diplomats and generals in the summer of 1914 were certainly making their own robust assessments about how to line up Kurds, Armenians, and Syriacs in support of Petrograd action, that is, when it was ready to give the signal.[168] Not surprisingly, the CUP was weighing up just how exactly to get its retaliation in first. As far as the Mar Shamun was concerned this seems to have involved an initial attempt to cajole or simply order him back into line, then to apprehend him. But by October this had given way to an order from Talât, now firmly ensconced as head of the Interior Ministry, to deport the *entire* Hakkâri community westwards, on the grounds that it represented a clear and present security risk. Insofar as it envisaged the community broken up into minute elements and thereby submerged within the wider, more Turkic-Muslim population of central Anatolia,[169] Talât's decision could be equally read as a first tangible attempt to implement the Nâzim scheme or, in more Lemkinian terms, as a case of genocide signed, sealed, and delivered. What these efforts *actually* precipitated, long before the Mar Shamun's open declaration of the fact in May 1915, was a war between state and community—a classic War Type Three—which equally rapidly degenerated into one of annihilation. Of the Nestorians, that is. As they retaliated against the opening efforts to terrorize them as the prequel to full-scale ethnic cleansing of Kohanes and its hinterland, it became open season for surrounding Kurdish tribes to attack and kill at will. Distinctions of age and gender proved no hindrance. Only in June 1915, however, did this war take on its final coherent form, as three Ottoman army groups invaded Hakkâri from different directions.[170] Like the Hereros on the Waterberg, eleven years earlier, survival could now only be secured by running the gauntlet of these armies: from the ancestral home, and in search of an escape route to territory beyond the enemy's control.

Estimates of those, the Mar Shamun among them, who made it across to the Russian lines on the Persian side of the border range from 25,000 to 50,000, suggesting at least a third of the community perished either in the effort, or within Hakkâri itself.[171] Russian-occupied Persia hardly constituted a place of greater safety, however. Ottoman forces had been advancing and retreating across this border since before the New Year, massacring Christians into the bargain on either side of it. These developments were not simply some unfortunate slippage of the conflict onto ostensibly neutral territory. The CUP leadership was quite deliberately intent on its own war of conquest in the east.

*

Going to war in 1914 at all, let alone imagining advance not just into the Caucasus but towards central Asia, in hindsight appears far-fetched, especially when set against the recent battering and humiliation the regime's armies had suffered in the Balkans. Looked at from a more contemporary perspective the most logical and sensible CUP course of action would have been to sit the war out, avoiding involvement at all costs. But how plausible was this really? The hegemonic world order of 1914 was predicated on Great Power threats of violence or their realization—deliverable, to greater or lesser extents, across the globe. Now these self-same Powers were engulfed in their own potentially lethal conflict but, at its end, the victors, whoever they were, were likely to be even more demanding and ruthless towards passive third parties than ever. To sit tight in these circumstances was to invite an even more abject neocolonial servitude for Ottomania. Or even outright liquidation; and this time without any possible room for manoeuvre, which had been the paradoxical benefit to the Porte of the fin-de-siècle power balance provided by the European bloc system.

The long-term goals of the CUP demanded something entirely other: a Turkey which was acknowledged as a partner, albeit a junior one, in the Western-dominated world order. There was only one non-Western country to date which had achieved that: Japan, and it had done so—in the process halting what appeared like an inevitable slide towards its own neocolonial thraldom—by giving one of the Great Powers a truly bloody nose. That the recipient in the war of 1904–5 had been Russia would have made Ittihadists even more fervent in their desire for Turkey to be the Japan of the Near East.[172]

This, perhaps, was the ultimate CUP martial fantasy. But we should be wary of reading into it the August 1914 secret alliance with the Kaiser as some foregone conclusion, or, by extension, some elective affinity—political, cultural, or whatever—with an authoritarian Germany, which might in turn explain the propensity of both countries to commit genocide. True, by going for the German option, the triumvirate did not simply burn their bridges to the West, or more exactly, to the British and French, who had been the Great Powers most consistent in shoring up and supporting a failing Ottoman edifice for the best part of a century. With them as enemies, in a critical sense all bets were off and anything now possible. But one has to equally wonder—from the degree of often racialized anti-Turkish invective which the Porte's decision for war now unleashed from Entente leaders—whether such statements actually acted as a goad for the CUP to do its worst.

British prime minister Asquith, a few days after the opening of overt hostilities in early November 1914, proclaimed that the Ottoman Empire had rung its own 'death knell'—not just in Europe but Asia; his then chancellor of the exchequer Lloyd George weighing in, days later, with the promise that the Turks had brought on themselves a 'final reckoning'.[173] But these ominous warnings also carried with them implicit—and in latter Allied statements quite explicit—subtexts. The empire had to go because it was barbaric: an entity, as one French official statement put it in early 1917, 'radically alien to Western civilisation, out of Europe'.[174] On 24 May 1915 the three Entente powers, with, by then, news of *Armenian* massacres increasing by the day, issued a declaration promising to hold Ottoman leaders and officials responsible for the atrocities to account. In its original Russian-inspired text, 'crimes committed by Turkey against Christianity and civilisation' were specifically cited. It was Anglo-French anxieties about the use of the word 'Christianity' potentially inflaming their own very substantial imperial Muslim populations which led to a word substitution—the final text referring to 'humanity and civilisation'.[175]

In terms of international law, the declaration is seminal: the first enunciation of its kind of the notion of 'crimes against humanity'. In its own more immediate context, however, Bloxham has pondered whether 'the Allied threat was responsible for precipitating the general deportation decision', which, at that moment, had yet to be made.[176] The notion that a megaphone war, alongside that of an actual military one, was part of the dynamic out of which Armenian catastrophe evolved, is necessarily disturbing. But it may also throw valuable light on the linkage between the CUP's motivation for war and the consequences for both Armenians and other Christians in the east.

The CUP went to war to free the country from *all* foreign political and economic controls, and in order to reassert Ottomania's sovereignty and independence of action. General war was taken to be the opportunity by seizing which these aspirations might plausibly be realized. This did not of itself make the war popular. Enver, as chief protagonist, faced quite vociferous opposition even from within the ranks of the Porte, including from within the inner circles of the CUP. Indeed, he had to organize what amounted to a German-backed subterfuge to get the Entente to declare war on Turkey rather than vice versa.[177]

Yet when, two months earlier, the Porte had announced that the Capitulatory system—in effect, the Great Powers' collective method for manipulating Ottoman tariffs to their own advantage—was revoked, along with the Ottoman public debt (all 2.4 billion francs of it), it was greeted with huge, largely spontaneous demonstrations of festive acclamation.[178] This is hardly surprising. The regime had dared to cock a snook at the whole edifice of international extra-sovereign controls on Ottoman independence, controls which were commonly perceived to include interference in the internal system by which the state-cum-caliphate self-regulated its relationship with its non-Muslim *millet*s. The implication was obvious—all these outside constraints were now null and void, just as those who acted as agents for them within the Ottoman polity were effectively also now outside of it.

On one level, this was also, for the Germans, a pointed reminder that Turkey was not about to become the Kaiser's Egypt. German acquiescence in the declarations and the subsequent hike in customs duties—as, later, in the actions the CUP were to take unilaterally against its Armenians—was the price the leader of the Central Powers was prepared to pay for having Ottomania as a member. There was a certain irony in this. From the beginning of 1914 the CUP, recognizing that it could not attain its objectives without at least one Great Power ally to assist it, had put out feelers to the Russians and French as well as the Germans, with the view to concluding a military pact. And the latter had initially (as had the others) turned Turkey down. A change of German heart began to be evident only when it was apparent that Britain was going to come into the war on the Entente side. And, as the military situation of late summer 1914 hardened, so the German High Command interest in a more extra-European prosecution of the war—striking at Britain and Russia within their imperial domains—equally began to take off as a serious facet of its strategy.[179]

The consequence was not simply that Germany was prepared to bail Turkey out of the reality of its immediate economic crisis as its markets and international credit collapsed—not to mention as the British naval blockade kicked in—subsequent to all those brave declarations of intent. A bankrupt Ottoman treasury was henceforth literally in hock to German financiers. Now more than ever it was dependent on the German military mission under Liman von Sanders, which it had appointed in 1913 to assist its military restructuring in the aftermath of the Balkan Wars, albeit to much international *scandale*.[180] One consequence was that German officers wearing Turkish uniform now became central to the defence of key weak points, not least at the Dardanelles,[181] and of the yet very incomplete Berlin–Baghdad railway—the great arterial route across the central-southern Anatolia—the tender for which the Deutsche Bank had won against intense, primarily British, competition back in 1903.[182]

The German alliance thus helped reposition Turkish political and military thinking. If, as the Germans were proposing, the Caucasus and beyond might offer fruitful terrain for covert military operations designed to disrupt Russian operations in their rear, this certainly also dovetailed with that strain of near-fantasy thinking which Enver and others had absorbed from the pan-Turkic idealists. But this was all highly contingent on the war itself. As we have already seen, CUP passions were particularly focused in 1914 on the possibility of recovering territory in the Balkans. There was no pre-war blueprint for some grand sweep to the east. When the War Ministry began planning in earnest, in the autumn, for a major Caucasus offensive, it was on an ad hoc basis and extremely improvised.

What gave all this additional emotional charge, however, was the November declaration of *jihad*. Again, the Kaiser's encouragement for the declaration was a key contributory factor. From the time of his trip to Jerusalem and Damascus in 1898, when he had ostentatiously offered himself as 'protector' of the world's Muslims, *some* German Orientalists had been running ahead of themselves with notions that Islam might be the key to mobilizing popular support against *Germany's* enemies.[183] Underlying the contention was a wider Western assumption that fundamentalist Islam was also inherently fanatical; and that, once suitably primed, 'Mohammedans' (*sic*) would start running amok.[184] As they presumably would do so against non-Muslims, and more specifically Christians, the proposition was inherently fissile—indeed, a serious case of playing with fire. As we have already seen, while the declaration itself served to frighten Entente colonial officials and intensify their paranoia, it generally failed to elicit its intended results, especially where it mattered most—in British India and the vast central belt of the Russian Empire where Muslims predominated.

Closer to home, however, the impact is less easy to assess. The very fact that the call to holy war came from a Caliphate operating under the auspices of a CUP government rather confirms not simply the latter's pragmatism but the degree to which—for all the modernizing aspirations of its leaders—they were still bound to the sinews of a traditional Islamic society. Enver and other officers who had fought in the Libyan campaign were perfectly aware, too, that serious resistance to Italian invasion had only come from the militantly devout Sanusi.[185] If the green banner of the Prophet was the emblem which could galvanize the Muslim tribes, peasants, and workers on both sides of the Ottoman eastern frontier into action against the Russians, this was surely to be encouraged, not restrained.

The problem was that the whole eastern border zone, even before the official declaration either of conventional war or *jihad*, was already wild with rumour— not to say rapidly degenerating into violence. There is evidence that tribal irregulars, organized by Cevdet Bey, the *vali* of Van, as an element of his scratch army, may have been fired up by what amounted to a sanction to slaughter, plunder, and—in their minds—take revenge on unbelievers. These participants seem to have been particularly responsible for a whole spate of atrocities, as Cevdet made an initial late-1914 lunge towards Tabriz by way of Urmia, where his troops were confronted by the Russian-armed self-defence militias, representing the 40 per cent of the local population who were Christian, and, predominantly, Nestorian. The worst of these massacres—in the Salmas plain—came in March 1915 as Cevdet's forces ran out of steam, were stymied in their advance by militia action in front of Tabriz, and then forced to retreat back across the border, precipitating a further series of indiscriminate attacks on Hakkâri villages or any Christians to hand, including Armenians, en route to Van.[186]

If due punishment for alleged traitors became the flimsy excuse for what was, in fact, their own signal military failure, the onslaught against communal targets, in autumn 1914 and through to spring 1915, was not isolated to Cevdet's ragtag forces. Nestorian Jilu tribesmen from Hakkâri took revenge for their own murdered kinsfolk by massacring Kurdish villagers. Nestorians and Armenian volunteer units also appear to have perpetrated massacres as they accompanied initial Russian probes around Bayazid, again from before the official opening of war— just as, on the Russian side of the border around Kars and Ardahan, *druzhiny* also carried out massacres against Muslims. But then so—against Armenians and others in the same arena—did Adzhar irregulars acting under Special Organization auspices.[187] We might interpret these events as evidence of a 'clash of civilizations', or even, following the Samuel Huntington line more closely, of Islam's 'bloody borders'.[188] More prosaically, however, we might read this epidemic of butchery— committed by those in or out of uniform—as the inevitable consequence of an already vastly destabilized border region ravaged by decades of worsening intercommunal conflict. By 1914, it was, as David Gaunt has aptly described it, 'loaded like an explosive device'.[189] That a Balkan Wars-style scenario of tit-for-tat atrocity might rapidly develop—with no mercy given or expected on either side—should not surprise, nor that the number of victims might run into tens of thousands.

Perhaps, however, to consider how the contingent nature of this crisis veered towards a wholly more systematic onslaught on the Armenians of the region, we need to consider some of the key political drivers and their objectives. One of these, undoubtedly, was Cevdet himself. The governor might be considered a critical provincial protagonist—in part working to his own assessment of the situation—or, if we wanted to put it in the terms of recent structuralist historians of the Holocaust, a mid-level 'man-on-the-spot' bureaucrat, whose actions, from his quasi-colonial 'periphery', helped, long with Special Organization operatives such as Ömer Naci Bey, to prepare the ground for and accelerate exterminatory decisions taken by the metropolitan 'centre'.[190] Alternatively, we might see him as a loyal outrunner for his brother-in-law Enver, a reminder in itself of the quite tight-knit, often family-connected nature of the core CUP inner circle of *génocidaires*—and of their political outlook.

Another critical player in the border war was Enver's uncle, Halil 'Kut'.[191] A high-ranking military officer and veteran Ittihadist, he had been one of the co-movers in Cevdet's mini-invasion of Persia, but in spring 1915 was under orders from Enver to strike further north into the Caucasus via 'Turkic' Azerbaijan. This in itself would identify Halil's own pan-Turkic proclivities. Like Cevdet, however, his expeditionary force—in this instance entirely composed of regular troops—was, in early May, seriously mauled in a series of bloody encounters around Dilman, to the north of Urmia. *Druzhiny* under the command of Andranik, a near-legendary Armenian revolutionary, certainly played a critical role in these encounters. Halil responded by liquidating up to a thousand unarmed Armenian and Syriac solders in his accompanying labour squad train, and, thereafter, in his retreat towards Van took retribution on non-combatant Christians at every opportunity.[192] Both he and Cevdet were to go on to play singularly grotesque roles in the extermination of both Armenians and Syriacs, the latter as instigator and director of what were aptly called *kesab taburi*, the butcher battalions.

At what point exactly Cevdet had made his mind up that Armenians in and around Van were *the* internal enemy is more difficult to ascertain. Cevdet had replaced another *vali* who ostensibly had been too Armenophile. So one interpretation might be that his wartime appointment could be seen as evidence of a hardening of the CUP policy in the Armenian provinces, just as, in a similar way, Halil's December 1914 transfer from military governorship of Istanbul to command of the 5th Expeditionary Force might also be taken as evidence of a murderous intent beyond Ottoman borders.[193] Cevdet's communication to Talât at the beginning of that month, in which he asserted 'I believe that the Armenians will be a problem',[194] is too ambiguous in itself to prove the case. But the manner in which he initiated and then directed brutal weapons searches in Armenian villages around Van from mid-April onwards leaves no doubt of his standpoint by then.[195] Indeed, by that juncture, the Ottoman state and society version of spy fever had crystallized into its own extended and utterly monstrous incubus: the threat of imminent, mass Armenian insurrection in the east.

Put that alongside what happened at the Dashnak Erzurum Congress the previous summer, however, and we are faced with an all the more frighteningly rapid and perplexing trajectory towards catastrophe. At the Congress Dashnak leaders had been approached by two key emissaries from the governing inner CUP circle, Ömer Naci Bey and Dr Behaeddin Shakir. They had come with a proposal: the creation of an autonomous Armenian statelet under Ottoman protection, primarily carved out of Armenian-populated lands on the Russian side of the border but also to include a slice of Erzurum, Van, and Bitlis, on the Ottoman side. The quid pro quo would be a Dashnak uprising behind Russian lines, coordinated by the Ottoman Special Organization. The proposal was turned down by Dashnak leaders, with the counter-proposal that it would be better not to go to war at all.[196] That said, those present also promised their loyalty in the event of war, as the Armenian Patriarchate in Constantinople, more publicly and enthusiastically, was to proclaim soon after, in its own Ottoman version of *union sacrée*.[197]

Whether the emissaries believed any of what they had been told by the Erzurum Assembly is another matter. American ambassador Henry Morgenthau, for one, thought that pro-Entente sympathies among Armenians at large were 'no secret'.[198] In a further closed Dashnak conclave in Erzurum, a few weeks after the Shakir confrontation, some participants argued for an open backing for the pro-Entente volunteer movement, even 'contrary to the decision and the will of the general meeting of the party'.[199] Enver, soon after, was receiving his own first intelligence reports of both Dashnaks and Hnchaks preparing with the Russians for insurrection.[200]

This, doubly, would seem to give the CUP proposal an implausible ring. It would also seem to go against the grain of Shakir's primary mission in eastern Anatolia in the high summer of 1914, which was to carry out reconnaissance work associated with the reorganization of the *Teşkilat-ı Mahsusa*; in other words, in preparation for covert operations directly accountable to the CUP—rather than the Porte per se. This necessarily makes the Special Organization of particular interest vis-à-vis its role in the Armenian genocide, even if, in August 1914, its exact objectives and lines of command had yet to be fully clarified.[201] What is equally relevant, however, about Shakir's mission is its longer-term implications. Whatever the Special Organization was required to do in the immediate term, underlying its purpose was the programme of Turkification which the CUP had been discussing in earnest at its own pre-war congresses, and now, under cover of war, was seeking tangibly to implement. This was not, then, specifically about Armenians per se, or at least not in isolation.

In 1916 and 1917 in particular, great waves of clearances, enacted through the most brutal terror and coercion, and with consequent mass fatalities, saw not only up to as many as a million Greeks from the Aegean littoral and Pontic region forced from hearth and home, but a whole range of other communal groups too. To be sure, most of the estimated 700,000 Kurds from eastern Anatolia who had, earlier in the war, been 'relocated', were initially refugees fleeing the Russians.[202] But that prised open opportunities for whole districts to be toponymically redefined, cleansed of their historically unreliable character, and with the entire exercise geared towards the elimination of heterogeneity, or—if one wishes to make a comparison—towards the equivalent of Nazi Reich-strengthening, Turkish style. While in the first instance it was communal groups, clans, and tribes considered particularly suspect or unreliable who suffered the full, sometimes lethal, brunt of this procedure, the underlying principle was that no group, *muhajir* or *indigène*, was automatically exempt. Indeed, under the auspices of the IAMM, any community was liable to be moved, split up, or thrown together with or next to some entirely alien people, and thereby—by order of the state—remade into worthy Turks. No wonder the CUP needed the Special Organization to smash internal opposition: alongside Shakir, the key person we associate with the *Teşkilat-ı Mahsusa*'s organizational direction was Nâzim, the key advocate of CUP demographic politics.

But if in this social engineering agenda we can read the authentic *intentionality* of the CUP ruling group it can only serve to make the Erzurum offer to Dashnak-sutiun all the more bizarre. Was this just a feint, a false offer, to see how the Armenians would react, and thereby confirm their contumacy? Or was this actually one last throw of the dice, one final attempt to resurrect the tacit understanding, tantamount to an alliance, the two parties had begun to forge in 1908? The evidence for and against is contradictory. On the one hand, there seem to have been further attempts after Erzurum—not least through Tahsin Bey, Cevdet's more tolerant predecessor—to win the Dashnaks to some sort of deal, just as there may well have been some similar effort made towards the Mar Shamun.[203] On the other hand, whether as a result of the initial rebuff or not, Shakir's response was to order the assassination of key Dashnak delegates at the Congress whom he suspected of betrayal.[204]

Whatever the truth, by winter too much water had passed under the bridge, and too much blood with it, for any further speculation on the actual state of the political breach to matter. But there were yet to be two more military explosions before genocide was fully enacted.

A DECISION FOR GENOCIDE?

In December, a full-scale Ottoman military operation was launched to prise open the Caucasus. It involved a complete army—the Third—and was led by Enver himself. He imagined the campaign as leading to a Turkish Tannenberg. What actually resulted was a military catastrophe. The 90,000-strong force was not simply defeated by the Russians, but little short of annihilated. To a considerable degree, however, the disaster was self-inflicted: Enver's campaign being hastily operationalized in the dead of winter and in the most extreme and hazardous of mountain terrain. Of a minimum of 75,000 Ottoman fatalities, not less than 30,000 of them—and possibly many thousands more—simply froze to death.[205] However, at a critical point in the actual battle around Sarikamish in the last days of 1914, rumour had it that Armenian *druzhiny*, on this occasion led by 'Garo' Pasdermadjian—the until recently Erzurum parliamentary deputy, though chiefly known to Turkish nationalists as an infamous 'terrorist'—played some considerable role in halting Enver's advance.[206]

Sarikamish was a critical watershed, in the sense that it blocked off—at least until the very end of the war—the pan-Turkic dream of the great military advance to the east. But for Enver—who survived the defeat—and other advocates of that forward policy, its denial was now increasingly linked to a proven Armenian culpability. Even before Sarikamish anxieties among some army commanders, citing the predictable justification of military security, had led to the disarming of their Armenian soldiers and their demotion into forced and extremely vulnerable labour squads. Similar anxieties on the civil side were reflected in the Interior Ministry's order removing all Armenian police officers and government employees from the three front-line 'Armenian' vilayets.[207] From early 1915, however, these localized 'precautionary measures' started to become more general. Towards the end of February, for instance, the Ottoman General Staff sent a directive to its various field commanders, removing Armenian officers and soldiers from all headquarter staffs and senior positions of command. Armenian treason and/or support of the Russians or French was specifically cited as grounds for this directive. It was rapidly followed by a general disarmament order from Enver, with regard to all Armenian draftees.[208] In a sense this decision from the centre was a simple relaying back to army commanders of their own heightened sensitivities. Nor were their concerns necessarily limited to Armenians. Large numbers of Greek soldiers were also disarmed and converted into labour battalions during 1915, as were—on a more patchy basis—Kurds and Arabs.[209] The notion of some sort of Armenian insurrectionary plot, however, was beginning to take on a particular and projectively potent hold, especially among Third Army officers in the eastern war zone, who were convinced of imminent attacks on rear depots and railheads—thereby cutting them off from distant and tenuous supplies of food, medicine, and armaments. The way German self-suggestion at the outset of hostilities in Belgium became prevalent and took on feverish dimensions comes to mind here by way of comparison. This may also explain, in turn, why some army commanders, as we have already seen in the case of Halil some months later, did not prevaricate about further orders but at particular crisis moments summarily shot or put to the sword their former Armenian comrades-in-arms.[210]

Can we ascertain that it was in these early winter months of 1915 that parallel decisions were being taken at the highest level for some comprehensive resolution of the Armenian question? Much attention has inevitably focused on CUP inner-circle discussions at this time as to the role of the Special Organization. There had already been moves towards its reformation and expansion for war-related activities in August 1914. Technically, this was under the auspices of the War Ministry. But an attempt at joined-up if covert coordination, especially involving the Ministry of Interior, also, critically, empowered Special Organization operatives to use the latter's ciphers. This in effect meant that an organization without accountability to any precise government agency, yet increasingly composed of thugs, criminals, and jihadists, was enabled to prosecute 'dirty' war not only with the resources of state—the telegraphic system included—but as if it were, somehow, acting in lieu of that state. For this, an already specially disbursed War Ministry budget had enabled the Special Organization to grow from a core of 700 Harbiye-led, 'professional' operatives to over 30,000 personnel. They came from all manner of social and ethnic backgrounds, many of them *muhajirun*, though, arguably, they did all have one thing in common: a seething sense of grievance. It is perhaps not altogether surprising, then, that the unilateral actions of many of these *çetes* excited friction with and the censure of some regular officers, including the one known

German officer, Lt-Colonel Stange, assigned to these units, at a time when the Special Organization was still operating under War Ministry licence.[211]

Sometime in late February or March, Shakir returned from his Erzurum operational base to Constantinople for a series of high-level but entirely behind-closed-doors CUP meetings to hammer out these problem areas. Something else was also fundamentally at stake. Should Special Organization energies continue to be directed towards operations against enemies beyond the border of the state? Or was the most pressing issue, at this moment of extreme crisis, rather the enemy within? If so, was now the time for the Special Organization—or at least a particular wing of it—to remove itself from War Ministry oversight and take on an essentially autonomous role? Martial law had already provided the key movers behind the Special Organization programme with a paradoxical freedom of action which, in normal times, might have been stymied by procedural blocking from other governmental ministers or parliamentary deputies. The only rubber-stamping needed now was determined by the inner-circle protagonists at these discussions. Crucially, Shakir's arguments both for an explicit reorientation of the Special Organization units under his control and for their structural autonomy prevailed. More crucially still, he seems to have convinced his colleagues, if convincing they needed, that the Armenians were the clear and present danger to both state and regime and, as such, had to be dealt with.[212]

Dadrian has taken these discussions as further proof positive that preparations began—or, indeed, had already begun in earnest—for the premeditated extermination of the Ottoman Armenian *millet* from around this time, and with the priming of the Special Organization as the main instrument for this purpose. He has, moreover, pointed to the existence of documents, most particularly an item known as 'The Ten Commandments'—which fell into British hands at the end of the war—as evidence of a clear, albeit draft, blueprint for destruction.[213] If authentic, this would leave no doubt that the CUP central committee meetings in late winter were indeed bent on genocide. The key problem is that the provenance, and hence reliability, of this and other such documents is questionable.[214]

This does not necessarily mean that Dadrian's case for a blueprint is wrong. Other evidence—some of which circulated at the time of the post-war Ottoman military trials of leading Ittihadists in 1919—include personal letters from Shakir in February and March 1915, which suggest not only that he was personally seeking a radical eliminationist solution to the Armenian Question but that he believed that the regime had the authority, command structure, resources, and, above all, the will to implement it.[215] A variety of other sources also point to something afoot. American missionaries in Sivas province later testified that they were told by a German officer, on oath, as early as September 1914, of some dreadful fate awaiting the Armenians. Stange also later wrote to his superiors in the German military mission claiming that a plan of 'thorough reduction, if not extermination of the Armenian population' had long been in preparation.[216] Morgenthau, too, recounts personal conversations with both Enver and Talât, later in 1915, in which both insisted that the actions that had been taken against the Armenians were the carefully considered result of prolonged deliberations by the inner committee. Enver, for one—offered the let-out by Morgenthau that the resulting violence must have been caused by too zealous subordinates—vociferously repudiated the inference and confirmed that responsibility was his and that of the Cabinet.[217]

None of this evidence, however, nails the case for a premeditated campaign of destruction of the *entire* Armenian community—and certainly not in February or March 1915. What it instead suggests is a deliberate set of actions being considered against the Armenians as a political entity. This, without doubt, was to involve mass violence—and, most likely, the deliberate beheading of the male leaders of the community, as well as the degrading of Armenian army units into labour battalions, pending possible liquidation; and, as a further corollary, the deportation of surviving Armenian communities from particular strategically sensitive areas within the six vilayets and Cilicia. In other words, the committee—having failed to win Dashnaks or broader Armenian political support for the war effort, and believing it had uncovered sufficient proof of their active and dangerous malevolence—had opted instead for an alternative plan: that of a targeted but nevertheless large-scale politicide.[218] The fact that CUP inner-circle discussions revolved around the role of the Special Organization would further emphasize this as the underlying goal, not least as its métier was that of political assassination.

Where Dadrian's meticulous research would tend to assist this line of enquiry—and is compelling—is in his identification of key political, military, and administrative actors who were both party to this policy shift and ready—as well as sufficiently empowered—to implement it. Two of these we have already noted as triumvirate members: Enver at the War Ministry, Talât at the Interior. Despite their well-known personal rivalry, the coordination of elements of their respective ministries for different aspects of the task was clearly crucial to its success. Yet the radical separation of the Ittihadist plan from regular administrative practice and policy, not to mention government administration at large, also presupposed that the support team had to be trusted to carry out the relevant directives in the utmost secrecy. As in all such cases, this rather narrowed down the possibilities for delegation to the more overtly political and politicized agencies of state, adept, in turn, at disinformation and misinformation. In Ismail Canbolat, head of the Directorate for Public Security within the Interior Ministry, on the one hand, and Colonel Seyfi, in charge of the Ottoman General Staff's Intelligence—Dept. II—as well as of its political section, on the other, the inner-circle protagonists were provided with the first tier of their support system. Seyfi, in particular, was responsible for the logistics, financing, and deployment of Special Organization units in the east. In this sense, too, he was also the centre's link with Shakir who, acting primarily from Erzurum, was effective director of operations at the periphery.[219] Nâzim was certainly also a key decision-making player, Dadrian going so far—perhaps rather unhelpfully—as to describe him as its 'elusive and invisible mastermind'.[220]

There were clearly others involved as part of this core CUP grouping. What is of most relevance here is not simply their cultural and political outlook, but their close social interaction and sometimes familial relationships. Seyfi, for instance, was a confidante of Enver. Another was General Mahmud Kâmil. The February appointment of this stridently Ittihadist officer as commander of an effectively replacement Third Army actually seems to have come about, however, through the energetic intervention of Sakir and Nâzim—against Enver's original nominee for the job. His subsequent appointment of Kâmil almost certainly sealed the fate of the Armenians in Third Army labour battalions. Later on, the general played an extremely proactive role in the extermination of Armenians in the area under his command.[221] In other words, having put resources and personnel in place for a particular emergency operation—the goal of which was extreme violence—the possibilities for a further ratcheting up of that violence to embrace all Armenians, or, more exactly, all Armenians in the rimland zone, was quite plausible. What is more difficult to demonstrate is that this followed as a *direct* consequence of the decisions taken in late winter 1914–15. Equally problematic is the assumption that the central committee behaved in a monolithic manner to this end, not least because we know that among its number was the third member of the triumvirate, Cemal. He was better known for his extremely draconian measures against Arab nationalists in Syria; but in this Armenian matter was apparently less than enthusiastic about, or even opposed to, the direction of flow. With regard to another other seminal figure—that of Gökalp—the jury also remains out.[222]

Undoubtedly, if we were seeking a moment when, with hindsight, we might expect a radicalization of the CUP's Armenian policy, it would be mid-March. The Anglo-French naval assault on the Dardanelles was in full swing and plans for the government evacuation of Istanbul for inland Eskishehir were in motion just as the fleet's action was fatally aborted on 18 March. Morgenthau reckoned that the whole Ottoman state was 'on the brink of dissolution' at this point, while there was further hysterical talk of using Entente residents of the metropolis as 'human shields' to deter any new bombardments.[223]

In all this we can discern something of an Armenian subtext. *Azadamart*, the leading Armenian paper in the city, had its presses confiscated on order of Talât.[224] Moreover, though no other Christian deportations—predominantly of Greeks—from the threatened sea of Marmara zone occurred until early April, further afield, in Cilicia, *local* Armenian deportations were ordered from late February.[225] Here, in the wake of Sarikamish and the escalating turmoil in the east, widespread draft-dodging had escalated into a more rebellious mood among some Armenian would-be enlistees. The evidence actually suggests that in Marash and, more particularly, Zeitun, where the young men's arguments for insurrection became most pronounced, this was opposed by most of the Armenian citizenry, who feared inevitable government reprisals. But, while some may have supported the rebels' behaviour as defensive, the regional officials were quick to read into it something more entirely offensive—perhaps not altogether surprisingly as Zeitun especially was a historic centre of Armenian resistance to Ottoman authority.[226]

Ironically, too, such rumours of revolt may have fed into post-18 March British military planning, which was now gearing itself up for a full-scale landing at Gallipoli, and, with this, warming to the idea of a secondary feint along the Cilician coast using partisans and raiding parties. In the overwrought atmosphere of spring 1915, it was thus not just Turks who were imagining armies of irregular Armenians striking at the Ottoman heartland. Armenian diaspora groups in Egypt and elsewhere were clamouring for the British and French to use volunteers they had at their disposal, or who they claimed would rise up in Cilicia when given the signal. In this way an irregular force of 15,000 Zeitunlis, pinning the Turks down in their rear, was confabulated into existence. Soon thereafter, thousands of Otto-man Greek insurgents, or an even larger number of turncoat Arabs, were equally plucked out of thin air to serve further fantasy British and French war plans (aided and abetted by the respective anti-Ottoman bidders for their attention) as their more conventional strategies failed to materialize, were aborted, or, for that matter, received bloody noses from the Turks.[227]

Yet what is equally notable is that orders for putting down the actually no more than semi-localized disturbances in Cilicia came not from Istanbul but from Cemal, from his regional military power base in Syria. Under his aegis all reputed malefactors were hunted down and publicly executed. This draconian trajectory took on sharper contours when all Armenian able-bodied men from the area were forcibly moved south to the desert district of Der Zor. Simultaneously the remain-ing men, women, and children were deported elsewhere, primarily to the Konya region in central Anatolia. This was an extreme and vicious case of collective pun-ishment. However, in terms of the contours of the genocide which were soon to become evident, Cemal's Cicilian directives are rather distinct. The main body of these deportations, which continued into April, was relatively orderly and did not involve direct violence. Moreover their (initial) Konya direction was *westwards*. This contrasts with the later, genocidal, deportations, which were largely by death march southwards towards Der Zor and Mosul. Similarly, while most Armenian army labour battalions would later be killed, under Cemal's Fourth Army aegis they would mainly survive.[228]

With hindsight, these discrepancies throw light on Cemal's ongoing variance from the thrust of CUP Ottoman intentions at the centre. The paradox lies in the fact that the deportations he ordered in spring 1915 were taken by observers soon after, and indeed historians later, as evidence of the first stages in a general pro-gramme of systematic extermination. Moreover, given all we know about Talât's—not Cemal's—obsessive micro-management of matters of the highest state sensitivity (insofar as they were within the Interior Ministry remit), it would be quite logical to assume that his desire for absolute control would militate against anything as serious as a deportation being determined by a governor at the periphery—even one as powerful as Cemal—acting on his own volition. Because Cemal was doing exactly that (albeit cooperating closely with Talât over the procedures and details) it has confused our awareness of the bigger picture. The fact is that after Cemal's localized deportations in April there were no further *mass* deportations, until late May and June, this time most definitively of a very different kind.[229]

Of course, if we were to revert to the standard intentionalist narrative in which linear development of the killing project is the key, the matter of some weeks between the Cicilian deportations and the wider programme may not sound *that* significant. Indeed, one might further argue that as genocide as a programme of state action would seem to require some considerable planning and organizational effort, not to mention allocation of resources and personnel for the task, one might expect there to be a specific time lag between decision and implementation. In these terms one could treat the Cilician effort as a sort of dry run. The problem with this interpretation lies in the fact that when mass deportation/genocide actually did take place there remained something extraordinarily improvizational and ill-resourced about it. Getting to the heart of the decision at the CUP centre to go down this route is all the more complex, moreover, when one remembers that the second military explosion arrived not in late May but a whole month earlier. On 25 April 1915, a full-scale British landing took place at Gallipoli. It marked not simply the second crisis in this immediate sequence of events but what, at that moment, appeared to be the very nadir of Ottoman fortunes—the point beyond which appeared to be the empire's extinction.

By the time of this second crisis, however, there was no doubt that the Armenians—and their alleged perfidy—were to the absolute fore in the regime's mind. Just five days earlier, the Armenians in Van had declared the formation of a 'provisional government' there, and—with the Russians advancing towards it—forced Cevdet to relinquish control of the city. Whether or not Van, geographically speaking, was particularly important strategically as a potential launching pad for the Ottoman advance into Persia or, vice versa, a critical first toehold for a Russian advance into Anatolia, the point is that at this juncture the CUP leadership chose to treat it as such. The uprising was thus taken as evidence that the Armenians were now actively and massively working to support a Russian invasion, the notion suitably embellished with rumours of 30,000 phantom Armenian insurgents massing to attack the rear of the Third Army.[230] Anxieties such as these were further heightened by fears that the Armenians in the capital were about to play a critical role in support of the British forces now near at hand. Recalling to Morgenthau, later in 1915, how only 200 CUP men had overthrown the Sultan, Enver said to him that if they could make a revolution why could 'a few hundred bright, educated Armenians' not do the same?[231] Talât's memoirs contain similar dark broodings.[232]

No wonder then that as panic swept the capital, the CUP—from the 24 to 26 April—arrested a swathe of Armenian leaders in the metropolis and other major centres.[233] The taking of 250 politicians and intellectuals in Constantinople on 24 April is now commemorated by Armenians as the beginning of the genocide. Yet what happened thereafter does not entirely support this assumption. The arrested were deported into the interior, but not immediately killed. And there undoubtedly was CUP outrage at events in Van. The likelihood that the Armenian uprising in the city was actually a defensive reaction against the increasingly wild and murderous provocations emanating from Cevdet—as recent, careful reconstruction of events has suggested[234]—would certainly have cut no ice with CUP leaders. Their firm conviction that what they were dealing with was a veritable Armenian stab in back is reflected in Talât's 27 April announcement to the German embassy: that the *millet* autonomy of all religious communities was to be abolished. More tangibly still, a whole series of Armenian deportations from strategic areas close to the front also ensued. Many Cilician settlements which had escaped the earlier round of deportations were now caught up in this dragnet, while the deportees previously sent to Konya found themselves re-routed towards the Syrian desert.[235] Even more ominously there were increasing reports of violence—or agitation for violence—against Armenians in the troubled eastern war zone, some of these emanating from CUP clubs. Evidence also suggests that the large-scale execution of army and labour units began around this time.[236]

In other words, there is no disputing that the late April emergency situation also saw a marked radicalization of CUP animus and, with it, exterminatory violence towards Armenians. However, had it reached the point of no return? Certainly, we can read a powerful desire for retribution for the alleged sins committed by the community against the state, mixed too, with a more calculated desire to 'get rid' of the problem once and for all. Enver's announcement on 24 April, for instance, that the Armenian population in the east was to be reduced to 10 per cent of its total while large numbers of Armenian menfolk would be relocated to the Euphrates valley area, speaks strongly to this desire. Yet at the same time it also harps back to the broader and more general Nâzim scheme of demographic engineering, which in itself did not assume the physical liquidation of communal populations.[237] That the regime may still not yet have fully made up its mind on the matter is also suggested by a top secret communiqué sent on 2 May by a member of the War Office staff—one İsmet (İnönü), later Kemal's closest political ally—to Talât. In view of ongoing Armenian revolts in the Van area, İsmet urged on him the army's earnest desire that the problem be resolved either by driving the rebel Armenians—as a communal body—over to the Russian lines, or relocating them elsewhere in the country, with their numbers replaced by Muslims.[238] The first suggestion is itself intriguing for its similarity to the Shcherbachev proposal barely weeks earlier, aimed at sweeping out the Jewish population of Russian-occupied Galicia: another clearly sub-genocidal proposition. But the İsmet letter is equally notable for moving the onus of what to do about the 'problem' away from the military and onto the Interior Ministry, as an essentially domestic matter. It further underlines the fact that if there was a comprehensive plan in readiness for a final Armenian solution senior elements of the War Office were entirely unaware of it—İsmet's proposal being for *local* deportations, not a general one.

Yet in the weeks that followed, the gradual ratcheting up of the deportations programme seemed to follow the İsmet approach. Thus when the Russian spring offensive finally did get under way—the secondary prong of which, with the assistance of Armenian *druzhiny*, reached and liberated besieged Armenian Van on 18 May—the Russian advance was met, stage by stage, with Ottoman evictions from areas in the line of its army's retreat. By this juncture there is no doubt that deportations were regularly accompanied or indeed replaced by massacre, with Cevdet's killers to the fore. But then this was not entirely one-way traffic. In Van, for instance, Muslims were also massacred before and after liberation by the other side. The Ottoman response appeared to reach its culmination on 23 May, with Interior Ministry instructions for a comprehensive deportation of all Armenians in Erzurum, Bitlis, and Van—the three vilayets in closest proximity to the Russian advance. The same also went for all of Cilicia and much of the coastal area around Aleppo. 'Military security' thus rings out as the essential stimulus to—and justification for—these draconian orders, though again with at least the semblance of orderly evacuation, not least in the formation of a scratch Deportations Department in Aleppo to supervise the southward flow of deportees to what was now a designated zone of Armenian 'resettlement' (in their words) in the forbidding Jazirah region between the rivers Euphrates and Kharbur.[239]

On 26 May, however, the whole process lurched into a new and much higher gear. Now, ostensibly on the basis of an oral decision emanating from the Supreme High Command, Talât not only issued orders for Armenian deportations from the entirety of eastern Anatolia but sought to give them legal character by promulgating a temporary law the following day, empowering the military authorities to order deportations themselves. A cloak of military necessity was thus put into effect to justify actions in areas where obvious military threat did not prevail. Indeed, by the last week of May not only had the Russian advance been stymied but so too had the British Gallipoli assault. The immediate crisis of state had passed. Yet as far as the Armenians were concerned Talât was now operating as if in two parallel universes.

On the one hand, while security became the undisputed premise for all anti-Armenian directives on movement or prohibition of movement—with public blaming and shaming of Armenian rebelliousness and treachery the catch-all justification for them—on the other, the various post-26 May legal enactments present the regime as not simply benignly but profusely concerned for the wellbeing of the deportees. Armenian persons and their property would be protected by order of the government, indeed the latter would be registered by specially *Emvale-i Metruke* commissions, which would not only ensure that the deportees' hearths and homes would be protected in their absence but, where sold, the proceeds would assist the deportees in their new places of settlement. The Ministry of the Interior even issued two manuals which promised that, en route, local administrators would ensure the provision of board and lodging, and that deportees would be able to take their valuables and furniture with them, or, if not, would be compensated. There were even assurances that items of great communal concern, such as church iconostases, would be sent on once communities had been properly resettled. All this would come to pass 'in places which suit public health, agriculture and construction', and where land would be allocated according to each family's 'previous economic condition and . . . present needs'.[240]

The manuals present not just an extraordinary and bizarre travesty of the reality then in the making but are noteworthy, too, for the almost surreal messages implicit in them. They were, of course, a blind; a subterfuge for international consumption only. And even putting to one side material such as the secret ciphers Talât is supposed to have transmitted to regional governors—on the grounds that they cannot be absolutely verified as genuine—enough alternative documentation is extant which confirms that the deportations were now no more than a cover for large-scale elimination.[241] Dadrian has hypothesized the emergence of a twin-track Ottoman state policy from this point on. The manuals, thus, were part of the official track in which relatively innocuous disinformation prevailed. The second unofficial track involved covert killing orders either sent by cipher or, sometimes, transmitted in person by *Katib-i Mesuller*—specially appointed CUP 'responsible secretaries', rather like the Jacobin couriers: the *répresentants en mission* at the time of the destruction of the Vendée in 1793–4. These latter orders were the ones that really counted.[242]

This still leaves us with something of an enigma. Why was late May the ultimate watershed? Could it be, as Manoug Somakian has inferred, the result of a kind of euphoria: Ottoman success in staving off the British at the Dardanelles galvanizing a CUP decision to go for an all-or-nothing drive towards a 'resurrected' Turkey—an argument not unlike Christopher Browning's on the Nazi launching of the 'Final Solution' at the height of Operation Barbarossa?[243] Was it, alternatively, the 24 May Entente declaration that was the straw which finally broke the camel's back: years of Great Power censure of Ottoman behaviour towards its Armenian population now being met by a CUP resolve to throw back this final reprimand in the interfering foreigners' faces?[244] Or was it actually the loss of Van to the Russians that was the real trigger to the CUP exterminatory response?

Each of these explanations may contain elements of the truth. But, equally, there is a danger in becoming too fixated on a particular moment when everything crystallized into a decision to launch genocide, as if by doing so we find the key to the whole process. Attempting to plot the countdown to the Holocaust has similarly taken up the energies of countless scholars. Yet, in the summer of 1941, mass killings of Jews already preceded any such definitive decision for systematic extermination. So, too, in the case of the *Aghet*: a cumulative slide towards mass murder was evident in the late-spring massacres of Armenians no longer only in the border zones or in Cevdet's Van, but in districts notably removed from the front, especially around the city of Erzurum.[245] This does not mean that identifying a final tipping point is not important. But concentrating on this alone may deflect us from reading causation through a somewhat different prism.

The documentary clue to this alternative approach may lie in the official deportation orders, more specifically those in some way relating to the role of the *Emvale-i Metruke* commissions for abandoned properties. These local commissions were established directly under the aegis of IAMM, the Interior Ministry Directorate also responsible for providing temporary shelter and sustenance and long-term provision of property and land for all displaced peoples, technically speaking the Armenians included. Transfer of Armenian property to other displaced people thus could not take place directly. But according to a September decree it could be put at the disposal of either the Ministry of Finance or religious foundations. The IAMM thus provided critical oversight of procedures whose ultimate result was the liquidation of Armenian assets. But this was not fundamentally driven by a 'duty of care' for *muhajirun*. It is evident, for instance, that Talât's deputy, Ali Münif Bey, played a key role in obtaining from the commissions' precise and very detailed information not only the number and location of Armenian emptied villages and urban buildings but—as his 22 June circular to the Erzurum authorities on Armenian schools in the area shows—the value of their real estate.[246] What Münif, in other words, was compiling, was an inventory: a sort of latter-day Doomsday book of Armenian assets. Outwardly, this was part of the façade of protecting Armenians' property rights. Its more exact purpose was to provide money for the regime as well as preventing anybody else from laundering off that money into *their* pockets.

This takes us rather dramatically back to the CUP's raison d'être. Talât and the others sought to create a strong, modernized, industrialized Turkey. Not only did they wish to bring in advanced technologies and a communications infrastructure for rapid economic development; they also saw as key to their modernizing aspirations secular reforms, which would subordinate the *sharia* courts to the state and equally emancipate women, giving them legal rights—including that of divorce—plus opportunities for education and employment within an opened-up labour market.[247] These aspirations were little different from other 'backward', latecomer states attempting to emulate an avant-garde West. What made the CUP distinctive within the Ottoman political firmament was their insistence on the rapid creation of the *milli iktisat*—a truly national economy run by and for Turks—as the only viable route to the achievement of these goals. This had been at the root, after all, of the declaration against Capitulations and the whole panoply of European financial control at the war's outset. The problem was that the declaration underscored in the raw the yawning gulf between aspirations and the complete lack of means to arrive at their realization.[248] It was all very well pontificating about a *milli banka*: a national financial institution which would trump and then make redundant the dominant Western-owned Ottoman Imperial Bank. But without any funds to turn this into reality the CUP ambition remained in cloud cuckoo land.

How then was the regime able to so dramatically turn the tables? And in wartime to boot? From *muhajir* settlement and tribal sedentarization—even under a forced-pace wartime programme of social engineering—might eventually accrue to the state some autarkic tax revenues, but only in the long term, and even then probably only after some decades of peace and stability. In the immediate term, the cost to the government of these programmes actually helped drain its central budget.[249] The 1916 windfall, and with it some embryonic basis for capital accumulation to kick-start, in turn, the *milli iktisat*, clearly came from some entirely different source—but one which is not hard to determine. As Gerlach puts it, 'the businesses, jobs, houses, land, possessions and valuables of Armenians (9–10 per cent of the population)...were equivalent to two and half state budgets, or more than all foreign investments in the Ottoman empire'.[250] In short, the regime's windfall was over the bodies of dead Armenians.

The proposition that the removal of the non-Muslim elements of the population—more particularly that significant middleman element, who, unlike the vast majority of Turks, were involved in commerce and industry—might provide a short cut to state-led economic take-off was not entirely novel in 1915. The notion had been implicit in Lichtenstädter's polemics, as in those of Halide Edib, the American-missionary-educated female Ittihadist outrider for a strictly Anatolia-focused Turkish nationalism.[251] Such ideas did not have to imply extermination. But for the state to get its hands on other people's wealth, at minimal or no cost to itself, at the very least implied massive coercion. In wartime conditions, the opportunities and indeed justification for such programmes of state-nationalized expropriation were hardly limited to the Turks. On the contrary, each of the belligerent powers sought in varying degrees to liquidate, without compensation, the businesses and properties of enemy aliens, and, to take only Britain as an example, provide capital for the creation of some its major post-war joint-stock companies.[252]

What made the notion doubly tantalizing for the CUP ideologues was not simply that it paid back the allegedly avaricious, money-obsessed Armenians for their siphoning off of national wealth but that, in the process, it provided an opportunity for an entire reformulation of the country's economic structure around a new 'Turkish' bourgeoisie. Or, to put it more brutally but honestly, a replacement 'native' (in their words) bourgeoisie for the one which was being expunged. By confiscating Armenian assets under the ruse of protecting them Talât sought to stimulate and develop entrepreneurship among at least elements of the Turkish population who previously had no background in, let alone taste for, capitalist enterprise. This call to *enrichez-vous* thus needs to be seen as quite distinct from the soon to be realized, strictly *dirigiste* Bolshevik route to capital accumulation, which would reach its apotheosis with Stalin's assault on the kulaks. By contrast, Talât's nationalization of the market through the state-sponsored sale, in 1916, of Armenian factories, workshops, property, machinery, goods, land, and accessories, to a mostly very limited circle of friends, clients, and assorted cronies, not only reinforced—ironically—the earlier Dashnak wisdom that the CUP were averse to any form of social, let alone socialist-orientated, redistribution of wealth, but led to the repeated popular outcry that they had simply created a new self-perpetuating financial elite, the '322 tuccari', otherwise known as the 'merchants', or even, more pungently, 'riches of 1916'.[253]

The more immediate problem for Talât was ensuring that the state was able to lay its hands on Armenian assets in the first place. There is, for instance, the famous case of his brazenly requesting from Morgenthau a list of Armenian policy holders with US insurance companies, on the grounds that as both they and their heirs were likely, by then, to be dead, their policies were escheat to the state.[254] With requests such as this bluntly turned down, the reliance of metropolitan *milli iktisat* proponents on their provincial officials' asset-stripping Armenian wealth on *its* behalf, rather than their *own*, became doubly imperative. An appointee such as Dr Mehmed Reshid as *vali* of Diyabekir in March 1915 may have been in part impelled both by his credentials as a radical nationalist modernizer and his recent critical success in violently evicting Greeks and Armenians from the Karesi district, in western Anatolia, the previous year.[255] As we will shortly see, Reshid's subsequent fervour in exterminating both Armenians and Syriacs would place him in the very front rank of CUP *génocidaires*. However, his appetites on this score would arguably be equalled by his prodigious efforts towards his own personal enrichment. Reshid eventually completed his tour of duty in Diyabekir in November 1915, leaving the province by carriage, then train, accompanied by two-score and more of boxes and baggage containing jewellery, precious stones, and fineries filched from his victims, the proceeds of which bought him a truly magnificent waterfront Constantinople home. Not surprisingly, once exposed, his covetousness would land him in serious trouble with the regime.[256] It would prove to be a far from an isolated case.

One might wish to go off at this point at some tangent as to the mindset of major and minor perpetrators—Turkish and, by extension others, in different genocides—and the projection of *their* avarice onto that of their victims.[257] Even putting aside the fact that it might suggest that the accomplishment of genocide could be dependent on either encouraging, or inevitably leading to, the venality of its more grass-roots actors, one might further wish to contemplate an inherent problem in the broader logic of state or societal financial gain by way of mass murder. In the process, what the CUP certainly appears to have either wilfully forgotten, or perhaps not even considered, is that bereft of the technical, commercial, and linguistic skills, and cultural, educational, and psychological factors which were at the root of Armenian 'success', plundering their wealth was likely to be a very finite exercise, and certainly not one which would simply lead to a replication, let alone a fast-track one, of further accumulation—and with it employment—for Turkish individuals, communities, or state.

None of this *alone* proves that underlying the genocide was some premeditated economic motive: some thought-out plan to declare war, commit a genocide in order to finance the war, not to mention provide the capital for post-war reconstruction. There is no evidence, for instance, that the liquidation committees initiated to wind up Armenian assets in the early summer of 1915 were anything other than rapidly improvised as the killing unfolded.[258] If, indeed, there was underlying intent to do *something* against the Armenians, the events of the first half of the year rather support the thesis in Michael Mann's *Dark Side of Democracy* that contingency kept getting in the way, leading to a series of default plans, each one more extreme than its predecessor. The consequences for our understanding of history can indeed be very messy. As for genocide, there is no reason why it cannot operate at different levels. On one—in the head—it might operate according to some conspiratorial idea in which a statist elite group of would-be perpetrators desires to eliminate a perceived communal enemy for any combination of political, economic, or ideological reasons. The group might even put its ideas on paper in some very bold, or, alternatively, nebulous plan of campaign. In practice, however, things might turn out rather differently as hastily improvised efforts by the group in response to unexpected events (even though these might be, at least in considerable part, of its own making) lead to some crystallization, that is, where idea and practice finally collide with explosive force. What the Armenian genocide suggests is that neither intent nor contingency *has to be* the sole explanation:[259] simply that process is crucial yet also very complex. What is equally crucial, however, is that the process, by summer 1915, had crystallized into one in which the CUP centre (with the important caveat of Cemal's deviation from this main script) were fully dedicated to the communal extirpation of Ottoman Armenians.

THE CONTOURS OF MASS MURDER

At the end of May Enver told Hans von Wangenheim, the German ambassador to the Porte, that the regime would not brook outside interference on behalf of the

Armenians.[260] It would be the first of many such regime rebuttals of diplomatic efforts aimed at softening the deportation or other anti-Armenian orders. Diplomats from the Central Powers and from neutral embassies had reason enough to be alarmed. What Wangenheim was hearing, for instance, through his vice-consul, Max von Scheubner-Richter, about the growing scope and scale of violence in Erzurum was being amply corroborated, especially by American, Danish, and other neutral counterparts throughout eastern and central Anatolia.[261] Such intelligence was finding its way too, to Entente countries in sufficient quantity for Lord Bryce, in Britain, to instigate the compilation of an official parliamentary dossier under the direction of Arnold Toynbee. In February 1916, this would commence bringing together some of the available consular reports—primarily from released US sources—alongside eyewitness testimonies and newspaper accounts in a massive, authoritative, and damning Blue Book.[262]

Today, we tend to think of the *Aghet* in terms of mass expulsions of entire Armenian communities; largely on foot, over incredible distances and extremely difficult terrain to climatically harsh and unforgivingly inhospitable frontier regions in the Syrian desert—literally 'beyond the pale'. In the process, the vast majority of deportees were either gruesomely killed or perished as a result of the vicissitudes they encountered. These were, in the fullest sense, death marches. Yet, paradoxically, concentration on the deportations and their effects, most obviously because there were some survivors who were later to recount the experience, diverts our attention from an equally significant aspect of this genocide: the vast numbers of those who died in massacres, in, or close to, their homes. Nor were only Armenians the victims of these in situ killings. So too were tens of thousands of Syriacs. Not surprisingly, there were few or no survivors to report *these* events.

The major part of this direct physical extermination in its initial stages took place in the east Anatolian vilayets closest to the war zone. Kévorkian's recent very full analysis and interpretation of the whole killing sequence in both its regional aspects and totality—effectively the first study of its kind to do so—lays stress on the CUP's preconceived organization for Armenian destruction.[263] That said, such pre-planning was only really possible where Russian proximity was absent. In other words, death marches in which massacres took place in transit were cut short where there was awareness of Russian forces being close at hand. The annihilation of such communities was undertaken in haste and, to a considerable degree, in a very ad hoc manner. The role of the military in these massacres, working in tandem with Ministry of the Interior-delegated operatives, was also conspicuous, in a way it was not outside the war theatre; in the latter case responsibility for liquidation fell more squarely on Special Organization personnel, militias, gendarmes, and the like. The coastal vilayet of Trabzon provides one example of the former method. Here the excision of some 14,000 Armenian inhabitants was accomplished in a period of a month, from late June onwards, by the local CUP's mobilization of not only all its own cadres, plus police agents and volunteer bands, but some 15,000 troops who helped round up the victims in conditions the Italian consul described as 'a state of siege'. The problem of dealing with this Armenian 'capacity' was then largely cut short by crowding thousands of them onto caiques which, towed into the Black

Sea, were then capsized. Only some forcibly converted women and children seem to have survived this Turkish equivalent of the 1793 Vendean *noyades*.[264]

Arguably even more gruesome were the massacres on terra firma—though with river drownings (another facet of the Trabzon province massacres) an additional instrument of liquidation—simultaneously perpetrated by the already seasoned military forces and auxiliaries under Cevdet in Van, and his then neighbouring governor, Mustafa Abdülhalik, in Bitlis. This region was the most populous and arguably most vibrant heart of Armenian traditional life. Here, undoubted attempts in the Mush and Sassun areas by Armenian *fedai* to hastily defend their villages, pending Russian relief, were met with the unrelenting fury of Ottoman retribution. These included wholesale conflagrations—usually, in practice, of the women, children, babies, and old people who had survived the initial onslaught—utilizing all available large buildings—churches, schools, orphanages, as well as in haylofts and stables—in which to pack and incinerate them. One survivor testified that, of 150,000 Armenians in this area, nearly all were wiped out during June and July.[265] Halil, again in his military capacity, was a major contributor to these exterminations, boasting in his post-war memoirs that, all told, he was responsible for the deaths of 300,000 Armenians—'it can be more or less, I didn't count'.[266]

Neither Halil's zeal nor his methods, however, proved idiosyncratic. Gaunt tersely reminds us of the common 1915 features of the latter: 'shooting, stabbing, stoning, crushing, throat cutting, throwing off roofs, drowning, decapitation', all of unarmed, tied up, or defenceless people. 'Witnesses talk of seeing collections of ears and noses and of brigands boasting of their collection of female body parts'.[267] If this is a sobering reminder of what genocide, writ large, regularly entails, Gaunt also present us with something rather more specific: the very public parading, humiliation, symbolic torture, and, finally, celebratory degradation of mutilated body parts of *other*—non-Armenian—Christians, most particularly of their communal and religious leaders. He cites, for instance, the slaughter of Syriacs at Sheikhan as human sacrifice and the case of the Midyat Jacobite leader Hanne Safar Pasha—whose head, after he had been decapitated by a ceremonial sword blessed by the Sultan, was then used as a football—again, not an isolated case.[268]

Anti-Syriac violence, with Reshid in Diyarbekir province consistently its most fervent exponent, poses us with an analytical problem. Our efforts to understand the events of 1915 have been implicitly predicated on the notion of some sort of political dynamic—however reified—between Armenians and Turks, and even of some form of—again however asymmetric—military confrontation. Nestorians, too, at least in terms of the Mar Shamun's leadership of the Hakkâri community, fall approximately between these brackets. Reading the Ottoman, or even CUP, relationship to the other Syriacs—Jacobites, Syriac Catholics, and Chaldeans—in these terms, however, lacks plausibility. These communities were simply part of a very rich and certainly religiously and socially complex ethnographic mix which, especially in their Tur Abdin mountain heartlands in the southern part of Diyabekir province around Midyat and Mardin, had rubbed along side by side with Muslims and other religious sects for more than a millennium. This is not to presume that these communities were not involved in the integral social and municipal life of the region. But they were, in essence, politically quiescent. Indeed, their immediate security was reliant on the dominant Kurdish *aghas* of the area, as, arguably, their long-term communal survival was dependent on Ottoman imperial stability.

Was their fate in 1915 thus an unfortunate result of being in the path of the more general human whirlwind—total war—which, in turn, tore away at the old pluralist sinews that had characterized the eastern rimlands for so long? It is for instance notable that in some of the massacres no distinction was made between Armenians and others. Uğur Ümit Üngör cites two notable August massacres at Nusaybin and Cizre in which hundreds of Jacobite and Chaldean men were viciously tortured and then liquidated alongside larger numbers of Armenian Gregorians, Catholics, and Protestants. The majority of their womenfolk and children were also terrorized, violated, and either enslaved or killed on the road or by the Tigris, within days. In Nusaybin there existed, however, a 600-strong Jewish community. This remained untouched.[269] The destruction of Syriacs, alongside or, as in so many other cases, independently of Armenians, was thus not accidental. Nor, to underscore the point, were there any Syriac deportations. These communities were butchered either in, or close to, their native hearths. Recognition of the Tur Abdin massacres has prompted Üngör to ask: 'How Armenian was this genocide supposed to be?'[270]

The interpolation in turn poses a further set of difficult questions. Was a key provincial actor such as Reshid leading the way, even operating in excess of Talât's orders; simply interpreting them elastically; or correctly anticipating and covertly carrying out what had always been intended? In mid-June there was a notable occasion when couriers acting on Talât's direct orders halted a mixed convoy en route from Mardin to Diyarbekir of 266 condemned Armenian and Jacobite notables and freed the Syriacs but not the Armenians amongst them. This stay of execution, for some but not others, appears to have had something to do with Walter Holstein, the German vice-consul in Mosul: his growing awareness of the killings in the neighbouring province, and his energetic efforts to prevent more through diplomatic supplication at the Porte. The part played by German officials such as Holstein and Scheubner-Richter, in turn problematizes the common charge that German diplomatic and military staff repeatedly turned a blind eye to the massacres, amounting to a form of complicity in them.[271] Indeed, just as one might argue that British officials did pretty much the same in wartime Russia when faced with tsarist anti-Semitic violence, so the German parallel might be read as a case either of avoiding antagonizing a shaky ally or of more proactive sympathy with and even active support for the CUP's anti-Armenian animus. A conclusion that it suited the Germans most of the time not to protest against the regime's worst excesses, however, cannot detract, in this instance, from an explicit July German embassy protest, which seems to have led Talât to issue a series of orders limiting the general *deportations* specifically to members of the Apostolic Armenian church. Reshid was also explicitly censured by the interior minister for exceeding his brief.[272] To be sure, if the effect was to halt the mass killings in the province's main towns such as Diyarbekir and Mardin—where the major bloodletting had *already* taken place—it was cold comfort for Armenians and Syriacs in outlying areas, especially those around Midyat—massacred in mid-July—and their equivalents around Nusaybin and Cizre—killed in August and early September—not to mention all those in the mixed Christian enclave of Urfa, who were exterminated in the middle of September.[273]

We are thus left with something not quite as absolute or coherent as Toynbee's contemporary characterization of events as following 'a fundamental uniformity of procedure'.[274] Certainly, his delineation of the approximate chronological boundaries of the deportation process is correct: 'April and May...assigned to the clearance of Cilicia, June and July...reserved for the east, the western centres along the (Baghdad) Railway...in August and September', and so on. Whether this amounted to 'a deliberate, systematic attempt to eradicate the Armenian population throughout the Ottoman Empire',[275] however, is dependent on *when* this 'systematic' deliberateness actually kicked in, which was almost certainly not until late May. To add to the irregularity of the sequence, there were no deportation orders for Van province, where, as in Erzurum and Diyarbekir, the mass killings preceded the main deportation orders. Similarly, we may note that in this latter province, Reshid, until brought back into line by his superiors, exceeded his orders, not least by going into overdrive against the Syriac communities.

Such instances would seem to make of the *Aghet* a process evolving out of a dialogue—perverse as it undoubtedly was—between protagonists at the centre and enthusiastic implementers in the spot. Thus, if we can identity Shakir in his peripatetic travels 'from province to province, exhorting the local authorities to ever more vigorous action against the Armenians'[276] as fundamental to the ongoing momentum of the killing process, equally we have to grapple with the mindset, and hence efforts, of those like Reshid and Cevdet, 'working their way towards' the idea of a purified Turkish state,[277] presumably relieved of all extraneous—for which read Christian—humanity. Their role is fundamental for another reason, too. In spite of the best efforts of the Special Organization it alone lacked the personnel for the Herculean task of mass murder across such a wide geographical vista. It could farm out its killers for key hands-on assassinations, it could act as organizing agent for exemplary massacres; but ultimately the regime needed many more teams of grass-roots enthusiasts to carry out a comprehensive 'cleansing' to the core. At one level, Reshid offers an almost textbook example of how this could be done.

*

Reshid arrived in Diyarbekir with a thirty-strong gendarme bodyguard of fellow Circassians—many apparently kith and kin—who effectively became the paramilitary strike force and exemplary model for future action. Reshid, however, quickly went one step further by creating an ominously entitled Special Commission of Enquiry 'for the solution of the Armenian question', made up of leading notables from the city, including the mufti, police chief, two parliamentary deputies, including Feyzi Bey, a CUP stalwart, plus other committed Ittihadists.[278] The aim of Reshid's commission was not so much to investigate as to promote a charge of Armenian conspiracy and 'high treason' of which Reshid himself was already chief believer and proclaimer. With the local bigwigs falling in rapidly behind him Reshid seems to have encountered little or no opposition in his efforts to create a militia from the city's Muslim citizenry who, in the heightened atmosphere of fear and loathing which Reshid had done much to promote, were now given authority by which to terrorize their Armenian neighbours in their frantic search for Dashnak and Hnchak arms. Additionally, support from the notables bolstered Reshid's other key task: the removal of unconvinced or obdurate district administrators in the localities—in favour of his own conformist appointees.[279] Whether this all proves that Reshid, from the time of his appointment in March, knew where he was heading is another matter. A few months later, ordered to account for his actions before the CUP general secretary, Midhat Şükrü (Bleda), Reshid claimed that:

> The Armenians in the Eastern Provinces were so aggressive against us that in their areas, if they were allowed to remain in place, not a single Turk or Muslim would be left alive... They possessed a fantastic organization... In this situation, I thought to myself, Hey, Dr Reshid! There are two alternatives. Either the Armenians liquidate the Turks, or the Turks them! Facing this necessity, I did not hesitate. My Turkishness triumphed over my medical identity... I saw that the fatherland was on the verge of being lost, therefore with my eyes closed and without looking back I continued in the conviction that I acted for the wellbeing of the nation.[280]

This startling confession aside, the key point at issue here is how Reshid created the foundations upon which an otherwise resource-starved state might implement a genocide at one of its far-flung peripheries, and, as Gaunt has put it, with 'literally thousands of perpetrators'.[281] The point is further underscored by knowledge of who these grass-roots killers were. With most of the able-bodied younger men in Ottoman uniform (the local Kurdish tribesmen being one exception), fighting on often far-away fronts, the fifty-strong paramilitary units Reshid created, often with red armbands as their only identification, were composed almost entirely of middle-aged men. German observers often assumed these killers to be from the lowest of the low.[282] But this view was mistaken. While there were certainly plenty of thugs, opportunists, or those such as butchers, used to killing, the units seem to have contained a wide spectrum of local citizenry, backed and urged on—where not personally led—by *agha*s or other local dignitaries, like Feyzi himself. Of course, while we have Reshid's self-exonerating post-war memoirs, we lack testimonies from most grass-roots participants and hence evidence of what motivated them to participate. Legitimized plunder may well have been one incentive, of which more below in this section. But, as in 1895, a sense that they were acting morally against those who had transgressed against not simply the political order but the religious foundations of the Islamic state seems to have played a powerful part. Indeed, oral history accounts point to the—albeit false—conviction, among at least some, that what they were doing had been specifically decreed by the Sultan.[283]

Certainly, Reshid's so-called *al-Hamsin* squads, like the Circassian butcher battalions in neighbouring Van and Bitlis, set about killing with an extraordinary energy. They also demonstrated an equally extraordinary capacity for inflicting prolonged pain and gratuitous suffering on their victims, not least by dreaming up different *methods* of killing. The earliest recorded exterminatory assault on entire village communities in the Diyarbekir area—those of Qarababash and Kabiye—not only involved mass burning in haylofts, as we have encountered earlier in this section, but saw the majority of victims hacked to death with axes and daggers. In the case of Kabiye many of its menfolk were thrown off a cliff face. However, prior to death these unfortunates were also bastinadoed or tortured using hot pins.[284] All this said, our *al-Hamsin* heroes were not sufficient for the completion of Reshid's task. To arrive there he also called on the 'good' offices of the Kurdish Reman tribe.

The involvement of many tribal Kurds in addition to those Kurds already involved in the Diyarbekir militia both widens the general range of perpetrators and complicates the bigger picture across eastern Anatolia. On the one hand, it reminds us that without strong Kurdish involvement in the genocide, the CUP would not have been able to fully implement it. Survivor accounts from the deportations all affirm the major role Kurds played in attacking, robbing, and destroying the convoys.[285] On the other hand, the subcontracting of *some* of the violence to Kurds rather suggests the degree to which the trajectory of the *Aghet* was dependent on forces which, to say the least, were operating semi-autonomously of the state. Back in the 1890s, Abdülhamid had sought to gain a tighter grip on some of the more truculent Kurdish tribes by elevating them into Hamidiye regiments, which were then given free rein to attack Armenians. But it was exactly this loose cannon element in the Kurdish equation that led the CUP to later abandon reliance on the regiments. To again attempt to co-opt armed Kurdish irregulars, as the regime did in 1915, thus had something of a hit-and-miss quality about it, success often having as much to do with inter-tribal or intra-tribal rivalries—perhaps indicative of the breakdown of the Kurdish social order in the east of previous centuries—as any obvious evidence of their loyalty to the state, let alone regime. Indeed, in 1915 some Kurdish tribes were in open revolt against the regime.[286] Paradoxically, the high Kurdish *profile* in the *Aghet* did have one advantage for both the CUP and for subsequent Kemalist and post-Kemalist administrations. At the time, the murderous role of someone like Reshid was assumed by German observers to be evidence of a provincial governor acting outside of state control.[287] By the same token, a post-1923 Turkish narrative of 1915 events has always emphasized the discrepancy between an orderly, non-violent CUP effort to deport Armenians to Syria and Mesopotamia to the best of its ability, and entirely lawless Kurdish interventions—alongside that of Armenian insurrection itself—which both undermined the CUP's good intent and led to massive loss of life.[288]

It is not only in this way that the Kurds become the convenient fall guy, not to say archetypal racialized 'other', in events for which the CUP were themselves primarily responsible. In the process they have also provided a cover, eliding from view those elements of the killing operation which the regime apparatus directly controlled. We have already noted how both in situ massacres and the killing of Armenians and Syriacs in Ottoman uniform have been largely lost from our historical vision. As the deportations themselves got under way, especially from June onwards, what happened to the remaining non-combatant Armenian menfolk is similarly obscured. If we take the town of Harput, for instance, from which

Armenian deportations began in June, we know from US Consul Davis, that hundreds of the community's leading luminaries—including elderly scholars he knew from the American-run missionary Euphrates college—were incarcerated in the town's prison where they were tortured and mutilated for weeks on end, *before* finally they were taken away, along with the men from the neighbouring town of Mamouret-al-Aziz. On the road to Diyarbekir, however, both groups simply disappeared.[289] This was not a singular case. All the evidence points to the disposal of the majority of the men by out-of-the-way massacres early on in the deportation process.

Any notion, thus, that Turkish administrators and gendarmerie (again with the exception of those in Cemal's Fourth Army area) were the thin line protecting deportees from the barbarity of wild Kurds is to be repudiated as simple subterfuge. However, the sequencing of the killing, with men massacred usually early on in the death marches by their military or police protectors, and Kurds playing a much fuller role later on, is itself revealing. The reports of Davis and others vividly portray communities in uproar, confusion, and terror after the public announcement of deportation: the Armenians rushing round trying to wind up businesses and desperately trying to salvage whatever they could, monetary or otherwise, from the wreckage of their lives. If this meant trying to dispose of now useless goods, furniture, and household effects for a song, or simply giving them away to neighbours—the counterpoint to which was that for the Turks this became a 'veritable holiday' and excuse to don 'gala attire'[290]—the other side to the picture was the deportees' own rapidly improvised survival strategy for what all now expected to be a long and hazardous journey. With the expectation that ready money or alternative items of value would be indispensable to bribe those on whom they would be utterly dependent for food, shelter, and security, survivor testimony suggests that all available jewels and valuables were not simply taken on the journey but carefully secreted in clothing or in the most private parts of the bodies of women and child deportees. This was entirely logical, not least in a society where, outside of the family, the integrity of the female person was considered sacrosanct. It was exactly this assumption which proved to be the fatal ingredient in what followed. It is also the ingredient which gives to the ensuing massacres their distinct, if wholly foul, flavour.

The majority of deportees from eastern and central provinces of Anatolia left their homes on foot or, where more fortunate, by cart. Usually within a few days, however, the officials and gendarmes accompanying them had extorted from the deportees whatever they could lay their hands on. With the men killed and the transport removed or filched, these long snake-like columns of marchers, weaving their way through ravines and gorges in blistering day-time temperatures, were thus essentially columns of women and their children. The basic unit was the surviving females in the family group. Mothers, mothers-in-law, aunts, sisters, grandmothers, and female cousins became the only protective shield to younger women carrying small babies or about to reach term—as many did on the route of the marches—plus younger unmarried girls and their prepubescent male siblings.[291] One thing that is immediately transparent in all this is the doubly gendered nature of this genocide. Already severely traumatized and with no male protection, not to say reduced by constant hunger, thirst, sleep deprivation, heat, cold, and basic visceral fear, these female groups would have very soon appeared to observers as an emaciated, disgustingly filthy, and lice-ridden rabble.[292] In this condition, the columns were not simply existentially exposed to danger, but radically so, by their degraded and effectively dehumanized appearance. And so they were further distanced from the broad societal and cultural prohibitions which might otherwise have stood as barrier of last resort against their violation.[293]

But there was also another element to this equation. The destruction of the Armenians in economic terms was akin to an inverted spoils heap. The greatest gain, in principle at least, accrued as fixed property, land, and bank assets to the state. Below that the opportunity for personal enrichment, à la Reshid, came through high- and then medium-level officials taking their pick of the most enticing commodities left in homes or stored under the auspices of the *Emvale-i Metruke* commissions.[294] By the time we reach the deportation columns a week or more into their plight, the gendarmes—having forcibly taken anything they could easily lay their hands on—were often quite ready to wash their hands of their charges by subcontracting any further stage of the 'journey' to local Kurds. It was thus they—the most impoverished and hence most ravenous and mercenary strata in our social heap—who were most repeatedly responsible for atrocities which brought so many of the columns to an early terminus.

In the remote mountainous area some distance from Harput, around Lake Goeljuk (Hazar Gölü), in the autumn of 1915, Davis, accompanied by an American missionary, Dr Atkinson, observed some of the results. Atkinson recorded that in this one place, between five and ten thousand women's and children's bodies were heaped, many on top of each other, all entirely naked and most horribly mutilated or burnt. Atkinson's report clearly implied that the women had been killed in a sado-erotic fashion, though he was too coy or traumatized to spell out his own inference that they had had their genitalia and breasts hacked off while still alive. Davis, by contrast, was able to confirm with certainty the underlying causation for the killing: the Kurds had paid to the gendarmes an agreed sum for the handover of the columns and, having butchered them, proceeded to burn the victims' bodies or simply rip them open as the most efficacious means to locate gold coins and rings either swallowed, or hidden in the vagina or rectum.[295]

In this way we can see that the method of dispatch employed in these killings, with rape as an integral element, was closely linked to a more overtly venal purpose. Nevertheless, at the same time it exposes an aspect of more traditional *normative* thinking and behaviour in operation during the genocide, which was hardly peculiar to Kurds. With the Armenians—that is, their men—charged and executed as traitors, and hence deprived of their conventional right to be protectors of their womenfolk, it was not simply the traditional rules of male–female relations that were radically reversed. Henceforth, taking the young and most attractive female Armenian, or Syriac, maidens became not simply a matter of opportunity but practically a duty: whether carried out against known neighbours—as commonly in the Tur Abdin events—or complete strangers, as in the majority of deportations.

It also carried one obvious once-in-a-lifetime windfall for otherwise impoverished Muslim men: it provided for brides minus a dowry, the major cost in the life cycle of traditional peasant and tribal households. That the intended victims themselves knew these implications is also evident in the manner in which apparently, day in and day out, hundreds of girls in the convoys would link arms or hold hands and commit mass suicide by throwing themselves into the Euphrates or other rivers, thereby defying this literal and shameful familial and communal dishonour.[296]

This did not prevent the abduction of many thousands of young women, girls, and sometimes boys too, by Kurdish, Turkish, and later Arab despoilers of the convoys for, if not sexual, then labour services. Others seem to have been sold for a few piastres at marts which appear to have sprung up in the transitional belt between the 'Kurdish' plateau and 'Arab' desert, or in larger slave markets which appeared in Aleppo, Beirut, Damascus, and other bigger centres.[297] The 'saving' of many thousands of young Armenians in this way, and their often thorough—if choiceless—absorption into Muslim households, would suggest that utilizing a Nazi racial template for understanding the *Aghet* would be to miss the point. By the same token, pointing to this substantial stratum of survivors as evidence that this was no genocide equally avoids the fundamental issue. As Bloxham tersely but correctly puts it, 'the death of every single Armenian was not crucial for the fulfilment of the aim of destroying the Armenian national presence in Anatolia and Cilicia'.[298] Indeed, a realization of genocide does not *necessarily* require either a state, or state regime's, intent, or attempted actualization of such intent, to kill every last member of a targeted community. It *does* require their physical elimination insofar, or until such time, as that community is 'no longer perceived to represent a threat' to the state.[299]

One could thus note that hundreds of thousands of deportees did make it (at least on paper) to the proposed Der Zor-Mosul government zone of resettlement. Kévorkian estimates total numbers of deported Armenians both here and more widely dispersed in Mesopotamia and Syria by late 1915 as numbering 870,000.[300] But relatively few of this number were those who had set out from the eastern vilayets specifically. What typically happened to most of them is conveyed by US Consul Jackson, Davis' counterpart in Aleppo, in his almost biblical description of the fate of two convoys from Sivas and Harput:

> On the sixtieth day when we reached Viran Shehir, only 300 had remained from 18,000 exiles. On the sixty-fourth day they gathered all the men and the sick women, and children, and burnt and killed them all. The remaining were ordered to continue on their way ... On the seventieth day, when they reached Haleb (Aleppo) 35 women and children were remaining from the 3000 exiles from Harput, 150 women and children from the whole caravan of 18,000.[301]

In other words, violent and painful death for all the deportees did not absolutely require direct massacre but might equally come about through a repeated but ultimately lethal cocktail of physical harm, exposure, exhaustion, and/or acute stress leading to bodily or psychic collapse. Equally, the very substantial numbers of Armenians present in the resettlement zone by late 1915 were, by and large, not from the

Armenian plateau heartlands, and not, hence, survivors of the death marches. Rather, they were from either Cilicia or from further west still, even as far as Thrace, having been ordered to relocate in the latter stages of the deportation process.

Yet again this reality presents us with something of a conundrum. While the western deportations had taken place under atrocious and wholly insanitary conditions, very often in boxcars along the Baghdad railway, this sequence of deportations had *not* been accompanied by direct massacre. Nor had the survivors been met with immediate extermination at the far end. Large numbers found clandestine work alongside enforced labour battalion workers on the unfinished Intilli section of the railway line. Much larger numbers still were incarcerated in a string of what amounted to open-air concentration camps along the Euphrates, southeast of Aleppo—which now, effectively, had become the administrative hub of the deportation agenda.[302] On the one hand, this might suggest that after the high point of killings in the summer of 1915, the CUP was going to allow a kernel of Ottoman Armenian life to be kept intact, albeit under the most extreme, not to say utterly alien, conditions. Such an assumption was also strengthened by the efforts of the local *Mutessarif*, Ali Souad Bey, to provide the deportees with what nominal care and provision he had at his disposal. Equally, further south, in Syrian districts such as Hauran, where survivors also more freely congregated, Cemal, as effective regional ruler, studiously avoided a repetition of the anti-Armenian actions of his fellow triumvirs.[303]

On the other hand, other factors intervened to suffocate such faint hopes. The most pressing of these might be deemed epidemiological. The whole process of deportation in the broadest public health sense had been an unmitigated disaster. Unburied, rotting bodies were strewn all over eastern Anatolia, not only along the major highways but particularly at sites such as cisterns, wells, and latrines, where they were heaped up in great numbers.[304] It was this relationship between corpses and water, more particularly running water, which created the greatest risk to public health. Arguably the single most publicized killing field had been at the Kamakh gorge near Erzindjan, where Kurdish tribes recruited by the local CUP club had committed scores of massacres. Further along the Euphrates, where there was a loop in the river, one survivor reported that thousands of dead bodies had created a barrage, forcing the river to change 'its course for about a hundred yards'.[305] With the major river systems overflowing with corpses into their downstream catchments, Talât's response to German complaints was long overdue in his when he sent an urgent coded message in mid-December 1915 to all *vali*s, ordering their underlings, on threat of dismissal for non-compliance, to clear up the mess.[306]

Was the great second wave of Armenian massacres in 1916, carrying right through to the very end of that year, a panicked CUP response to the fear of epidemic rapidly spreading beyond the Armenian camps? If so, they definitely came—in that respect—too late: one key observer noting in August 1916 that 50 per cent of villagers between Aleppo and Mosul had died from typhus, rising to a staggering 88 per cent around Ras ul-Ain, at the northern tip of the camp zone and the then terminus of the Baghdad railway.[307] As for the deportees themselves they had already been dying in literally tens of thousands, mostly from the combined effects of starvation, intestinal diseases, and typhus. Yet, in spite of this, there remained a substantial Armenian population in the camp area, demographically distorted towards the young—though not the youngest—and vast numbers of them orphans whose inbuilt resilience had kept them alive.[308] Could it have been, as Taner Akçam has posited, the 10 per cent rule, the CUP yardstick which determined an incoming group's acceptable size compared with that of their host population, which precipitated this new round of mass murder?[309] Was it again the regime's obsessive security fears about a dangerous population too close to critical strategic railheads and rail lines? Or was it, actually, CUP determination to eliminate as many Armenians as it could?

Whatever the exact justification, the 1916 camp massacres proved to be systematic, merciless, and, in some instances, entirely worthy of the title 'holocaust'. In one such incident, on 9 October 1916—as affirmed in a deposition by an Armenian lawyer, Mustafa Sidki—the police chief of Der Zor 'ordered [underlings] to pile great stacks of wood and spilt two hundred cans of petroleum on the whole stack. He lighted it and then had 2,000 orphans, bound hand and feet, thrown into the pyre'.[310] The scarcity of kerosene may have prevented other such identical infernos. But that hardly prevented the building of bonfires, or ingenuity in finding alternative pyromaniacal methods of dispatch. It is reported that as many as 60,000 people at the camp at Sabka were burnt to death. Meanwhile, the proximity of caves, as at Shedadi on the Kharbur, enabled the liquidators to herd thousands into them with the purpose of asphyxiating them by starting a bonfire at its closed head.[311] These killings point to a regime consciously dedicated to an exterminatory end goal. And, uncannily like the Holocaust, this is reflected in the way primary organizers of the early stage of the killings were redeployed to Der Zor to ensure the completion of the task. It was thus no accident that Ali Souad's replacement as governor was Salih Zeki, who had already distinguished himself as a torturer-cum-killer in the Kayseri region. His key counterpart in Aleppo was Mustafa Abdülhalik, previously chief perpetrator in Bitlis. For good measure, operating from Mosul was none other than our old friend Halil. According to Kévorkian, Cevdet, too, as a result of an impromptu visit to Ras ul-Ain, sealed the fate of camp survivors there.[312] These focused *génocidaires* certainly had their work cut out along the string of 'transit' camps along the 'Euphrates line' between Aleppo and Mosul. No wonder, too, that in a further foretaste of the Holocaust and its ethnic Trawniki cadres, large numbers of Circassians and Chechens—plus Bedouin Arabs—were deployed or redeployed to assist a coterie of experienced (again usually Circassian) Special Organization operatives to do much of the necessary 'dirty' work.[313] Massacre, indeed, remained their standard operating procedure. In Mosul, they were still committing them on a large scale as late as September 1917.[314]

*

Toynbee's detailed examination of the sequence of killing led him to conclude with a cautious estimate of the Armenian death toll as some 600,000.[315] But that was only to the end of 1915, and hence unable to take into account the second phase of killings in the Der Zor zone the following year. Kévorkian's extrapolations suggest that 200,000 more died in these particular massacres. However, these were not the sum total of Armenian deaths as many more died from famine and disease. Kévorkian proposes that no less than 630,000 Armenians, *including* those massacred, died in this second phase.[316] Most analysts of the Armenian genocide would today agree that the Armenian death toll was at the very least one million. How devastating that was in demographic terms depends upon the accuracy of the contested figures of the then Ottoman Armenian population. If there were only 1.6 million Armenians in the empire—the conservative figure Toynbee proffered— then fatalities amounting to more than 1.2 million in toto would be quite staggering. Even if the 1912 Armenian Patriarchate figure of 2.1 million were correct, the death toll would be hardly less terrible.[317]

Focusing on the east Anatolian rimland itself, however, provides us with a more dramatic picture still. Here, in the province of Dyarbekir, at the epicentre of the Armenian empire-wide catastrophe, over 90 per cent of the community was expunged.[318] In the neighbouring eastern border provinces of Bitlis, Erzurum, and Van the toll could have hardly been less severe, save for those able to flee to the Russian lines, or across the Russo-Persian border. This was equally the case for the Hakkâri Nestorians whose safety in their age-old mountain fastness came to an abrupt end with the summer 1915 slaughter.[319] But if, as we have seen, Nestorians were particular targets on both sides of the frontier, what of the other entirely quiescent Syriacs? The French Dominican observer Jacques Rhétoré compiled a report in late 1916 in which he gave some very precise figures of what each community had suffered in Diyarbekir province alone. Jacobite (Syrian Orthodox) losses he put at 60,725, or 72 per cent. Chaldeans, more closely akin to the Nestorians, though with smaller actual numbers, were even more completely destroyed their death toll estimated at 10,010, or 90 per cent. The Syrian Catholics, with 3,450 killed, or 62 per cent, were hardly less devastated.[320]

Certainly, a variety of caveats with regard to the overall picture can be offered. CUP fears about international media exposure of what was taking place may well have acted as a brake on wholesale Armenian deportations from the capital. As we have previously suggested muted, often dilatory, diplomatic protests from the Germans (and much less so the Austrians) seem to have played some belated, and in the upshot quite limited, role in exempting Armenian Catholics and Protestants from the deportations. In practice, even these exemptions, as with Talât's other assurances on the Syriacs' account, were more honoured in the breach than in the observance.[321] Strenuous counter-orders by von Sanders, as overall commander of Ottoman forces in the Aegean theatre, played a crucial though, as it turned out, temporary role in reprieving Smyrna (Izmir's) Armenians from deportation in November 1916.[322] Elsewhere, German military and officials also played a partial role in protecting some Armenians, especially so where they had a direct interest in the disarmed labour battalions and other deportees—some 50,000 of whom were believed to have worked as slaves on the Intilli section of the Baghdad railway. The labourers in the Taurus mountain work camps consequently survived. By contrast, in other places where the CUP intervened to ensure the liquidation of these labourers, on occasion sending in Special Organization brigades to ensure their slaughter, there was little German engineers or officers could do to stop it.[323]

More often than not Armenians and Syriacs were thrown back on their own devices for survival, whether in the form of their own humanitarian relief efforts, as in the Der Zor zone from late 1915,[324] or in the form of physical self-defence efforts. Some of these instances are well known, such as the defence of Van, or, more famously, that of the small Mediterranean coastal community of Musa Dagh.[325] There were, in fact, a range of such actions, as there were too among the Syriacs on the Tur Abdin plateau, most particularly at Ayn Wardo, Azakh, Hah, and the Za'faran monastery complex.[326] Against overwhelming odds, however, chances of survival were nearly always dependent on outside assistance: in some of the Syriac cases this came through local Yezidi Kurdish support; in the case of Musa Dagh, through eventual evacuation by means of a French warship. As we have seen in Van the proximity of the Russians also provided some slim opportunities for flight. Foreign citizenship, a consequence of the Capitulations system, also sometimes enabled Armenians to hunker down or seek protection within the walls of consulates. Elsewhere, some of the Kurdish clans, notably Alevis, safeguarded Armenian neighbours and deportees. Was this a matter of some historic sense of responsibility and hospitality? Perhaps, though there is also evidence that there was often a financial price attached.[327] Food and medical relief from Protestant German and, later, especially American church-organized sources also certainly kept alive thousands of the more radically displaced in the camp areas or—in the longer term—those who made it to the relative safety of Syria.[328] The possibility of survival through direct conversion to Islam may also have been an option in some instances, though cases—as we saw in the Balkan Wars—comparable with the Muslim Pomaks being forcibly converted en masse to Christianity have, to date, escaped scholarly awareness.

These examples all might suggest that the *Aghet* and *Sayfo* were not complete, just as, from the obverse side of the coin, one might equally venture the opinion that these events were simply part and parcel of a more widespread, wartime demographic catastrophe—the effects of which, through military violence, famine, and epidemiological collapse, decimated all communities in eastern and central Anatolia—including Turks and Kurds.[329] The key points of difference, however, are twofold. Firstly, there was no state attempt to eruct and then *destroy* any of these other indigenous populations, as there was with regard to Armenians and Syriacs. Secondly, at the war's end, while Kurds and Turks might seek to reclaim the Ottoman eastern rimlands as theirs, there was no sufficient nucleus of Armenians (let alone Syriacs, bar a small surviving remnant in the Tur Abdin) for them to do likewise. With very few exceptions, practically all of the latter population had been dispersed beyond the plateau or been killed on it, or in the Syrian desert, as, *after* May 1915, was the clear CUP aim. The province-by-province statistics in the confidential report Talât had compiled in 1917 simply confirm this fact.[330] Through this accomplishment, the richly pluralist nature of a region in which many diverse communities—Christian, Muslim, and others—had lived, interacted, and often flourished *together* for generation upon generation, came to a very abrupt and definite end.

IMPERIAL DISSOLUTION AND ITS VIOLENCE

In late July 1915, the veteran German consul in Aleppo, Walter Rössler, overwhelmed by the yawning gulf between CUP accusations of Armenian danger and the degraded and pitiable condition of the convoys he was seeing process before his eyes, could only ask of his Berlin superiors, 'how can women and children pose a threat'?[331] The stark answer is: when you reify them. Or, more exactly, when you project onto a communal group qualities and attributes that might, on the basis of the empirical evidence, normally be reserved for a much smaller, heavily politicized, mostly male element of that group.

Of course, there was nothing new about imperial regimes responding to insurrection—confabulated or otherwise—by meting out exemplary, even exterminatory, punishment on whole communities. In the ancient world, as in the great Central Asian belt of Islamic empires until historically quite recently, it was practically a standard operating procedure to slaughter the offending armed men and carry off the productive—and fertile—women, and children, as the legitimate spoils of a restated and divinely ordained order. For the Ottomans and their Persian neighbours, too, deportation—*tehcir*—of recalcitrant tribal groups was a further standard procedure.[332] It might be half-comforting thus to treat the events of 1915 as a case of *plus ça change, plus c'est la même chose*. Indeed, in the way that many grass-roots participants and bystanders to the slaughter also helped themselves to Armenian young women, girls, and boys with the full intention of absorbing them into their sexual-cum-economic units, and, equally, saw themselves as under no legal restraint from doing so, suggests clear resonances of time-honoured practice.

Yet to understand the *Aghet* and *Sayfo* requires us to look not only backwards but both historically (and geographically) sideways—and forwards—too. And what this presents us with is the dilemma of confronting thoroughgoing exterminatory violence as a primary product of a very *modern* type of struggle: for the would-be nation state. Ethnographic realities—in other words, the very complex plural elements embedded, stabilized, and hence endorsed within an imperial structure—should have made such a struggle a non-starter in the Ottoman eastern rimlands. The vertiginous pace of imperially uninvited nation-state creation and expansion on western Ottoman soil, which the protagonists of the Balkan Wars had brought to the empire's very heartlands, seemed to make it the *only* way forward.

Was the Armenian genocide—that is, the slaughter of an entire community of men, women, and children—therefore inevitable? Or, at the very least, was some extraordinary bout of bloodletting a necessary handmaiden to the gestation of one or more nation states in Anatolia? The broader question of whether, in our period, something other than competing and conflicting nationalized claims to parts of the same multi-ethnic territory could have been avoided by way of alternative political conceptions of post-imperial state and society, is something to which we will return in Chapter 4. Gerard Libaridian's consideration of Dashnak–CUP relations, in the wake of 1908, throws a rather tantalizing lifeline in this direction—and thus towards the, albeit tenuous, possibilities of what might have been.[333]

That, of course, assumes that the inner-circle CUP clique could ever have been willing partners in such a modus vivendi. Another way of deflecting a reading of late Ottoman developments as having within it an inherent genocidal logic, is by nailing entire responsibility for the *Aghet* on the focused agency—and intentionality—of this inner circle. The Young Turk tendency, as we have implied, was far from monolithic and, throughout the fraught period of its rule, even the Ittihad remained a conglomerate of groupings with 'different factions, loyalties and leaders'.[334] The prime movers had to go behind the parliament, and Cabinet, not to mention the vizier's back, to implement their agenda. And they had to confront, remove, or even eliminate high-ranking administrators on the ground who refused to play ball. Mann and Kaiser propose that as many as one-third were reshuffled in the main killing zones.[335] They even found themselves challenged in parliament for their anti-Armenian actions by none other than Ahmet Riza, the most prestigious, veteran, and arguably most uncompromisingly chauvinist of Ittihadists: though, one might add, not until 1917. Taken together this makes Dadrian's notion that the genocide was effectively an inner-party conspiracy sound all the more compelling.[336] If correct, it offers its own ultimate comfort, too: that only crazy, and, more specifically, ideologically crazy individuals do these sort of things.

By extension, making the most of Nazi parallels offers similar grounds for evasion. Many such comparisons *are* very pertinent. The use of railways for some of the deportations; the use of Armenian army battalions as little more than slave labour on major road and railway construction projects; the ciphers and linguistic euphemisms at which Talât excelled in order to expedite his secret killing orders; even the lurid Turkish medical experiments and vivisections on Armenian adults, pregnant mothers, and children in Trabzon and Erzindjan, to which Dadrian has sought to bring particular attention: all fall into this category.[337] Likewise, though from a rather different perspective, recent interpretation of the causation of the Armenian genocide has borrowed from functionalist thinking on the launching of the 'Final Solution', thereby more keenly priming an *Aghet* corollary to the intentionalist versus functionalist debate within Holocaust studies.[338]

However, CUP comparisons with the Nazis might be considered equally disturbing if they were to shed light on the degree to which the former (or indeed latter) were thinking and operating not so much outside standard progressive norms but, actually, very much *within* them. The CUP movers and shakers, for all their supposed pan-Turanism, saw themselves neither as fantasists nor fanatics but as radical progressives who were bringing *their* country into the light of modern day. One aspect of the party which is particularly noteworthy is the significant number of modern Tibbiye-trained medical practitioners who were either party founders or rose to senior executive ranks: men like Shakir, Nâzim, and Reshid. The last of these was firmly of the conviction that the problem with the empire was that it was diseased and thus needed the remedies which only a bacteriologist, or surgeon, could provide.[339] This sense that the country was like a body, and that only radical surgery could cure it, did not, however, just point to eliminating the extraneous elements which held it back or were perceived as acting as a slow but lethal poison from within. Taking the country forward also meant immunizing its poor and combating syphilis, malaria, and other diseases, not to mention eradicating the underlying social and economic illnesses which kept the peasantry exploited, impoverished, and uneducated. And who was the individual most associated with promoting these goals in the war years? Dr Shakir, the Ittihadist otherwise 'known as a humanitarian among Turks' yet also, arguably, the chief architect of the Armenian genocide.[340]

Nor were Ittihad's political, as distinct from social, aspirations in any sense off the modernist map. The fact that in 1915, or 1916, Ittihad amounted to a group of Turkish nationalists without a nation is immaterial. So, too, were the then promoters of the Czechoslovak, Yugoslav, and Ukrainian 'nations'. Yet within the next year or so, the Allies would be encouraging not only at least the first two of these but also (within an Ottoman Empire they were now blithely referring to as the Middle East) Arab, Jewish, and Armenian ones.[341] The fact that this clutch of so-called nations would have to be invented—and rather strenuously at that—does not seem to have deterred the Allied leaders, by this time with Woodrow Wilson first amongst equals, from pontificating on the rights of 'national self-determination'. Nor did it stop their Central Powers adversaries offering another clutch of national supplicants support where it suited them.

In this sense, the CUP, far from being at odds with a more general nationalizing tendency, was actually part of its self-professed avant-garde. One might even call it a vanguard party, but one committed not so much to rejecting—or for that matter even transcending, Bolshevik-style—the international hegemonic system as given, but rather to finding a way to punch their way through to an equality of status and respect within it. What did make the CUP unusual was the fact that they were attempting this nation-state building project from within a still existent imperial state. Looked at from this angle, there is indeed something quite astonishing—and very frightening—about not only the embryonic post-1910 formulation of the demographic programme of Nâzim and others, but also their determination to forge ahead with it, even under the most extreme and emergency conditions. Even here, however, we need to be wary of seeing these inherently inhuman elements of the CUP agenda in terms of complete exceptionality. The Ittihadist drive to replace a multilayered, segmentally organized, and heterogeneous polity with a centralized, monocultural, and homogeneous one was founded on the same basic imperatives that drove their upstart Balkan neighbours in their genocidal-style war-cum-ethnic cleansing of 1912 and 1913. This was also true for the post-1919 state elites of the 'New Europe', the only difference being that while they might have endlessly articulated and discussed the same nationalizing imperatives it was not until during or after the Second World War that they attempted to *maximally* implement them. By the same token, the reason why Talât today is denigrated on the world stage (though hardly in Turkey itself) while his successor, Kemal, is lionized, has less to do with the scale of their genocidal actions (*pace* that Talât's were worse) and more to do with the different contexts in which each tried to implement his respective but hardly dissimilar Turkish national programme.

And so, finally, to the relationship between idea, context, and actualization. Critical to emergent Turkish nationalism as propounded by Ittihadists and Kemalists alike was that it was founded in reactive mode. In part, this came through an almost adulatory desire to emulate the *strength* of the West, for which other forms of traditional people-solidarity, notably Islam, seemed unable to provide sufficient competitive tender. In other, perhaps more critical ways, it seemed to offer the *only* remaining instrument with which to defy Great Power humiliation, violation, and subjugation of Ottomania, and thereby reassert what remained of state and societal autonomy and integrity. From there on in, Turkish nationalism could begin formulating a plan for how to get even with those who had brought about this situation. The problem was there was no time—as Gökalp famously intoned—for standing still and philosophizing.[342] Operating instead on a continual emergency basis the CUP fatefully took the country again to war in 1914, in something akin to a national version of Trotsky's permanent revolution. In so doing, however, they not only, this time, brought to the fore the dichotomy in their relationship to the Dashnaks—the other major, nationally politicized group of Anatolians—but, in the process, wrenched the CUP's original homogenizing project away from its essentially anthropophagic intentions towards something wholly more catastrophic.

The Dashnaks, as we have suggested, in many respects were politically akin to the CUP. However, in other social and economic respects, *Armenians* writ large, represented to nationalizers—and especially proponents of the *milli iktisat*—the very model of what was fundamentally wrong, indeed sick, in the Ottoman body politic. Above all, Armenian success, or more exactly outward profile, was too closely bound up—correctly or incorrectly—with the concessionary regime imposed upon Ottomania by the West. It might inspire in nationally minded Turks a desire to achieve the same but it was much more likely to elicit jealousy, resentment, and wholesale fury that this population of *dhimma* was not simply making good on the terms set by the *frangi*—the foreigners—but doing so at their expense. Latent Turkish hatred of the Armenians was thus a very complex animus. It entailed, indeed, a form of schizophrenia: as if, on the one hand, one was berating a wayward member of one's own family who had broken all the codes of correct family conduct and, on the other, was constantly being left speechless by an alterior awareness that this was not in any sense a family member at all but a changeling who did things in radically different—and unacceptable—ways, and over whom, in practice, one had little or no control on account of the 'diplomatic immunity' sign over his front door. Moneymaking plus political insolence thus (not only for Turks) contravened the terms of Armenians' supposed subordinate and passive status under Ottoman Islamic law and moreover had a potency which seemed to derive wholly but illegitimately from the *frangi*. Akçam has made the sobering point that, unable to get back at the Western powers who had put them in their own subordinate situation, the Turks 'cast about for weaker groups upon whom they could vent their hatred'.[343] In the hysteria-prone and—in Turkey— apocalyptic conditions of war, that this hatred might fall in double measure on the Armenians should hardly surprise.

The other equally problematic side to this equation, however, is the behaviour of the Armenian nationalists. In 1932, Hans Kohn, a leading avant-garde historian of nationalism, charged that 'the Great Powers made use of the Armenians as a wedge to drive into the body-politic of the Empire and to weaken it. The Armenians were victims of that policy'.[344] But one might add that, in this process, their own radical elites, too, played an unconscionable role, willing on the carve-up of empire and anticipating an internationally mandated solution to the 'Armenian question' of which they would be chief beneficiaries. Turned on their head, it was exactly such prognostications which enabled Talât, Shakir, and the others to convince themselves that the Armenians were not only signing their own death warrant but entitling the CUP to sequester a community's entire financial assets so that their *own* elite-led, national developmental goals might finally and belatedly be realized. Was this an economic short cut to political catch-up with the West? Or was it actually a cruder justification for robbery by murder in the interests of an aspiring *national* bourgeoisie? Conveniently, nearly all the major recipients of this asset-stripping exercise were friends and nominees of the CUP.[345]

One might proffer that all that was needed in these circumstances was a charge of stab-in-the-back treason to light the match, to set the explosive fuse. The fact that the mine situated in east Anatolia happened to blow apart nearly all the Syriac communities of the region too rather suggests how jam-packed with explosive it was. For the victims, picking up the pieces after the event was indeed to prove a practically impossible task. Not that this was the end of the Ottoman sequence of ultra-violence—far from it, as we will see. But what 1915 had helped to catalyse was the zero-sum nature of what would, in future, be on the international table, even or especially as determined by the dominating West. The only post-Ottoman political units henceforth under consideration would be nation states. The Armenian nationalists, having failed to achieve one of these by way of Western imprimatur in 1920, found themselves faced instead with a treaty three years later between the new, self-proclaimed state of Turkey and the West in which:

> the absolute Turkish triumph, was reflected in the fact that in the final version… neither the word Armenia, nor the word Armenian, was to be found. It was as if the Armenian Question or the Armenian people themselves had ceased to exist.[346]

Talât, Enver, and the other leading CUP *génocidaires* were, by this time, mostly gone—dissipated to the winds, or gunned down by Armenian assassins for their sins. In place of them was Mustafa Kemal, the one who would anoint himself as Atatürk; in other words, the founder of Turkish national project stage two, ostensibly undiluted and without blemishes—one of which had been the Armenians. Kemal's great diplomatic victory at Lausanne in 1923 was, to a critical, a result of resurgent *Turkish* military success against the West and its cohorts. But it was to a further extent a matter of timing. Erasing the memory of the CUP era which had come before, Kemal could not only pretend that his national project had no predecessor, but at the same time profess that the wartime destruction of Armenians—of which *his* Turkey was the chief political and economic beneficiary—was entirely unconnected to the state-building about to commence.[347]

Kemal and his successors could reap the rewards from this sophistry in another way too. From now on Western politicians, businessmen, and scholars would come to Turkey's defence not only to proclaim the achievements of its progressive, modernizing regime but also to intone that what had happened to the Armenians had, after all, been for the best. As one American academic in the early 1950s could tersely—but entirely inaptly—summarize it:

> Had Turkification and Muslimisation not been accelerated by the use of force, there certainly would not today exist a Turkish Republic, a Republic owing its strength and stability in no small measure to the homogeneity of its population, a state which is now a valued associate of the United States.[348]

3

The First Crisis of the Rimlands

SETTING THE SCENE

Sovereignty is acquired by force, by power, and by violence.[1]
Declaration of Turkey's Grand National Assembly, November 1922

It is the state that makes the nation, not the nation that makes the state.[2]
Statement of Marshal Piłsudski

One by one the Central Powers, from late September through to early November 1918, sued for peace. Their defeat at the hands of the Western Allies, now with the USA much to the fore, carried with it fervent hopes from across the world that the inauguration of a new international order would lead to an era not only of peace but, with it, of justice. Early on in the new year, as preparations frenetically gathered pace for the Peace Conference in Paris, it seemed that a head of steam was building up to support these aspirations.

In mid-January, under the aegis of American secretary of state, Robert Lansing, the grand-sounding 'Commission on the Responsibility of the Authors of the War and the Enforcement of Penalties' began its proceedings. Geared primarily to bringing Germans and Turks found culpable of war crimes to book, its re-invoking of the 1899 and 1907 Hague Conventions on the 'laws of humanity', however, gave to it a potentiality for providing guidelines for international criminal law far into the future. 'Barbaric and illegitimate methods of warfare' might thus be its cover-sheet charge against the Central Powers—again with the Armenian massacres particularly in mind. That said, the initial report prepared by its sub-commission two months later was able to adumbrate a range of violations against civilian populations—systematic terror, murders, massacres, rape, deportation, forced labour, execution of civilians under false allegation—which might equally be understood as contravening universal standards of 'humanity and morality'.[3] It was as if an approximation of the Genocide Convention was being propounded at the end of the First, not the Second, World War.

Almost simultaneously, the first meetings associated with the founding of the League of Nations Covenant also convened in Paris. US President Wilson made early use of his prerogative as chair to propose a clause which would require state signatories to give freedom to all religious groups within their domains (with the notable proviso that no breach of 'public order or public morals' was involved).

In turn, this was given added value by the British diplomat and leading League enthusiast, Lord Robert Cecil, by way of his amendment requiring the League Council to respond to acts of 'religious persecution and intolerance' that 'endangered the peace of the world'. Soon after, Japanese delegate Baron Makino upped the human rights ante even further, when he proposed another clause, this one entitling all people, whether nationals or aliens, equal treatment within each respective League state, regardless of 'their race or nationality'.[4]

Both the Cecil and Makino initiatives demonstrated, as perhaps only such openly universalist propositions could, the very narrow boundaries within which the victors of 1919 *actually* saw themselves operating. The leaders of the West no more intended to box themselves in with political obligations that might require of them collective action outside the bounds of their own geostrategic or economic agendas than they sought to set up international juridical instruments which might one day rebound on themselves. As for the Japanese proposal, with its implicit glance at the West's racial barriers to non-white immigrants to their shores, this became the elephant in the room from the moment of its articulation. The overall consequence for the Peace Conference was inevitable: retreat on all fronts from the general to the particular, and with it from all abstractized notions of international society—let alone guarantees of *universal* security and justice—in favour of the real matter in hand: the defence and durability of a recast international system as won by a select group of the most powerful avant-gardist states, through the bloodiest of global wars.

Perhaps it is just as well that the early Paris Peace Conference debates on the future of humankind were essentially academic—and hence futile. Where Western power, expertise, and resources were most immediately needed in early 1919 was in combating and controlling soaring rates of contagious diseases, not least the lethal strain of influenza then decimating human populations worldwide. US relief efforts, under the broad aegis of Herbert Hoover, certainly played their crucial part by keeping millions of starving European and near-Europeans alive over the coming months and years. What Hoover was unable to prevent, however, was the microbial spread of disease in the first place, the key vector of which was the movement of a vast flood of humanity—the great majority of them refugees—fleeing or attempting to flee from east to west.[5] That reality brings us to the fundamental issue at stake in this chapter, and so to the deep gulf between the rarified, if of themselves repeatedly fractious, deliberations of the Big Three in Paris and the ongoing potential for genocide. The armistices had not, in practice, brought war to a termination in the rimlands. On the contrary, the end of the 1914–18 conflagration did not even represent a pause in the escalating tempo of violence then being visited on these vast regions. The only difference now was that its agents wore different uniforms, or none, and, indeed, acted on behalf of a myriad of competing national or anti-national forces, where previously there might have been—in any one theatre of struggle—only two imperial ones.

At the epicentre of this new reality was the implosion of the whole edifice of the Austria–Hungarian Empire in a matter of weeks, from late October 1918, effectively leaving a sort of political tabula rasa to be filled by whoever, in any given locale, had the nearest thing to a monopoly of violence. The collapse of the dual monarchy's territorial coherence, and with it of its discrete international boundaries, also ensured that political and social chaos here blurred into a further zone of uncertainty across the old frontier with what had been tsarist Russia, itself already reeling from a year of revolutionary and counter-revolutionary turmoil. Indeed, in the early months of 1919 practically the entirety of the rimlands from the Baltic in the north, to the Balkans in the south, to the Caucasus in the east and encompassing both 'Lands Between' and much of Anatolia in its central belts, had become one giant shatter zone. As if our tectonic plate had finally been so violently wrenched from its unstable moorings that nobody quite knew where it had come to rest.[6]

What ensued was a gigantic battle to impose some semblance of order over this entire arena. Viewed in suitably Manichaean terms this might be seen as one fought out between two dominant contenders: on the one hand, the peacemakers in Paris; on the other, their constant incubus, the Bolsheviks.[7] However, it was not this dialectic—this proto-version of the Cold War—alone which helped amplify the danger to already vastly exposed rimland peoples and communities. The Western effort to shore up the sequence of shattered fault lines and at the same time create an effective western barrier or, as the French premier, Clemenceau, put it, a 'barbed wire curtain', against the Bolsheviks,[8] was necessarily highly improvised but was still founded around certain *nationalized* premises as to what the 'New Europe' entailed. Why the new or reframed states of the East, and indeed Middle East, were assumed to follow these given contours and not others, may be sufficiently pertinent to our analysis as to demand further consideration, which we attempt as an aspect of Chapter 4.

Nevertheless, in 1919 the 'problem' of what would become of the vast swathes of peoples who having been de-imperialized were insufficiently readily repackable as members of nation states, was sufficiently serious and immediate for the Paris peacemakers to attempt to find a stop-gap solution. That the solution offered was the Minorities Treaties, an ad hoc series of bilateral treaties signed by each of the new or reformulated states as a form of codicil to their international recognition as sovereign entities within the League, seemed to signal a Western awareness of, and commitment to, protecting the most vulnerable ethnic and religious communities within the rimlands.[9] Yet if this provides us with a potentially positive starting point as to how the new post-1919 liberal order sought to identify and then counter states with persecuting agendas, or worse, our chapter concludes with another international agreement: that of Lausanne in 1923, which unequivocally gave Western imprimatur to the notion of compulsory 'exchange'—actually eruction—of 'minority' peoples from their indigenous hearths to some other entirely alien 'homeland' to which they were supposed—quite spuriously—to belong. Both sets of treaties, those of 1919 and 1923, were arrangements implicitly designed to prevent what later would be called 'genocide'. The paradox is that the four-year slope from one to the other came, in critical part, as a result of continued Western efforts to extend hegemonic control over the rimlands, and, more exactly in this case, against the other major unsubdued adversary in the East (over and beyond the Bolsheviks): the Turks. Our penultimate section, 'Anglo-French overreach in the East', traces Western, more exactly British and French, Anatolian adventures: their successful enlistment of Armenians and, more particularly, Greeks as proxies to their efforts, and consequences which were, at the very least, sub-genocidal.

These events in themselves offer a sobering reminder of the degree to which humanitarian good intentions were regularly sacrificed by the dominant powers to 'realist' ambitions. However, the dangers these ambitions carried in their wake were vastly amplified by Western dependency on rimland surrogates whose aims and methods bore notable resemblances to those of the Balkan predators of 1912–13. It is, again, part of the irony of the post-1919 situation that the West, unable to mobilize further human resources of its own to defeat Bolshevism, had little or no choice but to back regimes—whether pro-Allied and ostensibly liberal such as that of the Poles, or overtly revisionist and reactionary as in the case of Admiral Horthy's Hungary—whose similitude lay in their *militarized* ultra-nationalism. This not only provided international cover and military aid for these regimes but explicitly cut across guarantees of protection to 'minorities' either under the regimes' control, or likely to be so in the event of their territorial expansion. Worse still, throughout this crisis period decision-making and action was primarily in the hands of the most ruthless and impassioned defenders of these 'imagined' nation-cum-states: the men on horseback.

There was something else here, however, that cannot be marginalized from this examination: indeed, it is so central as to present us with a form of palimpsest over the primary text of the crisis. The struggle for control in the rimlands may have involved many players, each competing in overtly social-Darwinian terms for local-ized supremacy, but it was also, in its totality, intensely infused with anxiety about Jews. We have already emphasized in Chapter 1 the emerging potency of Judaeo-phobia as a political as well as psycho-social safety valve for Europeans unable or unwilling to confront their own Great War inner demons. The 'crude analysis' identification of Jew with a supposed Bolshevik alter ego not only now enabled the men on horseback to portray themselves as Eastern bastions of a Christian civiliza-tion on the point of being overwhelmed by this diabolic anti-system (or simply Antichrist) but, in turn, made the danger of direct physical violence to the already battered and traumatized Jewish communities of the rimlands all the more palpable.

If at the centre of this chapter, then, is the growing threat and actualization of mass anti-Jewish violence by anti-Bolshevik armies, especially Ukrainian and then Russian 'White', there is also the corollary and counterpoint of Bolshevik violence to be considered. The conspiracy-laden view of Bolshevism as 'Jewish' was, ulti-mately, a case of projective confabulation. That aside, Lenin and Trotsky's own con-scious militarization of both regime and society—war communism—was not simply in order to defend the revolution against those who were seeking to destroy it. It was unashamedly anti-systemic in its intentions—indeed, the revolution was read back to true believers not just as capitalism's *inevitable* but its *preordained* Nemesis. This certainty of mind and, with it, the actually explicit unction to carry out any act of violence, so long as it was authorized by the regime as a revolutionary act, is, again, something we need to explore further in the later, exclusively Soviet, Chapter 5. Here, in focusing on two Russian Vendées—the assault on Don Cossackry and the later, even more thorough, liquidation of the Antonov uprising—the aim is to provide some pointers towards a future, and, in some ways, uniquely Soviet, *genocide* trajectory, not least in the way social—as opposed to ethnic—formations might be collectively characterized as political threats, not to say abominations.

That a group such as Cossacks, or, for that matter, looking at our wider landscape, Anatolian Turks, might find themselves on a list of 'victims'—as opposed to 'perpetrators'—alongside more familiar Jews, Armenians, Greeks, Kosovar Albanians, or Caucasian Mountaineers—may suggest how the very attempt at incipient nation- and state-building across the as yet uncalmed fault lines of the post-imperial rimlands vastly exacerbated already toxic possibilities and potentialities. It hardly represents a consolation for those cut down in, or surviving the atrocities, of this period, that none reached the Richter-scale high point of the *Aghet* in 1915–16. What that might simply imply is the strongly contingent nature of the violence of 1917–23. Or, perhaps more pointedly put, of military men assuming the mantle of state leadership and decision-making, yet lacking the apparatus and resources of administrative support, let alone civil cooperation, to carry through systematic 'cleansings' of alleged communal dangers.

There is however, another possible—more structuralist—interpretation: not that the brass hats were out on a limb, but that they were actually representative of wider statist, political aspirations for dealing with irredeemable populations. In this sense, the sub-genocidal events had less of an ephemeral and more of a transitional nature; certainly constrained from a more complete delivery by resource weaknesses and ongoing social and economic turmoil, but at the same time indicative of where at least some of these new regimes—once suitably hardened and better organized—were heading in their longer-term agendas.

In which case, what we see being signposted in this crisis period are, on the one hand, an essentially Western-sponsored 'New Europe' system founded on nationalism, and, on the other, its Bolshevik antithesis. We also see that both are beginning to mark out their respective interwar coercive ground rules and discriminatory standards against intractable communal groups. Ironically, we have omitted from closer view here a third way—one which, in the upshot, would upstage all competitors in its fateful and unequivocally genocidal impact on the rimlands and their peoples. Like Soviet Russia, what would become Nazi Germany deserves further attention in a dedicated chapter. But as a point of departure for the unravelling of the immediate crisis we cannot but begin with the consequences of Germany's 11 November Armistice with the Allies.

ORDER VERSUS DISORDER

The jugular blow to Germany was delivered on the Western Front. The British and French generals had always believed this would be the upshot, their German counterparts conceding its truth when Ludendorff, in early October 1918, pressed

Wilhelmine Germany's last administration—that of the reformist Max von Baden—to negotiate with the Allies for peace terms. It is significant that it attempted to do so on the basis of Wilson's Fourteen Points: his January 1918 manifesto for a global peace founded on principles of liberal internationalism. Ludendorff's armies may have been facing defeat in the West but German expectations, by way of American adjudication, were still that the Bismarckian creation, as reformulated into a republic, 'would retain its great-power status and play its part in a reconstituted world order'.[10]

Such expectations were buoyed up by existential realities in the east. Here there had been no German defeat: on the contrary it had been the Kaiser's armies which had brought the West's Russian ally to its knees and forced its republican Bolshevik successors to bow to force majeure. At home a literally starving Germany may have been, by late 1918, on the verge of disintegration and revolution, as the impact of four years of British blockade drove its message home. Yet in the 'Lands Between' and, indeed, way beyond as far as the Caucasus, the terms of Brest-Litovsk were German terms and upheld in practice by German arms. If this Eastern reality was profoundly if not bizarrely contradictory for the Allies, it was made even more so by dint of the survival of the Bolsheviks in Petrograd. If the most serious threat to a Western-imposed settlement came ultimately not from the Germans but from this 'other' source—not just in terms of an advancing Red Army but equally through the Bolsheviks' own entirely subversive version of an internationalist peace (with far more radical and ostensibly populist signals than anything Wilson could offer)—who, then, was going to stand in their way? With only one Allied-led rimlands' force of any significance—that of Franchet d'Espèray, operating at this stage in the lower Danube region—entirely insufficient to the task,[11] and with Austro–Hungarian forces in meltdown, the only other *known* and *tried* troops with which to reliably keep order in the East, and, perhaps, if necessary, keep the Bolsheviks at bay, were the Germans. But if the Allies at this critical moment were to present Berlin—now actually Weimar—with peace terms which were clearly adrift from the spirit of the Fourteen Points then it was not inconceivable that the latter might make common cause with the Bolsheviks. And, if that was so, it would usher in Mackinder's nightmare: a new adversarial but doubly hegemonic sway across Eastern Europe that might completely wreck any anticipation of the West's new order.

The relationship between these geopolitical conundrums and the high-level Allied decision-making of early 1919 necessarily also had profound consequences for those rimland peoples who would be defined henceforth in the Western, non-Bolshevik sphere as 'minorities'. Nor were these consequences some marginalia to the main plot, but thoroughly embedded within it. In brief, to confirm German defeat in the West, and the denial of her victory in the East, and at the same time create, at the very least, a cordon sanitaire around the Bolsheviks, the Allies had to organize an improvisation little short of a conjuring trick. The Allied intention, of course—despite a common articulation by critics that what took place at Versailles was a Carthaginian peace—did not involve dismantling the Bismarckian legacy per se. The aim, however, was certainly to contain Germany politically and militarily which, according to balance-of-power theory, dictated that other *European* powers, over and beyond the obvious Western victors, would have to be brought into play in more than simply supporting roles. In classic Vienna Congress terms that would have entailed big, powerful states who were known quantities. The parties who traditionally fitted the bill were the dual monarchy, possibly Ottomania, most certainly Russia. However, on top of the fact that two out of three of these had been wartime enemies, by 1919 it was apparent that Austria-Hungary was history and the Allies had every intention of making Ottomania so, while Russia's future was so uncertain as to render her, at least for the time being, valueless if not downright counterproductive with regard to the task in hand.

Nor was there any obvious Plan B. The notion of creating a range of smaller states in place of large, defeated, imperial ones was not generally greeted in Allied chancelleries with enthusiasm. As late as August 1918 Robert Cecil stated in a Foreign Office memorandum, 'Whether a new Europe with two or three additional Slav states will be more peaceful than the old seems to me, I confess very doubtful'.[12] There had been those in wartime Britain, especially from the small but certainly very influential circle of intellectuals and experts in the 'New Europe' group, who had pressed for exactly such an aggressive territorial recasting, most particularly of Austria-Hungary.[13] But there were equally opponents, such as H. N. Brailsford, who formerly had been an enthusiastic partisan of the struggle for Balkan self-determination but was so shocked and disillusioned by the behaviour of the Balkan League that he read into any green light for the dissolution of the dual monarchy simply another invitation to 'half-crazed nationalists' to do their worst. Indeed, Brailsford's wartime proposals for a charter for the protection of linguistic and cultural rights of minorities, in the eventuality of such radical change to the European map, represents an early indication of some of the elite anxieties which were to be a critical background to the making of the Minorities Treaties.[14] The problem was that by the time of the Armistice neither of these lobbies, let alone the emissaries from the would-be autonomous nationalities themselves, were the ones determining the future shape of the European rimlands. High-level decision-making instead was essentially reactive, on the one hand to the implosion of Austria-Hungary; on the other, to the threat of the vacuum being filled either by the Bolsheviks, a still-to-be properly muzzled Germany, or even a combination of these two forces. In other words, the international imprimatur for the creation of the 'New Europe' was primarily dictated not by issues of national ethnography but by plain, political necessity.

In this, of course, there was a tremendous irony. While the Fourteen Points had carried no specific mention of the term 'national self-determination', this had, throughout the war years, 'dominated the vocabulary of propaganda and legitimisation among liberation movements and imperial powers alike'.[15] It was, moreover, doubly ironic that by 1918 it was not so much Wilsonian liberals who were making the populist running on this score, but the Bolsheviks. Not only had they enunciated, as part of their post-revolution pronouncements, the sovereign rights of peoples to freely determine their own futures, but they had also clearly gazumped comparable Western rhetoric on the matter by embracing reborn Muslim 'nations' in and beyond the Russian empire within this agenda.[16] They had further nailed their radical credentials to the mast of 'no annexations', something Western leaders could only pretend to do. Bolshevism's opportunistic seizure of the nationalist card thus further deepened the Allies' peacemaking dilemma. No longer were they faced only with the dilemma of how to create a durable peace—difficult enough in the circumstances; they also had to *appear* to do so as if it was in genuine response to demotic clamour: as if they were replaying Vienna 1815 but with the Jacobins not dead and buried but instead breathing down their necks.

In practice, the only thing the Allies could do was *not* offer genuine national self-determination, but only a rather disingenuous façade of it. This entailed giving endorsement to a series *of state-nations* whose legitimacy appeared to derive from 'a sense of ethno-cultural community' but, particularly in the cases of Yugoslavia or Czechoslovakia, only 'by stretching the definition of the latter to its limits—or beyond'.[17] That national rights themselves were not at the core of Allied concern in Paris, however, was made abundantly clear early on, as a consequence of the Czech seizure of the coal-rich territory of Teschen in November 1918. Here, according to the census of the former Austrian power in 1910, 'Czechs' were outnumbered two to one by 'Poles' while another considerable percentage of the population was 'German'. In other words, a classically mixed area of Central–Eastern Europe. Nevertheless, the Allies found in favour of the Czechs.[18] This, however, was not some one-off aberration. The power brokers repeatedly followed the same direction of travel wherever the issue at stake was the strategic viability, border defensibility, or territorial depth or of their Czech, Yugoslav, Polish, or Rumanian protégés. In the light of the Bolshevik and German 'threat' this clearly made political sense. But, paradoxically, it could only be achieved by replacing German militarism—the very thing the Western Allies had proclaimed they were fighting to end—by a conscious militarization of their proxies. And, more pointedly still, at the expense of all the ethnic and religious communities—national or decidedly non-national in their orientation—who now found themselves subject, but in no obvious sense party to, these self-proclaimed polities.

That this rapidly exposed some of these communities to tangible danger was highlighted by the leave the Allies gave to Czechs, Poles, and Rumanians, most especially the latter two, to extend their territorial range at the expense of the Germans, Hungarians, or Bolsheviks. The French, who were most vehement about the creation of a client-formed Eastern security system, were in the van of these developments. Their own grander plan to create a French-led super-force aimed at exterminating the Bolsheviks—strange, inverse resonances here of European coun-ter-revolutionary intentions in the early 1790s against Jacobin France—had to be drastically scaled down on account of its prohibitively high cost as well as spirited opposition from Wilson and the British prime minister, Lloyd George, who were both fearful of where it might all lead.[19] Yet no barrier or censure was put in the way by any of the Big Three as the Serbs made plain who was the master in the new Yugoslavia: enforcing their writ against insurrectionary Croat peasants, passive Bosnian Muslims, and truculent Kosovars by way of artillery bombardment, overt terror, and repeated atrocity.[20] Nor was anything but encouragement given for a

Rumanian invasion of Russian Bessarabia, on the one hand, or Hungarian Transylvania, on the other, given that both actions were deemed to be contributing to
the extirpation of Bolshevism.[21] As for the Poles, even while they prevaricated
over promised public announcements confirming their commitment to religious
freedoms and civil rights for non-Polish inhabitants, a Quai d'Orsay carte blanche
to them in early 1919 to invade both Lithuania and eastern Galicia—in the latter
case, as a stepping stone to crossing the former Austro-Russian border into the
Ukraine proper—elicited no immediate American or British countermand, or
attempt to halt Western military *matériel* bound for Warsaw.[22]

There was some further irony in all this in that many of the peoples most threatened by these developments would, in all probability, have found themselves both
more secure and more able to develop some modicum of communal autonomy
under an eastern pax Germanica. This is not a way of suggesting that German rule
in the East would have been benign. The key long-term goals of Brest-Litovsk were
the subordination of the mineral and agricultural resource base not just of the
immediate Russian rimland but practically the entirety of European Russia, in the
interests of a *Weltpolitik*-driven German state in alliance with its corporate business
cartels.[23] As German state-cum-empire in 1918 in effect meant Ludendorff and the
generals, the enactment of this new Eastern order would have been overseen and
supervised with an iron severity, as it already had been in the twilight months of
German rule in the East, not to say the previous three years of designated army
control in the Ober Ost.[24] And that particular experience suggested that draconian
controls, demographic reordering of the population, including migrant settlement
and deportations, as well as enforced labour to serve German infrastructural development, would have become a wider norm.[25] Yet—and it is a yet—the very nature
of this German intent, across such a vast swathe of ethnographically mixed rimland, dictated that the only way it might have been manageable for the long haul
would have been through *divide et impera*. In terms of an already partly nationalized population, that effectively meant reconceptualizing the human geography of
the region into smaller units, awarding territorial autonomy accordingly; also, in
so doing, hemming in big historically dominant groups such as the Poles, against
some of their weaker neighbours, Ukrainians and Lithuanians in particular; giving
a coherence to this programme by awarding all the various ethnic groupings, however small or large, some degree of national or cultural rights; and, finally, building
all these elements into a necessarily German-led federation. The German scheme
was no more nor less dictated by realpolitik than its Allied antithesis. It simply
had more possibility for maintaining a plurality of peoples within it than the
alternative.

Talking up that alternative, of course, one might conclude, as has one Eastern
European specialist, that the Western agenda 'still freed three times as many people
from nationally alien rule as they subjected to it'.[26] But, as we will more broadly
argue in Chapter 4, this is to assume as given that everybody in the rimlands
already saw themselves as a member of a nationality. Viewed more soberly, what
Western backing for the new state-nations in 1919 actually achieved was a situation
in which people who were not members of the now majority groups within them, or

who could not be easily submerged as such, became ipso facto '*foreign*'. Moreover, this was in a way that had rarely been the case under previous imperial systems, not to mention regardless of how many countless generations of those so designated believed the place they lived in to be their undisputed 'home'.[27]

The scale of the consequent human tragedy was immense. The peacemakers did not envisage or authorize mass deportations in 1919, as they would do in 1945. But for hundreds of thousands of Germans from Posen, West Prussia, or Upper Silesia, or indeed further afield from the Baltic, just as for equally large numbers of Hungarians from the now lost lands—as confirmed by the 1920 Treaty of Trianon—of Transylvania, the divided Banat, or the Vojvodina, the only logical recourse was flight to the residual 'homelands'.[28] Millions of dislocated people, of course, were already casualties of the Great War. Vast numbers of these, from 1919, found themselves literally 'stateless', a challenge in itself to a fledgling League of Nations, not least as with the multitude of new national borders came 'passport systems, alien registration and restriction rules'.[29] In short, what was emerging was the very apparatus by which the most hopelessly forlorn and impoverished human souls would either be kept out, very often even from their own erstwhile place of domicile, or prevented from moving on. With an overtly racial drawbridge also being firmly raised by the USA and the other 'Anglo' nations against poor migrants, not just from Eastern Europe but from anywhere outside a genetically north-European reservoir—and, of course, contra their own ostensibly laissez-faire rhetoric—the opportunities for flight for 'minorities' and hence for a continuity of migratory flow from overpopulated rimlands to the Neo-Europes—the crucial demographic safety valve of the fin de siècle—ceased forthwith.[30] This, in turn, emphasized the sheer number of those stranded within the new states which they had *not* loudly acclaimed. Indeed, an estimated one in four of the population of the 'New Europe'—some 25 to 30 million people—were believed to fall into the minority category,[31] in so doing confirming that the so-called 'nation states' to which they were subject were that in name alone. Significant among the irredentists—those who would be seeking the restoration of the former political authority over territories lost to a successor state—would be all the ethnic Germans and Magyars who had not joined the primarily middle-class and professional flight to Berlin, Budapest, or Vienna in the wake of Versailles and Trianon. But there were plenty of other peoples in the 'New Europe' who lacked even that solace.

*

While the danger of German minorities acting as a potentially destabilizing force in the 'New Europe' was one cause of anxiety for the Allied statesmen as well as the backroom planners of the peace treaties,[32] it was another minority in Paris which was uppermost in their considerations. The predicament of the Jewish rimlands might be described as an exquisitely agonizing one. As we have earlier suggested, the Jews were not the only ubiquitous Europeans, with a particularly strong though dispersed concentration in the 'Lands Between'. There were Roma too. We will note some of the comparative aspects of their situation in 'Anti-System Two', the final chapter in this volume. In 1919, there was one obvious difference: while the Roma were everywhere in the rimlands detested but politically submerged, the Jews were equally if not more detested but with a profile—real or alleged—which brought them quite literally to political centre stage. This was hardly, however, because the majority of Jews sought the limelight. With their strongest concentration in what had been Russia—more specifically in a Pale which now straddled many would-be states—being a considerable minority of 6 million within a big empire was, as one prescient commentator observed in 1917, much preferable to being 'a series of small minorities in many little countries'.[33]

In considerable part, this was a legacy of their historic Mercurian role as a middleman people. The elites of nationally minded states, once up and running, would be gearing themselves towards rapid economic development from a position of perceived backwardness. To get on the fast track meant doing what the Ittihadists already had proposed for Turkey: creating a truly national economy run by and for their *own* commercial and business class. The Jewish future in a country such as Poland was thus not simply bound to be compromised because the geographical range of business had been narrowed and limited by new national taxes and tariff borders. Over and beyond that, they stood to be dealt a mortal blow by the determination of the most nationalist elements in the political firmament—in this instance led by the rabidly anti-Semitic Roman Dmowski—to get the Jews out of Poland. And that determination was every bit as fervent as the exponents of *milli iktisat* intended for the Greeks and Armenians.[34]

If this was to be perceived as a straightforward issue of economic determinism, it would miss much of the point. Suitably *Polonized*, why could the Jews not become both vanguard and engine of Polish economic development? To which the answer was: *they were Jews*. Culturally and linguistically, the majority were very different from other peoples of the region—Poles or otherwise—while, religiously, they were not simply *not* Christians but, in Christological terms, their very antithesis. Encapsulating and assimilating Ukrainians, Lithuanians, or Belorussians into the fabric of Polish society was deemed by Dmowski-ites doable and ultimately necessary. The very idea that the same could be enacted with regard to Jews excited not so much derision as horror—how could one, after all, convert a 'subversive', 'alien' 'parasite' into an element of a 'healthy, strong body'?[35] Thus, when in July 1918 delegates of the Polish National Committee—the body authorized from late on in the war to speak in Allied capitals on behalf of a nascent Polish nation—proposed that the formula by which Polish claims to statehood could be reconciled with Jewish anxieties was 'equality before the law', the leading Anglo-Jewish interlocutor with the British Foreign Office, Lucien Wolf, correctly read it as a carefully prepared trap.[36] In fact, there was a small minority of Polonized Jews who would not have been disadvantaged by this seemingly innocuous invitation to citizenship. If legal equality, however, promulgated through laws and decrees, made Polish the only language of administration, law courts, school, and marketplace, and if, as seemed very probable, Sunday was decreed as a rest day, the vast majority of Jews—over two and perhaps as many as 3 million people, or up to 10 per cent of the overall population, depending on the eventual size of the country[37]—would find themselves unable to comply. Yet 'without any technical derogation from the principle of equal rights'.[38]

These seemingly theoretical debates before the Peace Conference had got under-way mattered, because it had already been accepted by all belligerent parties, from 1916 onwards, that an autonomous Poland, in some shape or form, would re-emerge as one of its consequences.[39] But the argument also particularly pertained to Rumania, a post-Ottoman state with an already significant Jewish population, but one likely to grow if the secret wartime treaty of Bucharest with the Allies was to be enacted. This would have seen Rumania expand to more than double its pre-1916 size, encompassing huge numbers of non-Rumanian peoples, most sig-nificantly Magyars, Bulgarians, and Ukrainians, as well as additional—especially Hungarian—Jews.[40] The French green light for further Rumanian military advances in 1919 only served to highlight Bucharest's undiminished appetites. Yet ever since the Treaty of Berlin in 1878, when the country had received its international cre-dentials, Rumanian politicians had cleverly manipulated its constitutional laws as a tool to, on the one hand, proffer absolute compliance with Western notions of inclusive citizenship, yet, on the other, debar the majority of its Jewish population from those rights on grounds that they were 'aliens'.[41]

With a British-backed Jewish national home in Palestine also an item of Great Power discussion in Paris, the Polish and Rumanian diplomatic position appeared to be further bolstered. If East European Jews already had not only a nationality but a home to which to go, the argument was simple: let them go there. Counter-arguments from mostly Zionist-orientated Jewish delegates in Paris that the new states should recognize Jewish national councils as the authentic voice of the Jewish populations within their boundaries; that this ought to involve providing a demo-graphically proportionate element of state resources for autonomous Jewish devel-opment; and that, over and beyond this, the councils represented an intended, internationally recognized worldwide Jewish parliament,[42] simply compounded the assumptions of East European leaders that the Jews qua Jews were intent on undermining the integrity, viability, and long-term stability of their envisaged states. The fact that, from a rimland Jewish perspective, the notion of national autonomy might have been a logical defence against statist anthropophagic or, more likely, anthropoemic tendencies directed against themselves, was increasingly lost, particularly on Polish and Rumanian leaders, who, on the contrary, believed they were witnessing the unfolding of a Jewish conspiracy *against them*.[43]

The charge was doubly ominous because it fed into both a broader and alto-gether more sinister accusation: that the Jews were not simply party to, but first cause of, the Bolshevik menace. It was easy enough in the spring of 1919 to make the equation. Béla Kun's regime had taken over in Hungary—and other emerging communist parties in Central and Eastern Europe, the Polish one included, were conspicuous by the Jewish backgrounds of many of their leading cadres. And with nothing in the continuing post-war climate of fear to dampen down that more deep-rooted European neurosis that what mattered about Jews was not whether they were socialists or capitalists but that *all* were intertwined in their inherently rootless, cosmopolitan animus against the nations, it became an almost logical next step to conclude that Bolshevism's declared internationalism had to be *Jewish*. Moreover, as we have suggested in the 'Blaming the Jews' section of Chapter 1, it was far from only Eastern European elites who were buying into this narrative. First reports of anti-Jewish disturbances in Poland and eastern Galicia, in the winter of 1918–19, had policymakers at the British Foreign Office rushing to make their own assessments. 'The Jews are determined to do everything in their power to prevent the foundation of a great and independent Poland', wrote one, while another sagely intoned: 'There is, I fear, some justification for the suggestion that Jews are the backbone of Bolshevism'.[44]

If such commentary represented a classic case of blaming the victims, there was, however, a different set of anxieties beginning to intrude into the Allies' high-level considerations of the situation. What if reports of widespread attacks on Jews in Poland and elsewhere proved to be correct? Worse, what if the attacks really started getting out of hand? With the Peace Conference in full swing, news in early April that soldiers from the Polish Fifth Division had lined thirty-four Jews up against the wall of the Russian Orthodox church in Pinsk and executed them, caused a veritable and very public outburst of grass-roots Jewish protest in Western capitals. Ominous in the reports of the massacre was evidence that those killed—actually members of an entirely non-threatening Jewish food distribution committee—were assumed to be Bolsheviks.[45] Western concern to mollify the protesters led to the dispatch of first a US, then a British, commission of enquiry, both led by prominent Jews; in the former case, Henry Morgenthau.[46] Reports of widespread Polish anti-Jewish violence, primarily perpetrated by the army and gendarmerie, however persisted. In May, a story that 2,000 Jews had been massacred in Vilna—inaccurately as it turned out—led Wolf to commit to his private Peace Conference diary his fear that the Poles were set on 'a deliberate attempt to thin out the Jewish population—by massacre'.[47]

Was it the reports of massacres, combined with the embarrassment of the public protests which finally forced the collective hand of the Big Three towards a review of the whole minorities question? Or was it more than that: some niggling doubt that 'the Jews'—Bolsheviks or not—were simply too critical, powerful, and dangerous a force, and that their situation in the 'Lands Between' could no longer be simply put to one side in the making of the peace?

A sense that Jewish power was behind actions inimical to the new states was taken as a given by most Eastern European diplomats. Within days of the armistice—as the first reports of Polish disturbances had begun to appear in the Western media—Balfour, on behalf of the Allies, issued a press statement containing a barely veiled warning to all of the new polities that the continuation of acts inimical to 'order and civilisation' would close off future Western loans.[48] During the Conference itself, further rumours circulated that Jewish bankers would retaliate against Polish disturbances by blocking the country's access to Western credit.[49] While new state diplomats might, more keenly than ever, see these developments as evidence of high-level Jewish sabotage—and fulminate accordingly—it was the same alleged evidence of Jewish power which had them quite regularly interceding with American and British Jewish delegates in Paris on matters of territorial boundary disputes before the Big Three—on the assumption they would be accordingly well-positioned to influence the outcome in their favour.[50] Not unlike the tsarist government's chop-logic calculations in 1915, on how to elicit Western financial aid, it may well have been that Warsaw, in 1919, attempted to put the brakes on specifically anti-Jewish violence for similar reasons.

All this was highly ironic. Jewish lobbyists, like Wolf, had some limited contact with the officials of the main Allied delegations but, despite months of urging on them the need for a specific minorities clause in the peace treaty, had had no prior success whatsoever. Whatever it was which finally galvanized the peacemakers to set up a specific committee of experts on the matter it came extremely late in proceedings, and carried little sense of having been properly appraised in advance. Wilson's own original idea of a universal minority clause to be included in the League Covenant was already dead and buried. The remit of the New States Committee, as created by the Big Three at the beginning of May, was, as its title implied, to limit itself to new states only, and to complete a Polish model minorities statute in time for the Versailles Treaty to be enacted with Germany, as scheduled for signing on 28 June. All this further underscores the extraordinarily on-the-hoof nature of the exercise.

Nevertheless, the Polish template was a significant milestone, if for no other reason than the fact that it did cut across notions of unfettered state sovereignty. In all likelihood, it was this symbolic aspect of the proposed treaty, more than its actual small print, which led to the staging of a diplomatic 'revolt' by all the leading 'New Europe' leaders in a secret plenary session of Allies and protégés at the end of May.[51] Paderewski, Brătianu, Trumbić, and Kramař—for the Poles, Rumanians, Serbs, and Czechs respectively—each and every one objected for the very reason that obligations were being imposed on them, and them *alone*. And, in that respect of course, they were absolutely right. As Sir James Headlam-Morley, the British delegate and one of the key drafters of the treaties put it in his own Peace Conference diary, these were 'definite exceptional cases' and in no circumstances would have applied to a state such as his. By implication, this would have given the League of Nations 'the right to protect the Chinese in Liverpool, the Roman Catholics in France, the French in Canada, quite apart from more serious problems, such as the Irish'.[52]

Conversely, however, could one not argue, following Headlam-Morley's own line of reasoning, that the application of these requirements only in respect of 'a new or immature state of Eastern Europe or Western Asia',[53] was as an enunciation of the West's determination to defend the rights and integrity of ethnic and religious groups against the possibility of persecution, or worse, genocide, by the states mostly likely to commit them? A Genocide Convention *avant la lettre*? The Minorities Treaties sought to guarantee to all inhabitants of the new states a 'full and complete protection…without distinction of birth, nationality, language, race or religion'.[54] In addition to ensuring their equality of citizenship rights, the recognition in further clauses that these states did indeed include racial, religious, and linguistic minorities, and that these were entitled to develop and manage their own institutions, schools in particular, suggested a quite definite Western acknowledgement, too, of the anthropophagic threat. The Treaties thus, at one and the same time, attempted to secure minority communities in the lands of their birth, with the same rights as members of other majority communities, and—albeit within quite strictly defined, primarily educational parameters—*further* rights to autonomous self-development. It was one of the Conference's 'notable'—even 'unprecedented'—innovations, and, as Zara Steiner has put it 'an attempt to expand the existing fabric of internationalism'.[55]

The problem is that this upbeat rendition rings hollow. Effectively a primary set of powerful states telling a secondary set of weaker ones how to behave with regard to a tertiary set of largely powerless communities, the proposition only made sense if the first tier—those with the big stick—were prepared to use it. In principle, having created both a Minorities Commissariat and Permanent Court of International Justice under League auspices, the war's victors had created a streamlined transmission belt by which aggrieved minorities could seek redress against treaty violations without recourse to the Great Powers themselves but, instead, through an impartial and entirely depoliticized legal mechanism. In practice, the model treaty-makers had studiously avoided giving its enforcement clauses any real efficacy or teeth: so much so, thought Pablo de Azcárate, the first director of the League's Minorities section, that if that body had not strenuously acted to 'create a right of petition for both states and minorities, then the whole document might have become a dead letter'.[56]

The reason for a conscious dilution of the Treaties' powers, however, was an obvious one: they were an anomaly. In terms of geopolitics, they were so because the aim in Paris, in 1919, was to provide for a durable, hegemonic peace, not an ethnic one. Or, to put it only slightly differently, realpolitik in the face of a potentially resurgent Germany and an imminently threatening Bolshevik Russia determined that Allied support for strong, large, rimlands' states precluded anything which in practice denied those states their freedom to do pretty much as they chose within their own domestic borders. Underlying this, though, was something more fundamental as to the nature of Western political philosophy. If, neither by complete intention nor by design, the victors had created a 'New Europe' of national states, conglomerate or otherwise, the settlement was underpinned by the premise that in each of these new states citizenship and nationality were indivisible, just as was the case—since the French and American revolutions—in the West itself. As such, there could be no official truck with the notion that an individual or communal identity might operate on two different tiers, any more than—to take one issue much debated among the treaty-makers—creating a notional Jewish nationality in a British Palestine could be deemed consistent with the recognition of Jewish national rights in a territorially sovereign Poland.[57] Any deference to the idea that sub-nationalities might have some special dispensations within any given state was thus deemed entirely provisional. Indeed, the only purpose of the minorities arrangements was, according to Alfrânio de Mello Franco, the Brazilian League rapporteur on the subject, at a League Council session in December 1925, 'to prepare the way...for the establishment of a complete national unity'.[58]

The fact that, in the interim, new states had no choice but to accept terms and conditions as determined by their patrons hardly prevented them from feeling anything but slighted, or indeed from giving voice to it by roundly blaming the Jews. It was Jewish lobbyists, after all, who had *appeared* to play the key role in instigating moves towards the creation of the New States Committee, rather unfortunately reflected in two doubly anomalous clauses of the finalized model treaty, which specifically mentioned Jewish rights. Whether being the centre of attention and primary cause for concern in an international statute was a restraint upon or an incitement to anti-Jewish violence in the 'New Europe' is a moot point. Certainly, none of the major powers had any intention, in practice, of seriously bringing offenders to book in the event of some gross treaty violation. But then none of the new states, in 1919, could be quite sure of that. Beyond the edge of the Treaties' remit—as one headed east, into lands which had been the domains of the tsars—the question was entirely academic.

RENEWED MILITARY ONSLAUGHT AGAINST THE JEWS

It was another irony that Western concentration on, and attempts to quell, the anti-Jewish violence perpetrated by the Polish military in the process took attention away from actually much more serious anti-Jewish atrocities committed in the same period in the Ukraine and southern Russia. There were two obvious reasons for this marked discrepancy: firstly, while the Polish centre held in the face of warfare and external threat, the Ukraine plummeted into an 'advanced state of social and political fragmentation'.[59] Secondly, the Ukraine was, in every sense, off the Western cognitive map anyway. In the chaotic conditions of 1919 this, combined with its inaccessibility and further notable breakdown of communications, not to say the dangers of reporting from there, ensured little short of a media blackout. Where reports on what was happening reached the Western press at all, they were usually months late and came in garbled form. The British 'Samuel' report on the Polish anti-Jewish violence was able to arrive (correctly or incorrectly) at a specific number—348—of Jews killed between late 1918 and summer 1919.[60] In Russia, more specifically in the Ukraine, the figures for Jewish deaths in mostly military pogroms range from 60,000 to 150,000.[61] In other words, nobody knows exactly how many died. However, a British Foreign Office official in 1920, referring to the efforts of one leading perpetrator, could quip, 'Grigoriev in the Ukraine killed more Jews in a single day than the Poles killed the whole time'.[62]

This should diminish neither Polish behaviour nor its significance for the wider incidence and morphology of post-war anti-Jewish violence. There was particularly in the transitional weeks around the Polish declaration of sovereignty on 11 November 1918, a wide spate of attacks on Jewish persons and property in major urban centres in which a wide range of Polish participants seem to have been involved. More alarmingly, outside reports of these events repeatedly refer to widespread Polish rejoicing at news of the pogroms.[63] In fact, the main cluster of really serious massacres occurred in the contested eastern borderlands (the *kresy wschodnie*), beyond the Bug and Niemen, from late 1918 through to the period of the Bolshevik–Polish War of 1920. And almost all of these assaults were committed not by nondescript members of the population but by uniformed troops operating under Warsaw's command.

That said, we cannot presume that any of the atrocities were committed on Warsaw's *direct* orders. On one level, many show evidence of something much more generalized: the result of 'emotional arousal of tired and probably poorly trained troops with the news of defeat or impeding defeat, nervousness engendered by fear of an avowedly hostile population, panic precipitated by an incident involving firearms and the injury or death of comrades and finally anger, leading to an act of retribution or revenge disguised as military necessity'.[64] We can discern these ingredients time and time again in the range of rimland wars of 1918–20, and they certainly played a role in, for instance, the Pinsk massacre, as they did too in the assault on the Jewish quarter of Lwów—the first major Polish military action of its kind, in late November 1918, in which no less than seventy-three Jews and possibly many more were killed.[65] Interestingly, from the Polish side the assault was variously described as 'a punitive expedition'; military 'pacification'; 'exemplary punishment'; a 'reprisal'; and 'revenge'.[66]

But revenge for what exactly? It is worth pausing here for one moment to examine these events a little further. Two things are immediately striking about the Lwów pogrom. In the first instance, this was the same Lwów that, under its former imperial title, Lemberg, had been the scene of another very similar soldierly rampage and pyromaniacal looting spree through the Jewish district, back in the second full month of the 1914 conflagration. Then it had been the Russian army which was responsible, as it struck across the frontier claiming to have 'liberated' the provincial capital of eastern Galicia from the Austrians. The new Polish invaders, of course, were claiming their arrival to be a genuine act of national liberation. In this instance they were opposed not by Russians, but the Western Ukrainian National Republic (ZUNR), who, in Polish eyes, were clearly not only an entirely illegitimate, upstart entity but had had the effrontery to appropriate an authentically Polish city. Which begs the question again: if it were the Ukrainians (Galician or otherwise) who were the enemy, why was revenge being taken out on the city's Jews?

The conundrum may take us to the very heart of the anti-Jewish violence across the rimlands' old imperial frontiers, and diverse, warring camps. A straightforward answer—by way of events in Lwów—might direct us to the existence of an independent Jewish militia, which, in turn, was operating on behalf of the regional branch of a Warsaw-centred Jewish national council, and which—according to the Poles—was collaborating with ZUNR against themselves. In other words, the Jews were not innocent bystanders who had had the bad luck simply to be caught in the crossfire, but were an adversarial party in their own right.

Certainly, it was true that regional Jewish groups had, at this juncture, tolerably good relations with both ZUNR in Lwów and the Directory in Kiev: the latter claiming to speak for Ukrainian independence on Russian soil. The same was also true of the embryonic Lithuanian parliament, the *Taryba*, which was simultaneously in bitter conflict with the Poles for control of Vilna. Positive Jewish interaction with these national movements is hardly surprising. Both Lithuanian and

Ukrainian leaderships had publicly declared their willingness to support Jewish national autonomy and to foster that development through Jewish participation in their administrations.[67] However, no less than with other would-be governments seeking recognition from the Allies, this certainly involved a standard calculation. Politically weak, not to say militarily beleaguered by enemies on all sides, both Lithuanians and Ukrainians saw the Jewish card as vital in their efforts to gain the ear of—and, with it, tangible support from—the West.[68]

Yet it was exactly such calculations—in themselves founded on an extraordinary misreading based on the *imagined* role of the Jews in the world—which represented such danger to *real*, corporeal Jews in an already highly unstable rimlands context. In actuality, the Jewish national councils were seeking to maintain, as far as they conceivably could, the integrity and safety of their communities, no more, no less than other self-styled national entities in the shatter-zone arena. The councils attempted to do so, in principle, by declaring a neutrality in the wider territorial struggle. The fact that, in practice, this began to fray round the edges as their militias began to be drawn into the street fighting, often in between the other contestants, should entirely disabuse us of any notion that Jews qua Jews had any power or influence with which to manage or manipulate the outcome of the struggle in favour of one side or the other. On the contrary, the ultimate inability of the militia to defend Jewish Lwów underscores how far this was from the truth. Yet, for the other contestants, it was exactly this truth which was the first casualty on so many repeated occasions when they were brought face to face with the concrete limitations on their *own* expectations. Instead, it was the Jews who had failed or *betrayed* them. And hundreds of Jewish urban and rural communities, most particularly in what once had been the historic frontier lands of the Polish imperial *kresy*, were now to pay the price.

Nothing quite like this had happened to Jews in terms of mass exterminatory violence for the best part of three centuries: not since the great anti-Polish uprising led by the *hetman* Khmelnytsky in 1648.[69] Was it coincidence that it was the main zones of violence, in eastern Galicia, Volhynia, Podolia, Zhitomir, and further east towards Kiev, which, in 1919, would again be the primary Jewish killing fields? And which again would erupt into repeated incidents of grass-roots anti-Jewish violence in 1939 and, more particularly, the summer of 1941? Was this evidence, in fact, that of all the 'Lands Between' this was the 'hot' inner core: the area with the most extreme predisposition towards anti-Semitism? The one, moreover, with a Cossack-inspired and sometimes led peasantry, who were, in the main, ready and willing to actualize their hatred in the most gut-wrenching of physical assaults?

There is no doubt that Ukrainian peasants, with or without a Cossack *hetman* to incite them, were a key factor in this new Jewish *khurbn* (catastrophe). But then, where assaults specifically on Jews began and more general looting, destruction, and murder ended is less easy to discern. The area, after all—claimed originally by the Rada in 1917, and now by the Directory, as an independent state of Ukraine—was nothing less than a war zone, where all central authority had broken down or ebbed away, leaving the rural masses to their own devices for security, or permitting strongmen and self-styled warlords of the ilk of *hetman* Grigoriev to fill the vacuum. There was, of course, the Ukraine's scratch army under the Directory's own strongman, Symon Petliura, but its inability to maintain even the capital Kiev under regime control—it changed hands during the course of the 1918–20 struggle, according to the writer Bulgakov, 'precisely fourteen times'[70]—is indicative of just how far the Directory's writ ran. Lawlessness, thus, was endemic, and Jews, either as property owners or in their own persons, were bound to suffer alongside other parts of the population.

This, however, is not a sufficient explanation. There was a definite specificity to the anti-Jewish attacks, just as there was a broader inability to staunch their flow, whether on the part of the avowedly socialist Petliura,[71] or the committedly anti-*pogromshchik* anarchist peasant leader Nestor Makhno, operating in southern Ukraine.[72] The question is, was this recrudescent wave of violent anti-Semitism all-pervasive and, if so, does this account, on its own, for the huge incidence of casualties? One might argue, of course, that anti-Semitism amongst rimland peasantry, as among its governing elite, had *always* been an intrinsic aspect of the Russian *mentalité*. The year 1919 was no different, except for the extraordinarily unstable, life-threatening circumstances of imperial collapse, revolutionary turmoil, and counter-revolutionary challenge: in other words constant day-by-day uncertainty, which was bound to have the population at large reaching for some form of projective psychological release. The Jews, as always, were on hand for such scapegoating purposes, though this time doubly so, through their assumed identification with the revolution and the Bolsheviks in particular.

The potency of this equivalence—this *Żydokomuna* as it became known—was, however, founded on a deeper psychosis still, and bears some parallels with Turkish anxiety about the Armenians. Maintaining a semblance of state and societal order in the Ottoman Empire was dependent on the Christian population accepting their position as subordinate *dhimmi*, and hence not transgressing the normative political space of the ruling *umma*. In Ottoman eyes—whether Hamidian or Ittihadist—the Armenians' cardinal sin was exactly of this nature. By identifying themselves with foreign powers and inviting those same powers to intervene on their behalf against the integrity of the Ottoman polity, they had effectively violated the sanctity of Ottoman life and order as it was *meant to be*. The Jews in Russia had similarly transgressed, though in their case the sin was far more heinous, not to say irredeemable. Nobody spoke of an international Armenian conspiracy to turn everything on its head or everybody in range into malleable puppets whose only purpose in life would be to dance to an Armenian tune. The American sin had been in being in cahoots with outside forces who sought the destruction of civilization—as 'good' Muslim Turks understood it. The Jewish crime was in being *themselves* the actual and merciless destroyers—in this case of Christian civilization, the very heart of which, for all 'good' Orthodox believers, was Russia itself.

That this dread caesura—this breaking with normative time—had actually come to pass with the revolution and the ascendancy of the Bolsheviks, moreover, was instinctively understood by ordinary peasant folk. In southern Russia between 1918 and 1920 a hugely popular ditty did the rounds: 'Sugar is Brodsky's, Tea is Vissotsky's, Russia is Trotsky's'.[73] It sounds almost quaint but implicit in the words was the sense that a sacred order had been overturned. And that could only mean by the forces of Satan and the Antichrist. Peasants may not have articulated the case quite so colourfully but those who sought to lead them in an 'anti-Jewish crusade' knew exactly what, in their view, was at stake. Grigoriev, in May 1919, issued a proclamation in which he called for 'the overthrow of the foreigners from Moscow and the country where they crucified Christ'.[74]

A broader proclamation of Cossack *hetmany* reinforced the point with its specific exhortation to Christians—in the name of the great national saints—'to exterminate once and for all the diabolic Jewish vermin'.[75]

These ominous religious undertones took on an added piquancy in the spring of 1919 as reports began to circulate on White investigations into the assassination of the tsar and his family the previous summer. Ekaterinburg, where the killings had taken place, was far to the east of the rimlands, but in the first half of 1919 was under the control of Admiral Kolchak, the supreme commander of White forces in Siberia and the West's best hope for Bolshevik defeat. It was hardly a dilemma for Kolchak to have a special pamphlet printed for his troops entitled 'The Jews have killed the Emperor'; Kolchak at the time appears to have been constantly immersed in his favourite book, *The Protocols*.[76] But the notion that the Jews had murdered an imperial figure who, in traditional Russian iconography, was himself the subject of intense, even mystical veneration fanned not just the inevitable martyrological flames but was a reminder, for anybody who wished to embrace the symbolic connection, that the Jews had once before severed the cosmic order, when they had 'killed Jesus'.

What matters, however, is not that Kolchak or his immediate entourage believed all this but the degree to which it suffused the ranks of thousands of not just White officers but those in the wider counter-revolutionary movement across the rimland zones of conflict, both in Russia and beyond. We know for a fact that British officers, in the person of Sir Alfred Knox, head of the British military mission in Siberia and a close Kolchak confidante, as well as in the isolated Archangel and Murmansk commands, played critical roles in disseminating anti-Semitic hate literature both in Russia and Britain on the back of the tsar murder story.[77] The propaganda office, OSVAG, operating under the authority of General Denikin's Volunteer Army in the south—the other major military threat to the Bolsheviks—also worked overtime in producing similarly inflammatory literature.[78]

Beyond Russia, other senior military figures and their supporters were equally hard at work in a like vein. Particularly alarming for some Western observers was the linkage between the eastern Galician violence perpetrated by General Haller's army—which, in spring 1919, had been transhipped from the Western Front for active service in Poland—and Dmowski's party, the National Democrats (the NDs, or Endecja) of which Haller's forces appeared to be a willing tool.[79] *Żydokomuna* hysteria in Poland actually peaked the following year when, with the Red Army advance on Warsaw and Polish war minister Sikorski's appeal to his countrymen to fight the Jewish commissar-led 'Moscow gangs', the insinuation was developed through a gendarmerie-distributed poster campaign.[80] News that the Bolsheviks had formed a Polish Provisional Revolutionary Committee in Białystok in expectation of their victory in which, unsurprisingly, some veteran Jewish socialists were prominent, had the Polish episcopate weighing in with their own anti-Jewish proclamation, warning that this was the 'race' whose previous efforts at Polish subjugation 'through gold and the banks' was now being superseded by a slogan of 'People, Workers, Freedom'—none other than masks, of course, 'to hide the true goal'.[81] A year further on, despite the tide having firmly turned against the Bolsheviks, the Polish general staff were still obsessing on the same theme, commissioning one of their number, Lieutenant-Colonel Stanisław Laudanski, to offer an analysis. His response, entitled 'Genesis of the Jewish Soul', repeated the usual canard as to international conspiracy but with the added twist that it was the kindly aspects of 'Christian character' which were the weak link against a concerted Jewish effort to manipulate world opinion and so subjugate its peoples.[82]

In Poland's case, there were fortunately *some* countervailing tendencies. While the strongest statist threat to Polish Jewry came both during and after the battle for Warsaw—when Tukhachevsky's Red cavalry assault was parried and thrown back—it did not quite materialize. For a while things looked like they might turn extremely nasty. There were mass round-ups of Jewish *intelligenty*—not just left-wing activists—plus some 10,000 Jewish officers and soldiers who had volunteered to fight with their fellow-Poles on the Vistula, along with many Jewish nurses and doctors. All were interned in two concentration camps at Jabłonna and Dasie, where they suffered repeated indignities from notably anti-Semitic guards from Posen. A convoy returning some of those incarcerated to homes in the Lublin region, in the wake of the emergency, also met with a mysterious and unexplained railway accident, which left scores dead.[83] Conscious, however, of being under constant international scrutiny, both military and civilian authorities made efforts to rein in the potential for extreme violence, report on excesses, and punish malefactors.[84] Much of the most serious anti-Jewish brutality was meted out far from central control, especially, in 1920, under commanders in the *kresy*—including a Petliura belatedly allied with Warsaw—only very nominally under Polish command.[85]

Yet what is equally significant about Polish generals of the ilk of Haller, Michaelis, or Dowbor-Muśnicki, whom one can clearly identify as key perpetrators, is in the degree of anti-Jewish animus shared with their opposite German, Hungarian, Ukrainian, and Russian numbers. In other words, being on the winning side of the Allies did not preclude intense frustration at what they perceived to be roadblocks thrown in the way of the attainment of national state goals. Nor of the persistence of the Jewish conspiracy trope which went with it. Some of these commanders, such as Dowbor-Muśnicki, had formerly been members of the tsarist officer corps, a fact which elicits parallels with leading figures of the post-1919 Iraqi military and state apparatus who—like their Turkish friends and brothers-in-arms with whom they had graduated from the Ottoman Harbiye—invariably held the same anti-Armenian or anti-Syriac prejudices.[86] The anti-Jewish animus, however, clearly transcended the division between military victors and losers and was much more pointedly a transnational phenomenon.

Certainly, we can see its more feverish expression in the behaviour of officers and officer cadets from the defeated Central Powers. In Transdanubia, of at least 4,000 people killed in the Hungarian White Terror in the summer of 1919, an estimated 3,000 were Jews.[87] The death toll can be directly related to the efforts of the ultra-right Szeged movement, that is, officers committed to the liquidation of all revolutionary elements associated with the deposed Kun regime. Revolutionary, of course, could mean anybody considered suspect or deviant by the leaders of the self-appointed counter-revolutionary militias: working-class men, intellectuals, left-wingers of any hue, 'politicized' women too. In Hungary, as in Germany and residual Austria, at the end of the war it was from these groupings that officers returning from the fronts had not only their first direct confrontation with imminent upheaval but a taste of their own medicine. Threatened not only with an insolence and insubordination from hostile, unruly crowds they identified as composed of rank, foul-mouthed inferiors, they experienced too a visceral apprehension of danger to their own persons.[88] At this moment, a time-honoured, recognized, and sacralized order founded on a closely controlled and thoroughly gendered hierarchy of crown, church, and estate—which included the rituals of court and military ceremonial, the emblems of regimental flags and insignia—had simply been smashed, fouled up, trampled on. It was a world turned upside down.

The explanation, here in Central Europe, as further east, however, remained the same. Which may in turn explain why the use of extreme violence against Jewish civilians subsequently became a common mark of distinction among White 'counter-revolutionaries'.[89] Political Jewish women were notable targets, as in the beating and murder of Rosa Luxemburg during the January 1919 suppression of the Spartacist uprising in Berlin, and the use of captured female activists for target practice by members of the Bavarian Freikorps after the subsequent crushing of the brief Munich *Räterepublik*.[90] As the Central European White militias struggled to regain both the streets of their cities and contested inner European borderlands, the sense of a common, cross-border solidarity and purpose amongst military officers and their acolytes became quite palpable. There were concerted clandestine, if ultimately abortive, efforts to create an ultra-right 'community of interests', a coalescence of the parties of national German, Austrian, and Hungarian defence, in which the names of senior military figures—not least Ludendorff, Max Bauer, and Horthy—bulked large.[91] Nor was there overt Allied opposition as such to the anti-Bolshevik leanings of these groupings. The Magyar militias' preparation of their revenge against the Kun regime under Rumanian protection, for instance, effectively went ahead with the say-so of Franchet d'Espèray.[92] When it came to the matter of the peace treaties, of course, the lines separating wartime Allied victors and their revisionist adversaries were clear-cut. This, in turn, might underscore why it was the officer class of defeated and humiliated states that was so utterly infused with a rage at those they charged with having delivered the stab in the back.

Freikorps, Heimwehr, and Magyar militia, as a result, might seek to cleanse their national sanctums of those who had violated them, and during 1919 and the following turbulent years would be responsible (in or out of uniform) for a spate of ritualized murders and assassinations in which high-profile political Jews, or those considered tainted by them, were prime targets. But the framework of the Allied peace also critically constrained and restrained the sort of blanket vengeance in the European heartlands which these self-appointed national guardians sought to enact. The 'day of reckoning',[93] of which so many of them spoke, would have to wait. Anti-Jewish passions in post-war Central Europe did not translate at this moment into full-scale genocide.

*

In areas of Russia under the sway of White generals, however, opportunities for retribution were of an entirely different order. There were again practical limitations of note. The nature of the civil war struggle meant that White authority in those parts of Russia not controlled by the Bolsheviks remained tenuous, not to say ephemeral. Moreover, the ability of the generals to maximize the resource potential of often vast regions remained pitifully weak and largely depended on non-Bolshevik but mostly leftist parties to supply the necessary cadres for administration. These factors in themselves ensured that anything quite as systematic as the exterminatory selection and/or incarceration of discrete but dispersed elements of the population was out of the question. A mass cull of Jews could only be accomplished in situ in the war zones, and by direct military methods. This again, however, raised complications—not least as the Whites' aspiration to an undivided Russia remained dependent on Western diplomatic, financial, and material support. An early indication was the appointment of Mackinder as high commissioner for southern Russia.[94] There could be no doubt that open Jewish massacre in the region would arouse Western censure. Paradoxically, however, the stored reservoir of specifically anti-Jewish resentment waiting to explode within the officer corps was, in 1919, closely if tortuously intermeshed with the legacy of Russia's wartime failure. Back in 1915 Stavka's own absurd, not to say risible, assessment of Jewish blame for the emerging military disaster—and the reckoning with the Jews which it had sought to deliver—had been held in check in significant part by a Russian civil government with its own bizarrely erroneous calculation of the adverse effect this would have on an Allied camp in thrall to Jewish power.[95]

Now, with generals as opposed to civilians in the ascendancy in the White camp, the possibilities for the open season which had been stymied in 1915 were given added impetus by the very nature of the life-and-death struggle with the Bolsheviks. It is in the connecting threads between Stavka's half-finished punishment of rimland Jewry and an emerging 'never again' resolve, four years on, on the part of a substantial element of its cadres to finish the job, that we have grounds for seeing a continuity of genocidal process. In other words, this was not a case of a new generation of peasant *pogromshchiki*, nor even the more politicized Russian ultra-national tendency we associate with the Black Hundreds, repeating the sort of anti-Jewish terror which had punctuated life in the Pale for the best part of forty years.[96] Instead, the prime mover was a professional military elite armed, deployed, and ready to execute a *thorough* elimination.

Genocidal process, however, need not lead to the implementation of total genocide. What actually transpired in the assault on the Jews of Ukraine and southern Russia in 1919 was at least as dependent on contingency as on conspiracy. Among the commanding White officers there was no counter-revolutionary blueprint to exterminate the Jews. Admiral Kolchak might have had in his head paranoid, projective urges in this direction, but with few Jews on hand in Siberia he had to make do with fulminations against Masons—the next best thing in the conspiracy-laden pantheon. General Denikin too, though operating from a south Russian theatre much closer to the Jewish centres of population, appears to have played no direct role in instigating or condoning attacks, claiming instead that his command structure was 'helpless' in the face of his soldiery's 'rabid fury'.[97]

But in that admission we may have a clue to how something akin to a 'Mexican wave' of military massacres developed in the Ukraine from early 1919 onwards. Reporting on the first major sequence committed not by Denikin's army but by troops loyal to the Directory, a Jewish relief committee noted that:

> Pogroms only commenced when the Directorate suffered defeat at the hands of the Communists. The more decisive these defeats were the more often the beaten Petliura troops had to carry out evacuations of territories which they had occupied, the more cruelly and irritated troops began to revenge their setbacks and hardships on the Jewish population and the more often they began to treat the Jews as communists. The battle cries 'Murder Jews and Communists' and 'the Jews are Communists' soon sounded throughout the Ukraine provoking sanguinary pogroms.[98]

What this narrative highlights is a trajectory of massacre closely correlated to the disintegration of first Directory, then Denikin, forces in this Russian rimlands theatre. Left to its own devices, or, even more likely, with the support of Western powers, the left-leaning Directory might well have achieved the political accommodation with its Jewish population which it had sought on paper. In practice, caught in the vice of not just opposing Bolshevik but also Polish, Rumanian, and White Russian adversaries effectively attacking it from all sides, the Directory's survival in any shape or form became dependent on the support Petliura could garner from quasi-autonomous *hetmany* already, as we have seen, utterly confirmed in their *Żydokomuna* phobias.

As such, the massacre of Jews in Proskurov, an ethnically mixed, medium-sized town in Podolia, ironically not far from Khmelnytsky, offers an insight into a broader pattern. Massacres of Jews initially in Volhynia in January had spread as Directory forces retreated westwards from Kiev in the direction of Vinnitsa. Proskurov, occupied by Petliura's deputy, *hetman* Semesenko, in the course of this retreat in mid-February, almost immediately suffered a mutiny of two Directory regiments acting in collaboration with local Bolsheviks, intent on fomenting an uprising. Some of these opponents undoubtedly were from the town's Jewish quarter. Semesenko responded with a blanket accusation against all Proskurov Jewry, and with an order for retribution, without respect to age or gender. Significantly, he also gave additional instructions that there was to be no looting or setting fire to the district—the troops were to be focused on the matter in hand. As it was the afternoon of the Jewish Sabbath, with most Jews in their homes, the casualties from these few hours of killing—that is, until Semesenko gave orders to halt the action in the early evening—were enormous. Something between 1,500 and 4,000 were killed or wounded, this from a town with no more than 5,000 Jewish inhabitants. The perpetrator troops, including Cossacks, were almost immediately responsible for a further massacre in Feltshin, another nearby town.[99]

Though most of the ensuing Ukrainian bloodletting was conducted on the orders of *hetmany* in this manner—that is, without reference to the effectively non-existent diktat of the Directory and usually in complete isolation from one another—what is equally striking is the number and density of such massacres within a limited geographical range. Arno Mayer delineates this as a rectangular zone bounded by Sarny in the north-west and Uman in the south-east, with Kamenets-Podolsk and Chernobyl as the other boundaries—though with Kiev too as part of the eastern boundary line; in other words, 'the core of the ex-Pale east and south of its Polish and Belorussian regions'.[100] Similarly notable is not only the fact that this, the western part of this same zone, would be at the rimland epicentre of local retributive killings of Jews in June and early July 1941—in addition to those perpetrated by German Einsatzgruppen—but that, just as at that latter juncture, anti-Jewish fury reached its zenith in the aftermath of some grisly revelation of Bolshevik atrocity. In March 1919, the example of this par excellence would be the discovery of 1,700 *Christian* bodies in Zhitomir, again after the town had been ephemerally retaken from the Reds. The consequence was a five-day orgy of violence, which left over 300 Jews dead.[101]

This Zhitomir example also suggests how military agency, in the perpetration of mass violence, could be supplemented by, or even merge with, demotic participation. Evidence on Grigoriev's killing rampage in Elisavetgrad in May 1919—the most egregious of his many atrocities—strongly suggests that the now regular menu of 'crucified Christ' imagery acted as a conscious incitement to townspeople and surrounding villagers. With the intentional release of criminals from the town's jail and the involvement of former supporters of the Black Hundreds, the result was a notably hands-on massacre which left not only 400 Jews slaughtered but hundreds more of the survivors severely mutilated or traumatized, not least from mass rape.[102]

Yet for all the blood-curdling rhetoric of the *hetmany* and the readiness of many ordinary folk to respond, the key sequence of mass killing in the western Ukraine—according to the available evidence—happened less at the beginning of 1919 than towards its end, when the Directory to all intents and purposes had been expunged as a player from the board and its place taken by Denikin's host. Better organized and equipped, backed by the Allies, firmly under the control of a professional, seasoned officer corps, the troops of the ascendant White general in the summer of 1919 should, in theory at least, have been the salvation of the Ukrainian Jewry, as they swept the Directory out of play and made ready for their lunge at the Bolshevik heart in Moscow. The initial advance, however, not only brought a new wave of anti-Jewish violence but one which could only intensify as the Whites faltered in the face of Red Army resistance. By the autumn, as the pace of the Volunteer Army retreat accelerated in the direction of Black Sea ports and the Crimea, the direction of retributive travel was also made crystal clear by the fate of the Jewish community of Fastov. This flourishing small town, a little south-west of Kiev, was occupied in late September by a brigade of Cossacks who proceeded, through an orgy of mass rape and plunder, to transform it, according to one Kievan paper, 'into a graveyard'.[103] One might say it was like Grigoriev's rampages all over again; except with two critical points of difference. Firstly, the violence was linked to a looting of the Jewish quarter which was altogether more methodical—Fastov's suffering proceeding over several days. Secondly, in spite of the clear lines of military authority and command, none of the perpetrators were disciplined nor, more importantly, was anything done to halt the outbreak.

Denikin might point to his record of proclamations forbidding his troops from anti-Jewish violence—one of which was actually enunciated in Kiev in October, *after* their most recent atrocity in the capital[104]—but there was nothing otherwise in his or his general staff's actions to suggest that they did not actually *approve* of the violence. OSVAG continued to churn out incendiary anti-Jewish propaganda, while the army hierarchy's idée fixe of Jewish responsibility for Bolshevism was further underscored by the removal of Jewish officers from its own ranks, again with clear resonances of the Trojan horse fears of 1915. One could not even claim this double-faced Jewish policy to be a case of projective paranoia. Rather, it was one that operated on two entirely distinct planes: one whereby Denikin's vapid promises to guarantee Jewish security were for international consumption only, and the other whereby his troops, defeated in battle, were permitted to vent their frustration and anger on Jewish communities in their path with impunity.[105] November and December were the high months in the Volunteer Army's Ukrainian retreat. They also marked the apotheosis of the military pogrom sequence, by which time at least 500 Jewish communities, large and small, had been laid waste, many on more than one occasion.[106]

There was, of course, one other component in this grim narrative: the Jews themselves.

Though no definitive breakdown exists enumerating their casualties, it seems likely that the contour of those killed, maimed, and traumatized was heavily skewed towards the very young, the very old, and females: mass rape being a further corollary of circumstances where a rampant military let loose on communities found few able-bodied male defenders to stand in their way. The reason is simple. Back in 1918, immediately post-Brest-Litovsk, Jewish traditional leadership had looked to the German military in the east as a protective buffer between themselves and the various nationalist forces most likely to menace them. With the withdrawal westwards of German armies—notwithstanding the infiltration of the thoroughly hostile Freikorps into the Baltic region—there was only one force in post-tsarist Russian unequivocally ready and willing to denounce anti-Semitism and pogroms: a force personified in Vladimir Ilich Lenin. As a result of his statements and broadcasts in 1918 and 1919 the Bolshevik regime was not only recognized by Jews as being the only one which would genuinely punish offenders. Beyond this—and perhaps more importantly—it was seen as the one which would embrace them as 'comrades in the struggle for socialism',[107] thereby offering a clear signal as to what able-bodied men in the Jewish communities should do. Politicized or not, the years of civil war in the rimlands saw their Jewish youth in flight towards the bastions of Bolshevik power, and from there flocking into the ranks of the Red Army, the Cheka, and other departments of the new Soviet state apparatus.[108]

TWO RUSSIAN VENDÉES

We must save Russia . . . even if we have to set fire to half the country and shed the blood of three-fourths of all the Russians.[109]

Kornilov speech, early 1918

We must carry along with us ninety out of the hundred million Soviet Russian population. As for the rest we have nothing to say to them. They must be annihilated.[110]

Zinoviev speech, September 1918

Juxtaposed thus, these two statements from leaders of counter-revolution and revolution might offer a sobering reminder not only of the lengths to which the contenders in the struggle for post-tsarist Russia were prepared to go to win through, but, with this, of the way in which the entirety of an empire, rimlands and heartlands alike, were engulfed in the flames. The resulting human losses were so catastrophic that the situation deservedly begs the question of whether we can single out anything quite so identifiable as *genocide* at all. Already, the Great War had taken a Russian toll of between 7.3 and 8.5 million killed or wounded. To this the sequel of revolution and overlapping civil wars from 1917 to 1921 is variously estimated to have caused another 7 to 10 million direct deaths, with a further figure possibly as high as 8 million as a result of the great famine of 1921–2, and the ensuing epidemiological collapse. Whether we wish to attribute to Lenin and the Bolsheviks *entire* responsibility for plunging Russia into this maelstrom and for 'hunger on a scale not seen for three centuries'—and that on the back of a revolutionary promise of bread and land to its peasants—the demographic consequences of the continuum of war and revolution are clear enough: a shortfall in the former empire's population—that is, those killed or not born as a result—of some 30 million people.[111]

Equally, we might seek to read the two statements in an entirely more provocative manner. Starting out from the backgrounds of the two speakers—the former Cossack, the latter Jewish—might we not perceive in their rhetoric a dialectic in which, if not two ethnic then certainly two communal populations, sought to exterminate not only each other but other populations caught in the draught of their mortal struggle? Cossacks had been the tsarist scourge of rimlands Jewry for centuries. In the context of the Great War all three of the main Cossack hosts—Terek, Don, and Kuban—had played disproportionately large roles among the uniformed tsarist troops who had terrorized and committed atrocities against defenceless *shtetlach* both within and beyond the Russian borders, just as they were again to do after the revolution. But by the same token, Cossacks, as a rule, hated Jews as the key 'inner enemies' who, they alleged, threatened their traditional way of life—an awareness to which the tsarist regime robustly responded by refusing Jewish settlement in the Don, even at the height of the wartime refugee crisis in 1915.[112] With the ascendancy of the Bolsheviks in Petrograd and Moscow, what was then to stop the Jews taking their *collective* revenge? The assumption might even be reinforced by the fact that in the high summer of 1919 there *were* those in leading revolutionary councils and committees subscribing to the view that 'sooner or later we will have to exterminate, simply physically destroy the Cossacks, or at least the vast majority of them'.[113]

As Peter Holquist has pointed out there was plenty in Russia's pre-revolutionary conditions, not to mention the amplified continuum of crisis from 1917 onwards, which made Manichaeism 'plausible and even appealing'.[114] And with a long shelf life too. The charge that the 1919 Bolshevik assault on Don Cossackdom—the first of our two Russian Vendées—was a case of genocide, with responsibility resting on Trotsky alongside Sverdlov, briefly head of the Bolshevik Central Committee (until his premature death in March)—their motivation being Jewish malice pure and simple—has been the stock-in-trade opinion of works on the subject in the late Soviet and post-Soviet period.[115] It also has resonances of the Jewish Bolshevik versus German Nazi conceptualization-cum-explanation of war and genocide on a larger European canvas, as more infamously developed by Ernst Nolte in the course of the 1980s *Historikerstreit*.[116] In 'getting it wrong', however, as crude analyses invariably do—there often remains some glimmer or kernel of insight, even where this is very different or even at cross purposes with the overwrought conspiracist mindset of its originators.

The Russian Revolution was not Jewish, any more than the ultimately sub-genocidal assault on the Don Cossacks in which non-Jewish figures played the critical decision-making roles. Nevertheless, there is no doubt that there was an attraction for many Jews in Bolshevism, just as there also was for others among the more urbanized, literate members of non-Russian rimlands groups: Georgians, Armenians, Germans, Latvians, and Poles in particular, on account of its essential colour blindness. Of all these groups, however, it is also clear that Jews responded to the Bolshevik call for support in proportionately the largest numbers.[117] Again, one might wish to understand this not as stemming from 'some inherent affinity with Bolshevism' so much as 'a collective instinct of self-preservation' in the face of possible neo-tsarist restoration.[118] Yet, more positively, one might add that what Bolshevism openly offered to committed, focused, educated Jews was the opportunity for participation in the political mainstream so blatantly and resolutely denied under the ancien régime. Indeed, just as the tsarist regime, for lack of a sufficient indigenous skills base, had turned particularly to ethnic German experts and professionals to provide the backbone of its civil and military apparatus, so, now, the Bolsheviks actively encouraged Jews to fulfil urgent administrative, military, and surveillance tasks which they considered essential to the preservation, defence, and security of the revolution. That, as a result, many Jews became not just commissars but operatives—including very senior ones—within the newly established political police, the Cheka, is, however one looks at it, an extraordinary and momentous departure, given a Russian Jewish history of largely defenceless passivity, not to say perpetual state persecution. Indeed, it was this very entrusting of power and, with it, of state-monopolized instruments of violence to a historically despised minority which would be considered a particularly heinous and quite unforgivable transgression by those in the dominant population who saw the ensuing Bolshevik bloodshed as both 'Jew'-organized and executed yet, paradoxically, also as having denied themselves—the 'true' patriots—the opportunity to be the unadulterated master-narrators of their own epic transformation. The legacy of these civil war memories would rebound later, with tragic consequences for Soviet Jewry.

There is something else, however, in this immediate post-1917 connection between 'progressive' elements of Russian Jewry and the revolutionary state which throws light on the much broader, unfolding disaster of Bolshevism. Critical to the appeal and attraction of Marxism *tout ensemble* to many, increasingly secular, mainstream-educated Russian Jews, was its claim to represent a coherent, rational analysis of how human society worked, as founded on its undiluted socio-economic underpinnings. With racial or indeed religious factors thus erased, Jews could be assured—or so they believed—that they would be henceforth embraced within the struggle for a better society minus the stigma of communal origin which had dogged the European Jewish condition for the best part of two thousand years. Indeed, one might go further and argue that while Marxists saw the problem of society in the relationship between those who controlled the means of production and those who were subjugated by it, this contained no inherent assumption that those among the subjugating capitalist 'class', Jewish or otherwise, were irredeemably, *genetically* damaged or damned. On the contrary, Marxism promoted the notion that bourgeois intellectuals who had come to a 'correct' understanding of the dialectic could be instrumental in its final proletarian resolution. By the same token, any individual who, through their own actions, sided with the proletariat was duly disaggregated from those identified as enemies; so too, under the Soviet political ecosystem, were the children of enemies: communist education and nurturing (at least in theory) redeeming them for the good of society. Even better, all these adherents would be on the winning side: the Marxist interpretation of history providing assurance that the seeds of capitalism's demise were built into the contradictions of the dialectic.

Bolsheviks as self-proclaimed, *good* Marxists thus anticipated an imminent end to human suffering and the creation, in its place, of a universally prosperous yet socially just world order, through the clear road map with which Marx had presented them. As Lenin portentously intoned, 'The Marxist doctrine is omnipotent because it is true'.[119] In a similar vein, in 1917, supported, critically, by the ex-Menshevik Trotsky, Lenin had presumed to *know* that the moment of destiny was at hand and that the Bolsheviks' seminal role was to act as trigger for the world revolution, which would proclaim its arrival by seizing power in Russia. The problem, as Menshevik critics would unceasingly remind their erstwhile cousins, was threefold. Firstly, this did *not* follow the Marxist script. It was instead a case of gambling on using a Marxist party as an 'organisational weapon' with which 'to bring Communism more quickly than history would do, if left alone'.[120] Secondly, it could only have any Marxist efficacy if the gamble—unorthodox as it was—paid off; that is, by precipitating revolution in the advanced industrial countries of the West where plausible socio-economic conditions could pave the way to Marxian transformation. Thirdly, if that failed the Bolsheviks would be faced with the dilemma of political control in a country which still had a long way go to reach its full *capitalist* stage of development; in other words, where conditions cut from under their very feet any justification for perpetuating a 'dictatorship of the proletariat', as proposed by Lenin.

The whole issue of this dread miscalculation and its societal fall-out is something to which we will return in Chapter 5. Here, what matters for our purposes is the immediate political consequences of the failed gamble. Two clear options were available to the Bolsheviks. The obvious one—once it had become clear by the time of Brest-Litovsk that revolution in the crucible of total war was not going to materialize—was to admit error and either relinguish control entirely or allow for an orderly transfer of power via the resurrection of a democratically elected Constituent Assembly, which the Bolsheviks, the previous December, had suffocated at birth. Bolshevik hubris ensured that this would and could not happen; even though Lenin himself privately conceded the party had no Plan B for rule in one country alone.[121] The second option was to unashamedly pursue the hubristic course, continuing dictatorial control as if it had become through the revolution a 'historical birthright',[122] even if this meant making up the rules as one went along. Whether this could be sustained with ultimately Marxist goals in mind or not, minority rule of this kind could only be perpetuated in practice by unadulterated violence. Indeed, violence harder, more calculated, more ruthless than anything any of the other contending forces could organize.

At this juncture, most commentators on Bolshevism in the era of civil war tend to adopt one of two postures, usually reflecting, in turn, a political position. They either extol Bolshevik actions as necessary but nevertheless contingent on the circumstances they found themselves in, or, alternatively, see their 1917–21 atrocities as clear conscious indicators or precursors of high Stalinism.[123] Both positions, however, to greater or lesser extents, see the violence as essentially instrumental, which, given the regime's ideological ground rules and sensibilities as to the nature of the human condition, rather negates the possibility of identifying any of this violence as genocide. Even the most perspicacious of recent experts confirm this view. Holquist, for instance, states: 'While sanctioning mass violence, the Soviet regime never set the extermination of people as an objective in itself'.[124] Amir Weiner agrees: 'Excision, even when carried out to completion, did not emanate from a genocidal ideology and was not practised through exterminatory institutions'.[125] In other words, however massive the scale of killing, the Bolsheviks and their successors never consciously sought to eradicate collective, communal entities.

Our thesis, however, does not require an assumed rational purposefulness or ideological clarity of a regime as necessary to determine whether it was, or was not, capable of genocide. This may sound counter-intuitive in the case of the Bolsheviks, given their own ultra-modern, ostensibly very clinical observation of the world, leading to 'audacious efforts to straighten out both nature and history, to make good their faults, to arrange human space and time anew'. The description is that of Zygmunt Bauman, though he is actually speaking of both Nazis *and* Communists. Each aspired, says Bauman, 'to do away with the messiness, haziness, contingency and uncertainty of human existence'.[126] Yet while we have no difficulty in ascribing to the former ultra-moderns the ability to commit genocide, on account of their 'audacious efforts' being framed within a racialized explanation of the human condition, we often too readily accept at face value the Bolsheviks' own solipsistic reading of themselves. We assume that their ultra-rationality remained internally consistent, when actually from the outset the very nature of what they were trying to realize—against the very grain of what was 'normally' realizable—was bound to lead to their own collective unreason; their own 'rupture with reality'.[127] In other words, Bolshevism's sociological ground rules proved as insufficient a prophylactic against slippage into delusional or phobic projection as did those of any less accomplished regime in conditions of perpetual, feverish, but nevertheless self-created crisis.

How much evidence is there to support this supposition? The bare facts of Bolshevism's creation of an apparatus of mass violence are clear enough. Faced with incipient counter-revolution from the Whites and a 'political economy of extreme scarcity',[128] Trotsky as war commissar strove to both meet the military threat and defend the 'citadels of revolution' by refashioning the tsarist instruments of total war into the service of what quickly became draconian one-party rule. In the process, he and Lenin contradicted not only everything they had said to either the peasants or the workers throughout 1917, but also what they themselves had held dear in terms of revolutionary precept—claiming instead the diktats of necessity as justification for a now tsarist-officered, forcibly mobilized Red Army on the one hand,[129] and the forcible extraction of grain from the countryside on the other. To feed the army and so save the would-be socialist, anti-system state, the makers of the revolution readily adopted the practices, if not the principles, of Hindenburg and Ludendorff. Indeed, war communism took Ludendorffian praxis to new heights of centralized command, control, and coercion.

Lacking the traditional ancien régime acquiescence of the majority of its populace, however, the Bolsheviks could only proceed towards these goals by the application of unrelenting mass terror. Their prime instrument was the Extraordinary Commission to Combat Counter-Revolution and Sabotage—Cheka—inaugurated on 20 December 1917, with the Polish-born Felix Dzerzhinsky its first chief executive.[130] Looked at objectively, one might argue, the Bolsheviks had absolutely no choice but to go down this route. The nationalization of the economy and concomitant suppression of private property and the markets, the enforced requisitioning of people and resources, the banning of dissent whether in the form of political parties, pressure groups, or independent trade unions, all pointed to the necessity for intensified political control, policing, and surveillance of the population. Moreover, over and beyond the external threat of the Whites and their Western backers, a growing internal resistance to Bolshevik rule, even in Petrograd and Moscow in the summer of 1918, was most obviously manifested in the efforts of erstwhile left-Social Revolutionary (SR) allies to destabilize the regime, assassinate its leaders, and attempt to overthrow its government. For a party which constantly saw itself through the Jacobin prism of the French Revolution, the 'never again' Bolshevik fear that the revolution would be swept aside—not because they had committed terror but because they had not committed enough of it, became an almost obsessive leitmotif.[131]

Quantitatively, it is easy enough to chart the consequent, increasingly bloody trajectory of the Cheka. Its personnel necessarily expanded exponentially, from 2,000 in mid-1918 to some 140,000 by the end of civil war, to say nothing of an additional 100,000 frontier troops under its aegis, in order to meet the counter-revolutionary challenge.[132] There was a parallel ratcheting up of its powers, too—beginning with a series of decrees in February, then again in September 1918—entitling the organization not only to arrest and detain suspects but to take hostages and isolate 'class enemies' in concentration camps. Above all, the Cheka was authorized by the revolutionary leadership, Sovnarkom, to execute at will not just Whites, but just about anybody suspected of economically or politically sabotaging Bolshevik rule.[133]

How many thousands or tens of thousands overall were liquidated as a consequence of this Chekist-led 'Red Terror' is difficult to estimate. But what concerns us equally here is the qualitative shift in the Bolshevik *mindset* as, from the time of Brest-Litovsk, the emergency deepened. We have already seen how under Great War conditions spy fever could take unremitting hold, whether in London, Constantinople, Belgrade, or Petrograd. With the Bolsheviks in 1918 there was an even more extraordinary multiplication of perceived enemies of all kinds—Whites, 'pseudo-socialists' (in other words any socialists or anarchists who did not submit to Bolshevik regimentation), the bourgeoisie and their unspecified 'agents', not to mention 'kulaks', 'marauders', 'speculators', 'hoarders', 'black marketeers', 'saboteurs', and other 'criminals'—all now declared 'enemies of the people' and hence firmly outside the regime's universe of obligation. Equally of note, however, is the way a rhetoric of righteous self-justification developed in tandem with the regime's determination to eradicate or suffocate all such subversive threats to the Bolshevik project. 'Proletarian compulsion in all its forms, beginning with execution by shooting and ending with the compulsory labour obligation is—however paradoxical this might sound—*the means for producing a Communist humanity from the human material of the capitalist epoch*', wrote the communist theoretician Bukharin, in 1920 (the italics are actually where Lenin had underlined his own copy of the text with the single word 'Precisely!' scribbled in the margin).[134] The renownedly clear-sighted Lenin had himself, at the very outset of Bolshevik rule, used even more colourful, not to say venomous, language: declaring in January 1918 that the regime's aim was to purge 'the Russian land of all kinds of harmful insects', and going on later to command subordinates, in one incident, to quell dissent by hanging a hundred 'of the rich bloodsucking kulaks'.[135]

With this sort of language as fair measure of its antipathies—whether deep-seated or recently realized—Bolshevism's supposedly firm strictures about 'unreliable' social categories being neither monolithic nor absolute begin to look paper-thin. In spite of the fact that 'nobody ever provided a clear description of what exactly a "class enemy" was supposed to look like', people were being sentenced to death or incarceration from this early period 'not for what they had done but for *who* they were'.[136] And if the actual identified malefactors were not on hand, exemplary punishment could always be meted out to their nearest and dearest. In 1919, when officers of the 86th Infantry Regiment in Petrograd defected to the Whites, it would be family members, including children, who were shot in reprisal.[137] This would prove to be just the beginning of the Soviet conception of justice.

*

The notion of 'unreliable elements' had been critical to an evolving tsarist military taxonomy of the social organism. Bolshevism was supposed to have, in its tool kit, more precise instruments by which to determine who exactly were the irredeemably dangerous individuals and who the saveable; that is, consistent with its own *particular* view of the good 'purified' society. By the late 1920s the wholesale ascription of the term 'kulak' to a great swathe of Russia's majority social formation—its peasantry—demonstrated the utter deformation of Bolshevik claims. Or was it actually that the tool kit was inoperable from the outset?

Through late 1918 and into 1919 a fierce debate was waged within and between the Bolshevik Central Committee (Orgburo), the regional party Don Bureau, and the Southern Front Revolutionary Military Council, as to how Soviet pacification and control of the southern Russian Don region was to be effected. At the core of the debate was the issue of *kazachestvo*, Cossackdom. Within the Don Bureau in particular, a grouping led by Sergei Syrtsov claimed that the Don Cossacks represented one of the most incorrigibly and irredeemably dangerous 'elements' of the counter-revolution, a problem to which only a 'radical' policy of de-Cossackization could provide a solution. What that policy should entail, as Syrtsov sought to develop it, appeared to be endorsed by Orgburo when, on 24 January 1919, it issued a striking directive to party and military officers on the spot:

> Considering the experience of a year of civil war against the Cossackry, we must recognise the only proper means to be a merciless struggle against the entire Cossack elite by means of their total extirpation. No compromises, no halfway measures are permissible.[138]

The circular went on to restate the case from a slightly different angle, emphasizing the need 'to conduct merciless mass terror *against all those Cossacks* who participated directly, or indirectly in the struggle against Soviet power'.[139] True, the explicit call for complete extermination was limited to wealthy Cossacks. Yet at the same time the circular insisted that all steps were to be taken to prevent 'middle' Cossackry similarly posing a threat. As the Soviets assessed the Cossacks as representing the top socio-economic tier of the Don population, the statement could thus be interpreted as evidence of a blanket extirpative intent. This happened to dovetail with Syrtsov's argument that only the swift and thorough liquidation of Cossackry as a specific *cultural* as well as economic group, accompanied by a mass socially engineered programme of dispersal and hence neutralization of rank-and-file Cossacks to other parts of the country—set against massive resettlement of the Don by Russian peasant elements—would suffice to meet the danger.[140] This, in turn, was interpreted by Bureau critics as evidence not of a correct class analysis but, on the contrary, as of a form of 'quasi-biological' stereotyping. Without actually mentioning the word 'race', Syrtsov effectively stood accused of having let that elephant into the room, and thereby threatening an aspect of Soviet policy by its 'degenerating into an amorphous zoological struggle'.[141]

However one interprets this internal party debate—something which, in itself, would not have been possible under Stalin—what is clear is that the whole issue of Cossackdom had touched a regime, and possibly more widely societal, raw nerve. That sense is reinforced by the knowledge that the hard-line Orgburo directive remained in force for the best part of two months. But if a genocide, even a partial genocide, of Cossacks was contemplated in 1919—even if this was then over-turned in favour of something less overtly exterminatory—we need, however briefly, to take stock of the issues at stake.

Cossacks historically had had an unusual position within the tsarist firmament, one entirely founded on their specialist military value as horsemen.[142] Conse-quently, Cossack 'hosts' had had been co-opted, through universal male military service, to defend the empire's vast steppe frontiers, facing both east and west, in return for which they had been granted land and economic privileges. Cossacks, however, were not an ethnic group but a corporate social caste, the Don host, for instance, being drawn in considerable part from people of Kalmyk origin.[143]

By the time of the revolution, however, questions were being asked not only about Cossack military utility but what was considered by most progressives to be an increasingly anomalous substratum of society. Judicial de-Cossackization was already firmly on the cards before the Bolshevik coup. In the Don itself, where only some two-fifths of its 4 million-strong population were actually Cos-sacks, but where landholdings were strongly skewed in their favour, angry peasants were reportedly demanding *istreblenie*—a clean exterminatory sweep of their adversaries.[144]

Bolshevik hostility to the Don Cossacks, however, appears to have been more than simply a question of pragmatically siding with the peasants against the sup-posed regional equivalent of a kulak class; or even against a body which supplied significant military manpower to the White cause. The very idea of Cossackdom excited emotions for and against, even where these were almost entirely based on what was imagined to be true rather than any solid, ongoing reality. It was certainly a fact that hundreds of years in the past when Cossacks had lived in the 'wild', disputed steppe lands between the Poles, Muscovites, Ottomans, and successor khanates of the Golden Horde, they had freely chosen their *hetmany* through war-rior assemblies—*krugy*—founded on an equal suffrage and in which women as well as men were participants. The very notion of the Cossack in this sense as a 'free man' practising his or her *vol'nost'*—freedom—through a form of primitive demo-cracy, thus appeared to stand in quite extraordinary counterpoint to an authoritar-ian tsarism dependent on serfs for its labour. It also may explain why one modern commentator has described Cossackdom as 'an alternative Russian ethnos, the embryo of a potential Russian nation with a quite different social structure'.[145]

Was it, above all, the May 1917 revival of the *krug* as an all-Cossack *voiskovoi krug* which stuck so stubbornly in the Bolshevik gullet? If the Cossack intent, in this action, was to reaffirm their historic, autonomous status within Russia, could it equally be interpreted less as evidence of Cossack liminality and more as a direct challenge to the political mainstream, especially after October when Bolshevik democratic centralism amounted to nothing more than a terminology for depriving the populace of power, autonomy, and freedom? But if this were the case, if it was the 'idea' of Cossackry which underpins those fevered Bolshevik debates of 1919 about the Don as a Russian Vendée, could this be not because the region had genuinely become equivalent to the site of the 1793 anti-Jacobin insurrection 'but rather because it was expected to be that'?[146]

What is so interesting—and alarming—is that such reified notions of the Cossacks thinking, behaving, and acting as a monolith were not peculiar to Cossack enemies. If, for leading Bolsheviks, they were an 'inherently unreliable' and 'intrinsically' 'counter-revolutionary bacillus' who threatened to pollute the entire Republic's body politic,[147] for White leaders—many themselves of Cossack origin—they were equally 'the natural bulwark of Russia's statist principle'. Indeed, the Don country itself was the obvious redoubt in which to gather all 'reliable' forces and from which to strike out to scotch the Bolshevik blasphemy for good.[148]

Yet time and time again, rank-and-file Cossacks, even those in mobilized units of Volunteer Army units, failed to behave according to either this or indeed any political script. They did not respond as required to calls from *hetman* Kaledin to march on Petrograd and Moscow and put down the Bolsheviks immediately after the coup, and proved so lukewarm in general towards the counter-revolutionary cause in succeeding months that White commanders were not only forced to abandon the Don as anticipated redoubt in favour of the Kuban, but—for lack of Cossacks to fill the ranks—had to find replacements from among students and military cadets.[149] In despair, Kaledin committed suicide. His successor as *hetman*, Krasnov, found so many Cossacks defecting to the Red Army or simply refusing to obey orders that he would end up hanging or executing an astonishing 45,000 of their number.[150] In the circumstances, grass-roots animosity against the elite leadership of the self-styled All Don Cossack Host is hardly surprising, nor the fact that it was a defection of Cossack units in January 1919 that enabled a second Soviet takeover of the Don.[151]

This itself, of course, is highly ironic, as it was exactly at this moment of Bolshevik liberation that 'high', potentially genocidal, de-Cossackization began. But then again, in a universe where there were apparently only two options, an earlier Cossack uprising *against* Bolshevik rule in the spring of 1918 was unlikely to have been understood, let along sympathized with, by Petrograd for what it actually was—a spontaneous combustion of grass-roots fear that it was *they*—not the elite but ordinary working *stanitsa* (community)-based Cossacks who were about to suffer expropriation and extermination at the hands of Bolshevik commissars.[152] What Orgburo had chosen to remember instead from this post-Brest-Litovsk moment was that both Germans and Whites had used the occasion of the uprising to kick the Bolsheviks out of the Don and so pave the way for Denikin's advance. And behind that, of course, were other bitter Bolshevik memories, not least of the first failed revolution of 1905, when Cossacks had been at the cutting edge of tsarist repression against party and proletariat. In short, just as the Whites preferred to ignore the complexities of the Jewish situation in Russia and to damn all Jews as a collective Antichrist, so now it was as if it were simpler, even comforting for the

Bolsheviks at their moment of crisis, to return to a stereotypical image of an irreducible enemy. And so pronounce their own 'never again' verdict and, with it, take righteous vengeance.

Yet at this point there is a twist to the story, one which is a reminder that even when state orders for mass murder are promulgated and rubber-stamped, contingent events can also work in favour of arresting their execution.

With the 24 January orders in place, commissars and military officers on the ground in the Don strove to carry them out to the letter. In the northern districts, where Cossack concentration was at its highest, isolating the richest Cossacks seems to have been largely dispensed with by some operatives, reports instead speaking of every fifth or tenth *khutorianin* being lined up and shot, and their *khutora*—settlements—then being burnt to the ground.[153] The operatives, however, were themselves under pressure from further up the chain of command. One commissar, Boguslavskii, operating in the Morozovskaia district, for instance, was reprimanded by a delegate sent from the Tenth Army for being too 'weak', even though local officials were angry at the level of killings he was initiating. But it was the superior order for more 'energetic' terror which won out: Boguslavskii responding directly to it by having sixty-four people held in the local prison summarily executed.[154]

The specific case is well known and became something of a cause célèbre in party circles. The irony is that it did so because, by late March 1919, the Bolsheviks were in retreat from their extermination policy, Lenin himself attempting to distance his good name (as he perceived it) from the bloodletting, just as in rather similar vein Stalin would do eleven years later in his infamous 'Dizzy with Success' article, when he denounced local officials for their 'excesses' in the first round of collectivization.[155] Back in spring 1919 it was Boguslavskii and two of his team who suffered the consequences, in the form of a closely orchestrated trial—an early Bolshevik example—followed by the death sentence. There were, however, two features of note in the Bolshevik change of heart for which Boguslavskii was the scapegoat.

Firstly, what reined in the Bolshevik agenda was not a sudden, unexpected surge of humanitarian compassion but a further grass-roots Cossack uprising centred on the Veshenskaia *stanitsa* in the upper Don—a direct response to the regime's ultra-violence. On this occasion, however, fears that this was truly the beginning of a new Vendée—the Cossack action, after all, enabled Denikin to recover the region and begin his, albeit unsuccessful, offensive towards Moscow—led the regime to steer a course exactly opposite to that taken by the Jacobins in 1793. Whereas at that earlier moment a revolutionary regime had responded to popular insurrection by attempting a vengeful elimination of the culpable region's entire population, the Bolsheviks in 1919 drew back from this fanning of the flames: arguably reading the lessons of the earlier Vendée as a corrective to their own mistaken policy. Henceforth there was no more terror against the entirety of Don Cossackdom as an 'estate'—a communal body; but *only* against those who, according to revolutionary tribunals, had committed counter-revolutionary acts.[156]

The second point of information, however, is considerably more sobering. One can focus on the period of high de-Cossackization and confirm that judicial executions in the Don accounted for a maximum of 10,000 to 12,000 victims.[157] This appalling death toll, nevertheless, was of men, not whole communities. And, as such, genocide qua genocide, in terms of *our own* reading of the phenomenon, did not take place. Bolshevik animus towards Cossackdom, however, did not dissipate. If anything the change of policy was purely tactical. It did not preclude the continuation of plans for the excision of the Don as a territorial-administrative unit—clear resonances here with the dismantling of the actual French Vendée—nor those for the dilution of the region's Cossack character by deportation of its most 'dangerous' and 'untrustworthy' elements, on the one hand, and their replacement with non-Cossacks on the other. Officially, this could be dressed up as the pursuit of the class struggle. But the regime's underlying antipathy was reflected both in the erasure of Cossack geographical place names and designations, followed, in 1920, by the abolition of Cossackdom as special substratum of society altogether.[158] Cossacks, in other words, had been pronounced as ceasing to exist. The point was reinforced the following year, when punishment for insurrection was meted out this time not to Don but to Terek Cossacks of the northern Caucasus. And not only against their men. Some 9,000 Cossack *families*—an estimated 45,000 people—or most of the population of five entire *stanitsy*, each a small administrative district in its own right, were deported to labour camps or regions far away, on the regime's orders.[159] An eyewitness would report in April 1921 of these events, and those in other major Cossack centres in the Kuban, thus:

> The Terek and Kuban oblasts have been subdued. The insurgent Cossack villages have been wiped off the face of the earth, the population has been removed—the men to forced labour in the mines, the women and children scattered everywhere. All living and dead stock has been seized or has rotted, or been pilfered.[160]

Indeed, of 3 million Cossacks in the main Kuban and Don areas of concentration, at least one-tenth and possibly many more were killed or deported in the high years of the civil war.[161] Lemkin certainly would have had no compunction in calling this genocide.

*

One might wish to interpose at this point the fact that the *broader* collapse of Don and Kuban populations in this period was less annihilatory in the direct sense and more a consequence of epidemiological breakdown, itself brought on by famine. But this, too, was an outcome of Bolshevik war communism; in other words, of a systemic violence of a state against its own majority population. By 1920, moreover, with Central Russia stripped bare of grain with which to feed the citadels of the revolution, it was the *khutorianin*, peasant, Cossack, or Mountaineer, of the recently re-'liberated' peripheries—primarily the rimlands of the Ukraine, southern Russia, and the northern Caucasus, as well as the Siberian interior—who now suffered the brunt of requisition and expropriation. Shock squads of military, party, and Komsomol cadres, very much like the *armée révolutionnaire* of 1793–4,[162] descended with brute force on communities, such as in the already devastated Don, with draconian orders to extract every last grain of food. For the Bolsheviks, their military struggle with Whites in the south may have been effectively won, as remnants of the latter's army had retreated into the Crimea. But an arguably even more murderous struggle—a genuine War Type Three—was about to commence, in which a ruthless and apparently unyielding regime found itself pitted against an empire-wide slew of peasant insurrections.

What made this insurrectionary sequence so potent and hence dangerous was the complete disjuncture between peasant and Soviet world views. For the latter this was clearly not a counter-revolution which they were facing. This was *anti*-revolution:[163] a wilful denial of Bolshevik or indeed *any* political elite's assumption that they had some superior or prior right to determine the lives and destinies of countryfolk. This was also clearly not in the Bolshevik script. Peasants qua peasants lacked the 'consciousness' with which to make rational, forward-thinking, progressive decisions on their own behalf. Their improvement could thus only come through a 'leading out' by those with a proletarian background, which, in turn, would render the backward-looking culture and mores of their peasant protégés redundant. In the interim, in the vortex of class struggle in the countryside—as in towns—peasants were expected to be malleable, to readily fall in behind what was expected of them by town-based revolutionaries, and, where they were clearly poor, to join revolutionary committees against supposed rich peasants—kulaks. *Divide et impera*: pure and simple.[164]

What this actually underscored was the Bolsheviks' intrinsic contempt for the peasantry and their way of life. Effectively, they were to the party what colonial natives were to settlers and imperial administrators: they could only be redeemed from their uncouth drunken sloth, stupidity, and slovenliness through assimilation into the Soviet model. Their ability to act of own volition, or for goals which were anything but reactionary, was nil. Coherent, organized opposition to the regime was also, by these standards, inconceivable: peasants, like natives, simply lacked the skills commensurate with the waging of a systematic struggle for coherent ends. When colonial peoples had done exactly that—and, further, through the tenacity and resilience of their response had struck at the very foundations of state power—even where this was driven by knowledge of this being, for them, a life-and-death struggle—the colonialist counter-response had been invariably one of massive, retributive, exterminatory overkill. So it was with the Bolsheviks. The assault on Tambov province in south Russia in the spring and early summer on 1921 proves the case. The peasant *Antonovshchina*, the insurrection named eponymously for its hero-leader, was not only a real Russian Vendée, it was a Soviet equivalent of Herero and other major colonial uprisings. And, in the manner of its military destruction, it bore the same colonial—genocidal—imprint.

But why Tambov, when great swathes of the Volga region, the Don, the northern Caucasus, Russian Armenia, and western Siberia were equally engulfed in starved but often incredibly tenacious peasant rebellion against Bolshevik seizures? There were instrumental reasons. Tambov was not so much a periphery as part of a strategic communications corridor stretching from Petrograd and Moscow down to the key grain supplies in North Caucasus and the Don to the south-east. Even if Antonov's insurgency failed to link up with the other major south Russian 'green' insurgency, that of Makhno—the latter having peaked in the late summer of 1919 (by the time of the *Antonovshchina* he was on the run from Red Army clutches)—the rebellion in Tambov still represented the potential to close off food supply and thus drive 'a knife into the back of the revolution'.[165] It also came at a juncture when Lenin himself acknowledged to close associates that 'We are barely holding on'.[166] Indeed, Antonov's timing proved immaculate. Just as the Algerian Muqrani revolt against French rule, or for that matter, the Herero revolt against German, were galvanized by colonial forces being drawn elsewhere, Antonov's embryonic movement exploded into full-scale action in late summer 1920 when Red Army forces were seriously tied up fighting the Poles.[167]

Nor did the movement fold up or wither away when confronted with superior Soviet firepower. Like many a native insurgency Antonov's, to a critical extend, was able to remain in the field and initially retain the upper hand because it knew its locality and thus could avoid direct confrontation in favour of elastic guerrilla encounters followed by rapid dispersal. But, to a further critical extent, the anti-revolution was sustained—again not unlike many a major colonial revolt—by its knowledge and *imitation* of its enemy. Far from being a scratch, non-politicized, inchoate 'rabble', the *Antonovshchina*—according to Tukhachevsky, its most serious Red Army opponent—could field 21,000 men in a territorial militia backed by a strong administrative base, in turn founded on a network of essentially independent rather than exclusively SR-organized peasant unions.[168] It also had its own security wing. This last point is particularly significant, not least because it demonstrated the insurgents' readiness to match terror with terror. Not only did Antonov have no compunction about terrorizing and murdering regime *apparatchiki* and cadres but he also struck back, blow for blow, against Order no. 130, issued with the authority of the centre in June 1921, which effectively gave the Red Army and commissars the licence to hostage-take or judicially execute insurgent family members. Antonovites responded in kind by murdering communist families in the Tambov area. There is thus no call to romanticize this insurgency, any more than the majority of native rebellions. As in most of them, the rebels indulged in conscious ritualized torture, including a wide range of bodily amputations or mutilations of victims before death, as well as in rape in the case of captured females.[169]

The death of some thousand Reds at the hands of the movement clearly acted, in turn, as a critical goad to Bolshevik revenge and to projective representation of the Antonovites as bestial savages. Yet this depiction happens also to be a convenient sleight of hand. If the base of the revolt was undoubtedly a desperately starving and hence brutalized peasantry—and Tambov, like the Vendée before it, was quintessentially that: a provincial rural society—the sharp edge of its violence was, to a considerable extent, the prerogative of former Red Army men who had jumped ship to repudiate the Bolsheviks as betrayers of the revolution for the liberation and empowerment of the people. Certainly, they carried many others, including draft resisters, with them. Antonov himself had not served with the Bolsheviks but was an SR-orientated opponent. Thus, superimposed on its wider peasant base, the insurgency here in Tambov, as elsewhere in other anti-revolutions of 1920–1, had an element of military mutiny; a resonance, if one prefers, of the more clear-cut and famous case—that of the Kronstadt uprising, which Tukhachevsky ruthlessly extirpated in March 1921. Tambov's profile was, to the outside world, entirely weaker; it was, after all, taking place in Russia's obscure backcountry. Yet like the Indian Mutiny, which embraced a population behind the men who had erstwhile been in the uniform of the oppressors, what actually caused the range of peasant insurgencies to be so utterly beyond the pale to Moscow was that they had, in considerable part, leaders who *knew* Bolshevism in principle and practice. The anti-revolution writ large could not thus be dismissed simply as peasant imbecility; or even, more cynically still, as a stalking horse for the counter-revolution. If that had been the case the insurgents would just have joined the Whites in 1918 or 1919. They had not. On the contrary, their leaderships often included former Red Army men who had been inducted into, and inculcated with, Bolshevik ideals of the better society. To then *choose* not to be on the right side—the side of the angels—and even to fight against it was—just like the charge levelled by the Jacobins against the Vendeans—proof of something *within* these opponents which was not just wilfully obtuse but even 'unnatural'.[170]

To add insult to injury, the contumacious insurgents in Tambov had presumed to run an organized, grass-roots entity of their own, with its own region-supplied army to boot, as if it were *the* authentic people's state. It may have been localized, and may never actually have spread beyond a limited zone in the south-east of the province, but the affront—and danger—to Bolshevik rule was crystal clear. If, as Tukhachevsky reported as late as July 1921, 'in five districts of Tambov province the Soviet regime no longer exists',[171] then why could the slate not be similarly wiped clean in neighbouring provinces or indeed anywhere within the Soviet firmament? Like the Whites, so, too, for the Bolsheviks: Russia was one and indivisible. There could be no exceptions to this rule, no unilateral declarations of independence, above all, no examples of how things might be if people were left to their own anarchic devices. Oliver Radkey, a biographer of the *Antonovshchina*, may have over-egged the pudding when he described it as the 'best organised peasant uprising in history', but insofar as it concerns a workers' and peasants' movement whose threat to the Bolsheviks surpassed 'by many times that of all the Denikins, Kolchaks and Iudeniches taken together',[172] his basic point may well be valid. Ultimately, the potency of the *Antonovshchina* was not on account of the material, or even human resources it could bring to the struggle—which were never going to be sufficient for military victory. Rather it lay—like that of grass-roots Don Cossackdom, albeit from a rather different starting point—in the idea, however absurd that might sound in post-tsarist Russia, of a genuinely free, grass-roots-based society. It was in this sense—of translating what was essentially symbolic into a formative actuality—that Tambov was, for the Bolsheviks, an anathema.

It was inevitable in these circumstances that Lenin would insist on the 'swiftest and most exemplary liquidation'.[173] Tukhachevsky, the ablest Red Army commander co-opted for the purpose would later, in 1926, openly and explicitly describe the planning and organization of his Tambov campaign as one of total war fought against not just 'bandits' but 'the entire local population'.[174] The kit he was accordingly allowed to marshal speaks for itself: three armoured trains, an aviation unit, sixty cannon, hundreds of machine guns, and some 50,000 Red Army personnel—a number sufficient to give the general a 2.5 to 1 superiority.[175] One senses, not unlike von Trotha in German South-West Africa seventeen years earlier, or, for that matter, Turreau in the Vendée, over a century prior to that, that Tukhachevsky was champing at the bit for this opportunity. It would be a classic textbook counter-insurgency campaign, the sort for which he, as a product of the tsarist officer academy, had minutely trained. He would have the pick of the best officers as his commanders on the ground. And he had what amounted to a blank cheque from the party to use whatever means he considered necessary, not least experimentation with poison gas to determine its efficacy, as an instrument for the elimination of the 'bandits' who retreated into the forests.[176] This, then, was not some small 'colonial' war but a massive statement to the natives-cum-peasants—all the ironies of who was making it notwithstanding—'never again' to mess with the party.

However, to really achieve such total goals involved not simply wiping out 'bandit' detachments, but dealing with the base of the insurgency, the core population of Tambov who had supported the rebellion. The genocidal implications here are just as immediate and fateful as they were for the Herero people or, for that matter, the communities of the original Vendée. The region having been tarred with the brush of bandit*ism*, the 'infection' could only be cured by a thorough cleansing which would eliminate any future recurrence forever. The aim, thus, was not simply one of *iz'iate* 'taking out'—in other words, killing—all suspects. It was also one of removing entire villages from the heartlands of the insurgency, dispersing their members to the far corners of the empire and/or incarcerating them in penal colonies, and replacing them with reliable elements.[177]

This may explain why the Bolshevik campaign in Tambov was, in its essence, never simply a military but rather a military-cum-Chekist operation geared towards a complete socially engineered solution. The task of stamping out banditism was considered to be of such priority in January 1921 that a Central Interdepartmental Commission for Combating Banditry was formed on the directive of Ogburo—the bureau responsible for maintaining order and dealing with the opposition—with Dzerzhinsky as chair and Trotsky's number two at the War Ministry, Skliansky, closely involved.[178] The very notion of treating all and any of the anti-revolutionaries as 'bandits', however, speaks volumes as to the way dissident political action was henceforth pathologized—and so criminalized.[179] The term 'bandits', of course, would take on an even more ominous significance when applied by the Nazis to Jews in the course of Operation Barbarossa, twenty years on. But the thrust behind the specific Bolshevik sub-commission 'for fighting banditry in Tambov province'—created a couple of months after its parent body—was not so very different from Nazi thinking. Under the aegis of Vladimir Antonov-Ovseenko, one of the most experienced and trusted commanders of Bolshevism's inner core, 1,200 Chekists and other officials were shipped into the Tambov district—in addition to military personnel—with the remit to undertake a giant surveillance of the entire population of the now quarantined bandit 'triangle'. Lists were drawn up of insurgent families and other alleged dissidents, and where these were caught they were then corralled into concentration camps where they were to stand as surety for the surrender of their bandit menfolk, before deportation elsewhere.[180]

Antonov-Ovseenko knew perfectly well, however, that the incarceration of families would only intensify the nature of the insurgent fight-back: Order 130 holding families accountable for resistance having its corollary in a further six-article-strong Order, number 171, which determined that all persons caught within the triangle were liable for exemplary—and lethal—punishment. 'Permeated', as various commentators have noted, 'with the principle of collective guilt',[181] the Order effectively translated the core of insurrectionary Tambov into a free-fire zone, with close parallels to Cromwellian Ireland at the height of the 1652 counter-insurgency campaign there, the *Vendée-Vengé*, in 1794, or, for that matter, the Mayan highlands of Guatemala in 1983. With the parameters of campaign and zonal targeting clarified thus, and the men and *matériel* in place from early May for its execution, all that was left for Antonov-Ovseenko and Tukhachevsky was to agree the fine details of demarcation between them and then do the equivalent of synchronizing their watches.

The result was predictable enough. At the centre of the insurgency in the Vorona valley, villages were obliterated, their populations massacred. With commitment to an 'implacable hardness' in force, at least 5,000 hostages were also executed in batches by late July. No estimate of total numbers of casualties exists but Radkey gives an approximation of 15,000 deaths in toto—of which perhaps a third were identifiably insurgents—in the villages and forests of Tambov, by the completion of the campaign the following month. Up to 100,000 survivors were deported far away to the Murman and Ural regions, or to around the Aral Sea.[182]

Of course, one can overstate the exceptionality of the Bolshevik assault against Tambov. The number of survivors as against those killed—deported or not—confirms a very extreme but not total genocidal event, even with the clearly collective attributes of the campaign exemplified in Orders 130 and 171. Furthermore, the orders made exemptions for feeding and pregnant mothers and sick people,[183] though, again, in the midst of intense counter-insurgency warfare, one questions the degree to which Chekists and soldiers would have halted to check the small print. Nor was this the only campaign of its type, though arguably Tambov was Tukhachevsky's template for the 'cleansing' of Saratov, Samara, the German Volga region, and, again, the Don, in the latter part of 1921.[184] And there was also the final extirpation of the White presence in the Crimea. This dated back to December 1920 when Chekists hunted down officers and collaborators associated with the last White regime of General Wrangel. Thousands were executed in Kerch, Sevastopol, Simferopol, and other towns, eliciting from Arno Mayer (a cautious commentator when it comes to Bolshevik violence) the view that the massacres had 'something of the avenging fury of Turreau's infernal columns in the Vendée'.[185]

Set against possibly as many as half million directly killed by the Red Army or Cheka in a range of state violence against insurgents or other suspects in the revolution and civil war period,[186]—excluding, that is, military deaths in the conflict with the Whites—the figure for Tambov, even combined with the Don, is clearly only a small fraction. However, we include two final points to conclude this section. Firstly, when Lenin, in March 1921, announced the New Economic Policy

(NEP), effectively an exhausted stand-down from war communism and, with it, a pragmatic drawing back from further conflict with the peasantry, this should logically and by rights have paved the way for peace—and, with it, amnesty—for the Antonovites. Instead, many months into the period when the NEP was being implemented, the regime made a singular point of saturating Tambov with not only an army of occupation but extreme, vengeful punishment. It had been the White supremo Kolchak, in spring 1919, who had extolled the Japanese extermination of the indigenous population of the Amur region of far eastern Siberia as the model for his generals to follow.[187] It was an irony that when peasants rose up against the Bolsheviks in the Russian heartlands in 1920–1, it was as if they were behaving like an indigenous people attempting to thrown off the shackles of colonial rule. And it was a further dreadful irony that the Bolsheviks responded to it as if they were themselves furiously implacable colonialists.

There is, however, a further aspect of the Bolshevik response to their Russian Vendées which brings us back more firmly to the broader crisis of the rimlands. The Reds were seeing, in mass excision of troublesome populations and the colonization of their regions by other, supposedly loyal, communal, or social groups, the key to social peace and transformation—as they determined it. The idea, however, was far from unique. In the Crimea, White generals toyed perhaps rather desperately with a mass recolonization of the peninsula by Don and other Cossacks as a way of strengthening the White hold on the region[188]—albeit based on the rather dubious notion that Cossacks were ipso facto loyal. Across the Black Sea, in Anatolia, Ittihadists had been first among equals in seeking to put into practice such grand, socially engineered designs. But now, as the Russian civil war wound down, the penchant for such 'solutions' as a route to state security, future development, and even international peace was on the cusp of being promoted not only by Ittihadist successors but with the acknowledgement, even recognition, of leaders of the Western system.

ANGLO-FRENCH OVERREACH IN THE EAST

The collapse of the White cause in Russia served to rapidly unravel the geopolitical game plan conceived by the Western Allies at the furthest reaches of their proposed rimlands security system in Anatolia—and across the old Ottoman–Romanov international border into the Caucasus. It had been a fundamental premise of their wartime position that it would be the Ottoman Empire, not the Russian, which would cease to exist at the war's successful conclusion. So long, indeed, as Russia remained within the Entente, there was only minimal Allied consideration of the role of subsidiary parties, indigenous or otherwise, in the future governance of ex-Ottoman territories. The notion of Armenian autonomy had always been, for Petrograd, little more than a vehicle for Russian penetration of eastern Anatolia. By the time of the Sykes–Picot–Sazonov Agreement its negative views on the Armenians, moreover, had become so entrenched that Sykes attempted to sell Petrograd the apportioning of the 'lesser' three of the six vilayets to a French sphere of influence centred on Cilicia, on the grounds that the Cilician Armenians—being alleg-edly less inclined towards 'anarcho-socialist' tendencies than those in the to-be Russian-controlled 'greater' Armenia—would exercise a moderating influence on their truculent cousins.[189] The French, however, had no intention of granting Armenians autonomy in their own zone. An explicit assurance to this effect from Picot to Boghos Nubar, the leading Armenian interlocutor on the international circuit—at a time when the latter, in anticipation of a quid pro quo, was attempt-ing to encourage Armenians to volunteer for the Légion d'Orient, the intended French military formation for the occupation of the region—was an 'outright falsehood'.[190]

It was the Russian collapse followed by Brest-Litovsk which saw Allied momen-tum towards a radical default plan, involving not only Armenians but a range of communal groupings, each with its own expansive national state or sub-state aspi-rations. At the centre of the change of plan in London and Paris was that little matter of the Mackinder nightmare: German advance into a rimlands political vacuum, delivering the Central Asian heartland to the enemy's advantage. An Allied buffer zone on its southern flank in 1918 thus became as urgent a priority as the creation of a similar cordon sanitaire on its western and south-western flank in the 'Lands Between'. The double blow which Bolshevism presented in the same geographical arena simply reinforced the Allies' search for a new road map. Equally problematic was the refusal of the Turks to lie down and die. The regime may have had to weaken the Palestine front for the purpose but, aided by the Germans, they demonstrated a renewed military vigour, not to say belated surge, in the Caucasus sector, even into the summer months of 1918. Turco-German success thus threat-ened to wreck key long-term Allied interests or objectives, which could only be parried by ensuring the control of Anatolian and adjacent theatres. First and fore-most was the small issue of oil, not just the fields in the Mosul region of northern Mesopotamia—which Whitehall considered firmly in its sphere—but also across the Russian–Caucasus border in the Caspian fields around Baku. If, however, secure access to and egress from this key locus of the emerging second phase of a global carbon economy was considered vital by the British, so, too, were French concerns to cement their economic hold on the Mediterranean littoral in Syria and Cilicia.[191]

The key problem, as high-level committees in Whitehall quickly identified, was a simple one of overstretch.[192] Even after the Turks sued for peace and acceded to the British-imposed Mudros Armistice in late October 1918, giving the Allies the right to occupy 'strategic' points anywhere in the empire, their actual ability to do so in the rugged Anatolian interior was severely limited. True, there were half a million British Empire troops in Mesopotamia and Syria. However, in practice, their ability to intervene in the Turkish heartlands never extended beyond a local-ized coastal range, while a direct British presence in the Caucasus and elsewhere—primarily the famous but tiny Dunsterville unit—was withdrawn in spring 1919.[193] This left only a handful of liaison and intelligence officers on the ground. In short, if the Allies wished both to continue their project for dismembering the empire—Anatolia included—and to pursue an ascendancy in the Caucasus, they had no choice, given the lack of friendly Russian muscle for the task, but to seek other proxies.

On paper, there was no shortage of potential helpers. There were Arabs, Jews, Assyrians (Nestorians), Greeks—both Aegean and Pontic—arguably at least some of the Kurds, possibly even some Circassians.[194] And then, beyond the Russian border, the three elements, Georgian, Azeri, and also Armenian, who had joined together to form the Transcaucasian Federative Republic in April 1918. True, no sooner had this been declared than it fell apart: the Georgians and Azeris being more prone to German or Turkish blandishments, respectively, than anything on offer from the British. But that still left the Armenians, while further afield there was the Mountaineer peoples' Union of North Caucasus, which had declared independence in May with initial support from the CUP, but, after Mudros, was inclined to look just about anywhere, including towards the Entente, for assistance.[195]

This plethora of would-be national entities also seemed to dovetail with the message coming from Washington, not least the twelfth of Wilson's Fourteen Points, which proposed 'an absolutely unmolested opportunity of autonomous development' for both Turks and non-Turkish nationalities within the empire.[196] By the time of a key Supreme Council meeting in Paris the following March, however, these inferences had hardened into a Conference resolution—very much at Wilson's initiative—'to separate from the Turkish empire certain areas'. These were to include not only the Arab territories earmarked for the French and British under the terms of Sykes–Picot but 'Armenia, Cilicia, and perhaps additional areas of Asia Minor'. The development of all these peoples would be put under the guidance of the Mandatory powers.[197] With the British and French having already weighed in with their own public declaration in November 1918, to the effect that Mesopotamia and Syria would have 'national governments . . . drawing their authority from the initiative and free choice of indigenous populations', expectations from communal groups in adjacent areas, especially the Armenians, Assyrians, Chaldeans, and Kurds rose accordingly.[198]

All this might superficially appear like benign and orderly progress towards a post-Ottoman national self-determination—in other words, doing for the Middle East as had already been proposed for the 'New Europe'—albeit, in this instance, under a more controlling League aegis. But putting aside the fact that the Anglo-French declaration was a thoroughly mendacious one designed to deceive on the issue of 'free choice'—not to mention its glaring omission of reference to Palestine, whose people were to be consciously denied any comment or veto on the implementation of the earlier Balfour Declaration—Allied signals actually served to vastly increase the danger to the religious and ethnic communities to which they were most obviously directed.

In practice, as Toynbee scathingly put it, the Supreme Council was encouraging 'inexperienced and unorganised entities'—he was speaking in this instance of the Transcaucasian republics—to look to the leading powers for 'guidance and a protection, which they had no intention of giving at any sacrifice to themselves'.[199] In other words, the Allies were asking weak, untried entities to do the Allies' own dirty work in a part of the world where, lacking any effective power of their own, they expected their protégés to take the hit if things went badly wrong. One might add that in terms of pure realpolitik the Allies almost entirely failed to bring on board the parties which really mattered. There was no chance, for instance, of the Armenians being able to secure for the British the critical oil and rail corridor between Baku and the Black Sea port of Batum, when in military terms they could hardly look after the very limited landlocked territory they had attempted to carve out for themselves around Erivan. Getting the military balance right would have actually required much more British emphasis on backing the Azeris and/or Georgians. That said, the very premise of looking to small peoples could be argued to be not simply strategically flawed but, worse, a case of pouring oil onto the flames of already massively destabilized inter-communal relations. Indeed, by seeking to encourage communal groups to behave as national and hence monolithic aggregates and to act accordingly in military–political terms, London, Paris, and Washington were effectively not only ensuring that chances of mutual reconciliation and hence collective recovery within the Anatolian–Caucasian shatter zone would be nil for the foreseeable future, but actually condemning some of the more exposed groups in the short term to the possibility of further genocide.

*

The post-*Aghet* struggle of the Armenians for political survival—its geographical range, after 1917, largely straddling the old Russo-Ottoman borders between eastern Anatolia and the Caucasus—is particularly indicative of where things were heading. Through to the time of the Bolshevik revolution, Armenian nationalists had looked to a stabilization of the Russian front to the west of Trabzon as a screen behind which an Armenian recolonization of the six vilayets from which they had previously been 'cleansed' and massacred might still be possible. The mass flight of Kurds and Turks from the Russian 1916 advance had encouraged this aspiration, though without any support whatsoever from Petrograd. With Russian troops withdrawn, however, in early 1918, the plateau descended into what can only be described as 'a war of all against all'. Kurdish tribes had undoubtedly sought to fill the vacuum left by the evisceration of the Armenians,[200] but now Armenian fighters in return sought, of their own volition, to cling on to or regain territory for the national cause on the Ottoman side of the border, as well as in formerly Russian-controlled eastern Armenia as far as Nakhichevan and Zangezur.[201] The immediate consequence was a range of Armenian atrocities against Muslims: the massacres in Erzinjan and Erzurum from late January to mid-February 1918—with close to 10,000 estimated to have been butchered in the two cities—being notable for their scale and ugliness.[202] These, however, were far from isolated incidents. In Van and Bitlis provinces on the one hand, and in the cross-border Kars region on the other, Armenian units—notably those led by Andranik in the latter case—went on a veritable killing spree 'emptying one Tatar (Azeri) village after another'. According to British reports, by May of that year 250 Muslim villages in the eastern Caucasus had been burnt down.[203]

It is perhaps significant that we can see in the actions of the Armenian military and proto-state at this juncture some similitude with the behaviour of the Directory contemporaneously in the Ukraine, more especially the following year. With no

choice but to attempt to fill the vacuum of a disintegrating Transcaucasian Republic, the Dashnaks, in May 1918, not only assumed provisional and actually entirely
nominal authority over what they deemed the 'Armenian provinces' but disavowed
the behaviour of Andranik.[204] But just as the Directory lacked the political or economic means to make their own entity viable and so were thrown back on Petliura
to wrest whatever they could from their sinking ship, so here, in putative Armenia,
it was Andranik and the other practitioners of extreme violence who became the
last bastion in defence of the idea of the nation. As in the Ukraine a year later, so
in Armenia it was headlong retreat which had acted as spark to the initial military
massacres. Acute famine throughout the region and the wider consequent population collapse were clearly, too, a goad to more mass violence in conditions where
life had become very cheap. On top of it all, the sheer desire for retribution for the
Aghet acted as justification for armed Armenians taking out their spleen on whatever Kurds, Azeris, Turks, or Turcomans they could lay their hands on—whatever
the circumstances. So much so that by the summer of 1919, with a slew of British
and American reports corroborating this information, one senior British intelligence officer in Transcaucasia committed to paper the opinion that 'the Armenians
should not be left in independent command of the Muslim population'.[205]

An almost identical picture, moreover, emerged from French-occupied Cilicia,
where Armenians were now constituted into a specific Légion Arménienne under
the authority of General Gouraud, French high commissioner for Syria and Cilicia.
From early 1919, however, these French-uniformed soldiers began taking their own
reprisals against local Muslims as well as arming returning Armenian refugees to the
region and assisting them to do the same, primarily in order to sequester property
for a growing Armenian enclave in the area, especially around Marash. The immediate consequence was a deteriorating relationship between the Légion and their
French commanders and, in turn, between the French and the overall British
command in the Syrian region, who protested against Armenian actions.[206]

Yet all this British or French horror was somewhat ironic, not to say meretricious, as both Allies had been looking to the Armenians, since early 1918, to bolster their own weak position in the Caucasus and Cilicia respectively. In turn, the
Armenians could continue to hope, in a way that the Peliurists could not, that
whatever the actions of their 'rogue' elements, the Allies would still come to their
rescue. On a basic humanitarian level, the Americans—with their very specific
commitment to the Armenian people and cause—were already doing this, the
charity Near East Relief (NER) attempting—largely against the grain of the possible—to keep hundreds of thousands of refugees alive through the feeding stations
it set up in the Erivan enclave and elsewhere.[207] Over and beyond this, reports that
the USA was committed to assisting in more direct political terms, through taking
on board a mandatory responsibility for Armenia as part of a post-war settlement,
were further buoyed by the dispatch to the region in August 1919 of a full-scale
and much publicized military mission under Major-General Harbord.[208] The
Armenian nationalists had, by then, already staked their future on Allied support
by declaring outright independence at the end of May. With Allied promises that
crimes against Armenians committed by the CUP would be brought to trial still

very much to the fore, and with many of the Allied leaders continuing to publicly voice a marked animus against *all* Turks, Armenian expectations were hardly illusionary.[209] On the contrary, even with the difficulties of communication, the presence of the Dunsterville force in the Caucasus back in the summer of 1918, and with it British promises to provide military training and *matériel* to the Armenians, strongly suggested that Western support was for real.

Paradoxically, it was exactly such support which played into a new, potentially intensified dialectic of violence between Turks and non-Turks in the region, in which the Allies, ultimately, could be little more than bystanders. Dunsterville, for instance, had arrived in Baku from Persia in August 1918, just after a major massacre of Azeris by a hastily created—and indeed ephemeral—SR regime, in which Armenian activists were among the primary perpetrators. Though the small British force had no direct responsibility for the massacre, this did not prevent them from attempting to coordinate with the local Armenians for the defence of the city against a joint German–Ottoman force, in what was clearly—at the Great War's twilight—a crude Great Power struggle for oil resources and control of pipeline. When the Ottoman forces, however—under none other than Enver's brother Nuri and his uncle, Halil—proved too great, Dunsterville was forced to retreat, with inevitable consequences for the city's Armenians. At the very least 9,000 were massacred by avenging Azeri militia in mid-September, this time as the Ottoman army either stood by or participated in the slaughter. The majority of the remaining 70,000 Armenians fled en masse across the Caspian, many thousands subsequently dying of epidemic and hunger.[210]

The events in Baku have been rather diminished in Western historical memory, when put alongside the final denouement of Anglo-French ambitions, namely the destruction and evacuation of Smyrna, precisely four years later in September 1922. The two events—which also happen to straddle a spatial (albeit invisible) fault line running between the Caspian and the Aegean—are nevertheless intimately linked. Indeed, they represent a connecting thread between the moment towards the end of the Great War when nationalist Turks refused to be cowed by Allied diktat, and a reassertion of complete Turkish independence in Anatolia. Again, however, it was neither the British nor French who were the victims of these catastrophes but their Armenian, then Greek, proxies.

That hard-line Turkish nationalists would not simply acquiesce in the Mudros Armistice—and hence defeat—should hardly surprise, given all we have previously apprehended as to their mindset. Ittihadists had already begun organizing a semi-clandestine organization, *Karakol*—the Guard—to keep their programme afloat against the oncoming tide, with former members of the Special Organization and Turkish Hearths to the fore.[211] Of course, Mustafa Kemal—the figure we most readily associate with the independence struggle—though one of the Macedonian-born, Harbiye-trained elite from which so many CUP cadres had been drawn, had been at personal odds with its inner core, and Enver in particular, almost since the party's foundation. Indeed, it was exactly his credentials as an army state loyalist rather than party activist which had provided his commission from the new Itilaf-orientated, peacemaking government of Damat Ferit in Constantinople in spring

1919 to act as newly appointed inspector-general of the Ninth Army, based in Erzurum. Kemal's required role, in effect, was to be enforcer of the new government's writ in central and eastern Anatolia, and so quell any military or civil dissent against the imposed peace.[212]

In practice, Kemal was no less sensitive than any of the dissident Ittihadists to the imminent demise of the Ottoman state. In particular, the likelihood of an Armenian entity emerging in its place under Allied auspices on eastern Anatolian soil was considered not only an affront to Turkish nationalism but like a red rag to a bull. What followed is well known. A 'Society for the Defence of National Rights in Eastern Anatolia' had already, in fact, been formed in Erzurum in February, just as similar regional groupings had been founded elsewhere in the country.[213] Kemal made this particular grouping the front for his own nascent political movement, also founded in Erzurum a few months later. Through the prism of Turkish state mythology this moment is applauded as Kemal's clear separation from the legacy of the CUP. Yet this can hardly disguise the fact that he was simply reiterating the constant Ittihadist refrain about the region as a bastion of Turkishness. Indeed, the emergence of a national resistance movement in the East, albeit under his leadership, in the summer of 1919, was not only a conscious shot across the bows of both Istanbul and their Allied minders but a quite clear restatement of the CUP's unconditional opposition to Armenian national claims to the region—regardless of what had happened in the *Aghet*. As such, it united Turkish secular nationalists and religious conservatives of multiple hues, including many Kurdish leaders. A stream of statements followed ranging from the plaintive—if Armenians, Chaldeans, and Assyrians had to be provided for by way of a homeland 'there won't be any left for us'[214]—to the downright belligerent—'not an inch of land, of our vilayets [would be ceded] to Armenia or any other country'[215]—the latter the Kemalists' direct response to the Armenian declaration of independence. Similarly strident statements about the non-negotiability of eastern Anatolia were made directly by Kemal to Harbord when they met in September, and even more forcefully the following year, when the Kemalists began negotiating in Moscow for a possible Soviet–Turkish friendship pact. So much so that when Chicherin, the Soviet commissar for foreign affairs, inquired of General Karabekir, Kemal's strongman deputy for the region, whether areas jointly inhabited by Turks, Arabs, Kurds, and Armenians might possibly determine their own fate, he received a very exact and absolute retort: 'In Turkey there has been neither an Armenia nor territory inhabited by Armenians...those [Armenians] living in Turkey committed murders and massacres...how is it possible to call back these murderers and give them the right to vote?'[216]

The comment was not only a snub, explicitly, to what the nationalists perceived as entirely illegitimate Armenian aspirations but equally, if more implicitly, to Western encouragement to them. Karabekir's remit was to crush that potentiality once and for all; indeed, at the height of his late 1920 offensive against them, Kemal's secret cipher instructions to his general were to undertake 'the political and physical extermination of Armenia'.[217] Here was a threat of a second Armenian genocide—but one in which Western commitments to the Armenians, without sufficient muscle or serious intent to support them, was proving to be the fatal ingredient.

*

However, it was not ill-considered Allied support for the Armenian political cause alone which was to help seal the fate of Ottoman Christian communities. Back in May 1919, at the very juncture when Kemal began marshalling the forces for his incipient revolt, the Big Three were on the cusp of an even more extravagant gesture bound to have the Turkish nationalist camp foaming at the mouth.

Under the leadership of the charismatic and forceful Venizelos—and since before the Paris Peace Conference—Athens had been making its own pitch for a sizeable share in the Ottoman carve-up. The personal standing of the Greek prime minister with Allied leaders was already heavily inflated. He had effectively engineered Greece's back-door entry into the Great War against the wishes of a neutralist king and country in late 1915, paving the way for the Anglo-French Salonika front. More recently he had also committed two Greek divisions to the ill-fated Allied intervention in support of Denikin.[218] The fact that this actually helped radically destabilize the position of the very significant Greek population on the Russian side of the Black Sea—leading to the mass flight of thousands of them from the Bolsheviks across the sea, in turn paving the way for further intercommunal conflict on the Pontic side[219]—does not seem to have unduly concerned the great man. On the contrary, Venizelos seems to have been much less interested in the wellbeing or fate of human beings per se than in his own big—nationalist— ideas. Nor was consistency his strong point. Throughout the Great War his big idea had been an 'ethnological settlement in the Balkans': in other words, a series of bilaterally agreed mass population 'exchanges' between the participants in the former Balkan Wars, eliminating, in the process, the 'problem' of national minorities.[220] With the end of the Great War however, Venizelos scented a much more exciting prospect still, and with it a big idea to trump them all: a Greek dominion on both sides of the Aegean.

Of course, this was in itself nothing new. The *Megali Idea* had been part of Hellenic wish-fulfilment for generations. What Venizelos strove to do in 1919 was make it real by selling it to the Big Three as if it were a fundamental aspect of their post-Ottoman security plan. Presented initially to the Council of Ten in February, the Venizelos bid did attempt an ethnographic argument, too, by reminding the Council of the significant Hellenic population in Asia Minor and of the additional 450,000 Greeks deported and expelled by the CUP from the region during the war who were now seeking restitution. Venizelos' figures actually were flawed—only by including all the Greeks in the already Athens-controlled Aegean Islands could one make an ethnographic case for Greek—as opposed to Turkish—preponderance in the strip centring on the port of Smyrna that Venizelos had proposed for Athens.[221] Venizelos, however, had something else in his favour. During the course of the Peace Conference there was a major falling-out between the Big Three and their fourth partner, the Italians, who, in the course of the war, had also staked a *prior* claim to Smyrna and a further chunk of the Ottoman interior; effectively getting this rubber-stamped in a 1917 codicil to Sykes–Picot. Italian exasperation at what appeared to be the stonewalling of this and other promises by their supposed partners in Paris led, in late April, not only to their diplomatic team—temporarily—seceding from the Conference in high dudgeon, but to the increase of their naval build-up outside Smyrna.[222]

A case of Rome behaving badly turned out to have momentous consequences for all the peoples of Anatolia. An aggrieved Wilson, in early May, backed Lloyd George—already thick with Venizelos—in a Supreme Council resolution to give the green light for Greek occupation of the Aegean port. Clemenceau also agreed, to his later regret. As Balfour acerbically put it, 'three all-powerful, all-ignorant men sitting there and carving continents with only a child to lead them'.[223] The immediate purpose had been no more than to slight the Italians, which was somewhat ironic given that Lloyd George, the prime mover in the stratagem, would have been perfectly content with an Italian occupation of Smyrna (notwithstanding the fact that, unlike the Greeks, they had no ethnographic pretext)—save for the fact that he *preferred* the Greeks. In the process he inadvertently, indeed almost single-handedly, created a very special British–Hellenic relationship which rested on the entirely flimsy Greek assumption that whatever they did in Asia Minor London would continue to back them, both in terms of political support and unquestioning credit for their spiralling military costs.

From the very beginning things went drastically wrong. The arrival of Greek troops in Smyrna on 15 May almost immediately sparked off a series of incidents which degenerated into local rioting, looting, and general disorder by elements of the Greek population against their Turkish neighbours—in which ill-disciplined Greek soldiery were also extensively involved. Toynbee, who, as we will see, became an eyewitness to ensuing atrocities in the region, put the Turkish death toll on this first day at 200, while other commentators believe there were many more.[224] All this took place under the watchful—if aghast—gaze of Allied observers and military detachments, which, in Turkish eyes, made them doubly complicit. Worse, news of events in Smyrna rapidly spread to other local towns in the vilayet of Aidin, not least as there were extensive railway links in this part of western Asia Minor. Turkish revenge attacks and the trashing of Greek quarters was followed by the Greek military occupation of offending towns, then further Turkish resistance, followed in turn by Greek military counter-massacre and the razing of the Turkish part of town, aided and abetted, of course, by local supporters. This was certainly the fate of the once prosperous centre of Aidin, which became the scene of mass carnage involving *both* communities in July.[225] Once initiated, the conflict thus became like the Balkan Wars all over again—this time, however, with what appeared to be the Allies' tacit support for the Greeks.

There was another dimension, however, to this emerging catastrophe. The Balkan War protagonists—for all their rampant aggression—knew, in the final analysis, what their territorial objectives were. By contrast, here, the conflict became increasingly open-ended. As self-propelled Turkish *çetes* responded to Greek occupation with murderous onslaughts on Greek military and civilians, the *evzonoi* advanced further and further beyond the littoral in an attempt to pulverize them. Not only was there thus no recognized halt line, but more and more of the Anatolian interior became drawn into the conflict, not least as communal groups in this once plural ethnic landscape rallied to respective national sides, or, failing that, to the one most likely to offer protection or security.

Already, in March, the Patriarchate, representing the Greek community through-out the empire, doubtless in anticipation of a new Hellenic dawn, had severed rela-tions with the Porte—in effect renouncing on behalf of its *millet* members their civic responsibilities to Ottomania. Greeks in the metropolis itself had responded by unilaterally declaring for *enosis*—union—with Athens. Concurrently, the Pontic community centred on Trabzon and led by their own Orthodox archbishop had sought to create their own independent Black Sea republic, an act which immedi-ately drew the ire of local Muslim Laz as well as nationalist Turks in towns along the Black Sea coastline, who began coalescing into an amalgam of scratch 'national forces': the *kuva-yi milliye*.[226] Many of these, in succeeding months, were however only nominally subordinated to Kemal and were more akin—as, for instance, in the case of Topal Osman (Lame Osman) operating in the Giresun area, or the Circas-sian warrior, Ethem, initially operating in Yozgat—to the freebooting warlords of the Russian civil war. Notwithstanding the fact that the localized pre-eminence of these warrior thugs and self-appointed vigilantes carried with it further potential for untrammelled violence and atrocity, Kemal, as long as he lacked his own undis-puted power remained highly dependent on them, until quite late in the overall conflict. This in itself would prove fissile, not least as Ethem—in a way reminiscent of Grigoriev's desertion from the Bolsheviks—was quite prepared to offer himself, and, in effect, his skills as a mass murderer, to the highest bidder; he eventually defected with a 700-strong band of fellow Circassians in January 1921, to the Greek side.[227]

This also ought to act as a sober reminder that the extreme violence visited on Anatolia and Thrace in the years 1919–23 developed within boundaries of conflict which were very far from clearly demarcated but rather represented a continuation of the 'war of all against all' which had already devastated the Russo-Turkish rimlands—in other words, the primary Armenian population belt—in preceding years. It meant too that the chances of being raped, mutilated, or slowly tortured to death at the hands of *muhajirun* who had suffered in the Balkan Wars, former *Teşkilat-ı Mahsusa*, dislocated Kurdish tribals, Greeks brutalized by years of immisera-tion and enslavement in labour gangs, or Armenian survivors of repeated mass murder, were at least as high as at those of the uniformed soldiery of the main competing Hellenic or Kemalist armies. Arguably, one might propose that the sheer chaos, law-lessness, not to mention desperate public health conditions resulting—not unlike the parallel, and in some respects very similar, situation in civil war Russia—para-doxically made the possibilities for anything so organized or systematic as genocide well-nigh impossible. But that would equally be to miss the point. A genocidal logic was emerging out of the larger framework of struggle: this increasingly centred on the outcome of the war—a classic War Type Two—between Athens and Ankara, the latter being, from late December 1919, the headquarters of Kemalist operations.

For these two parties, what was now at stake made for a titanic life-and-death contest. Athens could either militarily win through and impose its solution or, in all likelihood, collapse; Ankara, alternatively, with its back to the wall, had no choice but to win its war of independence or go under in a new even harsher era of colonial or neocolonial servitude. What was also painfully apparent as these two sides limbered up for a final military confrontation, was that the Allies—who had set the whole process in motion—were finding themselves with ever-decreasing options to adjudicate let alone find paths away from the most murderous zero-sum outcomes. It was, for instance, perfectly clear that the 'official' Damat Ferit government in Istanbul was in no position to restore order. Consequently, the British and French—the former more particularly—tended to intervene only where their own interests were directly at stake. Such actions, however, could have their own unforeseen but fateful consequences, just as had the original decision to allow the Greeks to occupy Smyrna. In March 1920, for instance, British troops unilaterally occupied the capital and a zone around the Straits. The move, galvanized in part by intelligence that Ankara was falling into the lap of the Bolsheviks, inevitably stiffened the Kemalist resolve, leading to a direct attack on British units around Ismid. With the British position precarious, Venizelos connived with Lloyd George to allow a Greek advance out of the Smyrna perimeter to help screen the British lines. With this decision Lloyd George effectively and quite consciously gave to the Greeks carte blanche to finish matters with the Kemalists by direct military means.[228]

True, the nemesis resulting from this decision would not materialize until the high summer of 1921, when Greek forces were finally, devastatingly defeated and routed by the Kemalists, on the Sakarya river, fifty miles short of Ankara. In the interim, as the British high commissioner for Istanbul, Admiral de Robeck—a vociferous opponent of the Lloyd George's line—correctly predicted, the green light for a Greek advance further into the interior could only mean that the danger to Christians would be 'infinitely increased'.[229] One immediate consequence was wholesale Kemalist round-ups of Greek men and boys in the Pontic area, based on not entirely imagined fears of a diversionary feint from the Black Sea area, perhaps even linking up with a Greek landing in the rear of the main nationalist forces. In this process there were uncanny resonances of what had befallen the Armenians six years earlier. Some 8,000 of an estimated 30,000 deportees force-marched towards Harput died en route, either from direct ill-treatment or dreadful conditions, with survivors set upon by irregulars and soldiery alike. Kemalist efforts of this kind, however, redoubled as the Greek Sakarya offensive got under way the following year—this time with systematic massacres by *çetes* licensed by the nationalist governor of the Pontus, Jemal Bey, especially in the Bafra district, with further atrocities committed against deportees, according to high-level British reports, extending into southern Anatolia.[230] The combined effect of direct massacres and reprisals, forced marches, disease, malnutrition, and hyper-exploitation in labour camps, accounts, according to one conservative estimate, for a death toll of 65,000 out of an estimated contemporary Pontic Greek population of 800,000—both natives and refugees from southern Russia.[231]

But it was equally Greek atrocities against Turks in the zones they sought to occupy in Thrace and Anatolia which were part of this picture of *mutual* exterminatory violence and terror. True, Greek deportations of Turks tended to be less in terms of mass aggregates and more selectively geared to removing communal leaders.[232] In Smyrna itself, after the initial sequence of atrocities—as confirmed by a first Inter-Allied Commission of Inquiry—Venizelos' appointment of fellow Cretan Aristeidis Stergiadis as governor proved an unusually astute choice for tough, not to say dictatorial, yet rigorously impartial enforcement of law and order, maintained until the final Greek collapse.[233] However, his writ only extended as far as the original Greek zone of control. Beyond it, atrocities committed by, or under the aegis of, the military command were equal to anything the Kemalists could offer.

We know this to be the case from a further Inter-Allied Commission of Inquiry (IACI), which reported on a specific sequence of events on the İzmit and Yalova-Gemlik peninsulas at the eastern end of Sea of Marmara, during the Greek offensive of spring 1921. What happened here was also corroborated in an International Committee of the Red Cross (ICRC) report and by Toynbee, as a firsthand observer of the Greek campaign in general and events on Yalova in particular. His careful reportage of what happened was subsequently published in the *Manchester Guardian*. It also cost him his chair of Medieval and Modern Greek at King's College, London, which was endowed by Greek shipowners.[234]

The IACI report found that Greek-organized forces around Yalova were operating a 'systematic plan of destruction of Turkish villages and extinction of the Muslim population'. Both Greek and Armenian irregulars were involved in the killings but were also found to be operating under military control and command, 'sometimes even with the assistance of detachments of regular troops'. This was underscored not only by findings confirming that there had been no cases where violations had been 'prevented or punished by the military', but by the fact that the underlying intention of the campaign, on the one hand strategic in order to secure the flanks and rear of Greek army, on the other appeared to be 'to create in this region a political situation favourable to the Greek government'.[235] In modern parlance we would call this 'creating facts on the ground'.

Beyond this crisply dispassionate account of events, Toynbee was able to fill in some of the more grisly details of what actually took place in and around Yalova. All the Turkish villages of the coastal area were pillaged, trashed, and then set alight, bar those which had some temporary use in terms of supplies. Toynbee himself was with an Allied naval flotilla that attempted to evacuate survivors from some fifteen Turkish villages. He became involved in a seven-hour stand-off on a beach to save these people from local *çetes* during which 'we had to wrestle for their lives, not only family by family but person by person'. He noted how the *çetes* were mostly ordinary locals, who were at one and the same time brutalized and fearful, yet vengeful. But he also recounted the behaviour of Greek and Armenian women, who gloated over their Muslim counterparts as they 'trembled and sobbed'.[236] In all likelihood, the only reason these Muslim women survived was the Allied officers' presence. Yet what is equally sobering is that these events were clearly far from being isolated or unusual but rather were part of a standard operating procedure. The slaughter at Yalova and İzmit shocked Western bystanders for the simple

reason that they could *see* it before their eyes, from Allied ships and in close proximity to the neutral, supposedly pacified, Straits zone.

By spring 1921, however, it was perfectly clear to all, bar the likes of Lloyd
George and Venizelos, which way the wind was blowing—and that it was not in
Greek favour. Most Greeks knew it too. Venizelos himself had been spectacularly
slung out of office, in winter 1920 elections. His successor, the pro-royalist and
hence historically wartime neutralist, Dimitrios Gounaris, was consequently seen
as a liability by both the British and French: their economic punishment of the
new regime entailed blocking credits formerly granted to the firmly pro-Allied
Venizelos.[237] As economic crisis loomed and the Hellenic kingdom seemed to
descend into a bout of mutual, even violent, denunciations and recriminations, the
terrible irony remained that Gounaris was no more able to extricate himself from
Asia Minor than his arch-rival. Staying the course was a matter of national honour.
Failing in that—as the prime minister intimated to Metaxas, a legendary general
whom Gounaris tried (unsuccessfully) to inveigle into taking over the Asia Minor
command—would mean that 'the English will cease to regard us as a serious
nation'.[238]

Gounaris' conviction that the Greeks would be obliged to continue the war to
the bitter end, catastrophe notwithstanding—in order 'to prove that we are a
nation on which a Great Power can depend', sits very uneasily, however, with
Toynbee's withering verdict that the powers themselves 'did not suspect how
quickly pawns in distress become an embarrassment', and that they little cared if
those pawns simply disappeared 'from the board'.[239] On paper, of course, the
Greeks, like the Armenians, were still due their prizes. The Treaty of Sèvres—and a
series of linked protocols concluded with the Damat Ferit government in August
1920—promised not only all of Thrace and any remaining Aegean Islands to
Greece, but also a plebiscite for Smyrna after five years of Greek rule, after which
it could be incorporated into the Hellenic polity. Armenia was to become a substantial state on both sides of the old Russo-Ottoman border: in all likelihood to
include the Pontus region, as the best way of protecting the Greeks there, but with
the exact boundaries of this 'greater Armenia' to be determined by none other than
President Wilson. There was even a notional possibility of a Kurdish state, or states,
in south-eastern Anatolia. All these entities, naturally, would be politically and
economically linked to the Allies and, moreover, would be part of a post-Ottoman
security belt which would include the regions Britain, France, and Italy had already,
earlier, apportioned to themselves under the terms of Sykes–Picot.

Sèvres, in short, was the very last in the sequence of great imperial carve-ups. An
Ottoman entity in Anatolia was to be allowed to continue to exist (the sultan even
retaining Istanbul—albeit under an Allied commission of control) but divided
into economic zones of influence, with Capitulations in force as previously, and,
indeed, with Tripartite supervision of Ottoman finances more rigorously applied
even than before 1914.[240] This might read all very justly if one were a Greek or
Armenian nationalist. But apart from the small fact that it inflamed Turkish patriotic anger, its other primary flaw was that it simply could not be implemented.
Save, that is, by Greek force majeure. It is then doubly ironic that the very first

IACI, which reported on the events around Smyrna in May 1919, had even then submitted that bringing the Turks to heel in this way—that is, by Greek military expedition *alone*—could not be attempted 'with any chance of success'.[241] As the whole purpose of the Allies utilizing 'the illusions of the local nationalities'—Armenian as well as Greek—was however to preserve rather than squander their own resources, and thereby 'salvage something from the wreck of their own schemes',[242] it logically followed that dumping the proxies would follow soon enough.

The French were first off the mark, withdrawing their troops from Cilicia in February 1920 without bothering to inform the Armenian resettlers. The result, not unsurprisingly, was a series of gruesome Kemalist-perpetrated massacres around Marash and Mersin over the following months.[243] They dwarfed anything the Légion Arménienne had previously committed against Muslim *indigènes*. That aside, French momentum towards a change of political tune gathered pace, hastened in November by the collapse of Wrangel in southern Russia. Realpolitik—in other words, preventing a Bolshevik–Turkish accord—now dictated that Sèvres was indeed a dead letter and that the only people worth knowing were those in Ankara. A French agreement was duly signed with Kemal in October 1921, ceding French claims to Cilicia for good, but not before wresting a French priority for 'economic collaboration' in the region, not least with some very specific mining concessions in view.[244]

This hardly made the French the particular villains of the piece. In many ways they were simply the avant-garde in an inevitable direction of flow. A British War Office supported by Churchill also wanted to go down the Kemalist route around this time but had an obdurate Lloyd George, backed by the Foreign Office, to contend with.[245] The Italians played their own game, not least to get their own back on British slights suffered in Paris. Their route to Kemal, and with that their own raft of concessions, was by providing Ankara with military *matériel*—in direct defiance of a British munitions embargo to all sides.[246] Even the Americans, in the person of Rear Admiral Bristol, their high commissioner in the Ottoman capital, had come to the conclusion that in the interests of 'open-door' business opportunities—not least those of Standard Oil of New Jersey—it was Kemal whom Washington should be backing.[247] This, alongside the Senate vote in June 1920 putting the lid on a US mandate for Armenia, doubly ensured that Wilson's gesture later that year—earmarking an additional 42,000 square miles of Turkish territory for the proposed Armenian state—became not simply another broken, entirely unenforceable, promise.[248] When, in the autumn of the following year, the British began covertly dealing with Kemal to allow for an exchange of prisoners, including a clutch being held in Malta for crimes committed against the Armenians,[249] it was quite clear that nobody among the Western Allies was now going to come to either Armenian, or for that matter Greek, rescue.

In that we reach the nub of the issue. There might have been plenty of outraged citizens, especially in Britain, even more so in America, who believed that the Christians of the Ottoman Empire—the Armenians in particular—should be assisted on humanitarian grounds and indeed for their *own* sake. But, in practice, there was never any question that any of the Western powers would support an independent Armenia for this reason *alone*. It may be that emotional support from Wilson, not to say his 'castle in the air'—as Eyre Crowe acerbically dismissed his Armenian award four days *after* Erivan's capitulation to the Kemalists—acted in the upshot as a form of brake on Kemal's extermination instructions to Karabekir as his forces poised for their final military onslaught on Armenian defensive positions around Kars in late October.[250] It was indeed a moment when a second full-scale genocide of Armenians *was* possible—though this time committed against not a subject population of the empire, but rather a militarily defeated—if in Turkish eyes entirely illegitimate—state. However, we will never know whether there was a clear Kemalist intention on this score because of a final irony of ironies. On the very day, 2 December 1920, that the Armenians accepted Turkish terms in the Treaty of Gümrü—a position from which the Turks might easily have annihilated what remained of Armenia—its starving, exhausted, almost entirely refugee population were saved by an ersatz miracle: the Red Army intervened. With the Bolsheviks thereafter incorporating the residual Erivan Republic into the Soviet system and Russia's frontiers again contiguous—if somewhat now to the Soviet disadvantage—with Turkey, as had been the case prior to the revolution, any Kemalist aspiration to irrevocably finish with the Armenians then and there had to be put on long-term hold.[251]

No such respite awaited the Greeks of Asia Minor or the Pontus, as the Western Allies jettisoned their Athenian prop. Toynbee, for one, had little sympathy with the players who had rushed into the initial Allied trap with 'their eyes open because they could not resist the bait'.[252] Nevertheless, the immensity of the catastrophe which followed, and in which the Allies were effectively nothing more than gaping bystanders, was, in its own way, truly shocking.

Everybody had been expecting the Greek military position on the Sakarya to unravel sooner or later. When it did so, in August 1922, its pace was vertiginous. The army's retreat to Smyrna and the sea became not simply a rout, but carried in its wake a mass exodus of hundreds of thousands of terrified Greeks and Armenians. If the majority were convinced that Turkish pursuit carried with it an unadulterated thirst for vengeance and murder their instinct was essentially correct. During the previous year both sides in the Greco-Turkish conflict had given licence to *çetes* to commit 'organised atrocities' on a scale far in excess of the earlier stages of the conflict.[253] Certainly, too, the Kemalists now saw the retreat as *the* opportunity to establish their own national facts on the ground—a complete ethnic cleansing of all the now remaining unwanted non-Turkish elements in Asia Minor. But the Greek army, abetted by its local supporters—often priests—also played its own critical part in this zero-sum game by, on the one hand, liquidating remaining Turkish villages in its line of retreat and, on the other, forcing recalcitrant *Greek* populations to retreat with them and burning their villages into the bargain.[254]

This scorched earth policy, strategically considered or otherwise, nevertheless proved utterly futile. While the Greek army and administration was able to evacuate Smyrna in relatively good order by 3 September, there was no salvation for the tens of thousands of refugees they had left crowding, panicking, and terrified on the waterfront. The following six days of hiatus before the Turkish army arrived were perhaps not unlike that dread moment just before the arrival of the Khmer Rouge in a beleaguered and wasted Phnom Penh in 1975—another jewel of Western cosmopolitanism in foreign parts, ransomed to extreme high-risk geopolitical calculations. Here, too, was a city at the very edge of its 'normative' time, its refugee victims waiting for deliverance, their would-be deliverers in the flotilla of Allied warships just outside the harbour watching and observing the escalating violence before their eyes but with no instructions to assist, bar those who could prove their bona fides as co-nationals.[255]

It was again the fact that what followed was so visible to the outside world which made it so shocking—not exceptionality. Extreme violence in Anatolia had become part of the everyday for years, just as it would become in Iraq as another consequence of unwarranted outside interference, in more recent times. Nevertheless, as the Kemalist army arrived and the already escalating level of Turkish demotic violence was given its full rein by military commander and former Smyrna governor, Nuraddin Pasha, American and British officers found themselves being drawn into efforts to put a brake on it, some intervening in incidents directly, some paying with their lives.

For the most part, however, Allied personnel remained bystanders to the sequence of mass killing which intensified from 9 September. It was surely no accident that the Armenian quarter was one immediate target. A US naval officer, Captain Hepburn, reported that every able-bodied Armenian man was hunted down and killed in house-to-house searches, with Turkish boys as young as twelve 'taking part in the hunt'.[256] There was Armenian resistance, which, in turn, precipitated the involvement of army units, who proceeded to systematize the killing, taking Armenians in batches to the *konak* for mass slaughter. System also prevailed in the round-up, court-martialling, and shooting of men—both Greeks and Armenian—listed on a Turkish registry as members of the Asia Minor Defence League. There was less system and more basic venality, however, in the way the Armenian quarter was completely looted and 'stripped bare' of absolutely anything worth plundering by soldiers and citizens alike.[257]

The counterpoint to arbitrary or focused massacre in port or city, on 9 September, was one singularly symbolic act of killing. Archbishop Chrysostom, strongly identified with Greek nationalist and certainly anti-Kemalist sentiment, yet also formidable in his protection of Christian refugees within the sanctuary of the cathedral church, was summoned that evening by Nuraddin, now installed in Government House. At the latter's clear behest, the archbishop was then handed over to a several hundred-strong Muslim crowd in the square below, where he was manhandled, dressed up in a barber's coat, and literally mutilated to death.[258]

There was one more significant act to follow, which in the circumstances one might consider to be the final, even necessary, coup de grâce. Who was responsible for setting fire to the Christian and foreign quarters of the city on 13 September is ultimately immaterial. In all likelihood it was the Turks, but then Greeks, Turks, Armenians, Bulgarians, and Serbs since the Balkan Wars had been making pyromaniacal statements with regard to what they clearly saw as contaminated built environments—almost as a matter of course. Smyrna, however, was a big city, and the inferno consequently awesomely striking: as one British journalist reported, 'an unbroken wall of fire, two miles long, in which twenty distinct volcanoes are throwing up jagged, writhing tongues to a height of a hundred feet'.[259] Under its cover the killings continued—perhaps 15,000 all told. Some further 30,000 Greek and Armenian men were marched off into the interior, with violence and death an inevitable corollary for many. Equally goaded, the Allies and Greeks also finally got their act together to evacuate the up to 200,000 surviving refugees still on the waterfront.[260] As for Smyrna, at least as that great 2,000-year-old centre of Christian Hellenism: it ceased to exist.

'THE UNMIXING OF PEOPLES': THE ROAD TO AND FROM LAUSANNE

The panicked Greek flight from Anatolia and then, equally, from eastern Thrace, marked the apotheosis in the process of conscious Kemalist eruction of non-Muslims. What Venizelos had envisaged as 'an ethnological wall formed out of the most healthy and the most profoundly Greek representatives of the race...Acarnanians...Aetolians and Arcadians' acting as a civilized buffer interposed between Europe and the Muslim world,[261] had been effectively turned on its head. Turkish power had been restored not only as far as the Aegean but to the European shore as far as the Maritza. How many had been directly killed in this 'unmixing of populations'[262]—Lord Curzon's memorable but unlovely phrase—is difficult to gauge. McCarthy, generally conservative on non-Muslim casualties, specifically estimates 313,000 Greek deaths outside of Istanbul, or something in the region of one-quarter of the Greek-speaking population eliminated from Turkey.[263] Even if this is an underestimate, broadly speaking one might suggest that the war of extermination had seen four Greeks removed for every one killed, with the slaughter heavily skewed towards men—not least judging from the overwhelmingly large numbers of women and children among the at least 1.2 million refugees who ended up in Greece.[264] Violence and dislocation, of course, had hardly been a one-way traffic. Again, McCarthy's estimate of 1.2 million Muslims who fled the Greek invasion in Anatolia—over and above those who left in the face of the Greek takeover in eastern Thrace—sounds curiously like an attempt at striking an equivalence with Greek suffering. All the more so when he proposes that as many as a third may have been killed or died as a consequence.[265]

Whatever the symmetry, or not, of the killing up to the high summer of 1922, the Greek military collapse thereafter dramatically increased the odds on the wholesale massacre of the population—or, more accurately, populations—associated with the defeated side. For those who could or would not flee, the situation was suggestive not simply of ethnic cleansing but wholesale genocide. At this juncture, the Western powers, so critically responsible and culpable for what had come to pass, intervened to save the day. Or so it seemed.

As an adjunct to new negotiations to replace the dead letter of Sèvres and so recognize Turkey—effectively for the first time—as an equal and sovereign partner in a Western comity of nations,[266] the Allies acted as third party to a Convention 'Concerning the Exchange of Greek and Turkish Populations'.[267] Actually, the initiative for the protocol came from the Kemalist side, evidence perhaps that the regime itself was looking to a future engagement with the outside world, cleansed of the classically Orientalist and thoroughly stereotypical image of the Turk as mass murderer. But by accepting a resolution to the 'problem' of unwanted minorities by compulsory, and apparently symmetrical, exchange between the Greek and Turkish parties, the Allies were themselves signalling—however much as an act of last resort—their official adherence to the principle. On both sides, a majority of the disaggregated, 'surplus' communities would be transferred to the nation state to which they (supposedly) *belonged*. There could, in principle, be no plea-bargaining (in fact there were some exceptional cases) and no tribunals before which the disaffected or truculent might seek redress. Neither individuals, families, clans, nor any other communal associations would be allowed any voice in the Convention's modalities.[268] Above all, the protocol's wording strongly suggested an exchange which was final and irrevocable. There would be no right of return to the country of one's original domicile except at the behest of the government of that country; which effectively meant no right of return. After all, at the heart of this Convention was a state *dirigisme*, which overrode and even negated individual human rights. If one can speak of a human right in the matter at all it was one offered in negation: the right *not* to be physically liquidated but only expelled from one's place of birth. Moreover as the protocol was drawn up after the main massacre sequence, the intrinsic value of this right was precisely nil.

What the Convention was actually enunciating, then, had nothing to do with humanitarian interests, but only with those of the states involved. Indeed, if there was an onus on anybody in this formulation, it was on the displaced persons themselves, through a double act of self-abnegation, or perhaps, more precisely, self-induced 'disappearance': physically from the country which had been real home; psychologically, culturally, and emotionally from all those traits which associated with their former lives, and thereby tainted them in their new ersatz ones. Only purged of these alien features might the transferee's life take on meaningful purpose. However, to imagine the displaced human to be thus, somehow, the ultimate object of the protocol would be a mistake. The Convention's bottom line was to create a 'realist' political framework for a durable peace founded on recognition of Turkey and Greece respectively, as authentic sovereign nation states. In turn, this would provide the necessary conditions for the fundamental domestic business of each: economic development, modernization, national progress, and so the creation of 'a brighter and better human future'[269]—within the context, of course, of the post-Great War international political economy.

Such a critique, with its implication that the exchange agenda actually entailed a state-demanded negation of human worth, not to mention self-identity, may at first sight read as Kafkaesque parody of the truth, not least when set against its cardinal, internationally mandated purpose of preventing what amounted to genocide.[270] One might further in its defence make the obvious rejoinder that it was better to be deposited in miserable squalor in an encampment or shanty town in Salonika, Piraeus, Sofia, or Ankara—as so many refugees were to live out their catastrophically alienated, psychically pulverized lives—than to be dead. In the real world, after all, there are rarely happy endings to human-induced catastrophes of such magnitude.

In response, and thereby by way of conclusion to this chapter, the seminal nature of the Lausanne settlement needs to be briefly contextualized as a further reminder of its significance in the history of genocide in the age of nation states, on two levels. On the first—that is, in terms of Greece and Turkey themselves—it is well to recall the radical nature of the caesura with the past. Within both Greek and Turkish cultural systems up to the time of the Balkan Wars, notions of social and ethnic plurality and diversity, contested as they may have been, were the norm. Certainly, if one thinks of the Hellenic version, even with religious and cultural boundaries, not to mention assimilative imperatives, it was still entirely possible for Albanians, Slavs, Vlachs, and others to be comfortably situated *within* Greek society.[271] Just as, in turn, Greeks of various hues within Anatolia might happily see themselves as part and parcel of a broader pan-Aegean Hellenic culture without compromising their *parallel* identities as *millet* members of Ottoman society. By the same token, even the Gökalpian turn—premised as it was on a form of cultural homogenization—assumed that Laz, Kurds, Bosnians, and Tobeshes—*indigènes* and *muhajirun* alike—might all be embraced within a larger Turkish family, sharing a *common* Ottoman–Islamic cultural heritage without racial, ethnic, geographic, or political preconditions.[272] Granted, these formulations of identity were already evincing elements of exclusivism, albeit founded on long-standing religious bonds. But equally, neither wrote out of the script altogether traditional realities of habitus, historic warps and woofs, or, if one prefers, communal peculiarities and idiosyncrasies.

The terms of Lausanne killed this idea of society as cultural mosaic stone-dead. And it did so by an extraordinary conjuring trick entailing the argument that the victim-survivors of the catastrophe were not refugees—*muhajirun*—at all, but, to use the Turkish linguistic euphemism, *mübadil*—exchangees—who were being 'repatriated' to their authentic national home where they would be reunited with other people of their kind.[273] That this was blatantly untrue is demonstrated by the mutual unintelligibility of the Greek spoken by Pontic Hellenes and Macedonians who found themselves in each other's nominal company when large numbers of the former were dumped in camps in the environs of Salonika.[274] Even more was this the case with the Turkish-speaking but Orthodox Karamanli from Cappadocia, though their 'transfer' to the Peloponnese had plenty of corollaries on the other side, including Greek-speaking Cretans, Valaades from south-west Macedonia, as well as many Albanian-speaking Chams from Epirus who found themselves deposited on Turcophone Aegean shores.[275]

It was, of course, a perverse if not supreme irony of the exchange that the yardstick used for determining who was to go and who was to stay was a religious one. Kemalists clearly saw an advantage in the formula as a means by which to get rid of as many Orthodox 'enemies' as possible. Only the firm veto of the League of Nations-appointed Mixed Commissions overseeing the transfer prevented Jacobites—mostly Syriac-speaking Orthodox—from inclusion in their numbers.[276] At the same time, a small group of Karamanli managed to avoid it also by claiming that they were part of a breakaway *Turkish* Orthodox sect, thereby affirming their politically reliable credentials to Ankara.[277] Underlying political calculations was clearly unease about the mutable, even wayward, background of some communal groups. On the Greek side the Valaades had not so long ago been Christians: a good reason one might think for saving them from the 'surgery'. As it was, it was their recent Islamic lineage that determined they were not to be spared.[278] Athens might well have wished to have used the occasion, too, to expunge another highly suspect 'Trojan horse': the possibly 60,000-strong, allegedly Turcophile, Sephardi community of Salonika. As Jews, however, they could not be included in the exchange formula. Instead, Athens had to make do with expunging the smaller 12–13,000 *dönme*, a distinct subsect who had opted for Muslim conversion back in the mid-seventeenth century.[279] Such efforts could also backfire. While the Greek mainland was being overwhelmed and economically devastated by the sheer weight of human flotsam, Turkey's strong interest in repopulating a devastated Anatolia did not run to embracing the Albanian Chams—of whom those who did arrive were considered sufficiently dubious, dangerous, and inherently unmalleable for Ankara to seek their removal to a third country.[280]

To suggest that all the refugees were incompatible with their new surroundings, or unruly in the face of the new homogenizing dispensation, would certainly be a sleight of hand. But the verdict of one commentator, that what actually was enacted through Lausanne—albeit using different terms of social and national classifica-tion—amounted to two deportations into exile, one of Christian Turks to Greece, the other of Muslim Greeks to Turkey,[281] speaks volumes in itself about how far down the road rimland states had gone by the early 1920s in imbibing Western-inspired nationalist discourses and categories in the face of the ethnological evi-dence before them.

This in turn begs the question of whether Allied intervention in the process could have either softened or somehow diverted its most toxic characteristics. Using Lemkin as guide, it would not be very difficult to read the implications and consequences of Lausanne as inherently genocidal, even putting aside the fact that the Convention's primary purpose was to act as a post-facto legitimization for the ethnic cleansing and massacre which had already occurred. It is clear, on one level, that the Allies were bowing to circumstances which they deemed in some way beyond their control. Lord Curzon, as head of the British delegation, was notably jaundiced—to the point of abandoning diplomatic etiquette—in his vituperative denunciation of the protocol's emphasis on compulsion.[282] Yet when push came to shove he, too, was ready to endorse 'the advantages which would ultimately accrue to both countries from a greater homogeneity of population and from the removal of old and deep rooted causes of quarrel'.[283]

Was this simply a matter of a senior British statesman attempting to put a good face on a humiliating situation in which, of all people, it was the Turks who were effectively dictating terms? Or was the Allied participation in the Lausanne process something more than simply a pragmatic retreat in the face of the inevitable? This takes us to our second and final level of discussion: that of the *international* significance of the Convention for future genocide.

Certainly, the Allies moved rapidly from a presentation of the Convention in wholly negative terms to one where their own role became centre-stage proof of their prescience in the face of humanitarian disaster, not to mention their ability to respond effectively through the good offices of the League. A mythology also developed around the undoubtedly energetic role of Norwegian explorer-cum-humanitarian Fridtjof Nansen. As the League's first refugee commissioner, it was Nansen who, in key respects, was the architect of the Mixed Commissions and of their efforts to ensure an orderly and safe transfer of peoples between the two countries.[284] As a consequence some 356,000 'Turks' and some 290,000 'Greeks' were successfully delivered.[285] Over and beyond this one can further see in the planning, organization, and implementation of the project aspects we might associate with conflict resolution and management in our own contemporary scene. Organizations that today we would call NGOs, not least the International Committee of the Red Cross, played a highly significant role sustaining life and limb and preventing the mass spread of disease in what otherwise could easily have descended into mass chaos and death. In the Convention itself there was, moreover, a carefully crafted second article which, in allowing for the preservation of the Greek community in the Istanbul area and the Turkish one in western Thrace, created a form of apparent mutual guarantee between the two states to uphold the integrity, security, and equality of their recognized 'minority' populations. The Convention also seemed to offer fairness and justice to the whole exercise by having the Mixed Commissions acting to evaluate and then compensate for the abandoned property of all exchangees.[286]

As a direct consequence of all this the Lausanne exchange was increasingly remembered in Western policymaking and opinion-forming circles thereafter as not simply one of the finest hours of the League but even as a case of best practice in the face of particularly knotty 'ethnic' problems. It was invoked in 1937, for instance, by the Peel Commission on Palestine, as a way of resolving the Jewish–Arab conflict in the British mandate territory (regardless of the fact that, if implemented, it would have involved an almost entirely one-way transfer of Arabs),[287] and became key precedent, if not legitimization, for the wave of ethnic cleansings which swept the 'Lands Between' in the build-up to and aftermath of the Second World War—of which more in later chapters. Even more alarmingly perhaps, commentators up to the present day have continued to read into it an essential benignity. Pavel Polian, an expert on Soviet forced migration, for instance, while acknowledging that it was '*not* an exchange of national minorities', nevertheless went on to characterize it as 'mutual *peaceful* ethnic cleansing'.[288]

Such interpretations are little more than sophistry. What the West actually presided over in 1922–3 was a largely genocidal series of ethnic cleansings, for which they attempted to absolve themselves of blame at Lausanne through the linguistic gloss of 'exchange'. Most of those ethnically cleansed, especially the

Greeks and Armenians, were, moreover, evicted *before* the implementation of the official Mixed Commissions-supervised scheme. However, because this did not begin until 1 May 1923, more than three months *after* the terms of the Convention had been completed, both Turks and Greeks were effectively given a window in which to accelerate removals by terror and violence.[289] The immediate result was that only a mere fraction of the 1.2 million Greek refugees were 'transferred' by way of the 'safe' Nansen programme. The wider result was that by having, in effect, given to both regimes that post-facto sanction with which to resolve ethnic problems by state violence, the West at Lausanne signalled that its prior commitment through the Minorities Treaties to the defence of vulnerable ethnic and social communities in the 'New Europe' (and beyond) was entirely specious, not to say null and void. How far this was the case was made abundantly clear by none other than Curzon, when he proposed that hardships suffered, 'great though they may be, will be less than the hardships which will result for these same populations if nothing is done'.[290] In other words, if there had already been a national onus on unwanted communities to 'disappear' there was now an international requirement, doubly to do so, for the sake of the stability of the new international order. The fact that issues of property compensation for survivors would also be, in the interim, shelved and then in 1930 conveniently cancelled altogether[291]—once general economic crisis had descended—simply reinforces the expendability of the human beings caught up in these games of others.

Indeed, what is most disturbing in this narrative is the degree to which the post-1919 West was ready and willing to dump whole communities when it became clear that otherwise its own interests might be adversely affected. Up to that point, schemes such as those of Lichtenstädter, or, more recently, those of the ironically Lausanne-based Swiss academic, George Montandon, for the compulsory mass transfer of 'minority' populations in the interests of nation-state homogeneity, had been mostly dismissed as the musings of 'political fantasists'.[292] Closer to the workings of the Paris peacemakers, the findings of the Wilson-mandated King–Crane Commission had made recommendations for the future of Ottomania in September 1919, envisaging population exchange as the basis upon which a small Armenia under mandatory supervision might achieve majority rule within five years. While using the language of 'repatriation', however, the report had fallen short of proposing that Muslims in the proposed state would *all* have to leave by coercion.[293]

Yet Western thinking in these terms was hardly squeamish when it came to native *colonial* peoples. On the contrary, the notion of territorializing ethnicity and thus forcibly moving people into administrative units according to their supposed 'natural characteristics' was tantamount to a standard operating procedure.[294] Complete, and by implication violent, ethnographic reordering with regard to imperial backwaters such as the Caucasus and eastern Anatolia had also actually been a facet of Great Power planning—whether the imperial arena in question was one's own or that of somebody else—for more than a generation.[295] In early 1919, the British military mission in the Caucasus had acted exactly on such geostrategic grounds to implement 'a mini population exchange' of Armenians and Azeris in the Karabagh and Elizavetpol regions—very much, in the former case, to the detriment of the Armenians. Overriding all objections, and regardless either of the short-term impact on the local population or what turned out to be long-term deleterious consequences, no sooner had the British done their worst than they withdrew from the region, leaving the populations to continue their inter-ethnic bloodletting.[296]

Looked at from this standpoint, Western acquiescence in population transfer looks less like radical innovation and more like a cynical redeployment of a time-honoured expedient. What was clearly different was that it was now taking place within an avowedly European or near-European nation-state context. And in this sense it was much more acceptable to assume a pretence of voluntarism and non-coercion. E. H. Carr, the British historian and backroom minorities expert in Paris, had mused on how minorities might be induced to migrate to their own nation state (as if they always somehow had such a thing) to resolve outstanding problems.[297] The answer seemed to be provided a few months later when, under the aegis of the Allied negotiations for the Neuilly Treaty with a defeated Bulgaria, Sofia and Athens agreed what was supposedly a voluntary population swap to resolve their long-term dispute over control of western Thrace. Except that in practice, the imminent arrival of Greek troops in the former Bulgarian zone the following May precipitated a mass flight of some 40,000 Bulgarians, many of whom were already the victims of Greek violence from the Balkan Wars. Bulgarian Prime Minister Stamboliski's plea to the Allies to let the refugees go on living in the region under a continuing inter-Allied administration, outside of Sofia's political jurisdiction, fell entirely on deaf ears. By 1928 it was estimated a full 5 per cent of Bulgaria's population—some 163,000 people—were refugees.[298]

The situation, of course, in metropolitan Greece—whose 4.5 million population grew by a full one-quarter as a consequence of the 'Asia Minor catastrophe'—was far worse, necessitating two successive emergency loans from the Bank of England just to keep a refugee-inundated Hellenic state from total collapse.[299] But then the Allies had also given short shrift not only to Stamboliski, but to another lateral, albeit emergency, plan which, if implemented, might also have prevented a mass eruction of humanity. In the summer of 1922, with Greek defeat in Anatolia looming, the incorruptible and far-sighted Stergiadis had put forward a proposal to the British whereby the Smyrna zone might be governed not by Athens but under the nominal suzerainty of the Ottoman sultan, backed by the Allies and, crucially, with a view to maintaining a genuinely multi-ethnic society and administration in which all parties—Greeks, Armenians, Muslim Turks, and others—would continue to live *together*.[300]

This 'humanitarian' proposal, however, was neither the brave new world of progressives and modernizers of the ilk of Venizelos or Kemal, nor, for that matter, of the new Western arbiters of the international political and economic order. The repudiation of the Stergiadis' proposal, followed by Lausanne, thus marked a definitive watershed between the old imperial, multi-ethnic world of the rimlands and their replacement by a system of homogeneous nation states—with all its implications for extreme violence against suspect, unwanted, or simply marginal communities. But why so? Was this the inevitable march of contemporary history? Why, instead, could the rimlands not have been a post-Great War beacon for an entirely different trajectory towards a true avoidance of genocide?

PART TWO

INTERREGNUM BETWEEN GREAT WARS

4

The Lost Peace

SETTING THE SCENE

It became clear to me that diversity of nations, religious groups, and races is essential to civilization because every one of these groups has a mission to fulfil and a contribution to make in terms of culture. To destroy these groups is opposed to the will of the Creator and to disturb the spiritual harmony of mankind.[1]

Lemkin's recollections from his unpublished autobiography point to a time in earlier life when his understanding of the nature of human collectivities was beginning not simply to take form but develop into firm convictions about their sacrosanct value in the grander scheme of things. As a budding young international lawyer these ideas would feed into his report to the 1933 League of Nations conference on international criminal law in Madrid, in which he proposed that attacks on such groups should be outlawed as 'a crime of barbarity'.[2] For Lemkin the need was urgent in the light of the recent 'Assyrian affair', in which a whole community—none other than the survivors from the Hakkâri holocaust of 1915—had again faced the possibility of annihilation, this time at the hands of the recently independent Iraqi state.

Lemkin's report, however, made no headway on the conference agenda. There were other, allegedly more pressing, dangers confronting the international legal community, not least the issue of increasing terrorism. It is significant that while the priority of the international commission on the unification of criminal law was the integrity and inviolability of state—which a growing wave of assassinations of public figures was avowedly endangering—Lemkin was going against the grain by arguing that a much greater danger lay in possible state threats to the lives of *peoples*. Whether a more positive response from his senior colleagues would have led to the implementation of an idea fifteen years before the Genocide Convention reached the international statute book is a moot point. What the stonewalling of crimes of 'barbarity' and 'vandalism' more vividly underscores is that mainstream juridical opinion in 1933 was closely attuned to a conventional wisdom that was, by this time, so standard that it hardly needed spelling out: namely that the best guarantee available for the protection of communities, national, religious, ethnic, or otherwise, lay in having one's own compact territory. Or, to put it more bluntly, if one wanted protection there was no point asking the international community to provide it but—as the revisionist Zionist Vladimir Jabotinsky had provocatively argued a decade earlier—one should instead create one's own 'iron wall' of 'bayonets'.[3]

For Zionists, as for Assyrians, in the 1930s, one could thus argue that a Lemkinian criminalization of statist bad behaviour was essentially irrelevant. The key existential issue in the face of communal vulnerability and potential defencelessness, rather, was how to gain powerful benefactors—through the League of Nations or otherwise—who might enable you to achieve territorial space within which to defend *your* people's integrity on a *self-organized* basis.[4] This implied sovereign independence: political autonomy within a broader federal arrangement was strictly second best. Either way, legitimizing such a petition carried one indispensable requirement: that you declare your communal group a 'nation'.

On this latter score, Lemkin was not at odds with contemporary system thinking, so much as one of its most enthusiastic adherents. Like Herder a century and a half earlier, Lemkin's starting point was to both accept and celebrate the existence of primordial national groups as an ostensible fact of humanity's natural history. Like Herder, too, what mattered about this 'reality' was enabling the sum of the nations' diverse parts to operate within an ecumenical discourse, the consequence of which would be the creation of a truly cosmopolitan, international civilization.[5] Lemkin's idea of the nation thus derived from a firm Enlightenment optimism. The need to temper such optimism by practical action related to instances where this 'symphony of nations' was threatened by forces intent on dissolving its discrete elements.[6] More mainstream interwar wisdoms suggested that such threats might be mediated by the League; in worst-case scenarios, perhaps, by a resort to Lausanne-style formulas. On Jews and Arabs both claiming Palestine as theirs, for instance, Peel Commission delegate and professor of colonial history Reginald Coupland declared, 'No two people who had developed national consciousness could live together as equal partners in a single state'.[7] In other words, the answer to the problem lay not in questioning the basic premise of the national idea but rather in managing the situation, if necessary by separating the two truculent 'nations' into their *own* territorial compartments. Where Lemkin was singular and arguably deviated from this standard position was in proposing that national cultures, *whatever their circumstances* or exact racial, religious, or ethnic form, needed the protection of international society—through the instrument of international law—to ensure their wellbeing and long-term survival.

It was certainly ironic that by the time that Lemkin sought to articulate such notions in the international arena, grounds for optimism about international relationships or even for a minimalist League management of inter-group disputes were receding fast. General economic crisis as a consequence of the 1929 Wall Street Crash had taken its toll. The rise of Stalin and then Hitler carried in their wake authoritative, as well as authoritarian, demands for all humanity 'to perform according to a new choreography'.[8] Advocacy of progressive liberal ideas of a Lemkinian kind, when set against an international climate darkening almost by the day, reads like a study in futility. If we are looking for a time and space in which a 'non-genocidal society' might have developed in the interwar period it would clearly not be in, or after 1933.[9] But is the quest in itself based on a false premise: at best, a naïve aspiration for the unattainable, and at worst, an unwarranted detour from what should be our primary focus of attention: that is, charting the preconditions for an extraordinary new sequence of genocide, if not enacted by the Nazi Germany or its acolytes, then by Soviet Russia?

This chapter, however, proposes to take a somewhat different tack. Its starting point is to posit that one cannot *know* the preconditions for genocide without a consideration of the available political and social alternatives most likely to either minimize or dampen its potential. As already intimated in this and previous volumes, those alternatives cannot however be assumed to be a ready-made given by reference to the structure, society, and international politics of the liberal West. Contra Lemkin, the Western *foundations* of modern nationalism—insofar as we are here specifically considering the fate of the rimlands—are critically perceived as intrinsically part of the problem. Considering the path to Lausanne and the West's responsibility and culpability in that regard, to propose even tentatively that the West offered some ultimate bulwark for damage limitation—that is, against ethnic cleansing *becoming* genocide—might indeed be considered charitable.

But, if not to the values and actions of the dominant West, where *do* we propose to turn? And *when* exactly? Given the fact that Lausanne was already formalized in 1923—and the ascendancy of Hitler ten years later—a window of opportunity for the non-genocidal society would already seem to be a diminishing one. Especially if we are to concur in a broadly held view of genocide scholarship, to the effect that conditions of general or 'total' war carry with them a much greater potential for the phenomenon. Doubly so if our focus remains on the rimlands, an arena which, whether we are speaking of Anatolia or the 'Lands Between', the Caucasus or the Balkans, had barely recovered from the violent convulsions of war, invasion, and mass dislocation before 1923. That would seem to leave an interregnum of something approaching peace in these regions of a matter of a few short years—if that. The rise of collectivization under Stalin, and with it the end of the NEP, would mark an end to Russian 'peace' no later than 1928 or 1929. Genuine parliamentary democracy survived even more briefly in some of the avowedly liberal states of the 'New Europe': Piłsudski's *Sanacja* (purification) dictatorship being inaugurated in 1926 in Poland, and Smetona's initial efforts of a not dissimilar nature in Lithuania in the same year. Paradoxically, such dictatorships may actually have acted as a brake on more radical demotic violence against minority groups in these countries, Jews in particular. Dictatorship, thus, even where it clearly spelt internal coercion—and violence—cannot *in itself* be assumed to be more *inherently* genocidal than liberal democracy. Any more than the label 'fascist'—given that the first state experiment in this avowed 'third way', as begun in Mussolini's Italy after 1922—automatically denotes a polity intent on annihilatory extirpation of *domestic* ethnic or religious targets.[10] All that said, and to iterate the main point of argument here, while peace for the West, more specifically in its relationship to Nazi Germany, was maintained until 1939, its precarious hold in the rimlands and (as we will see) the growing incidence of extreme, internal violence, especially in the case of post-Lausanne Turkey, would suggest that the search for genuine non-genocidal alternatives in this arena would prove elusive.

Could there, however, be a lateral approach to the question? One which, by considering the lost ideas, tendencies, movements, and leaders—the attempts to work within a rimlands reality of a multifaceted human geography which yet failed to become dominant or enduring—may serve to remind us of *what might have been*? The proposition is clearly counter-intuitive. But, equally, such an approach set against the rise and victory of nation-statism as a concretized norm may concentrate our minds on why the potentiality for genocide in these regions, over and beyond largely exogenous factors associated with Nazism and communism, was radically enhanced in the interwar years.

If this chapter's first section 'A world lost?' thus has something of the wistful about it, the second, 'A world restored?' is arguably more unexpected in its proposition that possibilities for an elastic, even benign approach to the national question during the most favourable 1924–8 years of the 'lost peace' came, on the diplomatic level, from a pre-Hitler Germany, and on a domestic one from the newly created Union of Soviet Socialist Republics (USSR). That these possibilities proved to be veritable cul-de-sacs will not in itself surprise, given our knowledge of what was to follow in these two great, disaster-prone, heavyweight polities. Nevertheless, in our final two sections, 'Genocidal "business as usual"' and 'A sobering sequel', we return to the contested post-Ottoman territories of eastern Anatolia and its hinterland to attain a full measure of how the new nationalizing dispensation dashed any residual hope for an alternative political or societal path which might have embraced the spectrum of rimlands peoples and communities. In the first of these, which surveys the Kemalist pulverization of Kurdish resistance from the mid-1920s, what is arguably as disturbing as the violence itself is the degree of 'international'—for which read Western—approbation of the Ankara line that the Kurdish movement amounted to a 'reactionary' drag on a progressive programme of Western-style nation state building. It should be then less of a surprise to encounter in our brief concluding coda on the Assyrian affair, that it was British and, by implication, League prevarication, not to say mixed messages, which led the nascent Iraqi political-cum-military apparatus to assume that they could massacre the Assyrians (aka Nestorians) with impunity in what, until a few months previously, had been a British mandate territory. More pointedly, the British refusal to robustly defend Assyrian, Kurdish, or anybody else's case for minority rights here, or anywhere else after 1932, underscores the yawning and ever-widening gulf between Lemkinian notions—that a Western-led international system of nation states would itself foster and provide a protective safety net for the world's most unwanted or reviled peoples—and a political reality in which those very same system leaders were intent on preserving the nation-state-based status quo at almost any cost.

A WORLD LOST?

Phase one of the modern nation-state *system* had developed in Western Europe by a convoluted process, over a period stretching back as far, if not beyond, the 1648 Peace of Westphalia. Diplomatic endorsement of each new state's sovereignty and integrity had not been some afterthought. Rather, such recognition was by reference and relationship to other discrete but likewise territorially bounded and internally pacified states of like nomenclature. After the arrival of Italy and Germany within this club, phase one of the process was largely completed and a new, chronologically shorter, second phase began, centred on the rimlands. Though the 1878 Treaty of Berlin was an important way-station in this process, culmination of phase two was actually reached with the post-war Versailles and subsequent peace treaties. However, one might identify a fundamental difference between this and the previous phase in the hegemonic and determining role played by first-tier Western states themselves. The new rimlands' polities were to be granted equal sovereign status with phase-one associates, on the Westphalian model, and provided with a framework template for a modern political economy, albeit as if from betters to inferiors; that is, from advanced, industrialized leaders of the world to their culturally, if not geographically distant, neighbours inhabiting a backward semi-periphery.

If this script rightly reads as problematic there is, however, another version which would forcefully (if itself problematically) reject the implications and inferences of the first. This would argue that there could be no legitimate Western oversight or supervision of 'New Europe' nation-state formation, for the simple reason that it was not in the West's gift. As countries such as Britain or France had required no outside endorsement to articulate their nationhood in the seventeenth or eighteenth centuries, leaders of new would-be states might thus be prone to remind their interlocutors that they were heirs to historic national polities which were much older still. As such, a recognition of state-nationhood could not be gainsaid, as ethnogenesis had already long ago taken place. All that was being demanded (supposedly) was a requirement that the Allies recognize the legitimacy of the historical title—with a further common invitation to the untutored among them to immerse themselves in the history, literature, and folk culture of the aspirants. The retort to the power brokers was thus an obvious one: sovereignty was derived from the people, which in turn was derived from *their* sense of deep-rooted national consciousness and belonging.

But this in itself was open to a wide range of questions. Why, for instance, did the new nationalizing regimes put such emphasis on folk culture—in other words, on rural, peasant-based life—as evidence of historical continuity, when they manifestly cared so little for the interests of present-day peasants themselves? Peasants, of course, made up the vast majority of all these societies. Yet, to take simply one example, that of Yugoslavia (its very name belying its national credentials) less than 1 per cent of its interwar expenditure was ploughed back into a heavily overtaxed rural sector; the vast majority was soaked up by defence. But Yugoslavia was by no means unusual in this respect. Throughout the Balkans—with the exception of Bulgaria, of which more later in this section—between 34 and 50 per cent of national budgets went to the military.[11]

Militarization, perhaps, offered a different route to ethnic solidarity, consciousness, and homogenization. The notion of the army as 'school to the nation' can be traced through French, German, and Turkish military thought throughout the nineteenth century. It was certainly the most streamlined way of marshalling the able-bodied men of a territory into a uniform and monolithic aggregate.[12] Repeated mobilizations by Balkan states were also designed to feed and nurture national consciousness, as, in the 'Lands Between', Great War efforts, especially by German occupation forces, were geared towards encouraging subordinate populations to think of themselves in ethnic terms. A further consequence of the Great War—the deportation or flight of population groups seen as security risks by imperial military commands—also enabled successor regimes to project themselves as representative of truly national constituencies—even ones which might aspire to be relieved of unwanted components in their entirety.

But these factors suggest that national identity and awareness was less a natural, inherent, let alone all-pervasive undercurrent of the 'New Europe' than something which was having to be constantly, perhaps rather crudely, even forcibly, instilled into populations by their elite guides. If it had been otherwise why, for instance, would the new Rumania have been constantly harping on about the *pan*-national goals of 'centralization, indigenisation and integration'?[13] If everybody in Rumania knew they were part of one indivisible Rumanian people whose epicentre was Bucharest and whose goal in life was to work towards some common, nationally collective goal, why should there be a need to go on about it at all?

Oppositional nationalisms in the new states might even more fervently, not to say ludicrously, bang on about the inherent vitality, unity—and essence—of *their* ancestral folk. The Slovak nationalist Tiso, for instance, defined the nation as 'a community of people who are of single origin, single physical type, single character, single language, single set of customs and single culture of equal goals, and they constitute an organic whole in a coherent territory'.[14] The very fact that such counter-national movements existed at all in some of the new national states—in this case Czechoslovakia—rather too obviously punctured the national oneness profile that they were attempting to present to the world at large. That challenges of the Tiso kind also carried with them, by implication, their own statements of ethnic exclusiveness—the authentic Slovak defined by contrast against some other 'type' (Czech, German, Jew) who clearly could not be a member of the wholesome community—only further highlighted one key underlying weakness which beset the rimlands' turn to organic nationalism *tout ensemble*. By appealing to uni-ethnic solidarity as the glue for the new society, the new political and cultural elites were attempting to find a compensatory formula to replace rule by institutionalized—and quite arguably fossilized—dynastic imperialisms which, nevertheless, had largely provided domestic order and stability for centuries. By contrast, through resorting to the notion of some historic national mission which preceded Habsburgs, Romanovs, or Ottomans as the foundational first cause of one's modern polity, the formula almost inevitably sowed the seeds for internal conflict either with, or from, all those in this actually still *poly*-ethnic environment who had been left out in the cold.[15]

The added paradox was that the new nationalizing elites, by this instrument, were not attempting to return to some golden age in the distant past, but to jump into the world of the Western industrialized avant-garde. After all, the name of the game was development: the ultimate point of having one's own integral but also dynamic and forward-looking state. The ebb and flow of traditional life—the folk-cultural aspects of the national image—thus only served a practical purpose if they could be turned into something else: not a subsistence agriculture, or one geared towards the selling of surpluses in historic but largely enclosed imperial markets, but an economic sector whose cash crops, sold for foreign currency on international markets, might supplement ready cash in the form of international loans garnered from the international money markets. By this route agriculture might help pay for industrial plants and hence provide accelerated momentum towards what later would be called 'economic take-off', and so to the creation of an advanced industrialized society.

From this perspective—putting aside all the issues of intensified, cut-throat interstate competition and acute Western dependency which the project negatively implied[16]—the essential instrumental purpose behind nationalizing the masses envisaged a familiar pattern: to build and make cohere a rudimentarily literate but also malleable workforce which, within the context of a harsh, indeed social-Darwinian, international economy, could nevertheless operate at a sufficiently streamlined level of efficiency and productivity to enable the state to become *strong*. Cynically put, demotic involvement in the life of the nation was the pay-off: the supposed quid pro quo for the 'colonization' of countryside by intelligentsia.[17] The method of national induction was entirely étatist, following more or less the contours, for instance, of post-revolutionary France. As such, primary and/or secondary schooling became the most effective apparatus—alongside inculcating linguistic uniformity and basic numeracy—by which to induct a country's mostly peasant (male but also female) youth into 'national' values. In so doing, school also became the suitable antechamber to further compulsory patriotic service for the country's young men in its military barracks.[18] One might indeed propose that in a 'New Europe' context all that was actually being attempted was a form of mimesis of a well-tried and tested Western formula, the end product of which was a broadly held and popular self-image of a single, coherent national community across town and village, metropolis and periphery, which was also uniquely distinct not only from its contiguous neighbours but all other national entities.[19]

In this sense one might argue, as has Anthony Marx, that making a distinction between a liberal Western civic nationalism and an Eastern—by implication distorted and hence toxic—ethnic variant is to miss the *historical* point. Western states in their earlier surge towards national coherence had followed coercive, including sometimes genocidal, paths towards the pacification or elimination of domestic (as well as more obviously colonial) linguistic, religious, and ethno-national communities out of step with or resistant to the states' modernizing trajectories.[20] No more nor less than their predecessors, the majority of the 'New Europe' elites 'who were trying to create a national community'—even where this entailed discrimination against minorities—understood themselves to be not reactionaries or fascists but progressive liberals, acting for the wellbeing and, indeed, betterment of society.[21]

The essential difference, thus, between them and the Western front-runners of phase one was one of time and space. Society in the rimlands was altogether more sharply differentiated and variegated, hence demanding apparently more wholly radical action to force it to cohere. The gradient up which the elites proposed to climb in order to take that society towards 'modernization' was altogether steeper than anything which the first phasers, at least, had been aware of, while the perceived time frame the second phasers believed they had at their disposal in order to make their catch-up effective was altogether shorter. Objectively speaking, these conditions spoke of either (the need for) social revolution, or failure. In a primarily rural environment—the Soviet route to collectivization aside—the obvious, logical, essentially non-coercive first step towards societal transformation would have involved empowering the peasants; more specifically, a programme of serious root-and-branch land reform. Barring the initial promise of the Stamboliski administration in Bulgaria, however, this option remained blocked off by political leaderships throughout the rimlands who were themselves dependent on property, including land-owning elites for the most part unwilling to part with an iota of their own economic leverage or power.

The discrepancy between new state aspirations and the limiting factors inherent in the unchanged socio-economic fabric of the rimland zone itself contained enhanced potential for internal state versus society—city versus countryside—conflict, regardless of any ethnic or other factor. It is important too to remember that one underlying 'time-bomb' aspect of this relationship was no longer contained by its pre-1914 safety valve. Overpopulation in the rimlands and the inability of imperial structures to soak up the rural surplus in sufficient urban, industrial development had found a major outlet before the Great War through mass emigration to the Neo-Europes, most obviously the United States. On this score, the war marked a major watershed. Thereafter, new US protectionist quotas and barely veiled racial restrictions on migrant movement from eastern and southern Europe were rapidly replicated elsewhere in the 'white' colonial dominions.[22]

The denial of free population movement from the rimlands to the Neo-Europes, set against imperatives upon rimland states to fundamentally integrate their economies with the proto-globalizing demands of the Western-led system, thus brings us back with a jolt to our key problem issue—the relationship between avowedly *national* states and the reality of their actual component parts. In the immediate pre-war period ethnic groups such as Jews and Armenians, even under imperial rule, had been heavily over-represented among the millions crossing the Atlantic to New World shores. Already marked out (correctly or incorrectly) as the classic *apatrides* of modern times—'ubiquitous, stateless and trans-national'[23]—the departure of so many of them suggests that intermeshed with economic-push factors were fears of state persecution and worse. One can overstate the specifics of their particular case. Other 'minority' groups such as pacifist Mennonites and Doukhobors were leaving Russia for the New World at this time, also under threat or perceived threat of religious persecution. And a more general, essentially peasant-based rimlands exodus at the fin de siècle, while most obviously motivated by acute economic hardship, was clearly in some areas, such as Macedonia, closely linked to political destabilization and, with it, the further threat or reality of endemic insecurity and violence.[24]

The point about the new uni-national visage of the state, whether in post-1913 Macedonia, 1919 'New Europe', or 1923 Turkey, however, is that far from either mediating tensions between different social and ethnic actors, or dampening down the inherent suspicion in which the state apparatus was held by specific communal groups, its effect was generally to exacerbate them. Certainly, the scope, scale, and intensity of disgruntlement varied according to the degree to which groups were prepared to acquiesce in, or protest against, administrative diktat, with all its potential consequences. For the majority of peasants of the Polesie, for instance, for whom the time-honoured badge of being simply *tutejszy* (from here), was as far as their sense of group identity extended,[25] knuckling down to being Polish represented just another layer of bureaucratic interference, albeit more intrusive than that under the tsars—but one with which they had little choice but to comply. Brailsford had equally spoken of pre-Balkan Wars' Macedonia as a region of 'anachronisms', 'withered customs', and 'dead ideas', where 'the centuries do not follow one another. They coexist'.[26] His description of Macedonian idiosyncrasy, however, only rings true by dint of the fact that its ethnographically rich yet essentially non-nationalized life had been usurped or overwhelmed in our period by exogenous *nationalizing* forces.

By 1923, whole swathes of firmly autochthonous but non-politicized peasant, mountain, and nomad peoples were having to comply—as those of the Polesie or Macedonia. On occasions, communities of this ilk with a strong sense of their own *internal* identity did take 'voice' in opposition to straightforward 'loyalty'.[27] For instance, the Lemkos, an estimated 150,000-strong Carpathian mountain people of the remote Beskidy region of what had been Austrian Galicia—and, in the months after Habsburg collapse in late 1918, an area which was contested by Poles and West Ukrainians—wanted neither one nor the other ruling over them, despite the fact that, linguistically speaking, they could be construed as part of the Ukrainian 'nation'. Instead, they insisted that they be included within the Russian family of nations, petitioned the Paris Peace Conference accordingly, and when this failed asked for inclusion in Czechoslovakia, whose boundaries were also contiguous with theirs. What they got, instead, was their least favoured choice—Polish overlordship; Warsaw's military suppression of their emergency statelet following in spring 1920.[28]

The Lemko dilemma underscores why, in the new climate of nationalism, it was arguably more pragmatic to go with the flow and articulate one's own case for independent political nationhood rather than depend on Lemkinesque-type guarantees. The post-1919 rimlands landscape was, after all, littered with examples of embryonic national movements who had not made their bids sufficiently forcefully. Again, as a further example, if one was just using linguistic criteria it was Belorussians who constituted the vast majority of some five ex-tsarist *guberniai*, including the all-important one of Vilna. Lithuanian-speakers by contrast, hardly counted here at all—representing a mere 1 to 2 per cent of the city's actual population. Yet it was the strength of Lithuanian national consciousness—not least emerging from a significant diaspora population in Germany—and their pugnacious determination that a state be carved out in their name which tilted the odds dramatically in Lithuanian favour, against a national Belorussian equivalent with a demotic groundswell (the attitude of the Polesians being one sound indicator) which was virtually nil. True, in their military competition for Vilna itself, with that other even stronger contender, the Poles, the Lithuanians could not but lose out: Lithuanian 'liberation' of the city finally coming—and at that particular moment only ephemerally—in 1939. However, in the wider intra-national struggle in the *kresy*, would-be Belorussian patriots paradoxically had to rely on the Soviets to create a national republic for them on only part of the territory of their 'imagined community', while their supposed compatriots who found themselves stranded across the Polish or Lithuanian borders were designated, respectively, as Poles or Lithuanians who just 'happened to speak' Belorussian.[29]

Of course, social-Darwinian competition by military means was in itself no guarantee of making good one's national credentials, as we have already seen by way of the fate of the Ukrainian national movement. A compact Ukrainian territory based on ethnography could conceivably have encompassed significant chunks of Poland, Czechoslovakia, and Rumania as well as what, under Bolshevik aegis, became the Ukrainian Soviet Socialist Republic. From this standpoint, the great travesty of the Allied-sponsored peace was the denial of the national rights of millions of people, by allocating them instead to somebody else's *national* state. By this reckoning, too, Hungarians, Serbs, and Bulgarians in Rumania; Ukrainians, Lithuanians, and Belorussians in Poland; and Germans just about everywhere in the 'New Europe' but in the Czech Sudetenland and Polish corridor in particular, became the true irredentist casualties of the lost peace and hence key cause—whether manipulated by the likes of Hitler or not—of the Second World War. But to adopt this line of reasoning is to assume erroneously that the only losers in this history were those who desired but failed to realize their legitimate national belonging, leaving by the wayside those *denied* their history altogether by dint of the fact that they evinced no interest in, or, alternatively, consciously chose to eschew participation in, the nation-state ethos at all.

It is immediately striking how many variants of these conscious or unconscious dissenters there were in the interwar rimlands, upon whom, however—to employ a famous Thompsonian phrase—'the enormous condescension of posterity' has descended as a consequence of the conventional narrative.[30] There were, of course, Roma, diverse in their composition, very far from all peripatetic, but sufficiently committed to *Romanipen* as a way of life, who, in many ways, were much more the 'stateless' and 'alien' *apatrides* than were Jews or other traditionally 'Mercurian' trading peoples. Equally, however, one could be or feel oneself to be a native of a particular region, yet be equally divorced from the dominant national tide. The peoples of Macedonia, for one, might have shaped a *composite* communal identity out of their diverse ethnic parts but were prevented from doing so by what amounted to nation-state colonization determined from Athens, Sofia, and Belgrade. Within a country such as Greece itself, a continuing process of forcible Hellenization only served to demonstrate how wide of the mark elite goals were in relation to local *mentalités* among actually very ethnically diverse communities, with only the most tenuous awareness of some supposed shared history.[31] Similarly, if there were former Habsburg Germans and Hungarians stranded on the wrong side of disputed borders, there were, by the same token, substantial groups such as Bosnian Muslims who—finding themselves post-1918 in a hostile and actually very menacing

Yugoslav environment (Serb military massacres of Bosnians at the Great War's end being one obvious cause for alarm)—would have asked for nothing better than a Habsburg restoration.[32]

Feeling communally safe within a large, multi-ethnic empire was neither illogical nor inherently reactionary. In the pre-1914 Bukovina, for instance, the political leaderships of diverse ethnic groups, conscious of their potentially centrifugal tendencies, had nevertheless sought to forge a common *regional* consciousness in which Ukrainians, Rumanians, Jews, Armenians, Germans, and other peoples might all have lived and worked together. They had even graced this notion with political expression by founding a 'Free-Thinking Union' of Bukovinan deputies within the Austrian parliament.[33] This very idea of a '*Homo buconvinensis*'—an inhabitant of Bukovina who, as one vociferous opponent put it, might 'melt together with the other peoples into an exotic Bukovinan species'[34]—had Rumanian chauvinists fuming at its negative implications for their own national project.

The fact that throughout the rimlands those often quickest to make vitriolic denunciations against Bukovinan-style deviance were themselves displaced by the very forces of nationalism is hardly surprising. Vociferous German or Austrian adherence to Nazism was notable among post-1919 Volksdeutsche refugees or those who felt under threat in Germany's new post-Versailles border zones in both West and East.[35] Their dislocation was as likely to be of a deeply emotional and psychically fractured nature as anything simply physical, as they attempted to come to terms with a 'normative' order of things which had been turned on its head. Likewise, Pontic and other Greek Thracian or Anatolian refugees with formerly little or no particular attachment to the concept of a unitary-state Hellenism were, early on, identified as eminently mobilizable cadres by Venizelist and other ultra-nationalist Greek politicians in their efforts to intimidate, muzzle, or simply swamp leftist resistance or—as, for instance, in the Salonika area—Jews or residual pockets of Slavophone speakers.[36] One can be overtly cynical and propose that in the search for security of housing and work, it was hardly in the interest of refugees such as these to challenge or snub the political hand that might feed them, especially in such a clientist-ridden, increasingly authoritarian state and society as that of interwar Greece. Everywhere, in fact, in the 'New Europe', with diminishing work opportunities and straitened economic circumstances, the most alienated or geographically displaced—including socially downwardly mobile aristocrats, rentiers, and professionals who had unwillingly chosen or been forced to abandon estates, property, and secure livelihoods in the place they had thought of as home under imperial rule—proved among the most prone to embrace chauvinistic and/or revanchist rhetoric.

Pragmatic, even opportunistic, getting on the gravy train in order to garner the patronage of a state official or bigwig who might provide a job—the new states, after all, replicated, and very often surpassed, the tendency towards overmanned bureaucracies of their imperial predecessors—constitutes one overtly functional explanation for this phenomenon. But then it was not refugees alone who increasingly shifted towards ultra-national, even fascistic, militancy. Grievance and resentment against 'foreigners' was part of the xenophobic climate of the new national Europe long before the Great Depression, though with identifiable groups such as high-school or university students very often taking a lead in demands for more overtly retributive or even violent action against them. Political elites could thus find themselves denounced as weak or even out of step for not being nationalistic enough. In Rumania, for instance, the so-called 'Generation of 1922' was primarily made up of university students inspired by Professor Cuza's National-Christian Defence League, which, as one historian has pointedly suggested, was mainly concerned with 'the alleged Jewish threat to the purity of Christian virgins'.[37] Among Cuza's student acolytes at Iaşi University—which was situated in a Moldavian city with its own very significant Jewish population—was Corneliu Zelea Codreanu, who became involved in foiled plots to assassinate Jewish leaders and allegedly 'Jew-loving' politicians before he attained real celebrity status by succeeding in murdering Iaşi's 'corrupt' police chief and then being acquitted. Codreanu's affirmation of the value of 'redemptive violence', however, carried with it quite definite political aims shared by all his 'Generation'; not least, the overturning of Jewish emancipation grudgingly conceded by Rumanian leaders in the new constitution in response to the peace treaties, plus efforts to drive out not just Jews but Hungarians from the Rumanian academic scene, economy, and society at large.[38]

That the undoubtedly charismatic Codreanu—who would go on to become leader of the notoriously violent as well as religiously-infused Iron Guard brand of Rumanian fascism—was himself of part-Ukrainian, part-Polish, part-German background may offer insight into how ultra-nationalist convictions might offer compensatory solidity, not to mention public cover, for someone confused or inwardly disarmed about their own origins—compounded by the diverse stimuli of growing up in the predominantly Jewish town of Huşi and, later, Iaşi.[39] We have noted such tendencies on the part of, especially, Balkan-born Ittihadists, also uncertain or anxious about their personal identities and eager to reach out for firm nationalist moorings. And, by the same token, we could find plenty of other ultra-nationalists of the interwar period with similar profiles. Ferenc Szálasi, the leader of the Hungarian fascist movement, the Arrow Cross—with a name redolent of a thoroughly pukka Magyar lineage—was another who may not have been well pleased with his part-Slovakian background—a despised people in the Hungarian hierarchy of races—or, worse, descent on his father's side from Armenians.[40]

Such arguably extenuating circumstances, however, clearly cannot act as an all-embracing explanation let alone apologia for every one of those who embraced virulent forms of nationalism in the 1920s rimlands. These movements were, after all, far from societally marginal. They were, in critical ways, fed by an often blatantly crude nationalism already instilled by the new regimes, yet at the same time threatened to gazump these very same regimes by challenging both their credentials and their ability to act on the basis of managed parliamentary democracy—in other words, borrowings from the liberal West—as either the appropriate or most effective way to accomplish the national mission. That mission was itself redemptive and made no bones about desiring to eliminate ethnic elements deemed to run counter to the country's 'purity' or national health. Above all, this implication of society as damaged or contaminated by extraneous influences always led a trail first and foremost to the Jews, whether the accusation itself emanated from the forerunners of the Iron Guard and Arrow Cross, or, as for instance in Poland, from the Endecja.

Yet for all the undoubted groundswell of aggrieved, intensely ethnicized nationalism, whether manipulated and managed by the state or demotically opposed to it, there remained tendencies—albeit largely survivors of pre-war ideas and movements—which swam strongly against this tide. *Sacro egoismo* was, of course, opposed by genuine socialists and anarchists as well as by what Daniele Conversi intriguingly calls 'counter-entropic' elements.[41] Resistance to what was being billed as natural and inevitable by the dominant forces of national and international society inevitably carried with it penalties and dangers. But the very reason such opponents were not so much sidelined as suffocated—or even physically battered into submission or to death—was that they struck a raw nerve. Opposition to nation-statism, while not of a piece, invariably clung to ideas of federalism and decentralization as the way towards a better society which would preserve intact, not to say enable, its diverse, plural parts. Self-organization by the people for the people was thus both critical to this tendency and anathema to its opponents—just as its very proposition that different peoples might share a habitus *together* was, for nationalists, the ultimate betrayal.

Yet indicators that rimlands society might be reconstructed on these alternative lines did show signs of budding in the blurred transition from Great War to the firm fixing of the new nation-state order. And, one should add, not just in the heads of a dreaming intelligentsia. Perhaps the most remarkable example emerged in the North Caucasus in the wake of the Russian liberal revolution in the spring of 1917. Mountaineers and lowlanders, Christians and Muslims, Slavic settlers and Turkic-speaking *indigènes*, not to mention an absolute plethora of other ethnic groups, when thrown together were—by standard nationalist logic—bound to be constantly at one another's throats. Instead, 300 delegates from among Dagestanis, Ossetians, Ingush, Chechens, Kabardians, Balkars, Circassians, Nogais, Adyghes, and Karachais came together in a congress in Vladikavkaz in May, not only to declare the freedom and unity of all Mountaineers from the Black Sea to the Caspian, but specifically to offer a welcoming hand of friendship to the Terek Cossacks.[42] These, as both an historic tsarist strike force and usurpers of traditional mountain land, were supposed to be *the* enemies. Yet the Cossack delegates invited to Vladikavkaz in turn helped facilitate a further effort at joint cooperation, this time with several different Cossack hosts themselves taking the lead, which, on 2 November—on the cusp of the Bolshevik coup—declared the existence of a 'South-Eastern League of Cossack Hosts, Mountaineers of the Caucasus and Free Peoples of the Steppes'.[43]

The aim was clearly not independence, or the false oneness of this ever-widening collection of peoples. On the contrary, what the South-Eastern League was proposing was effectively a formula whereby their multifaceted *differences* might be respected and upheld—preferably within a much wider and larger Russian federation. Nor were the founders of this proposition so starry-eyed as to assume that they did not have serious long-term problems to resolve: land seizure, mostly by Cossacks from Mountaineers, being the thorniest. What, instead, they were envisaging was a way forward which developed from the base level of the native village—or, in the Mountaineer case, *aul*—and thus carried with it as a first principle genuine communal self-determination. Linked to this was a further principled position of non-interference in the communal lives of others. The fact that the element providing for a broader combination and collaboration among the majority of Mountaineers was actually Islam, or that motivation and leadership for this came largely from the *ulema*, did not preclude collaboration with, and assistance to, Christian lowlanders. Significantly, even as the wider political scene darkened, and the Bolsheviks in particular strove to crush the Vladikavkaz Union, it remained committed to maintaining good relations with Terek and Kuban hosts until late autumn 1918.[44]

What defeated the Caucasus initiative was not dissension among its proponents but the impact of outside force majeure. As we have already seen, Bolshevism was relentless in its efforts to destroy any grouping, however large or small, which sought its own autonomous pathway: its main adversaries of this ilk—à la Makhno or Antonov—being primarily peasant-based. This was, however, equally the case in non-Soviet 'New Europe', where peasantries formed into their own constellations arguably offered 'the most serious challenge to the bourgeois ruling parties'.[45] Ironically, it was their militantly anti-militarist, often pacifist, as well as anti-developmental tendencies—in other words, opposition to breakneck, or hothouse, industrialization as the prescribed route to integration within a globalizing framework—in favour, instead, of a society founded on peasant ownership of land, which made them, in the 1920s, into the genuine third way between the urban capitalism of the West and urban communism of the Soviet state.[46] And, of course, it was exactly this which made them into the bogey par excellence of the nation-statists. The Croat middle classes had practically invited the Serb army into their region in November 1918 for fear of a green revolution, thereby sacrificing, into the bargain, their own chance of independence from Belgrade.[47] In those parts of Yugoslav Serbia, as well as across the Banat border in Rumania, parallel peasant movements were in part stymied by a limited land reform almost entirely at the expense of Hungarian or German landowners.[48]

Only in Bulgaria, with the post-war Agrarian Union-led government under Alexander Stamboliski, was there a serious attempt to implement far-reaching land reform. Significantly, this was closely aligned to a foreign policy geared towards peace, reconciliation, and a peasant-based (thus consciously non-Soviet) internationalism. Indeed, Stamboliski's aspiration to create a much broader and genuinely federal South Slav union than the travesty of the Yugoslav one under Serb tutelage represented a pluralist approach entirely at odds with the general trajectory of rimlands nation-statism. It also happened to be firmly opposed—in spite of Bulgarian wartime defeat and post-war loss of lands—to revanchist territorial revision. The predictable consequence for Stamboliski and his supporters was the undying hatred of both Sofia's military and an official IMRO organization now firmly shot of its own pluralist elements and closely in cahoots with the Military League (a menacing association of army officers demobilized under the terms of Neuilly). The resulting entirely successful coup in June 1923 saw Stamboliski himself viciously tortured and decapitated by IMRO diehards.[49] A genuinely alternative route for Eastern Europe by way of Sofia's beacon came to a complete terminus twenty months later, when a botched communist insurrection was drowned in a Bulgarian version of the 'White Terror'. The atrocities were reported to include the mass rounding-up and slaughter of hundreds of women and children, as well as men, in Sofia's working-class districts and surrounding villages.[50]

*

Does this leave the rimlands field to the nation-statists and, in so doing, confirm the antediluvian nature of their opponents? Arguably, not quite. Not all the politicians of the ascendant order were irreducibly uni-nationalist in their outlook. Masaryk, the lawyer-professor turned founding father and president of the new Czech republic, most fully represented an important 'realist' variant of 'New Europe' thinking. This firmly rejected the competing nationalist case for 'historic state rights'—in other words, the resurrection of the modern national state founded on supposed medieval frontiers and the subordination of other communities within it. Instead, Masaryk envisaged cooperation and cultural exchange *across* ethnic boundaries on the basis of 'shared interests and values'.[51] Paradoxically, Masarykian convictions regarding the possibility of a modus vivendi between different peoples may have owed something to the often fraught Czech efforts to achieve language rights and national acceptance within the pre-1914 Habsburg system. The Austrian parliament, for all the acrimony which accompanied this struggle, may have inadvertently provided a good 'democratic' education in how to mediate inter-ethnic disputes and carry on dialogue in spite of seemingly irreconcilable antagonisms. That, in practice, the half-Slovak, heavily Germanized Masaryk also presided over the (albeit rather slow) implementation of a land reform programme of particular relevance and urgency to its Slovak population may have been crucial to holding together what was otherwise intended as a firmly *unitary* and centralized state.

Interestingly, peasant party influence proved a decisive factor in Czech land reform. Elsewhere, Masaryk's acolytes, who, after the war, themselves spoke for politically subordinate or disadvantaged rimlands national groups, may well have looked to the connection between Prague's agrarian programme and continued Czech–Slovak cooperation for footprints by which to develop their own similar agendas. One of these was Mykhailo Hrushevsky, Ukraine's pre-eminent national historian, as well as president of its short-lived Rada in 1918. Hrushevsky returned home to a Soviet Ukraine in 1923, encouraged by the new communist policy of *korenizatsiia*—indigenization (of which more below in 'A world restored?'), despite charges of selling out from most of his fellow national émigrés.[52] If Hrushevsky's decision was spurred on by his belief that the 'peasant' nations of the rimlands were essentially kindred spirits, another nationalist leader, Stjepan Radić, two years later, equally caused consternation among the rank and file of his Croat People's Peasants Party (HPSS) by affirming that grounds for compromise could still be found between them and Serbs. By this juncture nearly all Croat nationalists had come to the conclusion that the so-called kingdom of Serbs, Croats, and Slovenes, formed in 1918, represented nothing more than an egregious Belgrade usurpation of what had been intended as an equal union of Yugoslav peoples.[53] By opting to go against the rejectionist camp and seek an accommodation with undisputedly hegemonic state actors, both Hrushevsky and Radić, in their separate contexts, were remaining true to a pre-war pluralist ideal.

One final strand of rimlands nationalism with more than a hint of pluralism is worthy of mention: that associated with Poland's Marshal Józef Piłsudski. Like so many other post-war leaders—ultra-nationalist as well as their complete oppo-site—this pre-war romantic socialist turned eventual military dictator came from a fluid cultural identity and geographical arena. A true son of the Vilna region, with half-Polish, half-Lithuanian parentage, the young Piłsudski gravitated first towards Polish socialism, then more openly to nationalism, before fighting for Polish inde-pendence in the Great War—just as his brother became an activist in the wartime national committee for an independent Lithuania.[54] Both Piłsudskis could argua-bly to be said to be operating within a historic legacy: that of the early modern Polish–Lithuanian commonwealth. In the case of Józef, certainly, this also carried with it notions of some wider Polish-led federation embracing Lithuanians, Belorussians, and Ukrainians. If this was undoubtedly inclusive in a way that a Dmowski-ite conception of Poland was absolutely not—including, in the Marshal's mind, ideas of 'national' cantons centred on regional capitals—one ought to be wary of reading into this approval of an equal relationship between these various communal groups. Snyder has described the Piłsudskian conception as more a case of 'a Polish political nation floating above the multinational borderlands'.[55] Like Masaryk's Czechoslovakia—where it was always the superior, progressive Czechs leading their more bucolic, even doltish Slovakian cousins towards modernity and enlightenment—Piłsudski's embrace of other peoples actually came with the rather aristocratic assumption that the Polish would always be the dominant culture and would bind all others together. It also meant that a city like Vilna would be forever Polish, whatever Lithuanians or Belorussians might have to say on the matter.

Even so, there is a certain tantalizing quality to imagining how a more thoroughly Piłsudskian Poland might have developed if Józef had chosen to maintain a firm hand on the state tiller at that critical moment, in March 1921, when not only was the constitution being enacted but the Treaty of Riga concluded, bringing to an end the Soviet–Polish War. Both events proved clear victories for demotic politics of the Dmowski-ite strain: the former slashing away at the possibility of strong presidential powers (for which read Piłsudski himself), the latter killing stone-dead Piłsudski's dream of a multi-ethnic federation. It was indeed ironic that the Soviets at Riga had been prepared to concede a swathe of territory at that point under Polish control, including Minsk. To Stanisław Grabski, staunch *endek* as well as head of the Polish delegation, this was taken to be tantamount to a poison chalice, as it would have brought within Warsaw's orbit so many more Belorussians (not to mention so many more Jews) as to cast doubt on the state's overall Polish majority—even if rejecting it meant abandoning hundreds of thousands of Poles of the eastern *kresy* to 'the tender care of Moscow'.[56] In declining the Soviet offer Grabski also underscored how much more modern the Dmowski vision of Poland was than the Marshal's: a country which put its integral ethnic constituency first, and, with it, a politics which assumed the need for a mass electoral mandate against Piłsudski's rather paternalistic, even traditionalist, conception of state governance.[57]

Even then, something of the Piłsudskian idea might have been salvaged given that within the borders of 1921 Poland the non-Polish nationalities—Ukrainians, Jews, Belorussians, and Germans in particular,[58]—were sufficiently weighty in demographic terms, if they worked together as an electoral bloc, to affect election outcomes. The following year, in the first election for president, this is exactly what happened when the just-formed Bloc of National Minorities (BMN) joined with centrist and leftist parties to defeat the Endecja. Piłsudski had absented himself from the contest. Nevertheless, he was perfectly content to see his friend Gabriel Narutowicz stand. A Pole of Lithuanian extraction—indeed, just like Piłsudski, a Pole with a brother immersed in high-level Lithuanian politics—Narutowicz had a concept of Poland which, while now unable as a result of the constitution and Riga Treaty to develop as a federation, might still have had a future as a state of nationalities as opposed to 'nation state'.[59] It was not, however, to be. Narutowicz was gunned down by a right-wing assassin a week after his elevation. It is an indication of where the country was heading thereafter that it was the assassin's grave—not the president's—which became, for ultra-nationalists, a shrine.[60] Only as a result of the storming back of Piłsudski himself, in his 1926 coup, and until his death nine years later, was the ring held between the forces of an increasingly chauvinist Poland and its similarly disaffected minorities.

It was, however, the assassination of Radić in June 1928, which, more arguably, marked the interwar end of any rimlands expectations that an alternative, home-grown path to peoples-coexistence might have been possible. Radić, as we have seen, had staked his reputation in 1925 on joining the Belgrade government, in the hope that he might thereby shift its inexorably centralizing path towards a more equitable, federalistic relationship with its non-Serb communities: the Croats, of course, in particular. Despairing of this possibility and returning to the opposition benches in the Skupshtina, Radić was one of three HPSS members gunned down there by Puniša Racić, a deputy from the Serbian radical wing whose main previous claim to fame had been as a leading and thuggish protagonist in the post-1918 'pacifications' of Macedonia and Kosovo.[61] This, along with the ensuing complete breakdown of parliamentary rule, the creation of anti-parliaments in Zagreb and Ljubljana by protesting Croat and Slovene deputies, not to mention the possibility of complete economic and fiscal meltdown to boot, all proved the perfect pretext for the Serb-turned-Yugoslav king, Alexander, to step into the breach and declare royal dictatorship.

The immediate consequence was the abolition of the fragile Vidovdan constitution, by which at least the façade of Serb–Croat–Slovene union—the Triune—had been retained. With it went not just parliament but political parties, trade unions, and all organizations founded on a regional and religious basis. True, the complete derogation of political rights was intended to be of a temporary, 'emergency' nature only, while a new, supposedly genuinely Yugoslav constitution was framed to replace its predecessor. But that, of course, takes us to the heart of the architecture conceived for the new Yugoslavia. Within it there would no longer be any basis or justification for being Croat, Slovene, or anything other than Yugoslav. The intention was clearly signalled, too, in the abolition of the previous thirty-three administrative regions of the state and their replacement with nine topographically named—and hence emotionally neutral—*banovine* (governorships), each run by a specially appointed military hardman, police security chief, or ultra-Serb nationalist. Each *banovina* was also designed to consciously cut across the historic boundaries within which traditional communities had rooted their cultural and social distinctiveness. The Croat regions were notably mutilated in this manner.[62] In short, this was a blatant, dynastic-led effort to engineer diversity out of the 'Yugoslav' population, in favour of a forcible homogenization organized around one single monocultural model: the Serbs. Or, rather, a Serb model as conceived and determined by a Belgrade elite.

What ensued was not so much pacification as a growing dynamic of violence between state terrorists—primarily the security police—and insurrectionary counter-terrorists, culminating in the latter's very public assassination of Alexander himself. This event, in October 1934, was to have very much broader geopolitical repercussions, for killed alongside Alexander on his state visit to Marseilles was French foreign secretary Louis Barthou, a key promoter of European collective security at a juncture when the Nazi menace was seriously looming. As a further consequence, Lemkin's argument that it was the vulnerability of peoples—not just 'very important people'—which was the root cause of the new instability, was pushed further into the long grass. Instead, the terrorism of those responsible for the Marseilles assassinations now came to the fore of the international agenda—in so doing putting under the spotlight the Ustasha, initially little more than a groupuscule of ultra-nationalist Croats who, having fled Yugoslavia in the wake of the 1929 state clampdown, had begun a shooting and bombing campaign against it.

Despite their violent tactics, Ustasha's growing support from Croat émigrés and *indigènes* alike showed how much Radić's Masarykian position was eroding. The Ustasha claimed historic state rights as their justification for an independent, Serb-free Croatia, which in turn made recourse to outside powers—notably Italy—to assist them quite acceptable. They were also prepared to make common cause with other disaffected ethnic elements—the Marseilles killings involved an Ustasha joint operation with IMRO—which further suggested that the 'Croat question' was only one aspect of Serbian internal colonization, and arguably not the most egregious at that.

In Macedonia as well as Kosovo—together designated, post-1918, as southern Serbia—where prying Western eyes were also much less evident, Belgrade's discrimination against and indeed open persecution of 'Bulgaro'-Macedonians and Albanians had been going on unabated throughout the 1920s. Much of this was in direct and flagrant violation of the minority rights Yugoslavia had acceded to in Paris, whereby Albanian speakers were specifically entitled to schooling in their own language. Complaints at the League of Nations about the non-implementation of these requirements were either studiously ignored or eventually met head-on by Serb diplomats in 1929—with the classic sophistry that the people in question were Arnauts and so simply in the process of being re-educated in their own authentic tongue.[63] At stake, however, was more than simply a dispute about language rights. Belgrade wanted not to encapsulate Albanians at all, but to eruct them in favour of a Kosovo repopulated with more 'reliable' elements. These did not have to be Serbs per se: one actually aborted scheme, consciously modelled on an Ottoman settlement of Circassians at strategic locations, involved 'planting' 7,000 of Wrangel's (fellow-Slav) White Army soldiers en bloc.[64] That failed effort aside, the process in the form of a scheme of creeping ethnic cleansing was familiar enough: intimidation and land seizures as part one of the programme; inducements and tax holidays, especially to Chetniks and Serbian demobilized soldiers, its latter facet.

This reinforces the sense that Kosovo, in some ways, was a rather special case: a region where the government was prepared to go to extreme lengths, including the sinking of state funds, not for development as such—Kosovo remained one of the most impoverished parts of Yugoslavia (and Eastern Europe)—but in order to reclaim it as integral Serbia forever. What this led to in practice was almost 'non-stop warfare'.[65] While IMRO became notorious in the wider international gaze for high-profile attacks on government officials, Kosovan *kaçak* rebels operating practically off the map, indeed from a demilitarized border zone with Albania (which was itself part of the unfinished business of the Paris Peace Conference), grew their own anti-Serb insurgency. The inevitable consequence was that Belgrade responded with an even more fearful counter-insurgency. How many thousands died in these operations, and how many of the dead were non-combatants, is uncertain.[66] Add to the litany of state violence, here and in Macedonia, the assaults on Rumanian priests and teachers in the Serb-controlled Banat; similar efforts directed against Hungarian speakers in the Vojvodina; plus those by subterfuge of land reform, also in the Banat, to 'encourage' half a million Volksdeutsche to leave, and the French parliamentarian Robert Schuman's assertion in 1934 that Serb terror was practically on a par with that of the Nazis would seem a perfectly just one.[67]

However, before we make a point of singling out Belgrade as the most serious human rights violator in the 'New Europe' pack, two things might be noted by way of context. Firstly, while Belgrade's efforts to sculpt Yugoslavia in its own Serb image was conducted in the most blatantly crude and—especially in its south—savage manner, what it was actually doing was, in many ways, simply a more radical extension of a general rimlands tendency. Across the border in Greece, politicians might have signed on the Allies' dotted line to provide Kutzo-Vlachs minority status; but the message to them, not to mention Albanians, Turks, Bulgaro-Macedonian Slavophones, or, for that matter, Salonika Jews, was a perfectly simply one: be Greek or get out.[68] In Rumania, initially hopeful experiments in regional administrative autonomy—which might have helped some 30 per cent of the country's population who were clearly non-Rumanian to feel at home (the figure had been 12 per cent in the pre-war Regat)—were almost immediately superseded by a crude étatist developmentalism aimed at bringing the dominant *ethnie* on, while doing just about everybody else—more particularly, all the more urban, more schooled, more 'modern' Jews, Hungarians, Germans, and Russians—down.[69]

As for Poland, the Endecja did not for one moment relent, Piłsudski in power or not, on their project of *odżydzenie*—the complete social and economic exclusion of Jews. Spokesmen such as Grabski twisted the knife in that little bit further with speeches in the Sejm intimating that 'the foreign element' might consider whether they might 'not be better off elsewhere'.[70] Piłsudski's ascendancy, of course, did represent the brakes on National Democrat intimidation of both Jews *and* Germans. As it did too on *endek* efforts within and without the *apparat* to speed up the Polonization of the eastern *kresy* and its peoples—Ukrainians and Belorussians being considered as little more than 'raw ethnographic material' to this end.[71] Piłsudski's 1928 appointment of his former Ukrainian comrade-in-arms and open federalist Henryk Józewski as governor of Volhynia was, if nothing more, a snub to the unadulterated Polonizers, not to mention a rare appreciation of the simple fact that here, as in eastern Galicia, Ukrainians outnumbered Poles at least four to one.[72] But for all the benevolence of Piłsudski to Ukrainians or, for that matter, the other non-Polish peoples, Jews included, he could hardly disguise the direction of Warsaw's nationalizing intent. Or the fact that, once Piłsudski was out of the way, the Polish colonization of the *kresy* would be resumed with a vengeance.

Yet this takes us to our second point. Eastern Galicia happened to be one region where the Allies in Paris were very concerned, in the wake of the failed West Ukrainian Republic, about the Poles overriding local national rights and interests. Recognizing the implicit warning, Warsaw in return had offered explicit promises that Ukrainian autonomy would be guaranteed, schooling in the Ukrainian language fostered, and a specifically Ukrainian university in Lwów (Lviv) founded. These promises were repeated in 1923, when the region was officially awarded by the Allies to Poland, only to be utterly ignored or repudiated in subsequent years as it became obvious that Warsaw nationalizers' key purpose for the province was indeed colonialist: upholding large Polish estate holders there against indigenous demands for land reform and encouraging the settlement of Polish ex-soldiers in the face of local need.[73] Yet what did those who had authorized the region's incorporation into Poland do? Precisely nothing.

The Allies, of course, were meant to be *for* national self-determination. And where, at the Paris Peace Conference, there had been disputes about whether a region had a majority of one people as opposed to another, the architects of the new order ordered plebiscites. Yet, as we have already suggested in Chapter 3, where these went against the general thrust of Western geopolitical interests in the 'New Europe', or perhaps, even worse, offered a result which suggested blurred ethnicities, the predictable Allied response was to enforce an outcome which favoured one of their clients. The 1921 plebiscite for the important Polish–German-disputed industrial region of Upper Silesia, at the furthest north-western reaches of our rimland zone, demonstrates this tendency rather well. The actual majority vote of the populace was for incorporation in Germany. However, this appears not to have been a reflection of consensual German identity as such but rather the opposite: uncertainty, ambiguity, even elasticity, as to whether being Silesian was equivalent to being 'Polish', 'German', or neither.[74] The majority vote for inclusion with Weimar thus appears to have had more to do with concerns about employment and long-term security (the Poles instigated no less than three revolts in the region to try and take it by force) than about any firm ethnic solidarity with one side or the other. What did the Allies, however, do in response—major dissensions between them notwithstanding? They shifted the goalposts so that the more industrially significant part of the region was hived off to Warsaw.[75]

On one obvious level this was all about the Allied, more specifically, French idée fixe about revived German power combining with the Bolsheviks to wreck their security system—so blocking that by giving more territory to their chief rimlands protégé. The same underlying rule, in other words, which enabled them to turn a blind eye to Polish avoidance of their eastern Galician responsibilities. But, in the case of Upper Silesia, it could equally be read as a clear repudiation of populations which sought their own social peace on the basis of 'ethnic osmosis'.[76]

If the Allies had been willing to venture down this route they would surely have done so by giving their support to the one immediately obvious, entirely friendly post-war leader willing to move rapidly towards a genuinely tolerant, multi-ethnic, and devolved federation of peoples in the post-imperial rimlands. That leader was Mihály Károlyi, appointed minister-president of Hungary on 31 October 1918, and otherwise known as 'the one totally sincere Wilsonian idealist in European affairs'.[77] Indeed, his favourable credentials extended beyond simply being anti-war and pro-Entente: he was also, very unusually, an establishment figure with a marked social conscience and commitment to radical land reform, which he personally demonstrated by parcelling out his own 50,000 acre estate amongst his peasant tenants.[78] Equally importantly, Károlyi, like Stamboliski, was for genuine peace, his government recognizing the new surrounding states—including that of the Poles, Czechs, and Ukraine—with alacrity. A Hungarian-led federation under Károlyi would have been liberal, democratic, and allied to the West. How then did the Allies repay him? They ordered him to evacuate a huge swathe of Magyar territory to the Rumanians, gave the green light to the Czechs and Serbs to invade, and thus paved the way for the instability and chaos of which Béla Kun would take advantage. Having done everything in their power to engineer the downfall of this liberal regime, and, of course, dismember Hungary to boot, Britain and France went on to authorize the anti-Kunist actions of, and give immediate recognition to, the utterly authoritarian regime of Admiral Horthy, elevated to power by naked force (actually on the back of Rumanian troops with the additional support of right-wing death squads). It was with this sort of gentleman, even as he presided over the White Terror (just as, a quarter of a century later he would preside over the destruction of Hungarian Jewry), that the West felt comfortable doing business.[79]

One acerbic but nevertheless thoroughly well-informed and acute British commentator, Charles Trevelyan, summed up the creation of the 'New Europe' thus:

> When Europe began to be repartitioned at Paris and a dozen new oppressions were substituted for the old ones, there was no protest in the name of principle or justice or liberalism against the fate of Germans annexed to Poland, Austrians to Italy and Czechs Serbs and Hungarians to Rumania...the liberal war to end all war...closed with an imperialist peace to perpetuate national injustice and armaments.[80]

Today, students of our phenomenon—where they recognize at all a relationship between genocide and its repeated incidence in our rimland shatter zones—normally assume that culpability lies squarely with Nazi Germany, though with the Soviet Russia sometimes also named and shamed. From a mainstream Western perspective this is logical and salutary. Genocide thereby becomes the responsibility of the West's great anti-system adversaries, in contrast to its own non-genocidal self. If Trevelyan was right, however, then the convenient analysis which blames these exogenous forces alone may have to make room for one which is more complex and certainly more disturbing. It might start with the consideration both of the crisis circumstances in which phase two of the international nation-state system was inaugurated in the rimlands, and of the underlying premises and structures upon which the West sought to authorize and helped to build it.

A WORLD RESTORED?

Bringing into play a set of new or reformulated nation states to fill the political void created by defeated or collapsed empires, the Paris peacemakers' underlying imperative had been to create a geopolitical framework for Europe and its hinterlands at least as durable as that dictated at Vienna in 1815. As little as possible could be left to chance. The demarcation lines between states had to be clear and precise. So, too, did lines of authority within each new territorial unit. 'National' spokespersons of communal groups upon whom the peacemakers' unction had not been bestowed were consciously prevented from travelling to Paris or making their petitions once there.[81] Nothing could be allowed to intrude uncertainty into the new order of things. Or perhaps, even worse, lead to localized arrangements between *peoples and communities* beyond the purview of Allied management. In short, everybody outside of the political and economic governing classes expected not only to know their place but to *be* in their place. Those who failed this test were consigned to a form of limbo: they became a 'minority' or, more unfortunate still, refugees. Such elements upset the new order's premium on order and predictability: their presence spelt exactly the opposite: a random, stochastic quality which identified them almost ipso facto as potential headaches, if not dangerous elements threatening to undermine not just the security of specific regimes but the system *tout ensemble*. The possibility that the impermeable nature of the new territorial frontiers themselves, or the required one-dimensionality of a person's status within such units might have significantly contributed to, or perhaps even been at the source of, the problem was, it appears, not open for discussion. To have admitted the possibility would have been to engage in a wholesale philosophical review of the fundamental operating premises upon which an Enlightenment, Linnean-style categorization of humanity had been founded. Worse, to have trodden this path in 1919, against the background of the peacemakers' fraught crisis management, might have been seen less as an exercise in academic futility and more as one tantamount to sabotage.

Yet in eschewing this interrogative mode, let alone 'imagining' an alternative conceptualization of post-war rimlands polity and society, the peacemakers found themselves caught between a rock and a hard place. The Károlyi episode alone forcefully demonstrated how liberal good intentions could readily be jettisoned when they got in the way of naked realpolitik. More by luck than good design, the peacemakers could still turn to a Masaryk-cum-Beneš Czechoslovakia or, latterly, a Piłsudski Poland, for confirmation of the essential benignity of the 'New Europe'. Czechoslovakia in particular was held up throughout the interwar period as a beacon of democracy, sanity, and civilized good governance, sometimes inviting comparison with Switzerland, as an example of diverse ethnic groups working within a shared polity. Yet the Czech state was not a cantonal entity but a unitary one, run by Prague and its largely Czech administrative class. The state's saving grace in communal terms was its positive encouragement of linguistic diversity in schooling, plus its laissez-faire attitude towards ethnic groups creating their own political parties (in effect, making Czechoslovakia a mini-version of its Habsburg predecessor), a situation which—given the multiplicity of its peoples—made coalition politics and hence compromise the order of the day. Even then, it was not just the second largest group, the Sudeten Germans, divorced from Austria yet disallowed their own republic in 1919, who felt they were not genuine stakeholders in the new entity. Large numbers of Slovaks, too, in effect the third largest group (but treated by the state as part of a single Czechoslovak majority) resented being subsumed within a national culture which was always Prague-centred and increasingly followed the Germans—especially with the onset of the Depression—in voting against perceived Czech hegemony and for ethnic separation.[82]

Poland under Piłsudski equally offered grounds for plurality, seemingly in spite of itself. Its unflattering interwar reputation as the 'most antisemitic state in Europe',[83] on one level appeared to be belied by the fact that a diasporic Ashkenazi Jewish culture, both religious and secular, reached its pinnacle here in the interwar years. And this in spite of a marked Polish Jewish economic decline as well as a background of increased violence against Jews from the Endecja and other right-wing groups. The contradiction is reinforced by reference to Poland's other minorities. Jan Gross, for instance, notes that in 1931, in the eastern city of Lwów, there were no less that sixty-eight periodicals on sale, in Ukrainian, Yiddish, and German, as well as in Polish, while seven years later there were eighty-three Ukrainian-language periodicals in the country as a whole.[84] This hardly speaks of a Poland where non-dominant communal groups felt so either marginalized or intimidated that they stopped expressing their identity or, more simply, their right to be different. Yet what we may equally understand is that the failure of the Polish nationalizing effort was not for want of trying, and lack of success may indeed point to Piłsudski as the inertial force—or, viewed from an alternative perspective, as the country's truly saving grace. Under him, state–community relations were expressed in the notion of 'state assimilation', in other words, a bottom line of loyalty was required of all citizens to the state but without further demands on their communal identities. As soon as Piłsudski was gone, however, his successors were back on the road towards 'national assimilation', putting the onus on Ukrainians in particular to become nothing less than Poles.[85] The consequences, not surprisingly, were to add grist the mill of an—until that point—muted Ukrainian national movement in Poland, and, with it, the first shots in what would become within a few years a truly genocidal Polish–Ukrainian confrontation.

But if *Sanacja* toleration thus represented a quirk of fate rather than a symptom of system design, this can only further reinforce a verdict that the Western liberal peacemakers' overall vision of phase two state-building lacked any intrinsic recognition of the value of plurality at all. To find that we would instead have to embark on a journey back to a pre-war Europe, where radical ideas about the future shape of post-imperial rimlands had yet to be hardened into nation-statist monoliths. With the key paradox that the most perceptive ideas geared towards avoidance of ethnic group competition, subordination, and hence violence in the rimlands emanated from Marxist, or *marxisant*, thinkers.

One proposal stands out. In 1902 the leading Austro-Marxist theoretician, Karl Renner, published *Der Kampf der österreichischen Nationen um den Staat*.[86] Its subject was the then intensifying nationality conflicts in the dual monarchy. Renner, however, did not simply regurgitate standard Marxist mantras which dismissed nationalist thinking out of hand as a false consciousness that thereby deflected progressives and proletariat alike from their proper focus on class struggle. On the contrary, Austro-Marxist thought was moving not only towards a recognition of the seriousness of the nationalist challenge within a multi-ethnic setting but, more provocatively, appreciated that it was potentially an agent whereby 'undeveloped' peoples and regions could be 'brought on' in the interests of a more *general* economic integration.[87] In other words, here was a line of reasoning which, instead of assuming that the rise of nationalism had to lead inexorably to the break-up of an entity such as Austria–Hungary, instead posited that if appropriately utilized and channelled it might act as the democratic engine not only for its transformation but, in the process, actually lead to its greater *coherence*. The tantalizing question, of course, was: how?

Renner hit upon a proposition which was simple to the point of obviousness yet at the same time almost gravity-defying in the way it overturned classic assumptions about the relationship between national identity and how that might be politically grounded. Why not, on the one hand, make citizenship the common privilege of everybody residing in the boundaries of the state, and nationality, on the other, a matter of one's *personal* identification and affiliation? And go on from this to recognize each of these nationalities as a distinct corporation under public law, and provide them with national secretariats who would be responsible for all matters pertaining to each group's national life, specifically those relating to language and education? In itself, the notion of separating out 'nationality' from 'citizenship' was not novel. Renner's particular advance on that was in proposing that national identity within the state could still be perfectly well accommodated, and indeed guaranteed, without the necessity of a compact territorial space. For instance, if you lived, say, in an industrial region, far from your native heartland but surrounded by other similar migrants from your own communal group—as well as from others—you would still be entitled to all the benefits of your nationality on a par with all other members of it—however dispersed your group was throughout the country. Significantly, too, the only limit on how much benefit—or, more precisely, how much of the country's resources—your group (and all others) would receive for its national needs, would be determined by the wealth not of each nation, but of the state alone. As each communal group would be entitled to the same level of resource, proportionate to its numbers, the way towards 'growing' that resource was through a general wealth accruing to the state. Renner's formula for the coexistence of peoples thus operated on two levels. On the national level each individual would help elect national officials to further national interests. On the civic level each individual would help elect state officials whose primary responsibility would be to further the interests of the commonweal. In this manner, Renner was effectively envisaging a dynamic but converging relationship between the interests of the individual as a member of a *community*, and the interests of the individual as a member of *society*.

If this sounds utopian one might equally counter that it only became so by dint of the triumph of nation-statism in the wake of Paris. Prior to that, personal, extraterritorial national or cultural autonomy was considered perfectly realistic and feasible by all manner of rimland parties, who recognized it for what it was—a major effort at maintaining the integrity of a post-imperial territorial polity against centrifugal and, by implication, destructive forces. To be sure, it tended to be the less dominant national groups who were its keenest adherents: Jewish socialist parties such as the Bund necessarily claiming to represent a community unusually lacking in a compact core; Georgian nationalists who were, ironically, 'perhaps the most sophisticated Marxists in the (Russian) empire'; the Belorussian socialist Hromada; and Dashnaksutiun, in both its Russian and Ottoman guises.[88] But it is equally interesting to note that when in the summer of 1917 the possibility of a Polish secession from the Russian Empire loomed, quite mainstream Russian parties such as the Cadets and Social Revolutionaries were also more than willing to engage with it: a federated bricolage of peoples within a single (Russian) state being considered far preferable to its potentially irreversible break-up.[89]

What all this boiled down to was a proposition that the welfare of peoples was best served by the preservation of large economic and social units, balanced by decentralized politics of human scale. It marked a distinction, if one prefers, between a 'language of national agendas, dominations and endgoals', and that of 'orientations, communities, regions', leading ultimately to a politics of 'together with' and 'alongside', not 'against'.[90] If this, meant à la Renner, divorcing nationality from the workings of state then that, too, was a price more than worth paying. If that, paradoxically, in turn meant the paternalistic governance of a Piłsudski rather than that of a modernizing Dmowski, then certainly for Jews of the Bundist ilk—steadfast in their continuing affirmation not only of cultural autonomy but of a truly socialist polity acting as a bridge across which all manner of peoples might cross together in harmony—that, too, even against the grain of post-war realities, was something worth fighting for.[91]

Against these genuine aspirations, the West's acknowledgement of plurality in the form of the Minorities Treaties reads as paltry and grudging. Indeed, as we have already suggested, the Treaties were considered to be a good idea not even by the peacemakers, who saw them purely as a firebreak—and not a very serious one at that—against the potentiality for violence and hence instability which nation-statism intruded into the world of the multi-ethnic rimlands. But could the Treaties still be made into a good idea and from that be transformed into something which gave to the genuine pluralists grounds for hope? The answer has already been confirmed as clearly negative, viewed through the prism of either the Allied record or—bar the blips or ephemera we have examined—'New Europe' thinking. The absence of the United States from the League clearly begs further questions as to whether American involvement would have made the necessary difference. That still leaves, however, one faint remaining possibility: that some other sufficiently potent outside element not aligned to the original formulation of the system might have impacted upon it in such a way as to force the system-makers to re-examine their modus operandi.

Enter Weimar Germany, the first of our two revisionist alternatives. Germany's position vis-à-vis the new Western-imposed order was clearly paradoxical. It had played no part in the making of the Versailles or other post-war treaties. It had been required to sign on the dotted line for what all Germans and many commentators considered a Carthaginian peace. It had then gone through a series of near-catastrophic internal political and economic convulsions, the upshot of which was a temporary but draconian Franco-Belgian occupation of its major coal-bearing Rhineland region. In foreign affairs German isolation led to a reappraisal of relations with Soviet Russia, which in 1922 led to the Treaty of Rapallo, ostensibly reinforcing the degree to which these two powers were outside and at odds with Western hegemony. That said, by the mid-1920s economic stabilization—significantly, with the aid of US loans—had led to a marked softening of Germany's relationship with the Allies. Moves towards German political rehabilitation as an equal partner within the new system—including as a member of the League—and, as a quid pro quo, German recognition of its *western* (not eastern) borders as determined at Paris, were concluded in the Locarno agreements of autumn 1925. Franco-British-German accord was made equally desirable if not imperative by London and Paris' awareness that the new post-Wilhelmine polity had democratic credentials at least as strong as any other state on the Continent, not to mention the fact that it was moving rapidly towards the most advanced social welfare system of the era. The man at the helm of the new Germany, Gustav Stresemann, was head of the centre-right German People's Party (DVP) and staunchly conservative by inclination. But the tenor of the Weimar regime, of which he was lynchpin in the mid-1920s, was decidedly liberal. One obvious indication of this leaning was both the support received and political participation in Weimar emanating from German Jews, which predictably led to the slur from all those other Germans unreconciled and hostile to it, that the Weimar Republic was a Jew republic.[92] Another indication of its leaning, again somewhat to the consternation and indeed provoking the opposition of unreconstructed German nationalists, was its movement towards the establishment of minority schools for the albeit relatively small number of Poles and Danes (but perhaps significantly not Jews) throughout the Reich.[93]

Stresemann, however, seemed to be formulating a minorities policy which was more than simply parochial in nature but instead, taken to its logical conclusion, stood to cut the Allies' limited minorities settlement from under their feet. Though not yet in the public arena, he was already, in 1925, toying with the idea of cultural autonomy as not only 'a natural right of every minority' but equally applicable throughout League states. This again was clearly a Lemkinian kind of notion, before Lemkin. And, somewhat akin to the Polish Jewish jurist's later thinking, Stresemann considered that the idea of bringing the protection of such groups to the forefront of League policy was not only key to the avoidance of 'further violent convulsions in Europe' but powerful enough to 'sooner or later, win over the opinion of the world'.[94]

It was certainly the case that Stresemann's proposition would have garnered support from the most forward-thinking elements associated with the League. The British-based League of Nations Union (LNU) was one very influential grouping—led by the Oxford classicist Gilbert Murray—which had been pressing the League secretariat in Geneva almost from its inception, not only for the formation of a permanent Minorities Commission but, equally tellingly, for all League members—not just those who had been on the receiving end of the 1919 Treaties—to adopt minorities provisions. The makers of the system found themselves further backed into a corner in the wake of Locarno, when a number of liberal and left-wing pressure groups began demanding an annual European Minorities Congress to be convened in Geneva. Covert support and funding for the proposal came from Berlin.[95]

The key question was whether Stresemann's growing public representations on the matter are evidence that he was in earnest, or was simply organizing a spoiling game to wrong-foot the League over the specific plight of the Volksdeutsche, especially in Poland. It was certainly the case that out of 1.1 million Germans on the Polish side of the post-1919 frontier, some two-thirds—and practically all the urbań class amongst them—were looking to 'voluntary' migration as the only way out of their predicament; a situation, however, which could have been significantly rectified by a border revision in Germany's favour.[96] It was also significant that when Stresemann finally made his critical move at a League Council meeting, at Lugano in December 1928, it regarded the small matter of the 'German' (in fact, German dialect-speaking) minority in that part of Upper Silesia awarded post-plebiscite to Poland, where, among other things, Polish language restrictions and the closing of minority schools was fuelling increasingly emotive anti-Polish sentiment in Germany itself. Thus when Stresemann took the floor to move from criticizing Polish actions to making the seemingly impromptu declaration that he intended 'to raise the *entire* problem of the League's protection of minorities' at the next meeting the following March, he predictably became the recipient of loud plaudits from fellow countrymen, who saw in the act evidence of Germany finally speaking as a strong nationalist power ought, and *in its own interests*.[97] That this also destabilized the tacit Locarno understanding that Germany's entry into the League would not lead to it launching a minorities crusade could only have fuelled further speculation that Stresemann's ulterior purpose was of a wrecking kind. That certainly was the case in early 1934, when the Polish foreign secretary, Colonel Beck, demanded the convening of an international conference to create a universal minorities system, again in the League Assembly. It proved no more than a cipher for, and prelude to, Poland's repudiation of its Minorities Treaty obligations.[98]

There is no obvious evidence, however, to suggest that Stresemann's project was not genuine, though there is equally no doubt that if Germany had continued to push for a comprehensive reformulation of the minorities system it would have led to increasing friction with the West's clearly hypocritical position on the matter. On the other hand, if Stresemann had strongly pursued his *Minderheitenpolitik* it would have most likely been backed by Jewish pressure groups at a juncture when the Jewish situation in many of the rimland countries was increasingly being jeopardized by a slew of legal and extra-legal enactments designed to discriminate against their economic position and/or restrict their access to higher education, particularly through the implementation of widespread numerus clausus measures.[99] The notion of a vocal international Jewish mobilization behind a German championship of minority rights is clearly a tantalizing, as well as counter-intuitive, one.

Such speculation, however, need go no further. Stresemann may have ephemerally ruffled the feathers of the upholders of the status quo, but in the upshot his efforts proved no more than a damp squib. The best he could offer by way of his March 1929 promised return to the subject was a study committee to look into possible improvements to the then current minorities system, which the League secretariat, in turn, was perfectly capable of burying. In effect, Stresemann had already renounced the issue as a major plank of his wider diplomatic offensive for a revision of Versailles. There would be no second chance. The onset of the global economic meltdown later that year, plus Stresemann's premature death the following year, ensured that further German *Minderheitenpolitik* would be pursued as an exclusively and consciously blunt confrontational instrument, until the advent of Hitler and Germany's League withdrawal blasted the minorities system to smithereens.[100]

*

If the years 1925–9 marked a brief window in which Germany appeared to take the lead in confronting the plurality versus uni-national dichotomy from *within* the Western-created minorities system, a more coherent, sustained, and arguably more radical challenge came from *without*: from the USSR. This must, retrospectively, read at least as counter-intuitively as the case of Germany. Certainly the Bolsheviks, by dint of having escaped the clutches of the Western system, were free to create whatever they thought appropriate to themselves. But Bolshevism, as well as being stridently internationalist at the time of its revolutionary moment, was also vehemently anti-nationalist. Its Marxism, unlike that of its Vienna cousins, had little time or sympathy for what it held to be a false, not to say reactionary, consciousness. And in lieu of the failed worldwide revolution in the immediately succeeding years, Bolshevik logic seemed to dictate that future purposefulness lay in building up the dictatorship of the proletariat in Russia, not pandering to the whims of bourgeois nationalists likely to secede their chosen territories from it at the first opportunity, let alone in preserving in aspic some quaint notion of ethnic diversity.

There was, of course, also the small matter of pragmatism. Just as Lenin had to make concessions to the peasants, first to win them over in 1917, and later, in 1921, to avert mass grass-roots insurrection, the party had no choice but to acknowledge the growing strength of nationalism, simply in order to survive. At the outset of the revolutionary period, the Bolsheviks—like other centrist parties—were clearly both surprised and unnerved by demands for self-rule from the imperial peripheries, the Ukraine, Baltic, and Caucasus in particular, and in the way this drained away support from what they perceived as their own urban, working-class constituencies.[101] Making declarations to the nationalities, as Lenin did in November 1917—promising them sovereign equality and the right to their own free development—can be viewed as a quite cynical attempt not only to go with the flow in regions where the party's power remained tentative or weak, but steal the clothing of primary competitors in the populist stakes, the Social Revolutionaries especially. A further proclamation to 'All Muslims of Russia and the Orient' the following month, urging them to join the Bolshevik-led struggle in return for the promise of national rebirth, can be taken as in a similar vein.[102]

The Bolsheviks were not coy in naming names. Chechens and other Caucasian Mountaineers, Crimean Tatars, and Kirghiz would all be supported in their liberation struggles, even where this involved backing these *ethnies* against others. Kazakhs, as they sought to roll back the Russian settlements in Semirechye—which had been a critical cause of the catastrophic 1916 rebellion—found themselves aided and abetted by the local authorities even where this involved 'excessive cruelty' and 'the character of revenge'.[103] A similar pattern followed in the North Caucasus where Stalin, as newly appointed commissar for nationalities, not only gave support to a Gortsy Republic re-formed and clearly less tolerant than its 1917–18 predecessor (as it confiscated lands from Russian and Cossack settlers) but, more amazingly, seemingly gave the endorsement of an overtly atheist patron to the *shariat* constitution of its protégé.[104]

None of this suggests altruism, only hard-headed political calculation, even—especially, perhaps—where this was clearly designed for maximum propaganda effect on the West. The upgrading of the Volga German Workers Commune, founded in late 1918, into an Autonomous Soviet Socialist Republic (ASSR) in 1924—alongside sixteen other German national districts throughout the length and breadth of the Soviet system—was clearly intended as a show case especially for the benefit of Weimar communists.[105] Similarly, after the violence visited upon the Ukraine, not least by the Bolsheviks in the civil war, efforts to encourage Ukrainian national culture—the appointment of Hrushevsky as head of the historical section of the Ukrainian Academy of Sciences being one key marker—was clearly motivated by a keen desire to demonstrate to Ukrainians across the border in Polish-controlled eastern Galicia how wonderful life was on the Soviet side.[106] By these criteria national groups might end up as losers as well as winners. Stalin's initial but actually ephemeral favouring of a united Gortsy Republic seems to have been impelled, at least in part, by awareness of the influence of the Naqshbandi and Quadiri *tariqa*s on neighbouring Iran and Turkey. By contrast, Georgians, Azeris, and Armenians, in their individual societal capacities, appear to have had no such geopolitical value, at least not in 1922 when they were forced, at Stalin's behest, into a single federated republic.[107] Other rimland communities received concessions when the regime took fright at the mass violence initiated by its *own* cadres and this violence proved to be utterly counterproductive to the securing of Soviet rule. One such instance was in the Crimea. Here, after receiving the 1921 report of the Volga Tatar communist, Sultan Galiev, on Béla Kun's post-Wrangel reign of terror (the same Béla Kun of the brief Hungarian Soviet Republic), Galiev's recommendation to come to an accord with the left-leaning Crimean nationalists of the *Milli Firqa* movement was acted upon, even while the organization itself was banned as counter-revolutionary.[108]

Again, all this could be taken as further proof that Bolshevism's nationalities programme had little or nothing to do with the interests of Russia's nationalities per se but was simply a reactive, where it was not an entirely opportunistic, set of short-termist policies—the ultimate aim of which was the creation of a single, streamlined proletarian state and society, not a federative or consensual one. Would-be national elites could only get on board in the first place by embracing, or at the very least tacitly accepting, the authority of the party. There was no question that the USSR was intended to be anything other than a centralized, socialist entity whose future development would be determined and supervised by a decidedly colour-blind communist apparatus based in Moscow. The famous dictum 'nationalist in form, socialist in content' further underlined the fact that issues of national culture would always be subservient to statist imperatives, and in no sense offered individual republics leeway to embark on their own autonomous development, let alone attempt to do so outside the Union's embrace. As for communities whose primary communal loyalty was to religion rather than nation, they were to be consciously left out in the cold where they were not overtly anathematized. One could have official status as a Greek, Finn, Ukrainian, or Kalmyk, not as an Orthodox, Lutheran, Uniate, or Lamaist. Jews, similarly, were entitled to a national culture not a religious one, meaning that while proletarian Yiddish of a communist-realigned Bundist variety was acceptable, the Hebrew of *hede*r, *yeshivot*, or, for that matter, anything to do with Zionism, was not.

Yet there is an alternative reading of early communist thinking on nationalities which must temper, if not entirely problematize, the straitjacketed, constrained, and essentially monochrome version outlined above. In the first place the very fact that Lenin took nationalism on board as a serious matter and one which could not be simply wished away by a wave of some magic Marxist wand is itself significant. Indeed, his pre-war concern about the position of what the party dubbed the 'oppressed nations'—rimland peoples in particular—within a tsarist 'prison of peoples', led him to delegate to the Georgian Stalin the composition of a party treatise on the matter. Interestingly, Stalin, in his 1913 response, *Marxism and the National Question*, did not dispute the historically based reality of nations, though he did propose that their existence was highly contingent on circumstances which could help bring them on to a point of fruition, or, alternatively, lead to them fading away.[109] Which, by implication, led to the question which really mattered for all good Bolsheviks: how did you then turn nationalists *into* socialists? The obvious Marxist answer was to make everyone cohere around a common proletarianism; which, in Russia, given its industrial 'backward-ness', was clearly unworkable. Alternatively, to try and mould all its diverse non-Russian peoples—in the early 1920s an estimated 64 million out of 140 million of citizens[110]—into one by way of a linguistic and cultural assimilation to a dominant Russian norm was to ensure that the country would be ungovernable. Indeed, to go down this route not only seemed to be a regression to coercive tsarist policies of *sliianie* (fusion); it also starkly confronted the revolutionary polity with an even deeper conundrum: how, having swept away a defunct reactionary empire, did you still legitimately claim rights to maintain that empire's territorial integrity and unity?

Finding the answer would inevitably take Stalin and the Bolsheviks back to the same question posed by Austro-Marxists with regard to the dual monarchy. To which the latter's answer had been to propose a symbiosis of interests between the economically integrative purpose of the workers' state and the national cultures of its peoples. Or, to put it in more firmly Russian terms, if the first helped the second—more specifically the weaker, more 'backward' national elements at the peripheries—to 'catch up' with the more 'advanced' Russians at the centre through the *medium* of national autonomy, the end result would still be unitary fusion.[111] In other words, the point at issue in the internal Bolshevik debate was not the end but the means—as well as timescale—by which you arrived there. The notion that enabling these nationalities was only a transitional stage en route to the society of *Homo sovieticus* offered a sop to those in the party who remained essentially at odds with the policy's unsocialist characteristics, just as, more inad-vertently, it harked back to an older imperial script in which an 'enlightened' *sblizhenie*—rapprochement—between tsarist state and peoples was simply imag-ined as a gentler way-station on the road to an ultimate Russification.

The point, however, about what Stalin, backed by Lenin, put forward at the criti-cal Tenth Party Congress in spring 1921 (the one at which Lenin's NEP diktat was also delivered), and endorsed as firm policy two years later at the Twelfth, was that it committed the party to a here-and-now policy that was the absolute reverse of Rus-sification. Instead, the order of the day was *natsionalizatsiia*, nation-building, or, as it more generally became known, *korenizatsiia*—implying something which was local, native, and intimate.[112] A new breed of Soviet ethnographers, ethnologists, and lin-guists rapidly got to work to determine to which nation obscure tribes, clans, and obscure rural dialects *belonged*. In the Caucasus, for instance, this meant that it was no longer possible to be a Turkish-speaking Muslim. Henceforth, one was a member of a designated national people, such as Azerbajani. Institutional implementation necessarily followed: 'Each Soviet nation, no matter how small, was granted its own national territory, national schools, and national elites. Dozens of written national languages were created for national groups that lacked them'.[113] As a consequence the patchwork-quilt-like nature of the tsarist empire's actual human geography—again more especially in the rimlands—was given legal-political reality in the form not just of a dozen large national republics but within them—initially at least—thousands of smaller *oblasti*, national-territorial regions, districts, and even national townships. Translated onto a map the USSR looked positively 'Byzantine' or, for that matter, like the Holy Roman Empire in its medieval heyday.

In more contemporary terms, however, its significance was twofold. Firstly, it demonstrated that the USSR was the *only* state emerging out of the shatter-zone chaos of the rimlands which made national diversity the basis for a plurality within its political system; and indeed, positively encouraged communities to think of themselves in national terms, even where—in the case of myriad nomadic peoples in Central Asia and Siberia—this was entirely remote from their cultural self-understanding or consciousness. In contrast, thus, to the very best examples of the Western dispensation—Czechoslovakia or Estonia, for instance, where demographically less strong communities were given firm minority rights against the power of the majority *ethnie*—in the USSR there were no minorities, only *nationalities*. One might go further and suggest that what Lenin and Stalin did was bend over backwards to ensure that the possibility of 'Great Russian chauvinism' within the state was blocked off, by actually denying Russians (until 1936) the one thing proffered to all the other 'oppressed' nations—national autonomy.[114] From this angle one might even say that what the communists sought to do was the very reverse of nation-statism as authorized by the West and practised by the 'New Europe'.

Which takes us to the second, and more important, point of relevance to this study. By recognizing the right of communities to a national existence, the Lenin–Stalin formula was, at least on paper, able to steer a course between the Baumanesque Scylla of forced assimilation and the Charybdis of eruction. Safeguards against the latter were reinforced by the requirement to embed national existence within a given, officially mandated territory. This was, of course, a critical element which departed radically from the Austro-Marxist concept of personal–national autonomy—as well as presenting a particular challenge to Roma, Jews, or other groups which were small in number, dispersed, and lacked an obvious homeland. In fact, in practice, elements of both territoriality and extra-territoriality intruded into the Soviet system, for better or for worse. For Jews, for instance, there was both a Jewish Commissariat and Jewish Sections of the Party—the Evsektsia, with purported roles to promote a strictly secular, communist version of Jewish life and culture. Equally, however, there was an entirely artificial effort to create a small Jewish ASSR far away from the historic Jewish centres of the Pale, in Birobidzhan, in the Soviet Far East.[115] Large numbers of Jews responded to these doubtful blandishments, as well as the requirement from 1932 to have nationality entered onto internal passports (on the basis of *jus sanguinis*—that is, parentage not place of birth), by opting for some other nationality altogether, usually Russian. This was all the more necessary given that, as a consequence of attempting to fix, as far as possible, so-called 'titular' national communities within their given territorial compartments, the predictable consequence for other 'national' groups was restricted access to earmarked jobs and educational opportunities.[116] If all this, however, is a reminder of how, by 1932, the whole nationalities project, alongside everything else in Stalinist Russia, had turned sour, perhaps we need to be reminded of what Terry Martin has said regarding the original 'commitment to ethnic proliferation', namely, that it 'would seem to have made the Soviet Union a highly *unlikely* site for the emergence of ethnic cleansing'.[117]

In the initial start-up years, from around 1924 to 1927, there is, moreover, evidence of the tangible benefits which accrued to at least some rimland communities from the policy. These were, for instance, years of relative independence for the Ukrainian Republic, while in the Crimea, after the mass bloodletting at the end of the civil war, its Tatar element sufficiently recovered under the presidency of its formerly *Milli Firqa* leader, Veli Ibrahimov, for this time to be remembered as a 'veritable golden age'.[118] Further east, on the steppes of the lower Don, a cultural revolution saw Kalmyk literacy expand from a mere 2 to a more than respectable 91 per cent of the population.[119] In all these instances, as also in the Mountaineers' Caucasus, these were societies essentially as antithetical to the diktat of Bolshevik commissars as they were to Whites. Yet in each instance, *korenizatsiia* along with the economic latitude offered under NEP provided opportunities for nation-building as—more specifically in the case of the Kalmyks and other like communities of the 'Asiatic and semi-Asiatic periphery'[120]—it gave to the Bolsheviks grounds for self-congratulation on their civilizing mission. Bolshevik justification on this latter score, moreover, might repudiate the charge that this was simply some Soviet version of a well-worn colonial enterprise by pointing to the contrast between Western assumptions about nationalism and the purpose of *its* nationalities pro-gramme. A leading Western commentator on the subject, Alfred Zimmern, for example, had recently argued that nationalism was 'a safeguard of self-respect against the insidious onslaught of a materialistic cosmopolitanism...the sling in the hands of the weak undeveloped peoples against the Goliath of material progress'.[121] Yet the USSR could claim quite legitimately to be fostering exactly the opposite process: providing the tools for the historically dependent and marginal to catch up with the metropolitan core and thereby pave the way not only for a genuine accommodation between the peoples of a post-imperial Russia but on basis of an economic streamlining which would have them all marching arm in arm towards a happy, proletarian future.

Of course, this utopian mirage was itself founded on some rather standard West-ern assumptions as to the nature and trajectory of progress, not least in the require-ment that 'poor', 'benighted', 'backward' peoples would have to be transformed into something else—a process that usually involved turning nomads into peas-ants, or nomads and peasants into industrial labourers. Even then it was founded on an even more thoroughgoing premise that loose tribal and clan communities, necessarily operating in their own local habitus and often on the basis of multiple social, linguistic, and ethnic interactions, were, nevertheless, 'redeemable' as single national categories. Which rather begs the question: was the failure of the Soviet experiment—and with it the turn towards the very thing that Martin suggested *ought* to have been unlikely—a function of a false operating premise, leading to classic anti-colonial resistance, at the hands of native peoples? Or arguably, equally disturbingly, was the Bolshevik nationalities' commissariat in some sense a victim of its own hubristic success?

As suggested, once conceived, Soviet eagerness to pump resources into *koreni-zatsiia* and thereby make it sustainable for the long haul undoubtedly did produce early quantifiably verifiable results. But, paradoxically, this rapid achievement can also be said to be a product of the one thing the Austro-Marxists had warned against: territoriality. Renner's formula had looked to the creation of a Danubian federation of peoples, which was both considerably more elastic in conception and more mass-movement-orientated in its appeal. By plumping for a spatial compartmentalization of the idea of the nation, and in the absence of Bolshevik cadres willing to carry it through at the grass roots, the commissariat had had no choice but to fall back on those who *believed* in their national destinies. And these people tended to be the equivalent of the overtly socialist or left-leaning elements of the national elites of the 'New Europe', with the critical proviso that they had been prepared to go with the flow of Bolshevik supremacy. Even so, what Soviet *korenizatsiia* in the mid-1920s seemed to most obviously celebrate were the achievements of national republics and, hence, of local cultural and political leaders with whom those achievements were most clearly associated.

In a system which deemed itself to be politically as well as nationally plural this could have been a major benefit: indeed one might envisage it as a libertarian socialist solution as good as any to the problem of how to successfully frame a coherent, but non-violent, post-imperial society. But giving power and prestige to 'national' elites, however much they proclaimed (or disguised) themselves as good Bolsheviks, not only cut across the top-down, control-freak nature of Soviet decision-making; it also carried with it the implicit threat that these same leaderships would start treating their respective republics as in some way sovereign, and so entitled to develop agendas of their own. Similarly, nationality as an 'obligatory ascribed status' allotted to each Soviet citizen from birth was there to serve state interests of 'social accounting',[122] not to provide a resource for local bigwigs. In the Soviet script, only the party had the maturity and wisdom to know what was good for the people. Republic functionaries who appeared to think or act otherwise by initiating their own self-help schemes not only became suspect in themselves but stood to be accused of infecting much larger sections of their base population with the same—national—virus. When, in 1927, the first purges of Ibrahimovists began in the Crimea, encompassing so-called 'bourgeois nationalists', and the *ulema*, along with all surviving members of the pre-revolutionary Tatar intelligentsia,[123] it was as if their crime had been to play the Soviet *korenizatsiia* game far too capably, successfully, and well. It was not yet mass ethnic cleansing. That was still to come. But the buds of plurality had already been trampled on and would not be coming up again until the very twilight of Soviet rule.

However, if the Crimea's crime lay in not playing the game according to Soviet rules, there were already other Soviet rimland societies who had suffered its wrath for not playing at all. For the Bolsheviks the only game in town was the one it devised. To refuse it was to declare oneself outcast. In Turkestan, more especially in Semirechye and the Ferghana valley, openly anti-Soviet *basmachi* bands cut across communist blandishments to local populations—both during and after the civil war period—to come on side. Attempts to reassert an independent *khanate* in Kokand, which had last ruled in the nineteenth century, had led to a major urban massacre in the course of the civil war in which thousands had been mown down—somewhat ironically by Armenian units.[124] One of the last casualties of the *basmachi* struggle in 1922 had been none other than Enver Pasha, still pursuing pan-Turanian dreams. But hardly had the *basmachi* insurgency flickered out, and Central Asia submitted to Soviet rule, than another insurgency began, this time in the North Caucasus. As with Kokand and Bukhara, as with the *Antonovshchina*, so here, too, in 1925, the Red Army marshalled an enormous array of artillery, machine guns, aircraft, and ordnance with which to pulverize and liquidate the Chechen-led rebels. Close to half of the 242 communities of what had been the Gortsy Republic were bombarded, strafed, and razed in this way.[125]

Why had this new insurgency taken place? In significant part because the republic of which the Mountaineers had been so proud had been broken up into smaller autonomous zones at the behest of Stalin. *Divide et impera*, pure and simple. But Mountaineer anger was also consequent upon another Soviet broken promise: to let Muslims, their *sharia*, and *tariqa*s be. Was it significant that the most serious domestic resistance to Soviet rule came from some of its most independent-minded Muslim rimlands? Or that, in turn, the Soviet response closely mirrored that of colonial powers at the fin de siècle as they had striven to wipe out once and for all communal movements which, having looked upon the new merciless face of progress, had chosen to defy it? Today, the sub-genocidal consequences of Central Asian and Caucasian defiance are largely forgotten because they took place in out-of-the-way locales, off Western cognitive maps—not to mention that they would soon to be dwarfed by truly gargantuan sequences of mass murder. But then, in terms of pattern they were not so singular. In another rimland zone close by, another very similar sequence of part anti-Muslim, part anti-national violence was being meted out by a polity with its own sense of undeviating and utterly ruthless mission.

GENOCIDAL 'BUSINESS AS USUAL': KEMALISM VERSUS THE KURDS

> That population is neither peaceful not civilised. It lacks national consciousness and is only capable and willing to work as hired murderers.[126]
>
>> Official Yugoslav response to Albanian émigré appeal to League of Nations to enforce Minorities Treaties and to protect the Albanian minority in Kosovo, 1924
>
> Their cultural level is so low, their mentality so backward, that they cannot be simply assimilated in the general Turkish body politic...they will die out, economically unfitted for the struggle for life in competition with the more advanced and cultured Turks. As many as can will emigrate into Persia and Iraq, while the rest will simply undergo the elimination of the unfit.[127]
>
>> Foreign Minister Tevfik Rüştü Aras, speech to Turkish Cabinet, 1927

Each of these statements evokes a dread chill in its own right. Juxtaposed, they present us with a troubled theme across time and space. Well before the 1920s, Kurds and Albanians already had a reputation as truculent, recalcitrant recidivists in the face of either the imperial or the national projects of their respective 'masters'.

Albanian nationalists, including in Kosovo, had played a critical pre-war role in undermining Ottoman rule in the Balkans, just as, a decade later, the Kosovans presented a martial thorn in the side of Serb-led Yugoslavia. In the immediate decades before the great conflagration, Kurds—just like Albanians—lost their historic standing as a largely loyal Muslim element of the Ottoman frontier population and instead became perceived as troublemakers, and even outriders for interfering foreign powers. Within the new Kemalist version of Turkey their position as a largely compact non-Turkish bloc threatened to be even more troublesome still. Ottomania may have ended but its submerged fault lines at Balkan and eastern Anatolian extremities appeared to be as unstable as previously.

Taking the comparison a stage further, it is also notable how both Yugoslav and Turkish nation states sought—entirely unsuccessfully—to resolve their respective Albanian and Kurdish 'questions' by the expedient of encapsulation. We have already come across the sophistry of Albanians as Arnauts; in other words, Serbs who had forgotten who they *really* were. Kemalist Turkey went to similarly extravagant lengths to scientifically 'prove' that the Kurds were really Turks (albeit of a mountain variety) who had gone astray in earlier centuries of Persian dominance.[128] The conceit was hardly peculiar to the policymakers of Belgrade or Ankara. In Rumania, for instance, Ukrainians became Ruthenized Rumanians and Magyar-speaking Szeklers ('hidden' Rumanians) as Bucharest's way of getting round its minority rights schooling provisions while at the same rigging higher school entrance in favour of its own *known* Rumanian group.[129] From a statist perspective, the trouble with the Kurds and Albanians was that they simply didn't know when they were beaten. The same was true of the Muslim Chechens and Dagestanis. From the time of their *Ghazawat*—their Holy War against Bolshevik rule in 1921—they battled on for their independence, against all the odds and even against hope.[130] The equivalent result in Kurdistan was an interwar period of supposed 'peace' in which warfare was actually the norm: seventeen of the eighteen Turkish military operations of the period 1924 to 1938 took place in the Kurdish provinces, all but one of them against Kurdish combatants.[131] One of these, the Shaikh Said rebellion of 1925 was of a scope and scale to actually threaten the Kemalist regime, consequently registering concern in world capitals. Even in the wake of this Turkish Vendée, more localized though still extraordinary convulsions rocked the Kurdish east well into the 1930s—culminating in the great Dersim bloodbath of 1937–8.

But if this pattern of actually asymmetric Turkish–Kurdish conflict might already suggest genocidal possibilities, there is something else which must pose difficult questions, not so much about the Turks as about the mindset and behaviour of supposedly 'more civilized' Western onlookers. A decade earlier an attack on 'human diversity' in exactly the same geographical arena—that is, on Armenians and other Christians by the Kemalists' immediate predecessors—had led to a torrent of vituperative international denunciation against Ittihad for their attempt 'to preserve a decaying hegemony over populations'. Yet when it came to the Kemalist assault on the Kurds, far from the West frowning or wringing its hands, no such moral censure was recorded. On the contrary, either by conscious omission to act or commission, France, Britain, even the United States, actively gave succour or support to the effort. *This* attack on human diversity was thus countenanced as being a perfectly acceptable 'way of bolstering society in the name of progress, by the elimination of elements that had no place in the new order'.[132]

The dread question—how could this be?—becomes all the more telling, however, in the context of the mid-1920s years of promise and opportunity. These were years, after all, as we have seen, in which a still revisionist Germany was making its peace with the Allies, and even the USSR looked to be re-establishing its credit with the West. Add Turkey to this list and the self-appointed successor states to three out of four of Europe's pre-1914 land-based imperial powers start looking like a line-up of model polities on their way to an economic and political convergence with the leaders of the mainstream system. In brief, we have the first, albeit false, dawn of contemporary globalization: a globalization whose fundamental twin engine involved the ideas of development and progress.

Nowhere was this recipe embraced more fervently than in Kemal's Turkey. Nor were any of the 'new' sovereign states embraced with quite the same degree of elite enthusiasm in the West. It is not very difficult to see why. The early years of Kemal's post-Lausanne leadership were ones of a veritable cultural as well as political revolution. All the institutions which related the country back to the Ottoman past were overthrown or eliminated. In rapid succession went the sultanate, the Caliphate, the Şeyh ul-İslam, *sharia* courts, Sufi lodges (including, of course, the dervish orders) *waqf* (religious) property; anything, in other words, which harked back to Islamic governance and culture. In came Western-style education and Latin script, Western dress (and, with it, intimations of female emancipation), Swiss civil and Italian penal and commercial codes, ultimately even, in 1928, the removal from the constitution of the clause proclaiming Islam as the religion of the Turkish state.[133] Turkey—said the man who seven years later would nominate himself Atatürk—'Father' Turk—could no longer afford to be 'a land of mystics and witch doctors', nor could anybody in a civilized society be 'so primitive as to seek their material and spiritual wellbeing through the guidance of any old Shaikh'.[134] That this particular autumn 1925 public statement was a very pointed reference to the revered Naqshbandi spiritual leader, Shaikh Said, who had been at the head of the just crushed rebellion, was quite intentional. In his speech, Kemal contrasted primitivism with the 'learning and science of civilization'. That this actually meant a path of secular modernization on Western, European lines, was practically the leitmotif of the Kemalist revolution just as, in more Gökalpian terms, any resistance or refusal to follow this path was denounced as tantamount to a denial, even betrayal, of the nation's 'glorious future'.[135]

Of course, healing the wounds of Western versus Turkish enmity did not happen overnight. The British in particular had issues with Kemal over Mosul, the largely Kurdish province which, for geostrategic reasons as well as more obviously for its oil reserves, Whitehall wanted in Iraq, not Turkey.[136] Before resolution of boundaries in 1926, the Turks, not without good reason, believed that the British continued to incite Kurdish unrest in their own interest. If a complete end to outside interference in its internal affairs was a sine qua non of all Turkish negotiating positions of this period, so was the absolute abrogation of Capitulations, the cornerstone of the former neocolonial subservience of Ottomania to the West. All these bitter memories continued to fuel, on the Turkish side, the perpetuation of what has aptly been called the Sèvres syndrome: the ongoing fear through to the present day that Turkey's historic 'enemies' would conspire to extinguish through partition the resurrected Kemalist polity.[137]

Losing Mosul to the British—a territory which Kemalists deemed integral and indispensable to Turkey—was bound to heighten precisely such anxieties. Yet what is more striking even than the British quid pro quo guarantee not to agitate on behalf of either Kurds, or Armenians,[138] is the simple fact that on this score the Turks need not have worried unduly anyway. By opting to be a mirror to the occident, Turkey provided Western policymakers and opinion formers with an alibi for dumping the Kurds; and thus, for falling into line with Turkish minimization of or, alternatively, justifying the extreme, exterminatory violence meted out to, Kurdish communities. In the very wake of Shaikh Said's rebellion, for instance, not only was US High Commissioner Bristol alluding to the necessity of 'stringent measures' to re-establish order, but the newly formed Council on Turkish–American Relations extolled the supposed fact that 'peace now reigns within her [Turkey's] borders': these comments, remember, representing an America which had previously been vehemently hostile to 'barbaric' Turks.[139] As for Kurds, they would continue, for decades to come, to be characterized in an emerging Western historiography of Turkey as the 'forces of reaction' resisting the 'progress of Westernisation'.[140] Or simply required to suffer the ignominy of being patronized, as was Shaikh Said, as a 'picturesque and illiterate overlord'.[141]

Such highly contentious comments perhaps should not surprise, coming as these do from Bernard Lewis and Patrick Kinross, two notable Western apologists for the Kemalist legacy. But while the largely tunnel-visioned 'orientalist' tendency to define Kemal as 'a good thing', on account of Turkey's break with a wider Muslim world supposedly mired in anti-Western obscurantism, has continued to the present day—notably in the writings of Samuel Huntington[142]—what is altogether more worrisome is the way other, more critical writers have also been prepared to endorse Ankara's Westernizing credentials and, in the process, elide or simply airbrush out the layers of Kurdish corpses which bedecked Kemalism's triumphal path. Stanley Payne, a leading authority on fascism, for instance, describes the regime in contrasting manner, as 'neither militarist nor imperialist' but rather 'the most positive example of a developmental dictatorship in the process of creating a sort of "guided democracy"'.[143] Even Michael Mann has deflected direct responsibility for the repression of the Kurds by blaming instead—*pace* Payne—the country's 'military authoritarianism' and 'organic nationalism' on Kemal's Ittihadist predecessors, compared with Kemal's own 'stable rule', which 'eased tensions in the region and led Turks to deny rather than complete genocide'.[144]

It was, of course, the case that what Kemal created in Turkey—certainly in an interwar context—had its sui generis quality. It was, as Kadro, the early 1930s quasi-independent, theoretical mouthpiece of Kemalism, claimed, neither fascist, nor communist, nor even exactly capitalist, but an anti-colonialist, anti-imperialist national liberation movement geared towards the creation of a state-run national economy, founded on a homogeneous population, without classes.[145] The rhetoric of this alleged fourth way certainly positions Kemalism as a precursor of other elite-led (very often military elite-led) 'guided democracies' which exploded onto the African and Asian scene in the wake of post-1945 decolonization. Like them, Kemalist state-building was, in practice, determined, authorized, and supervised in thoroughly top-down étatist terms by a tight clique of individuals around the person of the *Gazi* ('great leader'), and with a developmental programme bound to favour and so enrich a socially very narrow group of loyal clients. It also brooked no dissent. The military, police, and juridical instruments used to liquidate the Shaikh Said rebellion itself provided pretext and cover for a much wider range of draconian emergency measures, most particularly in the form of the so-called Independence Tribunals. Their drumhead sentences of death proceeded over the following year to eliminate a slew of opponents, including some of Kemal's former comrades-in-arms now perceived to represent a threat to the *Gazi*'s personal authority. More precisely, the two show trials of 1926 against those charged with anti-state conspiracy were designed as weapons of terror and intimidation with which to silence all aspects of parliamentary and extra-parliamentary opposition.[146]

This was, quite simply, dictatorship at the point of the gun, and in its consciously anti-liberal actions should have had Western commentators recoiling with horror. Indeed, it was perfectly obvious to see Kemalism at this point for what it actually was: a more coherent, sustained, and streamlined—though certainly more personalized—version of Ittihad. All the more so given that Kemal sought to cover his tracks in 1926 by the elimination of leading CUP contenders, though in a like position they would have done exactly the same.[147] It was not just, however, in his authoritarian propensities that Kemal followed a well-trodden Ittihadist path. His national population policies equally revisited well-established Gökalpian contours. True, in the new Turkey all were now *Turkish* citizens regardless of religion. That would have been difficult under Ittihad with its Ottoman legacy of *millet*s, not to say multi-ethnic realities. But then both the CUP and Kemal had *between them* irrevocably changed the country's religious composition, to the point where, by the early 1930s, it had become 97 per cent Muslim.[148] Being Muslim however, did not automatically equate with being Turkish, begging the same fundamental question for the new regime as had beset the old: how did you inculcate everyone with a sense of having the same Turkish identity and with it, hence, a commitment to the state?

Kemalism's response operated on two levels. The first was seemingly inclusive, utterly bizarre but at least, at face value, not inevitably toxic, provided it was contained within Turkey's domestic context. This involved inculcating school children with a foundation myth of their shared origins in which their supposedly racially Alpine—in other words, 'white'—brachycephalic-endowed forefathers had, for millennia, not only roamed across the Central Asian steppes but bequeathed to other Indo-European peoples just about everything worth having, not least all the civilizations and languages of the ancient Near Eastern and Mediterranean world.[149] The fact that, in the process, Ankara had created for itself a construction 'devoid of history and symbolic weight' not to mention a 'geography of nowhere'[150]—having

somehow mislaid, or, more exactly, blanked out, the normal nationalist requirement to cherish the 'sacred landscape' of its people/s—may in itself speak volumes
about the inherent problem of creating a monolithic identity founded in, and on,
Anatolia. That the regime opted instead for an entirely mythic (indeed nonsensical)
narrative of unbroken (but geographically unanchored) ethnic continuity—and,
with it, historic greatness—rather too obviously points to its psychic compensatory needs in the wake of *Ottoman* defeat and devastation at the hands of others.

The regime's institutional and educational overhaul in this direction, however,
did not properly get under way until the 1930s. In the meantime, its behind-doors
population policy continued to grapple with the realities of a still very ethnically
mixed and diverse society. As with the Austro-Marxists, this still turned on the
segmented relationship between citizenship and nationality: the difference being
that Kemalism plumped for what amounted to a dystopian version of the Renner
formula. Everybody, granted, was a citizen. But their value as citizens, *in practice*,
seemed to cut diametrically across the supposed racial inclusivity of the constructed
foundation myth, being determined instead by more measurable indices of ethno-
cultural origins. Thus, as Soner Çağaptay has demonstrated, one might speak of
three concentric zones of citizenship in the new order.

In the first zone were 'true' Turks—their position in society bestowing on them
preferential treatment in terms of education and occupation. Then there was a
secondary, in fact much more substantial, zone, such as the Turks religiously
Muslim by background but of culturally disparate, including *muhajir*, background.
A cursory consideration of government policies towards *different* ethnic groups
within this category would bring to mind the Russian military manual of the fin
de siècle. In other words, there were communities such as the *muhajir* Bosniaks
and Pomaks who were considered essentially sound, loyal, and hence easily assimilable as Turks. Then there were other groups, some *indigène*, such as the Laz, others
immigrant, such as the Albanian Chams, who were viewed as altogether more
problematic and certainly less malleable. It is notable that from the time of the War
of Independence even the Circassians began to fall into this more suspect category.
The mere enunciation of Circassian minority rights—as in the 1921 appeal by a
group of Anatolian Circassians then convening under Greek-occupied aegis in
Smyrna, calling for the 'Great Powers and the Civilised World' to support Circassian self-preservation against Kemal's Turkifying programme—would have been
warning signal enough for Ankara that among not just with the Circassians but
such communities more generally, a strong sense of proto-national identity might
develop rapidly both in counterpoint to, and at the expense of, Turkey's homogenizing goals.[151]

If zone two categorizations were, in effect, an internal government acknowledgement of the country's intrinsic plurality, this not only carried an implicit
hierarchic ordering of groups ranging from loyal to disloyal (or simply good to
bad), but fed into issues of spatial planning which were a direct consequence of
Ittihadist, more specifically Nâzim-style thinking, dating back to the CUP Salonika
conferences. The old chestnut of how to make the country Turkish throughout its
length and breadth demanded that the more insubordinate communities either be

resettled in locales where they could not cause trouble or, alternatively, be swamped by 'loyal' incomers. As *muhajirun* were still arriving in Turkey in the 1920s and 1930s in large numbers from the Balkans[152]—in itself evidence of the exclusionary, inherently violent interwar policies of those rimland states—there was no ostensible problem for Ankara in terms of human resource. As, moreover, the whole purpose of the exercise was—in the words of the British ambassador, Loraine, in 1934—to bring 'all Muslim elements into one whole, entirely Turkish in character, speech, manner of life and outlook',[153] inducting different communities *together* made a lot of sense. It was a little like the Nazi notion of Reich strengthening avant la lettre. Or perhaps more mundanely, akin to the post-1948 Israeli challenge of assimilating hugely diverse 'ingathered' Jewish diasporic populations under a single Hebraicized umbrella.

That still left a third zone, however, primarily made up of the residue of the old 'non-Muslim' *millet*s. Jews were considered just about assimilable as Turks; Christians, not. Here, then, was an instantly disruptive factor not only in the Kemalist grand scheme of things but with regard to any pretence that the overall project could be conceived of as benign. In 1925, Kemal's right-hand man, İsmet İnönü, had stated the government position abundantly clearly:

> We are frankly nationalist and nationalism is our only factor of cohesion. In the face of a Turkish majority, other elements have no kind of influence. Our duty is to turkify non-Turks in the Turkish homeland no matter what happens. We will destroy those elements that oppose Turks or Turkism. What we are looking for in those who are to serve the country is above all that they are Turkish and Turkist.[154]

The regime proceeded to eruct those who, in its mind, did not meet these criteria—namely Christians. They did so not by outright genocide but by creeping cold pogroms. On the one hand, there was legal cover—a 1929 decree, for instance, preventing Armenians from the right 'to sell or bequeath property'; on the other, sheer intimidation: the death of two Armenian priests in police custody soon after the decree leading to the panic exodus across the border into Syria of not less than 10,000, and possibly many more, of the 25–30,000 'submerged' Armenians still remaining in the east.[155] Where Armenians—whether in eastern Anatolia or the country's western metropolises—clung on, they tended to do so in spite of the climate of fear and intolerance. Syriacs, after the Armenians the most reviled of communities, found themselves similarly targeted, threatened, directly expelled, or encouraged to flee. There were, of course, enclaves which, under the terms of Lausanne, were meant to be safe havens, including the largely Greek-inhabited islands of Tenedos and Imbros. Venizelos' visit to Ankara in 1930, initiating something of a thaw in Greco-Turkish relations, not least because it came with Athens' revocation of Greek 'exchangee' compensation claims, was meant to bolster such feelings of safety. For the islanders, however, it proved cold comfort as Turkish discrimination and then repression were the inevitable prelude to slow-motion ethnic cleansing.[156]

One might pause at this point to offer some brief remarks on the Kemalist nationalizing project. Firstly, it suggests criteria as to who were 'in' and who were 'out' that were hardly empirically based but founded on subjective, emotional, if not entirely projective cultural underpinnings. A US diplomat, in the wake of the 1929 Armenian exodus, accurately noted that the Armenians were actually 'better able to harmonise with the Turks than the Greeks and the Jews; they have similar tastes and speak Turkish almost universally'.[157] In other words, just as strong Jewish acculturation in Germany should have provided objective grounds for an interwar accommodation between the German state and its Jewish community, the same—at the very least on cultural terms—could have been possible between a Kemalist Turkey and its now much smaller and entirely politically emasculated Armenian population—even *after* the Ittihadist genocide.

Secondly, a distinction is in order between the Turkish classification of its population and any direct cross-reference to Nazism. It is clear that despite the former's attempt at a racial self-imagining this did not translate into a Turkish form of racial hygiene, or a state effort to eruct or eliminate people on racial grounds. Equally evidently, however, Kemalism was quite capable of targeting human collectivities—short of outright genocide or not—regardless of racial discourses. Thirdly, in the case of the remaining Christian communities, while Ankara had no objective need to commit genocide when it clearly could employ other means of easing them out (*pace* Lemkin, who might argue these were in themselves part of a genocidal battery), its novel need for international approbation may have acted as an inertial factor on open violence—even while, in an entirely contradictory vein, the most common populist accusation against Christians was that they were fifth columnists working in the interests of foreign powers.[158] Fourthly, and this is clearly the most problematic remark of all, in spite of the stack of evidence confirming flagrant human rights violations, the Western response to the Kemalist regime remained firmly sanguine where it was not positively adulatory.

Again, one has to ask the question: why? The cynical answer has to be that having been beaten at their own military game the Western Allies decided they could do business with a newly reformulated Ottomania after all. The Kemalist slogan 'Peace at home, peace in the world', with its implied renunciation of territorial claims, suited the West just fine. One could, however, go further and argue that, after all the trials and tribulations of the period up to Lausanne, the Western powers did not simply like what they saw in a country consciously if not ostentatiously imitative of themselves, but recognized in its planned homogenization the exact model for the global semi-periphery which they had been seeking ever since Versailles. Here was a state which had not simply cleaned up its act: its proposed action plan would henceforth be geared towards a monocultural unity. To the authoritarian aspects the West could simply turn a blind eye. Of course, there had to be a veneer of probity; the Lausanne Treaty contained clauses stipulating the protection of *non-Muslims*, their religions, even their right to use non-Turkish languages in public as well as in private.[159] But beyond that, there were no stipulations recognizing rights to schooling in 'minority' languages as there were in the other rimland treaties the West had dictated. By mutual agreement, Turkey and her interlocutors had simply dispensed with the notion of minorities or, for that matter, plurality.

*

Which, at last, brings us back to the Kurds. They, not the Armenians or other Christians, were the primary casualty of the new post-1923 Turkish order to which the West had given its assent. There had been no reference to Kurds or Kurdistan[160] (any more than Armenia or Armenians) in the Lausanne protocols, which was itself ominous. This, after all, was a 180-degree turn from Sèvres, in which the articulation of Kurdish statehood in some form or other had been quite explicit. The reason for the Western volte-face, however, was quite transparent. The Kurds, who, like the Armenians and others previously, had been perceived as a useful prop—temporary or otherwise—in the bolstering of the Allied game plan geared towards the dismantling of Ottomania, had lost all utility now that the Allies had come instead to an agreement with Kemal. Actually, their situation was even more exposed, as, unsubdued, they remained not just the spanner in the works of Turkish developmental modernization but 'a threat to the national integrity of the Republic'.[161]

In Kemalist eyes, as we have already intimated, 'the very socio-political structures of Kurdish society...tribes, religious orders, shaikhs, aghas, sects, nomads and bandits',[162] represented the very antithesis, not to mention the bête noire, of the regime's normalizing process. These purported characteristics helped confirm regime portrayal of Kurds as economically backward and religiously fanatical, which in turn reinforced the regime's case for arguing that within its grand Turkification scheme the Kurds qua Kurds simply did not and could not fit. The only way, thus, that they could be assimilated at all was by becoming something *other* than what they were. This line of thinking already pointed to the Resettlement Laws of the 1920s and 1930s, and their corollary in the 'Eastern Reform Plan', which envisaged mass 'dispersions' of Kurdish tribes outside of eastern Anatolia to designated zones elsewhere. It also followed the already established CUP formula that in no district would deportees be allowed to constitute more than 10 per cent of the overall population.[163] In other words, the new Interior Ministry programme was not in itself novel but rather represented a more thoroughgoing commitment to the earlier nationalist goal of extinguishing the 'Kurdish question', through isolating and disaggregating Kurds from habitus, clan, and community. Only through this method could they be made to submit to the rules, behaviour, and, ultimately, identity of the already pacified and 'Turkified' people around them.

The charge of cultural (or actual) genocide—assuming the plan had been fully implemented—aside, two further things are immediately striking about Ankara's Kurdish policy. One is clearly cultural. Kemalists stigmatized everything Kurdish because it reminded them a little too closely of what actual Turks had *also* once been—a set of tribal, nomadic peoples. Kemalism was thus caught in a cleft stick of its own making. 'Turks' were extolled—provided it was in the past tense—for being free, independent, and certainly utterly martial warriors of the plateau and steppes; Kurds, in the present tense, were the object of absolute abomination on exactly these same grounds. One might put the projective quality of this dilemma thus: what upset Kemalists was the image of their uncouth, untutored, and certainly rowdy 'Oriental cousins' embarrassing their own efforts to be suave, well-mannered, neatly-suited Ankara gentlemen as they sought out the polite company of *other* Western gentlemen.[164] This, of course, notwithstanding the equally enervating fact that they were simply following in the more successful and accomplished footsteps of the Armenians, who had been playing this game for decades.

However, if this feature of Kemalist hostility to Kurds could be argued to be a banalization of the serious issues at stake there was, arguably, something more immediately political which struck at a much rawer nerve. Prior to the Armenian genocide an awareness had begun to emerge among contending 'national' elites of the triangular nature of the relationship on the eastern Anatolian plateau. Dominated by the better mobilized, savvy, and certainly internationally much better connected Armenian revolutionaries, the largely (though not exclusively) tribally based, fractious, and internally quarrelsome Kurdish *shaikh*s and *agha*s had repeatedly been beaten into third place as the struggle with the Ottoman centre intensified. The Kurdish position seemed particularly shaky in the immediate pre-Great War period, as Dashnaks and CUP appeared to get closer to their own two-way compact, with land-reform implications which particularly threatened to endanger the *agha*s' 'as well as Kurdish urban notables" economic hold. *Some* Kurdish tribal leaders, as we have seen, reacted by accepting the blandishments and guns of the Russians, in opportunistic or indeed desperate efforts to carve out or simply hold on to their diminishing frontier assets. However, in the wake of war, defeat, and Kemal's calls for defence of the Ottoman homeland from his initial Erzurum and then Sivas bases, Kurdish elites on the plateau appeared much better positioned to influence the direction and outcome of events. Kemal now clearly *needed* them in their military capacity. And, in return, Kurdish worries about the Armenians regrouping militarily at their expense—not to mention with revenge in mind—clearly had many of them willing to reciprocate in kind. While these relationships proved fluid—there were, for instance, countermoves in far-away Paris in 1919 to create an Armenian–Kurdish accord[165]—most Kurdish leaders in the period before Lausanne opted for Kemal.

The point thus, is simply this. The Kemalist regime, post-Lausanne, in order to cement its unitary, uni-national notion of Turkey, had to pretend away or completely cover over the tracks of the arrangements and understandings it had made directly—or possibly indirectly, via secret CUP or even *Teşkilat-ı Mahsusa* channels—with Kurdish leaders, in the critical phase of the independence struggle back in 1919. These included some open declarations which were more than simply appeals to fellow Muslims but which specifically named Kurds as 'equal partners and allies'. 'Committees for Turco-Kurdish Independence' were another consequence. Kurdish leaders certainly seem to have believed that they had been offered, at the very least, a devolution of powers to an autonomous Kurdish region. In other words, there is at least some evidence to suggest that in the emergency conditions of 1919 Kemal had not flinched from the possibility of a consociational rather than unitary state.[166]

The notion, moreover, in 1919, had been far from ludicrous. While, as Martin van Bruinessen has pointed out, it was the massacre of Armenians which 'made a Kurdish state feasible',[167] Kurds were, thereafter, the dominant element in the east or, put another way, in control of a third of Turkish territory—some fourteen contiguous provinces—even if they only constituted a fifth or less of the country's population overall.[168] Whether Kemal ever really intended to share Anatolia with Kurdish leaders is a moot point. A canny practitioner of realpolitik, he was as willing as the British or Russians to make fulsome promises when the need was greatest, and then as easily break them when the crisis had passed. Making friends with Kurdish *agha*s, and giving them leave to hang on to the lands and property they had stolen from the Armenians under CUP aegis, was par for the course.[169] Kemal, after all, was the great master of biding his time, waiting for the right moment to come out into the open with his real position. When he finally did so, on matters Kurdish it became abundantly clear that not only was there going to be no accommodation whatsoever but that of all the rimland nationalisms, this one—led by once proud empire men—was going to be quite the most thoroughgoing and non-negotiable of all.

Was it the Kemalist overruling of the possibility of Kurdish nationalism per se, however, which was the fundamental goad to Turco-Kurdish conflict, or, more exactly, the denial of an alternative conceptualization of the state? There are good grounds for believing that what most Kurds in the east wanted was the perpetuation of a polity which did not ultimately distinguish between Turks, Kurds, and other *Muslims*, but instead provided for a universe of obligation founded on the community of the *umma*. After all, Kurdish society was itself very variegated, even more so in the complexity of its languages—not to mention, in the view of one sympathetic expert, 'fatally disadvantaged' in the nationalizing stakes, due to a lack of both 'a civic culture and an established literature'.[170] There were, of course, elite Kurds, not just in the metropolitan mainstream or military trained, but among the provincial urban notables, who considered these problems not insuperable. There was, too a small handful of foreign, more precisely British, observers, who agreed.[171] But then the actual situation that Kurds—whatever their background or level of sophistication—found themselves in post-Lausanne, was one of being squeezed from at least two directions.

The abolition of the Caliphate in April 1924 not only symbolized an end to a 'multi-ethnic polity and authority' but has been described as being perceived by many as an 'eschatological intrusion into the collective identity of the Kurds, the state and the fraternity between Muslim groups'.[172] Later that year, the specific abrogation of Kurdish (and other) language rights in the constitutional settlement confirmed that without the Caliphate there would be no space in the new Turkey for 'diverse loyalties and local autonomy'.[173] Of course, some Kurdish leaders, particularly those who had aligned themselves previously with the CUP, were able to make a relatively smooth transition to the new normality. But for many others who had held out for a restoration of 'what once had been' on the plateau, the dawning realization that *all* historic inter-communal relationships were now null and void and had been superseded by a single 'one size fits all' *Turkish millet*, must have registered not just as shocking but quite literally blasphemous.[174] Worse, there was, increasingly, nowhere to escape to.

In the past, nomadic Kurdish tribes had avoided direct confrontation with interfering or menacing government through migration elsewhere, most especially across the border into Persia. Looked at in terms of the *longue durée*, Kurdish tribal survival had practically been a function of this liminal existence in the frontier zones of historic Middle Eastern empires. The declaration of Turkey as a republic, by contrast, carried with it implications of a very Western-style demarcation of boundaries—and of a repudiation of any administrative or other distinction between centre and periphery. Indeed, the very fact that the republic was now, in its south and south-east, bounded by French Syria and British Iraq, not to mention on its east by the consciously modernizing Iran of Reza Shah, radically ate away at the notion of a porous frontier as a tribal Kurdish safety valve.

Paradoxically, the delineation or re-delineation of these state boundaries also keenly drew attention to the notional existence of an entity called Kurdistan. Yet even as this was being articulated, any hope of its concrete political attainment was being strangled at birth. This was doubly paradoxical—and hence doubly toxic—because the idea of a Kurdish entity was brought onto the international agenda at Sèvres not by the Kurds themselves but by the *British*. Whitehall, of course, had no interest whatsoever in helping to create Kurdish independence in the estimated 200,000 square miles of territory—straddling several actual or would-be states—where Kurds were the majority population. The British project, on the contrary, was of an entirely fragmentary as well as provisional kind. Its aim was to create a *localized*, British-supervised, Kurdish statelet, or perhaps even tribal zone, in south-east Anatolia, contiguous with a notional Armenian state to the north, as part of its wider containment effort aimed at keeping the Turks isolated and prevented from linking up with the Bolsheviks.[175] The Kurds, at the time, for the most part, had appropriately repudiated the Sèvres scheme as a sham. Yet the very fact that the idea had been articulated at all—and by an outside power—had Kemalists lining up, just as had their CUP forbears vis-à-vis the Armenians, to reify Kurds as the cat's paw of a foreign interest (even long after that had actually dissipated), and hence by definition another Trojan horse community of would-be traitors.

Kemalist worst fears seemed to be realized, moreover, within months of Sèvres, when a Kurdish rebellion broke out in part of the Dersim and Sivas provinces, where Kurdish and Turkish populations overlapped. Though the rebellion took the name of the leading protagonists, the Koçgiri tribe, it notably drew support from across historic linguistic and religious divides within Kurdish society, and—in its specific demands for Kurdish autonomy—raised the spectre of a modern political consciousness which, up to that time, had been associated with the more rarified discussions of the pre-war town associations *Hiva-ya Kurd Cemiyeti* and the *Kürd Teavün ve Terakki Cemiyeti*. Indeed, the rebellion was fomented by a closely linked successor grouping, *Kurdistan Taali Cemiyeti* (The Society for the Elevation of Kurdistan), which not only had chapters in Istanbul and major eastern Anatolian towns but, clearly, was able to incite many tribes to actively back its demands.[176] Ultimately, when push came to shove, sectarian interests did impede the insurgency. It remained relatively limited to the Dersim area, with its mostly Alevi protagonists finding a distinct lack of broader tribal support—partly due to the fact that many chieftains had simply been co-opted with bribes and patronage from Kemal.[177]

Equally significant with regard to these events are both the nature of the rebellion's destruction in spring 1921, and its aftermath. The Koçgiri challenge to Ankara came at the height of the struggle with the Greeks, with rumours spreading thick and fast that not only were the rebels in cahoots with Athens but that behind this collaboration lay none other than perfidious Albion. The rebellion thus elicited a classic perpetrator charge of 'stab in the back'. Ankara's immediate response was not a general assault on all Kurds; Kemal needed to keep as many on side as possible. However, the localized military repression was of such ferocity that, in angry debates in the National Assembly, the government was accused of perpetrating atrocities which would have been unacceptable even for 'African barbarians'.[178] This was hardly surprising: the campaign was spearheaded by Lame Osman, whose cut-throats already had a bloodcurdling reputation for their exploits on the Black Sea coast every bit as loathsome as those of more contemporary paramilitaries operating under licence of the state, such as Arkan's Tigers of the post-Yugoslav wars of the 1990s.

*

That the Turco-Kurdish relationship had moved in short steps from one of allies in a fraternal struggle to one of outright enmity, not to say to a classic War Type Three situation, tells us much not only about Kemalist intentions but about the belated crystallization of out-and-out Kurdish *nationalism*. From imagining that the triangular relationship on the plateau might be replaced by one of dual control, many Kurdish leaders had woken up after Lausanne to the realization that—bereft of an Armenian screen—they themselves were fatally exposed to playing a zero-sum game, defeat in which meant much more than simply subordination to Ankara. In a report which another newly formed, military-based nationalist group, Azadi (Freedom) submitted to British intelligence, in November 1924, they stated at the top of their list of anxieties and grievances a primary fear of a generalized 'transplantation'—in other words, ethnic cleansing—of *all* Kurds in the eastern vilayets to western Anatolia. Azadi could also confirm that a softening-up process in preparation for this denouement was already under way. A month earlier the constitution had prohibited the use of Kurdish in all public places: Kurdish publications were banned, Kurdish place names were in the process of being changed to Turkish ones, and the administration of eastern Anatolia was being taken over by government appointees who were from Turkish not Kurdish backgrounds.[179]

The issue of loss of patronage is itself highly indicative of this sea change. Back in the formative years of CUP rule—and at the time of the problem of the triangular relationship in eastern Anatolia—Talât and crew had ultimately eschewed an accord with the Dashnaks in favour of continued reliance on Kurdish tribal leaders and urban notables, a decision which, in turn, locked the CUP into handing out traditional sweeteners and honours to them. Kemalist co-option had followed a similar course, greased with sequestrated Armenian properties and lands for good measure. The new slew of laws in autumn 1924, however, included one which made it possible for large Kurdish landowners to be expropriated and their lands given to Turkish and other settlers in the region.[180]

The penny had finally dropped among Kurdish elites. Not only was there to be no Ankara compromise but, as a result of the belated recognition of the fact, the more prescient, including the Azadi grouping, worried that they were about to miss the nationalist bus altogether. Preparations were hastily put in train for a general Kurdish rebellion before the gate was firmly bolted against the possibility. Azadi, like its Kemalist and Ittihadist counterparts, had at its core serving army officers, some with a background traceable to Hamidiye tribal regiments from the 1890s. This substantially raised the threshold of any possible military confrontation to one of Anatolian civil war. This was doubly the case as Azadi was able to draw on connections with a broad range of Kurdish tribal chiefs and spiritual leaders, including Shaikh Said. This, too, provided the opportunity to present any uprising less as a bid for Kurdish secession and more as a legitimate Muslim protest against the irreligious blasphemers in Ankara who had trampled on Caliphate and *sharia* alike.[181]

Yet it may be as well to remember at this point some of the uncanny resemblances between what was now unravelling in 1924–5 and events in eastern Anatolia a mere decade earlier. This, after all, was *exactly* the same territory as that in which Armenian revolutionaries in 1914 had been faced with an imminent crisis as to what to do, or where to turn for help. Establishing how many of the Azadi cohort were among those who had sealed the Armenians' fate in those earlier years would require a detailed study of its own. That aside, they were, in key respects, retracing in 1924 the same Armenian steps. Azadi had been founded in Erzurum, a key political symbol of control in the east for Armenians—and Turks. Looking out from there, the key existential issue became which of the foreign powers would back their cause? The Armenians had looked primarily to the Russians, and to the British too. Azadi knew the Soviets would not commit against the Ankara regime and so fatally put all their eggs in the British basket. But without any concrete commitment from this source, Azadi was effectively operating on a desperate all-or-nothing throw of the dice—just as had the Armenian radicals in 1914. Yet, just as the Dashnaks, at their Erzurum Congress in the high summer of 1914, had listened to the CUP emissaries who promised them a statelet of their own in return for backing the CUP cause—before some had committed themselves to revolt anyway—ten years on to the month Azadi and other Kurdish leaders had met with Turkish delegates in a congress at Diyarbekir where, again, the latters' emissaries seemed to offer a route out of conflict by way of a special Kurdish administration for the region. Was this apparent concession a case of history repeating itself: the government waving a carrot as a ploy with which buy time or trap the Kurds in their own traitorous intentions? Certainly, fears haunted the follow-on Azadi gathering (as they had the latter stages of the Dashnak Erzurum one) that the Turks would use the occasion to arrest or eliminate their leadership.[182]

In the event, two singular developments emanated from Azadi's internal debate. The one which Kurdish society best remembers and celebrates is the Shaikh Said rebellion itself. Galvanizing a communal mobilization, as no Kurdish revolt in eastern Anatolia before or since has done, the rebels not only took the offensive against regular Turkish forces but, from February through April 1925, wrested from government control a swathe of central-eastern Anatolia. Yet if this demonstrated a singular resolve there was also an appalling downside to the Kurdish effort. Essentially reactive in causation, and botched in implementation, the rebellion was actually founded on a narrow segment of Kurdish society, primarily Zaza-speaking tribes especially disaffected by threat of land seizures and known for their religious devotion.[183] Turkish divide-and-rule policies successfully prevented many other tribes, including Alevis, from joining the insurgency, which also did not touch any of the sedentary Kurdish population or townsfolk. The Shaikh's declaration of *jihad* equally proved insufficient to inciting broader, active support across ethnic boundaries. In short, the revolt qua revolt provided evidence less of an upswelling of Kurdish national consciousness and more of a desperate, millenarian-tinged last stand of traditional Anatolian tribalism.

To which, of course, once it had been suffocated, then crushed, the Ankara authorities showed no mercy. Failed internal rebellions throughout history have nearly always led to the full force of state retribution against their leadership and followers alike. In this case an official figure of 420, mostly Kurdish notables, sentenced to death by the regime's Diyarbekir Independence Tribunal in May masks the much larger number of extralegal and summary executions, particularly of Kurdish intellectuals, that took place in the following months.[184] But in a sense this only shows us a small, essentially urban fragment of the picture of state reprisals perpetrated against Shaikh Said's real and alleged mass, rural following. Van Bruinessen speaks of the 'hundreds of villages...destroyed, thousands of innocent men, women and children killed'—without trial.[185] Üngör cites more specifically a range of targeted atrocities perpetrated by middle-ranking commanders in the Lice and Palu districts, where both participating tribes such as the Zirki (according to survivors massacred by the same *kesab taburu* butcher battalion as had exterminated Lice's Armenians a decade earlier) and entirely innocent communities, such as the villagers of Karaman, were mown down in machine-gun executions or driven into sheds and haylofts and then set alight.[186] Robert Olson also refers to an army round-up of Zaza tribesmen in the Diyarbekir area, who were then corralled and subjected to an hour-long bombardment until their complete annihilation.[187] All in all, there is no doubt that the military commanders in charge of the operation, if not their superiors, sought to exact punishment through the mass, indiscriminate slaughter of entire villages; that air power was part of this battery of extreme violence; and that at least 20,000 Kurds were deported as the state attempted to take firm control of the rebel zone.[188]

Is the destruction of the Shaikh Said revolt, then, a case itself of genocide, or the beginnings of a wholesale campaign of the same by the Kemalist regime against its Kurds? Five years after the revolt, US diplomatic sources reported that the Turkish authorities were planning 'to exterminate the Kurds and to repopulate Turkish Kurdistan with Turks from across the border in Azerbaijan and other parts of Soviet Russia'.[189]

It was no secret that the regime wanted to colonize the region with incoming Turks, and that previously attempted CUP efforts to remove as many Kurds as possible to other non-Kurdish regions remained integral to the Kemalist solution to 'the Kurdish question'. Reports written by members of Kemal's inner circle in the wake of the revolt's suppression not only looked forward to a long-term process of 'resettlement' by which eastern Anatolia's population became predominantly Turkish, but considered how this programme would be in practice implemented. The consequences included the creation, in 1927, of the first of three military Inspectorate-Generals for the east, to administer the region by martial law directly on Ankara's behalf. This was a statement as blunt as any of the regime's internal colonization programme.[190] But equally telling were two Settlement Laws, the more significant one, in 1934, starkly stating that non-Turkish nomadic life in the eastern provinces as founded on 'tribal chieftaincy lordship, squirearchy and shaikhdom' was to be abolished forthwith.[191] We might read these developments as the logical carry-through of the original CUP intentions for the destruction of Kurdish power, which, of course, predated either the Shaikh Said or, for that matter, Koçgiri revolt.

From this perspective, the possibilities of an autonomous Kurdish administration—ostensibly still on the table in the wake of the Koçgiri events—were never more than a meretricious Kemalist smokescreen.[192] And, by this reckoning, we might even read Ankara's project as rather akin to the British state's eighteenth-century taming of the Scottish Gaeltacht. Here, too, an autonomous socio-economic power base represented by the Highlands' tribal chieftains was closed down as prelude to London's visible, militarily enforced encapsulation of the region; the building of roads, bridges, and eventually railways throughout it underscoring the complete, irreversible permanence of a new hegemonic and modern order. The fate of the majority of the Highland natives was displacement to the Lowlands, or deportation overseas.[193] It was as good a social engineering model as any for a Kemalist response to its last serious domestic threat. But with the added value that *its* civilizing mission would not simply deal anthropophagically *and* anthropoemically with its insolent Kurds but ensure that, in their place, eastern Anatolia would be rurally repeopled with its *own* nationalized population.

If such *Lebensraum* goals thus speak to a genocidal process, one might nevertheless argue they lack any direct exterminatory *intent*.[194] However, what is missing from this explanation is the contingent aspect. Just as one cannot understand the nature and intensity of the British violence against Highland Scots except in the context of the very real Jacobite challenge to the Hanoverian ascendancy represented by the '45 rebellion, so we cannot rule out the intensity and scale of the Kurdish threat to Ankara both accelerating and amplifying the Turco-Kurdish dialectic towards a *more* zero-sum outcome. In the wake of the Shaikh Said defeat in 1926, British intelligence reports led ambassador Sir George Clerk to fear that the forcible removal of Kurdish tribes was 'on a scale which to some extent recalls the mass deportations of Armenians in 1915'.[195] That this proved not to be a general trajectory, however, might equally, if paradoxically, point to the ongoing evolution and resilience of the Kurdish *national* movement. Indeed, this takes us back to the Azadi factor and the second set of developments, which fatally handicapped the Shaikh Said revolt while yet ensuring it an afterlife.

A *general* Kurdish revolt in spring 1925 was meant to be galvanized by an Azadi-inspired signal from *within* the army. This does not seem to have been well coordinated: instead leading to a premature garrison mutiny in the Hakkâri area, a month after the Diyarbekir Congress.[196] Kemalist repression of suspected officer collaborators necessarily followed, but not before a large number of them and their men had fled, with their weapons, across the border into British-controlled Mosul province, and then later on into French Syria. What this meant, in effect, was the continuation of a Kurdish resistance outside Turkey that also acted to galvanize ongoing localized guerrilla insurgency within Turkish Kurdistan itself—especially in the Dersim region, which was contiguous with the Syrian border.[197] One effect of this insurgency was to significantly sabotage the Interior Ministry's efforts to implement wholesale Kurdish deportation. During the 1930s, presumably mostly in the wake of the 1934 Settlement Law, over 25,000 *were* removed.[198] Yet the following year, in the face of the Dersim-centred resistance, Ankara had to abandon—at least temporarily—its deportation programme.[199]

Another effect was that while Azadi had failed to meet its 1925 objectives, its efforts transmuted into the new, overtly Kurdish, eponymous independence movement Khoybun (Independence). It was led by Nuri Pasha, chief instigator of the earlier army mutiny and flight into Iraq. Nuri sought to create a new military strategy which, in later revolutionary theory, would be best represented by the idea of a *foco*: a small liberated zone from which the struggle could be expanded and developed towards a general grass-roots insurrection.[200] The area chosen was that around Mount Ararat, home to Nuri's own Çelabi tribe, who became the key standard-bearers of the new revolt. But Ararat also had great symbolic significance for Armenians, and it was no coincidence that the formation of Khoybun in Lebanon in 1927 not only had Dashnak backing but represented a restatement of Kurdish–Armenian accord, this time directed—in terms of the old triangular relationship—*against* the Turks. However, it also more objectively underlined how weak the two once-dominant communities in a multi-ethnic region had become and, equally, how dependent they now were on whatever exogenous support could be garnered, whether from fellow Kurds in Syria and Iraq, or Reza Shah now playing his own realpolitik game in the Turco-Iranian border zone.[201]

All this aside, what is significant about the Khoybun insurrection, as it developed from positions around Ararat from 1928 onwards, is that, far from being some sort of poor man's sequel to Shaikh Said, its tenacity and developing military success not only carried in its wake possibilities for exactly the sort of wildfire popular support which had eluded the earlier revolt, but, in the process, once again threatened to undermine Kemalist rule in eastern Anatolia. The very fact that it was able to create a self-administered zone, the so-called Republic of Ararat, beyond the control of Ankara or any other contiguous state—not to mention, through its military action in 1929–30, actually extend itself into parts of Van and Bitlis—could not but invite an even more violent Turkish response. As in all such struggles, the initiative initially lay with the insurgents. Ankara's early summer 1930 counter-insurgency stalled. What took its place was a massive military build-up of men, *matériel*, and ordnance worthy of the Red Army against its peasant insurgents, or, for that matter, any colonial power whose determination to be the 'one lord and master' in the land had been questioned.[202] Spearheaded by the Turkish air force, with lessons clearly garnered from, among others, British blanket bombing of tribal villages in Iraq and Afghanistan,[203] the Turkish campaign this time set out to liquidate insurgency, supporting villages, and *all* Kurdish communities in the proximate area. Putting aside any question mark over Ankara's intentions in the wake of Shaikh Said, this time round the aim was to commit a clear, unadulterated Turkish Vendée.

Drawing a ring round Ararat, the Turkish aerial bombardment revved up in July and August, and was joined by a ground offensive. The result was a bloodbath all the way up the Ararat mountainside. According to an excited Turkish newspaper report, at the epicentre of fighting around Zilan 15,000 enemies had been eliminated and the Zilan River was filling up with corpses. It added, 'the possibility of escaping this cannot be imagined'.[204] Participants in the massacres themselves or in the 'pacification' campaign continuing until the end of the year, moreover, were forgiven for having committed any crime by a new law: number 1,850. It very specifically stated that 'murders or other actions committed individually or collectively' in the area of the First Inspectorate 'will not be considered as crimes'. It even went to the trouble of including local authorities, guards, militiamen, and civilian auxiliaries in its absolution.[205]

Two final things about these events stand out. First, despite the ratcheting up of the Turco-Kurdish conflict, the result was not the same as that which befell the Armenians. The degree to which the Kurdish struggle burst into life in the midst of the most hopeful peace years of the interwar period may have some passing bearing here—though clearly with little or no consolation for the Turkish Kurds themselves. Too substantial in number; too resistant to deportation, dispersal, and forceful assimilation; too resilient to be entirely subdued (the Ararat rebellion, even after being militarily crushed, flickered on in the immediate hinterland throughout 1931 and 1932), their fate instead was to suffer a long-term genocidal process through to the present day—a creeping genocide, if one prefers, punctuated by spasms of extreme, exterminatory violence. One might also add for good measure that the very nature and manner of Ankara's essentializing efforts, to make Turks out of Kurds, arguably acted as the most powerful recruiting agency for the evolution and development of their consciousness and modern identity *as* Kurds.[206]

Second, was the response of the outside world. There was rhetorical condemnation from those who cared but could do little to help. The socialist (but anti-Soviet) Second International, following Dashnak intervention, adopted a resolution at the height of the fighting at the end of August 1930:

> Peaceful Kurdish populations who have not participated in the insurrection are being exterminated just as the Armenians were. The degree of repression extends far beyond containment of the Kurdish struggle for freedom. Yet capitalist public opinion has not in any way protested against this bloody savagery.[207]

The irony is that the International's grasp on the geopolitics of the Kurdish struggle was shaky. Nobody was seriously going to come to the defence of the Kurds. Certainly not the British. They had made their peace with the Turks over Mosul, they had developed a strategy in the form of forward air power for containing any possible Turkish or other belligerence across mandate Iraq borders, and they had, in any case, a loyal ground force—none other than the Assyrians—who they believed they could count on in the event of serious trouble.[208] The Kurds had served their purpose in 1919 and 1920. While the British, or at least some of their political elite, felt that they owed them in some shape or form,[209] that certainly was not going to stand in the way of Turco-British rapprochement.

The French from the Mandate of Syria were of a like mind. They had their own insurgencies to contend with, not least that of the Druze, contemporaneous with that of Shaikh Said. They did not want the threat of a further bad example encroaching on their zone of influence. Indeed, they had made their position perfectly clear during the Kurdish rebellion when they placed at Kemal's disposal their north Syria railway to speed his troops to the scene.[210]

There actually remained one other regional player waiting in the wings but eager to flex his muscles. In the initial phase of the Khoybun revolt, Reza Shah had been quite willing to allow Khoybun supply of their Ararat positions by way of Persian territory. But his purpose was the entirely cynical one of reminding Ankara of the real power on its eastern flank. The point having been made by way of the Kurds, the two states did a deal: Turkish troops were given the green light to complete their encirclement of the rebels on the Persian side of the border, and the insurgency was crushed. Tehran was duly rewarded with border adjustments in its favour.[211] It would be no more and no less than what Reza's son would do in the 1970s, this time with the Iraqi Kurds of Shaikh Barzani as both cat's paw and victims.[212]

That leaves, of course, the two latter-day superpowers of the Cold War era. Back in the 1920s and 1930s the Soviets wanted their extended southern flank secure and, as a consequence, were not willing to meddle on behalf of the Kurds, whatever the Second International might have to say on the matter. As for the USA, they had already firmly opted for what we might today recognize as 'constructive dialogue' with Ankara (in other words: concentrate on the business opportunities, ignore the human rights violations). Later, where they would meddle on the Kurdish question, as they did in 1970s, it would be at Iraq's, not Turkey's, expense. On the contrary, with Ankara's full integration into the Western geopolitical orbit by way of NATO, Washington would adopt a firm hands-off policy with regard to all matters of Turkish domestic policy, past but smouldering, present but fissile.

A SOBERING SEQUEL: 'THE ASSYRIAN AFFAIR'

The Kemalist war against the Kurds underscores how exposed and vulnerable the rimland peoples and communities who had not achieved nation-statehood in the critical phase between 1919 and 1923 had become. The brief years of quasi-peace which were to follow would not redress the balance in their favour, and unless they could look to their own internal resources to achieve the necessary breakthrough— improbable in itself—they could forget succour or assistance coming by way of some supposed liberal humanitarianism. In fact, the situation was starker still: Western policymakers actually felt themselves duty-bound in their own states' interests to throw overboard 'peripheral' peoples when they stood in the way of realpolitik.

The statement sounds inordinately cynical. But, in the context of the diminishing returns of interwar peace, there is one final, albeit ephemeral, rimlands episode which firmly hammers the nail into the coffin of liberal hope and expectation.

*

In the early hours of 11 August 1933, a motorized machine-gun detachment of the newly independent Iraqi state entered the Assyrian village of Summayl, in the Dohuk district of the predominantly Kurdish vilayet of Mosul, and proceeded to systematically, cold-bloodedly massacre its male population, either by machine-gunning or bludgeoning them to death. In addition to 305 men and boys—the entire male population—four women and six children were killed. Many of the surviving women were raped on following nights. In both preceding and succeeding days Assyrians (i.e. Nestorians) throughout Dohuk, mostly but not exclusively men, were shot out of hand, hunted down and killed, or taken away in trucks, to be turned out and machine-gunned. Kurdish, Arab, and Yezidi tribesmen were also participants, with primary responsibility for the looting and destruction of sixty-four Assyrian villages.[213]

These events were monitored by London's 'man on the spot', Lieutenant-Colonel R. S. Stafford. His report emphasized the fact that the massacres were not some rogue attack perpetrated at the lower levels of army command but had been 'definitely decided' upon by the Iraqi army leadership with a view to the Assyrians being 'as far as possible . . . exterminated'.[214] The military had, at the very least, the backing of the civil authorities—evident in the fact that at no point did the police intervene to quell the wider sequence of disturbances. Stafford was also able to demonstrate how broader state and society was implicated in these events. For instance, in the following weeks the troops of the Northern Command—in other words, the prime perpetrators—were the focus of rapturous attention in victory parades held in Baghdad, Kirkuk, and Mosul. In the last, triumphal arches were constructed in which decorated melons stained with blood and with daggers stuck in them were intended to represent the slain Assyrians. There were, too, celebratory speeches from the Iraqi crown prince and other dignitaries, and decorations and promotion for the commander, Colonel Bakr Sidqi, and other officers who had participated in the campaign.[215]

Shocking as these details are, the immediate reverberations of the Assyrian affair have not carried through to the present day. And the reason is hardly surprising. The killings, of which Summayl was the apotheosis, possibly accounted for some six hundred dead, according to Stafford; a maximum of 2,000 to 3,000, according to the Assyrians' own, probably highly inflated, estimate.[216] Compared with the welter of violence visited upon Iraqi communities in later years, especially by Saddam Hussein, these figures are small fry. Put in the wider annals of twentieth-century massacre and genocide and the Assyrian affair hardly registers.

That said, it is a fitting place to end this chapter. At first sight, the affair would appear to belong to the space of a colonial or imperial history rather than that of our nationalizing rimlands. Geographically speaking, the vilayet of Mosul *is* at the very far south-east reaches of our east Anatolian shatter zone. However, its (albeit contested, later legitimized) transfer from Ottoman control to that of the British Empire at the end of the Great War—with the additional guarantee of coming under the terms of the League of Nations-supervised mandate system—should, by rights, have placed the Assyrians firmly out of harm's way. Alternatively, one might argue that this itself is a misreading of the situation, given that the assault on the Assyrians was indisputably a product of an Iraq which had just relinquished its mandatory status. In other words, the Assyrian affair was not just the action of a newly independent, post-colonial state, but that of a state which was making a demonstrative point on the matter by attacking those it deemed the 'tools and creatures of imperialism'.[217]

However, this is also insufficient to explain the full picture of what happened in 1933. The British were not just horrified bystanders. They had created Iraq and, even as they negotiated their withdrawal in 1932, they ensured that the future modalities regarding their relationship with the former mandate included maintenance of control over not only its oil resources but many other aspects of Iraqi domestic, foreign, and defence policy.[218] This included a monopoly of experts and advisors to the regime, of which Stafford, as administrative inspector of northern Mosul, was one. If this points to a British responsibility of either commission or, alternatively, of omission, as to what transpired a year on, there is something else here which matters with regard to the British-conceived architecture of the new relationship. Iraq, in 1932, stood poised between the political economy of empire and that of the rimlands. The former still contained within it possibilities for a multi-ethnic plurality: the very factor contemporaneously being expunged from a post-Ottoman Turkish neighbour. Plurality did not in itself of course make for benign rule: on the contrary, it was pragmatically conceived and managed—with some particular acumen by the British—through divide and rule. By contrast, the new world of rimland nation states had no place whatsoever for such complexities; there was only one organizing principle and that was uni-national. In turn, this was the type of governance which the metropolitan states of the hegemonic West accepted and indeed valorized as the norm in their new semi-periphery. And here, precisely, is the point: Iraq's transition in 1932 was from old imperial (hence peripheral) to the new, semi-peripheral type of political economy. And it is in that unstable transition that what Stafford called 'the tragedy of the Assyrians' can be found.

We do not need to detain ourselves with its finer details. But there are some notable, not to say poignant, ironies en route. The Hakkâri community of Nestorians—that is, Assyrians—as we may recall were casualties of the CUP centrist drive, under emergency wartime conditions, to take control of *their* east Anatolian periphery. Hakkâri communal survival, in the face of this maximalist assault, was, in turn, predicated on their bellicose, tightly organized tribal solidarity, which enabled a substantial portion of their number to fight their way out from the jaws of annihilation and across the Persian border, or, if one prefers, from the world of unforgiving, emergent nationalism *back* into the world of disparate and—in modernist terms—chaotic empire. The circumstance of the Russian Revolution and, with it, Petrograd's retreat from the Caucasus theatre, largely determined that it would be under British protection that the Mar Shamun's flock would place themselves. And, in turn, they would find themselves, in the early 1920s, not simply as protégés but as proxies in British efforts to pacify an unquiet and troubled Mosul where many Kurdish tribes were acting as a stalking horse for a possible Kemalist recovery of the province. This itself had immediate implications and complications, not least as the British reliance on the able-bodied Hakkâri menfolk as imperial levies was a signal of their special protected status—as well as of separation from an embryonic Iraqi army—and also cut across and had the potential to destabilize parallel British efforts to turn the tables on Kemal by way of encouragement to the Kurds both in Mosul and across the Turkish border.[219]

In a classic imperial landscape of *divide et impera* this was all par for the course. And, from an Assyrian viewpoint, it had immediate and manifest advantages. In recognition of services rendered, the British doled out land grants in the Dohuk and Amadiyah area to their ethnic soldiers, allowing them effectively to rule themselves through their own headmen, under the continuing authority of the Mar Shamun. The community was also, in practice if not in principle, exempt from taxation. In return, they were more than willing to act as a stalking horse for a British bid to extend their northern buffer zone into Kemalist-controlled Hakkâri. It was another irony that the Azadi mutineers who crossed into Iraq in late 1924 were members of the garrison sent to quash the Assyrian attempt to recover their homeland.[220] The realization that this was not going to happen appeared to more firmly ensconce the community as a permanent feature of Mosul's human landscape. Not, however, without consequence for inter-communal relations. There were some serious flare-ups, not least when, as a result of a dispute in the bazaar in Kirkuk, again in 1924, the levies ran amok—killing possibly fifty people. A British court martial handed down notably lenient sentences.[221] Anti-Assyrian hostility, especially among the Kurds, was clearly on the rise, and with knock-on effects too, for the indigenous Syriacs of Mosul. Yet a conviction that the British would always back them seems to have fed an almost insouciant disregard among the Hakkâri incomers of the need for either conciliation or even constructive fence-building with their new neighbours.

Assyrian expectations were short-lived. Once it had come to a resolution with Kemal on Mosul's borders, Whitehall was looking to withdrawal from Iraq at the earliest opportunity. That, of course, was predicated on the preservation of what amounted to a neocolonial control of the country and its communication routes. However, the Mar Shamun's hope that this would also involve continued reliance on the levies proved quite illusory. Instead, the British were attempting to imagine Iraq—against the grain of its own wider sectarian, tribal, and ethnic fissures—as a genuinely unitary state. Having thus given a green light to the idea of an Iraqi *nation*, the notion of subcontracting the protection of British interests to a separate proxy force was clearly going to be counterproductive, not least as emerging nationalist sentiment was already evincing a marked anti-imperial disposition. London's conundrum, thus, was how to manage—and moderate—the national idea while at the same time encourage a durable pro-British regime. The imposition of an ersatz, albeit Arab, protégé, the Hejazi Sharif Faisal, as king, was clearly insufficient to the requirement, as was the extent of any significant—let alone robust—civil society. Whitehall, however, found—or thought it found—the answer to its problem by looking to Iraq's northern neighbour as model.

Who had pulled Turkey together, out of its potential chaos and fragmentation? The answer was its officer class. And they had done so, to a critical extent, by making the army the school for the nation. The thinking and mindset of Iraq's nascent military elite was practically identical to that of the Turks—bar the obvious fact that they saw themselves as custodians of an Arab rather than Turkish nation. There is no coincidence here: practically all of the first generation of Iraqi officers were educated and trained at the Harbiye, often graduating alongside contemporaries who became Turkey's governing class. In the same way their opposite numbers in Baghdad, from the very onset of the mandate in 1922, filled all the senior political as well as military posts in Faisal's administration.[222]

The British thus calculated that just as they had come to an external modus vivendi with Ankara's military nationalists, they could arrive at some approximate equivalence with Baghdad's. In this the British, and, by extension, Western liberalism, were about to be hoist by their own petard. Throughout the rimlands, as we have seen, an implicit tension in the West's efforts to integrate societies into their international political economy by means of nation-statism lay in the urge of the new national elites—one might say their logic—to organize their own politically (if not necessarily economically) independent state-building programmes. The Harbiye graduates who reached maturity in the early years of CUP ascendancy—whether ultimately Turkish or Iraqi—were notably driven on this score and, with it, intransigently opposed to patchwork solutions which might have yielded any degree of sovereignty or 'national' resource to sectarian or communal interest. To have done so would, in their minds, not only be to regress to the perceived weakness of Ottoman plurality but provide renewed openings for foreign interference. The problem for the British, by the late 1920s, was that having conceded the principle to Baghdad, they now were forced to unravel the very understandings—indeed, binding commitments—they had previously willingly made with Iraq's 'minority' peoples.

This was not just a matter of the Assyrians. Five out of every eight people in the population of Mosul province were not Arabs (or Syriacs) but Kurds. They had been promised some form of sovereignty at Sèvres. Under the terms of the League-supervised mandate the British were bound to protect their national and cultural rights. The notion too, of a Kurdish national home, not unlike the Jewish national home in Palestine, lingered on into the late 1920s. All these promises were kicked off the board as the British cleared the way for their 1932 agreement with Baghdad. Six years earlier, in the Mosul Treaty with Ankara, Kurds had been referred to in sixteen of its eighteen articles. Now there was not a single mention.[223] This was quite conscious. Kurds and other minority groups were pointedly advised by the British that the solution for the future lay in them thinking of themselves as Iraqis.[224]

At least, one might, say the Iraqi Kurdish plight was on their own home soil. Assyrian exposure was much more palpable. When the Mar Shamun, in 1924, had petitioned for the creation of a *millet*-style, self-governing enclave under British jurisdiction—whether in Hakkâri or somewhere as close as possible to that in Mosul vilayet—he had some inkling not only of British support but that of the

League's special Commission on Mosul, whose recommendation for Assyrian autonomy was reaffirmed as British negotiations for a 'treaty' with Iraq drew closer in 1930. By then, however, the British had done a complete volte-face, declaring the Commission's proposal to be 'inoperable'.[225]

The Assyrians—like the Kurds, like the Greeks and Armenians, not to mention the Circassians, before them—were in the process of being unceremoniously dumped. Running backwards and forwards between the British and League for a reconsideration of their situation altered their existential plight not one jot. In the circumstances, there was only one logical thing to do: declare oneself a sovereign nation. It is again of no surprise that the Assyrian national pact of 1932 modelled itself on Kemalist precedent and formula.[226] The only problem was that it was as suicidal as the first attempt, back in 1915, if not more so, for the Hakkâri community to declare its belligerent self-defence against the state. At least then the Assyrians had had the known fastness of Hakkâri from which to mount their potential *Götterdämmerung*. Now they were reduced to a quasi-mutiny of the levies as the British withdrew. Recognizing that assistance from that quarter was null and void, several hundred of them—with their arms and kit—made the fatal and probably entirely panicked decision, in late July 1933, to attempt to cross the Tigris into the French Mandate of Syria. It was this and the subsequent fighting that flared between them and Iraqi troops at the border crossing which provided the casus belli for Bekr Sidqi's exterminatory campaign.[227]

There is no doubt that the Iraqi military were champing at the bit for the opportunity to declare open season on the Assyrians. They did so to demonstrate their independence from the British; to indirectly hurt the British by assaulting their erstwhile protégés; to make plain their contempt for the British argument that Iraq had insufficient enemies to warrant a large standing army; and to make visible their own warrior prowess—not least against the threat to state security which the Assyrians supposedly posed.[228] Behind this was clearly a matrix of other underlying grievances, one of which was the implied British slur to Iraqi virility of turning to Assyrians as their preferred soldiery. One can only assume that the officers who led and murdered the levies in cold blood justified it to themselves as sweet revenge against a group who had dared to challenge their nascent state, not to mention a desire to convince themselves that they were as hard and ruthless as their Turkish Harbiye counterparts in the killing stakes. We can equally treat the affair as a culmination of nearly a century of Kurdish–Assyrian mutual antagonism, or as just the beginning of Iraq's long history of military dictatorship: the Kurdish Bekr Sidqi using the affair as something of a launching pad for his 1936 coup.[229]

In short, the Iraqi government's response to the shrill and frenetically aggressive behaviour of the Assyrians was itself utterly projective, phobic, and hysterical. But then what of the British: what did they do in the wake of Summayl? Did they come running to the Assyrians' aid; openly censure the Iraqi government; force the League to support a revocation of Baghdad's authority? Not a bit of it. At the height of the crisis they put their available bomb supplies at the disposal of the nascent Iraqi air force and informed interior minister Hikmet Suleyman that 'British policy was not to support the Assyrians but...the Arabs in the maintenance of the integrity of the Iraqi state'.[230] These decisions were taken *after* the first killings. Earlier on, the British authorities were implicated in and possibly directly responsible for the detention of the new, young, and inexperienced Mar Shamun in Baghdad, thus depriving the levies of their legitimate leadership and arguably galvanizing them into their desperate action. It is true that British sotto voce intervention with Hikmet did prevent further massacres. But faced with demands at the League for an inquiry into the 'affair', the British response was to warn that if pursued it could lead to the collapse of Faisal's regime; to his replacement by extreme nationalists who would incite an outbreak of xenophobia directed at foreigners and their property; even to a repudiation of the recently signed treaty itself.[231] There was no enquiry. Only a rather belated and half-hearted effort, in association with the League, to find an alternative home for the Assyrians. Nowhere was found, though British Guyana was rather ominously cited as one possible 'home': ominous because this same territory would, not long after, likewise be considered as a possible 'home' for eructed Central European Jewish refugees.[232]

Displaced communities were, by their nature, disruptive of the real political business conducted between sovereign states. And doubly so when their existence uncomfortably reminded leading states of promises and commitments previously made. But in a world where the choice was between the modernity of the streamlined polity and the intrinsic humanity of plural society there was actually no longer any contest. As Sir Francis Humphrys, the British high commissioner in Baghdad wrote home to the colonial secretary, in June 1932, 'Assyrian demands...if granted would be followed by similar claims from other communities such as the Kurds, Yezidis, Chaldeans, Shia and even the people of Basrah. It is realised in Baghdad that to grant such demands would result in the final extinction of the authority of the Central Government'.[233]

The Allied peace as a space in which the potentiality for genocide might have been forestalled had been irrevocably shattered. The iron years of the 1930s and, with them, the clash of systems beckoned.

5

Anti-System One: The Emerging Stalin State

SETTING THE SCENE

The history of Russia is one of ceaseless beatings. She was beaten by the Mongol Khans. She was beaten by the Turkish Beys. She was beaten by Swedish feudal lords. She was beaten by Polish–Lithuanian pans. She was beaten by Anglo-French capitalists. She was beaten by Japanese barons. She was beaten by all—for her backwardness. For military backwardness. For cultural backwardness. For political backwardness. For industrial backwardness. For agricultural backwardness...You are wretched, you are abundant, you are mighty, you are powerless, Mother Russia...We are fifty to one hundred years behind the advanced countries. We must make good this lag in ten years. Either we do, or they crush us.[1]

Historians of the USSR and beyond will instantly recognize this gobbet from a very famous speech, as too the speaker, audience, date, and wider context. But let us instead just for one moment, suspend our knowledge and pretend that we have had a memory lapse. And, further, have temporarily forgotten what happened in, and to, Russia after November 1917. How then would we attempt to understand our piece? As the impassioned fulminations of a new tsar? Of some priestly demagogue seeking to resuscitate the medieval idea of Moscow as the Third Rome? Or perhaps, entirely more soberly, of a patriotic intellectual reminding his receptive, nationalist audience of what needed to be done if 'mother Russia' was to survive and fulfil her mission in an international political economy dominated and determined by others?

If the third is our best guess, perhaps it is because we have made a cross-reference to a very similar type of declamation made in 'Esnaf Destani', Ziya Gökalp's celebrated poem of around 1912, following the mauling Ottoman Turkey received at the hands of Italians and Balkan states. If the protagonist in our extract speaks of making up the shortfall between 'us' and 'them' by a relentless increasing of the pace, Gökalp, too, demands that there be no standing still. Indeed for both 'little time is left'.[2] Essentially the only difference is that they are speaking of their respective mother-cum-fatherlands. Otherwise, their messages are practically identical: without a rapid and urgent forced march towards a strong industrialized country founded on a technologically advanced base, *national* enslavement beckons.

At which point we have no choice but to take a reality check. The date of our speech is 4 February 1931; our audience one of Soviet technocrats and industrial bigwigs assembled together in the midst of the great collectivization surge; their interlocutor none other than Stalin, the leader of a state which did not even have Russia in its name; whose very raison d'être indeed, was derived from, and comprehensively guided by, the principles of historical materialism. Which would seem to make the speech—restated for public acclamation in *Pravda* the following day—not simply anomalous but entirely out of sync with all our received wisdoms about communism. Ten years on we know that, in the face of Nazi invasion, Stalin enunciated the Soviet response in terms of a 'Great Patriotic War'. But from the vantage point of 1931 it is what had happened in the decade or more prior to that which surely counted: the creation of a revolutionary state that had buried its tsarist predecessor, and upon whose ruins was going to be built a proletarian paradise from which every last vestige of 'chauvinist' Great Russianism was going to be swept away.

And thus we are presented, at least as far as the terms of our study are concerned, with not simply something of a contradiction, but, more exactly, a conundrum. A traditional reading would tell us that the potentiality of genocide derives from xenophobic prejudice, discrimination, and hatred of ethnic and communal others. This would usually be informed, within a state context, by a predisposition towards ultra-nationalism—even more so where overt racism is intrinsic to political self-definition. Yet these were the very aspects of society which the USSR, ostensibly, or at least on paper, had set itself against. Which rather begs the question: did genocide—assuming that we can, in the first instance, isolate it as a phenomenon—develop under Stalin as part of a slipping away from the state's internationalist profile towards a more nationalist set of priorities? Or, more exactly, towards a deeper-embedded tsarist set of imperial imperatives and anxieties which might, in turn, explain a rising trajectory of genocidal violence, especially in the rimlands? Alternatively, is it actually possible to identify the potential for genocide in the USSR in the state's *objective* ambitions and aspirations?

Standard answers would not seem to get us very far in this specific quest. Stalinism was responsible for as much if not more violent death than Nazism in an equivalent time frame.[3] We could read this as a consequence of Stalin's drive for absolute power, or, more provocatively—à la Bauman, Holquist, or others—as evidence of a high modernist, sociologically informed, even aesthetic drive to sculpt the perfect society attuned to the regimes's own platonic ideal.[4] These are perfectly plausible explanations, though they would also seem insufficient to a full understanding of the incidents of mass bloodshed we have already encountered—such as the 1919 anti-Cossack drive, or the crushing of the *Antonovshchina* two years later. Of course, these events preceded the (seemingly) anchored, Stalin-led Soviet state of the late 1920s onwards, and could be seen instead as indicative of the Bolsheviks' initial life-and-death struggle for power. But that can only underscore the question: why, on the one hand, was there so much violence in the apparently post-crisis USSR; why, on the other, is it so difficult to pin the label genocide on at least parts of it?

It is easy enough to adumbrate the forms of violent death from the late 1920s. There was death through famine, deportation, executions at the hands of the Chekist security police—as it transmuted through GPU, then OGPU, to NKVD—as well as as a result of hyper-exploitation, most particularly associated with the Gulag, the state-wide, security police-run, forced-labour camp complex. Then there were the mass casualties in the wake of interstate war—a subject to be returned to in 'Wars of All Against All' in Volume Two—much of the wastage of which can be laid at the door of the regime itself, rather than its main Nazi adversary.

How much such death there was has been the subject of great scholarly dispute. The truly gargantuan figures running into tens of millions reported by Robert Conquest, and paralleled by the quantitative extrapolations of R. J. Rummel,[5] were notably contested by an emerging school of US-based revisionist history in the 1980s.[6] These revisionists, for good measure, also challenged received wisdoms as to the role of Stalin himself as grand master puppeteer, and hence of a clear intentionalist programme of mass murder as, for instance, associated with the Great Terror (otherwise known as the *Ezhovshchina*) of 1937–8. As with similar Holocaust controversies, a resolution to these debates must, in the first instance, be a matter for the experts, to which an author writing at second hand can only add cursory comment. That said, two things stand out. Firstly, the number of deaths—as revealed through the opening up of the Soviet archives in the 1990s—while not reaching Conquest-style proportions, remains huge. The archival expert Michael Ellman for instance, cautiously puts the range of victims of direct Stalinist repression at between 3 and 3.5 million 'from shooting, while in detention, or while being deported, or in deportation'.[7] But these are figures for one category of violent death only. Fatalities from the more catastrophic of the two sequences of Stalin-period famines, in 1932–3 for instance, at the very least doubles the figures for direct repression: the contemporary Soviet analyst N. A. Ivnitskii claiming 7.7 million famine deaths.[8] At this point what becomes the issue is not the scale itself, but the culpability of the regime for it. And, read more closely, culpability can be regarded as either of two things: negligent omission—through failing to assist the starving in time—or commission, that is, poor weather conditions being consciously utilized in order to punish and destroy particularly recalcitrant groups of peasants opposed to collectivization.[9]

Secondly, none of the above helps make the charge of genocide any the less elusive. Holocaust comparison—where it might most obviously be applied, in relation to the camp system—at closer inspection falls down on one fundamental issue: there were no Soviet *death* camps. As Nicolas Werth has pungently put it, in 'the vast and multiform penal universe' of the Gulag, 'waste, sloppiness, randomness and improvisation' were always to the fore but not 'a specific will to exterminate'.[10] Similarly, while the 1932–3 famine sequence was certainly more catastrophic in some regions than in others—something to which we will return—its devastation was not limited solely to these regions. Even where we can identify the state homing in on specific targets—people identified as peasant 'kulaks', or 'bourgeois nationalists', or some other possibly all-embracing catch-all designation, such as *sotsvredelementy* ('socially harmful elements')—not until the 1940s did these become entire communal cohorts, and, even then, evidence that this amounted to a will to physically annihilate these groups in toto remains debatable.

To be sure, the will to place people in negative categories is an important indicator of the possibility of genocide. The USSR was awash with all manner of such problematic 'elements'. There were *byshvie liudi*, all those who were associated with, or simply harboured, nostalgia for the tsarist ancien régime. They were certainly considered suspect, even dangerous. Then there were *chuzhdye elementy*, whose 'alien' background at various moments made them equally so. On top of that there was an ever-expanding group of *lishentsy*, people who, for whatever reason, had been disenfranchised, and hence, to use Helen Fein's terminology, had been cast outside of the communist state's universe of obligation—thus deprived not just of civil rights but of the basic means of sustenance in the Soviet state in the form of housing, rations, and medical and welfare care. These might be kulaks but they could equally be peripatetic artisans or seasonal workers, those of no fixed abode, people of independent mind, or, for that matter, single women.[11] All these human beings were not 'our' people, *good* people, but elements who failed to conform or were considered unlikely to be to redeemable as authentic members of species *Homo sovieticus*.

The fact, moreover, that the family ties of tainted individuals were tied into ascriptions of guilt would suggest that there was an underlying genealogical aspect to the Stalinist state's assault on its supposed enemies. The proposed 1930 'liquidation of the kulaks', for instance, involved not only a three-tier system of categorization—from most dangerous to least—but also tagging in terms of households. While this might involve the separation and physical elimination of male individual heads, it was much more likely to involve the deportation and exile of that head with his whole family. Removed to 'special settlements' in some distant, remote, and entirely inhospitable territory without proper food, shelter, or medical facilities, such family groups were exposed to the potentiality and actuality of lingering death, often en masse.

Nor was the kulak instance an aberration. During the assault on real or imagined political opponents, as it rose to a crescendo in the late 1930s, wives, children, and extended families were invariably caught up in the dragnet. In this case family units were broken up: the women being sometimes liquidated as 'enemies' in their own right, or, more likely, sent far and wide into Gulag enslavement, while their children were usually placed in state orphanages. This fate befell almost the entirety of the Trotsky clan, down to the second or third generation, as it did most of Stalin's own extended family, the Alliluevs and Svanidzes, and countless members of Bolshevism's purged political and military elite.[12] The very fact that Stalin famously declared that the guilt of the fathers could not be visited on their sons, could actually be taken as evidence of exactly the opposite being true.[13] The standardized abbreviation 'ChSIR' in official documents—for 'members of the family of a traitor to the motherland' as also 'children of the enemies of the people' in party jargon—underscores the degree to which hereditary guilt had been bureaucratically normalized within the system. It was upon this basis, too, that one of the most infamous NKVD orders, number 00486, of mid-August 1937, proposed at the behest of its new boss, Nikolai Ezhov, meticulous screening of all family members of male suspects—taking it as a given that wives, including divorced ones, were implicated by association, that their children over the age of fifteen were likely to be 'socially dangerous and capable of anti-Soviet activities', and that, in the circumstances, only babies should not be parted from their mothers and placed in orphanages.[14]

Add to all this the Chekist predilection for making and remaking 'associational maps of Soviet society'[15]—as in some fabulous Venn diagram—and a case for reading the fatal consequences in terms of the social anthropological connectedness of at least large numbers of the victims would seem clear enough.

Yet, if this would appear to bring us within a whisker of a bona fide case for a charge of genocide, there is nearly always something in the Soviet experience to sabotage its uncontested affirmation. Deported kulaks who had survived the original liquidation had the opportunity to work their way back towards societal 'rehabilitation'; their children were allowed to go to school and leave the special settlements on reaching the age of sixteen; while, with the implementation of the new Soviet constitution of November 1936, their parents were also, at least on paper, restored to their full citizen rights as were all 'former people'.[16] In the face of the *Ezhovshchina* this proved to be no defence against further arrest and possibly execution. Even so, there remained constraints that prevented these secret state killings spilling over into *communal* bloodbaths. Decisively, Ezhov's order on family guilt, which could have provided the obvious green light for this outcome, was cancelled three months after its inception.[17] Some months further down the line, and the Great Terror was itself unravelling *against* its leading NKVD perpetrators. Large numbers of *Chekisty*, including Ezhov, were themselves liquidated in this final macabre denouement which some (anti-revisionist) commentators have always regarded as a controlled Stalinist exercise.[18] Whether this makes the killings of the 1930s less stochastic and more a case of a shifting range of assaults on real or imagined social, occupational, or, increasingly, ethnic groups, what still remains clear is that the individuation of targeted 'enemies'—even where this involved them as household heads—complicates a standard genocide narrative founded on the notion of an untrammelled assault upon entire communal bodies. We may end up with whole *cross-sections* of communities being arrested and killed, but rarely communities in toto. At least, that is, until the sequence associated with the 'punished peoples' of the Great Patriotic War period.

Is this the point at which to give up on genocide as a critical element of Soviet mass murder and plump instead for Rummel's broader terminology of democide?[19] In this way we are absolved from worrying too much about the specifically Stalinist dynamics of conflict at particular moments, or with particular groups, and can concentrate our attention on an overall death toll whose common causality is Soviet totalitarianism. In other words, what matters most is the culpably terroristic nature of an ideologically driven regime against its entire population, which is thus explanatory of the fatal consequence.

This would, in turn, lead us somewhat closer to a case for a sui generis interpretation of Stalinist mass violence; though, following this same line of argument, with some acknowledgement of Nazi 'totalitarian' parallels. Interestingly, on this latter score, detailed information and research would suggest a differentiation between Nazi sequences mass murder, some of which would fall squarely into a genocide category, others of which might require alternative nomenclature. The so-called 'euthanasia' or T-4 killings of physically and mentally handicapped people, both German and non-German, is one such case where, in spite of mass murder being self-evident, *communal* aggregation is absent. In the T-4 programme we have an aspect of the Nazi's own racialized anti-system which, singular to itself, is clearly exterminatory but not obviously categorizable as genocide. Likewise the mass shooting, or alternatively starving to death, of hundreds of thousands of mostly male Soviet POWs in the course of Operation Barbarossa is another instance which demonstrates singularly Nazi characteristics, and is much more overtly genocidal in its operation al fresco; even so, because of its mono-gendered nature, it falls somewhere wide of, if close to, genocide per se.

The point, thus, is even in the case of the twentieth-century state-regime recognized as genocide perpetrator par excellence, we have exterminatory trajectories and overlapping episodes, some of which fit a standard genocide yardstick, while others do not; the latter category perhaps being interpretable as variations on a theme. The very nature of the German anti-system may, in part, be an explanation for this variation, just as that of the Soviet anti-system may equally help elucidate its own divergences from genocide 'norms'. If, by this route, we might even go further—to posit that the existence of our Soviet anti-system offers a basis upon which we might reformulate our understanding of its mass killings to *include* examples of genocide *Soviet-style*—it is equally important that we do so by reference to a broader context within which this anti-system sought to survive and develop.

The Soviet experiment emerged not in a vacuum, but out of a conscious effort to fashion a political economy which was distinct from and necessarily at diametrical odds with its dominant Western adversary. Indeed, the very formulation of the USSR as a 'system' was predicated on the development of a transformative agenda, the purpose of which was not simply to challenge, but ultimately supersede its Western antithesis. Thus Lenin's successors had no choice (whether they liked it or not) but to look to their Russian imperial inheritance—its territory, people, resource, and infrastructure—as the essential clay out of which victory would be attained. But this in itself sets up an almost classic inbuilt tension. On the one hand, and at each step of their developmental path, the emerging communist leadership looked fearfully outwards at the Western enemy in the full expectation that their experiment would be attacked and extinguished before it could reach its necessary military-industrial take-off. On the other hand, it looked equally fearfully inwards, at those sections of the population—those 'elements'—most likely to disrupt, or at the very least act as inertial drag on, their great leap forward—and who, by implication, were perceived to be in the 'camp' of, or acting as the proxies or stooges of, that same Western enemy.

Stalin's 1931 speech is all the more striking because it offers a very conscious and emotionally charged presentation of what was a stake. *Russia's* potentiality for strength was undermined by historic structural weakness—or, expressed more pungently, 'backwardness'—compared with the West. Yet its possibilities, as an entirely new (Sovietized) state, to overcome these limitations still remained dependent on the social, ethnic, and cultural wellsprings of what had come before. The very fact that Stalin appeared to be declaiming like a tsar, not to mention retreading the, at once, both utterly angst-laden yet also exaggeratedly expectant ground of tsarist predecessors, can only underscore the nature of the dangerous path upon which his project had embarked. In *The Meaning of Genocide* we characterized the tension between old–new and weak–strong components of modern polities as the critical preconditions from which genocide regularly emerges in the context of developmental urges in the modern world.[20] In our specifically Soviet case we might discern two arenas which particularly emitted these danger signals. In the first, the very demand for forced pace, rapid structural overhaul in favour of industrialization *within* a very largely traditional peasant economy, served as its own basis for a dynamic of state–societal conflict. In the second, the potentiality for outside interference destabilizing the effort was bound to be felt mostly keenly at the contested peripheries of the Russian-cum-Soviet 'empire', and, more exactly, at those points of geographical contiguity with the world of the dominant West. In effect, that meant largely, though not exclusively, in the rimlands; in other words, within western Soviet territories across from the 'New Europe' or, as a south-eastern extension of that, in the Caucasian border regions adjacent to the 'new' Kemalist Turkey.

These aspects, of themselves, do not make for a ready-made recipe for violence, let alone genocide. What this chapter in part turns on, however, is the manner in which historical legacies—of 'time'—alongside realities of political and ethnographic geography—of 'space'—penetrated and thereby helped sabotage the Soviets' running jump at transcendence. And, in the process, made exactly such violence, *including* genocide, much more likely. Certainly, as we emphasized in *The Meaning of Genocide*, genocides cannot transpire out of *inert* preconditions alone. They require trigger mechanisms which can only be supplied by state-cum-societal responses to real, ongoing contingencies of a crisis nature. The major paradox of the Soviet experience under Stalin was that it was in the regime's extreme efforts to make the fundamental break with the dominant Western system in favour of its own authentic alternative that the possibility for self-inflicted crisis increased exponentially; the psychological fall-out of which in turn amplified projective and phobic tendencies—the scapegoating and blaming of supposed (in this case largely *imaginary*) internal enemies, fifth columnists, and traitors—which have always been an essential ingredient of genocide. In other words, far from escaping the burden of actual overreach and consequent psychic disturbance which we have associated with recognizable patterns of genocide in the world of the metropolitan-led system, Stalin's anti-system offers an *extreme*—if also distinctive—variant on the same.

This still requires the caveat that, insofar as we can speak of contours of genocidal violence in USSR, these involved aspects, including, as we have already suggested, a morphology, which do not always translate into simple comparisons elsewhere. It is highly significant, for one thing, that the call for the 'liquidation' of an enemy group designated as 'kulaks' had little or no relationship to any actual social body as such. In many ways, thus, 'kulak' is code for something else—or, more exactly, a pretext by way of semiotics for a *general* subordination of the peasantry. Here, though, is a genocidal thread which demands further examination, not least because, on the one hand, it carries with it no immediate (at least synchronous) parallels outside of the Soviet system, and, on the other—through its USSR-wide universality—it would appear to disrupt our previous emphasis on the rimlands as the critical site of genocide in this period.

But that, in turn, begs a further question, as to the degree to which the assault on the peasantry in practice was accompanied by, or perhaps even became subsidiary to, an assault on perceivedly dangerous *national* groups. What is interesting, if certainly tortuously complex, is that in charting the course of the state's extreme violence during the 1930s it is not always so obvious where the two are entirely separable. Thus, while our section 'Smashing the internal enemy', on the assault on kulaks-cum-peasantry, merges into a discussion on the degree to which the 1932–3 famine involves a more targeted attack on rimlands nationalities, the following section, 'Smashing the external enemy', which charts the much more transparent and open assault on these and other peoples at the Soviet peripheries from *c.*1935 onwards, can hardly do so without reference to the wider scope of NKVD 'mass operations', not to mention elitocide, of the Great Terror. By reconnecting these two elements—a) the 'peasantry', that is, the people writ large, and b) national groups, more precisely the 'periphery' peoples at the imperial rim—we return to the problem/question we posed at the outset: was Stalinist genocide a function of its misplaced drive towards fashioning a new, supposedly Marxist-informed and guided society, or, rather, of its inability to master its own pre-Soviet history? Or, perhaps, as we suggested in our Introduction, 'a particular combination and configuration of *both*'. Whatever the answer, we cannot interrogate it further before we have briefly considered the developmental goals (in other words, the crisis elements) of the Soviet anti-system—and its discontents.

THE STALIN STATE: ASPIRATIONS, LIMITATIONS, INCUBI

'Lenin had invented a cul-de-sac for communism: Stalin drove the party down it'.[21] So proposes Robert Service. In late 1917 the Bolsheviks had taken it upon themselves to light a spark which they believed would inaugurate a new dawn for humankind. They did so against their own Marxist runes, which told them that the historical trajectory could not be forced in this way. Even from within their own Bolshevik ranks, ten years earlier, the renegade Alexander Bogdanov had warned that a socialist state facing a hostile capitalist world 'would be profoundly and lastingly distorted by the many years of its besieged condition, of unavoidable terror, and of a military regime'.[22] But Lenin had not heeded the warning. Instead, he had staked everything on one, fateful, autumnal throw of the dice. The gamble failed. There had been no worldwide revolution. The Western capitalist-cum-imperialist system had not collapsed. Proletarians in the advanced states had, in the main, not rallied to the cause. Nor, with the outcome of the Soviet–Polish War had there been a military solution to the impasse. In short, the historical dialectic, beloved of Marxists, had not been resolved.

It had faced the new regime in Petrograd with a very odd situation indeed. It was not unlike that of the very earliest Christians. They, too, had seen the word made flesh. Or so they believed. For a moment, normative time—and space—had been ruptured. Or so it seemed. But an imminent Second Coming had not followed. For true believers, of course, the 'eschatological clock' might still be ticking. They were duty-bound to carry on and to bring the glad tidings of a society finally and irrevocably unshackled, 'conflict-free and harmonious', to all humankind.[23] Their responsibility was immense. If they failed now the human species would once again descend into the pit. There would be no second chance. It was not just a matter of historical birthright; the party was, said Trotsky in 1921, 'obliged to maintain its dictatorship' in expectation of the final victory.[24] But victory over what, or whom, exactly? Was this going to be, essentially, an ideological battle between capitalism and communism? Was it really, as some latter-day Cold War commentators would suggest, one between the forces of light and the forces of darkness?[25] Or was it something at once both equally awesome yet altogether more mundane: a struggle between *Russia* and its historic state adversaries?

Even as 'true' Bolsheviks attempted to circumvent this latter possibility, by repeating at every turn the mantra of permanent revolution, it was entirely clear from 1921, if not much earlier, that the party had not escaped from 'normative' geopolitical realities. And that if even the task remained the same as before, to *change* those realities they were still going to have to secure their apparatus in the interim, albeit for the longer haul. At least—unlike the early church, which would have to hold on for another three centuries to arrive at this point—the Bolshevik party-clergy had the advantage of having a state from which to consolidate their position. The key problem (in some ways, again, not unlike the Christians in fourth-century Rome) was twofold. The Russian imperial state was not simply weak (at the beginning of the NEP, all socio-economic and demographic indicators suggested a situation much closer to free-fall). Rather, the vast majority of its population were entirely hostile to the new imposed order. Or, put another way, even if the Bolsheviks' real, historic mission remained the capture of the hearts and minds of the peoples of the industrialized, avant-garde West, their first evangelical call still had to be to the peoples of Russia itself. But as that had already been tried and the response found to be wanting the irony was that the only remaining post-1921 route by which the Bolsheviks might prove *to the West* the efficacy of their message was by some practical demonstration that Russia itself could still be transformed into a wholly better, more socially just, indeed more advanced place than anywhere else on Earth: in other words, made fit for its *own* inhabitants.

If this sounds wholly convoluted, it should also further underscore why the effort to attain what was logically unattainable not only ensured that it would come up against its own self-inflicted dead end but one bespattered with blood. The only issue at stake here is how this should be read: as a facet of Bolshevism's 'internationalist' imposition on Russia, or rather as something more to do with the interpenetration of its agenda by the empire's historic discontents. In 1925, the dissident writer Mikhail Bulgakov outlined the case for the anti-Bolshevik prosecution in his satirical, and, for many decades unpublished, novel *A Dog's Heart*. In this barely veiled allegory an innocent Moscow stray is turned, Frankenstein-like, into 'a loutish man-hound' at the hands of a professor, who implants into it the sexual organs and pituitary gland of an evil man. The 'good' mongrel is, of course, the Russian people; the professor and his assistant, intellectual types of the ilk of Lenin and Trotsky, who are thereby implicitly accused of treating Russia as a giant laboratory for their hubristic, even blasphemous, experiments.[26]

The notion of the Bolsheviks as a group of marginal 'cosmopolitan' intellectuals who had nothing intrinsically to do with 'mother Russia' but, having captured it by devious stratagem, had sought to remake it according to their own ideological blueprint, has an obvious appeal for anybody who would prefer to imagine the USSR's communist leadership as an alien plant. At its extreme end this blurs into an anti-Semitic slur which, interestingly, the Stalin state in its own twilight years was perfectly willing to promote—not as an example of its authentic Soviet self but as the ultimate menace to it. Of which more in the 'Stalinist Reordering: Russian Peace' chapter of Volume Two.

But in that very act of Stalinist deflection by means of classic scapegoating, we may have found our way into a more complex truth. The Bolshevik leadership in power ostensibly represented a complete break with the tsarist past. While Lenin pragmatically engaged many former military officers as well as bourgeois 'experts' in the running of the country, as in its defence, the people in charge were an entirely new breed. An Ottoman comparison is in order here. The Ittihadists (and later Kemalists) who brought about the Turkish revolution were still essentially loyal children of an empire from which they derived many of their values and norms, even while they opposed the Hamidian regime. They also happened to be functionaries and military officers of the state, albeit at a secondary and tertiary level and hence, in normal times, with every likelihood of remaining there. Not so the Bolshevik elite. They were complete outsiders, very usually in their social, their *intellectual*, and their often strikingly rimlands-based ethnic profile. And they were entirely and vehemently at odds with the structural, and indeed moral, operating premises of the ancien régime, which they sought to dismantle brick by brick. They also happened to be driven, energetic, focused, and, as it turned out, administratively capable and competent in ways which—with a few notable exceptions—meant they were a breed apart from their tsarist counterparts.

So far, one might propose, we have offered no case for a Bolshevik relationship with what to them was a redundant tsarist past. However, by the late 1920s nearly all the leading figures of the Old Bolshevik elite were no longer at the helm. They had, slowly but surely, been removed from key offices of party and state and been outmanoeuvred from involvement in central decision-making roles by the party secretary, Stalin. In turn, he had formed an increasingly tight new leadership clique around himself, whose power derived from his person. Which might rather conveniently lead us to the conclusion that whatever change of emphasis occurred from this period onwards—and, with it, statements like the quote at this chapter's outset—had little or nothing to do with Bolshevism per se but were peculiar to Stalin.

This would certainly be the position of all those, especially Trotskyists, who, far from blaming the party for Russia's woes, would instead staunchly defend *its* record until Stalin's ascendancy put a spanner in the works. Chapter and verse has also regularly been deployed in support of this argument in the form of Lenin's December

1922 'Testament' and a subsequent addendum, in which he drew attention to the party secretary's capricious nature and potential abuse of power. In short, Lenin wanted Stalin removed from office.[27] The fact that a dying Lenin was never able to effect this sacking, while his 'Testament' (actually intended for open party congress consumption) remained under lock and key, thus explains how it was that the others named in it as potential successors—Trotsky, Zinoviev, Kamenev, Bukharin, and Piatakov—were the ones forced out of office; in Trotsky's case, forced out of the USSR. The fact that, a decade on, these same party leaders were the targets of a Byzantine set of conspiracy charges culminating in a series of show trials, simply underscores the verdict that it was Stalin—a man with a 'gross personality disorder'[28]—not Bolshevism, which was the aberration.

Yet, as we have already seen, as far as genocidal violence was concerned the Bolsheviks, with or without Stalin, were already extremely successful practitioners. Stalin was simply one of them—a leading and certainly very ruthless Bolshevik. Nor did he initiate some coup which took over or superseded the party. The various tendencies within it were simply played off one against the other—Stalin himself, in the 1920s, holding to no fixed position either on ideological matters or developmental imperatives. As a result, while he was able to accumulate power by isolating his adversaries, he did so without any notably serious opposition from the rank and file, nor—at this period—by fomenting internal fratricidal bloodshed. In other words, the party remained the party, committed ostensibly to the same goals towards which it had been impelled in 1917.

This is not to propose that Stalin's tyranny was inevitable and that the party, therefore, deserved what it got. It is to suggest that the programme which became associated with Stalin represented the perversely logical endgame to the problem which had confronted it since the failure of world revolution. Rather than reading things, in Bulgakovian terms, as a matter of 'had the Bolsheviks taken over Russia?' the question might be turned on its head to read 'had Russia— by 1928, or 1929—taken over the Bolsheviks?' This, as posed, is both too essentialist (as well as too dualist) to provide us with an answer which does full justice to the complexities of Stalinism—and its violence. But it is posed, nevertheless, in order to highlight the non-viability of *anything other than* a statedirigiste-led and determined project of accelerated industrial development which confronted our party of would-be Marxist evangelists in its 'treading water' years of the 1920s.

In short, the party opted for a Stalinist version of itself because it had nowhere else to go; one with which the term 'Socialism in One Country' is synonymous. Except that the term is an oxymoron. Marxist socialism could not operate in one country. What the Stalinist project was instead proffering—and the party accepting—was a redefinition of goals, the bottom line of which involved securing and strengthening *the state*. Not for its own glory alone, but in order to take on the more advanced metropolitan polities whose industrial baseline, not to say momentum, was exponentially already that much greater. Stalin's imperative to 'overtake and pass'—*dognat' i peregnat*—signalled from late 1928,[29] was thus predicated on acceptance of not only a social-Darwinian race for survival, but of one which could not only be entered into on the briefest of lead-in times. Which in turn, given Russia's actual limitations, could only be done by the wholesale abandonment of both NEP and fully fledged *korenizatsiia*: the elements by which the party had sought accommodation with a post-imperial population. What was now being proposed in their place was a timetabled plan of all-Union industrialization, supported by agricultural collectivization according to the diktat of the Russian centre. And, without putting too fine a point on it, over the bodies of the population, peasant peoples and entire national communities alike.

But does this therefore mean that 'Socialism in One Country' should really be read as a case of 'the empire strikes back', thereby placing Stalin himself in the company of either the most power-hungry, or aggressively modernizing tsars? One might argue, to the contrary, that nothing quite like this had ever been proposed or developed before. Industrialization under the last Romanovs had involved the gradual, tentative enabling of a bourgeois and technocratic class which looked to the civil society of the West for its political and cultural inspiration; a stop–start attempt at slow, capital accumulation to pay for the process by bringing peasants out of serfdom and into the market; in practice a high degree of state dependency on foreign loans; and, finally, an almost schizophrenic attitude on the part of an essentially closed ruling elite as to whether they considered industrialization (and hence modernization) a good thing at all. One might add that while tsarism fed on a long tradition of absolutist compulsion over the people, it also had ingrained and indeed cherished views on the fundamental basis of society founded on the peasantry. Tsarism would never have consciously sought to emasculate or destroy that bedrock.

But that is exactly the point. The party under Stalin did for Russia what tsarism would never have *dared* to do. Or been capable of organizing. Here was an entirely new, maverick ruling class which, through its own peculiar transmutation, had put itself in a position to tackle head-on the ultimate problem of Russian 'backwardness' in 'its unusual conjunction with acceleration'.[30] To do so, it would drive a coach and horses through all obstacles, it would never take 'no' for an answer, and it would arrive at its goal by sheer political will. Who got trampled on in the way was ultimately of no consequence; it was simply a symptom of what *had* to be done. The fact, moreover, that there was an ideological and, with it, anti-system rationale for all this provided extremely valuable cover for the element, of ultimately, continuity. And, of course, the paradox which went with it: the Stalin state in the context of a Western-dominated international political economy was an entirely radicalized, more fit-to-purpose, Mark 2 version of its imperial predecessor.

It is further of note that it was exactly these features which enamoured many *national* movements in post-colonial states of a Soviet-style programme and template for their own short-cut drives to development.[31] To consider these consequences—including genocidal consequences—here, would be to stray unduly from our more immediate subject, and must await a further study. What is striking, however, in the Soviet case itself, is that commitment to state development under the aegis of its official—universalist—Marxist-Leninist line complicated and in key respects continued to act as an inertial drag on, a full-blown enunciation of a *Russian* nationalism as the ultimate justification for the Stalin project. In this respect Kemalist Turkey's privileging of the nation as its first principle—regardless of whether or not this was an entirely manufactured conception—arguably represented a more coherent station from which to drive *its* developmental train, and, in turn, offer an alternative model for many future Third World polities. But then, the great success of the Kemalist conjuring trick had been in ridding itself of its imperial husk and removing or pulverizing those non-assimilable elements who remained. To be sure, comparable success here is not measurable in terms of the avoidance of human violence and suffering.

The Bolsheviks, by contrast with Kemalism, had consciously fought to hold on to as much as they could of their predecessors' empire and to preserve control of it, as we have seen, by way of their own *korenizatsiia* conjuring trick. Having committed the regime to this path (he was, after all, its major architect) not even Stalin proved capable of a comprehensive back-pedalling, or, for that matter, of circumventing the historic impediment of tsarist ambivalence towards an unadulterated Russian primacy in a multi-ethnic setting. Yet a shift towards the extolling of all things Russian is quite clear in the official propaganda from the early 1930s, as is the inference that it was the Russian people who were the loyal heartbeat of the communist state. As with all things Soviet, much of this propaganda was carried on through barely coded messages. It was the Russian *working class* who were, above all, lionized as the heroes of the Great Leap Forward, just as the introduced terminology of 'Friendship of Peoples' became another route by which to demote the importance of *korenizatsiia* on the one hand, and, on the other, to elevate Russian culture as the gelling and unifying force in Soviet life.[32]

Yet, as his 1931 speech also amply demonstrates, the erstwhile Georgian revolutionary was perfectly capable and indeed comfortable in locating the Great Leap Forward in terms of a *longue durée*, which linked its glory not so much to an uncertain Russian national as to a fully recognized Russian *imperial* past. It was not only party detractors and oppositionists who muttered among themselves that Stalin was like an 'Asiatic' despot, a Genghis Khan, or an Ivan Grozny.[33] Stalin himself seems to have been more than willing to promote his own likeness to the dread sixteenth-century tsar, as is evident in his developing personality cult in the 1930s and beyond: the regular usage of *vozhd*—'chief'—and the extraordinary, ultimately part-aborted, heavily state-sponsored Sergei Eisenstein film project, 'Ivan the Terrible'.[34]

The imperial and the national, however, cannot be so easily disentangled. Nor were they meant to be. Stalin's quite conscious demotic appeal lay in promoting the notion of the return of the imperial strongman, unflinching in his determination to carry through the forced march to victory just as an Ivan would have done, or a Peter the Great, in earlier centuries. Russians—very particularly Russians—were thus being encouraged to buy into a recognizable 'deep' historical model dating back to the time of the Mongol hordes, in which the notions 'unquestioning submission of the individual to the group' and 'the state is everything and the individual nothing',[35] was being not simply justified and presented as legitimate but celebrated as a facet of a very special Russian way. By this route, too, a loyal populace—the historic *nas narod,* 'our people'—was effectively being groomed to give its dutiful assent to terror, a secret police primed to kill regime opponents (Ivan Grozny, of course, had already had his own in the form of the Oprichniki), and the absolute authority of an autocratic ruler who would determine, and as necessary dispense with, the lives of others.

Here was something clearly much cruder and more visceral than anything that had as it starting point notions of historical materialism or even class struggle. One might argue for or against the proposition that the implicit millenarianism within Marxism predisposed *some* Russians—in the absence of a now reviled and rejected Orthodoxy—to see in it a transmuted version of a Russian salvationist mission. There was, as we have already suggested, a limited constituency of true party believers. What Stalin was effectively doing was casting the net much wider and giving it a much more populist twist by putting the patriotic into proletarian, the national into Bolshevik, and, indeed, the overtly chauvinist, even xenophobic, into an ideology which was meant to be entirely colour blind. By these means ordinary Russians were being encouraged to view the Stalin project as *theirs.* And, obversely, to view those who either did not fit this prescript or, perhaps worse, dissented or cavilled against it as, at best, dubious malcontents, at worst, enemies of the people.

The question often posed is whether these tendencies could have been softened, even avoided, under different management, most obviously that of Trotsky? Stalin's self-aggrandisement towards the status of medieval tsar not only provided cover for the emergence of entirely personalized, even sacralized despotism—plenary meetings of the supposedly all-powerful party Politburo, for instance, shrank from eighty-five in 1930, to three in 1938, just two the following year[36]—but ensured that regime policy became completely determined, not to say overdetermined, by the predilections, anxieties, and obsessions of this one clearly very phobic individual. The consequence was not just a matter of the withering away of checks and balances on the *vozhd*'s autocratic rule, or, more exactly, the extinguishing of all zones of administrative autonomy in favour of a heavily micro-managed system worked through his own tightly organized secretariat, with official Politburo resolutions simply ciphers to this end. Stalin's extraordinary achievement also lay in the manner in which he rolled back the centuries to a conspiracy-laden milieu where traitorous enemies lurked in every Kremlin shadow, hatching plots in cahoots with encircling, vulture-like outside powers, and where 'Muscovite hatred and suspicion of foreigners and foreign influence bordered on the pathological'.[37]

In these respects, the gulf between Stalinism and its supposed Marxist-Leninist underpinnings seems a catastrophically yawning one. And it may be, as Aronson has suggested, that in Stalin's fearfulness of the emperor's new clothes being exposed as betrayal, sham, and utter lie, that we have the roots of the regime's very particular rupture with reality.[38] By the mid-1930s trumpeted confabulations of a bountiful and already attained socialist state repeatedly jarred against the latest saga of yet more party members, Old Bolsheviks in particular, apparently stopping at nothing to subvert or sabotage this same glorious entity—even to the extent of being in league with British, German, Japanese, Polish, or other foreign enemies. Nor can one avoid the manner in which the figure of the exiled Trotsky—'conscience' and, according to his son 'living embodiment of the ideas and traditions of the October revolution'[39]—appears to have haunted Stalin, leitmotif-like, and certainly demonic, as the single fixed point around which swirled the myriad confabulated *international* conspiracies against the worker's state.

The problem, however, with putting all our emphasis on this intentionalist 'blame Stalin' argument is that while it might serve to explain the Soviet elitocide it hardly suffices with regard to the much more sustained and demographically significant assaults on the peasants, not to speak of the nationalities. Once we return to this central issue, Stalin's path starts looking less like radical deviation or deformation and much more like something—however upwardly calibrated— consistent with the boxed-in dilemmas and projective fantasies of the party writ large. For one thing, one might note that it was not only in deep tsarist experience that one can find legacies of a conspiracy-laden world view. Bolshevism was born in a Russia where to voice any form of disagreement with the state was effectively to brand oneself a revolutionary. In turn, this implied operating in underground cells and according to closed rules and codes. It was par for the course for the Okhrana to try and infiltrate such groupings, as it was for competitors to try and sabotage them and even shop them to the authorities. Assassination of tsarist officials, as of informers, was also considered both a standard and entirely justified operating procedure. After the revolution, the Bolsheviks in power did not throw off such notions of *konspiracia*; instead they assumed opposition parties, especially those most like themselves—Mensheviks, SRs, or, for that matter, turncoat Bolsheviks—would carry on plotting, whether proscribed or not, just as the party would itself have done in similar circumstances. Equally to the point, however, in the early 1920s the party way of dealing with a largely hostile population was to routinely shield its actions behind a screen of disinformation, if not downright lies.[40] In such circumstances it is hardly surprising if party loyalists—indeed, quite wide sections of the population (whether hostile or supportive)—were receptive to official news, as well as to a more subterranean rumour mill in which explosions in mines, and damage to industrial plants or agricultural produce in transit, let alone cases of actual shootings and bombings, were all put at the door of malevolent wreckers and saboteurs in foreign pay. Nor that, when the regime found itself in a serious state of emergency, the conspiracy narrative went into a frenzied overdrive.

As a phenomenon in itself this was hardly unique to Soviet Russia. For instance, Soner Çağaptay describes the 'almost paranoid' atmosphere in Ankara in 1935, after the discovery of a plot to kill Kemal. There had already been something like this in 1926, in the wake of Shaikh Said, when an assassination attempt had provided the *Gazi* with a pretext to judicially eliminate a slew of rivals. Nine years on, however, it is significant that the alleged new plot rapidly snowballed—including a cast of Hoybunists, Dashnaks, Circassians, Laz, and Lezgins all supposedly linked into some vast Western-coordinated intrigue, with Athens as its operating hub, and with the successful assassination primed to trigger a dastardly insurrection which would bring back the Caliphate.[41] In other words, the regime did not so much fashion the plot story as feed it on the basis of its own worst, including ethnically aggravated, nightmares. That this sort of narrative could also be fed by collective hysteria welling up from below we have already confirmed by reference to the Europe-wide 'spy fevers' of 1914–18. Even supposedly calm and collected Britons could be swept up in such moral panics, not least during the 1918 libel trial of the MP Noel Pemberton-Billing, when he successfully defended the allegation that the Germans were capable of bringing the country to its knees on account of a 'black book' they possessed and which—he alleged—contained 47,000 establishment names, all of whom were sexual perverts![42] By contrast, US Senator Joe McCarthy's famous 1951 speech claiming to have uncovered 'a conspiracy so immense as to dwarf any previous such venture in human history'—though admittedly involving claims of long-term communist infiltration of US government and high-level administration, not to mention cultural subversion by way, especially, of Hollywood—seems almost pedestrian.[43]

What is at stake, therefore, is not some unique Soviet state (or societal) proclivity to conjure up flesh-devouring spirits and soul-destroying demons at every turn, despite the fact that the discrepancy—not unlike a Nazi Germany—between that in high-modernist, scientifically grounded self-image and repeated recourse to the cosmic conspiracy motif is an especially marked one. What is most striking in the Soviet case is that the party saw itself as, and indeed monopolized its position as, vanguard of the entirely rational (of course, atheistic) *good* society that it proclaimed to be imminent; yet, while proposing it as the clear-headed and clinical instrument of this new Jerusalem, and simultaneously trumpeting its progress in terms of often crass hyperbole ('there are no fortresses which Bolsheviks cannot storm' was one particular favourite[44]), the party's zealots had no choice but to block out their awareness of the gaping mismatch between resource allocations on paper and those on the ground. Added to that was the actual implementation of goals repeatedly, especially at a distance from Moscow or Leningrad, carried out in an irregular, haphazard, and often incompetent or negligent manner by lower-level operatives whose own solace lay, more often than not, in venality, pilfering, depravity, cruelty, and drink.[45] In this light, to have been even moderately sceptical about the fabulous quota-determined programme of infrastructural development which, from the late 1920s, was the essence of the Great Leap Forward would have been to question one's own individual—as well as the party's—raison d'être. Even at the height of his final struggle with Stalin before his exile, Trotsky was still insisting, 'The party is always right because it is the only historic instrument which the working class possesses for the solution of its fundamental problems'.[46] Thus, retreat could never be entertained. Nor could open criticism. To have so much as murmured the possibility would have been tantamount to betrayal—like Judas selling his soul to the devil.

In spite of this self-denying ordinance, post-*perestroika* evidence confirms that there *were* some brave party souls prepared to poke their heads above the parapet. Significantly, the group we know most about—the so-called Ryutin Platform (who took their name from an exceptionally far-sighted and fearless middle-ranking party official)—were expelled in October 1932 on the charge that they were 'degenerates who have become enemies of Communism and the Soviet regime'

through having 'attempted to create a bourgeois-kulak organisation for the restoration of capitalism and particularly kulakdom in the USSR'.[47] Their actual crime
was that they had written a detailed critique of Stalin's crash-course collectivization
at its 1930 height, in which their cardinal sin was most certainly to propose that
the party should indeed 'retreat', not least by giving back the peasantry their freedom. In uttering such blasphemy, however, Ryutin not only put himself beyond
the pale but, according to Robert Conquest, initiated the 'original conspiracy'.[48]

*

What makes the party's behaviour towards the peasantry a complex matter is the
fact that this was one area where a lethal obsession was, at least in significant part,
based on empirical realities. The Russia which the Bolsheviks had wrested from the
Romanovs and their ephemeral liberal successors was a country in which 82 per
cent of population were peasants or nomads; mostly, in fact, peasants.[49] Among
this latter majority the figure translated into a visual landscape of 25 million primitive smallholdings whose level of productivity has been described as comparable
with fourteenth-century England or France.[50] Whether one wishes to read this
positively or negatively it does confront us with the 'problem' as viewed from a
Bolshevik perspective. The party represented no more than an urban island in a
rural sea, and was starting from a position in which it lacked any real understanding
of, engagement with, or indeed sympathy with what was effectively beyond its
shoreline. This was hardly surprising given that the Bolshevik vision of the human
future was of an industrial proletarian kind, supported by a mechanized—and collectivized—agricultural hinterland. In 1917 Lenin's reaching out to the peasants to
promise them 'land' had been an entirely cynical exercise, on the one hand involving the filching of the central plank of the SR platform, on the other, simply giving
the nod to what peasants were then doing anyway, namely expropriating the land
they already worked from aristocrats and more recent 'bourgeois' owners, and dividing it up among themselves through the *obshchina*: the historic peasant commune.

The Bolsheviks, however, had had no intention of allowing this 'black partition'
to be the final word. Instead, they had sought, through war communism, to bring
the countryside and its people under their own firm, draconian grip. The consequence was the collapse of the 1917 accord, the first phase of what Andrea Graziosi
has called the 'greatest European peasant war',[51] which was paralleled by the catastrophic famine. But the consequence beyond that was the signal failure of the
Bolsheviks to get their way. While the peasants paid the most colossal price in
blood, they defied the proletarian state and—seemingly—won. The NEP, as one
Tenth Party Congress delegate described it at the time, was a 'peasant Brest'.[52] Or,
seen from that alternative perspective, a peasants' victory unlike any other, not even
the ephemeral one achieved by their Bulgarian counterparts under Stamboliski.

Here, then, it could be argued, was the *genuine* revolution. And one which
threatened to completely shipwreck the grandiose, even millenarian, claims of the
Bolsheviks. The primitive commune (the *mir*), with its implications of egalitarian
democracy, had regularly been held up by nineteenth-century *narodniki* as proof of
the possibility of a genuine grass-roots communism. Now it was if the idea had been

translated into practical action, not within the Soviet system but beyond it, through a network of more than 400,000 autonomous *obshchiny*.[53] This was not only a direct affront to the much smaller number of rural soviets where mandated power from the centre was meant to reside. It also threatened the moral credentials of the system writ large. The party organ, *Izvestiya*, gave the game away in 1927 when it accused the communes of too much emphasis on 'equalisation' and not enough on class struggle.[54] In other words, the *obshchiny* did not *need* to struggle for communism because, by implication, they were already there.

Worse, they seemed to be heading down this route while, at the same time, strengthening their own independent economic wherewithal through the benefits of the market as allowed under the NEP. The upshot might be conceived of as not unlike the dual power situation which had characterized the stand-off between the provisional government and the Petrograd soviet in 1917. However, this could arguably overstate the case. Local communal solidarity hardly translated automatically into demotic, all-Union, anti-Soviet politics any more than the growing tendency towards *obshchina* self-taxation—while it clearly undercut the function of the rural soviets—did not in itself constitute a declaration of peasant fiscal as well as cultural separation. Yet while the Bolsheviks' own repeated mantras proclaimed that the peasantry were incapable of serious self-organization in any shape or form, the very fact that this is exactly what they were achieving in the mid-1920s starkly posed the question of whether, as a bloc, they might possess 'the aggregate capacity . . . to make or break the national economy'.[55] In a country, moreover, where the quotidian flow of grain from the countryside to the city was the bedrock upon which the polity qua polity functioned—witnessed most dramatically by the Petrograd and Moscow demonstrations of February 1917—the peasantry were actually well positioned to accomplish the latter by doing precisely *nothing*. They did not need to conjure up a Makhno or an Antonov: simply by refusing to participate in the Soviet-supervised and regulated market and in doing so forcing the revolutionary citadels to forfeit their daily bread, they could hold the regime to ransom.

That this could conceivably happen had already been demonstrated in the so-called scissors crisis of 1924. With state-determined grain prices too low and those of factory-made goods too high, the peasants simply, and entirely logically, reacted by stopping bringing their produce to market, concentrating instead on maximizing their own home-grown self-sufficiency. For the Bolsheviks this did not just amount to a case of selfish 'hoarding' of grain: it was further proof that the peasants were irredeemably reactionary when it came to the issue of progress. The charge of what Moshe Lewin has dubbed 'archaisation'—namely, a peasant retreat into a rural shell,[56] was not in itself peculiar to the Bolsheviks. The urban political elites of all the yet-to-be-modernized states of our rimlands' semi-periphery also saw the 'primitive' lifestyles and economic practices of their majority rural populations as the fundamental obstacle to their own programmes of industrializing salvation. What made the peasantry doubly the 'Achilles heel of Soviet society' lay in the very discrepancy between this being the only polity of the time which staked its entire existence on the creation of a proletarian 'new' man,[57] and its providing, in actuality, a unique space in which the peasantry might have conceivably mapped out their *own* special path to self-determination.

This searing contradiction would have been unacceptable to any self-respecting modern or modernizing state. For the Soviets it was intolerable for several further reasons. It was so because the dictatorship of the proletariat understood itself as the wise arbiter and controller of all economic, as political and social, matters. A private peasant sphere completely contradicted a situation in which all individual as well as company-owned assets, including landholdings, had technically already been sequestered, nationalized, and put at the disposal of a Supreme Council of National Economy (VSNKh) specifically created to organize and finance the direction of state-determined economic development.

It followed that if the NEP offered a somewhat different route to the same ultimate goal, it only had validity if it could deliver. While peasant accommodation may have been deemed in 1921 a matter of absolute political necessity—and from this had followed something more than simply a tacit encouragement to rural self-enrichment—this was of no intrinsic value to the state if the peasants failed to keep their side of the bargain. They could only do so by selling sufficient quantities of grain on the state market, which could then be sold on to foreign markets, from which hard currency necessary for the state's purchase of industrial plant, in turn, could be derived. Soviet self-exculpation thus might read that it had been prepared to prioritize the peasant sector and, through its Commissariat of Agriculture, build a bridge to the rural masses (especially through provision of technical and agronomic assistance to increase agricultural yields and efficiency),[58] but had in return received little short of peasant ingratitude. Palpable Bolshevik frustration with what, in its view, was not so much peasant immaturity as delinquency, speaks volumes as to the enormous psychological gulf between these two worlds. The fact that peasants, since the 1861 emancipation, had been finding their way into the market economy but *'on their own terms'*,[59] thus became entirely immaterial if not irrelevant to Soviet purposes, just as, in fact, had also been the case two or three decades prior, under tsarist ministers such as Witte and Stolypin. From this perspective one might read the NEP as the very last effort in a much longer governmental struggle to cajole or entice the peasantry, or elements of it, towards engagement with state-modernizing imperatives as set against what the administration—tsarist or Soviet—perceived as a monolithic wall of, at best, peasant inertia and at worst wilful—even perhaps SR-inspired—sabotage.

However, as we have seen, the Soviet timepiece was entirely more tightly sprung than that of its predecessors. And it was on its uncoiling that the state versus commune contradiction ultimately, irreversibly, and irrevocably shattered. The regime, in short, perceived itself as running out of time in its preparations for conflict with its truly powerful external enemies. Slow, primitive accumulation of capital by way of peasant wealth creation—in essence as advocated by Bukharin and the gradualists within the party—was not going to provide nearly quickly enough for the unvanquishable military-industrial complex which the party demanded. In 1926 it might celebrate the country's return to 1913 industrial production levels.[60] Yet it was perhaps no coincidence that in the autumn of that year its Fifteenth Conference was also declaring for 'the strengthening of the economic hegemony of large-scale socialist industry over the entire economy of the country', further emphasizing the supreme urgency of this task in order to 'surpass the most advanced capitalist countries'.[61]

Nobody publicly said so, but the judgement being passed on the peasantry was a momentously damning one. In 1917 the Bolsheviks claimed to have ruptured time in a progressive sense. The peasants' refusal to synchronize with that forward momentum was tantamount to their own rupture, but in a regressive sense. Again, nobody yet publicly accused them of being traitors to the Soviets' historic mission. But then, in another sense, nobody needed to articulate what was taken as a given. In the summer of 1927 the party resolution of the previous year began being translated into what would become the First Five Year Plan for the transformation of the entire USSR into an industrial mega-state. Six months later, at the next party congress, Stalin signalled its commitment 'to uniting and transforming the small individual peasant holdings into large collectives'.[62] Again, nobody, not even Stalin at this juncture, openly articulated compulsion or terror. Yet nobody, not Bukharin, nor anybody else in the so-called Right Opposition, challenged the basic collectivization premise.

But then, by the early winter of 1927, the collective position of the party had significantly hardened. For one thing there had been a serious war scare in the summer, with rumours rife—following the explosion of a bomb in Leningrad and the assassination of the Soviet minister in Warsaw—that behind alleged émigré plotters the Poles were preparing the ground for a possible invasion, with—behind them in turn—a grand British design to internationally isolate Moscow and bring the regime to its knees.[63] A sense of heightened emergency was thus already prevalent when it became evident, towards the year's end, that not only was economic transformation at a virtual standstill—underscoring the general lack of foreign investment—but, more unexpectedly, that there was precious little grain available for export to meet the fiscal shortfall, let alone to feed basic urban needs. The 1927 harvest had been a perfectly sound one. Yet the Soviet regime, in the upshot, was compelled to buy grain on foreign markets, followed rapidly by a rationing of bread and other essential staples. Where the peasants fitted into this picture was actually very simple. Under the impact of tightening price controls on grain (and other commodities) and an increased tax burden, especially on the most productive peasants—in other words, kulaks—the countryside had once again simply switched off the supply.[64]

There was, of course, a transparently obvious answer to the party's dilemma, and indeed, one which could have resolved the problem at one stroke: increase official grain procurement prices. But for the party to have done so at this critical juncture would have been to even more emphatically confirm the city's dependency on the countryside. Or, put in more apocalyptic terms, the party's capitulation to the people. This time though, if the peasants were not prepared to voluntarily part with their surplus grain for the benefit of an omniscient party, its leadership was more than ready to contemplate not just forcibly taking it from them but pulverizing the peasantry entirely and bending it forever to its will. A declaration of war was in the offing, though no ordinary one.

SMASHING THE INTERNAL ENEMY: THE
WAR AGAINST 'THE PEOPLE'

'We will make soap out of the kulak'[65]

    Cadre in dekulakization drive

'They are not crates, not cargo, but living people'[66]

    Commissar Tolmachev, Bergavinov Commission, 16 April 1930

'We have gone over from a policy of limiting the exploiting tendencies of the kulak to a policy of liquidating the kulak as a class', announced Stalin in his infamous *Pravda* article just after Christmas 1929.[67] In essence, here was the regime's justification for its great assault on the countryside to both Soviet society and the world at large. Its quarrel was not with all Russian peasants, just a small group of rural exploiters and troublemakers who stood in the way of, or sought to sabotage, the country's legitimate striving to both feed itself and become strong. A Sovnarkom Commission in 1927 found kulaks constituted 3.9 per cent of peasant households across the Union. Or, put more concretely, some 782,000 households—an estimated 4.9 million people—who made their living on the land by practices which included hiring labour and renting additional land for their own entrepreneurial purposes, hiring out labour to others, leasing land, lending grain or money, livestock, and agricultural machinery at interest to other peasants, and—most significantly and heinously—selling surplus grain or animals on the private NEP-sponsored market at moments when they could reap a maximum return from high seasonal prices.[68] In short, kulaks were wealthy 'bourgeois' peasants who were taking advantage of both the system and their poorer neighbours. The very term *kulak* not only meant 'fist' but implied an usurious extortion and rapacity whose brutal imposition on village life upset its moral order and wellbeing.[69] Soviet explication in terms of class-based exploitation simply updated the terminology. If greedy, venal, rural capitalists were removed from their properties and sent elsewhere it was, therefore, natural justice. If some who were particularly malicious terrorist-types were dealt with more severely by OGPU, it was a case of getting what they deserved. But whatever was done would be done by the law. There would be a Politburo commission of oversight, under comrade Molotov, to determine which category of danger each kulak household head and his family represented. Only a small number of first-category kulak heads would suffer the severest penalties. Their families, and entire households from a further, larger second category would be exiled to special work settlements, sufficiently far away that they could cause no further harm. A third category would not even be removed from their immediate surroundings. They would simply have their property and wealth expropriated and their citizen rights withdrawn. Even then, peasants who were wrongly accused would have a right of appeal through a further specially formed commission. This, under the headship of comrade Bergavinov, would, in particular, register petitions from those who claimed they had been wrongly exiled, and would have full powers to return innocent parties or orphaned children to their original homes.[70]

Thus ran the official version; according to which, clearly, 'liquidation' was not to be read as meaning blanket physical extermination but rather as an appropriate 'social' cleansing of the countryside's most unreliable, suspect, and nasty elements. In which case, it could not be construed by latter-day commentators as a case of genocide or anything like it. But then this itself would be to take the official version at face value, including the stated premise that the fundamental purpose of the exercise was dekulakization. To be sure, it *was* integral to the Great Leap Forward; nevertheless, dekulakization's *primary* purpose was not of a freestanding kind but rather to provide a smokescreen and pretext for something altogether much grander: the transformation of Russian society by way of the blanket super-exploitation of its peasant aggregate mass. The method—collectivization of *all* peasant holdings—was not simply a matter of robbing Peter to pay Paul, a peasant surtax, or even a 'tribute' (as Stalin had ominously couched the proposed financing of industrialization to the party's Central Committee plenum back in 1928).[71] Rather, it was the Soviets' unique formula for the sort of resource maximization which had been practised by other states hell-bent on modernization by way of the radical short cut. In North America and Australia this maximization had been achieved by Anglo incomers through the simple expedient of expropriating the indigenous inhabitants of these continents, albeit cumulatively, through subjugation, eviction, or outright mass murder. In other words, genocide. More recently, in CUP and then Kemalist Turkey, it had also involved expropriating assets, but this time more in the form of capital, property, land, and industrial infrastructure from their legal owners—primarily Armenians and Greeks—for the needs of the projected 'Turkish' national economy. Also genocide.

One might riposte by arguing that this is to take the comparison too far. The Soviet intention was one of internal *colonization* of its peasantry, not their mass physical destruction. But then, could one not equally suggest that if Native Americans, aborigines, or Armenians had submitted to the demands of state or settlers, they too would have been spared? All they had to do was hand over their assets, do the bidding of their new masters, and, as required, clear off. The same was equally true of Soviet peasants, down to handing over their last 'chickens, rabbits, hoes and buckets' to the secretariats of each newly organized *kolkhoz* (collective farm).[72] Only refusing to submit made violence inevitable. The likely variation in the contours of this violence compared with our other proffered cases, thus, does not lie in some intrinsic difference in the Soviets' accounting exercise. In this case, just as in the others, the state wanted something for free, totally at the expense of a perceived 'outsider'—and, by implication, redundant—population. What made the implicit genocidal trajectory of the Soviet example different rather lay in the respective weights of the opposing state versus community forces. In the prior examples, the state could contemplate the successful application of maximum violence because—putting it crudely—behind it was an overwhelming demographic advantage. In the Soviet case the asymmetric equation went entirely the other way: the minority element, albeit in control of the apparatus of state, finding itself pitted against a very substantial majority of the population.

It was not, then, that state did not expect violence in the face of collectivization. On the contrary, it knew with absolute certainty that the peasantry qua peasantry were bound to resist *à outrance*. Nor at issue was some basic squeamishness about committing mass murder. Again, putting aside 1918–21, historic state behaviour against peasant insurrection carried with it something close to the certitude of bloody and merciless overreaction. This was very far from peculiar to the Russian experience—the scale of the extirpations of early modern uprisings such as that led by the Don Cossacks, Stenka Razin, and, later, Pugachev notwithstanding. Right up to the twentieth century, European *jacquerie*—albeit by now largely confined to our peasant-dominated rimlands zone—were crushed without compunction. In landowner-dominated Rumania, for instance, in spring 1907, unfulfilled promises of land reform had seen rural unrest met by Bucharest's General Averescu, who, in just three days, was responsible for the military massacre of some 11,000 peasants.[73] The Bolsheviks were in good company. But again—as they geared up for their own fateful showdown—with one critical difference: the possibility, in the ensuing conflict, that the peasants might *win*.

It had already happened once, in 1921, in spite of the extirpation of the *Antovonshchina* and other insurrections. At stake was not simply the fact that it could happen this way again. At the 1928 party plenum, where Stalin delivered his 'tribute' speech, the risks were clearly on a lot of comrades' minds, not least as proven in a heated exchange between Stalin's close confidante, Voroshilov, and the increasingly marginalized Bukharin, when the latter warned of a repeat performance should the state attempt a renewed anti-peasant drive.[74] In a sense, however, there was no need for the 'right oppositionist' to press home the message. Everyone perfectly well knew how close the anti-revolution had come to bringing the Bolsheviks to their knees. Makhno had been particularly astute in the way he had specialized in terrorizing and eliminating grain procurement convoys to the point where Red Army units themselves were threatened with hunger.[75] Stalin clearly had similar personal memories in mind when, corresponding with the writer Sholokhov, he reminded his interlocutor of the peasant's 'quiet war'—including non-violent tactics such as sit-down strikes—which had left not only the Red Army but the workers, too, 'without bread'.[76] One can draw some obvious parallels here. Nazi military planning for Operation Barbarossa in 1941 was equally obsessed with food security, firstly for its soldiers, and secondly for the German urban population at large. And, just as with the Soviets, it was the nightmarish memory of starvation potentially precipitating political collapse at the hands of a vicious internal enemy (in the Nazi instance, of course, not the peasants but the Jews) which was the goad to their promise to themselves that 'never again' would this even be contemplated. Instead, in this second round, the enemy in question would be punished, smashed, and destroyed forever.

What this narrowed down to for the Soviet leadership was a *strategic* question. How could the peasantry be prevented from mobilizing against collectivization with such force as to stop it in its tracks? The obvious tactical answer was to get one's retaliation in first. This pointed to neutralizing the most dangerous elements of the rural population—those who were deemed to be most likely and able to foment and amplify its insurrectionary potential. By 1930, the Soviet authorities should have felt more confident than they had been a decade earlier that they were ready for the task. For one thing, the moral and religious leadership of the countryside had all but been extirpated. A veritable onslaught on the Orthodox clergy, especially in 1922—evidence in itself that the NEP offered not the slightest political, let alone cultural, softening—had seen at least 8,000 of its priests, deacons, monks, and nuns slaughtered, not to mention many times that number of followers.[77] With the church's senior hierarchy already mostly expunged and other religious groups and sects cowed or themselves emasculated, a major plank of any anti-Soviet front had already been removed. Yet to read OGPU intelligence reports as they filtered back to *apparat* head Genrikh Iagoda, on the cusp of the collectivization drive, one would think that this was not the case at all. On the contrary, OGPU was convinced that a vast 'bloc' consisting of SRs, bandits, counter-revolutionaries, nationalist intelligentsia, White Army officers, *and* clergy was on the point of coalescing in order to unite the rural masses, subvert the Red Army, and establish contact with allies abroad—'all in preparation for an uprising against Soviet power'.[78] At the very heart of Iagoda's octopus of conspirators, however, was one consistent enemy: the kulaks. 'If we do not strike quickly and decisively', he declared, it would be from this kulak source that counter-revolution would arise.[79]

The fact that *kulachestvo*, as we have already suggested, was as much a projection of the party's ideologically driven yet at the same time highly agitated world view, as anything neatly definable in terms of a social category, *in this sense*, is beside the point. The party, true to its own sociological strictures, made repeated efforts to put flesh and bones on its subject, as equally to extrapolate its demographic weight. But the statisticians tasked to do so found their efforts repeatedly confounded by the desire of their political masters to expand the scope of kulak menace. The result was not simply a discrepancy of a mere '2.5 million souls' between the figures advanced by various state agencies and research bodies over the period 1927–9.[80] It underscored the fact that repeated anti-kulak statements had much less to do with the possibly concrete emergence of a richer and more firmly embedded class of peasants—a subject which is perfectly discussible—than it had to do with party members' individual and collective need to have a catch-all enemy upon which it could vent its emotional frustration and spleen. Even Bukharin, in an unfortunate secret approach to the disgraced and redundant Kamenev soon after the 1928 party plenum, while defending to him the case for conciliation of the 'middle' peasants, proposed that the 'kulaks can be hunted down at will'.[81]

Yet, viewed from the security imperative, all this avoids why the Stalin state, as it geared up for collectivization, *had to* both identify and then demonize kulaks. It was the only *technique* available by which to divide and rule a dangerous and threatening peasantry *tout ensemble*. Or, to put it another way, if a military-style OGPU operation of such magnitude could be mounted *pre-emptively* against the most dynamic section of the rural community—beheading, on the one hand, its natural leadership; terrifying, on the other, the rest of the peasant mass into abject submission—not only might the threat of mass peasant resistance—a veritable

War Type Three—be nipped in the bud, but the regime's *own* 'necessary', premeditated war against the peasants might yet be won.

So far, one might say, so simple. Except that it is not quite *that* simple. Why, if the kulaks were the preordained target did Stalin, in late 1927, censure 'those comrades...who believe we can and should do away with the kulaks by fiat'?[82] Was this another one of his devious subterfuges? Had he changed his mind by the following January anyway, when the extent of the grain deficit became clear? If so, this verdict would sit somewhat uneasily with the efforts through the subsequent months, led in considerable part by Stalin himself, to forcibly extract grain not so much from this specific 'class' but from *entire* if selected regions—the so-called Urals–Siberian method. The sending of tens of thousands of urban cadres into key regions to intimidate and terrorize the peasantry—whether charged as kulaks or not—into handing over grain, may have been billed as an extraordinary and 'emergency' measure. But it equally smacked of a regime which did not know quite where it was going or how it was going to arrive there. As far as neutralizing the peasantry was concerned it was a catastrophic failure. The rural masses correctly read it as a reversion to war communism, with the result that not only did the NEP as a policy crumple but, in the face of a mounting tide of rural resistance to grain seizures, local requisitioning authorities proved quite incapable of meeting their new grain targets. The year 1928 has been quite rightly described as a year of drift.[83]

All this would further suggest that if the regime had clear intentions on paper it was still prey to its own prevaricating, very often haphazard response to contingent circumstances, not to mention actually quite intense ongoing Politburo disputes behind closed doors as to how best to proceed. In part, this may perhaps explain why, as late as spring and early summer 1929—the best part of two years on from its declaration of intent to implement an autarkic route to industrialization—the party, through its official gatherings and media, was still articulating an essentially voluntary code of relatively slow-pace collectivization, even with occasional nods to the NEP, and with shock therapy tactics supposedly in strict abeyance.[84] To be sure such pronouncements can only underscore the degree to which party behaviour had become truly schizophrenic, as the generalized application of the Urals-Siberian method, the steepening of taxes on richer peasants, and the arrests or property confiscation of those who failed to comply were equally aligned to measures to 'persuade' as many 'middle peasants' as possible into the *kolkhoz* embrace. Bukharin had, by now, the full measure of what was being enacted, speaking of it as a 'military–feudal exploitation of the peasantry'.[85] As for the regime's main enemy, from early on in the year both centre and regional authorities were repeatedly referring to 'kulak-terrorists'—presumably anybody in the countryside caught disrupting their programme—with the first of many *localized* deportations being enacted in late June.[86]

Even so, what is clearly most remarkable about the growing campaign for *combined* collectivization and dekulakization is the dramatic lurch towards wholesale acceleration of the process heralded by Stalin's article announcing the 'Great Turn', on 7 November 1929. Why Stalin signalled 'full steam ahead' towards industrial take-off and, as its corollary, a crash course in compulsory collectivization at this juncture,[87] is a matter for some critical speculation. Taken together with his *Pravda* directive on kulak liquidation six weeks later, it certainly constitutes a paradigmatic moment in its own Soviet way, on a par with the launching of the 'Final Solution'. Clearly, it did not come entirely out of the blue. There had been an openly denunciatory, anti-kulak campaign in the press throughout the summer. The growing isolation of the Bukharin faction and their sacking from the Politburo weeks after the 'Great Turn' announcement not only removed the final internal party bulwark in the peasant's defence but resistance too, to 'the optimal variant': the maximalist fast-tempo version of the Five Year Plan. From within Gosplan, the responsible planning commission, economists such as Strumilin gave their weight to the achievability of the project on the argument that collectivized peasant assets and (their) ongoing human resource (on the proviso of good harvests) would provide the internal combustion for industrialization.[88] One might further speculate that Stalin and his team also gambled on one sheer, extraordinary opportunity. Just over a week prior to the 'Great Turn' speech, on 29 October, capitalism suffered its own gigantic, antithetical spasm in the form of the Wall Street Crash. In the days that followed, the possibility that the whole Western economic system might fall apart seemed quite plausible. Was it this, the immediate tsunami-like effects of the Great Depression, which induced—to use Christopher Browning's terminology—a 'euphoric' response on behalf of the Soviet anti-system?[89]

If such speculations are really outside the scope of this study, what cannot be gainsaid is that the seismic shift into *wholesale* collectivization and its accompanying dekulakization not only came 'suddenly and without warning',[90] but seems to have caught OGPU—as the agency with primary responsibility for the latter process—largely unprepared. In other words, while it was perfectly logical that there should have been a blueprint for exactly this scenario, Iagoda and his senior echelons found themselves, in early January 1930, having to respond to Politburo needs and directives largely on the hoof. Given that the agency's own assessment of unfolding events, however, pointed to a massive peasant uprising, OGPU was required to demonstrate that it was both ahead of the game and, at the same time, in control of events—not least by getting in there to destroy the kulak 'menace' rapidly and efficaciously.

This was no straightforward matter. For one thing, as we have seen, Politburo directives on dekulakization did not infer extermination of the entire kulak cohort. While OGPU was certainly tasked with physically eliminating dangerous category-one elements as indicated by the Molotov commission, its major task was to oversee the deportation of an earmarked 150,000 families in category two from their homes to places of new domicile in some of the farthest and most remote regions of the USSR—the Northern Territory, Siberia, the Urals, Kazakhstan, and the far east. This then, in some ways, was more akin to a grand social engineering project of the Ittihadist/Kemalist kind. Except that the numbers were much greater and the proposed timetabling was much more condensed. On 10 January Iagoda set his completion date for the destruction of the kulaks as March, or, at the latest, April. Having laid out his timescale, the agency's 'shadow government planning' became, in bureaucratic terms, one frantic effort: on the one hand via coded telegrams devolving detailed implementation of campaign to regional security units, on the other, a much larger paper chase as the agency strained to the far reaches of its capability and competence to coordinate with other party, transport, and regional authorities and departments to meet the logistical and resource needs of the intended programme.[91]

Various things are immediately noteworthy about the genocidal implications of these Herculean efforts. One is the perpetrators' own struggle for self-preservation. While regional party heads protested at the influx of deportees they knew they could not hope to feed or house, many regional OGPU commanders nevertheless strove to radically increase category-two quotas by regularly doubling or trebling their numbers—to the point where, ultimately, some 1.5 million people ended up as deportees.[92] The repeated 'overfulfillment of quotas' might have been the result of OGPU officers' efforts to demonstrate their resolve, capability, and enthusiasm for the task, even with an eye to promotion. Yet, perhaps equally or more so, their concern may simply have been a more fearful and desperate one of being caught out by more senior officers, peer-group colleagues, or even those junior to them with accusations of slackness, or worse, right-deviationist sympathies for the victims. There is no doubt that at the coalface of these operations—whether involving the security apparatus or otherwise—those cadres who prevaricated were now rapidly replaced by younger, more eager comrades ready to seize the opportunity of what was now being likened to a new 'revolutionary moment'.[93]

At the Moscow centre of OGPU operations core anxieties were different again. Credentials, here too, were on the line. As a result, nothing could be left to chance. Category-one *kulachestvo*, as a consequence, was expanded far beyond the Politburo Commission definition, to include all manner of real and imagined enemies—'bandits' repeatedly and ominously appears on the charge-sheet—while category two now encompassed 'local kulak authorities and the whole kulak cadre':[94] in other words, anybody OGPU deemed as a troublemaker or malcontent. Nevertheless, the agency's insistence that it could handle all disturbances was reflected in its operational directive at the beginning of February expressly forbidding the involvement of the Red Army, except in cases of insurrection. Again, part of the worry was how peasant recruits might react to 'atrocities' in the country; Iagoda claiming that there was a 'kulak mood' permeating the army.[95] And, of course, there were certainly memories here of Red Army men who had been leading anti-revolutionists a decade earlier. Even so, by effectively confining army units to barracks, OGPU was offering itself as a hostage to fortune.

But what then, of *other* perpetrators' attitudes towards the victims? There is no doubt that among tens of thousands of very often young, usually urban, cadres, especially those mobilized through Komsomol—the party's youth wing—to enter into the countryside and enforce the *parallel* drive towards collectivization, ferret out grain hoarders, and achieve party targets, there was some extraordinary zeal, mirroring Stalin's own declarations that through the cadres' actions Russia would be finally freed from her age-old backwardness.[96] The cadres' internalization of the party's propaganda caricature of the kulak as the embodiment of everything that was not only archaic, vile, and loathsome but also standing four-square in the path of Soviet progress, thus translated into repeated intimidation, terrorization, plunder, and worse—as an unconscionable city took its ugly revenge on a countryside it neither understood nor wished to understand.[97] The security police, of course, were required to carry out their remit through an entirely more professional modus operandi. Kulaks were simply statistics, cargo, 'ballast' to be eliminated or exiled as orders demanded. For those at the cutting edge of operations, clinical indifference combined with contempt was the general, though not universal, rule.

One cannot help noting, both here and closer to the pinnacle of the planning security hierarchy, some uncanny resemblances with a much better-known genocide record. For one thing, the notion of eructing what actually turned out, in the two major 1930 and 1931 deportation sequences, to be over 1.8 million people to some of the most inhospitable terrain in an always challenging Russian landscape[98]—the Siberian wastes of Narym; an either freezing or alternatively torrid Kazakhstan; an Arctic *taiga* whose true inhabitants were among the world's most resilient 'native' peoples—seems almost a harbinger of Heydrich's Wannsee projections. The notion of the far east, or the Arctic north, as zones in which deported European Jews would be put to work, and then 'undoubtedly disappear through natural diminution',[99] may, or may not, have been code for an actual programme of direct physical destruction. Yet, read *literally*, its wording very much represents the *prior* fate of a substantial element of the exiled kulak population.

Of course, there is a major difference. There was no OGPU reception party at the railheads or the entrance of the special settlements to corral the arrivals into some quarry, ravine, or industrial warehouse in order to execute or otherwise eliminate them en masse. Nor, as in the Armenian case, were they butchered either before transit or en route. Though, of course, some *were*: the security police records state that some 20,000 first-category kulaks, nearly all male heads of households, never made it onto the deportation trains but were shot out of hand. Another 10,000 would die in similar circumstances, in the second sweep the following year.[100] Beyond that, we know very little about the exact circumstances of these unfortunates' demise. For the rest—the vast majority eructed from their homes and communities—OGPU calculated an 'acceptable' loss of 5 per cent in the process of journeying and resettlement.[101] Such figures proved a significant underestimate of fatalities. Though how, *objectively* speaking, the agency could have so radically failed to anticipate the lethal consequences of its actions is less easy to gauge.

The fact is that once set in motion, however rigorously planned the whole dekulakization campaign was meant to be, it rapidly descended into chaos. Brought to collection points by carts or forced march, from February onwards, with the minimum of possessions—though supposedly with enough food to sustain them for an initial two-month period—deportees found themselves rail-freighted in cattle wagons for days and weeks, in utterly cramped, freezing, entirely inhumane and degrading conditions. For survivors, however—that is, for those not 'abandoned in deportation'—the journey was only the first part of a living hell. Arriving in distant destinations, very often in the middle of nowhere and without any shelter or food to rest and sustain them, they were put to work, usually scores, if not hundreds, of kilometres from their yet-to-be built settlements: mostly in felling and hewing timber, mining, and other extractive projects organized under OPGU commandants. This was Iagoda's initial plan, which would make sense of the whole exercise. By putting the deportees to work, the upheaval would be justified in terms of an intrinsic productive value, making the project self-financing, perhaps even remunerative, as well as opening up historically inaccessible wastes and wilderness to Soviet internal conquest. In fact, it was Russian-style hyper-exploitation pure and simple: shambolically implemented, viciously brutal, vastly under-resourced. Starvation for the able-bodied—this, remember, before the famine sequence of 1932–3—rapidly kicked in, as either insufficient food to hand or operating regimes in which deportees were only fed if they fulfilled their production quota inevitably created a vicious circle. The more exhausted and ill they became from overwork, the more they failed to deliver, the less gruel they received.[102]

However, the steeply ascending rates of mortality in the first months and then year of the special camps did not come primarily from among the able-bodied, large numbers of whom, paradoxically, succeeded in evading capture or even incarceration at every stage of the dekulakization, deportation, and resettlement process. It was instead, inevitably, the weakest, most vulnerable, most utterly 'innocent' members of families and communities—the babies, children, suckling mothers, old, crippled, and ill people—among whom death rates soared. Especially the children. What deportation provided from the very first was a lethal matrix of conditions in which life-threatening communicable diseases were bound to wreak havoc. As one pleading letter of petition among the tens of thousands addressed to Kalinin, the titular head of the Soviet state, reported with regard to families deported from the Ukraine and Kursk:

> They were packed off into the terrible cold—infants, pregnant women piled into cattle cars on top of one another, and right there women gave birth (could there be a worse indignity); then they were thrown out of the cars like dogs and put in churches and dirty, cold sheds, lice-ridden, freezing and hungry, and here there are thousands of them, left to the mercy of fate, like dogs no one wants to notice.[103]

Herded together thus, in these insanitary conditions and with few medical carers to tend to their misery let alone drugs available to check the rampant spread of measles, diphtheria, pneumonia, and whooping cough, public health collapse did much of the work which direct genocidal shooting or gassing might otherwise have done. A little further on in this section we discuss whether such non-intervention to save people from death amounts to the same thing as genocide. What cannot be gainsaid here is the sheer numbers of those who died. In the Northern Territory, health commissioners sent to report on a situation in and around Vologda, in March 1930, where temperatures had plummeted to -36 or -37 degrees Celsius, confirmed that mortality amongst the children was 'colossal': indeed, it was the largest element of the 21,000 reported deportee deaths in this region in this first year, in spite of the fact that large numbers of the youngest had already been repatriated home. If not less than 15 per cent of deportees were victims of unnatural deaths in Northern Territory, Kazakhstan was not far behind, with estimates ranging between 13 and

15 per cent.[104] No deportation zone escaped mass mortality. Some post-Soviet statisticians, moreover, have proposed that 1931 death rates overall were actually worse than the previous year, though how many fatalities there were in toto is less easy to clarify. Andrea Graziosi, for instance, notes that while 250,000 deportees certainly died in the famine sequence of 1932–3, in his opinion (more nebulously) 'at least several hundred thousand peasants and as many nomads had…*already* died before the famine struck'.[105] Werth, equally uncertainly, proposes that of the 1.8 million deportees from 1930–1, half a million perished or *fled*. However, as regards the children transported to the settlements his proposition is far balder: half of them died.[106]

The thousands of letters to Kalinin and others which found their way into the Soviet archives, alongside more recent oral testimonies, bear this out—albeit anecdotally. A Ukrainian child exile to Narym recalled the conditions in cramped, breathless barracks, where the children and old people—having begun to die—were piled in stacks. The bodies were then taken away by horse and cart for mass burial elsewhere. She concluded her story, 'In our family, there were six children, three died'.[107] Another, Anastasia Lavrovskaya, tersely tells her tale thus:

> Our family of nine (my sister got married and wasn't rounded up) was exiled…We lived in the special settlement of Kopanka, then in Kosolbanka. Between 1931 and 1934, the family was virtually wiped out; my father died in 1931, then five of my sisters and brothers. In 1933 they took me away from my ailing mother and put me in an orphanage in the city of Verkhoputiye. My entire family died of hunger. That would have been my fate, too, if they hadn't taken me to the orphanage.[108]

Such belated efforts to 'save' surviving kulak children may underscore one obvious distinction between Soviet and Nazi methodologies in relation to supposed 'enemies'. Yet Soviet determination to destroy the kulaks *as a class* clearly, *in practice*, had a physical eliminatory certitude too. For instance, by autumn 1931, the fact that less than 10 per cent of 'special settlers' were able to engage in productive work at all not only wrecked Iagoda's aspirations that something productive might come out of kulak 'liquidation',[109] but suggested that the regime's duty of care in the matter (except in terms of its own public reputation), was precisely nil. The fate of category-three kulaks further informs this conclusion. Testimony from a member of one such unfortunate family, the Andhokins, suggests that being deprived of rights, expelled from commune, home, and school, while still being allowed to 'exist' within the locality may have been equally if not even more a sentence of death than the extreme rigours facing those in the special settlements: 'There we would have had the right to work and earn some money and thus had some kind of life'. Instead, the large family was presented with a lingering death with 'nowhere to live, nothing to eat, no place to work', not to mention being hounded by local activists who 'made deliberate efforts to wipe out the whole family'. Both parents were sent to the Gulag, either for failing to plant grain for which they clearly had neither equipment nor seed (everything of theirs having been confiscated) or for gleaning grain to fend off starvation. As for the small children, even the alms they received from begging were confiscated.[110] No wonder that, in 1934, the Politburo set up a commission to focus on homeless children and attendant crime.

One obvious irony of all this is that regime anxiety regarding the rapid rise in juvenile delinquency was a direct corollary of its own best efforts. An even greater irony, closer to our immediate interest, is the spectacular failure of the dekulakization strategy. If it was intended not only to destroy the most recalcitrant element of the rural population but, at the same time, thus to terrify the rest of the peasantry into embracing collectivization with open arms, the consequences in February and especially March 1930 seemed to point in entirely the opposite direction. To be sure, the explicit Soviet tactic to divide and rule the countryside via the *kombedy*—the poor peasant committees—undoubtedly brought into play a destabilizing and thuggish rural element willing to play the Soviet game. The tactic had been used with partial success during the years of war communism as, for instance, in the assault on Don Cossackdom.[111] It can also be compared with Ittihadist mobilization of the most distressed Kurdish tribes, Circassians and others, in its attack on the Christian communities of the east, there with an overt ethno-religious dimension. In a degraded rural economy, or simply one where communities lived year to year with the reality of scarcity, a political manipulation of peoples' baser desires to covet what belonged to their neighbours was bound to have some knock-on effect.

Yet what is equally surprising and revealing about the Soviet countryside, as it reached its moment of truth in the harsh early months of 1930, is the degree to which it did not crumple, fragment, or turn in on itself but, instead, attempted, against all the odds, to stand together against both regime blandishment and regime ultra-violence. To be sure, in the face of the terror emanating from *kombedy*, local Soviets, and the incoming collectivization brigades, there had been a panicked rush into the collectives throughout late 1929—just as there had been efforts at self-dekulakization by peasants fearful of what might otherwise happen to them. But the very fact that large numbers of 'kulaks' were able to 'disappear' into the peasant crowd—perhaps for a bottle of *samogon* or some other material inducement—rather than being shopped to the authorities is a testament in itself to the ongoing solidarity and resilience of the *obshchiny*. As one peasant complainant was perfectly willing to point out to a newspaper: 'If we are kulaks, then all Siberia is kulak'.[112]

This naked truth stands in marked contrast to the obsessive nature of the Stalinist projection. The most significant aspect of Soviet rural society in the 1920s is not how far it divided into rich and poor but rather how far it went towards levelling itself. By the same token, while there is little evidence to suggest that kulaks responded to the Soviet attack as a class, there is plenty to suggest peasants responded as *communities*. To be sure there was no *Antonovshchina*, no mass generalized uprising, as Iagoda had anticipated. In this sense, the Soviet-cum-OGPU pacification and disarming of peasant society, including the political emasculation of its inherent SR tendencies, had achieved its aim in the preceding years. Resistance in 1930, as a result, was largely localized, fragmented, and almost entirely dependent on traditional agricultural implements to withstand the ultra-modern weaponry of the security state.

However, this made the struggle no less a War Type Three: a fight to the finish every bit as bitter and contested as any between some imperial-colonial hegemon and a native people making a last-ditch effort to defend their historic right to life, land, and liberty. The evidence is provided by OGPU itself. According to their notably detailed documentation there were getting on for 1,400 disturbances in 1930—ten times those of the previous year—with the majority bunched at the height of the collectivization drive between February and April. OGPU believed that not only did some 2.5 million people participate in these anti-state riots—a quite staggering figure in itself—but that some 200 of them took on an insurrectionary character in which the security apparatus lost local control.[113]

Equally revealing is OGPU's confirmation that while the majority of this resistance was against collectivization, a considerable proportion involved communal efforts to prevent or impede the arrest or deportation of those targeted as kulaks. Women, and sometimes children, featured prominently in these efforts, as, repeatedly and persistently, women also took the lead in efforts to prevent the vandalization of churches and, in particular, of bells, iconostases, and other church relics.[114] This, then, was not only about an *entire* peasantry convinced it was about to enter into a second serfdom, and struggling as such to defend hearth, home, livestock, and seed store—the fundamental peasant equivalents of capital. It was, in an even deeper sense, a struggle for the last, residual vestiges of everything these people held dear. Lemkin, in his developing formulations of genocide as cultural vandalism and physical barbarity, would have instantly recognized what was taking place.

The peasant fightback thus, not surprisingly, involved its own fierce retaliation. Some 1,500 Soviet functionaries and activists were killed, another 7,000 wounded or roughed up. Absent from the OGPU record are peasant casualties in these clashes.[115] That said, the scale and intensity of this first spring round of peasant opposition is also significant for what followed. For one thing, as the countryside plunged into chaos and posed once again the possibility of Vendée-like scenarios—this time writ large across the entirety of the Soviet rural landscape—Stalin, from on high, attempted a diversionary tactic. Hardly more than a month in from the commencement of campaign, on 2 March, a new article appeared under his single name in *Pravda*. 'Dizzy from Success'—depending on how one views it—suggests either a desperate bid at damage limitation before the whole edifice of his creation came tumbling down around him, or, alternatively, a brilliant subterfuge by which to lull the peasantry into the notion that they had won the war. The article certainly was cunning in the way it distanced the great leader himself from the *manner*, up to this moment, of collectivization—the 'excesses' of which were laid firmly at the door of cadres in the field, along with those who had been tasked with its crash-course implementation.[116]

Certainly, by calling for what appeared to be a 'retreat', not only did Stalin achieve the entirely improbable but certainly tsar-like feat of presenting himself as thaumaturgic saviour of the people, but, in the process, he also manipulated the peasantry into totally relaxing their guard. In this sense, the *Pravda* article may represent a critical watershed in the collectivization crisis. While the peasants now left the collectives in droves, OGPU were equally freed up to move in, arrest, and, indeed, eliminate suspected opponents—'kulaks' or otherwise—with something approaching impunity. Nearly 143,000 arrests were made between mid-April and early October, on top of the 140,000 already made from the commencement of the programme in early

January.[117] All manner of confabulated kulak types were now paraded as elements of the many-headed Hydra, 'ideological kulaks', kulak-accomplices and hirelings ('*podkulachnyk*'), sub-kulaks, even kulak 'choirboys'.[118] In other words, the regime's planned extirpation of the 'awkward squad' within the peasant cohort was able to press ahead, but now without the fear of it sparking off a full-scale confrontation with the peasantry. In turn, not only was the regime able to accrue—through con-fiscation of property and chattel—assets from which to finance the new collective farm system—again providing obvious parallels with Ittihadist, Nazi, and other expropriations for whichever state project—but this also paved the way for a new wave of unimpeded collectivization-cum-dekulakization which, from the autumn of 1930 and into the spring of 1931, accelerated to full throttle.[119]

Thus one might conclude that the Soviets, by stratagem, luck, or a mixture of the two, were able to reach their goal while yet avoiding genocidal mass killing. Except that, once again, the verdict is insufficient. The peasantry certainly knew by 1931 that the game was up, and that, tricked, they were now defeated. Something new and terrible, however, was already developing out of their despair. The first warnings had come in 1929, with self-dekulakization: peasants with that little extra wherewithal attempting to submerge themselves in the general throng by selling or giving away their property to family and neighbours. What had followed was a mass flight to the new townships and construction sites where, de-identified, these internal refugees became, paradoxically, a critical if—by the nature of their situation—floating element of the very labour source demanded by the 'Great Turn'. But there had also been another, harsher, side to the kulak response: *razbazarivanie*, literally 'squandering', or, more exactly, denying to the authorities anything which might be of value to them. This was, in effect, peasant Luddism, a classic weapon of the weak. But also a last-resort one. Its ultimate manifestation was the slaughter-ing of livestock, the most precious possession of all peasants and at the very core of rural family-based autonomy, dignity, and pride. To kill very often beloved animals upon which peasant life and culture were built and sustained was not just a state-ment of despair but of an obdurate and stubborn refusal, even in the face of force majeure, to bow down to bureaucratic diktat.[120] It was as if the *razbazarivanie* practitioner was saying, 'You won't ever lay your hands on what belongs to myself and mine, even if we have to take the knife to our own horse and oxen, even if that means, in turn, our own annihilation through starvation'.

With the full-scale resumption of collectivization, it was, however, no longer kulaks alone who were practising *razbazarivanie*. The slaughtering of livestock became endemic among whole sections of the peasant population and, from this point on, the countryside began to topple over into wholesale collapse. Far from 1930, or 1931, marking Stalin's final victory against the peasantry, the whole land-scape of the state-versus-people confrontation was about the lurch into a new, even more viciously deadly, phase.

*

Thus far, we have sketched the broad contours of the regime's war against the countryside and of its key paradox: that while ostensibly seeking to avoid mass extermination of whole strata of peasant society, this—by a process something akin to a cumulative radicalization—is more and more what it did achieve. Nevertheless, something remains missing from this account. That something becomes increasingly self-evident as our attention moves towards the catastrophe of the famine, from late 1932 and through into 1933, and more especially the region we have come to most associate with its full impact, the Ukraine.

However, a marked rimlands' dimension was already strongly in evidence in the 1930–1 sequence of events. Terry Martin confirms the point: 'In theory collectivisation was not supposed to have an ethnic dimension, in practice it quickly developed one'.[121] One obvious reason for this was the particularly large percentage of peasants targeted as 'kulaks' coming from the Soviet western and southern border regions. Of the total 2.25 million deportees designated as such—the 1.8 million we have already noted plus those added in further Politburo-ordered sweeps in 1932 and 1933—the first and third largest cohorts came from the Ukraine and North Caucasus.[122] Belorussia, despite its relatively smaller population also figured heavily in the kulak statistics, even more so in respect of its Polish element, a rhyme of the time—*raz poliak, znachit kulak*—reading less catchily in translation as 'All Poles are kulaks'.[123]

In fact, this did not in itself presuppose that OPGU set out to blanket whole ethnic groups as enemies. But, equally, by targeting large swathes of their number as kulaks, an OGPU idée fixe that areas such as the Ukraine and North Caucasus—more particularly its Cossack element—would be the seedbed for counter-revolution practically became a self-fulfilling prophecy. In March 1930, the high month of peasant resistance, 45.1 per cent of anti-state disturbances—nearly 3,000 out of over 6,500 separate incidents—took place in the Ukraine.[124]

Nor was this just an internal security issue. Some of the more serious uprisings took place closer to the Belorussian or Ukrainian border with Poland, in some instances leading to the localized collapse of Soviet authority for weeks on end. As OGPU strove to restore its control, resisters—often, unsurprisingly, Poles—fled across the border, exciting the Politburo in turn to specifically stipulate the March deportation from these two border republics of an additional 18,500 families: 'in the first line, those of Polish nationality'.[125] If this might be read as a desperate Soviet attempt to dam a flood already in full spate, behind it was an even more obsessive geopolitical anxiety about the peoples of the border regions making common cause with Warsaw. In fact, the regime's sensitivity on the matter was not entirely unfounded. At this moment of acute state vulnerability and crisis, there is evidence to suggest that Piłsudski's intelligence agencies had more than a toehold in the Ukraine, even having infiltrated some OPGU, Red Army, and Black Sea fleet units in the republic.[126] So-called *smenovekhovtsy*, bourgeois intellectuals of the Hrushevsky ilk who had returned from exile in the years of *korenizatsiia*, were simultaneously being charged in a show trial in Kharkov (the then Ukrainian SSR capital) with having used their favoured positions within the Ukrainian Academy of Sciences to infiltrate and undermine the republic's communist leadership and stir up a 'new national revolution'.[127] The accusations in themselves may have been part of a carefully planned Stalinist stratagem to quash some of the leading lights of

Ukrainian *korenizatsiia* before it became too strong and independent-minded. Equally, however, the notion that the true *smenovekhovstvo* purpose was to organize 'a popular uprising as a prelude to foreign intervention' had already taken on, within the party leadership—as Martin shrewdly suggests—the power of 'a psychological truth'.[128]

Thus, for a Polish conspiracy-obsessed Kremlin, behind peasant foot-dragging in the face of collectivization, or the delivery of new Moscow-set annual grain quotas, lurked secessionist movements—the Union for the Liberation of Ukraine (SVU) and its Belorussian equivalent, the SVB—who, for all their alleged demands for independence, were actually themselves the dupes of Warsaw's sinister game. But equally bleakly, looked at the other way round—through the prism of grass-roots behaviour—the open display of national slogans in peasant demonstrations, and the emergence of a new wave of primitive, rebel-like sabotage and revenge attacks against Soviet rule in the Ukrainian countryside, suggested that the distinction between national cultural elites who led and a populace who followed was redundant anyway. The sin of the Ukrainian peasantry was no longer that they simply were, or supported, the kulaks: they were *Petliurist*-kulaks. Stalin in 1925 had sagely intoned, 'The nationality question is by its basis a peasant question'.[129] Five or six years later, the *vozhd* might have rued his words: large sections of the Ukrainian, if not necessarily Belorussian, peasantry voicing not loyalty but demands for a national exit, even by way of Warsaw.

Worse, the Ukraine's disease seemed, to Moscow's fevered imagination, also to have spread to the North Caucasus—in particular to the Kuban, a largely Cossack area. Here, paradoxically, as a consequence of the initial powers which *korenizatsiia* had conferred on the non-Russian republics, a proposed Ukrainization of the districts' schools had been, in the late 1920s, a cipher for a Ukrainian republic versus Russian federation struggle for control in the area, with local Cossackdom keenly looking to the former as patron.[130] With the onset of collectivization, the Kuban *stanitsy* flared into a particularly serious case of open insurrection, so much so that OGPU strictures confining the Red Army to barracks for the duration were over-ruled through the urgent dispatch of the 'reliable' 14th Moscow Rifle Division to the region.[131] In fact, quasi-militarized uprisings in wide swathes of the Caucasus belt—embracing Chechens, Ingush, and Karachai amongst others, as well as Azeris further south—led to the withdrawal of both OGPU units and other military contingents from their normal duties guarding the Turkish and Iranian borders. In the Caucasus, as in Central Asia, where *basmachi* bands were once again in operation, a clearly panicked Politburo decree in late February, ordering a drawing back from full-scale collectivization in the so-called 'National Economic Backward Regions', failed to put a lid on revolt.[132]

However, if this confirms that southern and western rimlands—alongside the Kazakh steppe—were major 'ethnic' hot spots, just as they had been a decade earlier, it was the Kuban which was to receive the full weight of Moscow's wrath. Was it rekindled anti-Cossack animus from the civil war period, with the Don and Terek as the main focus of regime ire, that explains why, in late 1932 and early 1933, the Politburo decreed three entire *stanitsy* in the Poltava area were to be ethnically cleansed? Already, the previous year, some 60,000 of the young and able-bodied from the region had been forced into road-building labour battalions: of whom one account claiming that only 15 per cent survived.[133] The new decree, however, was not selective but a sentence on an entire communal cohort as the homes of another 60,000 Cossacks were to be vacated in favour of Red Army soldiers and their families—the iron-fisted nature of the pacification and deportation confirmed by the presence of *Antonovshchina* hardman Tukhachevsky as overseer. Stalin's other trusted man on the spot, Lazar Kaganovich, contemporaneously articulated the 'never again' parallels: 'All the Kuban Cossacks must be reminded how in 1921 the Terek Cossacks were deported. It's the same situation now'.[134]

But while the Kuban's crime, on the one hand, was playing the Ukrainian–'Peliurite' nationalist game and thereby being implicated in the alleged Piłsudksi stratagem, on the other, the actual accusation on the charge-sheet was 'the sabotage of grain delivery'.[135] Which might suggest that while the Kuban deportations certainly represent an extreme example of Moscow's response to peasant opposition, they were, at the same time, part and parcel of its determination to impose the totality of its new command economy on the entire countryside. The key question at this point thus becomes: is the descent into famine, from late 1932, a consequence of the level of compulsory grain targets as set by the centre? And, if so, more pointedly, were those targets consciously ratcheted up to impossible levels with regard to specific regions, or peripheral republics, in order to precipitate the intentional death by starvation of millions of their inhabitants?

Here we step into a minefield, not only of the historical evidence but of the scholarly disputes which have been fought over it. Nor has the opening up of the Soviet archives done much to soften these. Ranged on the one side are some eminent structuralist historians who, having trawled through the economic statistics as well as new archival material, conclude that while Stalin's collectivization policies were 'ruthless and brutal' they do not carry with them any evidence of a conscious plan to use famine as a weapon either against the peasantry writ large, or specific ethnic elements of it.[136] This necessarily poses wider historical as well as moral questions. Are we to presume from the lack of a *written* Hitler order Hitler's innocence, or perhaps bystander role, in relation to the destruction of European Jewry? Are we to take the Ottoman Porte's *official* May 1915 decree on Armenian deportation as proof of what Talât actually intended? In such instances finding a historical middle way may not be possible, or, at the very least, easy. The same is true in this case. At the opposite pole to the structuralists is a radical intentionalist position, which directly accuses Stalin of a premeditated purpose to destroy the *Ukrainian* 'nation'. Its advocates have freely adopted the neologism *Holodomor* 'death (or murder) by hunger' as shorthand for the 1932–3 famine as it occurred in the Ukraine. The argument—as one might expect—is closely aligned to that of Ukrainian memorialists and diaspora groups bitter at the prevarication and/or silence of the international community when it comes to recognizing their national suffering as a bona fide case of genocide. In this respect, as with similar Armenian and Syriac efforts with regard to 1915, it is not always easy to disentangle processes of historic causation and context from the emotional charge.[137]

What is not a subject of contemporary contention (as it had been in the face of the Soviet denial of the time) is the existence of a famine which killed millions. Exactly how many millions, it is true, is not agreed, and the lack of consensus on this score certainly plays into and often amplifies the more fractious areas of debate. Putting aside some of the more implausible numbers running to 10 million or even 20 million deaths,[138] this author is not equipped to professionally adjudicate between recent extrapolations by Soviet and Western demographers attempting to 'read' the truth of the population shortfall between the census of 1926 and the entirely more 'dodgy' one of 1937. Observing these extrapolations, a cautious Stephen Wheatcroft, while disputing some of the very large figures adduced by Robert Conquest prior to the opening of the archives, confirms that a nationwide death toll as high as 4 or 5 million *is* plausible.[139] The Soviet researcher Ivnitskii, however, paints an altogether starker picture, proposing that from the autumn of 1932 to April 1933, the USSR's population collapsed to the tune of 7.7 million. The breakdown of major fatalities he ascribes as follows: 4 million in the Ukraine, and 1 million each in the North Caucasus, the Volga region, and Kazakhstan.[140]

Among the experts, thus, while the largest numbers of deaths in the famine is confirmed as being Ukrainian—whatever the exact percentage from an estimated population of over 29 million in 1926—equally clearly there is agreement that starvation was very widespread, with other areas of extreme severity beyond the USSR's second largest republic. Pavel Polian, for instance, notes that 25 to 30 million souls were without food in early 1933 in the Ukraine, North Caucasus, and the lower Volga.[141] However, in per capita terms, what is most striking is the impact of the famine not in these places, but further east: in the historic steppe lands. Here nomad peoples' traditional lifestyles, livelihoods, and, ultimately, lives were quite simply swept away. Those among the Kirghiz of Central Asia, as well as the Bashkirs of western Siberia, who survived the onslaught, found their only recourse was to flee elsewhere, or across into China.[142] For the more substantial Kazakh peoples, however, the consequences of the complete obliteration of their flocks was in communal terms even more catastrophic. Alec Nove suggests figures of between 1.5 and 1.7 million deaths or, put statistically, 42 per cent of their number. Other commentators broadly confirm that between 1 and 2 million Kazakhs died in the famine, while somewhere in the region of another 2 million migrated across the Chinese border.[143]

Viewed from where the Soviet southern rimlands bleed into Central Asia, our perspective on the overall causation of this human disaster would thus be bound to be somewhat different from one which concentrated on the singularity of the Ukrainian experience. Unless we chose to keep them off our cognitive map (which would certainly be consistent with most modern, Western-orientated scholarship) we would have to acknowledge that the events of 1932–3 were even worse for the Kazakhs and other nomads *as communities* than they were for the peasants of the grain-rich black-earth provinces.[144] This position would certainly carry with it the problem that our 'thick' knowledge of the Kazakh catastrophe is almost non-existent by comparison. But accepting with honesty this reality, we are still left with the same underlying question as before: what grounds are there for assuming that what happened at this moment, whether in the Ukraine or Kaza-khstan, amounted to genocide? Here, I propose briefly to develop three approaches to the question. Each takes us in a slightly different direction. Nevertheless, each also leads towards an affirmation of the 'guilty' verdict.

Our first approach borrows from the work of the British political scientist Eric Herring, who made a major study of the 1990s sanctions policy adopted by the USA and Britain against Iraq, in the wake of Saddam Hussein's invasion of Kuwait. Herring has not been alone in arguing that both the ensuing epidemiological crisis and massive mortality increase in Iraq between 1991 and 1998, including—according to UNICEF—some half a million deaths above the anticipated rate among chil-dren under five, was a direct consequence of the embargo on purification plant equipment to maintain clean water from the Tigris and Euphrates, medical sup-plies including vaccines, and basic humanitarian aid.[145] Where Herring has gone one crucial step further however is in proposing that in adding to, and thereby reinforcing, 'the effects of US bombing in 1991 and Iraq's long war with Iran in the 1980s', the practitioners of sanctions fully *anticipated* this result. Herring, indeed, has been quite unequivocal in his charge: 'Those policymakers who backed the sanctions cannot say *they did not know* what was going to happen. Whatever the political purpose, it was a conscious and callous choice to deny an entire society the means necessary to survive'.[146]

What is particularly pertinent about Herring's argument is the way it can equally be applied in the Soviet instance. Stalin did not have to consciously send the OGPU or the Red Army into the peasant heartland or nomad steppe in order to ensure mass death would result from his collectivization drive. Just as he could have anticipated that large numbers of people, especially children, would die as a consequence of the unsafe conditions of the kulak deportation programme, he could equally have expected that there would be a large-scale resort to *razba-zarivanie* as the peasantry made a last-ditch effort to deny to the state their moral and physical assets. To be sure, the collapse of peasant resilience in this way could be imputed to the peasants' own obduracy. They did not *have to* slaughter their livestock or eat the following year's grain seed. But then, as we have already seen, genocide also occurred in the 'Anglo' imperial record where native peoples defied the state's command to them to submit. The convenience in these instances to the perpetrator is an obvious one: regime exculpation reading 'this was not our fault, we were simply attempting to apply a legitimate state-sanctioned pro-gramme'. But in that lies the rub. Rather than blaming the victims, what today we would call the precautionary principle would require anticipation of the statis-tically probable danger of adopting an unsafe policy and, on that basis, choosing to *avoid* it.

Similarly, the argument that the mass mortality was an unintended conse-quence of some other unrelated piece of contingent bad luck—more exactly the drought of 1931 or further bad weather conditions in 1932—also lacks credi-bility. The drought was undoubtedly very serious, but so too was that of 1936, which did not result in famine. True, 1933 was also unseasonably bad. In which case, there was all the more reason for the state to make provision, very much along the lines followed by both traditional and contemporary strong states, by preserving the residual harvest for native consumption, applying *across-the-board* rationing, and under no circumstances allowing grain to be exported abroad. In the context of 1932, this might have also been an opportunity to call a halt to a vicious downward spiral in the state–peasantry relationship, and the beginning, instead, of a slow process of reconciliation. The clincher for a Herring-style indictment lies in the fact that the regime did exactly the opposite. Knowing full well that the countryside was on the brink of mass starvation, procurement demands (*zagotovki*)—especially on the main grain-growing areas—continued unabated with entirely unrealistic quotas. The requisitioning shock brigades were sent in again, with redoubled encouragement and powers, to ransack their way into uncovering concealed stores and force remaining recalcitrant peasants back into the collectives.[147] Meanwhile the drive to increase grain sales on foreign markets, in return for ready cash to fuel industrialization, remained firmly the order of the day.

True, the manner in which the state ratcheted up its 1932 *zagotovki* drive has some apparently self-contradictory elements. For instance, under anxious pleading from party secretaries in the Ukraine and North Caucasus, grain quotas were actually lowered consecutively four times in these regions, from late 1931 through into 1932, but then increased just as mass starvation took hold, in the latter part of the year.[148] This volte-face appears to have been directly related to the appearance on the scene of senior party military and OGPU representatives acting under the direct authority of Stalin's enforcers, Kaganovich and Molotov, in order to maximize procurements regardless of the sensitivities of regional party leaders. The cleansing of the Kuban *stanitsy* was one direct consequence of these developments. So, too, were entire confiscations of other crops, such as beet or potatoes, in the absence of grain. By contrast, while rationing by this time was taking place in the cities, the food reserves put on standby for Moscow and Leningrad remained greater than those for the entirety of the Ukraine.[149] Indeed, very specifically here, and in North Caucasus, a slew of draconian new decrees was applied with maximum severity. This began on 7 August 1932 with the infamous colloquially entitled 'law on the wheat-ears', making it potentially punishable by death to take from the state its 'sacred and inviolable property'—even in the form of spilt grain from the field. The Ukrainian countryside in particular, not unlike the veld under Kitchener at the time of the Boer War, became a grillwork of controlled districts, increasingly guarded by watchtowers whose primary purpose was to prevent peasant malefactors—now officially designated as 'enemies of the people'—surreptitiously gleaning from the fields.[150] The threat of being shot for their crimes, however, did not prevent the starving from roaming further and further afield—even to major cities—to beg for food and, very often, simply collapse and die on the streets. The state's response was again unequivocal: a Politburo decree in December specifically singled out and censured the Ukraine and North Caucasus for failing to reach their grain quotas. The following month a new directive, carrying Stalin and Molotov's signatures, closed the borders to peasant movement from the two regions.[151]

The denial of access and egress 'for bread'—except at the state's behest—from the Ukraine and North Caucasus points to a second approach to our question: indicating that these were regions specifically and consciously targeted by the state to suffer the full effects of famine. What the turn-of-year decrees suggest, moreover, is how, in the Kremlin's mind, the charge of grain-requisition sabotage in both regions was linked to a more heinous crime: *Ukrainization*.

At first sight, this has to read as nonsensical. *Korenizatsiia* may have been whittled down but it was still the official nationalities policy of the USSR, with the Ukraine the jewel in its crown. Not only was it Moscow's guarantee that the second most substantial group after the Russians—at 21.3 per cent of the Soviet population (in fact, a staggering 45.6 per cent of non-Russians in the USSR)—would remain loyal; the policy was equally geared towards presenting the region as a showcase—the so-called Piedmont principle—to Ukrainians across the border in 'New Europe' Poland, Czechoslovakia, and Rumania.[152] As already implied, part of the Kremlin's problem on the cusp of the 'Great Turn' was that, by its own criteria, the policy may simply have been *too* successful. The Ukrainian SSR was effectively ruled by its own national communist elite and had its own relatively strong industrial and agricultural power base, not to mention, by dint of its rimlands position, a window on the wider world. What above all the Kremlin feared, however, was that this might be the basis for the creation of a better, more efficient *Soviet* alternative to that on offer by way of Moscow.

Here then was a Stalinist neurosis which went even deeper than its chronic fixation about an independent, Polish-sponsored Ukraine on its doorstep. Look for the origins of the Russian state and one would have to go way back beyond the tentative foundations of Muscovy under Mongol tutelage in the late thirteenth century, to the emergence, and then efflorescence, of Kievan Rus five centuries earlier. The contrast between isolated, wintry Moscow and the sunnier metropolis founded on the banks of the Dnieper—linked thereby to the civilizations of Byzantium and the Christian West—is a striking one. The Ukraine, long after Kiev's collapse, maintained its association with aspects of the 'West', more recently through Polish cultural, as well as political, influence. One critical legacy was the creation, in 1921, of a westwards-looking autocephalous church; that is, an Orthodoxy distinct from Moscow's tutelage. Another more deep-seated one was the general absence of either *obshchina* or serfdom. Ukrainians on the land proved to be part of an integrated rural society without the necessity for the ties of the commune. And in that lay the Kremlin's headache. The Ukraine, since the late Romanovs, was Russia's grain-basket, and so not only the source for feeding its growing cities, but with the potential for a US-style export sector from which to finance its industrializing goals. But, it happened also to be worked by an essentially free and free-spirited peasantry who might be described—for want of a better word—as kulaks. With their own consciously national language—realized, ironically, through *korenizatsiia*—and their separate religious base, as well as private farm ownership, the Ukraine presented, as one commentator has pithily put it, 'the peasant antithesis of the new Soviet identity'.[153]

A showdown between Moscow and Kharkov over the direction of Ukrainization was thus almost inevitable, with or without the collectivization crisis. A regime as control-obsessed as Moscow was not going to stand for a competitor. And especially not one which, by successfully going its own ostensibly 'soft' communist way, might threaten to take with it a much wider swathe of the non-Russian periphery. That Kharkov's leadership was in no position to parry Moscow's diktat was already evident in 1930 from the snowballing of arrests which followed on from the initial SVU trial and, indeed, the complete extirpation of the autocephalous church—some 20,000 of whose members, 1,150 priests included, were deported and/or killed.[154] That all this was intended as a clear signal to Ukrainian comrades to forego any thoughts of 'cultural counter-revolution' by making common cause with the *smenovekhovtsy* is also perfectly clear.[155]

What the heightened crisis from the summer of 1932 seems to have done, however, is lurch the Kremlin leadership into an even more obsessive and paranoid focus on the Ukraine as the weak link in its wider project: 'The *chief thing* now is the Ukraine . . . if we don't make an effort to improve the situation in Ukraine, we may lose Ukraine'. The way Stalin repeated the very name in this 'holiday'-time August missive to Kaganovich—one of several, in fact, all on the same theme—is highly indicative of his state of mind. As is the inference to be drawn from his remarks. Improving the situation did not mean seeking emergency grain shipments—even, if necessary, from abroad—to avert famine. No, it meant clearing out 'the rotten elements, conscious and non-conscious Peliurites, as well as direct agents of Piłsudski' within the Ukrainian party so that the region might be transformed 'into a true *fortress* of the USSR, a truly model republic'.[156] The failure to deliver grain—and the particular 'sabotage' of the Ukrainized Cossack Kuban on this score—is thus read here as the fault of the local party leaderships and of behaviour—whether intentional or inadvertent—favouring the 'enemies of Soviet power'.[157]

Stalin's immediate emergency solution was to send in Molotov and Kaganovich to so browbeat the leaderships of the Ukraine and the North Caucasus that, suitably terrified, they would cave in to the impossible grain quotas now demanded of them. In effect, they became collaborators in the mass murder of their own populations. As for the commissioners themselves, they fulfilled a role not unlike the Jacobin *répresentants en mission* in the Vendée and elsewhere in 1793–4. They ruthlessly enforced the writ of the centre and emasculated local cadres by leaving them as helpless bystanders while the starvation and deportation punishments of the Kuban were carried out. The Kuban's indictment was further emphasized in December, with the Politburo decree bringing to an end the creeping Ukrainization of the North Caucasus on the grounds that it had become nothing other than a legal cover for the work of grain-sabotaging traitors.[158] Regional comrades had to take it on the chin just to stay alive. For many, it was already too late. A mass purge of the Ukrainian party began with the arrival of Pavel Postyshev, Stalin's new 'viceroy' in Kharkov, in January 1933. He set about his task with a vengeance, eliminating 'entire commissariats, judicial boards, university faculties, editorial departments, theatre groups and film studios'. In a report to Stalin the following November

Postyshev boasted that 'almost all the people removed were put before the firing-squad or exiled'.[159]

But if this points towards a quite intentional, even clinical, elitocide—the beheading of an increasingly luminous element of what might have been a diverse Soviet cultural scene—one is bound to remember that these were not the *mass* casualties of this sequence. Instead, what the policy radicalization from August 1932 suggests is a quite conscious Kremlin effort to use the growing grain shortage as an instrument against the *entire* national peasantry of the Ukraine and its hinterland.

The evidence for Ukrainian population collapse thereafter is not in question, By March 1933, not only were starved and emaciated corpses a regular sight for Ukrainian city dwellers but a descent into cannibalism in some areas had become the subject of common knowledge.[160] Yet how did the state authorities respond to these realities? With the Ukrainian OGPU empowered, that month, 'to deal with insurgency and counter-revolution by applying the death penalty',[161] a crescendo of executions followed. The January decree forbidding peasants from crossing the Ukraine and North Caucasus borders into other regions had already assumed that the peasants' search for bread was bogus, and what those making the journey were really doing was agitating on behalf of SRs and Polish agents 'against the collective farms and against Soviet power as a whole'.[162] Shooting adult grain pilferers, or children stealing from railway cars in sidings, thus became almost a standard operating procedure—always accompanied by the justification that the criminals in question were really kulak saboteurs. Desperate peasants attempting to swim the Dniester into Rumania were similarly dealt with by OGPU guards.[163] The vast majority of deaths, however, were not from the barrel of a gun. One report speaks of some 3000 'kulak' orphans, aged between seven and twelve, held in a camp on the right bank of the river at Verkhnediprovsk until every last one died of starvation.[164] Even more common was death in, or close to, people's homes: often whole village communities dying in excruciating circumstances but always with the youngest, the babies and little children, not only the first casualties but the largest number. The dissident Soviet demographer M. Maksudov has suggested that no fewer than 3 million Soviet children born between 1932 and 1934 died in this way.[165] Meanwhile, foreign correspondents reported huge grain stacks, from which the starving had been denied access, rotting in the fields.[166]

While this last bit of information may be anecdotal, overall there is sufficient corroboration of evidence on the facts of the famine to lend weight to Michael Ellman's contention that starvation appears to have been consciously utilized as a weapon by Stalin to punish the peasantry: in the first instance, for their unwillingness to submit to collectivization, in the second, for their alleged withholding of grain as their *own* 'terror' weapon against the cities. He refers to this as a case of 'accusation in mirror', in other words, as an action whose justification lies in blaming the other side for having the truly malevolent intentions to which one's own response becomes legitimate self-defence. This kind of projective demonization of the victim is actually standard fare in cases of genocide, as we have repeatedly seen. One might note, however, that Ellman's conjecture is not Ukraine-specific. Nor is it based on an attempt to prove some conscious, premeditated blueprint for the organization of a man-made famine. Instead it proposes that Stalin's actions were contingent upon knowledge of massive food shortage as it fully emerged in summer 1932, which *thereafter* produced the intention to use these circumstances to deliver a 'knockout blow' against the peasantry.[167]

Which brings us to the third approach to our question: an argument to the effect that 'famine as weapon' was the consequence of an already primed developmentalist agenda, but one which only tipped over into this specific outcome as a result of the series of complex but interconnected contingencies which arose in the course of attempted collectivization—one crucial element being the depth and extent of ongoing peasant resistance. Comparative cases may offer some insight. For instance, we might consider the decision of the German East Africa governor, in 1905, to meet the Maji Maji—the ongoing cross-communal peasant insurrection against the production of colonially imposed cotton as a cash crop for the region—with the creation of a conscious, systematic, military-induced famine. Up to 300,000 people are believed to have died as a consequence, through into 1906. However, what is also of gruesome note about this strategy is its contrast with the better-known case of the German response to the Herero and Nama insurrections in their South-West Africa colony, over the previous two years: where the initial emphasis had been on direct physical extermination. Genocide could be said to be the outcome in both situations, but, in the East African instance, the decision to opt for starvation as a technique arguably derived from what had been *learnt* from the previous colonial experience. The punishment of the Tanganyikan peoples certainly proved less 'newsworthy' than that visited on the Herero. Meanwhile it was logistically less challenging, less onerous on the German treasury, and—with the full capitulation of the survivors—clearly, for the perpetrators, more effective.[168]

It was not the premeditated intention of the Germans in their African colonies to wipe out native subjects upon whom they depended for labour, any more than it was Stalin's with regard to Soviet peasantry. But in the Russian, as colonial, examples, the frustrated inability of the state to get its way translated into a quite fearful urge for mass retribution. Indeed, Stalin's anger against peasant obduracy is intimated at this time in his references to 15 per cent of pre-collectivization households 'belonging to the past'—by which he meant increasing deportations to a total of some 10 or 12 millions. The tack of Stalin's thinking is mirrored in early 1933 in internal leadership discussions about immediately deporting another 3 million to western Siberia and Kazakhstan.[169] One reason why this may have been radically reduced to 'only' 268,000 was possibly because officials in the reception regions vigorously protested against the unrealistic nature of these plans. Ellman, however, argues that the scaling down also came out of the realization that starvation offered a more *efficient* substitute for dealing with the 'problem'.[170] Or, put entirely more cynically, Stalin could have his cake and eat it: having the satisfaction of punishing the peasants on the one hand, while achieving his 'final solution' for the countryside on the other.

There is no doubt that food deprivation provided the decisive weapon by which those peasants and nomads who had not already died or fled to the towns or abroad were forced to do Stalin's bidding. Just as with the special settlers, the only way one got to eat on a *kolkhoz*, henceforth, was through daily piecework. Otherwise one continued to starve. This linked to a new, more formalized passport system, introduced at the end of 1932, which prevented peasants simply moving—as they had been doing previously in their hundreds of thousands—to the bleak but safer refuge of the towns. As a consequence, further peasant resistance was futile.[171] As M. M. Khatayevich, the key architect of collectivization in the Volga region, boasted to a fellow party activist, 'This year was a test of our strength and their endurance. It took a famine to show them who is master here. It has cost millions of lives, but the collective farm system is here to stay. We've won the war'.[172]

He was correct. The logjam had been broken. For a regime which had also effectively dumped *korenizatsiia*, except as an instrument for keeping the peripheral peoples in their isolated place and space, other benefits which spoke to its Russianizing preferences also ostensibly followed. A leading party official in Chelyabinsk, for instance, told a foreign communist visitor:

> The famine has been of great benefit to us in the Urals, in Western Siberia and in the Trans-Volga. In these regions the losses from starvation have mostly affected the alien races. Their place is being taken by Russian refugees from the central provinces. We are, of course, not nationalists, but we cannot overlook this advantageous fact.[173]

In other words, in regions where, in the early years of Bolshevik rule, the regime had sought to adjudicate in favour of the native populations against Russian incomers and, in the process, mitigate the worst effects of colonial violence against them, it now seemed to be moving in a reverse direction. The Kazakh steppe, a region imagined as a 'virgin' territory ripe for turning into a US-style, prairie-like granary was the most obvious casualty of this tendency. But then, attempted—though actually in many instances aborted—resettlements of tens of thousands of Red Army soldiers and other Russians from the central provinces, in parts of the Ukraine and its hinterland, especially around the Black Sea, the Sea of Azov, and the Kuban, were also indicative of post-famine Soviet social engineering.[174] Had this all been preordained? Very probably not. It was the famine that opened up opportunities—'advantageous facts'—seized upon by the state, through the depopulation of whole districts. But then, the regions which suffered the famine most severely were, as we have already seen, not simply the victims of an act of God. As William Chamberlin, one of the most seasoned contemporary observers of the Soviet scene, concluded:

> The unquestionable fact is that collectivisation wrought greatest havoc in the main just where the peasants were more intelligent and more progressive in farming methods, where the pre-war standard of living was the highest... The worst famine regions in 1932–1934 were in many cases the most fertile and prosperous districts... the rich North Caucasus, the German colonies on the Volga, and in Ukraine, where the population was always noted for their good farming—the fertile 'black-earth' Ukrainian provinces of Kiev and Poltava. It was not the more backward peasants, but the more progressive and well-to-do, who usually showed the greatest

resistance to collectivisation, and this is not because they did not understand what the new policy would portend, but because they understood only too well.[175]

What Chamberlin's verdict also rather suggests is that the thrust of famine-punishment was not *exclusively* directed at rimland nationalities but *any* region which showed marked signs of independent action and opposition. Of course, the co-relationship between the two can hardly be ignored. If Stalin's 'solution' in the North Caucasus and Ukraine was sealing-off of the borders, in the Crimea it was the targeted deportation of Muslim–Tatar clergy as well the most successful peasantry, while in the Karakum desert regions close to the Iranian frontier, a full-scale military campaign of scorched earth included the closing up of wells and the razing of villages.[176]

But then, perhaps, what underlies this willingness to punish and murder writ large is the paradoxical requirement to fashion a new *Homo sovieticus* whose primary purpose in *life* was to fulfil the needs of the state and its historically ordained mission. For 'socialism in our country' to fail, said Stalin in a significant speech in May 1935, entailed not just the loss of independence but Russia becoming 'an object for the games of imperialist powers'.[177] The problem, thus, with both unreconstructed peasants *and* nationalities lay either in their lack of understanding of what was at stake or, worse, a wilful refusal to participate in the solution, in spite of that knowledge. Only by chains could the peasantry be 'attached' to socialism, or so thought the leading communist and one-time Stalin confidante, Sergo Ordzhonikidze, of the sentiments of his fellow party activists in 1930.[178] Like colonial governors with regard to their natives, the Soviet regime thus started out with a view of its rural masses—whether at the centre or in its rimlands—which was contemptuous where it was not downright antagonistic, as well as fearful. Necessary for their labour, peasants could not all be eructed, but neither, except in the longer term, could they be truly assimilated to the Soviet cause. One day, the whole Soviet countryside would be a giant motorized tractor station—an MTS—in which a truly proletarianized class of 'heroic' agro-industrial tractor drivers would harvest grain for the country's flourishing industrial cities. In the meantime, like the equally dangerous, secessionist-minded, insurrectionary-prone peoples of the periphery, the peasant masses had to be pummelled into submission in much the same way as the 'savages' and 'barbarians' of colonial empires. This is no parody. Post-collectivization, in other words post-Stalin's victory, the remaining peasantry in the countryside—still 70 per cent of the population—found themselves corralled, isolated, marooned in their *kolkhozy*, legally discriminated against,[179] and with no option but to work and provide for their city masters. Those who murmured objection, after all, could always be sent to the burgeoning Gulag.

In that respect, one might argue that Stalin's achievement in his drive to transform *Russia* into a modern, progressive, industrialized power was in simply carrying out what his tsarist predecessors might have dreamed of but never dared do. Witte, the finance minister we most associate with the pre-1914 drive to industrialization, might, too, have talked about the need for peasants to make sacrifices in order to provide for the creation of industry. Nor was any tsarist regime, then or earlier, squeamish about the application of *katorga*—forced labour—or, for that matter, the expendability of human flesh in order to arrive at its destination. Where such regimes stopped firmly short of Stalin was in their refusal to consciously privilege the new industrial working class over their peasant base, not least when it came to food entitlements. Stalin, however, was prepared not just to do that but to practise what amounted to triage when it came to the collectivization crisis of 1932. His euphemistic reference to this in his 1935 speech referred to the necessity to economize on food 'in order to accumulate the necessary resources for the creation of industry'. Or, as he more pointedly added, in order to get rid 'of our *technological famine*'.[180] What, of course, he did not expound further upon was the intentional peasant punishment which went with it. Six years later, another leader, stymied in his efforts to transform Russia, this time through conquest, also took out his anger on the Russian people, though, in this instance, more specifically by denying bread to the rimland *cities* he had so far conquered. Those like Kiev, from autumn 1941 onwards, starved, their populations plummeting. The justification repeated throughout the Nazi military, secret police, and bureaucracy was that those so targeted were 'useless eaters' anyway and that to give them sustenance would be to deny it both to German soldiers on the Eastern Front and to the people back home.[181] For the Nazis, of course, over and beyond Jews and Roma, all Russia's Slavic peoples, Ukrainians included, were *Untermenschen*, to be subjugated, starved, or obliterated as appropriate to Germany's aims and needs. But that begs the question: were Stalin's operating premises—albeit founded on the supposed cultural rather than overtly racial backwardness of his own base population—so very different from that of his arch-rival, Hitler?

SMASHING THE EXTERNAL ENEMY: THE WAR AGAINST THE 'FIFTH COLUMN'

So Stalin had won his victory. So much so that he could joke at the Seventeenth Party Congress in early 1934 that 'there is nothing more to prove and, it seems, no one to fight'.[182] Two years later, the new 'Stalin constitution' would proclaim the victory of socialism. There was no more class struggle and no more bad bourgeois or kulak people to be brought into line. The 'most democratic' constitution in the world could afford to be magnanimous. 'Former people' could even have their citizen rights back, just like everyone else. This did not mean that all kulaks could pack up their bags, leave the special settlements, and go where they fancied. But, even for them, the embrace of the workers' and peasants' state beckoned. Everyone would be looked after, everyone could look forward to a better life.[183] Mission accomplished.

Hardly. With hindsight the only important issue for students of Stalinist violence is how the brief pause between the end of the famine and the onset of the Great Terror should be understood and interpreted. Was the Stalinist state preparing itself for a next round? Is it appropriate to talk about a pause or interregnum at all? The Russia of, say, 1935 may seem peaceful, even 'normal' when compared to

1933 or 1937, but even that relative judgement would have to be a very superficial one. For one thing, the Gulag—acronym for the Main Administration of Corrective Labour Camps—was burgeoning under the auspices of the newly reformulated secret police, no longer OGPU, but NKVD. There may have been an economic rationale to their programme, as the most infamous hyper-exploitative complex of all—the Dalstroi camps in the Arctic far east of the Kolyma peninsula—was the location of a vast cornucopia of mineral wealth, above all gold, with which to help pay for Soviet industrialization. But the tens of thousands of inmates sent there in these first years of major expansion just happened to be coming to one of the most inhospitable places on earth. Huge numbers of them simply perished from the often –45 degree Celsius temperatures on the final leg of the journey across the Sea of Okhotsk to the port of Magadan—before they could even be put to work.[184] A few years later one of these boats, caught in winter pack ice and not freed until the following spring revealed 12,000 people on board, all of whom had frozen to death.[185]

The very nature of the Gulag system, operating at the very furthest reaches or most out-of-the-way places of the Soviet empire—certainly off most people's cognitive maps—at least meant that its contribution to a mid-decade climate of fear was, to some extent, held in check. The same could not be said of what was actually repeatedly broadcast by the regime itself, in complete contradiction of its avowed declarations of normality. The threat of foreign invasion remained pervasive and, from the mid-1930s onwards, with the rise of Hitler and the flexing of Japanese muscles in the Far East, in some respects quite real. But internal cases of sabotage and disruption, while always something to do with foreign intelligence agencies—if not the Germans or Japanese, then most regularly the Polish, British, or sometimes Turkish—were equally always linked to malevolent and evil people acting from within. There were, of course, very public enemies in the form of all those supposedly embittered Old Bolsheviks such as Zinoviev and Kamenev, who had not just lost the socialist plot but who had conspired with the renegade Trotsky and the foreign vultures to bring the regime down. In 1936, according to the Soviet propaganda machine, they were to get their just deserts in the first of a series of very public show trials, with at the head of the charge-sheet their responsibility for the assassination of popular Leningrad party boss Sergei Kirov, two years previously.[186]

But was this simply a diehard core of wreckers and malcontents? Not a bit of it. On top of thousands of officials removed from their posts—*not* killed—during this period, for incompetence and corruption,[187] there was a whole slew of entirely more sinister forces constantly being flagged up to the Soviet public. At the head of Stalin's blacklist was anyone with Trotskyist sympathies. Within the economic bureaucracy alone the *vozhd* claimed that 6–9 per cent were of this inclination.[188] When, a little later, in January 1937, during a further public trial of yet more disgraced, formerly leading Bolsheviks, one of them, Karl Radek, confessed to the existence in the party of 'semi-Trotskyites, quarter-Trotskyites, one-eighth Trotskyites'.[189] The point could not have been better publicly broadcast by Stalin himself. If all roads, however, ultimately led to the exiled enemy number one, a spate of trials of usually non-party industrial experts—dating back to the Shakhty affair in 1928—was also a reminder to the public that there were those at senior technocratic levels who seemed intent on spiking or discrediting the USSR's method and pace of industrial development. The experts' supposed weapon was industrial sabotage. When a series of explosions at the Kemerovo mines in western Siberia, in September 1936, was revealed by Ezhov—appointed in their immediate wake as head of the NKVD—to be the work of Trotskyist infiltration of the Commissariat of Heavy Industry,[190] again it simply added to the burgeoning file of evidence that the USSR was under many-sided, potentially lethal, attack.

Not only were there secret agents everywhere. Their scope of operation was as wide as it was deep. Beneath the Old Bolshevik turncoat conspirators there was clearly a mass base of *sotsvredelementy* willing to do their (and foreign powers') bidding. Far from having seen the error of their ways, reprieved or simply dissembling kulaks remained as their most probable strike force from within this larger group of delinquents. But then kulaks could also be nationalists, doubly intent on disintegrating the Soviet entity. Ever since the arrest of Volga communist Sultan-Galiev in 1928, on grounds of inciting Muslim-Tatar secession, there had been a steady spate of 'unmaskings' of supposedly loyal national communists. 'We can always provide evidence provided he wears a Caucasian hat!' an NKVD chief in the region is said to have quipped to an inexperienced assistant when the latter protested that he had no proof with which to make arrests.[191]

Yet, from the late 1920s onwards, the danger of national breakaway was considered by the state as no laughing matter. Especially when it came to the rimlands. Soviet sensitivity to the supposed threat from these areas was expressed as far back as 1923, when the entire Soviet land and sea frontier was demarcated into variable but 'increasingly high security border strips', where secret police powers of search and seizure were unlimited.[192] By the mid-1930s, however, the supposedly colour-blind workers' and peasants' state was increasingly deporting swathes of border people on transparently ethnic grounds. Repeated eructations, in 1935 and then in 1936, of tens of thousands of Poles and Germans from the border zones of Kiev and Vinnitsa *oblasti*, were clear indicators of this trend. Another was a sweep of a whole range of indigenous people—Finns, Estonians, and Latvians in particular—from in and around Leningrad: itself clearly within a border zone.[193] The proposition that such ethnic populations were seeking common cause with the military and intelligence wings of the neighbouring nation state to which they owed their real, genuine allegiance, was underscored in a December 1933 plenum announcement portentously declaring that 'the remnants of the bourgeois-kulak and nationalist elements of Karelia have united with the interventionist circles of Fascist Finland with the goal of annexing Karelia and uniting her to Finland under the slogan of "Great Finland" extending all the way to the Urals'.[194] Though the supposed cross-border machinations of the Finns was clearly a matter of particular, almost feverish, anxiety, as it was so close to the heart of Soviet power,[195] other groups, in the 'quiet' mid-1930s, also found themselves under intense suspicion and NKVD surveillance. The Tatars of the Crimea, for instance, were adjudged through their national behaviour to be threatening the USSR, supposedly by encouraging

Turkish intervention. As for the Germans, in a late 1934 decree, they too, across the range of their agricultural colonies in the rimlands and beyond, were deemed by the Politburo to be responsible for harbouring 'counter-revolutionary fascist elements': mass arrests and show trials following.[196] Nowhere—at least not before 1937—did this lead to blanket ethnic deportations. By that time, however, non-Russian ethnicity, especially that of some rimland groups, had become an undoubted marker of unreliability and potential danger.

*

Did Stalin then *know* that the river he supposedly was navigating had rapids ahead? Indeed, did he consciously engineer matters so that, from mid-1937, the aim was to pass directly over them? There is a strong tendency, especially within Russian scholarship, to confirm this viewpoint. Roy Medvedev, for instance, argues that Stalin's behaviour at this time was one of 'great self-control', guided by 'clear-cut political...considerations and calculations'.[197] What has become known as the *Ezhovshchina* was thus really the *Stalinshchina*, a controlled exercise organized by a dictator with clear strategic objectives. Oleg Khlevniuk is another leading Moscow-based expert who sees the Great Terror as fundamentally about Stalin's 'careful manipulation of the equilibrium in relations between...party and...secret police'.[198] Having cut the first down to size by means of the NKVD, he then simply turned the party tables on Ezhov and his closest echelons, and thereby brought the relationship between the two pillars of his rule back into balance, but now under his even firmer tutelage.

A strikingly revisionist view, however, advanced by Robert Thurston and others, proposes that the rapids came up unexpectedly and without warning; the pilot was far from properly in charge of his boat, with the result that crew and passengers were plunged into a chaotic unknown in a state of unadulterated panic.[199] If this sort of analysis is correct it certainly might help explain why the consequences in 1937–8—the mass operations—went far beyond a bloodletting confined to an essentially closed political elite, albeit with the same caveats about whether this can be described as a prima facie case of genocide—or of something akin—even while peculiar to the Soviet (anti-)system.

To these possibilities we might add a third. This, as Sheila Fitzpatrick has expounded, would eschew a reading of the Great Terror as either unitary process or 'simple phenomena' but instead as 'a number of related but discrete phenomena'.[200] What Fitzpatrick thus points to is the necessity for a synthetic analysis which might meld the ordered, and certainly murderous, intentionalism of Stalin with a set of contingencies which did not simply throw him radically off course but led to a wholly unprecedented eighteen-month spasm of violence: in which arrests increased by 700 per cent, and actual executions a staggering 315.8 times.[201]

The point, perhaps, is that without understanding the course Stalin appears to have consciously set himself it is well-nigh impossible to understand the radical deviation from it. Or, more prosaically, while we cannot by this account explain the sudden appearance of the rapids we are at least alerted to the fact that the boat had been quite intentionally set on course down a river already in full spate. At the heart of this trajectory was a Stalinist project to eliminate the many political rivals who had crossed his path in the previous twenty years of Bolshevik hegemony. The psychological dimension to this urge—important as it clearly is—need not in itself unduly detain us. We can read Stalin quite simply as a supremely calculating person who, having clambered to the top of an already ruthless, dictatorial oligarchy, could not rest while active individuals who could not only make at least as strong a claim to the ultimate prize as he, but who might at some stage contemplate or actively challenge him for it, remained alive. Nor, in terms pointing more closely to the nature of his psychotic disturbance, could the inner Joseph Dzhugashvili put aside real or imagined slights which had necessarily beset his otherwise carefully calibrated rise to power in the 1920s. From this perspective, like a modern Ivan Grozny, Stalin was both a power-obsessed megalomaniac for whom possession of the throne was all, and an 'emperor' inwardly terrified that his monomaniacal pretensions to absolute rule would be exposed not only as illegitimate but as a preposterous travesty of the—in this case Bolshevik—truth. Hence, the obsession with Trotsky, on account both of the latter's coruscating intellectual barbs and of his freedom from afar, which he could mobilize into a wholly alternative Marxist-Leninist camp. Hence too, Stalin's overwhelming fear that he was surrounded by closet acolytes of this tendency, who, given half an opportunity, would all acclaim the exiled leader.

Stalin's own counter-strategy is equally notable for the calculated purposefulness with which he set out to unmask and then publicly parade the 'omnipresent conspiracy' against himself.[202] The very fact that Stalin initially circumvented the body most obviously suited to this role—Iagoda's NKVD—in favour of Ezhov—from 1935 head of the Party Control Commission, the inspectorate with oversight of abuses of power in the economy, party, and government—is itself evidence of Stalin's cunning. Ezhov was an apparently one-dimensional if entirely obnoxious Stalin *apparatchik*, yet had at the same time a singular reputation as a relentless, utterly zealous harrier of bureaucrats, experts, and 'bourgeois' specialists who failed to adapt themselves to the requirements of the Great Turn.[203] By appointing Ezhov as his creature, and with a precisely timetabled task of reopening the party files and thereby uncovering the alignments which linked apparently disparate groupings and social circles within the elite to a central conspiratorial hub, Stalin sought to prove to a public at home and abroad that it was he, head of the legitimate socialist state, who was threatened by 'an array of evil forces'. In one stroke the *vozhd* had his justification for whatever action he might deem necessary for its sure defence. Those, like Bukharin, who recognized the stratagem for what it actually was—the 'medieval principle', as he put it at his own 1938 trial, extrapolated by Moshe Lewin to mean the Soviet equivalent of 'witch trials and the inquisitorial persecution of schismatics'—were already too browbeaten or implicated in the alleged conspiracy web to do anything to unmask the unmaskers.[204] Indeed, by early 1937, with the first two of the show trials successfully completed and the 'guilty' dispatched (this, in itself, a major departure for a party so outwardly conscious of the dangers of fratricide) Stalin was poised to publicly invest himself with the full powers of life and death.

This duly happened at the late February–early March 1937 party plenum in Moscow, with several hundred of its leading figures in attendance. Ezhov's podium denunciation of one of them—his NKVD predecessor, Iagoda—for failing 'to protect the party and country from the threat of political sabotage', not least from those 'diversionaries and spies who hide behind the mask of loyalty to Soviet power',[205] paved the way for Stalin to deliver his own broadside of even more withering proportions. At the end of the plenum the party elite could be left in no doubt that Trotskyite agents of German–Japanese counter-intelligence had infiltrated party, NKVD, and industry alike, while Bukharinites, whether or not they were in direct cahoots with the Trotskyite conspirators, were themselves equally accused of being wreckers, diversionists, and spies. The leaders of the Ukrainian SSR were also singled out as guilty of 'incorrect leadership'.[206] That a figure such as Postyshev, elevated by Stalin to the Ukrainian satrapy for his staunch party loyalty, was now being branded a potential enemy of the people could only imply that the anti-state set of conspiracies had penetrated the entire apparatus. That such accusations were intended for public consumption, moreover, is made very clear by the full text of Stalin's speech being widely published in the press at the end of March, and succeeded by a brochure later that year.[207] That this manner of media broadcast implied a form of (almost Mao-like) appeal over the heads of the bureaucracy to the demos is doubly extraordinary in the degree to which it seemed to invite the grass roots to agree with the *vozhd* that his own party could not be trusted and was rotten through and through. Only lock, stock, and barrel replacement with truly reliable proletarians could save the day.

The consequences of this aspect of the Great Terror are infamous. Indeed, they were at the core of Khrushchev's 1956 denunciation of Stalin's crimes at a closed session of the Twentieth Party Congress, three years after the latter's death. Khrushchev stated that of 1,966 party delegates who attended the Congress of Victors in 1934, only fifty-nine returned to the Eighteenth Congress five years later.[208] A whole swathe of the Old Bolshevik faithful had, by then, been eliminated—nearly all in 1937–8. They included staunch pro-Stalinists and individuals like the regional collectivization enforcer M. M. Khatayevich. Within the non-Russian republics, the rimland ones in particular, such outcomes were even more devastating for the party itself. In the recently created Chechen-Ingush republic, for instance, the NKVD operation on 31 July 1937 to clean out the local apparatus not only left the region entirely bereft of an administrative class but ensured that the secret police themselves had to take over running it until an alternative indigenous echelon could be imagined (or rather forced) into existence.[209] In a very similar vein, the extinguishing of the Ukrainian Politburo—only 3 out of 102 central committee members or candidates survived the purge—left a hole so gaping in the executive, not to mention further down the line in administrative and technical positions, that, again, it had to be filled by parachuting into post either NKVD personnel or very obviously Moscow appointees, Ukrainian or not. Interestingly, the new first party secretary was one Nikita Khrushchev.[210]

The elitocide element of the Great Terror is thus, for all its gargantuan proportions, at least on one level quite interpretable, even understandable. It represents

an entirely conscious cleaning out from the ruling party, administrative, and economic *nomenklatura* of anybody whose position did not owe itself to Stalin, and
their replacement by protégés—in effect 'yes men'—who could be counted on to
do his bidding. This certainly spelt the end of a sophisticated, intellectual, worldly
stratum of Bolshevik 'society', traceable to pre-revolutionary days. It could hardly
be otherwise when almost the entire Leningrad party echelon—the crème de la
crème of the Bolshevik milieu—was swept away.[211] Not, of course, that their
urbanity had prevented such types from supporting, participating in, or at the
very least acquiescing in the smashing of the peasantry. In this sense, the fact that
the new ruling class was a wholly cruder entity—younger, educated under Soviet
auspices, and hence more attuned to Stalinist method—is beside the point. Rather,
the problem is twofold. In the first place, while we are clearly speaking of tens of
thousands killed in these 'familiar' *nomenklatura* purges, they cannot account for
the many times that number eradicated—without occupational replacement—from
other, much more lowly, strata of the population.[212] In the second place, it does not
explain the sudden take-off in this wider wave of killings which—following hot
on the heels of the already snowballing elitocide from late spring—exploded onto
the scene with a spate of Politburo and NKVD decrees in the high summer of
1937.

To get to the heart of this broader sequence does not necessarily mean jettison-
ing its close relationship to the party purges but perhaps involves unravelling the
latter's origins in a slightly other than one-dimensional way. For instance, it is
agreed by commentators coming at the issue from different perspectives that the
February–March plenum represented a major watershed in Stalin's accumulation
of personal power.[213] Not only can one imagine that the majority of delegates actually present were quaking in their boots, but that anyone in the party cognisant of
where things were heading would now have understood that the situation was
reaching the point of no return. *Unless*, of course, they took matters into their own
hands. Is this the moment, then, when opposition from within the party hatched
into the embryo of a *real* plot to remove Stalin?

Why does most commentary on this period treat this notion as implausible?
After all, Stalin's conviction that Trotsky *had* had high-level sympathizers within
the party, especially in agencies such as the internationalist Comintern, was not
just a figment of his imagination. The Trotskyite *Bulletin of the Opposition*, though
produced outside Russia, had been far too well informed on the quotidian state of
Soviet affairs not to suggest a steady stream of information coming from high-level
sources.[214] Trotsky's son, Lev Sedov, is often taken to have been the interlocutor
between his father and clandestine supporters travelling to and from Russia on
official business.[215] True, the internal party dissidents hardly amounted to a coherent grouping, especially after all the trials, tribulations, and ultimate elimination of
known oppositionists. Even so, the notion of a 'reserve centre'—an *alternative*
leadership which might have taken control in the event of Stalin's demise—may
not have been solely the subject of NKVD fabrication. Especially in early 1937. In
the face of a growing war scare, particularly, at that moment, coming from Japan,
surviving old guard Bolsheviks would have remembered the once revered war

commissar's call from ten years earlier—with, at that time, the potentiality of Polish invasion in view—for exactly such a grouping.[216] And it is difficult to imagine that such trenchant criticisms would not have had some privately uttered resonance within that highly prized and protected element of the Soviet apparatus: its military. Look to other countries, Nazi Germany in particular, in its period of high war emergency, and the idea of at least a section of its senior military becoming involved in plots against Hitler—on grounds, above all, of pragmatism and competence—is entirely accepted and understood. To be sure, in Russia, the communist party certainly had a very profound aversion to what it called Bonapartism. But where else, in spring 1937, could it hope to turn, firstly to neutralize the NKVD, and then decapitate the Stalin entourage?

Was there then a growing consonance of interests between dissident elements of both party and military? Was there, as Isaac Deutscher has firmly pronounced, a plan for a coup d'état, in which the leading plotter was none other than Marshal Tukhachevsky?[217] To over-speculate on the motives or indeed organizational readiness of the coupists is, in some ways, immaterial to our discussion. Or even, for that matter, whether the plot *really* existed at all. The story in itself is certainly an extraordinarily Byzantine one, not least because there was at least one other foreign intelligence agency—Heydrich's SS—with a direct interest in confirming its veracity for the benefit of the NKVD.[218] What *does* ultimately matter brings us back once again to the issue of 'psychological truth'. Stalin, in April or early May 1937, had information in front of him indicative of a military plot whose causation lay not only in the plotters' fears of being exposed for their contacts with Trotskyists, White Russian generals, and foreign intelligence agencies but was founded equally on their supposition that in the event of war a more competent leadership than that of the Stalin clique was absolutely necessary for the USSR's survival. Which meant, from Stalin's point of view, not only stamping out the coup (real or confabulated) from top to bottom, but stamping out the insinuation of not being either ready, or capable, of dealing with a *genuine* emergency. Put more starkly, while up to this point, it had been Stalin calling the shots in an orchestrated and entirely instrumentalized campaign against the party, the post-plenum events point to an overtly, if desperately, dynamic response from a largely unexpected quarter—the military—in turn bouncing the Kremlin into an entirely reactive, indeed, defensive set of countermeasures.

To be sure, the fact that no coup—as far as one is aware—took place suggests the NKVD was highly successful in its own pre-emptive strike. The immediate consequence was a hastily organized trial of the most implicated generals, followed by a cascade of equally rapid executions, the death toll ranging from possibly 20,000 to as high as 50,000 military officers—a percentage of Great Terror casualties notably greater than that for any other elite professional grouping.[219] But arguably, having been thrown off course once by a radical contingency, there was no reason why the regime could not be thrown again. In June, a report from Sergei Mironov, head of the west Siberian NKVD, claimed to have found evidence of a series of underground organizations running under the umbrella of something described as ROVS—the Russian All-Military Union—which was itself working closely with Japanese intelligence services. 'A revolt and a seizure of power' by the former would be timed to coincide with a Japanese invasion, the report stated. In itself, this was a case of almost standard NKVD suggestibility, combined perhaps with the zealotry of another provincial secret police chief 'working towards' the *vozhd*. But, in the context of the already massively heightened fears and tensions of preceding months, the report's findings were well-nigh explosive. Here was evidence of linkage between the émigré White generals in ROVS—to whom, in the Kremlin's book, the Red Army military coupists were also in hock—and other foreign military powers, in this particular instance, a Japanese imperial army limbering up for a major onslaught on northern China.[220] Later that year, in early November, at a Kremlin reception on the twentieth anniversary of the Bolshevik revolution, Stalin gave full vent to his anger at this turn of events, claiming that leading oppositionists had been planning exactly such a territorial disintegration of the USSR in league with a slew of predatory foreign powers. Anybody who attempted such a thing, Stalin declared to the assembled dignitaries, whether Old Bolshevik or not, would suffer not only their own annihilation but that of their entire clan.[221]

On one level, this trope of a fifth column from within prising open the national gates to invasion from without provided all the ammunition needed for repeated post facto justifications for the Great Terror. Molotov, from his dotage in the 1970s, was quite candid on this score, proposing that the issue was not only one of known Trotskyists and Rightists but of 'those who did not firmly follow the line and in whom there was no confidence that at a critical moment, they would not desert, and become, so to speak, part of the fifth column'. In other words, as a precautionary principle in a time of national emergency, anybody half suspect had to go, even if 'one or two extra heads were chopped off'.[222] During the actual Second World War itself, even foreign commentators were prone to accept this verdict. Sir John Maynard, a British specialist on Russia, for instance, in 1942 remarked, 'However much falsity of detail there may be, the trials of the leading personages in 1936–38 were substantially justified by facts: and were probably the means of saving the USSR from an attempted revolution which would have given to the Nazi government an earlier opportunity'.[223]

But if this tells us much about the degree to which Stalinist apologetics came to be believed *as if they were true* by their creators as well as onlookers, returning to the Mironov report takes us much closer to the *real* connection between the fear of a foreign-inspired insurrection and the mass killings which followed. Mironov proposed that the foot soldiers who would initiate the revolt in Siberia would be a mix of bandits and convicts but, more especially, the more than 200,000 exiled kulaks in settlements spread across the Narym and Kuzbass areas of Siberia.[224] A bad element of society which had supposedly been marginalized, emasculated, and pacified was now being written back into the script once more as part of a military equation. Nor was this just another recrudescence of a distant *Antonovshchina* memory: Narym had been the site of a quite genuine week-long uprising by kulak 'special settlers' back in July 1931.[225] Six years on, the regime's response was almost instantaneous. A Politburo directive signed personally by Stalin on 2 July 1937 named kulaks, either in the settlements or who had returned home, as among the primary ringleaders of the counter-revolutionary conspiracy uncovered in western Siberia. The directive's implications, however, went far beyond this single region. The next day Ezhov set in motion a massive Union-wide round-up of 'hostile elements', nearly 76,000 of whom were slated for immediate execution. The operation 'to repress former kulaks, criminals and other anti-Soviet elements', otherwise better known by its 'top secret' order number 00447, was about to explode into action.[226]

We can hardly treat this response as some reasonable prophylactic measure to nip an incipient security threat in the bud. But is it the piece of the jigsaw that suggests that the regime's increasingly paranoid inability to distinguish not only between the real and the confabulated but between cause and effect had finally tipped it over into a frenzied spasm of bloodletting? Two factors strongly suggest this to be the case. Firstly, as David Shearer pithily puts it, the 2 July resolution 'on which order 00447 was based, seemed to arise out of nowhere'.[227] Before this moment there is nothing to suggest that the regime had been discussing a major campaign of mass murder directed *outside* the apparatus. This, then, speaks of a rupture with the intended trajectory. Secondly, the element of repeat violence, against those parts of the wider population who were meant to be already pulverized or exterminated, provides the 'never again' signature of a perpetrator now focused on 'a bloody, final reckoning'.[228] One grisly symptom of this radical new direction is the killings which took place following a further Ezhov order in late August, for the elimination of the most counter-revolutionary elements within the Gulag. There appears, to have been at least one specially designated killing site—a brick factory in the Vorkuta complex of camps in the Arctic Komi region—where known political oppositionists had already been dispatched at the behest of special Kremlin-authorized NKVD commissions the previous autumn. Here—at least on one selected site along the line of BAMlag railway construction camps in the Soviet far east, certainly in the original Gulag complex on the Arctic Solovetsky archipelago, as well in the Kolyma region, and very probably in the range of Gulag camps elsewhere—the autumn and winter of 1937 saw NKVD-organized selections and mass executions.[229] How many died in this 'purge within a purge' is not certain.[230] Operation order 00447 specified 10,000, but in a new surge of executions in spring 1938 this number seems to have been exceeded threefold.[231] Yet what must equally shock is the very idea that among the most wretched and defeated of the inmates of these vastly out-of-the-way high-security camps anybody might conceive of the existence of a tangible threat to this or any other regime.

Ezhov clearly, however, was in earnest 'once and for all' to get rid of 'the entire gang of anti-Soviet elements'.[232] This is how he himself described the purpose of 00447 operations. Beyond the camps, what this particularly amounted to is what Lynne Viola has summarized as a second dekulakization.[233] The NKVD were put to round-the-clock work hunting down and arresting 'kulak enemies', not only in the special settlements, but those who had escaped the round-ups in 1930 and 1931, as well as those who had been taken but later released or amnestied. Major sweeps of communication hubs, especially railway depot areas, became—as in Ottoman Anatolia in 1915—a significant feature in this supposed race to defeat the fifth column insurrectionists and saboteurs. Alongside kulaks they embraced all manner of dubious social elements, ranging from the petty criminal and marginal to all those former White army officers and enlistees, political opponents and members of the clergy, *ulema*, or religious sects who had gone to ground, taken on new identities, and somehow survived in the interstices of a surveillance-ridden Soviet society. But whether in countryside or city, special settlements or labour camps, the most significant feature of these round-ups makes them very different from 1930–1: of some 650,000 people arrested in this single operation, most were not automatically sent to camps. On the contrary, around 320,000—*almost half*—were executed.[234] Yet that is not the sum total of fatalities as a consequence of the mass operations. According to official statistics NKVD arrests ran to 1,575,259 people, through to the winding down of the *Ezhovshchina* in November 1938. Only a fraction of these were released. A much larger percentage were sent to the Gulag. The remainder—681,692—were executed. Indeed, according to some recent studies of the data on executions, the figure may be higher still.[235]

To be sure, while we have here a clear case of state mass murder of a swathe of its own population, we might at this juncture wish to note features which do not conform to the usual contours of *genocide*. The very fact that NKVD arrest led to the interrogation of each and every suspect, involving as standard procedure psychological and/or physical torture, speaks of a modus operandi not well suited to rapid mass slaughter. The torture, of course, was highly purposeful: the aim was not only to extract confessions of guilt but also to force people to implicate others. Thus, as each individual prisoner reached their inevitable breaking point—most obviously through sleep deprivation on top of humiliation, beatings, and threats, usually directed at family members—other people were named. The snowballing consequences are rather obvious. They also, inevitably, gave to the regime's fevered conspiracy narrative an air of self-fulfilling prophecy, while, paradoxically, doing almost the exact opposite of resolving the apparent crisis. The more the Politburo became convinced of the scale of the conspiracy, the more the dragnet had to be widened, and the longer became the timescale for completion of the campaign, as it drifted from its initial four months towards its actual fourteen.[236]

Again, the extraordinarily time-consuming Soviet bureaucratic process, with its own peculiar conception of doing things, including mass murder, correctly and by the book, proved a further brake to the rapid expedition of campaign. Superficially, the granting of extraordinary powers from the centre to a troika of *oblast*, *krai*, or republic officials—usually consisting of party secretary, procurator, and local NKVD head—was meant to facilitate and indeed streamline the in camera process. However, in the case of the so-called *natsoperatsii*—national operations—which came hot on the heels of 00447, the names of those found guilty of category-one crimes and thus sentenced to be executed had then to be sent to Moscow, more specifically to Ezhov, for signature, and to Stalin or another member of the inner governing circle, for countersignature. Again, to be sure, lists of such names were bound up into albums to expedite the process. The fact that signing albums was then delegated to much more lowly departmental heads in the central *apparat* in itself was not intended to lead to a bureaucratic paper chase. But, equally, it is clear that such micro-managed control from the Kremlin led to major overcrowding of regional prisons and holding centres, while the local authorities awaited a decision from the centre. This particular logjam in the system was finally broken in September 1938 when the album procedure was abolished and new special *troiki* given the unusual power to clear up the backlog without further clearance from Moscow.[237]

This is not to propose NKVD and party officials in the localities were disallowed any initiative. They could, for instance, request additional quotas of those to be repressed and were frequently given the green light for this. Barry McLoughlin, for instance, highlights the case of one comrade Gorbach, appointed just before Operation 00447 officially began, as head of Omsk NKVD. He petitioned Moscow to have his 'shooting' quota raised from an initial 479 to 8,000(!) on grounds of the 'Stakhanovite work practices of his men', and played the same argument again when he was elevated to NKVD head for western Siberia.[238] Gorbach got his go-ahead from Stalin no less, but his clear efficiency at ratcheting up the execution statistics again underscores two further aspects of the mass operations which certainly run against the grain of genocide 'norms'. In the first place, while the Nazis were equally obsessed with compiling the numbers of those killed, they certainly did not operate on the basis of prescribed quotas as the route to solving the problem. Soviet implementation of the quota method can certainly be read as a quintessential example of the banalizing of evil. Conquest notes, for instance, the following telegraphic order from Ezhov to the NKVD chief in Frunze, capital of Kirgizia: '"You are charged with exterminating 10,000 enemies of the people. Report result by signal". The form of reply was "In reply to yours of . . . the following enemies of the people have been shot", followed by a numbered list'.[239]

This 'figures mania', as it had been aptly described,[240] certainly has its own peculiarly morbid fascination. As if, by settling on a given number of people to be eliminated, one could magic the underlying problem away. Its inherent flaw was that if it failed to work the only obvious default position was to increase the quota figure once again. Why, for instance in January 1938, when, to all intents and purposes, the 00447 operation seemed to be being intentionally wound down by the Politburo, did they then suddenly wrench it back into an overdrive—this time with a 5:1 emphasis on category-one over category-two sentences—in other words, 48,000 death penalties as opposed to 9,200 to be gulaged?[241] The expert commentators remain largely mystified.[242] In a sense this does take us back, albeit uneasily, onto more familiar genocide terrain, where a panic response to a crisis contingency (in this case determining whether it was well grounded or not is largely immaterial) leads to an ever more frenzied spasm of bloodletting. But then one would not expect as its denouement (in the autumn and winter of 1938–9) the murder of comrade Gorbach and most of his ilk.

This, then, is that second element of the Great Terror which radically subverts a standard genocide script. The key perpetrators, Ezhov at their head, were ultimately as vulnerable to elimination as those they themselves had targeted—in the process hopelessly blurring the line between 'perpetrators' and 'victims'. Again, we might wish to read this in a number of ways. One might be as a special kind of Russian morality tale in which the most enthusiastic mass killers (or, alternatively, those most fearful of failing to demonstrate their vigilance in the face of the 'enemy') were—deservedly or otherwise—hoist by their own petard. But then the very idea that secret policemen, alongside poets, writers, artists, and entirely ordinary people, could be consumed in this manner might suggest an orgy of violence without rhyme or reason, save perhaps as a method of inducing population-wide terror for its own sake.

Yet this too remains entirely unsatisfactory as a conclusion. While it was possible to be caught up quite stochastically in the *Ezhovshchina*, it is also quite clear that large swathes of the population remained relatively untouched by it, and, indeed, firmly believed that arrests—where they had occurred at all—had nothing to do with them. The popular saying of the time, 'He's not a party member and he's not a Jew, so why has he been arrested?'[243] has more than a little pertinence to the broad base of Soviet society in this period, if only anecdotally. Where the anecdote falls down, or more exactly suggests the myopia of those who did not know, or chose not to know, what was really happening around them is most amply demonstrated in the case of the *natsoperatsii*.

*

We have already seen that the take-off of the mass operations aspect of the Great Terror in the summer of 1937 was precipitated by a security alert (real or imagined) in which foreign agencies were purported to be working hand in glove with a range of fifth column elements within the Soviet Union—all, in various ways, supposedly intent on its dissolution. Even before Operation 00447 had received its go-ahead at the end of July, Stalin had, just a few days previously, kicked into touch a separate NKVD directive, no. 00439: geared towards the Union-wide arrest of Germans working in sensitive military and public installations. Ezhov's subsequent directive for the operation cited the combined role of German military headquarters and the Gestapo in organizing a large network of spies and wreckers whose efforts were to be focused on the sabotage of defence industries, railways, and 'other strategic sectors of the national economy'.[244] Hot on the heels of this directive appeared another, in early August, whose target this time was much more all-embracing: this alleged a 30,000-strong spy network operating to the malign orders of the so-called Polish Military Organisation (POV)—again working in tandem with the intelligence department of the Polish general staff. On this occasion Ezhov's order no. 00485 was unusually (and quite extraordinarily) supplemented by a sealed letter to regional NKVD chiefs, setting out in no less than thirty closely detailed pages the scope and scale of the supposed POV operation in Russia all the way back to the revolution, and citing not only the organization's complete control over the KPP, the Polish Communist Party, but its infiltration of all sections of the Soviet *apparat*, the diplomatic corps, Red Army, Comintern, collective farms, defence industries, and, indeed, the NKVD itself.[245]

From the more tentative and limited scope of the 'German operation', its Polish successor thus carried with it a charge-sheet against 'Polish spies', which put practically any Pole living in Russia—native or foreign-born—under suspicion of espionage and, hence, treachery. The regional NKVD chief, with responsibility for Moscow, went as far as getting his agents to scour the Moscow telephone directory for 'Polish last names'.[246] More ominously still, Operation 00485, while it dwarfed similar national operations, in both framing and self-justification, nevertheless became the model for a succession of others: Finnish, Estonian, Rumanian, Bulgarian, Greek, and Chinese from October, followed, in turn, by a major Latvian operation put into operation in early December, with further round-ups of Afghan and Iranian 'suspects' not being fully operationalized until the following February.[247]

It is easy to read too much into this new trajectory. The operations were *not* in themselves intended to be assaults on the entirety of ethnic or national groups. Indeed, until May 1938, the NKVD data on the national affiliation of prisoners was not yet fully standardized, and then more as a consequence of a new state directive which required the nationality of parents to be indicated in all new passports and official documents. If, from this point onwards, a particular national background in itself could be grounds for suspicion, the initial targeting of individuals—in line with the prime *natsoperatsii* objective to smash alleged foreign spy rings—was much more about whether individuals had had 'contact with abroad' and, more specifically, a hostile country.[248]

In the case of the 'Polish operation' what was thus critically at stake was whether the person under suspicion had had some connection with Polish state or society, regardless of whether he or she was actually ethnically Polish or not. This necessarily put under the spotlight often very poor Polish Galician refugees as well as deliberate immigrants (both of which were now embraced under negative NKVD nomenclature as 'defectors') who had crossed the border eastwards in the post-1917 turmoil, just as it also did Polish leftists who had been exchanged for Catholic priests after the Polish–Soviet War. Equally, however, it could mean Russian Red Army men held in captivity by the Poles during that war, or, entirely more banally, someone who might have been a cleaner or a messenger in a Polish embassy or consulate, an amateur radio operator, a philatelist with Polish stamps in their collection, or a Belorussian or Ukrainian whose parents had passed themselves off as Polish so that their children might study in a 'better' local district Polish-language school.[249] It was no coincidence that large numbers of those arrested came from the western border zones. However, while 70 per cent of those ultimately tried and executed in the entire course of the Polish operation through to November 1938 were ethnic Poles (whether born in the USSR or not), Belorussians and Ukrainians, and, to a more limited extent, Russians and Jews, made up most of the rest.[250]

By the same token, in the 'German operation', while most German citizens working under contract in the USSR were expelled, 39 per cent of all those arrested (again whether Soviet or German-born ethnic Germans or not) were domiciled in the Ukraine, more particularly in the border areas—representing a figure in percentage terms closely in line with the 'Polish operation'. Yet Germans in the Volga ASSR—actually the main single German concentration in the country—were hardly affected at all.[251] Nevertheless, if this suggests an emerging geographical plot in which being a member of a particular national group certainly exacerbated one's chances of being arrested and subsequently killed, the so-called Kharbinsty Operation is a potent reminder that the *natsoperatsii* were not, at heart, about seeking ethnic enemies as such, but rather alleged fifth columnists of *any* hue. The misfortune of those caught up under order no. 00593, the third largest of the national operations, promulgated in September 1937, was that they were primarily Russian engineers, railwaymen, and other personnel who had operated the Soviet-owned and controlled Chinese–Manchurian railway centred on Kharbin until 1935, when it was sold to Japan, and they resettled in Russia. But, by summer 1937, Japan represented a major political–military threat, a reminder in itself that it was not just the rimlands facing west and south which were keeping the Politburo on tenterhooks. The fate of the Kharbintsy thus hinged not on who they were, but where they had been; with their 'Russianness' no protection at all against their Soviet re-identification as creatures of the Japanese and, consequently, another discrete category of 'enemy nation'.[252]

Being in the wrong place at the wrong time could also, of course, affect genuine ethnic aggregates. The one blanket national *deportation* of a whole people in this period involved close to 172,000 Koreans, deported in some 124 train echelons from the far east to Kazakhstan and Uzbekistan, following the ratcheting up of an originally more partial Politburo security directive to this effect in August 1937.[253] Like the Kharbintsy Operation, the ethnic cleansing of the Koreans was precipitated, in part, by anxieties that the Koreans might act on behalf of Tokyo (Korea, after all, was Japanese-occupied territory) in the event of a new Russo–Japanese war. The removal of the Koreans as a precautionary measure actually had a certain level of rational plausibility to it. With mounting evidence that war was imminent, the Japanese were themselves deporting Koreans from their side of border.[254] Moreover, in a strikingly comparable instance, in the wake of Pearl Harbor the entire Japanese-American population of the US West Coast was deported to concentration camps in western desert regions on the grounds that they 'could not be trusted to refrain from sabotage, divulging military secrets and other practices intended to aid and abet Japan in its war against the United States'.[255]

The fact that in neither the US nor the Soviet instance there existed any intent to exterminate the deportees could hardly have offered consolation for the misery and hardship both sets of people suffered. Though in the Korean case they were meant to be provided with logistical support to enable them to start again as *perselentsy* (agricultural settlers)—supposedly distinguishing them from the negative 'kulak' status of special settlers (*spetsperselentsy*)—conditions of cattle-truck transit and lack of facilities on arrival decimated them to the tune of some 40,000 people: around 23.2 per cent of their total number in the first year.[256] Other ethnic groups qua groups also suffered in a similar vein, albeit in smaller and more partial measure. Some 1,325 Kurds in Armenia, Azerbaijan, and, more particularly, the autonomous republic of Nakhichevan, for instance, were deported to Kazakhstan and western Siberia on grounds of their 'unreliability'. The sites of these people's former habitus became, instead, 'special restricted areas'. Forty such zones—along almost the entirety of the USSR's Central Asian and southern rim—were created, with the consequent closure of schools, village councils, collective farms, newspapers, and other 'national' institutions.[257]

However, for all these peoples' travails, and indeed the genocidal implications, the methods do not display the entirely more lethal tendencies we associate with the national operations. This separate subset of the Great Terror thus offers a pattern of destruction which, far from being stochastic, confirms a common repeat motif: state anxiety usually combined with acute antagonism against *particular* rimland ethnic communities. It is important to note that most non-Russian nationalities were not subject, at this moment, to this ethos or rationale. The very high incidence of Turkmens killed as a result of 00447 and related directives certainly offers an exception to the rule, but one which tells us a great deal more about the enthusiasm of the region's NKVD, in both overfulfilling its quota and killing prisoners 'without due process', than anything else. In Moscow's book these were 'excesses' which themselves demanded investigation and censure.[258] There were no national operations in Turkmeniya. Nor were there in border republics such as Armenia or Georgia where we might, perhaps, have expected them. To be sure, as in nearly all other republics and regions these suffered their share both of the general terror and the more specific purging of the party apparatus. As in 1932, so again in 1937 Stalin's henchmen—this time Zhdanov, Andreev, and Malenkov in particular—worked overtime, scouring the expanse of the USSR in order to carry out the great leader's writ.[259] But it was neither in all border republics, nor indeed against those communities such as Chechens, Ingush, Karachai, and others who just a few years later would be collectively indicted as 'enemies of the people' that the 1937–8 national operations were directed.

What gave to the hard core of *natsoperatsii* their specific bite was an implication of irredentism. In other words, the charge against alleged fifth columnists was not simply one of working for a foreign power, even one intent on the USSR's destruction—as in the German- or Japanese-orientated Kharbinsty operations—though clearly this was bad enough. What was rather at the heart of the matter was an accusation of being ethnically attached or, alternatively, in some other way culturally or politically inclined towards, a neighbouring country whose original sin lay either in having wrested its sovereignty in whole or in part at the expense of *imperial* Russia—hence the black mark against Poles, Balts, Finns. Or, in the case of Bulgarian-Macedonians, Rumanians, Greeks, Chinese, and Afghans, of being associated with countries which *ought* to have owed their existence to Russian patronage and should have continued to remain in its orbit.[260] This would suggest that underlying the reactive and highly contingent origins of the national operations was something more profound at work which actually links us back to Stalin's proclamation of statist-imperial mission at the very outset of this chapter. By 1937, the *vozhd* was clearly thinking of himself as a great Russian leader not only within the historic, territorial domains of tsardom but on a much wider world stage.[261] One obvious signal of this new direction was the USSR's involvement as chief military and political supporter to the beleaguered Spanish republic in its war against the Mussolini- and Hitler-backed Francoist insurgents. Yet the immediate arena for the securing of this ambition was Russia's hinterlands which, in the context of the heightened *European* tensions of 1937–8, could only mean, more specifically, the 'Lands Between'.

We are thus back with a jolt at the problem of the rimlands, or rather, the inherent instability of projected geostrategic agendas in regions where the indigenous populations, for whatever reason of ethnic idiosyncrasy or contested loyalty, failed to play their prescribed role in the authorized script. The very notion of a 'fifth column' had arisen out of the partially Soviet-backed, last-ditch—but actually successful—defence of republican Madrid being potentially undermined by Franco sympathizers within the city. Stalin's own riposte, and indeed the price for his continued (if temporary) support of the republic, was to extend the struggle not against the Francoists but rather internally, against the republic's wider leftist but non-Stalinist supporters, especially, of course, against the Trotskyists. Oleg Khlevniuk has seen in the emerging Stalinist fear of the fifth column in Spain something of the immediate origins of the Great Terror.[262] Correct or not, closer to home the price of the USSR's security in the face of increasingly hostile or suspect regimes to its west, on the one hand, and the stabilization it needed for the projected flexing of its Great Power muscles, on the other, was paid, above all, by a handful of rimland peoples. Martin contextualizes their position starkly: though they represented a mere 1.6 per cent of the Soviet population, he estimates they accounted for up to 26.8 per cent of arrests in the totality of operations, that is, both 00447 and national operations, with figures higher still if we were to concentrate on executions.[263]

And, indeed, focus on the killings provides much more explicit evidence of an ethnic dimension to the mass operations, especially in the latter half of 1938. Certainly, Operation 00447 was, in toto, responsible for more deaths than the national operations, the latter of which accounted, according to NKVD records, for 247,157 fatalities or 36.3 per cent of total executions in this period. Yet once *natsoperatsii* got fully under way in early 1938, the figures again suggest that such executions radically overtook those of their more long-standing predecessor. This would have been facilitated, too, by the nature of Ezhov's orders for these operations. For one thing, there was no quota. Individuals were targeted on grounds of suspicion alone and regional NKVD units were encouraged to use their initiative in this regard. Secondly, suspicion was much more likely to lead to death. In fact, 73.7 per cent of those arrested in these operations met this fate. These figures were not entirely consistent across the board. They reached, for instance, the 80 per cent mark in Greek, Finnish, Estonian, and Polish operations, while there seems to have been less enthusiasm for the death penalty in the Afghan and Iranian episodes.[264] However, the median figure does provide an approximate benchmark of the process. For example, in the Latvian operation—in the eleven months following its commencement in December 1937—of around 25,000 people arrested, over 22,000 were tried by *troiki* and, of these, 16,573 were sentenced to death: some 74 per cent of the total.[265]

We can all too easily fall into the trap of reading all this as an exercise in statistics, losing sight, in the process, of the immensity of the individual and collective human tragedy. Because so many people were caught up in these operations

(national or otherwise) the mere problem of where to house them prior to interrogation, sentencing, and execution threw up immense logistical challenges. The
Lubyanka, the NKVD headquarters in Moscow, has come to symbolize the Terror.
But it actually had relatively few cells, and, beyond old, often fetid tsarist prisons,
all sorts of buildings—mills, garages, barracks, even monasteries—had to be commandeered for banging up the prisoners, providing cells for interrogation and torture, the space indeed in which to carry out executions.[266] Local NKVD chiefs
were ordered to adapt buildings as appropriate. Part of this remit was strict secrecy
of operation: cells being specially adapted for 'quiet' night-time executions. One
report on killings in the North Caucasus notes the existence of a special hermeti-
cally sealed execution hall, improvised with concrete, in which 'revolving firing
positions were fitted into the walls and ceilings from the exterior'.[267] But it is also
clear that the sheer scale of the killing exercise overwhelmed such in situ efforts,
even where—as in the case of the (political prisoner only) Lefortovo prison in
Moscow—there was a crematorium.[268] Instead executions sites al fresco became
the norm.

However, this carried its own logistical headaches. Where could sites be found
sufficiently near to the NKVD reception centres, but sufficiently far away from
unwelcome public attention? The Gestapo exhumation, in 1943, of some 9,432
corpses from a site embracing an orchard, a cemetery, and part of the municipal
park within the city limits of Vinnitsa underscores the potential for the regime's
secrecy to be undone where concealment was inadequate.[269] Much later, discover-
ies in the era of *glasnost*, or after the collapse of communism, by the organization
'Memorial' revealed killing fields, usually several steps removed from prying eyes.
They might contain relatively small numbers of bodies—a forest outside Voronezh,
500 kilometres south of Moscow, for instance, had 460 believed to have been
executed in the first three months of 1938; others, like Kuropaty, near the Belorussian capital of Minsk, no less than 50,000.[270] All this, of course, is also testament
to the number and range of perpetrators involved. Simply taking prisoners to Moscow's main killing site, twenty kilometres to the south at Butovo, in lorries surreptitiously marked 'meat' or 'vegetables', required somebody to do the driving. As
Service reminds us, 'The Great Terror required stenographers, guards, executioners, cleaners, torturers, clerks, railwaymen, truck drivers and informers'.[271] Executioners, in particular, would have been needed aplenty as the victim's death was
usually laboriously administered by a single heavy-calibre bullet shot from a
revolver to the back of each individual's neck, though German forensic evidence at
Vinnitsa of regular second or third shots, or even the use of blunt instruments to
finalize the dispatch,[272] may suggest either inadequate weapons, professional
incompetence, or both. Or, alternatively, the drafting in of less experienced NKVD
operatives, not least as so many executioners were themselves eliminated in the
course of the Terror.

These features may suggest also a rather gender-specific delimitation of these
killings, further raising a question mark over the use of the term genocide. The
rescinding of Ezhov's order 00486 denied the even more terrifying direction of
flow in which wives and children of *mostly* male suspects would conceivably also

have been sucked up into the killing process. But what perhaps with hindsight is equally alarming about the order is its relationship to Ezhov's immediately preceding 00485 Polish operation directive. Even putting aside the fact that 00486 was cancelled, the targeting of the menfolk of relatively small ethnic cohorts is bound in itself to have had the most devastating effect on the coherence and sustainability of their wider familial and communal networks. McLoughlin refers to the execution of at least sixty-seven out of seventy-one Greeks in the Krymsk tobacco-growing region of Krasnodar, following their arrest on the charge of being part of a Greek counter-revolutionary organization in December 1937.[273] But we know nothing from this statement of what happened to their spouses, or whether their children ended up in orphanages; how many, indeed, of these 'survivors' survived.

Returning to the statistics, it is very clear that the impact of the Terror on the 656,000-strong Polish community (according to the 1937 general census) was more quantitatively devastating than on any other single community. Those who have done the necessary number crunching confirm that of the 143,000 people arrested in the Polish national operation, some 98,000 were Poles. But if we add to this those arrested in the entirety of the national and other operations, including 00447, we arrive at a communal deficit of something between 118,000 and 123,000 people. Not all of these were executed, but a very high proportion were, suggesting a staggering one-fifth of Poles living in the USSR 'repressed' in this brief 1937–8 window.[274]

Considering the Polish tragedy, however, points to something broader and arguably even more menacing still. Eight per cent of those killed at Butovo, mostly in 00447 operations, were Poles: over 1,600 of the 20,765 murdered there.[275] The high figure is certainly no one-off aberration. Soviet or foreign-born Poles alongside Finns had become, by late 1937, the particular butt of a widespread grass-roots phobia associated with the fear of imminent foreign invasion, in which Warsaw and Helsinki were seen, as in earlier instances, as vital lynchpins in a wider conspiratorial chain. The state's draconian behaviour towards these and other alleged fifth columnists, in other words, hardly developed in political isolation but was actually, in some ways, a *reflection* of a Soviet societal 'spy mania' of the sort we have otherwise previously noted in the context of Great War collective hysteria and paranoia.[276]

But this reflex was also apparent in the wider state repression of those perceived as foreign, or foreign-connected. One-fifth of those who met their ends at Butovo were from abroad. Forty per cent of these, in turn, were Polish, followed by a contingent from Latvia. However, in all, people from twenty-eight countries outside the USSR were unwillingly represented in this single mass graveyard.[277] In the 'German operation' people from thirty-five different national groups were victims.[278] In Leningrad, 30 per cent of those executed between August and December 1937 were foreigners.[279] Again, a large majority of these had rimland connections. But among the kaleidoscope of foreign nationals were also large numbers of communists or ex-communists from Poland and the Baltic states as well as from other countries too, especially Germany.[280]

The supposed crimes of this latter group could not thus be objectively construed as in any way to do with some *class* misdemeanour. The perceived threat they represented came from their foreignness, just as, in a similar way, having outside artistic, musical, or literary connections made intellectuals suspect, as it also did those who, in practically blanket terms, had served in Spain, in consulates, trade delegations, or in any other capacity abroad. We can certainly read some historical parallels here. Jacobin France—from having been the most proud and vociferous banner waver for a cosmopolitan future for all humankind—faced, in September 1792, with the potentiality of many-sided foreign invasion, flipped over into the most strident xenophobic—and violent—reaction against practically *all* foreigners, as it equally did against all those perceived as socially undesirable.[281]

Russia *as* Russia, as we have noted, had deep xenophobic undercurrents of its own. And these very obviously reared their head at a grass-roots level in the early 1930s; for instance, in Russian post-famine 'revenge' attacks on Kazakhs in Central Asia—clearly with the events of 1916 in mind.[282] The key issue by the time of the 1937–8 crisis was whether Stalin, through his own distorted, phobic outlook on his country and the world, could have conceived of any good reason *not* to give such Russian chauvinism its head. Lenin would certainly have a put on a lid on it; indeed, would have fiercely punished the protagonists. But then Lenin had not conceived of Socialism in One Country.

Was, then, the evolution of the Great Terror 'into an ethnic terror', as Martin has proposed,[283] the logical corollary to a repositioning of Russia, and indeed all things Russian, as the now clearly undisputed fulcrum of Soviet life? Can we thus view the mass deportations of Koreans as not simply a security policy but Stalin's tacit way of demonstrating his agreement with a groundswell of demotic Russian antipathy in the far east towards them? Much closer to home was the blanket closing down, in December 1937, of the schools and national soviets of the rimland peoples then under attack in the *natsoperatsii*:[284] again Stalin's way of signalling his oneness with *nas narod*? Might we even consider, as one commentator has suggested, that the formal termination of mass operations, eleven months later, was not on account of the destruction of the alleged rimland 'agents' of foreign intelligence services, but rather because too many 'honest' Soviet citizens—again, 'our people' not 'alien elements'—had been repressed in the course of Operation 00447?[285]

There are certainly pitfalls in reading too much into this argument. Stalin, by the end of 1938, through an unquestioned elitocide, had remade the apparatus of the Soviet state into one of 'yes men': 'comrades' who did his bidding. They were still cosmetically—even absurdly—'comrades', nevertheless. He may, too, have found ways of making Russians the national—and natural—centre of the Soviet communist universe; but it was still a *communist* universe, at least in the eyes of true believers. In this realization we are clearly faced with an intense paradox. Here was a state which saw itself as legitimate heir to the revolution, which extolled and celebrated itself, first and foremost, for its destruction of tsarism and for the ascendancy of proletarian man which was its promised gift to all humankind. It was this which Soviet propaganda projected to anybody in the wider world who cared to watch and listen. The future was bright: the future was red. *Korenizatsiia*, and alongside it repeated campaigns to promote the brotherhood of Soviet peoples, was simply part and parcel of this same *fraternal* message.

Yet Stalin had already long broken with the internationalist course of communism. He had instead created a very special anti-system: one which portrayed itself as having, perhaps even in some peculiar way believed itself to have, through its claimed universalism, bypassed, even transcended, the primacy of the liberal world order. In practice it had given itself up to the very same state systemic obsessions and geostrategic fears as its tsarist predecessors. The Great Terror represented the culmination of this process. The assault on the peoples of the rimlands represents unadulterated evidence of where the Soviet experiment under Stalin was, in reality, heading, in terms of its internal *ethnic* politics. But, in the attack on foreigners and foreignness more generally in the course of these events, this anti-system demonstrated that genocide—even sui generis Soviet genocide—always has, at its core, external as well as internal drivers. While public declarations of the unity and solidarity of the international communist movement might remain part of its ongoing persona, behind the mask the destruction of German, Polish, and other leading East European communists on its soil prepared the ground for something which, in all leftist manuals, was meant to be not just impossible but unthinkable: a pact with that other anti-system, Nazi Germany. A pact, of course, which not would not only set a Halford Mackinder's heart racing, but act as the starting pistol for genocide in the rimlands—from two directions.

6

Anti-System Two: The Emerging Hitler State

National socialism professes...the heroic teaching of evaluating blood, race, and personality as well as the eternal laws of selection and thus consciously puts itself in unbridgeable contradiction to the philosophy of pacifist-international democracy and its effects.[1]

Hitler, Nazi party convention speech, Nuremberg, 1933

If the nascent USSR's relationship to the wider world was defined by its determination to create a universally classless society, Nazi Germany was defined by its intention to realize one founded on a German-led and dominated hierarchy of race. These two systems, thus, though diametrically opposed in their visions of the future, had notable aspects in common. Both believed themselves to have knowledge of the driving forces of human development since its earliest prehistoric existence. Both were profoundly teleological in their belief that humanity was moving towards something better, albeit with their own leaderships as the key agents and guides towards that final stage of humanity's realization of its potentialities. Both saw themselves as fundamentally at odds not only with each other but with what they viewed as the decayed and decadent principles of the post-1918 dominant Western liberal system.

In the Nazi case, race as guiding principle has been treated normatively in standard post-1945 histories and textbooks as the key to the regime's actions: both in the way it sought to legitimize expansionist war as necessary for the provision of *Lebensraum*—'living space'—for its *Übermenschen*, and, as corollary to that, the destruction of racially inferior peoples who stood in the way of that purpose. At the centre of this was the Nazi mass murder of the Jews. As all serious scholarship confirms the unequivocal nature of this sequence of events as geno-cide—in other words, without any of the caveats we have felt necessary to inter-pose, for instance, in the case of Soviet mass killing—we are rather conveniently provided with a clear and straightforward explanation for what we have come to call the Holocaust.

Yet, like it or not, this simple postulate poses problems. If the concept of race is founded on a notion of hierarchy, why go to the effort of killing inferior peoples at all, if they can be otherwise subordinated or, alternatively, removed from the arena of the racial hegemons' rule? The only *logical* reason to do so would be if those same races collectively, and hence in some sense militarily, attempted to challenge or resist their imposed status. Such an induced dynamic of violence underlay much of the Western colonial-cum-imperial behaviour of previous centuries. Applied to the Nazis, the scenario would certainly be more than plausible if our focus rested entirely on Hitler's drive to the east, with the consequent resistance of diverse *Slavic* peoples, most (though not all of whom) had been branded by the Nazis as *Untermenschen*. Indeed, this would reinforce a case for the rimlands as a more geographically concentrated and intensely social-Darwinian locus of genocidal violence as earlier meted out in its global fin-de-siècle sequence.[2]

However, if this line of approach dovetails with aspects of our own argument, its untrammelled pursuit is handicapped by one rather inconvenient truth. The *primary* Nazi attack was not on Slavs, but on Jews: a minority group who, in their transnational dispersal in the rimlands and beyond, could pose no obvious physical challenge to Nazi overlordship. The same, of course, applies equally to the Roma, acknowledged as the group second most keenly targeted for Nazi destruction. Yet if neither of these groups offered any perceivable existential threat to the Nazi agenda—and certainly not the basis for some empirically observable 'race struggle'— why do scholars of genocide unanimously agree that the Nazi war against the Jews, in particular, was of an entirely extraordinary nature? So extraordinary, one might add, that the consequent lorry loads of post-event literature on the subject hardly provide grounds for adding anything further at all.

To be sure, our own purpose is still to consider the wider historical connections between the gamut of genocides in the age of the nation state, including this one at the extreme end of the 'Richter scale'. Notwithstanding the exceptional qualities of the Rwanda genocide in 1994, 'the Holocaust'—whether we wish to consider it as a composite matrix of *genocides* or not—when viewed through the prisms of perpetrator commitment, geographical scope, organizational and resource alloca-tion, not to mention sheer scale and longevity of the projected and actual annihila-tion process of an entire yet ubiquitous communal aggregate: men, women, *and children*—provides us—again, putting aside all the heavy-duty debates of the 1990s about 'uniqueness' versus 'universality'—with the 'ultimate' example of our phenomenon to date.

But reiterating this point, in some respects, simply compounds the problem. If the Nazi-led Jewish genocide (or genocides) was both more thoroughgoing and more gargantuan than anything else comparable, how are we to explain its/their wellsprings if we cannot do so either by reference to Nazi race theory, or a broader history of racially informed colonial violence? Again, to be sure, there could be a danger of throwing out the baby with the bath water. Most of the mass murders of Jews took place in the ethnic mosaic of the 'Lands Between', synchronous or near-synchronous with a range of other closely related mass murders committed by Nazis and others. In other words, 'the Holocaust' was not only *not* a genocide hap-pening in isolation, but one which took place, at the very least, in an, albeit extreme, *colonial-like* context. Similarly, if we were to chronologically rewind to the Hitler years prior to the launching of either expansionist war or Holocaust, it is absolutely clear that race theory did *inform* Nazi policy or attempted policy towards the Jews. The regime, for instance, completely set itself against any *anthropophagic*-style resolution to the 'problem': the standard technique adopted by most new nation-state regimes, at least with reference to some of their perceived misfit or recalcitrant ethnic communities. By contrast, the way the Nazis set themselves against any form of assimilation, forced or otherwise, and, as an extension of that, evinced intense fear of racial mixing, was not just a product of their peculiar policies towards Jews. It was also, as we will develop in this chapter, in line with an intense and ongoing policymaking debate about so-called *Mischlinge*—children of mixed 'race'—in which people with part-Roma, and black, as well as Jewish backgrounds, found themselves exposed to the possibility of sterilization or worse.

All this said, what we cannot simply elide is that as far as the Jews were concerned, the Nazi *Weltanschauung* never considered itself to be simply dealing with 'congeries of biological degenerates'.[3] Insofar as the Jews were a race at all, they were an anti-race: a race of demons, which, in the words of Auschwitz commandant Rudolf Hoess, required their destruction 'without exception'.[4] The Hitlerian movement, from its elementary origins to its institutionalization as a state-embedded anti-system, to its final *Götterdämmerung*-like paroxysm, breathed every breath as if engaged in a mortal struggle with them. Like millenarian Christianity, it was as if it were fighting both Antichrist on Earth and entirely more cosmic forces of darkness beyond. Indeed, as one of the more astute writers on the subject has ventured, Nazism was nothing if not 'a messianic movement that endowed nationalism with an elaborate terrestrial eschatology'.[5] In this one sense—of its theodicy—Nazism was indeed unique: all the corruption and alienation of the world being laid by it at the door of what it proclaimed was the 'eternal enemy' of all humankind. Only by expunging it/them—the Jews—could the world be liberated from evil; and this only through the saviour in the person of Adolf Hitler:

> If the Jew, with the help of his Marxist catechism, triumphs over the peoples of the world, his crown will be the dance of death for mankind, and, as once before, millions of years ago, this planet will again sail empty of all human life through the ether…
> I believe that I am today acting according to the purposes of the almighty Creator. In resisting the Jew, I am fighting the Lord's battle.[6]

But if we follow this terrifying prophecy to its logical conclusion of some global Holocaust—in which, that is, 'the Jew' is himself annihilated—it is almost as if we have entered into a realm entirely beyond historical time; leaving us in the process with this further yawning conundrum: if 'the Jew' enemy is both the 'metaphysical' proposition around which Nazi self-understanding of its salvatory mission revolves,[7] yet also, somewhat more prosaically, the clear and present danger to be confronted and defeated in order that the 'power and glory of the German people' can be rightfully redeemed,[8] how do we explain a historical reality of the *early* years of Nazi rule, when, despite frightful anti-Jewish violence and persecution, *no* genocide was enacted?

The very simple answer might be this: for Hitlerite intent, in its fevered imagination, to be translated into successful, practical accomplishment, still required not only the most propitious circumstances—in effect, a question of timing—for the 'forces of light' to take on this supposedly most cunning of all enemies and, in

Hitler's words, cast him back to Lucifer,[9] but furthermore the creation of a—in 1933 as yet non-existent—phalanx of Christ-like soldiers who would unflinchingly prepare for and dedicate themselves to the task. Then again, this proposition itself might be questioned as too readily falling into an assumption—or, more exactly, trap—that a Nazi blueprint for genocide was by process, crafted into existence for a final 1941 unleashing, when most of the empirical evidence suggests that the descent into total mass murder was entirely more contingent, improvisatory, even contradictory.

However, in a critical sense this is to run ahead of ourselves. If, as we propose, there was clear genocidal *intent,* yet nevertheless no programmatic *plan,* we have, at very least, to do ourselves the justice of trying to understand the nature of the Nazi trajectory from no genocide to ultimate genocide. Which would rather suggest, too, that we would need to sketch in a modicum of the wider German social and political context. Not least perhaps since, compared with the Soviet anti-system for much of the 1930s, the Nazi one, for all its very palpable and public incitement to violence, appeared—odd as it may sound—*relatively* calm, even constrained.

What, then, were the conditions which enabled a Nazi party with its open anti-Semitism to come to power? And how much was that anti-Semitism—or, more starkly, Judaeophobia, as we might prefer to label to it—intrinsic to Nazism's popular appeal? Our first subsection, 'The legacy of 1918', proposes that the answer to that question may lie less in the actual 'moment' of 1933 and more in that legacy. Defeat and/or collapse were suffered not only by Germany, of course, and this in itself begs the question of the degree to which we can make parallels with other states—notably the USSR and post-Ottoman Turkey—in their own defiance of the Western liberal system. Nor was German nationalist and ultra-nationalist opinion alone in the post-Great War period in its ongoing fixation with the international Jewish conspiracy motif as explanation for the country's supposed undoing. Practically all 'New Europe' nationalists and ultra-nationalists, and a sizeable proportion in Western Europe, too, were of a similar opinion, reminding us that anti-Semitism in the interwar period was very much a pan-European phenomenon. What made the person of Hitler so potent is the manner in which he was able to make his own intensely personal Judaeophobic fixation a point of entry into an element of the collective German psyche and, at the same time, present himself as the true path towards a cleansed and hence redeemed *Volksgemeinschaft*—a truly pure national–racial community.

Iteration in our second section, 'The Hitler phenomenon and German longing', of the most salient features of Hitler's political career—and mystagogy—is thus necessary to our purpose, notwithstanding that these elements have been the subject of almost endless recitation in either magisterial or plain crass studies of the demagogue. In our third, however—'A regime and its "enemies"'—we seek to consider the realities of Nazism in power. These realities threw up statist constraints on open season on German Jewry while, at the same time, posing issues of confrontation with other elements of society—not least the dominant churches and, more problematically still, the Jehovah's Witnesses, who, until that moment, were entirely off the party's radar screen.

Paradoxically, it was through the apparatus of the traditional German state, more particularly its bureaucratic, legal, police, and public health organs, that Nazism was not only rescued from having its anti-Semitic aims derailed by the more radical proclivities of its *sans-culotte* activists, but given a framework within which to both ground and develop its race policies as if as they were not simply normative but at the cutting edge of modernism. Indeed, our fourth section, 'Race in place of people', proposes that it was through the state's scientific and medical elites that Nazi Germany came closest, pre-war, to enacting genocidal-type policies. What is doubly paradoxical is that the experts' drive towards this brave new world of a hereditarily pure community posed lethal dangers to a much wider range of Germans than simply its Jewish population; though, in this first instance, it was Roma who bore the full brunt of its sterilization programme.

However, this turn towards genocide by the back door would prove unsustainable; for the basic reason that the whole thrust of the Hitlerite mission was ultimately not towards a radical domestic reordering but rather a renewed politico-military challenge to the 1918 Western-imposed order. Indeed, it was the Wilhelmine victory in the east in that year which was the primary Nazi goad, twenty years later, towards its own fateful march in the same direction. That march began with the absorption of Austria—the *other* Germany and, of course, Hitler's own birthplace—into the embrace of the Third Reich. Once that was achieved, the intertwined relationship between Nazism's broadest geostrategic, anti-systemic goals and its desire to be revenged on a cosmically hostile Jewish power—supposedly responsible for the thwarting of pre-Nazi German efforts in this direction—began to unravel. Simultaneously, the implicit tension between the German state and Nazi party began to be circumvented by a new locus of power: the security apparatus of Himmler's Schutzstaffeln (SS). We thus finish this chapter in the transitional year of 1938: a year in which it became abundantly clear that the renewed turn towards the rimlands by the Nazi-combined 'Two Germanies' also represented for Europe's Jews, as well as Roma, the gravest existential threat.

THE LEGACY OF 1918

'We want to have compassion only for the German people...others have no compassion for us'. So Hans Frank told a group of his own senior General Government officials in Cracow, following a fateful meeting in Berlin of Nazi party leaders and their Führer in mid-December 1941. Frank was actually speaking about the question of the Jews. There could be no question of compassion for *them* if they were to 'once more succeed in unleashing a world war' he told his audience, in effect repeating what Hitler had told his, just a few days earlier.[10] That Hitler speech is now widely accepted as *the* major staging post in the all-Europe implementation of the 'Final Solution'.[11]

Can one speak of a German collective neurosis about the Jews? And how far does it link us back the events of 1918? A month prior to his December speech, Frank, in a confidential press briefing, had harped back precisely to 'the 9th of November

1918...for us a day of fate and decision. At that time Jewry revealed that it was geared to the destruction of Germany. Thanks only to the Führer and the strength of character of the German nation, they did not succeed'.[12] Encapsulated in this statement we have a succinct rendition of the *Nazi* 'perpetrators' "never again" syndrome'. Objectively, we know that Germany was defeated in the autumn of 1918, on the battlefields of the Western Front and equally through the impact of the Allied blockade: the West's own ugly weapon of mass civilian destruction. In these circumstances, in which Ludendorff's 'silent dictatorship' faced the prospect of military annihilation on the battlefield and societal collapse through literal starvation in the domestic rear, OHL (the German Supreme Army Command) had no choice but to go cap in hand to the Allies and seek an armistice. They did so behind the screen of democratic civilian politicians, which OHL initially appointed in the hope that somehow this might lead to gentler Wilsonian terms and, in so doing, let them—the generals—off the hook. This was not the story, however, which German 'patriots' told themselves, either then, or for the next quarter century. Refusing to accept the actual verdict they instead opted for an alternative fantasy rendition of events: the repeated idée fixe of their own, or, more exactly, Germany's *victimhood*. The Germany army had never been defeated— a story which, from exile in Sweden, Ludendorff quickly embroidered in order to popularize the already widely prevalent notion of *Dolchstoss*: the stab in the back. It was from the machinations of the enemies within—those who were intent on Germany's destruction—that all her subsequent tribulations sprang: the Versailles 'diktat', the imposition of war guilt, territorial loss, the radical downsizing of the army, reparations and, with it, the disastrous inflationary spiral, and Rhineland occupation.

To be sure, defeat was no abstraction. Nor the apparent demise of the Wilhelmine order. For those for whom the Reich was everything, especially for those in uniform who felt they had sacrificed their all for the sake of German victory, the insolence and insubordination of mere enlistees and the vulgar populace alike— the declaration of workers' and soldiers' councils, the uprising in Berlin, the Räterepublik and Soviet in Munich, the deaths of comrades at the hands of revolutionaries in some of these events, the possibility of the Baltic arena or, even closer to home, Hungary, falling to the communists—provided evidence not just of a world turned upside down but of a threat to one's very raison d'être.

The nationalist narrative read into these events its own retrospective exculpation. If only the Kaiser had listened to those like Heinrich Class, the leader of the Pan-German League, or General von Bernhardi, who—before the war—had been insisting not only on the need for a pre-emptive strike to break out of Entente encirclement but, equally, a muzzling at home of all those negative forces who stood in the way of *Weltkrieg* and victory.[13] Even during the war, with the backing of the newly formed Vaterland party, and firmly loyal supporters such as the Young Germany League, OHL could still have grasped the nettle, shut down the Reichstag, silenced the 'pacifist' press, and smashed the socialists for once and for all.[14] Above all, they could and should have finally dealt with 'the pernicious and destructive influence of Jewry':[15] the source of all Germany's woes.

Anti-Semitism, of course, had been seminal to the pre-war German and Austro-German right, and more especially among a multitude of *völkisch* exponents and ideologues. However, as Geoff Eley has argued, in the period 1917–19 it took on a far more virulent and unrestrained character, providing 'quite suddenly' for 'a vocabulary of counterrevolutionary desperation for individuals who had treated it far more fastidiously before 1914'.[16] That note of desperation should remind us, once again, how much anti-Semitism has acted as a barometer of a broad range of European cultural responses to circumstances where assumed state or societal control of one's own destiny has been dramatically exposed as mere conceit. As we suggested in our Introduction, 'The Structural Underpinnings of European Genocide, 1912–1953', it was, more exactly, among European political elites and their nationally conscious supporters—whether in Berlin or London—that the idea of a 'Jewish' arch-control and manipulation of events amounting to the imposition of 'a master-plan for history' became the projective alibi as the Great War reached its final, yet still into late 1918 highly uncertain, conclusion.[17] In Germany, 'unexpected' defeat made the need for a psychological refuge for those unable to face up to their own, or their state's, failings all the more urgent—and all the more difficult to then relinquish. Given the nature of the alibi, too, it was inevitable that those who were impelled to action in response would carry it out in the most violent and destructive of fashions.

Yet the 35,000-strong volunteer Freikorps units who bore down on the Munich Soviet republic, in the spring of 1919, to mete out revenge and initiate a reign of White Terror for the handful of ultra-nationalist hostages murdered by the revolutionaries there—or, for that matter, the Deutschvölkischer Schutz- und Trutzbund (the German Nationalist League for Protection and Defence) similarly formed on the cusp of Weimar with similar intent—cannot simply be dismissed as gangs of freebooting thugs. The nationwide Freikorps—made up primarily of otherwise demobilized soldiers comprising, amongst others, many thousands of elite army officers—prided themselves on being a last bastion of German defence and honour. Considerably more broadly based, the Schutz- und Trutzbund (whose very name might remind us of a latter-day Rwandan one—*Interahamwe*: 'those who stand together'), consisted of professionals of all types, including teachers, civil servants, and white-collar workers, just as had the Pan-German League before it.[18] As for the last major effort, bar one, of such ultra-right groups to repudiate Versailles by force—the Berlin-centred Kapp putsch of March 1920—it was, again, very much a Prussian Junker-inspired and, in large part, military-concocted affair: behind the naked show of Freikorps force were the machinations of former Vaterland party leaders, Ludendorff included.[19]

That right-wing German nationalists should have sought hard, authoritarian, military-led solutions to their perceived problems is, in itself, hardly surprising. In the wake of Ottoman collapse it had been that almost quintessential 'man on horseback', Kemal, who had ridden to the *nation's* rescue. In Russia, in 1917, Kornilov was only the first of several 'old-school' military men who attempted to turn back the revolutionary tide and restore legitimate 'order'. The parallels but also disjunctures between these and the German situation may have some relevance to our discussion. The Western-backed, liberal-orientated Damat Ferit regime in Constantinople, after 1919, was increasingly isolated and quickly overshadowed by Kemal's alternative power base, initially constructed in the Anatolian east. Like Weimar, the Constantinople administration (while claiming to be a continuation of the sultanate-cum-caliphate) was tainted from the first as collaborationist and in hock to—in its case—the Sèvres diktat. As a largely phantom government it lasted just three years, entirely dependent throughout on the backing of Allied troops, and then only in the zone around the Straits. That said, the liberal Western-orientated Russian regime we most associate with Kerensky—in Petrograd's Winter Palace—lasted only a matter of months; perhaps again not surprisingly, as the alternative Red Guard-backed Soviet power base was literally across the way in the Smolny Institute, getting in its own pre-emptive strike before an army-led 'third force' could take its own decisive action.

If both Russian and Turkish situations underscore the limitations of pro-Western, liberal governments without a 'hard' power base to support them, Weimar's survival until 1933 can be, in part, attributed to the fact, that, on paper at least, it did have exactly this feature. One might indeed add that there was no need for a Kapp or a Ludendorff to 'restore' order—either from near or afar—when the old Wilhelmine apparatus, including its core military element, was already firmly embedded within the *new* regime. Democratic Weimar had only come into existence because the generals had allowed it. A long line of them—Noske, Seeckt, Schleicher—usually through their role as defence ministers, underwrote its continued existence, with the most senior commander of all—the by then thoroughly gerontocratic Field Marshal Hindenburg—ensuring something more than simply symbolic continuity with the ancien régime when he was elected state president in 1925. That did not prevent leading military and ex-military officers, Hindenburg included, from participating in all manner of thoroughly Byzantine manoeuvres and backstairs intrigues, the ultimate purpose of which was the removal of the Weimar constitution and its replacement by some form of military-led directory or dictatorship. The two major attempted putsches notwithstanding, what the senior echelons of the Reichswehr soon grasped was that they could have it both ways. They could denounce the treasonable acquiescence of Weimar in the Versailles humiliation and, by implication, excoriate its liberalism as proof of its illegitimacy, while, at the same time maintaining a veneer of loyalty to what kept them in their jobs. Their behaviour thus was that of a *genuine* fifth column: as if they were priming a giant underground mine for the appointed day when the whole edifice would be blown sky-high.

Nor was this just a matter of the military busily loosening the brickwork in this manner. The personnel of ministries, universities, *Länder*, police forces, and gymnasia were heavily populated by those whose true allegiance was to Weimar's authoritarian predecessor. The tendency was particularly striking within parts of the judiciary. Some judges had a habit of demonstrating their true views on 'bourgeois' justice by either failing to convict or often giving very light sentences to members of secret ultra-nationalist groups such as Organization Consul, or the *Schwarze Reichswehr*, who had tasked themselves with the assassination of the so-called 'November Criminals', and whose killing sprees ran into the hundreds.[20] When one Adolf Hitler was similarly found guilty for his bit part in a complex, military-inspired but (bar the *völkisch*, paramilitary, Munich element) abortive 1923 plot to attempt to overthrow Weimar by force, his sentence was to enjoy the privilege of a brief and gentle sabbatical in the Landsberg fortress, from which he would pen *Mein Kampf.*[21]

The defeat of the Munich putsch, however, is also a reminder that there were factors other than simply the prevarication of the generals—or the inability of any one of their fractious number to cohere and stamp their authority, Kemal-like, on the nationalist movement—which may explain the relative longevity of Weimar. The Kapp putsch evaporated in the face of a general worker-led Berlin strike. The proposed Mussolini-style 'March on Berlin' by Ludendorff and his acolyte, Hitler, did likewise when faced with a robust wall of Bavarian state police. Five years to the day from the abdication of the Kaiser and the Reichstag declaration of the republic, the failure of the putsch illustrates the fact that Germany, despite defeat and economic chaos, was in many respects more like the West than like Ottomania or Russia. Already, under Wilhelmine rule, it had a growing sense of itself as a *rechtsstaat*—a constitutional state. It had strong civil society traditions, and was led by a highly educated, motivated, and culturally sophisticated middle class. It was, of course, an advanced, industrial country as much as a traditional peasant one, but the latter element was also in no sense monolithic: the authoritarian tendencies associated with the huge aristocrat-run Junker estates in the east were balanced by smallholder interests elsewhere among the diverse and localized mosaic of the *Länder*. In short, Germany was notably pluralistic in social, occupational, religious, and political terms: the traditionally conservative *Mittelstand*, one aspect; the left-leaning working class another; with a political centre-ground occupied by a range of parties—the Catholic Centre Party and Social Democrats in particular—committed to the preservation of Weimar as a going concern.

That this concern *could* conceivably have delivered Germany into firm membership of the Western system was, paradoxically, aided by the terms of Versailles. Post-1919 Germany was more like an authentic nation state, in significant part because it had been hewn of a significant rump of its 'imperial' eastern rimlands. Bereft thereby of much of its former Polish population—giving to the country a much more homogeneous character, from a liberal perspective—this also undercut the economic power of the Posnanian-Junker military caste, who had done so much to take Germany into the Great War. Under Stresemann, another once-staunch acolyte of Ludendorff, the German orientation seemed to be firmly westwards. Reconciliation with France brought political fruits in the form of the Locarno treaty. Equally importantly, it brought economic ones—through, first, the Dawes Plan, which balanced the country's reparations payments with US loans and aid, and, on the cusp of the financial crisis of 1929, the Young Plan, which generously extended the terms of the offset, not to mention radically reducing the reparations bill itself.[22]

Conventional wisdom tells us that it was the spiralling effects of the Wall Street Crash, not least the withdrawal of US credits to back the Young Plan, which wrecked these possibilities. As German unemployment soared to unprecedented levels and deep social malaise set in, the mere exercise of government became increasingly dependent on emergency presidential decree—the implicit authoritarianism of which paved the way for Hitler's ascendancy. Yet vitriolic opposition to the Young Plan had *preceded* the withdrawal of credits. Indeed, the very fact that the Plan smacked of a tacit acceptance of Versailles and, with it, of 'war guilt', meant that it was bound to be repudiated by any 'true patriot', with or without any economic crisis.

Explaining the rise of Hitler and, as its corollary, the demise of Weimar purely in terms of that Great Depression would thus seem to be a case of reading too much into the immediate symptoms and not enough into the deeper causes of the German crisis. The first perspective would certainly have no choice but to concentrate on the years of the Brüning administration, from 1930 to 1932, which had to deal with the economic storm, and which is easily indictable—primarily through its emphasis on fiscal probity rather than government-sponsored reflation—for mass unemployment, not to mention the cutting of what, until then, had been generous welfare state benefits to millions of ordinary families. Brüning's economic policy, however, was clearly not one of outright failure. On the critical issue of reparations it was Brüning who was able to arrange a US moratorium which, in effect, killed the whole issue of future payments stone dead. And, in expectation of the crisis bottoming out, the chancellor did eventually begin developing a reflationary package which included job creation schemes—not only, famously, the autobahn system later picked up by Hitler, but a plan for a modest redistribution of Junker land to the unemployed.[23] It was Brüning's boldest scheme, however—his proposed Austro-German customs union in March 1931—which notably reconnects us to the deeper ramifications of Versailles as it affected the German national psyche and, hence, to a longer-term perspective.

The customs union idea cut across a French proposal for German economic cooperation as one route out of the general crisis. Paris read into Brüning's efforts a countermove, whose longer-term goal was a matter of bringing not just Austria into Germany's economic and political orbit but, in the process, much of the 'New Europe' too. The result was not just vociferous French opposition to the union—backed by its East European allies 'the little entente'—but a run, very probably Paris-inspired, on the Austrian schilling, which, two months later, led to the collapse of the premier central European bank, the Vienna-based Creditanstalt.[24] This, in turn, precipitated the wholesale collapse of the Austrian banking system, a situation only immediately retrievable with the assistance of French gold reserves. Not only did this sequence of events mark the nadir of the European economic crisis—the Creditanstalt bankruptcy inevitably having knock-on effects on other, especially German, banks; in its wake, it foreclosed for good both Brüning's customs scheme and his other big idea: a multilateral agreement providing for German equality of arms.

For nationalists of all hues, however, Brüning's ignominy was nothing as compared with Germany's shame and the conviction that, once again, she was the victim of some omnipresent plot to deny her the greatness which was hers by right. Indeed, what the episode equally highlighted was how quickly this latent persecution complex could resurface and, in the process, become an open, all-consuming psychological wound. Solipsism, narcissism, hubris—call it what one will—its projective mechanism had the ability to block out all sense of proportion: to see, for instance, that the terms imposed by OHL on Russia at Brest-Litovsk were altogether more all-encompassing and cruel than anything the West had meted out at Versailles. Worse, the frustration it bred inevitably carried with it a baggage of sadomasochistic fantasies—even, eventually, in the context of the initial victories of the Second World War, fantasies of omnipotence—which, short of professional therapy, could only be redeemed through violent actions.[25]

Of course, not all Germans gave themselves up willingly to this psychosis. The very fact that the period of Weimar, as Richard Bessel has described it, was 'a fourteen-year latent civil war',[26] is testimony enough that for every German who subscribed to a persecution complex or a cult of violence as its expiation, there were plenty of others whose thought patterns ran in very contrary directions. The problem is that we are not comparing like with like. Bar the opposing paramilitary associations of communists and Social Democrats, the weakness of those Germans who were not looking for a fight lay in their very passivity. By contrast, what the nationalist *Wille zur Macht* offered was a very palpable escape mechanism out of humiliation, out of angst—out of Weimar. The path of violence would be the path of Germany's redemption.[27] Through it, a heroic future beckoned. Here was fascism in the making. But in this German case—unlike that of its Italian progenitor—with a very particular focus on who would pay the price.

*

By any objective criteria, the Creditanstalt episode should be grounds enough for exploding the nonsensicality of Jewish responsibility for German woes. The bank was Rothschild-founded and owned and thus was as much a victim of the economic crisis as any 'Aryan' business. The Rothschilds, in their personal capacity, moreover, proved instrumental in the rescue and revitalization of the bank. The crude analysis of the conspiracy-minded, however, read into these events, as so many others, a perfectly logical and consistent example of Jewish manoeuvring towards their ultimate goal of world domination. This explanatory device, as we have seen, had been endemic to nationally-minded European society writ large during the Great War and its aftermath. A renewed bout of societal angst in the eye of the economic crisis between 1929 and 1932, especially in the most economically ravaged countries of Central and Eastern Europe, was bound to lead to its recrudescence. But in Germany's case, it was not so much latent crisis but the *persistence* of the motif which begs the question: why the Jews?

Looked at in terms of straight socio-economic indices, anti-Jewish animus in Germany is potentially explicable in terms of standard envy or jealousy elements but completely fails to take us beyond that. Demographically speaking, German Jewry was insignificant. The 564,000 members of local synagogally based *Gemeinde*, in 1926, represented less than 1 per cent of the total population. It was certainly true that at the top end of the communal pyramid there were some seriously rich people who, proportionate to their numbers, also played a highly significant role in the economic life of the Germany. If bankers of the ilk of the Rothschilds and

Speyers had a particularly high profile on this score, the same was hardly less true in the world of media, publishing, and cinema. Jews owned four out of five of the major department store chains. Thirteen per cent of German doctors, 16 per cent of German lawyers, were Jewish.[28] As Jewish concentrations were largely urban, not to say metropolitan, their association with modernism, and hence the world of business, was, without doubt, very strong.

But where does any of this get us? For every Jew in Germany who was rich or comfortably off, there was several more who were extremely poor, almost all *Ostjuden* refugees who had fled from the East, before or after the Great War, as a consequence of economic impoverishment and/or the prevailing political insecurity. They were, of course, heartily detested by German xenophobes, with all the standard accusations that all xenophobes everywhere level at the most vulnerable incomers. But they could hardly be accused of economic takeover, any more indeed than could the well-embedded Jewish elites. Even where Jews were involved in key financial institutions, as board members, for instance, in the great Deutsche and Dresdner banks, there was no Jewish interest per se, let alone a hegemonic one. Nor could they be charged with being some comprador class, a charge repeatedly levelled against Armenian and Greek businessmen in pre-1914 Ottomania. Jewish commercial orientation in Germany was always decidedly towards the liberal ethos of the West, as, in fact, it was among Ottoman empire 'middlemen'. But Germany was already a strong, heavily industrialized society by 1914. There was no question of Jews acting as the agents, unwitting or otherwise, for some foreign economic penetration. Nor was there any ambiguity on the matter. High-profile 'Germans of Jewish faith'—the very terminology is itself revealing—were often quite embarrassing in their protestations of love for and loyalty to Germany. The leading industrialist Walther Rathenau, in 1916 wrote:

> I have—and I know—nothing but German blood, German ethnicity and German people. If I were to be driven from my German land, I would continue to be German, and nothing would change that…My ancestors and I have been nourished of German soil and of the German mind…and we have had no thoughts that were not German or for Germany.[29]

Yet this is the same Walther Rathenau who, as Germany's first Jewish foreign minister, was assassinated in June 1922, on the grounds that he was one of the alleged 'three hundred Elders of Zion whose purpose and aim was to bring the whole world under Jewish influence'.[30] So ran the corroborated testimony of one of the surviving accomplices of the assassins. 'The murder was timed to coincide with the summer solstice' and, after the young men from the Schutz- und Trutzbund and various other ultra-right groups had committed the deed, students and other 'young Germans gathered on hilltops to celebrate simultaneously the turning of the year and the destruction of one who symbolised the power of darkness'. Rathenau, in other words, had been 'offered up as a human sacrifice to the sun-god of ancient Germanic religion'.[31]

If this is the genuine motivation for the assassination we seem to have entered into a collective mindscape in which rational, empirical observations about Jews have no bearing or value whatsoever, as if requiring deferment to the perpetrators' own fevered *völkisch* imaginings on the matter. That this mindset was certainly nothing new is attested by the range of *völkisch* groups in existence on both sides of the Austro-German border from before the fin de siècle. In *The Rise of the West* we noted the connecting threads between such disparate organizations and networks, not least in the way their deep-set anxieties about the state of the modern, industrial world were luridly projected onto the Jews as purveyors of bodily contamination and societal decomposition. In pictorial representation Jews were serpents nestling at the trunk of the German tree of life, or hooked-nose spiders with their tentacles round the world—the sort of imagery which would later become standard fare under the Nazis. Virulent Judaeophobia of this sort also claimed one could always tell Jews by their distinct, overpoweringly nauseous body odour.[32] And, in a remarkable metamorphosis of that most potent of all medieval horror stories, the ritual murder—in which Jews sucked blood out of children in order to revitalize themselves—the 'body snatcher' trope now made its way across the 1914 divide with the lecherous but also money-grubbing 'banker' Jew not simply vamping the blood of his always maiden female victim but, through the process of sexual defilement, spreading his syphilitic contagion far and wide.[33]

All this sounds like a form of lunacy perfectly at home in the exclusive company of unhinged marginals, perverts, and fantasists; but hardly representative of any mainstream society, certainly not one whose self-regard was founded on a profound sense of its own innate respectability. The fact that the other side of the *völkisch* coin—as touted by the Austro-German, swastika-bedecked, fin-de-siècle magazine *Ostara*, or, after 1918, by the equally swastika-infested Thule Bund—centred round an amalgam of occult elements and esoteric mumbo-jumbo, the main thrust of which amounted to the need to recover, from the mists of time, the cosmic relationship between an *ur*-race of German supermen and their very own pagan sun god,[34] would also hardly seem to make it the stuff around which a sophisticated, modern body politic might frame its self-understanding, let alone organize itself.

However, such a view would be to fatally dismiss the potency and relevance of the delusional and paranoid in the inner life of states and societies under stress. The career of Theodor Fritsch comes to mind as significant here. Before the First World War, Fritsch already had a long pre-war history as a rabid, at times exterminatory-sounding, but very popular anti-Semitic publicist with a finger in a range of *völkisch* pies. Just before the war the political success of his message seemed to bear fruit with the founding of the *Mittelstand*-orientated, openly anti-Semitic *Reichshammerbund* in 1912, and the Cartel of the Productive Estates the following year.[35] But in a sense these political constellations also confirmed the limitations of Fritsch's petit bourgeois background and the social barriers to making common cause with other, more elite, ultra-nationalist, social formations, as represented by, for instance, Heinrich Class' Pan-German League. Anti-Semitic parties in the pre-1914 period were notable too for their electoral failure. All this changed, however, at the war's end. And the key to the *mood* change was the arrival of the *Protocols*.

The conspiracy narrative gave answers as to why the war had taken place; why Jews were apparently at the head not only of revolutionary Bolshevik government in

Russia but also of the would-be soviets and republics at home; and why, indeed, normative time had been fractured. Fritsch got to work at his Leipzig publishing house producing a popular edition of the *Protocols*. By the time of Hitler's takeover it had sold nearly 100,000 copies, though, in fact, Fritsch's was only one of thirty-three such pre-Nazi editions. Even so, it was he, above all others, who would receive plaudits from the Nazis as *Altmeister*—master teacher—for informing the world of the imminence and urgency of the Jewish danger, and whose own 'classic' 1887 diatribe, *The Anti-Semitic Catechism* (later retitled as the *Handbook on the Jewish Question*) would become a standard element of their school curriculum.[36]

But the key question remains: why did so many Germans, *respectable* Germans, buy into the Judaeophobia of the Fritsch type, not to say its openly violent projections? For there is no doubt that, after 1918, respectable, educated people were doing so in droves. A Jewish observer who attended several Berlin meetings in the early 1920s entirely devoted to the *Protocols* wrote:

> The speaker was usually a professor, a teacher, an editor, a lawyer, or someone of that kind. The audience consisted of members of the educated class, civil servants, trades-men, former officers, ladies, above all students, students of all faculties and years of seniority… Passions were whipped up to boiling point.[37]

The observer was particularly struck by the students '… eyes flashed, fists clenched, hoarse voices roaring applause or vengeance'. The connection between such students, their reading of the *Protocols*, and the gunning down of Rathenau is well attested.[38] Nor was it just in the early 1920s that audiences of this ilk proved to be the most enthusiastic imbibers of the message. A Weimar secret police report on a meeting in the upper-class Berlin district of Charlottenburg in 1932, during which a Nazi speaker called for Jewish extermination, noted that the gathering was made up of the 'better bourgeoisie' who greeted the speech with 'stormy applause'.[39]

One could, of course, try and pin all this down to a particular sequence of extraordinary and unexpected events consequent on war and the Russian Revolution. The *Protocols* had come into Germany in the kitbags of ultra-right, usually rabidly anti-Semitic White Russian officers, who were part of a much wider exodus of Russians and other peoples dispossessed, terrorized by, or simply fearful of Bolshevik rule.[40] Among the refugees were also many Russophobe, ethnic Germans from the Baltic area and the wider rimlands zone, including one Alfred Rosenberg, who would rise within Nazi ranks to become the chief promoter of the *Protocols* narrative and self-styled theoretician on the 'Jewish question'.[41] Just as with the many émigré Turks from Russia at the turn of the century who compensated for their often complex, fraught, usually rimlands' backgrounds and experience by immersion in the notion of a redemptive pan-Turanism, those *Auslandsdeutsche* of the ilk of Rosenberg—and there appear to have been a great many in Nazi 'perpetrator' ranks[42]—were amongst the most fervent promoters of the pan-German creed, on the one hand, and Judaeo-Bolshevism, on the other.

Yet while this might provide the most likely vector for the initial spread of the *Protocols* into the German mainstream, it hardly, on its own, explains its potency. For Russian subjects to blame Jews for what happened in their country, erroneous as that may have been, could at least be understood as a form of chop-logic for events happening all around them. In Germany, however, the entire Jewish–Bolshevik connection was altogether more tenuous and distant. Of course, *there had been* that searing moment in November 1918, when revolution had nearly happened and in which many of the leading figures were, indeed, of Jewish background. Perhaps we should take this as quite sufficient in itself—a moment when, for true believers, the mist had lifted from their eyes and the whole sordid truth had been revealed in an instant, yet forever. The only minor problem is that, thereafter, there is scant evidence to confirm the ongoing nature of this supposed menace *within* Germany. For instance, while there were Jews involved in radical politics, especially in the German Communist Party (KPD), few were very prominent and, by 1931, not a single one was among the hundred party deputies elected that year to the Reichstag.[43]

To be sure, there had been a handful of notable Jews in mainstream, pro-Weimar politics. There had been Hugo Preuss, the founder of Weimar constitution. And, of course, Rathenau. But to have embraced them within the Jewish–Bolshevik conspiracy narrative would have been truly to engage in convoluted mental gymnastics. Which is exactly what the Volkists did, after Rathenau's critical role in the making of the Rapallo Treaty. Perhaps, though, the point is that it was not politics alone which kept alive the fevered Judaeophobic imagination throughout the Weimar years. It was something deeper and entirely more angst-laden.

Nationalists loathed the republic in its own right, and the reason for this was not only because they saw it—actually, quite incorrectly—as the illegitimate child of Western imposition, but because it seemed to subvert a received value system in which order, place, and, hence, continuity in the world were both known and assured. Without these elements there could be no purpose: at least not as traditionally understood. That would have required a restatement of clear—and, one should, add unnegotiable—social, religious, and moral, as well as political, boundaries which, in turn, could only be determined by hierarchy and authority. In fact, Weimar did not go about consciously removing these pillars of certitude. But, by creating a democratic, free-thinking cultural climate in which it was possible to question received wisdoms, it did enable those who wished to do so to push at the boundaries and, in the process, acted as a seedbed for a range of cultural, artistic, and scientific innovations. The result was an explosion of cultural modernism: a perfect environment for what Yuri Slezkine might describe as intelligent, quick-witted, and instinctively provocative Mercurians to take the lead—even (God forbid) intellectually excel—over their somewhat slower, more dull-witted Apollonian neighbours. In short, this was indeed the moment in which a developing 150-year-long interaction, even symbiosis, between Jewish *Haskalah*-orientated education and German *Bildung* bore an extraordinary crop of fruit.

It was, of course, not *only* Jews who were involved in the Bauhaus movement, compositional atonality, or the Institute of Social Research. Four German *non*-Jews received Nobel prizes, as did the five Jewish winners in physics and medicine under Weimar.[44] For the Jews involved, anyway, the accolades first and foremost went to their country and their culture. Here was the great paradox. Most German

Jews felt thoroughly rooted in their homeland. The nearest Weimar Jewish equivalent to the radical Armenian disposition vis-à-vis the Ottoman state were the German Zionists. They wanted explicit minority status and Jewish national rights. They also sought to prepare German Jewish youth for migration and settlement on the land in British-controlled Palestine.[45] The vast majority of Weimar Jews, however, recoiled with horror at this negation of their hard-won *German* identity. The philosopher Hermann Cohen, in the Wilhelmine era, had gone to great neo-Kantian lengths to demonstrate how the German spirit and the Jewish spirit were thoroughly reconcilable. Now German Jews were freed from the need to have a philosophical touchstone to prove the point. They did it in a much more natural way. By the late 1920s an estimated one in three Berlin Jews—and this, after all, was the major Jewish concentration in Germany—were marrying out. Indeed, if this demographic trajectory had been continued—assuming no further Jewish migrations from the East—a specific German Jewish community would have ceased to exist within a couple of generations.[46]

Even after 1933, the record is replete with examples of both Jewish leaders and ordinary Jewish men and women declaring, in the most fulsome terms, their love for and loyalty to Germany. The Centralverein deutscher Staatsbürger jüdischen Glaubens, the chief organization for the defence of the community, declared in the face of Hitler's tightening grip in March of that year, 'Germany will remain Germany and no one can rob us of our homeland and our fatherland'.[47] The following month, when the Nazis attempted a boycott of Jewish businesses, countless Jewish Great War veterans appeared at their shopfronts, their campaign medals proudly adorning their breasts. Some of them, it has been said, 'but for Nazi antisemitism would have become avid followers of Hitler'.[48]

But this is exactly what nationalists of 'the German ideology' themselves recoiled from with horror. The very last thing they wanted was to assimilate Jews: that is, to resolve 'the problem' through some metabolic transformation of 'them' into 'us'. For more than half a century anti-Semites had been warning that to attempt to go down this path would actually result in 'us' becoming 'them'—a veritable *Verjudung* ('Judaization') of German society, the consequence of which would be 'a race of pseudo-hebraic mestizos, beyond all doubt degenerate physically, mentally and morally'.[49] But, for Houston Stewart Chamberlain, the fin-de-siècle writer of these gentle words, at stake here was not just the fate of the 'beautiful saving Aryan': the victory of the Jewish anti-race would also ensure that Western civilization would be cast adrift from its firm and sure moorings into a pointless, mechanistic universe in which nothing would be sacred.

Here, at last, we are back with the fundaments of the German nationalists' inner neurosis: the loss of control. The culture of Weimar rubbed their faces in it, above all in the theoretical physics of Nobel laureate Albert Einstein, and, perhaps even more alarmingly, though the pyschoanalytical method founded in Vienna by Sigmund Freud.[50] One did not have to know anything about the Oedipal complex, or the theory of relativity, to recognize that what these pathfinders were actually doing was taking apart received science—that is, as one *thought* one knew it—and putting instead, in its place, uncertainty, instability, fluidity, and doubt. The emerging disciplines of which Einstein and Freud were the leading, most brilliant exponents were not simply 'subversive' but ipso facto 'Jewish', and thus like everything else which Jewish intellect espoused: dangerous, decadent, deceitful, and destructive.

More than simply as a disturbance of their physical, or emotional, peace, which the new sciences clearly were, the anti-Weimar ideologues thus read their Einstein and Freud as a pointed, mocking, sarcasm-laden affront to the very concept of Germanness. If the Jewish Marxists and Bolsheviks were going to literally over-throw Germany and enslave her politically, 'Jew' science and culture was part of the softening-up process, the creeping paralysis designed to breed scepticism, emasculate German manhood, spread moral and sexual degradation, and so pave the way for the tyranny of Zion. There was no point engaging with any of it: the only logical riposte was obliteration, getting it out of the system like every other *undeutsch* element with which the Jews had contaminated the ersatz republic. Indeed, for nationalists the point was that Weimar was a *Judenrepublik*.

Its striving to be included in institutions such as the League of Nations and the Permanent Court of International Justice, its very espousal of a liberal philosophy of human rights, were all evidence—as Hitler would have put it—of the way 'the Jewish spirit' had carried 'the three plagues of humanity'—internationalism, democracy, and pacifism—into the very heart of the nation in order to destroy its ' race value'.[51] No wonder the zeal with which his supporters, at the moment of Nazi takeover, vented their patriotic spleen by destroying Magnus Hirschfield's Institute for Sexual Research in Berlin: an open example of supposedly 'Jew' pseudo-science, proclaiming homosexuality, of all things, to be natural and innate.[52] No wonder too, that at the core of this assault—as of the much more stage-managed public burning of 'un-German' books, organized nationwide in early May by the new propaganda minister Joseph Goebbels—were German students.[53]

More than a century earlier the great German Jewish poet Heinrich Heine had mused that it was but a short step from the burning of books to the burning of people. But the fundamental question for us here is how much can we read back, into the immediate years *before* Hitler, clear evidence of an eliminationist desire, evinced by at least a substantial number of Germans against their fellow German Jewish neighbours? The very simple answer is that, in quantitative terms, we can-not. What we have instead is some specific examples where individuals publicly enunciated such thoughts, nearly all in response to the immediate conditions of post-war alienation and the fear of direct Allied invasion or retribution. For instance, an army officer penned recommendations to the Bavarian state president, in 1920, in which he proposed rounding up all Jews and incarcerating them in concentration camps, executing those who resisted—alongside Germans who tried to protect them—and then starving the rest of the Jews to death at least as long as Allied anti-German action continued. Once the threat ended, he proposed, all Jewish property and assets were to be forfeited and the survivors vomited out to Palestine. The officer's unwarranted intervention actually was the subject of repri-mand, though not before a prominent state-assembly representative had provided an affidavit supporting this 'thoroughly well-meaning and honourable young man'.[54]

In another instance, three years later, one of the early Nazi acolytes, Hermann Esser, proposed that, in the event of a French invasion, a German Jew should be shot for every French soldier who set foot on German soil.[55] These examples evince similarities in terms of thought process with Hitler's much better-known, indeed infamous, *Mein Kampf* assertion that a million decent German lives could have been saved if 12,000 to 15,000 Jews had been exposed to poison gas near the Great War's outset.[56]

The issue at stake, however, is not whether this or that individual German openly espoused Jewish extermination, or even whether this was something altogether new given that the motif is acknowledged as 'part and parcel of *völkisch* oral and pamphlet tradition'.[57] Rather, the deeper issue is whether the psychological tensions set in train by the circumstances of the1918 defeat provide a sufficient connecting link between what appears to have been *thought* by many other Germans under Weimar was only *acted upon* through Hitler. The social group which would seem to provide us with the most concrete evidence of such a link is the German student body. Under Weimar it became one of the 'hardcore constituencies of antisemitism',[58] increasingly veering towards open and explicit support for the Nazis, and undoubtedly aided and abetted by an older generation of academic gurus. Intense upset and frustration at Germany's defeat, compounded by the fact that this so-called 'wartime generation' had been too young to offer their own bodies in sacrifice to the military struggle, translated into equally intense desires for vengeance against those deemed in every sense responsible for their personal and political woes. It was exactly from the most elite, Weimar-educated circles and, more exactly, by way of the Deutschen Hochschulring—the 1921-founded umbrella for a range of radical, anti-Semitic student groups—that a majority of the leading practitioners of Jewish genocide in the rimlands would later be drawn.[59]

Of course, there is one small impediment: while student unions, just like many other 'patriotic' organizations, adopted Aryan clauses excluding Jews from their number and, in their own particular case, with the added insult of refusing Jewish access to their duelling fraternities, relatively few students participated in assassinations, beatings, desecration of cemeteries, or the other anti-Jewish 'excesses' of the 1920s. This has led Ulrich Herbert, a leading and critical Holocaust expert, to conclude that most of the anti-Semitism of the Weimar years was not of the 'shrill' or 'truly fanatical aggressive species'—by which he refers to the overtly pornographic kind touted in Julius Streicher's Nazi rag, *Der Stürmer*—but was instead, while albeit virulent, still essentially 'passive'.[60]

This argument is perplexing, however, because it suggests something essentially contradictory: that there was a high level of interiorized anti-Jewish animus, especially in elite sectors, with students always at the cutting edge; yet that so long as it remained detached from large-scale, direct *physical* anti-Jewish violence, also lacking was serious exterminatory—or, as Daniel Goldhagen would put it, 'eliminationist'— intent. The argument is doubly perplexing because Herbert also goes on to assert that after 1933 'anti-antisemitism...could no longer be expressed in public'.[61] Which can only mean one of two things: either the Nazi state created a climate in which groups or individuals were too cowed or frightened to express their dissent from statist policy—which does not entirely fit with what we now know about the somewhat less than absolute authoritarian modus operandi of the regime's pre-war years—or, alternatively, Nazism in power provided the legitimization for what for many, *though certainly not all*, Germans, was already implicitly there, in their heads. From this perspective the role of Hitler, not so much as vector but more precisely as authentic 'voice' of German Judaeophobia, becomes all the more crucial.

THE HITLER PHENOMENON AND
GERMAN LONGING

> Once I am really in power, my first and foremost task will be the annihilation of the Jews…I will have gallows built in rows—at the Marienplatz in Munich for example…As soon as they have been untied, the next batch will be strung up, and so on down the line…Other cities will follow suit, precisely in this fashion, until all Germany has been completely cleansed of Jews.[62]
>
> Hitler to Josef Hell, 1922

One can hardly get away from the centrality of Hitler's Judaeophobia. It is very publicly in evidence right from the start of his political career in September 1919, first as a Bavarian Reichswehr observer of, at that point, the Munich-based German Workers Party (DAP), then as its leader. Shot through with sexual angst, Hitler's feelings towards Jews were utterly projective. They were also a supreme, as well as extreme, case of the personal as political. Jewish sadism, cruelty, deceitfulness, not to say desire for absolute power were simply the inside-out expression of Hitler's true self: a real-life version of Oscar Wilde's Dorian Gray.[63] Obversely, all the things Hitler longed for, for the German people—purity, communal cohesion, longevity of history and existence—were attributes which seemed to be possessed by the Jews, even while their 'mongrel depravity' was infecting and decomposing the German nation. It was hardly the only contradiction in Hitler's peculiar analysis of the world around him. But then, longing and loathing were inextricably mixed up in his inordinately complex psychopathology.

All this, of course, has been minutely mined and documented, explored for its childhood and adolescent wellsprings, exhaustively interpreted and reinterpreted by Hitler scholars from diverse disciplines.[64] As well it ought, as regarding the person most responsible for the ultimate genocide of modern times. But then Hitler's rantings—the above 1922 quote is one of his more transparently exterminatory statements for public consumption—were hardly, in any sense, original. Nor was the anti-Jewish argument, insofar as there was one, anything but derivative. To be sure, Hitler's reading, within a certain tightly defined medium- or low-brow confine, was eclectic. We know of his debt to Fritsch, on the one hand, to US ideologues—in particular Madison Grant—on the other, for much of his race hate, which extended beyond Jews to blacks, and Asians in particular.[65] The clear wedge of *Mein Kampf* accusation regarding Jewish sex defilement of German maidens and the consequent contamination of the German blood pool can be equally traced to some thoroughly scatological, pornographically smutty writings from the war, or immediate post-war period: most obviously Artur Dinter's 1918 novel *Die Sünde wider das Blut* ('The Sin against the Blood') but also by way of Wilhelm Bölsche's 1921 *Vom Bazillus zum Affenmenschen* ('From Bacillus to Anthropoid Ape'), which promoted some thoroughly science-fiction-type examples of Jewish contamination, for good measure.[66] Fears of infection through sexual contact and the consequent possibility of miscegenation run as a consistent thread through Hitlerian neurosis. As for the Jewish plot to take over the world, Hitler hardly had to invent or even imagine any of that. It was there to be read at every street corner, in the pocket editions of the *Protocols*, and was directly on tap through fanatically *völkisch* and anti-Semitic individuals in the original DAP—notably Dietrich Eckart, acknowledged, until his death in 1923, as a key mentor in the development of Hitler's conspiracy world view, not to mention the person to whose memory *Mein Kampf* would be dedicated.[67]

Yet for all the delusions of grandeur and convictions of thwarted artistic genius to boot, the supreme irony is that Hitler, while a suitable case for mental treatment, by rights should be instantly dismissible for what he *actually* was: an ill-educated 'ignoramus at a *Bier Keller*' spewing out 'gangsterish threats and murderous flights of fantasy'.[68] His humble origins certainly should have made him, in political terms, a nobody; an irrelevance from the word go. And for some this is exactly what he remained. Hindenburg, for one, memorably referred to him as the 'Bohemian corporal': the reference to Hitler's ancestral background in the impoverished Czech–German lands of the Waldviertel a pointed put-down on ethnic as much as social grounds.[69] Yet this was the same Hitler who not only superseded the neo-kaiserian field marshal to become Germany's supreme ruler, but went on from there to convulse all of Europe and beyond, in so doing drawing all the global powers into another world war. How could this be? How, more exactly, could this preacher of open hate come to be embraced by so many Germans as their *redeemer*?

There is, of course, a way of responding which, by disaggregating Hitler from his anti-Semitism, whether intentionally or otherwise, exonerates the majority of Germans from Jewish mass murder. Most Germans who voted for Hitler in the key elections between 1928 and 1932, it has been argued by Sarah Gordon, for instance, did not do so in support of anti-Semitism but from other motivations—most obviously to do with dire economic circumstances to which Nazism, with promises of state-sponsored jobs, claimed to have the answer.[70] As also did the KPD, the other end-of-the-spectrum radical party, to which the unemployed turned in droves, and which, while anti-wealth, was not in itself anti-Jewish. Even many of those who joined the Nazis (the National Socialist Workers Party, refashioned out of the original DAP in 1920) may not necessarily have done so for its anti-Semitic vitriol. Becoming a Brownshirt clearly gave otherwise very dislocated people a sense of barracks-like belonging and purpose. It was clearly quite possible to engage with Hitler's opportunistic appeals on grounds of self-interest while divorcing that from any personal relationships one had with Jews one knew in a social or economic context. Ian Kershaw has for instance noted that peasant smallholders in Bavaria, many of whom would have voted for the party, were still—once Hitler was in power—among the most socially resistant to the easing out of local Jewish cattle traders with whom they did business or, indeed, who were looked to as trusted providers of small-scale credit.[71]

All this may be true, even while, at the same time, we ought to bear in mind Theodor Abel's careful contemporary assessment, based on a detailed study of Nazi supporters, that anti-Semitism had struck a popular note, and 'in so doing contributed to a considerable extent to the success of the movement'.[72] One might add that many Brownshirts had already had a previous incarnation in the openly anti-Semitic Freikorps. But, in a crucial sense, all this misses the point. Our aim here is not to corroborate Goldhagen's claim that more or less all Germans were 'eliminationist' anti-Semites looking for the first opportunity to enact their most deep-felt inner desires. Even if all the people who did vote Nazi *were* either closet or open anti-Semites, one still has to bear in mind the fact that, at the high point of the 'free' electoral swing towards them, in July 1932, 62.7 per cent of the franchised population did *not* vote for the party.[73] Yet what this underscores is simply that voting patterns alone are clearly insufficient to explain underlying societal drives, let alone provide evidence of a country's approval for genocide.

In fact, genocide does not of itself necessarily require an assumption of societal acceptance anyway. In this case it was clearly carried out through Hitler as dictatorial head of the Nazi state, not as freely chosen leader of German society. Moreover, it took place at some clear spatial and chronological distance from his accession to power. Yet, modern states—even ones sometimes erroneously described as totalitarian—are dependent for their ongoing legitimacy, cohesion, and ability to govern on social groups willing to identify with them. Throughout previous volumes we have identified the primary gelling agent in this process to be nationalism. Taking our own cue, thus, what matters is not whether all of the people living in Germany supported Hitler or his anti-Semitism but whether the already more nationally-minded elements—the ones to whom the sense of German belonging was at the core of their personal sense of identity—connected with Hitler and imbibed what he was saying to them. One might object that the whole point of Nazism was that it did not seek to speak *only* to some, but to all *echt* (real) Germans; to be, as Goebbels put it, 'a genuine party of the people'.[74] That would have mean cutting across all sectional, class, or localized interests to create, or, rather, as its leadership imagined, to recreate, one single *Volksgemeinschaft* marching together, according to one single iron will.

If the notion of transcending historic classes to provide for a mobility and opportunity in society and state regardless of one's background clearly had a very broad and potent appeal—in some ways mirroring the appeal of communism in Russia—what I want to propose here is that it was to those who already felt intensely national (and so intensely at odds with the experience of Weimar) who most thoroughly surrendered themselves to the intoxication of the brew. And who, in the process, subliminally or otherwise, endorsed its most violent anti-Semitic underpinnings. Victor Klemperer, that critical observer and sane interpreter of the whole Nazi era in Germany, put his finger on it when he proposed that it was fellow-countrymen who were most educated, well read, and well versed in the history of both literature and Christianity who most profoundly bought into Hitlerism. And one of the reasons they did so, Klemperer argued, was because Hitler so all-encompassingly appropriated the vocabulary of traditional Christianity.[75] Living in Hitler's Germany thus was not simply an *ewig* experience—one linking individual and community to 'the path to eternity': the very supplication in the Lord's prayer *Dein Reich komme* ('Thy Kingdom come') could now be read through the Third *Reich* as the fulfilment of an historical promise. But, as Klemperer points out, this could only have meaning if you already had some sense of the medieval Holy Roman Empire and so could make the connection to its proposed resurrection, or rather legitimation, for a new—supposedly holy—'universal order'.[76] For Germans of the likes of Paula B., Klemperer's rather serious, introverted, ivory-tower colleague at his Dresden university, the effect seems to have been altogether overwhelming: the woman suddenly appearing in his room one day soon after Hitler had become chancellor, to announce her new-found German 'duty':

> Everything is related to the issue of being German or non-German, that is all that matters; you see that's what I, what we all, have either learned from the Führer, or rediscovered having forgotten it. He has brought us home again!...I belong entirely to the Führer.[77]

By any standards, this is remarkable stuff. It is as if this cautious, intelligent woman, presumably alongside many thousands of other similar men and women, had been caught up in a form of religious revivalism. At first sight, moreover, it would seem to have less to do with the modern, secular European world and more with something akin to the world of possession we associate, for instance, with the ritual, magical formulas of the mystical secret society cults of West Africa.[78] Uncannily, Hitler, in his initial self-promotion as 'the Drummer' may have been closer to the shaman prophets of such movements than even he could have imagined. Except, in a notably inverted and distorted sense, Hitler's chiliastic framework is clearly Christian. In 1924, one prescient observer, Carl Christian Bry, published a little-known study, *Verkappte Religionen* ('Masked Religions'), in which he proposed that Volkists were seeking to metamorphose Christianity into a new, racialized form of mystical religion, with Jews cast as the eternal antithesis.[79] A decade later the French Jewish philosopher Emmanuel Lévinas ran further with the argument, proposing that Nazism was specifically seeking to invert the Western hierarchy of soul over body, the latter becoming 'the bearer of absolute spiritual value...conferred by birth and unalterable by any act of speech or thought'. The result was to place 'every human being irrevocably inside or outside of an "authentic" community of blood'.[80]

If this is a keenly perceptive reading of the Nazi world view, the equally astonishing paradox is that large numbers of German Christians, especially within the Protestant Evangelical Church, embraced it fervently, even—to use that favoured term of Nazi years—'fanatically'.[81] Indeed, quite lacking irony, the leader of the majority part of it, which reformulated itself in spring 1932 as the German Christian Church—before the Nazi takeover—proclaimed its followers 'stormtroopers of Jesus Christ'.[82] Yet one can also see, following Klemperer's lead how, even against the obvious blasphemy, so many educated people could willingly have given themselves up to the idea that Hitler was not only Christ-like, but in some very specifically *German* way the embodiment of Jesus' promise to return to the world.

Who, after all, was Hitler, but, like Jesus, a rank outsider from the back of beyond who had appeared on the scene at the moment of the country's ultimate paroxysm? And who, like Christ, had taken upon himself all the pain, anguish, and despair of its (German) people, even as he, on 9 November 1918, lay in his Pasewalk military hospital bed, blinded and overcome by the hallucinatory visions consequent upon his wounding in a British mustard gas attack? He had suffered, yet he had returned from the dead: a very corporeal proof that the sacrifice of all those other young men in uniform had not been in vain.[83] Spared yet again, five years to the day later, from the bullets of the Bavarian state police, the miracle of his survival could only reaffirm that this time, *through* Hitler, a truly millenarian redemption and transfiguration would soon follow. Thus, Hitler's presence among the Germans was treated for so many as akin to a Pentecostal experience. As an SS Gruppenführer would later put it, Hitler was greater than Jesus, who had only twelve loyal disciples, for 'the Führer stood at the head of a nation of seventy million sworn to loyalty'.[84] Messenger, prophet, epiphany-like fount of Germany's rebirth, Hitler was received and accepted as Führer not primarily as a politician or even statesman, but as a messiah. Here was the one who would confer grace on his fellow Germans and, in so doing, not simply guide them to a safer place—beyond danger, beyond sin—but restore them to their God-promised glory.

What, however, is also crystal clear is that embrace of this message carried an equal embrace of its explicit urge to redemptive violence. To be restored was not only to turn the tables on the Allies, but specifically to cleanse the national community of the contamination which had brought it so close to seeming obliteration. On the altar of war, on which Germans had made their sacrifice, there would now be a national awakening, followed by visionary retribution. And that could only mean through the prism of Hitlerite eschatology against the Jews. This is the point at which educated Germans should have recognized that this could not, in any sense, be squared with either clear objective reasoning, on the one hand, or normative Christian theology on the other. Instead, however, vast numbers chose to imagine their idolatrous rapture of Hitler as some fulfilment of the Christian millennium. This is interesting in itself because it would seem to be so fundamentally at odds with the assumed drivers of either individual or collective social behaviour in modern societies. Nor can it simply be explained as nationalism in some form of extreme overdrive. Victor Klemperer's wife Eva thought that Hitler was actually most comparable to the sixteenth-century Anabaptist leader, Jan of Leyden, a charismatic figure of the Reformation who preached hellfire and brimstone but who nevertheless swept up great numbers of the populace of Münster by means of his impassioned, vision-laden oratory.[85]

The suggestion is equally bold because demagogues of the ilk of Jan, at the onset of the early modern age, very clearly represented a challenge to political norms by way of a prophetic sanction, which was, at the same time, a clear repudiation of the religious rule of the priesthood. Though it was the conservative radical Moeller van den Brück who had given the term currency in the 1920s, Hitler's appropriation of the medieval idea of the Third Reich—'with its echo of a thousand year empire before the Last Judgement'[86]—can be viewed as similarly antinomian. By wrapping himself up in the mantle of prophecy, Hitler was effectively proclaiming his own abilities as thaumaturge; not thereby to return Germany to the lost Wilhelmine era, but rather to transcend time altogether, thus bringing together Germany's golden past and an even more effulgent future.

Of course, it was *normative* time which the Jews in 1918 were alleged to have ruptured. Turning distorted time back on itself, it was as if God himself had come down from on high to proclaim the new dawn, and hence to dispense grace where it was rightly due. The fact that Hitler's restorative promise came from outside the system—that it was not only *not* tainted by involvement in the politics of Weimar but was consciously presented as an anti-Weimar *movement*—made it all the more compelling. When, finally, Hitler did throw the Nazis into the parliamentary fray, the party's purpose was, quite openly, like that of Christ among the money changers in the temple. And when Hitler became chancellor, in January 1933—actually through the machinations of Hindenburg's inner circle—this was greeted by supporters as if they were at the onset of some millennial reign.

We have here all we need to understand why so many nationally-minded Germans were prepared to follow Hitler, even through the adversity of war, even to the bitter *Götterdämmerung*-like end. In the sense that Hitler's Nazism visualized a Germany complete, a society organized as a coherent and centralized whole, beyond class, or party, or regional interests, or even deference to traditional hierarchies, the appeal was intensely nationalistic yet at the same time thoroughly modern. As a nationwide communal cult, its potency, however, was of an entirely different order. Reinforced at every turn by its symbolic manifestations, whether in the form of mass uniformed rallies and parades, the appearance everywhere of the swastika, or the everyday use of the Hitler salute—above all, of course, in the nationwide broadcast speeches of the prophet-leader himself—Nazism was, for all its obvious paganism, affirmed by millions of German Christians as a profoundly ethical experience.

That alone still does not explain the leap to genocide. The gap between apocalyptic rhetoric and focused, eliminationist state practice, especially in the first five years of Nazi rule, requires further comment, which we seek to develop in the section, 'A regime and its enemies'. There is, however, one other passing matter of consequence before we arrive there. There is little doubt that in the immediate run-up to 1933 the nationalist groupings, whether Nazi-orientated or not, were clearly heading towards a conception of Germany in which Jews were excluded from public life, perhaps even from society altogether. This is detectable, for instance, in the way a major section of the previously liberal-leaning German Democrat Party hived itself off in 1930 to form a German State party, part of whose purpose was to take a fundamentally and stridently anti-Jewish stance; and is even more apparent in the pre-Hitler chancellorship of Franz von Papen, under whom legal regulations were devised to purge Jews from the civil service, deny naturalization to *Ostjuden*, and even prevent name changing which might disguise Jewish identity.[87] These tendencies were also much in line with the arguments of

Carl Schmitt, the much-vaunted leading jurist of the day, whose assertion of Germany as a 'total state', and hence of its absolute right to defend its interests versus those of internal or external 'enemies', was clearly directed, above all, against the Jews.[88]

However, this begs the question of whether, for the upper echelons of the state apparatus—that is, for the army, corporate chiefs, and aristocratic-run presidential inner circle—operating behind the Weimar façade, Hitler actually offered the best, most efficacious route to this Schmittian goal. The Nazis may have repeatedly called for a national revolution, entailing a *Gleichschaltung*—an integrated, state-planned streamlining of society—but there was little in place to indicate how this was going to be carried out. The leadership of the party moreover were, like Hitler himself, untried political outsiders with no experience of government at the national level, albeit with some early indications of what might follow in the form of recent Brownshirt bully-boy aided victories in *Länder* elections. However, for the traditional ruling elite the obvious direction for a reassertion of pre-Weimar order was not the elevation of the Bohemian corporal and his thuggish crew but the introduction of a more firmly based, top-down leadership, most obviously under the tutelage of an army general and, if not founded on absolute dictatorship, then at least involving some form of co-option of the most important movers and shakers within the statist firmament. This appeared to be the actual direction in which Germany was heading in 1932, with Schleicher in the role of self-appointed national saviour.[89] As is well known, backstairs political intrigues, swirling around the figure of the now probably senile Hindenburg, conspired to wreck that particular ambition, just as, over the previous two years, Brüning's efforts to punch Germany out of its economic quagmire were ultimately emasculated by the president's refusal to go on granting him further emergency powers to rule without the consent of the Reichstag, something that was allowable under the Weimar constitution.

Why then did the ruling, technically Weimarian, yet implicitly anti-Weimar, elite ultimately conspire to put Hitler, not Papen, Schleicher, or, for that matter, Brüning in the driving seat? The obvious if disastrous answer is that they believed the demagogue could be ridden, and that behind a Hitlerian façade there would actually be a neo-Kaiserian regime under which the ill-tutored Nazis would essentially do as they were bidden. The paradox, however, is that by the end of 1932 there was no direct presidential need to bring Hitler in from the cold. His success in the polls had bottomed out in November and the man was threatening suicide, as he had done at other crisis moments in the past when his personal–political ambitions had been thwarted.[90] For all that, at least some of the forces of big business and the landed estates had been coalescing around him for some time.[91] Now, as the crisis deepened, the corporate shift to Hitler gathered pace, while the major newspaper tycoon, Alfred Hugenberg—who happened to be leader of the competing Nationalist Party—also embraced the Nazis within the Harzburg Front, which aimed to have the entirety of the right and ultra-right singing from the same shrill song-sheet. If all this was clearly geared towards embedding Hitler within the system—not dismantling it—when it finally came to the crunch, the Byzantine manoeuvres of Germany's supposed custodians delivered the chancellorship to him on a plate, ostensibly as head of an ultra-nationalist coalition administration.

One might wish to treat this as a fatal error of judgement, hubris, or, indeed, stupidity. But perhaps we can discern something else at work here, something which ultimately has a critical bearing on the relationship between state formation—or, in this case, conscious *re*formation—and the gruesome subject of our actual focus. For the arbiters of power, the crucial issue was not how to beat the economic crisis as such, but how to wrest Germany from the Versailles system and thereby recommence an independent course in which, among other things, it would assume full unilateral control of its military–political destiny. In geopolitical terms, in the years between 1929 and 1932, this could only be set against what was happening in Russia. The sheer dynamism of Stalin's Great Leap Forward offered not just a striking contrast to Germany's economic and political drift, but made clear that authoritarian rule was the only answer if Germany—through the rebuilding of a full-scale military–industrial complex—was to reassert its power *against* the liberal system. Army generals and heavy industry magnates alike would thus have looked to the Soviet example as the necessary riposte to Versailles. Equally, however, they would have feared the consequences of the Soviet drive to mastery, not, of course, on account of the innate violence and barbarity of Stalin's paradigm shift but, more obviously, for the existential threat it posed to Germany itself. That said, there was something even more fundamental at stake here. Russia's rise forced recognition of the degree to which Germany now found itself in the equivalent of the last chance saloon: that is, in a situation where either the country succumbed to acceptance of being locked into the Western system or, possibly worse, in thrall to a Soviet anti-system; or, alternatively, chose to use this moment to break out of the impasse altogether. After all, where, further down the road, would there be another opportunity like this?

Here, then, is the further paradox. The chaos, misery, and consequent social conflict of the recession actually gave the German inner establishment the pretext for its great escape. Just as the 1923 inflation may well have been in part engineered by the regime to defeat reparations,[92] so now caving in to Hitler gave it the excuse for allowing a complete political rupture with the terms of Versailles. Brüning himself, of course, had attempted to manipulate the crisis towards ending reparations, not to mention towards a much wider reformulation of Germany's military–political standing vis-à-vis Anglo-French hegemony. Through having Hitler dismantle Weimar altogether, the old establishment, by contrast, could justifiably claim that they were helpless in the face of the popular will while at the same time getting exactly what they wanted out of the procedure: a complete renunciation of all the treaties and instruments to which Germany answered under Versailles, Locarno, or the League of Nations.

Of course, what they did not bargain for was that Hitler was a shrewder, more calculating player at these high-risk stakes than they were. Within weeks of taking office, the Reichstag fire, whether Nazi-instigated or not, delivered to Hitler another emergency which now could be played not towards a conservative restoration—that moment had already come and gone—but for the benefit of rank-and-file nationalists now clamouring for '*ein Volk, ein Reich, ein Führer*'. With open intimid-ation and straight terrorizing of parliamentarians and other dissenting voices per-fectly allowable—the police, after all, were now under the chancellor's authority, not to say supplemented by 50,000 hastily organized auxiliary supporters—Hitler could press ahead towards what had always been *his* focused goal, an Enabling Act—freezing the Weimar constitution and thus clearing away the parliamentary, democratic detritus. For supporters of the Kaiserian state there was nothing too much to fret about, provided the economy did not go belly up again. Hitler, after all, had provided them with a more radically reshaped, Mark 2 version of what they had always dreamt. Mainstream opposition melted away: 52 per cent of voters in early March giving their endorsement to the new dispensation.[93] More signifi-cantly, perhaps, in addition to the one million Germans who had joined the Nazi party in the rush to belong by the summer of 1933, there were, by now, 2 million in the ranks of the *Sturmabteilung*, the Brownshirts—or, put another way, some 10 per cent of the civilian male population over the age of seventeen, ready and will-ing to dish out Nazi writ on Germany's streets.[94] No less surprisingly, Germany's Jews were quaking in their beds.

A REGIME AND ITS 'ENEMIES'

Klemperer's diary entries for the early months of 1933 make it abundantly clear that during this period the Jewish population of Germany were in fear of their lives. Rumours of imminent pogrom were interspersed with more concrete evi-dence of fellow co-religionists who had been abused, terrorized, kidnapped, shot; who had committed suicide, or had simply fled the country. One is equally struck, however, by Klemperer's sense of a country which was rudderless and had given itself up in an absence of mind to the intrinsic, demotic violence of the Nazis. Inbuilt into his analysis thus is a faint hope—one can't put it much more strongly than that—that the regime would prove so unequal to the task it had set itself, indeed, would so rapidly descend into chaos, that the forces of traditional law and order, the army at the helm, would come running to the rescue, remove the Nazis, and so restore sanity and stability.[95]

With hindsight, we can perfectly well see that Klemperer was not simply clutch-ing at straws but, in one critical element, had seriously misconceived the line-up of forces for and against the regime. There was a Nazi threat to stability but it came not from Hitler himself but from within the Brownshirt ranks of the movement, as led by the potential *sans-culotte* Hitler contender, Ernst Röhm, and as geared towards a 'second', more overtly anti-capitalist, revolution than the acknowledged *Machtergreifung* of January–March 1933. When order against this grouping was restored, in a spectacular but short-lived nationwide bloodbath—the so-called 'Night of Long Knives'—on the cusp of July 1934, it was the party's inner security SS forces who expedited the majority of the several hundred-odd murders, through operating in close liaison with the office of the Reichswehr's chief of staff. A variety of other targets, including two senior-ranking generals, one of them Schleicher, were victims of this reckoning. However, in a sense this all the more clearly high-lights the complicity and involvement of the military in the operation, in turn signalling its willingness to offer its wholehearted allegiance to the Nazi state, which it subsequently did in the form of the Hitler oath. With the death of the aged Hindenburg a month after the 'Night', and Hitler's further, official self-aggrandizement as Führer, there could be no question from this point all the way through to the 1944 anti-Hitler plot (even that led by a distinct minority of dissi-dent army officers) of anything but Nazi hegemony within the German polity. Henceforth, when Hitler spoke and acted he did so not only for the mass ranks of party faithful but equally for the military, bureaucracy, industrial, financial, and agro-business establishment—and *their* state.

The Hitler dictatorship, however, did not mean state and party cohered into one, any more than the great German corporations surrendered their independ-ence and interests to Nazi control. The political revolution may have been far-reaching but it never—bar with those, like the Jews, deemed 'alien'—took on the character of a Soviet-style assault on property rights. Nor, actually, can we discern any communist parallel in terms of the primacy of party. There may have been those who sought such a direction: very belatedly during the war, Hitler's trusted (but by everyone else thoroughly hated) head of the party chancellery, Martin Bormann, being the chief promoter of the idea. But by that juncture, the true arbiters of power, and, with it, of life and death, were neither state nor party anyway, but the SS. All this is by way of confirming that the picture of amor-phous incoherence which Klemperer was implying at the very outset of Nazi rule was in some sense true yet never resolved.[96] It was, for instance, quite pos-sible to go on being a relatively senior civil servant within the state apparatus without necessarily being a card-carrying Nazi; though, of course, it usually helped. What matters here, and thereby explains why Klemperer's expectations of an early Nazi demise were wishful thinking, is the fact that Hitler initially turned to the state apparatus not only to steady the boat, but to develop and carry through policy.

Hitler's pragmatic and 'rational' side—that is, in notable contrast to his violent neurotic other self—thus may also tell us something as to why Nazi actions towards the Jews in these early years did not lurch rapidly and cumulatively towards either eruction or worse. The notion is certainly counter-intuitive when set against not only the barely subliminal messages to act out a sadistic street violence emanating from *Der Stürmer* but actual *party* plans, set out in late 1931 secret documents, which detailed, for a future Nazi state imagined as beset by communist threat, 'emergency measures', which included Jewish mass starvation and expulsion.[97] Similar thinking is also transparent in Goebbels' actually not very original idea, in March 1933, that German Jews should be held as hostages against any anti-Nazi response emanating from the Western powers.[98] At this exact juncture, the propa-ganda minister was laying the final touches to his 'big idea' to initiate a boycott of German Jewish businesses, in response to the alleged 'atrocity propaganda' and 'mischief-making' which 'World Jewry' journalists were supposedly disseminating in the international media in order to destroy the Nazi 'reputation'.[99] The irony is that despite the menacing presence of uniformed Brownshirts outside Jewish-owned stores on the boycott's opening day—1 April—few shoppers seem to have been either taken in by Goebbels' disinformation or dissuaded from making their normal purchases. The boycott's almost immediate surcease, however, may have had as much to do with the leadership being spooked by its own conspiracy fears, as Jewish organizations abroad, especially in the USA, took steps to initiate their own worldwide counter-boycott campaign against German business.

What all this actually reveals is the degree to which Hitler and his inner circle, in early 1933, were stumbling around in the dark as to how they might *systematically* implement their intended attack on the Jews. If it all rebounded on German economic prospects, they themselves would get the blame. If Jews were rounded up, or worse, assaulted en masse, that would simply worsen German international standing at a moment when the country was clearly weak and vulnerable. It is ironic, then, that it was the state's bureaucrats who came to Hitler's rescue. And they did so through 'regulation by statute', in other words, dressing up the Nazi intent in suitably clinical, legal-administrative measures. Thus, less than a week after the failure of the boycott, the grandiosely entitled Re-establishment of the Career Civil Service Act came into force. Under its terms, Jews who were public servants were summarily dismissed from office. The numbers affected were relatively small, perhaps 2,000 initially, and this despite the fact that any scientist, professor, or teacher in public service with a single Jewish grandparent was encompassed within the act. The law was certainly weakened by exemptions written in at the behest of Hindenburg, excluding those who had served Germany in the Great War, had lost family members in the fighting, or whose public service had preceded the onset of hostilities.[100] But in another sense this pill sweetener simply reinforced the notion that what was being promulgated was entirely legitimate and in the best traditions of thought-through German rationality, orderliness, and even fair play.

Moreover, the bureaucrats having set the precedent in their own occupational arena, 'Aryan' doctors and lawyers—in professions where Jewish colleagues were altogether more numerous—were eager to follow. Here, occupational restrictive interest combined with party aspirations could be realized in the same way as for the civil service. In these early cases of 'legalized' exclusion, the state thus provided a formula for what would eventually become a huge corpus of *Judengesetzgebung*: anti-Jewish law. And it would be almost constantly added to right up to the July 1943 decree which finally and irrevocably terminated German Jewish legal rights and protection under Nazi rule.[101] By then, of course, the law as legitimizer, or as some fabricated basis for legitimate anti-Jewish practice, was entirely irrelevant, not least as the vastly greater part of the country's remaining Jewry had been deported east to their deaths. It was, indeed, an interesting example of how diverse elements of the regime could operate, almost surreally, on quite different, even contradictory, planes.

In these early months and years, however, the gradual, piecemeal exclusion of Jews from the social, economic, cultural, and sporting life of the wider community suited the regime's purpose rather well. As did a scheme such as *ha'avera*, which enabled German Jews to leave for Palestine. Some 52,000 migrants, a not insignificant proportion of the community, were willing to take the opportunity so provided up to 1938—regardless of whether they were enthusiasts for, or distinctly lukewarm towards, the Zionist project. Again, however, what is striking about the programme is its twofold nature. Firstly, it was voluntary: this was no wholesale or systematic disgorgement comparable, for instance, with what befell the Greeks of Turkey in 1922–3. Secondly, it was not designed as a complete fleecing exercise either. The mechanism by which those departing paid into a trust company was actually rather ingenious, as it underwrote German industrial and other exports to the British mandate territory, and provided a return to the German economy in the form of much needed foreign currency, while, at the same time, through the sale of goods, leaving something by way of reimbursement for the immigrants themselves. The procedure was hardly 'fair' in the sense of giving the departees a market-price return on their liquid assets yet, in the context of the time, it offered them some-thing entirely more precious: an orderly escape route out of Nazi clutches. And again, it did so not through the offices of the party per se but through a deal struck between German Zionists and the Reich Economics Ministry; Hjalmar Schacht, the fellow-travelling yet non-party president of the Reich bank also playing a lead-ing role.[102]

One is in danger, to be sure, of painting this emerging German technocrat-led direction on Jewish affairs as somehow acceptable and hence pardonable. The foundations of *ha'avera* preceded the Nazi takeover anyway, so could not actually be taken as a firm indication of Nazi-period policy. That said, sponsored Zionist migration to Palestine most certainly served Nazi interests inasmuch as it neatly sabotaged the simultaneous efforts to isolate Germany through the counter-boycott campaign. The Nazis either did not notice or chose to ignore the blatant evidence from this saga, that Jews were as incapable as any other communal group of responding to a crisis in a unified, let alone monolithic, fashion. Meanwhile, the very poorest Jews, nearly all *Ostjuden*, who found themselves threatened, intimid-ated, or simply leant upon to sell their businesses at nonsense prices by venal neighbours, chancers, and the like, almost never had the liquid assets to fall back upon to enable them to get onto the *ha'avera* ladder. Furthermore, they found that a new juridical pronouncement gave them no defence in the law courts either, if they tried to file for bankruptcy.[103] Underneath the pseudo-legal canopy then, is a picture of cumulative impoverishment and immiseration especially focused on the already most vulnerable elements of the community, and only held at bay by a necessarily ever-expanding, if increasingly stress-driven, programme of Jewish national and international charitable relief efforts.[104] Then there was the further variable: that Brownshirt activists would find some pretext to go on an anti-Jewish rampage, with or without the say-so of the party hierarchy. In August 1935, this more demotic tendency seemed to be on the rise once again, with Streicher doing much of the stoking by way of what the political state police, the Gestapo, referred to as a 'race defilement psychosis'. *Ostjuden* districts received the full brunt of the consequent hooliganism.[105] The regular police, by now, were little more than bystanders, while the growing incidence of denunciation of Jews to the Gestapo, for imaginary or fabricated crimes,[106] precluded any possibility that they might look to the authorities for protection from, let alone redress for physical injury, vandalism, or pillage.

The evidence, moreover, that Hitler, Goebbels, and company were now more than ready to pick up the cudgels themselves as tossed to them by the gallery seemed further confirmed when Hitler used the occasion of the Nuremberg party rally in mid-September to deliver two major anti-Jewish legal enactments: the Reich Citizenship Act and the Law for the Protection of German Blood and German Honour. In the popular mind, these have come to be seen as the acme of pre-war Nazi legal persecution against the Jews. The Citizenship Act stripped German Jewry of its political rights as Germans, in effect overturning at one fell swoop 150 years of liberal emancipation process. The second law was entirely more cutting in its implications, prohibiting not only further marriages between Aryans and Jews but any form of sexual relations between them. For good measure, a clause prohibited the employment of German domestics under the age of forty-five in Jewish households, thus carrying into law a standard *Der Stürmer* slur about the predatory instincts of the Jewish male, while failing to recognize the equal slur it placed on German women of all ages.[107]

The origins of the legislation, however, suggest the need for some considerable assessment and reassessment of how we might interpret and contextualize the laws. Previously assumed to be not so much part of any specific Nazi blueprint but drafted in extreme haste by Interior Ministry functionaries because Hitler was short of a headline-grabbing pronouncement for his rally address, more recent consideration has instead emphasized the continuity and consistency of the state-led assault on the Jews. Put on the spot, civil servants may have quite literally cobbled together the legislation in less than forty-eight hours, in the process failing to nail the thorny issue of who exactly was a 'Jew'. Nevertheless, a high-level interdepartmental conference on the subject, in August, suggests an administrative consensus, the SS included, on the broad direction of travel, prior to Nuremberg.[108]

It may be true that Hitler treated the laws as purely provisional and that, by the same token—at least if we were to judge the matter by way of Klemperer's lack of reference to them in his diaries—they were not perceived by German Jewry as representing any major shift amidst their daily litany of tribulations.[109] However, arguably what matters most about the laws, in the short term, is the way they were received by the majority of 'law-abiding' Germans. Up to this juncture, the very visibility of palpable baiting or violence against Jews on the streets, in shops, or in school classrooms, had clearly been a subject of some unease. What the laws appeared to do was take away the *need* for such public displays of distastefulness. By clarifying the situation—and, again, as if it came through some higher juridical sanction—the laws thus resolved the 'objective' relationship between Germans and Jews. Or, at least, *appeared* to do so. The latter had been demoted to a secondary tier of German society, where they were now not citizens but 'state subjects', with their involvement henceforth in the social and cultural life of the whole clearly cordoned off. Majority acquiescence in this Interior Ministry-led fait accompli was clearly quite capable of blocking from view the denial of civil, economic, and political rights to people who, until recently, had been fellow Germans, and often neighbours. Yet, and it is a 'yet', through the laws Germany seemed to have arrived at its own special formula for regularizing its 'Jewish question' without the recourse to Russian- or Turkish-style deportations, or worse.

With hindsight, such a statement sounds risible to the extent that it is not actually blasphemous. However, viewed from, say, the Germany of mid-1937, there is something striking about the stay of execution. The cumulative effect of ongoing acts of Jewish legislation had become tantamount to creating a form of social quarantine. Yet even then, the constraints were not as absolute as they had become for most German Roma through enforced spatial isolation in designated quarters, or behind strictly guarded camp fences. Jews could walk the streets—mostly without harm—where they had the means, to shop, go to cafes, or even go to the theatre. To be sure, with diminishing economic wherewithal the possibilities for such normal social intercourse were rapidly declining, especially for the poorest amongst them. But by creating the possibility of this alternative, if highly constrained, sphere of existence, the state apparatus had created the possibility for a form of Jewish neo-normality. Indeed, the other side to this odd coin is, on the one hand, the initial return of some 10,000 of the initial 60,000 German Jews who left the country in 1933,[110] not to mention the relatively slow haemorrhage thereafter—up to 1938, that is; on the other, the notable Jewish renaissance which occurred within the confines of the community during these twilight years. Again this sounds counter-intuitive, as if we somehow ought to be thanking Hitler for enabling individuals who previously had shown faint interest in their Jewish background or religion to now do so. The fact remains, however, that the Jewish community, while numerically diminished and increasingly materially impoverished, did not collapse but rather, under the auspices for the first time of the all-German Reichsvertretung der deutschen Juden, found itself looking to its inner, including spiritual, resources, for sustenance and survival.[111]

All this is equally perplexing given Hitler's obsessive and concentrated hatred of the Jews. The lack of a more forceful follow-through can be put down to various factors in the mid-1930s, the most overriding of which, perhaps, was the regime's calculated efforts to keep the Western-system leaders from interference in Germany's domestic affairs—at least, that is, until it had caught up with and then surpassed them in the military balance of terror. Again, it sounds odd to speak of Hitlerian pragmatism winning out over principle, but in the years of the Führer's, albeit ambivalent, international fence-building—the cornerstone of which was the 1936 Berlin Olympics—the immediate heat was off the Jews. This certainly cannot but remind us at the same time how much their fate ultimately rested on the demagogue himself. If he changed his mind—if, for instance, the fence-building proved provisional, or, alternatively, some other contingent factor intervened to upset the Hitlerian agenda—then the resumption of anti-Jewish actions could be assumed to follow as night follows day. As it did: in 1938. However, as long as the Western system versus emerging Nazi anti-system stand-off remained relatively calm, or rather—given the reality of the Spanish Civil War—was at several removes from Germany itself, one can discern not so much a Hitler- but rather an apparatus-led Jewish policy.

This tendency also fits in with what we know of the Führer's aloofness from the day-to-day running of state. Unlike Stalin, Hitler was no micro-manager and was perfectly willing to let often competing interests propose and pursue policy, even while these polycratic tendencies had the ability to undermine the overall coordination of national effort: a supposed Nazi priority. A facet of the situation was the proliferation of Jewish 'experts' within the various ministries. Dr Bernhard Lösener, one of the Interior Ministry officials tasked with drafting the Reich Citizenship Act, for instance, had no prior experience in this field but went on ultimately to draft, or help draft, some twenty-seven 'Jewish' decrees. He also had no particular Nazi leanings, going so far in his own post-war testimony to insist on his anti-Nazi credentials.[112] It was Lösener, backed up by the Ministry's state secretary, Dr Wilhelm Stuckart—an avowed party stalwart—who was responsible for amendments to the citizenship law which proposed German half- or part-Jews to be separate categories outside the immediate terms of the Act. Later, the status of these *Mischlinge* would become a bone of contention with Reinhard Heydrich, as the 'Final Solution' became operationalized under the Sicherheitsdienst (SD), the SS-controlled security and intelligence agency of which he was head. However, in the mid-1930s neither Heydrich nor his boss Himmler essentially demurred from the Interior Ministry's efforts at 'regularizing' Jewish matters. Indeed, when Hitler came down from on high to adjudicate between the Interior Ministry's stance and the opposing maximalist view—emanating primarily, at that time, from the party radicals—it was to support the former.[113]

The apparent primacy of the Interior Ministry on the Jewish question at this juncture is also reflected in the lead Stuckart took in attempting to coordinate other ministries and departments towards a complete solution of the 'problem'. In September 1936, for instance, he convened a conference in which officials from the Ministry of Economics and the Office of the Deputy Führer were also participants, and in which wholesale German Jewish emigration to Palestine, or elsewhere, was discussed. In fact, it came to no conclusion on the matter.[114] Nor did any other department of state. Perhaps this suggests that the issue had simply lost its sting. Or even that the supposed Jewish threat to German society had somehow evaporated. The SD, for instance, though a few years on the driving force behind the implementation of systematic Jewish mass murder, considered the issue of so little importance that they did not have a Jewish department until the summer of 1935. Even then they initially maintained just three desks to monitor the activities of the German Jewish community.[115]

The fact is that German Jewry by this time was so materially weak that the more immediate issue was not the supposed threat it posed, but rather whether it might become a financial burden on the state. Back in 1933, the idea of some Jewish–communist takeover had proved to be exactly what it was: Nazi fantasy. To be sure, the party's efforts to get its retaliation in first against the possibility of a KPD backlash in the crisis weeks which followed Hitler's elevation to the chancellorship can be accepted as a form of rational anticipation. That said, this was as much a pretext for the sweeping emergency powers—as wrested from Hindenburg—used to end Weimar's civil freedoms and replace them by unrestricted police powers of surveillance, arrest, and detention. Armed accordingly, the SS and SA, as legitimated agents of state, were able to declare open season on *all* suspected political opponents of whatever hue, the consequences of which were that some hundred thousand were taken into custody, beaten up, and terrorized across the length and breadth of Germany.[116] This period was most definitely a time of 'wild' actions, of arbitrary terror, of the hasty improvisation of holding units as the police cells and prisons failed to cope with the onrush of inmates, of selective revenge killings, and the initiation of the first of many concentration camps. But where were the Jews in the equation? Practically nowhere. To be sure, there were some Jews among activists in the KPD, trade unions, and other parties. Some were imprisoned, some killed. Many fled. But what the spring of 1933 proved unequivocally was the entirely chimerical nature of the supposed Jewish *threat*. Equally, however, what it also exposed was the frailty of general German political dissent in the face of the Nazi triumph.

*

So complete, in fact, was the pulverization of standard opposition that only a few thousand politicals were still in detention by the end of the year. For hard or unrepentant cases, of course, there was indeterminate 'protective custody' on offer in Dachau, chief testing ground for what would grow into an SS camp system of refined brutality and murder. Open support for the Jews had disappeared. The building up of the Hitler Youth, the most obvious and high-profile of the party organizations designed to induct an entire nation towards the thinking and practice of *volk* politics, suggested that the fearful legacy of 1918—a populace in opposition to the state—was dead and buried.

Or was it? Another paradox of Nazism in its early years of power was that it found opposition emanating not so much against its political programme but on its more symbolic turf. This was, fundamentally, an issue of the clash of world views. Nazism was at heart viscerally anti-Christian. What is surprising, however, is the muted nature of the clerical response. Few church leaders, Protestant or Catholic, made an issue of the regime's racial ideology, let alone its anti-Semitism. The German Christian Church, as we have seen, went in entirely the opposite direction, not only embracing Nazism as its own but consciously undertaking the quite monumental task of de-Judaicizing its theology—including all connections between Jesus and his Jewish reality—in order to prove the point. The partially breakaway Confessing Church stood firm against this path, though equally it took no united stance on the anti-Jewish persecution, except where it involved Jewish converts. Indeed, its primary concern was the implications of *Gleichschaltung*: in other words, its autonomy as a church as set against the totality of the Nazis' homogenizing agenda.[117]

If the Protestant half of the German nation was thus either largely behind Nazism or failed, with a few valiant exceptions, to articulate a strong dissenting position, what of the Catholic half? By rights, notions as to the immortality of nation, or, for that matter, the proposition that only through the *volk* could Germans arrive at a relationship with God, ought to have been recognized by all believers as an anathema, though by Catholics in particular, as inherently at odds with the church's universalism. 'There is only one Führer and that is Jesus Christ', thundered the Jesuit priest, Josef Spieker, to a packed Cologne congregation in October 1934.[118] Spieker has the dubious honour of being the first Catholic priest to be sent to a concentration camp. Others were to follow. That said, despite eventual arrest, trial, and a nine-month spell in camps—which Spieker survived—the authorities, Gestapo included, were clearly at pains to avoid confrontation with the church hierarchy over this or any other priest. The feeling was reciprocated on the part of the German bishops, who had already cut the ground from under the feet of their own Catholic Centre party at the time of the Enabling Act, when they had met in conference to back the Vatican's interest in favour of a concordat with Hitler.[119] What this meant in practice was that there was no renewed *Kulturkampf* in Germany as there had been in Bismarck's day. And, by the same token, while the Gestapo remained on constant alert for signs of dissension within Catholics ranks, at least for now, the path taken by those such as Spieker was a very lonely if courageous one.

Again, what has to be emphasized is that objections of the Spieker kind tended to be tightly theological, where they were not in defence of more parochial church interests. Perhaps it might have been different if Pope Pius XI had followed up his 1937 encyclical 'With Deep Anxiety', which was tentatively critical of the Nazis, with the further one he had in mind condemning racism and anti-Semitism. Since awareness of the proposed encyclical surfaced in the 1990s, it has become one of the great 'ifs' of Holocaust history. A text had been prepared at Pius' behest by the campaigning American Jesuit, John LaFarge. It unequivocally declared anti-Semitism to be 'inadmissible' while reaffirming the strong spiritual ties between Christians and Jews. But the text was re-routed through the openly anti-Semitic general of the Jesuit order, and arrived on the pope's desk when he was mortally ill, in early 1939, subsequently disappearing into the Vatican archives. Under the new pope, Pius XII, the church retreated into abject silence on the matter.[120]

If we were looking for a case where the Nazi regime found itself genuinely pitted against an entire religiously-based communal group, we would have to put the Catholics aside to consider opposition from an unexpected quarter. The Jehovah's Witness were a small if tightly cohesive church. Their heartland was North America but there were an estimated 25–30,000 members throughout Germany, nearly all in the lower classes.[121] The sect was stridently against war, condemned all other religious groups as false, and specifically affirmed that the civil law had to be resisted wherever it conflicted with the church's own views. This stance, in itself, was actually *not* a recipe for social conflict. In normal times, the community was firmly quietist and law-abiding. But it also happened to be overtly millenarian, expecting not only Armageddon but a subsequent end of days with some imminence.

Here, then, we have the exact conditions for a genuine non-compliance with Nazism founded on *religious* grounds. Indeed, one expert on the movement in Germany has described the situation as one of battle lines being drawn as if between 'two competing unmalleable world systems'.[122] Yet Nazism's adversary here was unequivocally *not* the Jews. Jehovah's Witnesses may have held to the eschatological notion that, at the millennium, the Jews would return and reign in Jehovah's kingdom, but they otherwise evinced no particular sympathy for the contemporaneous Jewish (or Roma) plight, were known to be thoroughly against the atheistic communists, and clearly could not be demarcated as racially non-German. These were sufficient grounds for the Nazis logically to have navigated incipient conflict with the group into calmer waters. The regime, after all, had no prior interest in them, and was indeed disinterested if not bemused by people they mostly regarded as 'mad'.[123]

If anything the gauntlet was thrown down by the group itself, most especially in response to their banning in the wake of the Reichstag fire. This, alongside a few early arrests, was read not simply as persecution, but as a prophetic sign of the times. Witnesses responded by going on the offensive, not only by making a point of meeting in defiance of the ban, but openly proselytizing with their literature and calling on their fellow Germans to repudiate the false prophet Hitler, in favour of 'the true saviour, Jesus Christ'.[124] The Brownshirts responded with open violence, while the Gestapo weighed in with arrests and brutal interrogations. As this, in turn, simply emboldened the Witnesses as to the rightness of their convictions and cause, the scene was set for a developing, albeit entirely asymmetrical, dynamic. This culminated, in June 1937, with an attempt by Witnesses to mass leaflet by hand the entirety of German households with an 'Open Letter' enumerating personal stories of violence, persecution, and death committed by the Nazis against them. It was inevitably followed by mass arrests and concentration camp incarcerations.[125]

Was this, then, the *real* pre-war story of a persecuted but fearless David of a community versus a merciless Goliath of a police state, leading to an all but forgotten case of genocide? The Gestapo hunting down of Witnesses was conducted with a sadistic zeal, the force also going to efforts to circumvent leniency, as often proffered in the courts, by simply transferring accused Witnesses directly to the camps. That the practitioners of state violence, both in the police and in the camps, developed a heightened animus against Witnesses is evident in the very high level of the latters' suffering. Early studies in the 1960s found that least a third of them were imprisoned and, of these, somewhere in the region of 4,000 to 5,000 died in custody, very often as a result of repeating beatings or torture.[126] A more recent study has been a little more circumspect, agreeing that though as many as one-third were imprisoned, the figure for concentration camp inmates numbered 2,000, of whom 1,200 were killed.[127]

The particulars of the assault on the community qua community, on closer inspection, also prove to be notably at variance with the fate of Jews and Roma at the height of their paroxysm. For instance, according to a 1935 Cologne Gestapo directive to all city police stations, where married partners proved to be equally recalcitrant Witnesses, only one of them was to be taken into custody on grounds that their children would otherwise be a burden on public welfare and cause 'emotional as well as economic damage'.[128] The fact, however, that what befell Witnesses, women and men alike, proved to be of a lesser order what befell other targeted groups hardly diminishes the scale of what was clearly martyrdom, nor its broader significance. There were other small sects, notably Seventh Day Adventists and Mormons, who attracted Gestapo suspicion, mostly on account of their foreign connections. Yet, with a few individual exceptions, these churches found themselves able to tack to the prevailing Nazi wind. By contrast, the absolute refusal of Witnesses to bend the knee to a system which they could not possibly by normal physical means hope to overcome, was quite remarkable. It even brought a strange accolade from Himmler who, in 1944, recognizing the resilience of their obduracy, proposed that at the end of the war they should be resettled in the east as part of a defensive wall against the Asiatic tide, and even have their pacifist creed propagated among the suppressed nations in this region![129]

Himmler's comment is telling on a further account. There have been some considerable efforts within latter-day German historiography to conjure up a picture of what has been termed *Resistenz*: namely, localized, day-to-day non-conformity or non-compliance with the diktats of the Nazi system.[130] This has been especially attributed to Catholic or proletarian circles, though clearly inbuilt into this quest has been a retrospective need to find some exculpation amongst groups who *ought*—so the assumption goes—to have objected to the regime where they did not resist it in an outright manner. The problem is that while *Resistenz* may have occurred in the manner described, little or none of this adds up, in macro terms, to evidence of a society in opposition. Indeed, nothing compares to the single example of the Jehovah's Witnesses consciously pitting themselves, regardless of their lack of material resource or line of retreat, against the might of the Nazi state.

And it could be that there is a disturbing reason for this singularity. We have already suggested that *many* nationally conscious Germans were already favourable to, or cajoled by, Nazism because of its impassioned, rhetorical message to them as *Germans*, and because this perhaps opened up and legitimated a form of emotional release which, in other times or circumstances, the vast majority might have self-consciously kept closely under lock and key. The Witnesses simply did not buy into any of this, because their millenarian starting point was both different and equally authoritative. It uniquely gave them an ideological framework and hence a *moral* strength with which to contest Nazi claims. However, the reason why arguably the majority of 'ordinary Germans' may have settled down to Nazism may have had little or nothing to do with ardent nationalism at all, or at least not be due to this alone. They may have enjoyed all the fascistic pomp and pageantry, they may have even been swayed by the creed's undoubted fervour. Large numbers, especially among the previously unemployed, would have picked up with alacrity on the promise of state-provided jobs. Yet the real clincher for many was—entirely paradoxically—the Nazis' promise, or so it seemed, of a return to an idea of society in which one's behaviour followed a very tight social, cultural—and sexual—code of conformity and, hence, uniformity. In fact, the apparent Nazi position in this regard was made quite explicit when the Prussian Ministry of the Interior issued a decree in December 1937 adumbrating classes of people who were considered 'asocial' and thereby liable to police preventive measures to combat crime. The decree pronounced the term 'asocial'—'deviant' will perfectly well do as an alternative—to apply to:

such persons...who, through behaviour which is inimical to the community (but which need not be criminal) show that they are not prepared to be members of the community...who, by virtue of petty but repeated infringement of the law, are not prepared to comply with the order that is a fundamental condition of a National Socialist state.[131]

The decree went on to list examples of such misfits: vagrants, gypsies, prostitutes, drunkards, the work-shy, as well as those with contagious, especially sexually transmitted, diseases. Interestingly, the decree's wording seemed to be suggesting that such 'asocial' types were not *necessarily* criminals, but if they failed to change their tune they would become so. Jehovah's Witnesses were not part of this choice range (nor indeed were Jews) but they might as well have been. They, too, were people who clearly did not fit in, whose behaviour and ideas were odd, the sort of people one didn't quite want one's children mixing with. And, their harping on about how nastily they were being persecuted only reinforced the conviction that the best place for them was in a camp where a bit of iron discipline and drill would knock them into shape.[132]

The Nazis, of course, had a ready-made formula for making how the age-old tendency to exclude the strange, the threatening, and the unknown into a workable but entirely modern basis for organizing both state and society. It was called racial hygiene. What so many Germans failed to realize was that by buying into this actually elite-led agenda, they were exposing themselves to an implicit exterminatory danger.

RACE IN PLACE OF PEOPLE

'National Socialism is applied biology'.[133] So intoned a leading Bavarian *alter Kämpfer*, Hans Schemm, after the party's elevation to power. The Nazis proclaimed at every turn their goal of a racially homogenized community. But it was, above all, university-trained scientists and professional practitioners who sought to implement it as medical and social praxis.

This poses an interesting historical problem. Did this trajectory represent some uniquely regressive, even lunatic, deviation from the standard norm on the part of the German academy and its acolytes? Or was what it began to put into practice in the 1930s simply at the cutting edge of the modern? In this sense could one even say that it was not unlike what was taking place in Soviet Russia, albeit founded on a radically different methodology? If we assume the standard norm to be the West, these questions would seem to be at cross-purposes. If the highest expression of modernity was based on liberal precepts which gave value to all human beings, regardless of their social or ethnic background, culture, or religion, how could one conceivably cast Nazi racial ideology as, in any sense, an extension of a liberal best practice? A considered answer might refer, however, to the degree to which racial ideas were already well-embedded in Western science. Post the Darwinian revolution, the classification of the human family by way of racial categories was normative. This did not mean that emerging schools of university-trained anthropologists, ethnic geographers, and geneticists all subscribed to a view that racial difference was either rigid or hierarchical.[134] However, many leading academics in these fields, especially in Britain and America, were exactly of this opinion. Nor was eugenics, as we suggested in *The Rise of the West*, in any sense a minority position. On the contrary, German race scientists working from the mid-1920s at the highly prestigious Kaiser Wilhelm Institute of Anthropology, Eugenics and Human Heredity in Berlin, found some of their most vociferous support coming from fellow eugenicists in the West.[135] The US Rockefeller Foundation, for instance, put major funding into the Institute's research programme, despite the fact that this included not only projects for improving racial stock but others suppressing supposed damaged or weak human genetic material.[136] Nor should Eugen Fischer, the Institute's director and a leading advocate of the state-administered sterilization of the weak and inferior be seen as an isolated voice crying out against the civilized grain. Some US states were already, in part, practising what Fischer and his German colleagues were preaching. When Nazism in effect adopted the latters' recommendations, like-minded US eugenicists were the first to applaud and propose that their own legislators more firmly follow suit.[137] In early 1930s Britain, too, a high-level committee of experts, operating under the aegis of the Ministry of Health, proposed the sterilization of some quarter of a million 'defective' and 'feeble-minded' Britons. Only government fear of a hostile popular reaction killed the scheme; albeit not the scientific argument, nor, indeed, the hereditarian assumptions which went with it.[138]

From this perspective one could argue that the inbuilt violence of 1930s eugenic practice in Germany was not novel *because* it was Nazi but rather because the Nazi acquisition of control of the state enabled a set of its otherwise frontier-less academic advocates to pursue its aspirations in an untrammelled fashion. As Fischer himself celebrated the case in 1943, 'It is rare and special good fortune for a theoretical science to flourish at a time when the prevailing ideology welcomes it and its findings can immediately serve the policy of the state'.[139] The synergy between this elite discourse and the Nazi state is certainly striking. Even before the formation of specialist outfits such as the SS Hygiene Unit—mandated to act as the cutting edge of an all-embracing, Nazified version of preventative medicine[140]—the party could count on the widespread support of the German medical establishment. With Jews cut out from the public health scene, one in two doctors were Nazis, while one in ten would join the SS.[141] These professionals did not need Nazism to be convinced of the need for tough biological as well as legal remedies for perceived social ills. Nor did they need the party to tell them that 'Jewish science' was bogus. They wanted biopolitics as an absolute priority of national development just as the party wanted them to legitimate its plans as if this were all a matter of 'sober and dispassionate calculation'.[142]

Between these two pillars of state and medical science were not only the grounds but the capacity for turning Germany into a giant experimental laboratory. Which, by implication, meant that the entirety of the population would henceforth be under scrutiny for their alleged genetic strengths and weaknesses. The question was how the experimenters would determine—indeed, how far they would go in determining—who was good for the stock, and who bad. What procedures would they propose for encouraging the former and for removing the latter? Nazism was nothing if not collective in its implications. Individuals could only be worthy within the context of the wider racial community. True, an individual's abilities might be more than the sum of his or her genetic background. But the firm— supposedly scientifically supported—assumption of the Nazi biopolity was that these facets could be evaluated through physical characteristics on the one hand, hereditary history on the other.

Yet here the would-be creators of this brave new world came up against a kink whose implications threatened to sink the whole project. What if a large section of the German population proved, through screening, to be already contaminated by weak or unsatisfactory elements? As pure Germans were strong, blond, and beautiful, it could only be racially extraneous matter which could be to blame. Or so the mantra went. But the conventional wisdom equally adopted by race scientists from the work of Felix von Luschan stated that the first cause of the problem—namely racial miscegenation—could not be righted by breeding out the 'bad blood' over the space of some generations.[143] On the contrary, these unwanted characteristics, said von Luschan, had an inbuilt hereditary dominance. Logically that would seem to suggest that these traits were in fact, 'better', 'stronger', 'more resilient', than Aryan traits. Pursuing the Nazi's own chop-logic, however, the obvious solution was blocking off these traits altogether. Or, as Dr Achim Gercke, the Interior Ministry's race expert, tersely put it: 'extinction'—*Ausmerze*—which, translated into practical action, meant 'sterilisation of those hereditarily inferior'.[144]

But this is exactly where Gercke ran into a little problem with some of his own Ministry colleagues, in particular those who had the task of drafting the Nuremberg laws. If one started adding to the known Jews from the *Gemeinde* records all the people with perhaps a half, or a quarter, or one-eighth Jewish ancestry, one ended with a much more considerable number. Gercke's genealogical assistant Wilfried Euler, a veritable anorak of a card indexer, turned up a figure of one and half million all told.[145] Lösener, for the drafting team, parried with some calculations of his own—among other things noting that if one included half-Jews in the Jewish total one would immediately lose to the armed forces 45,000 men of military age. In fact, even more thoroughgoing extrapolations coming from the party's own Racial Policy office suggested a deficit of 308,000![146] Fantastically inflated or not, the sheer headache of trying to include anybody with part-Jewish ancestry as *Jewish* proved too much for the Interior Ministry, though, significantly, it did not attempt to defy the general thrust of the new racial ordering. It simply interpreted it differently: as the late Raul Hilberg pithily but famously put it, by protecting in the part-Jew 'that part which is German'.[147] The consequence was a series of socially constructed *Mischlinge* categories in between full Jew and full German. There were those of the first degree with two Jewish grandparents (those with three were determined to be Jews). A second degree had one. And finally there was a third category, *Geltungsjuden*, who were also offspring of mixed marriages but—unlike the other two categories who were assumed to have no Jewish religious connections—were registered prior to the Nuremberg laws as being members of the Jewish synagogal community.[148]

The impact of this quasi-pragmatic bureaucratic response to Nazi biopolitics, as we have already hinted, was ultimately to act as a significant brake on the encompassing of those deemed *Mischlinge* within the 'Final Solution'. Nor, though it was discussed on many subsequent occasions—most notably at Wannsee—was the path of mass *Mischlinge* sterilization carried through into practice. However, by focusing on the twists, turns, and, ultimately, peculiarities of the German Jewish case we are—paradoxically—in danger of losing the main thread of Nazi pre-war race thinking. The main place to re-find it, indeed, is not with the Jews, but with the 'gypsies'—the Roma.

*

The Roma have, in recent years, become more seriously acknowledged, alongside Jews, as the main genocidal victims of Nazism. But while the ultimate sequence of their respective mass murders in the rimlands has spatial and chronological links, bracketing them together as similar products of Nazi racism or, for that matter, Nazi phobia, is more problematic. We can, of course, point to some similarities between the two groups. Both were, within a European context, ubiquitous, at least from the High Middle Ages. Yet both were considered quintessential outsiders: communities which failed to fit into a picture of sedentarized, 'rooted', essentially peasant-based society. One might argue this made them both equally marginal. But their marginality expressed itself in rather fundamentally different ways. Classic *Romanipen* was founded on seasonal perambulations from place to place, which underscored the fact that Roma life and livelihood involved moving *by choice*. And always, in the process, maintaining some degree of social, cultural, and, indeed spatial, separation from *gadze*: non-Roma. One could make something of a similar statement about traditional Jewry, except that Jews were rarely, if ever, anything if not in the interstices of the mainstream, even where they chose to maintain or preserved a socio-religious otherness. Moreover, Jews were, as we have seen, also key agents of modernity—the very process of which inevitably undermined their ability, even where it was desired, to stay on the 'outside'. This was particularly, inevitably, so in countries undergoing rapid change, such as Germany. This is not to assume that Roma life did not also undergo considerable transformation, including, sometimes, forced or voluntary sedentarization as a consequence of these wider changes. Very few Roma, however, began to come to the centre stage of modern economic, cultural, and political life, as Jews increasingly did.

It is again an irony that what the two groups supposedly had in common in Nazi typecasting tells us much more about Nazi angst than anything particularly about what genuinely linked gypsies and Jews. Both were guilty of an apparently clannish cohesiveness across time and space which, in itself, affronted the Nazis' elusive aspiration for the preservation and perpetuation of their own *Volksgemeinschaft*. That Roma, like Jews, had their own elaborate purification rituals, demarcating them from majority society, again amplified the Nazi sense that the two communities had appropriated to themselves what rightly belonged to an uncontaminated German self-image. Worse, both groups seemed apparently to carry off this feat of inner purity while at the same time contaminating the German bloodline. In the

Roma case, their normal, quotidian practice of what the Nazis extolled as Aryan open-air wanderlust clearly so touched a raw nerve that Roma roaming was rewritten as a pathological condition, founded itself on a genetic disorder.[149]

Here, however, we are already straying into areas where the supposed racial characteristics of Roma underscore the Nazi distinction between them and Jews. If the latter were wholly evil, the problem for Nazi race science, at least as proffered by Himmler's 1935-founded research institute, the Ahnenerbe (ancestral heritage)—tasked with investigating the origins of the 'Indo-Aryan'—was that studying the Roma might actually bring it that much closer to its holy grail. Again, part of the irony of this situation is that Nazis were not simply race ideologues with highly contradictory views about a range of communal groups. Rather, when it came to the Roma, some dubiously sympathetic notions that *pure* gypsies were actually 'descendants of the primordial Indo-German people' had to jostle with a much more general baggage of which Nazis,[150] as Germans—and Europeans—also happened to be inheritors. And nearly all of this general baggage was deeply, sometimes viscerally, anti-Roma.

Roma numbers in 1930s Germany were so small that, alone, they could not have represented any existential threat to the majority community. An estimate of between 20,000 and 30,000, a number which, in demographic terms, made them similar to the Jehovah's Witnesses, constituted no more than 0.1 per cent of the total population.[151] Even then, German Roma were hardly monolithic. The most significant element—the Sinti—were part of an early wave of Roma in-migration, though actually there were at least another five other Rom communities, especially if one includes Austrian territory embraced within the Reich as a result of the Anschluss.[152] That certainly should remind us that German Roma were part of a transnational phenomenon. They had arrived in Europe in a series of migrations from the East—originally, in all probability, from the north-western reaches of the Indian subcontinent—during the Middle Ages, with concentrated areas of dispersal in the rimlands, especially the Balkans. The physical distinctiveness of Roma, including their usually dark complexion, compounded by their itinerant lifestyle, made them strangers everywhere. *Gadze* response could include fascination and attraction to the ostensible 'exoticness' of the 'gypsy', even sometimes to the point of romantic identification. But, for the most part, it took the form of fear and distrust, bordering often on feelings of extreme repulsion.[153]

How persistent these feelings regarding 'gypsies' remained over a period of hundreds of years is perhaps gauged from standard near-contemporary lexicon definitions of them. As late as 1952, the *Dictionary of Czech Language* described the term Gypsy as, among other things, 'a symbol of mendacity', and the people themselves as 'jokers, liars, imposters and cheaters'. Even a relatively recent edition of the *Oxford English Dictionary* notes them to be 'cunning', 'deceitful', and 'fickle'.[154] What this points to is a dark, often subterranean history of non-Roma/Roma relations in which violent persecution of the latter radically preceded the Nazis. One might argue, indeed, that, far from beginning at this point, an ultimately systematized Nazi drive to genocide was simply a culmination of centuries of pent-up, continent-wide, anti-Roma hatreds. In this respect, it was not simply that 'gypsies' were Europe's 'other'; rather they were the nearest domestic equivalent to the wild, savage peoples of the colonies, or, more exactly still, the aborigines of the post-conquest Australian scene. Thus, just as Tasmanian aborigines had supposedly proved immune to the humanizing efforts of missionaries such as George Robinson, so the 'enlightened' efforts of the Austrian emperor, Joseph II, to assimilate Roma to the normative labour force as 'New Hungarians' or 'new peasants' had failed on the ostensible grounds that their very primitiveness acted as an incurable block to the inculcation of civilized values.[155]

'Worthless and shiftless',[156] as they supposedly were, it was no wonder that the standard response of state or local magistracy was to move them on—often after facial or other mutilation—or even to transport them actually to the colonies. In Prussia, in 1722, it was declared a capital offence to be a gypsy. In Rumania, they could be legitimately enslaved and would have gone on being so had it not been for the small question of international recognition of the two principalities in 1856.[157] Toleration by way of stringent utilitarian thinking, or, indeed, international protocol, was making some inroads. Yet even in the age of the Enlightenment and beyond, too much on the Roma account (unlike the Jewish parallel) seemed to be pointing in the reverse direction. Even on the cusp of the Josephine reforms, sensational, though, as it turned out, entirely unfounded charges of cannibalism led to torture being committed by local Hungarian authorities against an entire Roma community, the culmination of which was the very gruesome execution of forty-one of their number.[158] The charge of cannibalism, however, did not disappear. In 1927, in Slovakia, this time under the liberal Czech republic of the period, a Roma group was again tried—if this time acquitted—for the same alleged crime. The following year, in the same region, six Roma—including two children—were caught and killed for pilfering.[159] This was nothing new in itself or, in the historical run of anti-Roma assaults, notably shocking. 'Gypsies', like aborigines, had been a constant pretext, or simply excuse, for gratuitous vigilante violence, with recurring frequency. And not just in out-of-the-way parts of the rimlands. In 1830s Jutland there had been a gypsy hunt for sport in which scores of their number, a women and suckling babe included, had reportedly been massacred.[160] Indeed, as with the aborigines in Australia, Gypsophile tendencies, usually emanating from professional or amateur ethnographers, were often motivated by fears that 'gypsies'—whether through being hunted down, miscegenation, or simply being unable to cope with the burden of modern society—were in danger of becoming a dying race whose folklore, hence, had to be preserved while there was still time.[161]

While the romanticizers underestimated Rom resilience—a classic example of scholarly getting-it-wrong—there is little evidence that their admiring interest translated, post-1918, into a wider state or societal shift towards Roma acceptance, let alone accommodation. States which purported to have universalist or even plain humanitarian underpinnings proved little different on this score from others. In the USSR Roma were typecast from 1929 as *sotsvredelementy*, 5,000 of them being rounded up and deported four years later from the environs of Moscow to remote regions.[162] In liberal Czechoslovakia just a few years earlier, new legislation required non-sedentarized Roma over the age of fourteen to register that they were travellers.

In turn, this meant having a licence and special papers which included finger-prints, as well as a registration book which, signed by the local mayor, determined how many days each gypsy could spend in any single locality.[163]

If this was clearly not equality before the law, nor was it any different under Weimar. Again, one might even offer an acerbic reading of Himmler's December 1938 decree 'for combatting the Gypsy plague'—for all its very threatening-sound-ing title—as less a radical new departure than simply a logical extension of the anti-gypsy policies of National Socialism's democratic predecessor. After all, the decree's requirement that all Roma, sedentary or travelling, should be registered, and that data on each and every one of them should be held in a special criminal police unit in Berlin was, on one level, little more than a systematization of the permanent police surveillance of Roma initiated in 1928.[164] For years, police authorities in the *Länder* had been consistently urging an extension of powers so that they could keep tabs on, as well as segregate, Roma from the rest of the popu-lation. The inauguration of *Zigeunerausweis* in Bavaria, Prussia, and other regional states, around the same time as they came into force in Czechoslovakia, was evi-dence enough that legislative bodies were finally falling into line with police best practice.[165] And clearly, too, with an eye to cross-border cooperation. When the grandly titled International Centre for the Fight against the Gypsy Menace was founded in pre-Anschluss Vienna, in 1936, it was not at the behest of the Nazis. Berlin's Interior Ministry was simply one of its many endorsers.[166]

One might infer from all this that Nazi anti-Roma policy was less a consequence of cutting-edge thinking than one of regime responsiveness to other, including notably grass-roots, pressures. Gypsies appear to have played no part in Hitler's worldview; nor do they appear in *Mein Kampf*.[167] The leading state-sponsored Roma field researcher, Eva Justin, as late as 1942, equally confirmed that 'the gypsy problem cannot be compared with the Jewish problem, because the gypsies are not able to undermine or endanger the German *Volk* as such'.[168] By contrast, societal anti-gypsy feeling was ever-present in what came down to a recurrent round of fears. Begging and loitering, shiftiness and the avoidance of normal work all pointed to one thing only: that Roma were *hereditarily* criminal pickpockets and thieves—not to say degenerates to boot—and, thus, a constant menace to the personal wellbeing, safety, and property of upright, decent Germans. Popular demands to local authorities, and, from those same authorities, to Berlin to *do* something on the matter could, consequently, take on quite a shrill quality.

Take the case of Austrian Burgenland, an almost entirely rural, relatively impov-erished eastern border region of Austria but the one with the largest number of Roma, estimated at 8,000. Barely months into the Anschluss, the new Gauleiter, Dr Tobias Portschy, wrote a memorandum on 'the Gypsy Question', trotting out all the usual anti-Roma accusations, but supplementing these with lurid warnings as to how the eight thousand would become at least 60,000 within fifty years as a consequence of their alleged sexual promiscuousness. This, he claimed, would have knock-on effects in terms of prostitution and the blackmailing of Germans who fornicated with them and, in the process, 'devour the industrious and plagued border Germans'. For good measure the Roma were also the 'train-bearers' (as he put it) for social democracy and Bolshevism. However, as Michael Zimmerman has particularly noted, what stands out about Portschy's memorandum is the way it 'was shot through with repressed sexual fantasies and anxiety regarding racial mixing'.[169]

Portschy's demands, however, for a tranche of measures to punish the malefactors and prevent intercourse—especially sexual intercourse—between Germans and Roma, did not go unheeded. The following year orders from Berlin led to the rounding up of large numbers of the Burgenland Roma and to their preventative custody in Dachau, Buchenwald, and the newly created women's concentration camp at Ravensbrück.[170] In fact, the clearing out of Roma from particular localities and their forced removal to special *Zigeunerlager*, or from there, often, to the concentration camps, had been going on, by this juncture, for some time. Some of the initiative came from the municipal authorities who wanted their districts cleared of Roma; some came from on high—as during the Olympics when Berlin's six hundred-odd community found themselves confined to a sewage dump in the suburb of Marzahn where, not surprisingly, they began succumbing to disease.[171] In the middle, the onus was on the Kripo, the criminal police, to clear the streets and countryside of travelling 'hordes', a remit supposedly clarified, post-1938, by the coordination of effort emanating from Himmler's special Gypsy unit in Berlin. But all this still rather begs the questions: was this simply a more hard-edged, Nazified version of traditional state harassment? Or were there novel elements in the practice which lead us into the new biopolitical territory of race?

The answer could conceivably be summed up in two words: Robert Ritter—the expert most closely associated with the 'scientific' study of German Roma in the Nazi period. The immediate problem, however, is that the more Ritter's involvement in the 'Gypsy question' is assessed, the more we become aware that his working premises and methodology were somewhat at variance with standard Nazified race science. Ritter himself was not a Nazi per se. He was, instead, essentially another (this time glorified academic) anorak, who saw the opportunity which the regime provided to build up his own research empire. With a background in educational psychology and the study of anti-social 'problem' children, the move into gypsy research provided the possibility of state patronage and funding for what he had already chosen as his lifetime's work: the (supposed) relationship between heredity and criminality.[172] What, from the mid-1930s, Ritter thus—as 'his own duty to science'[173]—sought to demonstrate was how the entire gamut of 'gypsy' asocial behaviour, not to say 'cultural impoverishment', lay in genetic failings, including hidden forms of mental deficiency. The research programme was predicated on the creation of a huge family tree, a genealogical record in effect of all 30,000 or more itinerants in Germany.

This more exact emphasis on descent rather than race, however, proved little obstacle for his initial main sponsors: the Public Health Department of the Interior Ministry of Health, and Arthur Nebe, the powerful Kripo boss to whom Ritter became a special adviser and later head of Kripo's own Criminological Biological Institute.[174] Indeed, by way of Ritter, the synergy between scientific researcher and Nazi state becomes rather clear. Ritter's team, including Justin, 'equipped with syringes, calipers, eye-colour charts, and pots of wax to take masks of gypsy faces',[175] were able to enter the Roma camps and concentration camps, prisons, hospitals— anywhere, indeed, where they could lay hands on their subjects—and, with police protection, take their craniometric and other measurements, not to mention con- duct their interviews 'unrelentingly' and to their hearts' content. The authorities, in return, gained access to the huge, increasingly detailed genealogical archive which Ritter was amassing. As a consequence, Ritter's institutes became 'the deci- sive influence on the concept and practice of National Socialist Gypsy policy'.[176]

There was just one little complication. The emerging genealogical data just hap- pened to turn racial essentialism on its head. In other words, if there was—as all authorities in Nazi Germany agreed—a gypsy problem, it did not reside in any clearly delineated gypsy race line. How could it, given Ritter's assessment that less than 10 per cent of the Roma screened were 'pure' Roma through and through? But in this sense one was also back with state and society's fundamental race angst: that of *Vermischung* and *Verfliessen*—miscegenation and blending.[177] It was all very well, as the Interior Ministry proposed in March 1936, to prepare the ground for a Gypsy law which would bring about a 'total solution of the Gypsy problem on either a national or international level'.[178] An interim remit included kicking out all the stateless gypsies, packing off the rest into a special reservation, and steriliz- ing the *Mischlinge*. But then, if most gypsies were *Mischlinge* how deep did the infection into German society actually go? Given von Luschan's prescription that the bad blood would always turn up sooner or later, that would seem to require of the state a very total solution indeed. Precedents on hand, such as the contempo- raneous efforts of Australian aboriginal administrators to 'breed out the colour' of half-castes by removing (i.e. 'stealing') the children from their mothers and native communities and 'absorbing' them, by calculated degrees, into the white popula- tion, were, for all their own genocidal implications, not even considered by the Nazi experts.[179] Closer to home, Swiss public policy towards its own 'racially degenerate' *Jenische* travellers, through a brutal mix of banging them up in mental hospitals, prisons, and the like, abducting the children (as delegated though vari- ous supposedly child-orientated organizations such as Pro Juventute), and com- pulsory sterilization, demonstrated strong Ritterian influence. Even so, the Swiss attempt to forcibly assimilate the *Jenische* children into 'gajdo culture',[180] again fundamentally contradicted a key tenet of Nazi eugenics in principle—and practice.

What the Nazis appeared to be seeking was a solution which would eradicate the problem for all time, by making the Roma *Zukunftslos*, that is, biologically 'future- less'. It was also clear that the proposed method for arriving at this point was mass sterilization. To this end, even before Ritter's role as key scientific adviser on these matters was cemented, hundreds of male Roma from Bavaria, during the Olym- pics period, were transported to Dachau for the clinical procedure.[181] The fact that the agents for this round-up were not Roma 'experts' but the police, and that their method for determining who were their targets had nothing to do with scientific method at all, suggests that in 1936—as indeed, throughout the entirety of the Nazi period—the question of who, or, for that matter, what, was actually driving the battle against the Gypsy menace, was far from clear. Were the Roma, at heart, a social problem? One of domestic security? Or a matter of supreme public hygiene? Ritter appeared to be the man to square the circle through the criminality-equals-heredity formula. But Ritter's interpretation of his own findings—for instance, his insistence that the problem was *not* the 10 per cent 'pure' if 'primitive' Roma who, he thought, should be allowed to continue to freely roam, but the 'parasitic' half-caste *Zigeunermischlinge* and *Jenische* rest[182]—hardly squared with the much broader view that *all* gypsies were inherently threatening and dangerous.

Nevertheless, where Ritter's research findings were more far-reaching, they related to the supposed hereditarily determined 'asocial' tendencies among the Roma *Mischlinge*. For example, Ritter claimed, in 1937, to have found a high degree of what he described as 'disguised mental retardation' among gypsy children. What exactly he meant by this is rather opaque, given that it did not amount to a lack of intelligence but was a 'disorder' with 'a mask of' quick-talking 'cleverness'.[183] In other words, the empirical grounding for what was no more than an assertion about behaviour *as if it were biology* was dubious in the extreme. What mattered, however, was the use of the term 'mental retardation' which, in Nazi science-speak, had become a catch-all for any 'sign of a degenerate inner condition' and, hence, 'hereditarily determined' and therefore 'irremediable *attitude*'.[184] The argument was a clearly circular one. But at its root was the requirement for a biological-cum-racial explanation for people whose behaviour was deemed, as a matter of straightforward prejudice, to be 'asocial'—with the same sanction in all cases: sterilization.

*

The trouble was that as soon as one started going down this route the more one was bound to find any number of conditions which amounted to some either hereditary or congenital mental or physical failing in whole swathes of the population; with the eugenicist logic that the more you found the more you needed to almost literally cut out. This carried with it, moreover, a logic beyond mere sterilization. Ideas from the turn of the century most keenly developed in an infamous 1920s tract, 'Permission for the Destruction of Life Unworthy of Life', by two supposedly 'liberal' German university academics, Karl Binding and Alfred Hoche, looked forward to the involuntary termination of the lives of all those who represented a burden, or, as Hoche put it, *Ballastexistenzen*—'a human ballast' upon the limited resources of society as a whole.[185] The proposition—including Hoche's nebulous references to those suffering from psychiatric disturbance, brain damage, and 'retardation' as those who would be the most suitable cases for treatment—had been firmly taken up by mainstream elements in the medical establishment by the time of Hitler's chancellorship.

While euthanasia as such remained in abeyance until the onset of war, the medical profession offered its services four-square to the protection of 'the German nation from biogenetic degeneration'.[186] The first, most immediate, public consequence was the July 1933 act for the prevention of hereditarily diseased progeny. The nine conditions specified as liable for *compulsory* sterilization of the patient included Huntington's chorea, as well as severe physical malformation where the hereditary character had been 'sufficiently established by research'. But if these *were* hereditary conditions, others including epilepsy, schizophrenia, and manic depression were, at the very least, discussible. As for chronic alcoholism, a late addition to the list, this was no more than a sleight of hand.[187] There was, of course, nothing of which the population at large needed to be fearful. All these developments were being guided by some of the leading, most learned scientific and medical academicians in the land. The Expert Committee for Population and Racial Policy, operating under the Ministry of the Interior, would certainly not allow anything arbitrary or untoward to befall its fellow Germans. This, after all, was all being done for the benefit and wellbeing of the whole *Volksgemeinschaft*, as was the reorganization of the public health system in July 1934: when 650 new countrywide bureaux were tasked with the collection and registration of data about the genetic antecedents of the population at large.[188] Everything would be done by the book. There would be proper card-indexing systems which, in due course, would become a nationwide hereditary archive. There would be properly constituted Hereditary Health Courts, which would ensure that there would be no miscarriages of justice. As for the party, its new Racial–Political Office, with 3,600 staff members, would work overtime to ensure that the public at large knew what was happening and why.[189]

Not that many ordinary people were asking too many difficult questions about what *exactly* was hereditarily wrong with gypsies or, for that matter, the five hundred to eight hundred so-called 'Rhineland bastards': the children of African or Asian soldier-fathers who had been part of the primarily French and Belgian occupation forces in the early 1920s. Surely it was just what scientists would later call the precautionary principle which was determining that these half-castes should be prevented from having children of their own? Indeed, the Bavarian Interior Ministry had already proposed as much during the Weimar period. When the Nazi state decided unequivocally to act on the matter in 1937, unsurprisingly it was with the imprimatur of Fischer and a bevy of other scientific experts. Even so, the decision came outside the remit of the Nazi's own progeny act, was decreed in secret, and was implemented by the mass removal of four hundred of the children to Bonn and Cologne hospitals by the Gestapo, operating under secret orders. After sterilization, many of the children appear to have disappeared, some as a result of medical experiments conducted on them.[190]

Could it be, that on matters such as these, a fine line was being drawn between what the mass of population was prepared to stomach from the Nazi-sponsored eugenicists and what the regime instinctively knew they might well recoil from with horror? This returns us to that, albeit problematic, proposition mooted at the end of our section, 'A regime and its enemies', in response to the question of why so many *ordinary* Germans *liked* Hitler and his regime. This had little or nothing to do with some radical take on modernity; it had everything to do with a promise of social order. It was transparent that under Nazism there was no place for shirkers and skivers: the police would make sure of that. As for gypsies and other layabouts, what did it matter if, following a major police clampdown in the spring and summer of 1938, some 10,000 of them were behind the guarded perimeters of concentration camps—or that from these and the *Zigeunerlager*, inmates were

commandeered for highway construction and other projects in which hard, unremitting labour was the order of the day?[191] If it meant the streets were clear of
beggars and other licentious riff-raff, and that ordinary decent folk could sleep
easily in their beds without fear of robbery, so be it. And if this also entailed forcible sterilization for such people, again, this was a perfectly acceptable price to
pay. Indeed, it promised a future in which all those elements which had disgraced and endangered German society through their unkempt slovenliness and
unruliness, and, by extension, filthiness (which everybody knew, in the wake of
the post-bacteriology revolution, brought with it lice-carrying disease),[192] would
become a thing of the past.

Sexual backsliding, too, deserved just punishment. One can imagine the relish
with which many would have greeted the November 1933 Law against Dangerous
Habitual Criminals, in which sex offenders, including perceived paedophiles—
whether they had committed crimes or not—could be not just locked away more
or less indefinitely in prison or asylums, but castrated.[193] As for those Rhineland
women who had consorted with not just foreign but *black* foreign soldiers, one can
hardly imagine much general sympathy for them when their children were removed,
however distraught the mothers may have been.

Here then, we perhaps have grounds for extending what Goldhagen might provocatively describe as a 'cultural cognitive model'.[194] In Goldhagen's argument,
demotic German cultural antipathies revolved primarily around the Jews. We
might concur with at least that most minimal element of the thesis insofar as a
great many Germans wanted rid of their presence, or at least to have them isolated
at arms' length from the rest of society. But then, for many at the grass roots, Hitler
was a good thing because he was perceived to be dealing with *all* the bad eggs, even
the 'degenerates' in the party, such as Röhm and his ilk. Nazism could thus be
acclaimed for the state-led restoration of a conservative morality and, with it, of a
sanitized public space—and hence perceived normality. It is telling on this score
that the much older, entirely regressive German catchphrase, *Kinder, Küche, Kirche*
was never contested as such by the Nazis. Indeed, the secret of Nazi success on the
social plane may actually lie in the way that its recycling of traditional (patriarchal)
aspirations seemed to confirm the party's lack of desire to intrude into 'ordinary
Germans'' private lives—provided, that is, those lives remained within
acceptable—monochrome—bounds.[195]

This would seem to amount to a form of trade-off. Overt Nazification of the
public arena placed onerous responsibilities on each individual towards state and
national community. Race and heredity, for instance, became part of the general
school curriculum just as, out of school hours, there was the Hitler Youth—albeit
not in fact compulsorily until 1939.[196] And, as in Wilhelmine times, so now again
under the Third Reich—unfettered from the terms of Versailles—there was male
military service. All this, of course, could bring pride, a sense of belonging, even
career advancement. Yet at the same juncture, a semi-autonomous sphere *appeared*
to remain sacrosanct. People went to church, as in previous times; they could travel
abroad; they were not, as a rule, bullied or harassed for not being Nazis—though
if they tried to interfere with their children's commitment to the youth organizations

it could be different. The police presence for most people, however, was not all-pervasive. Perhaps it was actually this *absence* of totality which explains why the Nazis were 'able to accomplish much of what they set out to do without acquiring unquestioning allegiance or imposing complete control'.[197]

Yet here's the rub. When it came to the question of 'applied biology', Nazi policy clearly did not only interfere with the racial outsiders or the *bad* people. Its impact could be felt across the board anywhere in society—and often devastatingly so. At the self-consciously elite level of party and SS, the requirement to provide proof of Aryan ancestry back to 1800—a Nazi version, in effect, of the old Castilian obsession with *limpieza de sangre*[198]—while providing a veritable bonanza of work for the likes of Euler, also had the potential to hoist the Nazis by their own petard. Heydrich, no less, remained dogged by persistent rumours of Jewish background, while Hitler himself, post-Anschluss, went to the trouble of having his ancestral Waldviertel village of Döllersheim blown to smithereens by the army, the cemetery included, for no less all-consuming fears.[199] For other, lesser, mortals within the *Apparat*, 'reclassification' from the taint of Jewish *Mischling* blood could only come by way of a special 'liberation' from the Führer.[200]

If this suggested party and state were not above ways of getting around the racial strictures they themselves had invented (even if recipients of 'liberations' had to increasingly prove their 'positive merit'), the populace at large found themselves with little or no appeal when members of their families were deemed biologically wanting. In the four years from the onset of the Progeny Law, a staggering 300,000 people were subjected to what, with gallows humour, was called the 'Hitler-cut' (*Hitlerschnitt*), and another 100,000 by the onset of war.[201] To be sure, a significant proportion—some 30 to 40 per cent—were 'invisible' in the sense that they were banged up in mental asylums or other institutions for the incurably ill. In other words, in places of confinement where their opportunities to reproduce were close to zero.[202] But, nonetheless, they could still be Auntie Ulrika or cousin Hans.

Being on the outside of an institution, however, proved no prophylactic against the range of hereditary and congenital failings that the august architects of the sterilization programme had dreamt up. Indeed, leading protagonist and psychiatric expert Professor Ernst Rüdin made a point of linking feeblemindedness with that all too ubiquitous if annoyingly undefinable deficiency: being 'asocial'.[203] Rüdin and his colleagues got round the problem by devising a set of intelligence tests, which at least 50 per cent of those screened for sterilization conveniently failed.[204] For those who passed the tests, however, there were always other criteria to fall back on to confirm the correct verdict: 'moral insanity' being the one most usually to the fore. As a result, it was quite common for a case like that of Anna V. to come before the Hereditary Health Courts where, having been in effect found 'guilty' of teenage promiscuity, the reasons adduced as proof of her 'feebleminded' condition were 'the inability to earn a living through regular employment or to adapt to society; an uncritical approach to one's actions; weakness of will; the dulling of ethical sentiments; and gross defects of character'. Anna was accordingly sterilized in an asylum in May 1938 shortly after having given birth to a baby girl which was immediately put into care.[205] The baby was, in one respect, lucky: in 1935 eugenic abortion was sanctioned for women up to and including the sixth month of their pregnancy.[206]

But if the doctors and psychiatrists had this much power, where exactly did it end? One leading psychiatrist, Franz Kallmann—ironically of Jewish background, which rather put his opinion out of court—proposed in 1935 that all those carrying the putative recessive gene for schizophrenia should be sterilized. Kallmann was rebuked by colleagues: he was in effect proposing that the procedure be adopted for 20 per cent of the population![207] Even so, five years later, in July 1940, the Ministry of Interior published formal guidelines detailing how the German population would be categorized in the future. There were to be four categories, including one at the top which, because it contained 'genetically especially valuable' material, would receive positive support and encouragement for its reproduction. Then, considerably lower down the hierarchy in category two, were biologically 'average' Germans, followed by category-three families, who were also characterized as 'still acceptable' if not exactly 'an asset to the national community'. The guidelines stated that they could be subjected to forcible sterilization. As for category four, at the lowest rung of all, Götz Aly states that what was intended for these people in terms of 'negative population policy' was not actually spelt out in the guidelines because it included deportation, slave labour, and extermination.[208] What is significant, however, is that eugenicist opinion had become so standard as the state organizing principle that it was now taken as a given that heredity was at the root of all social behaviour: the best people ipso facto came from genetically superior stock; by contrast, the biologically retrograde were one and the same as 'asocials'.

Were the Interior Ministry guidelines, then, evidence of formulations towards or even a form of sketch blueprint for auto-genocide? The notion sounds ludicrous; but is it? With the onset of war, the sterilization programme against those 'unworthy of life' had already been largely superseded by a new, more radical programme, which was to result in the direct murder of as many as 200,000 mentally ill or physically disabled adults and children.[209] And just as Hitler had forbidden the publication of the figures for those sterilized, so now Aktion T-4—the team of medical practitioners and support staff drawn together to organize and implement the new programme—would do so in the strictest secrecy, operating on the single authority of the Führer's personal chancellery. There was a cover story, of course: that what was being conducted were 'mercy killings' for severely disabled children at the behest of their beseeching parents. But news as to what was really going in the dedicated asylums and clinics spilled out soon enough into the broader population. As early as November 1940, SS security experts were filing reports of growing, anxious rumours from the grass roots that the measures would be extended to encompass the elderly, invalids, workers past their prime, as well as wounded or mentally disturbed soldiers.[210] In fact, there is perpetrator testimony to suggest that in the early stages of Operation Barbarossa T-4 operatives were involved close to the front in killing severely traumatized German soldiers with lethal injections.[211]

Clearly, however, we have to be extremely wary of assuming that popular perception amounted to the same thing as regime intent. On some levels, the latter may even have sought to row back from the chop-logic of its own hereditary strictures. It is, for instance, highly ironic that had the Jewish gay campaigner Magnus Hirschfield's advocacy of homosexuality as an inborn and immutable trait been comprehensively appropriated by Nazi racial hygiene—that is, in a *negative* sense— the assault on men in German society would have reached truly horrifying proportions. Nazi violence against homosexuals is unquestionable. Wearers of the pink triangle in pre-war concentration camps were more vulnerable and, in all probability, more exposed to violence than any other group. Of the possibly 5,000 to 15,000 German men who were interned in concentration camps on grounds of sexual orientation, as many as 60 per cent were killed.[212] But while Röhm and his coterie's known homosexuality may have been a factor in the subsequent ratcheting up of a more general assault on gays, the regime clearly did not attempt to *systematically* screen the male population for 'queerness' as it did, say, for epilepsy or feeble-mindedness.[213] Again, an irony of the situation is that had it been more conservative, more like, for instance, Franco's regime in Spain, or Pétain's post-1940 France, the consequences could have been very different. The Nazism of the *alte Kämpfer* was anti-bourgeois and, to say the least, ambivalent about its sexual values. Putting that aside, simply on pragmatic grounds it would have made little sense to have started applying the thumbscrews to 2 million men—Himmler's 1937 guestimate as to the number of homosexuals in Germany—at a moment when the country was moving rapidly towards a war footing.[214] If the regime had done so families (whatever the level of their homophobia) throughout the length and breadth of the country, from the most wealthy and powerful to the very poorest, would have found themselves tainted and traumatized.

Nazism's let-out on the issue was to circumvent the possibility of homosexuality's grounding in nature, thereby both isolating those who were the hardened core of punishable 'seducers' while enabling those so 'seduced' to be 're-educated' or 'cured' and then returned to 'normal' society.[215] Even so, there were clearly contradictions in this position. Homosexuality was regularly included in administrative and police lists of asocial behaviour, alongside other recidivist disorders such as alcoholism, promiscuity, work avoidance, and the like. While the state, by way of the Interior Ministry, failed to arrive at a law encompassing all these deficient, 'valueless' traits, or what exactly it proposed to do with individuals (or, by its own hereditary logic, families) who manifested them, the ascendancy within the regime of the overtly puritanical Himmler carried with it the possibility for all manner of *attitudes* to be equally marked down as asocial. In late 1944, for instance, the Reichsführer-SS cited examples which included 'indifference toward the war; preference for English ideals, speech, behaviour, and clothing; and attraction to jazz, "hot" music, and swing dancing'.[216]

It seems likely that had a more tightly SS-run Nazi Germany somehow survived the war, or even won through, its card indexers—not unlike their Soviet counterparts—would have been working flat out, not to say in overdrive. Whether the eugenicists would have been able to accommodate their supposedly tightly defined racial science to Himmler's altogether more elastic rubric is perhaps an open question. How this would have actually impinged on the German population *tout ensemble* is even more a matter for speculation.

What is for certain is that the pre-war ascendancy of the bureaucrats, medical experts, and scientific academy within the Nazi state, and their commitment to translating eugenic ideas into social practice—however contradictory, inconsistent, and illogical that practice often turned out to be—took Germany to the brink of a biopolitics which, even where it may not have fitted squarely into a definition of genocide, was clearly exterminatory. State-determined euthanasia would become a logical extension of state-determined sterilization. But it is also significant that the transition from one to the other crystallized out of crisis conditions which the regime itself consciously set in train. As it took this course, Nazism found itself firmly back on its primary genocide track.

THE YEAR 1938

It is ironic that in the midst of all the attempts to delineate the asocial in German society, nobody seemed to notice that the country was led by a bunch of individuals who fitted the description to a T: Hitler primus inter pares. Which makes the issue of German submission to the will of the Führer all the more remarkable. Through the early years of his rule one can see how the elite sectors of society willingly lent themselves to the Hitler project. It was, after all, their project too: 'the complete reshaping of Germany, militarily, economically socially, and spiritually'.[217] The plausibility of it all started to be realized with the military and foreign policy successes; rearmament in defiance of the West; the unopposed march into the previously demilitarized Rhineland; the way in which the Luftwaffe was able to use the conflict in Spain as a testing ground for total war. At every turn France and Britain blinked, evidence in itself that without the USA to back them, the frontline states of the liberal system seemed incapable of halting the German tide.

But then came 1938—and it was the turn of the traditional German elite to blink. Hitler's plans for future war were laid before a small coterie of senior military and foreign policy advisers at the end of the previous year. The principles of Hitler's forward policy were not, in themselves, new. When he had spoken in *Mein Kampf* of how Germans would turn their 'eyes towards the lands of the east',[218] he was, in one respect, simply enunciating standard Wilhelmine goals whose previous high-water mark had been Ludendorff's 1918 drive far into the rimlands. It was well understood that timing would be of the essence in any future war and that this would probably require getting German retaliation in first against any threat emanating from the fast industrializing Soviet anti-system. It also assumed that the Western powers would themselves have to be politically if not militarily neutralized. All this looked forward to a resurgent Germany in which the liberal system would, in effect, be overthrown or at least subordinated to Nazi dominance in the Eurasian arena.

Hitler, however, did not conceive of victory simply in standard geopolitical terms. In *Mein Kampf* he had already enunciated the justification and projected development of the imagined empire in the East. It would not follow 'liberal' colonial policy as in pre-war times but would be founded on the conquest of new *Lebensraum* for the German *Volk* in the 'heartland of the world'.[219] Hitler's vision thus seemed to suggest a regression to a model of earlier world empires, on the one hand involving German colonies and settlement at the expense of native populations, on the other an autarkic economy which would deliver the resource base of the entire imperial region for the sole benefit of the German nation. If this sounded altogether atavistic, this was no leap back in time. Hitler's proposed medium-term expansion to the east should be conceived of, amongst other things, as taking control of rimlands' oil for an already highly mechanized Wehrmacht, while powering the industrial–technocratic base upon which Germany's ultra-modern military machine would be constantly refined and developed.

However, the November 1937 conference at which Hitler outlined some of these ideas also set out a series of potential scenarios for possibly imminent conflict. And it was at these that the conservatives balked. One was a lightning strike on Czechoslovakia and Austria, which Hitler characterized as removing a threat to Germany's flank in the event of war with the French.[220] Even so, it is important to note how the acquisition of these core historically 'German' regions of former Habsburg Austria would have fitted into Hitler's wider *Ostraum* vision. By the union of the 'Two Germanies' into 'one common fatherland—the German empire'[221]—he was imagining more than simply a launching pad for further dismemberment of the 'New Europe' nation states. The 'Two Germanies' between them, after all, embraced within their separate compasses the entirety of the 'Lands Between' to the east, and the Balkans to the south-east. Joined together and truly 'coordinated' a pan-German *Drang nach Osten* took on a potential never previously realized, even under the Holy Roman emperors. But, in going for broke, Blomberg and Fritsch for the generals and Neurath for the Foreign Office sensed that Hitler's ambition could now be the nation's undoing, not least as it could bring about the one thing they were striving to avoid as their key lesson from 1914–18: war on two fronts.

That it was the dissenters who were retired or dismissed, the regime which survived, speaks volumes about the degree to which the Nazis had, in the previous half-decade, taken firm control of the apparatus of state and, conversely, rendered the initial platform of traditional elite mentoring redundant. There were enough up-and-coming military and civilian technocrats to take the place of the old guard. And as nothing quite succeeds like success—between spring 1938 and spring 1939 both Austria and the entirety of Czechoslovakia fell into the Nazi lap without recourse to war—Hitler's way also seemed to be Germany's good luck.

One can hardly imagine such a policy radicalization from an old-school politician or military man. Threatening war and forcing the West into contortionist acts of appeasement and accommodation, Hitler set his own bar against which pragmatic caution, or even retreat in the face of overwhelming odds, were simply dismissed as unacceptable weaknesses. To take such policy forward necessarily carried with it the need for a new breed of high-level personnel with unswerving commitment to the cause. But the very process crystallized obstacles or threw up contingencies which were neither expected nor necessarily welcomed.

*

By moving into conquest mode what Hitler ensured, above all, was a full reactivation of the Jewish spectre. Indeed, this was a case of the regime being firmly caught on the horns of its own mythically conspiratorial dilemma. If 'the Jews' were the ultimate threat to the wellbeing of the German people, logically they had to be removed from the body politic. But if the Third Reich's rise to world greatness was predicated on a drive into the rimlands and beyond, it inevitably added to its subject population the main global concentration of Jews—to the tune of millions. The scale of this self-induced crisis was already evident even in the relatively small numbers of Austrian and Czech Jewry—195,000 and 357,000 respectively.[222] There was no preconceived Nazi plan for how this 'problem' would be overcome. On the contrary, it simply amplified what was already starkly obvious: the regime's failure to free itself of its still existing core German Jewish population. True, by early 1938, having seen the writing on the wall, large numbers of the wealthier, more skilled, and dynamic elements of the community had decamped to other countries—including, ironically, Austria and Czechoslovakia. But this in turn underscored the nature of an ongoing domestic reality: the older and poorer elements of German Jewry who did not have the wherewithal to cope with either the regime's currency restrictions or its flight tax were not going to be able to leave any time soon. Indeed, with the emigration of the more able and/or expropriation of broader communal funds—they even threatened to become a residual burden on the Nazi state itself.

So long as Germany was contained within its Versailles boundaries this eventuality could—in functional, if not ideological terms—arguably be put off to another day. The victories of 1938, however, brought the regime face to face with the wider consequences of its anti-Jewish goals, in the way these enmeshed with its expansionist agenda and so forced it into further, even more radicalized anti-Jewish action. The immediate catalyst was the mid-March invasion of Austria. The Anschluss proceeded unopposed but, even before German forces had entered Vienna, a pent-up, demotic fury against Austrian Jewry was unleashed. The animus expressed itself most infamously in the way Viennese Jews, young and old, men and women alike, were rounded up by their neighbours and forced to scour the city streets with toothbrushes, nailbrushes, or even their bare knuckles. Visible public humiliation, however, was only the half of it. A pandemic of gratuitous violence so terrified the main concentration of the Austrian Jewish community that an estimated 1,700 committed suicide in the immediate wake of the pogrom.[223] Viennese anti-Semitism, of course, had a long lineage and was hardly something the leadership in Berlin was now going to admonish. How could it when the local SS and SA were involved in the plunder and violence, the Gestapo was busily arresting Austrian Jewish community leaders prior to sending them to Dachau, and the entire corpus of Germany's own anti-Jewish legislation was being railroaded through the Austrian statute book?

Even so, there was one immediate headache for the Nazi 'liberators'. Over and above, that is, the fact that the visible contours of Austrian street violence were in notable contrast to its relative containment in Germany proper. The proceeds of the Austrian open season were falling into the wrong hands. The Anschluss moment had offered a licence and impunity to rob and plunder at will and, as a result, gave some 25,000 largely self-appointed 'commissary administrators' the opportunity to appoint themselves as liquidators of Jewish properties and businesses. One consequence was that some 40,000 apartments had new inhabitants almost overnight, their former Jewish ones literally kicked out onto the street.[224] One might add, moreover, that all this came not only with the blessing of the Austrian wing of the party—indeed many of the administrators were Nazis—but was thoroughly in keeping with an old-style Nazi rhetoric, which sought to restore the things supposedly stolen by the alien Jews from the people, to the 'people'.

The critical stumbling block for the regime, however, was that with war looming its need to maximize capital as well as industrial resources for *that* purpose was becoming a priority of state over and above all others. Behind full-frontal genocidal drives often lie other practical, statist considerations of the moment. We have seen that in Ottoman Turkey in 1915, the CUP urge to provide a quick independent financial fix for a Porte treasury which, if it had not been heavily mortgaged to the Germans would have been empty, proved one critical factor in the reckoning. So, too, were the benefits of binding leading elite actors to the state through the cheap sale of Armenian factories, businesses, and properties. The procedure, needless to say, was predicated on the annihilation of the Armenians themselves, thus rendering their assets available at no extra cost to the regime's coffers. In 1938 the drive to wholesale expropriation of all Jewish concerns within the Nazi Reich, of course, *preceded* the wholesale annihilation of their owners by at least three years. But then, equally, the state-sanctioned redundancy of those owners' property rights in 1938 may suggest a signposting to their irrelevance as people.

What matters here, though, is not whether expropriation was, at the time, an intended prelude to genocide—as there is no specific evidence to advance the case. Rather, it is the manner in which state intervention sought to limit the demotic interest as attempted by the Viennese interlopers in favour of a much more controlled exercise, the ultimate purpose of which was to channel sequestrated Jewish wealth towards the Four Year Plan.[225] With all its apparent resonances of the Soviet model, the Plan was the nearest the Nazis came to organizing a command economy. Its sole purpose, indeed, was to pave the way for Germany's military-industrial complex to prepare for the launching of war. At the helm of the commission project was Hermann Goering, the—in every respect—larger-than-life Nazi leader as well as voracious accumulator of fiefdoms in his own right. Where Jews came into this equation, consequently, had little or nothing to do with the 60 per cent of an estimated 160,000 German Jewish small businesses—a large number of them one-man operations—which, by April 1938, had already been wound up or Aryanized, largely through opportunists acting in a similarly intimidating manner to their later Austrian counterparts.[226] What instead mattered to Goering about the free-for-all in Vienna was the likelihood that much larger and more heavyweight banking and industrial concerns would fall outside his commission's purview. Gauleiter Josef Bürckel, the man on the spot tasked with integrating the economy of Austria with that of Germany, was particularly under orders to ensure that major Jewish industrial holdings—most obviously the Viennese Rothschild-owned Witkowitz mines and ironworks in Bohemia—passed directly into the state's portfolio. Bürckel amassed a team of economists and human resource planners to help him expedite this remit.

They were not above hostage-taking and ransom to achieve their objective, proving in the process that the difference between them and the small-time gangsters was simply a matter of the power at their disposal.[227]

Nevertheless, the Austrian experience set both a precedent and model for a much more systematized and streamlined all-Germany programme of state-organized plunder.[228] Within six weeks of the Anschluss, the Interior Ministry was responding to an initiative from Goering in the form of regulations requiring the compulsory registration of all Jewish businesses and assets over 5,000 marks. Up to this juncture many of the really significant Jewish-owned concerns had weathered the storm of threat and intimidation by reconstituting managing boards with 'Aryan' representatives; in top-flight cases, often with members from the Dresdner and Deutsche, the two leading national banks. Given that, in former times, many leading Jewish magnates had themselves been on these boards, looking to their still ensconced Gentile colleagues after 1933 to do right by them seemed plausible. In the case of the Dresdner it soon proved to be disastrous, the largely state-owned and increasingly Nazified operation quickly learning that backing Aryanization brought with it definite benefits, at least in the form of handsome profits from brokering the sale of Jewish stock packets from asset-stripped companies. It was also not above collusion with the Gestapo, such that internal documents could be furnished to 'expose' Jewish entrepreneurs of shady dealings: the case of Ignatz Nacher, the philanthropic owner of Germany's second-largest brewery, presenting a particularly vicious example of the bank's entirely amoral willingness to assist in a farrago of lies in order to asset-strip Nacher of his business and livelihood.[229]

That had been back in 1934. Four years later, who would remain steadfast against the latest slew of Nazi desiderata? Not the Deutsche bank, with its eye on its more internationally oriented business and supposed pride in its political independence and financial rectitude. How could it afford to eschew participation in the break-up of Jewish concerns when the sizeable brokerage commissions or, for that matter, valuable stock, would otherwise go to its arch-rival?[230] Nor were the big Gentile-owned German industrial conglomerates any different. Here, after all, was a once-in-a-lifetime opportunity to gain key empire-building assets at minimal cost. Major corporates, especially in the field of armaments production, including I.G. Farben, Siemens, and Krupp, were necessarily among the major recipients. What sense was there for them to spite themselves by refusing to play, while at the same time getting a bad reputation with the regime? The whole process of divesting Jews of their wealth, moreover, could still be presented by the regime as a genuine redistribution. Everybody could gain something: luxury motor cars auctioned at knock-down prices to party stalwarts, bicycles, nice furnishings, all manner of moveable items more or less given away to ordinary folk.[231] It might only be crumbs from the rich man's table but here was surely one arena in which *Gleichschaltung* had a genuine meaning. State, party, police, banks, corporate business, and people all could have a stake in this national clearance sale, and therefore all had some interest in cooperation towards this end. All we have to remember is that despite the voluminous rake-offs, property confiscations, and embezzlement on the side—to the personal enrichment of thousands of profiteers, not least of

Goering himself—it was the Nazi state which was the ultimate arbiter and coordinator of process. Its own rake-off was an estimated 60 and 80 per cent of proceeds from the large-scale domestic property transfers, that is, some 3 billions-worth of the 7.1 billion marks derived from the compulsory registrations of Jewish wealth, not to mention, as Peter Hayes notes, 'increased tax proceeds on stock transactions throughout 1938–39'. Or, put another way, sufficient receipts to contribute 5 per cent of the national budget in the final year prior to war, or, yet again, the difference between acceleration or cut-back on German armaments production.[232]

That overall figure, in fact, might suggest that German Jewish wealth was rather far from representing the economic stranglehold in the land that Nazis and Volkists had always claimed. Yet conversely, and more soberly, it might remind us that genocide can be studied in cost-benefit terms; that one might indeed speak of an 'economics of genocide'; that there was—however twisted—a path from Vienna to Auschwitz. Even so, the caveat remains: in 1938 the new Nazi goal was mass expropriation, not a considered programme of extermination.

But expropriation carried with it its own inexorable logic: a complete removal of the suitably impoverished Jewish burden. Eruction beyond the borders of the Reich was now conceived of as being entirely non-negotiable. At stake, however, was a question of praxis. How was mass removal of the Reich's Jews going to be achieved in a world full of emigration barriers against the poor and unwanted? Nobody knew the answer. The testing ground for the new proposition, nevertheless, remained Vienna, though it is perhaps significant that the man we remember most for it was not Bürckel, technically responsible for creating a prototypical Central Office (*Zentralstelle*) for Jewish Emigration,[233] but one of his minor underlings, Adolf Eichmann.

In terms of the wider contours of the Holocaust the focus on Eichmann—its key organizational operative—makes sense. Yet at the start of 1938 the Austrian-born Nazi was nothing more than a lowly desk operative in the SD, with a role monitoring and analysing the activities of Zionist organizations within a small bureau which was compiling information on the alleged ideological Jewish threat to state security.[234] Certainly, the bureau was crucial to Heydrich's insistent efforts to find a comprehensive 'solution' to the Jewish problem. And with the SD, since mid-1936, an emerging force in a unified German police under Himmler, the bureau's star was in the ascendant. Yet Eichmann's specific innovation, when he was pitched into the Vienna maelstrom, was more a matter of organizational method than brilliant idea, and, furthermore, to a considerable degree not his idea at all, but that of his Jewish *victims*. Their key desideratum now, practically to a man and woman, was to flee Austria as fast as possible. What conspired to block their exit was—paradoxically—bureaucracy. At every turn the multitudinous papers which required stamping, the different offices which needed to be visited, the administrative snarl-ups and loss of relevant forms—a consequence in itself of paperwork overload—acted against both (albeit entirely differently motivated) Nazi and Jewish interests. As a leader of the community put it to Eichmann: what was needed was a streamlined, *centralized* emigration system. And this is exactly what the SD operative, on Bürckel's authority, set about creating. He took over the

Rothschilds' Vienna palace on Prinz-Eugen Strasse, mobilized a team of local Nazis to set up shop in it, and then proceeded to move Jews through it as if on a conveyer belt. As Hannah Arendt later summarized, 'Like a flour mill connected with a bakery you put in a Jew who still has some property...at one end...He goes through the building from counter to counter, from office to office...and comes out at the other end...with only a passport'.[235]

Arendt's reference to propertied Jews turns out to be particularly relevant to what was at stake here. With the majority of Viennese Jews by this time practically destitute—robbery and extortion on top of final state and municipal bill demands having done their bitter work—Eichmann came up with one seriously provocative improvisation. He made the *Zentralstelle* the financial hub of the emigration process; in other words, one which took responsibility for the emigration of *all* Jews, whether rich or poor. Thus, now treated not as individuals but as part of a collective aggregate, those Jews who could paid their money into SD coffers. The SD, in turn, used these same funds to furnish the necessary papers and minimal monies with which a much larger, anonymous Jewish mass could be 'legitimately' removed from the country.[236]

One might cynically read this as egalitarian to a T. In fact it amounted to daylight robbery not only of all Austrian Jews with regard to whatever wealth they had left but also of foreign Jewish welfare organizations, whose relief revenues to the Vienna community were also duly misappropriated to finance the *Zentralstelle* operation. The humiliation was, in fact total—as the 'emigrants' found to their personal cost as they ran the gauntlet of 'desk-bound bandits',[237] who continued to intimidate as well as fleece them at will. Eichmann, however, had not only found his preferred modus operandi but could proffer figures to his superiors to demonstrate that it worked. By November he was claiming a removal rate of 350 a day, 50,000 all told, as compared with a German Jewish emigration in the same period amounting to only 19,000.[238] Bureaucracy could work as an engine for efficiency: not least when combined with unadulterated terror.

*

Eichmann's success, however, carried with it its own further complication, but now with wholly more destabilizing international ramifications. Indeed, even before his processing method had got into full swing, the surge of Austrian Jewish *refugees*— that, after all, is what they actually were—had propelled President Roosevelt, no less, to step out of standard US isolationism and call an international conference on the matter. It duly took place at Evian on the Franco-Swiss border in July and confirmed what more or less everybody knew: that no major power on the world stage was going to come to the Jewish rescue, least of all the Americans. This is not quite the sum total of the picture, given that Britain, soon after, began easing its immigration restrictions: the major consequence of which was the rescue of nearly 10,000 mostly Jewish *children* from the Reich in the countdown to global war.[239] On the obverse side, the general failure of the conference could be argued to have actually exacerbated the Jewish refugee predicament. While, for instance, rather too refreshingly honest comments from the Australian delegate to the effect that his country had no racial problem but also had no intention of importing one amounted to a form of collusion with Nazi anti-Semitism over and above straight-forward appeasement, the general Western refusal to budge on its admissions policy would have had the Nazis less than celebratory, however much the SD tried to ease the problem by ratcheting up illegal immigration to mandate Palestine.[240]

Worse, German policy was providing encouragement for its eastern neighbours to tighten the screws on their own more substantial Jewish populations. Hungary was already heading towards overtly racialized anti-Semitic legislation, while the Polish state's lurch to its own version of para-fascism was mirrored in a wave of populist anti-Jewish pogroms, which in turn helped strengthen government calls for mass Jewish emigration. In March, Warsaw passed a Denaturalization Law primarily aimed at barring the estimated 50,000 Jewish nationals who had taken up domicile in Germany from returning to Poland.[241] It was, in effect, the Polish regime's attempt to get its retaliation in first against any post-Anschluss German effort to force its hand on the matter. But it was also an invitation to an international stand-off. In the wake of the Munich debacle in September and the consequent entry of German forces into the Czech Sudetenland, 25,000 Jews living in the region were immediately expelled. Towards the end of the following month, in anticipation of Warsaw's law coming into effect, some 16,000 to 17,000 Jewish Polish passport holders in Germany were brutally rounded up by the authorities and dumped in what was effectively a no man's land close by the border at Zbąszyń. Warsaw retaliated by refusing them entry onto Polish soil, the inevitable consequence of which was the refugees' rapid collapse into illness, degradation, and squalor, in full view of the world's media.[242]

Here, then, we have the critical ingredients of what Götz Aly has described as a 'chain reaction',[243] the immediate outcome of which was *Kristallnacht*. The Nazi rank and file had been working themselves up into a lather against Jewish enemies of the state throughout the tense, conflict-laden months from spring onwards. Towns and villages were now vying to be first in the region to be 'Jew free'; where that failed, authorities were going out of their way to ensure that remaining Jews in their locality were debarred from all public facilities, often down to park benches. Moreover, whereas previously the threat of overt, grass-roots violence had to some extent been contained through juridical measures, state propaganda was once again consciously whipping up anti-Jewish fury.[244] If much of the drive, thus, for more direct action was clearly coming from below, it is also significant that when a flimsy pretext presented itself, it was, above all, Goebbels who ran with the possibilities it presented.

A Jewish youth, Herschel Grynspan, living illegally and by his wits in Paris, and whose family were among those suffering the Zbąszyń purgatory, had, on 7 November, opted to take his revenge on the German ambassador, though in the event he mortally wounded a more lowly German official. There had been an event like this before, in 1936, when a leading Swiss Nazi had been gunned down by an equally desperate young *Ostjude*. Both murders were, unsurprisingly, treated by Berlin as conspiracies, though on the earlier occasion—perhaps more surprisingly—no further Nazi retaliatory action was taken, for fear of inflaming foreign opinion. The whole international climate now, however, was entirely different. And the official also happened conveniently to die two days later on 9 November, that particularly sombre anniversary date in the German calendar, especially for Nazis commemorating the fallen 'martyrs' of the failed 1923 Munich putsch. Goebbels urged Hitler on to consent to a 'spontaneous demonstration' of popular outrage at Jewish perfidy. One can quite clearly read this as an attempt by the self-styled Nazi revolutionary and propaganda minister to inveigle himself back into the Führer's favour at a juncture when his position at the executive centre of state policy on Jewish matters was fast losing ground to the technocratic likes of Himmler and Heydrich. Described by Karl Schleunes as 'the result of a last-ditch effort by the radicals to wrest control over that policy',[245] Goebbels' hasty improvisation was a far cry from the detailed, often meticulous calculus of SS-organized genocide.

Indeed, the events of the night of 9–10 November were, in some critical respects, less a prelude to systematized mass murder than akin to a last fling of the pogromists. Through peremptory telephone calls from senior party and SA officials to their local branches throughout the post-Anschluss Reich, Goebbels provided a green light to the party faithful to do their worst, though preferably not in their Brownshirt uniforms. If the aim, thus, was to present the night-time and early dawn rampages as evidence of popular anti-Jewish indignation on a national scale, no domestic or outside observer was fooled into believing that this was anything other than state-sponsored thuggery, even if Hitler himself had conspicuously retired into the shadows.

That said, there was something quite spectacular about *Kristallnacht*. Adam Tooze has noted how violent, pent-up Nazi energy during the summer months of the Sudeten crisis was now unloaded not in war, but in this 'unprecedented assault on the Jewish population'.[246] On 9 November, Jewish life in Germany and Austria literally went up in flames. Homes and businesses were smashed up, synagogues torched.[247] It was the smashed glass from these often very beautiful, once honoured buildings which gave the event its name. The vandalism of it all fell quite squarely into what Lemkin, in the 1930s, had been attempting to understand as genocide. But then there was the barbarism too. Lives had been lost. Nobody has done an inventory as to how many pet dogs, cats, other animals, and birds were set on fire, tortured, and murdered as a way of traumatizing their Jewish owners. We would not even consider these aspects if it were not for the likes of Klemperer reminding us of this ongoing facet of Nazi terror throughout the Hitler years.[248] But, of course, human lives were lost in this mini-Holocaust too. The official figure for Jewish dead is ninety-one. Most of these were knifed, burnt, or battered to death. But then, that again fails to take into account all the suicides—680 alone in Vienna,[249] or, for that matter, all those who also succumbed within weeks or months to broken limbs and broken hearts.

Certainly, the morning after, when the world was treated to a landscape of urban, including metropolitan, devastation, there was shock, even disbelief. Roosevelt recalled his ambassador, while the international condemnation even had senior Nazi figures, including Himmler, ruing the event as a 'disaster and a humiliation'.[250] There was palpable disquiet, too, on the German street—that is, from those elements of the population who had not participated in the orgy of destruction or the subsequent looting. Indeed, 'Reports on Germany' compiled by SOPADE—the Social Democratic organization in exile—make it perfectly clear that there was widespread indignation at what had taken place. What is more disturbing, however, is that relatively little of this had to do with sympathy or compassion for what had happened to the Jews. Rather, the repeated plaint regarded the wanton destruction of Aryan (as opposed to Jewish) property; the futile waste which went with it—not least given that Germans were being daily reminded to conserve and save everything for the needs of the Four Year Plan; the disgrace to Germany's 'civilized' reputation in the eyes of the world.[251]

While *Kristallnacht* thus hastened Goebbels' and the radicals' departure from the making and implementation of Jewish policy, the one thing that it did not however do was bring about a regime reconsideration, let alone contrition for the consequences of its actions. On the contrary, Goering—very much the man of the moment—now seized the opportunity not only to indulge in some overt *Schadenfreude* but to ensure that German Jewry, now down on its knees and broken, would never be allowed to get up again. Just two days after the pogrom he convened a high-level conference, the prime purpose of which was to bring to completion the transfer of all residual Jewish assets to the state. To make clear the non-negotiability of his intention the first requirement upon the Jews was to accept *their* liability for the events of 9 November, in the form of an atonement tax, amounting to 1 billion marks.[252] Just in case there was any domestic or, for that matter, international objections to this demand with menaces, 30,000 Jewish men, particularly targeted because of their wealth,[253] were already in the process of being rapidly hauled into concentration camps without trial or knowledge of their ultimate fate. It was, in effect, Goebbels' hostage fantasy from the time of the failed 1933 boycott. Now, however, it was Himmler and Heydrich stepping into the breach to oblige. They had stood by during the events of *Kristallnacht* itself, though, to be sure, without doing anything to impede its excesses. The logistical headache of where to put all the additional prisoners notwithstanding, they were only too willing to support Goering's latest initiative.

They had good reason. At the meeting Goering informed his audience that he had received a letter from Bormann, written at Hitler's behest, requesting a coordinated, once-and-for-all solution of the Jewish question.[254] The supremo thus could claim absolute authority for a comprehensive and systematic sweep of Jews from the Reich's social and economic life. Any Jews remaining in German schools were to be excluded henceforth. Social intercourse between Jews and Germans was to be pared to a complete minimum—a prolonged exchange at the meeting between Goering and Goebbels on how to keep Jews separate from Germans in railway carriages evidence of the degree to which the leading Nazis continued to obsess over every last ugly detail of their cleansing project.[255] As a consequence, new regulations would rapidly come into force to deny Jews access to all public places and leisure facilities. And all this, of course, was now pointedly geared to a final eruption of Jews from the Reich. That, after all, was the explicit point of the concentration camp imprisonments: to so terrorize and mentally destroy those incarcerated in them that the survivors—let out weeks or months later—would be begging to leave Germany, whatever the financial cost. All Jewish communal organizations now came under the direct supervision of the Gestapo. A decree giving the state authority to wind up Jewish businesses—on terms set by itself—was a further direct consequence of Goering's diktat. Jews would no longer be able buy or sell through legitimate business dealings, nor on their own individual account. In an ominous resonance of Ittihad thinking from nearly quarter of a century earlier, a representative of the German insurance companies, at Goering's invitation, was present at the conference. Not only were Jewish insurance claims for the destruction wrought on 9 November to be redirected towards meeting the atonement levy but all other Jewish insurance policies at home or abroad were to be escheat to the state.[256]

Checkmate in two moves? Goering had acted swiftly to prevent any further economic Aryanization from below. Now only the state had expropriation rights and prerogatives over and against the Jews. And with the delegation of Jewish removal to Heydrich's team—the *Zentralstelle*, founded early in the new year, and the logical all-German follow-through of Eichmann's Vienna scheme[257]—the regime seemed to be within a whisker of bringing Germany's Jewish 'problem' to successful closure.

But there was a hitch. Or, more exactly, a yawning gulf between the theory and the practice. To where were all these Jews going to be vanished? Evian had already demonstrated that the West was not going to offer any serious reprimand to Germany's anti-Jewish actions but neither was it going to accept waves of impoverished Jewish refugees, even under duress. More to the point, there was one searing inbuilt contradiction in the Nazis' 1938 'Year of Destiny' plans: a promise to themselves of expansion into the very rimlands where several millions of Jews resided. It would be as if all the 'cleansing' efforts of the previous five years were once again set at nought. Nobody, moreover, was going to come to the Nazis' aid to find a comprehensive humanitarian way out of this impasse: not the Western liberal system, certainly not the Soviet anti-system. Resolution of the Jewish problem, instead, would have to come by and through the Nazis finding it themselves. Heydrich, for one, seems to have understood the logic of where Nazi anti-Jewish policy was heading, as far back as 1934:

> The methods of 'rowdy antisemitism' are to be rejected. One does not fight rats with a revolver, but rather with poison and gas. Foreign political damage has no relationship to local success.[258]

Notes

INTRODUCTION

1. Sir Halford J. Mackinder, *Democratic Ideals and Reality: A Study in the Politics of Reconstruction* (London: Constable & Co., 1919), 194.
2. Arnold J. Toynbee, *The Western Question in Greece and Turkey: A Study in the Contact of Civilisations* (London: Constable & Co., 1923), xxiii. Toynbee himself took the reviewer's comment to be an exact and succinct summary of his argument.
3. See Brian W. Blouet, *Halford Mackinder: A Biography* (College Station, TX: Texas A&M University Press, 1987). Also Brian W. Blouet, ed., *Global Geostrategy: Mackinder and the Defence of the West* (Abingdon and New York: Frank Cass, 2005).
4. William H. McNeill, *Arnold J. Toynbee: A Life* (New York and Oxford: Oxford University Press, 1989).
5. James Bryce and Arnold J. Toynbee, eds., *The Treatment of Armenians in the Ottoman Empire: 1915–16 Documents Presented to Viscount Grey of Falloden* (Princeton and London: Gomidas Institute, 1916; 2nd edn, 2005).
6. Toynbee, *Western Question*, 15.
7. Geoff Eley, 'What are the Contexts for German Antisemitism? Some Thoughts on the Origins of Nazism, 1800–1945', in Jonathan Frankel, ed., *The Fate of the European Jews 1939–1945: Continuity or Contingency? Studies in Contemporary Jewry XIII* (New York and London: Oxford University Press, 1997), 116.
8. Steven T. Katz, *The Holocaust in Historical Context*, vol. 1: *The Holocaust and Mass Death before the Modern Age* (New York and Oxford: Oxford University Press, 1994), 27, for this terminology.
9. The thesis as originally expressed in *Geographical Journal*, 23 (1904), 421–37; the paper was later reprinted as Sir Halford J. Mackinder, *The Geographical Pivot of History* (London: John Murray, 1951).
10. See, for example, David E. Omissi, *Air Power and Colonial Control: The Royal Air Force, 1919–1939* (Manchester: Manchester University Press, 1990).
11. Toynbee, *Western Question*, 267. Interestingly, Maria Todorova, in her more recent study of Western perceptions of the Balkans, has mirrored Toynbee by arguing that ethnic homogenization, culminating in the ethnic cleansing of the 1990s, was less a residual anomaly of an imperial legacy or of some supposed Balkan 'essence' than a case of 'the ultimate Europeanization of the Balkans'. Maria Todorova, *Imagining the Balkans* (New York and Oxford: Oxford University Press, 1997), 13.
12. Snyder, *Bloodlands*, quoting from dust jacket.
13. Norman M. Naimark, *Fires of Hatred: Ethnic Cleansing in Twentieth-Century Europe* (Cambridge, MA, and London: Harvard University Press, 2001); Benjamin Lieberman, *Terrible Fate: Ethnic Cleansing in the Making of Modern Europe* (Chicago: Ivan R. Dee, 2006).
14. Terry Martin, 'The Origins of Soviet Ethnic Cleansing', *Journal of Modern History*, 70:4 (1998), 813–61, more esp. 817–21.
15. Immanuel Wallerstein, *The Modern World System*, 3 vols (San Diego and New York: Academic Press Inc., 1974–89).

16. See Mark Biondich, *The Balkans: Revolution, War, and Political Violence since 1878* (Oxford: Oxford University Press, 2011), for the Balkans as a discrete zone of violence.

17. Fikret Adanır, *The Caucasus and Its Hinterland: Imperial Borderlands in the Grip of Great Power Rivalry, Ethno-Religious Conflict, and Nationalist Secessionism, c.1770–2009* (Oxford: Oxford University Press, forthcoming), for an equivalent, transnational study of the Caucasus–Anatolia zone of violence.

18. I have used the term 'Lands Between' as do Alan Palmer, *The Lands Between: A History of East-Central Europe since the Congress of Vienna* (London: Weidenfeld & Nicolson, 1970) and Alexander V. Prusin, *The Lands Between: The East European Frontiers in Wars, Revolutions and Nationality Conflicts, 1900–1992* (Oxford: Oxford University Press, 2010). However, in some ways the designation remains as elusive as the region's exact demarcation, as captured in Kate Brown, *A Biography of No Place: From Ethnic Borderland to Soviet Heartland* (Boston: Harvard University Press, 2005).

19. See Levene, *Rise of the West*, 302–22.

20. See Shimon Redlich, *Together and Apart in Brzezany: Poles, Jews, and Ukrainians, 1919–1945* (Bloomington, IN, and Indianapolis: Indiana University Press, 2002), for a searching micro-study.

21. Quoted in Z. A. B. Zeman, *The Making and Breaking of Communist Europe* (Oxford and New York: Basil Blackwell, 1991), 24.

22. See, for instance, Snyder, *Reconstruction*, 50, who, referring to the Vilna region at the end of the nineteenth century, opines: 'Belorussian speakers were calling themselves "Russian" if they were Orthodox, "Polish" if they were Roman Catholic, and "local" if they were watching out for themselves'. The term *tutejszy* has indeed become particularly associated with an indigenous rejection of national designations in this region.

23. See Brown, *Biography*, 'Introduction', for an excellent overview.

24. Quoted in Vejas Gabriel Liulevicius, *War Land on the Eastern Front: Culture, National Identity and German Occupation in World War 1* (Cambridge and New York: Cambridge University Press, 2000), 34.

25. Liulevicius, *War Land*, 35.

26. Rogers Brubaker, *Nationalism Reframed: Nationhood and the National Question in the New Europe* (Cambridge: Cambridge University Press, 1996), 3.

27. The very ethnographers' 'naming of peoples', giving them 'labels' as such and thereby dividing them for purposes of censuses, (multi-coloured) maps, and museums into 'knowable groups' designed to give order, coherence, and state or imperial control to the European/Western global project is developed in Benedict Anderson, *Imagined Communities: Reflections on the Origins and Spread of Nationalism* (London: Verso, 2nd edn, 1991), esp. ch. 10, 'Census, Map, Museum'. Conversely, failure of local people to fulfil these criteria, or, worse, election their own ethnicity against the grain of Western designation was bound to cause, at the very least, a perplexed administrative response.

28. Quoted in Brubaker, *Nationalism Reframed*, 3.

29. Palmer, *Lands Between*, 14.

30. See Uğur Ümit Üngör, *The Making of Modern Turkey: Nation and State in Eastern Anatolia, 1913–1950* (Oxford: Oxford University Press, 2011), 20–5, for examples.

31. George F. Kennan, 'The Balkan Crises 1913 and 1993', in *The Other Balkan Wars: A 1913 Carnegie Endowment Inquiry in Retrospect with a New Introduction and Reflections on the Present Conflict* (Washington, DC: Carnegie Endowment for International Peace, [1914] 1993), 13.

32. Todorova, *Imagining*, 14.
33. Todorova, *Imagining*, 13.
34. See *Crisis of Genocide*, vol. 2, Appendix.
35. See, for example, Timothy Snyder, 'The Life and Death of Western Volhynian Jewry, 1921–1945', in Ray Brandon and Wendy Lower, eds., *The Shoah in Ukraine: History, Testimony, Memorialisation* (Bloomington, IN, and Indianapolis: Indiana University Press, 2008), 102, who speaks of the violence in this area in 1943 as 'not quite a war of all against all but of most against most'.
36. A. Dirk Moses, 'The Holocaust and Genocide', in Dan Stone, ed., *The Historiography of the Holocaust* (Basingstoke and New York: Palgrave, 2004), 536.
37. Paradoxically, the term was first used by German socialists to describe what was being done to the western fringe of the Russian empire as a consequence of the Brest-Litovsk peace. See Toynbee, *Western Question*, 25.
38. I am thinking here particularly of Paul Weindling, *Epidemics and Genocide in Eastern Europe, 1890–1945* (Oxford: Oxford University Press, 2000).
39. See Volume 2, 270–2.
40. Why it chose to do so, however, is a matter of some controversy. See Davide Rodogno, *Fascism's European Empire: Italian Occupation during the Second World War* (Cambridge: Cambridge University Press, 2006); Jonathan Steinberg, *All or Nothing: The Axis and the Holocaust 1941–43* (London and New York: Routledge, 1990), for key studies. The issue is pursed in *Crisis of Genocide*, vol. 2, Chapter 3.
41. See Michael Burleigh and Wolfgang Wipperman, *The Racial State: Germany 1933–1945* (Cambridge: Cambridge University Press, 1991); Friedländer, *Nazi Germany and the Jews*; Daniel Jonah Goldhagen, *Hitler's Willing Executioners: Ordinary Germans and the Holocaust* (London: Little, Brown & Company, 1996), for three key renditions of these themes.
42. Hannah Arendt, *The Origins of Totalitarianism* (New York: Meridian, 1958).
43. See Jürgen Zimmerer, *Deutsche Herrschaft über Afrikaner: Staatlicher Machtanspruch und Wirklichkeit im kolonialen Namibia* (Munster, Hamburg, and London: Lit Verlag, 2nd edn, 2002); Wendy Lower, *Nazi Empire-Building and the Holocaust in Ukraine* (Chapel Hill: University of North Carolina Press, 2005); Peter Holquist, '"To Count, to Extract and to Exterminate": Population Politics in Late Imperial and Soviet Russia', in Ronald Grigor Suny and Terry Martin, eds., *A State of Nations: Empire and Nation-Making in the Age of Lenin and Stalin* (Oxford: Oxford University Press, 2001), 111–44, for key examples.
44. Alain Besançon, as quoted in Richard J. Golsan, 'Introduction to the English-Language Edition: The Politics of History and Memory in France in the 1990s', in Henry Rousso, ed., *Stalinism and Nazism: History and Memory Compared*, trans. Lucy B. Golsan, Thomas C. Hilde, and Peter S. Rogers (Lincoln and London: University of Nebraska Press, 2004), xxiii.
45. Pierre Hassner, 'Beyond History and Memory', in Rousso, *Stalinism*, 293.
46. Krzysztof Pomian, 'Postscript on the Ideas of Totalitarianism and of the "Communist Regime"', in Rousso, *Stalinism*, 299.
47. Lieberman, *Terrible Fate*, xii.
48. Michael Geyer and Sheila Fitzpatrick, 'Introduction: After Totalitarianism—Stalinism and Nazism Compared', in Geyer and Fitzpatrick, eds., *Beyond Totalitarianism: Stalinism and Nazism Compared* (Cambridge: Cambridge University Press, 2009), 26.
49. Omer Bartov, *Mirrors of Destruction: War, Genocide and Modern Identity* (New York and Oxford: Oxford University Press, 2000), 159.

50. Bartov, *Mirrors*, 6, my emphasis.
51. Üngör, *The Making*, 108–22, more esp. 112.
52. Zygmunt Bauman, *Postmodernity and its Discontents* (Cambridge: Polity, 1997), 18.
53. Bauman, *Postmodernity*, 18.
54. Eric D. Weitz, *A Century of Genocide: Utopias of Race and Nation* (Princeton and Oxford: Princeton University Press, 2003).
55. See Michael Mann, *The Dark Side of Democracy: Explaining Ethnic Cleansing* (Cambridge and New York: Cambridge University Press, 2005). See also Prusin, *Lands Between*; Naimark, *Fires*; Lieberman, *Terrible Fate*.
56. Bauman, *Postmodernity*, 18.
57. See, for example, A. Dirk Moses, ed., *Genocide and Settler Society: Frontier Violence and Stolen Indigenous Children in Australian History* (New York and Oxford: Berghahn Books 2001); Alfred W. Crosby, *Ecological Imperialism: The Biological Expansion of Europe, 900–1900* (Cambridge: Cambridge University Press, 2004), for the concept of neo-Europes.
58. Bauman, *Postmodernity*, 18.
59. See Levene, *Meaning*, more specifically 49–51.
60. Đorđe Stefanović, 'Seeing the Albanians through Serbian Eyes: The Inventors of the Tradition of Intolerance and their Critics, 1804–1939', *European History Quarterly*, 35:3 (2005), 485.
61. Slawomir Kapralski, 'Ritual of Memory in Constructing the Modern Identities of Eastern European Romanies', in Nicholas Saul and Susan Tebbutt, eds., *The Role of the Romanies: Images and Counter-Images of 'Gypsies'/Romanies in European Cultures* (Liverpool: Liverpool University Press, 2004), 218.
62. Michael Mann, *Sources of Social Power* (Cambridge: Cambridge University Press, 1993), vol. 2, 740.
63. Todorova, *Imagining*, 17.
64. Mackinder, *Geographical Pivot*, 30.
65. Quoted in Joshua A. Sanborn, 'Unsettling the Empire: Violent Migrations and Social Disaster in Russia during World War 1', *Journal of Modern History*, 77: 2 (2005), 90.
66. See, for instance, Gavan McCormack, 'Reflections on Modern Japanese History in the Context of the Concept of Genocide', in Ben Kiernan and Robert Gellately, eds., *The Spectre of Genocide: Mass Murder in Historical Perspective* (Cambridge and New York: Cambridge University Press, 2003), 265–86.
67. See Silvio Castro Fernández, *La Masacre De Los Independientes de Color en 1912* (Havana: Editorial de ciencas sociales, 2002); Edward Paulino, 'Forgotten Atrocities: The 1937 Genocidal Haitian Massacre in the Dominican Republic', in Roger W. Smith, ed., *Genocide: Essays toward Understanding, Early Warning and Prevention* (Williamsburg, VA: Association of Genocide Scholars, 1999), 79–99.
68. Levene, *Rise of the West*, 275–6; A. J. Barker, *Rape of Ethiopia, 1936* (New York: Ballantine Books, 1971).
69. See Paul Preston, *The Spanish Holocaust: Inquisition and Extermination in Twentieth-Century Spain* (London: W.W. Norton & Co., 2012), for a significant recent corrective.
70. Sybil Milton, 'Non-Jewish Children in the Camps', in Michael Berenbaum, ed., *A Mosaic of Victims: Non-Jews Persecuted and Murdered by the Nazis* (London and New York: I.B. Tauris, 1990), 85.
71. Alan Kramer, *Dynamic of Destruction: Culture and Mass Killing in the First World War* (Oxford: Oxford University Press, 2007), 2, offers a succinct if discussible distinction by which mass killing is distinguished from 'genocide by reciprocity, for both sides conduct it'.

72. Donald Bloxham, 'From Streicher to Sawoniuk: The Holocaust in the Courtroom', in Stone, *Historiography*, 414.

73. Levene, *Meaning*, 196–202, for the concept of a 'perpetrators "never again" syndrome'.

74. See Léon Poliakov, *History of Anti-Semitism*, vol. 4: *Suicidal Europe 1870–1933*, trans. George Klin (Oxford: Littman Library and Oxford University Press, 1985), 49, referring to Mann's August 1966 Brussels lecture to the World Jewish Congress: 'Germans and Jews: An Insoluble Problem'.

75. See Geoffrey Hosking, *Russia, People and Empire, 1552–1917* (London: HarperCollins, 1997), 5–8, 483.

76. See, for example, Clive Foss, 'The Turkish View of Armenian History: A Vanishing Nation', in Richard G. Hovannisian, *Armenian Genocide: History, Politics, Ethics* (New York: St. Martin's Press 1992), 250–79.

77. Levene, *Meaning*, 186–90.

78. Robert F. Melson, *Revolution and Genocide: On the Origins of the Armenian Genocide and the Holocaust* (Chicago: Chicago University Press, 1992), for an emphasis on revolutionary caesura.

79. See the essays in Amir Weiner, ed., *Landscaping the Garden: Twentieth-Century Population Management in a Comparative Framework* (Stanford, CA: Stanford University Press, 2003), for further critical lines of enquiry.

80. Quoted in Raymond Pearson, *National Minorities in Eastern Europe, 1848–1945* (London and Basingstoke: Palgrave Macmillan, 1983), 230.

81. Pearson, *National Minorities* 136.

82. Mann, *Dark Side*, 67. It is surely significant that Macartney was a rather sympathetically inclined historian of a multi-ethnic Habsburg Empire.

83. See Robert Bidelux and Ian Jeffries, *A History of Eastern Europe: Crisis and Change* (London: Routledge, 1998), 345–6.

84. Quoted in Randolph L. Braham, *The Politics of Genocide: The Holocaust in Hungary* (New York: Columbia University Press, 1981), vol. 2, 605.

85. John. H. Morrow Jr, *The Great War: An Imperial History* (London and New York: Routledge, 2004), 36.

CHAPTER 1

1. Quoted Yuri Slezkine, *The Jewish Century* (Princeton and Oxford: Princeton University Press, 2004), 159–60.

2. Quoted in Panikos Panayi, *The Enemy in Our Midst: Germans in Britain During the First World War* (London and New York: Berg, 1991), 233.

3. See Vahakn N. Dadrian, 'Bibliography of Published Works. Updated January 2006'. <http://www.zoryaninstitute.org/bibliographies/Vahakn%20N.pdf>.

4. See, for instance, the sleeve notes to Jay Winter, ed., *America and the Armenian Genocide of 1915* (Cambridge: Cambridge University Press, 2003) or, similarly, Peter Balakian, *The Burning Tigris: The Armenian Genocide and America's Response* (New York: HarperCollins, 2003) for not unusual but standard renditions of a common error. See Levene, *Rise of the West*, for earlier twentieth-century genocides in a colonial context. For ongoing, acute critique of this type of conventional genocide studies' wisdom and the 'memory politics' which goes with it, see the work of Dominik J. Schaller, most recently, in Schaller, 'From Lemkin to Clooney: The Development and State of Genocide Studies', *Genocide Studies and Prevention* (hereafter *GSP*) 6:3 (2011), 245–56.

5. Morrow, *Great War*, 36.

6. See Joanne Bourke, *An Intimate History of Killing: Face-to-Face Killing in Twentieth Century Warfare* (London: Granta Books, 2000), esp. ch. 3, 'Training Men to Kill', for the classic study. However, see also Barbara Ehrenreich, *Blood Rites: Origins and History of the Passions of War* (London: Virago, 1997), for a radically different view on war as a continuation of more primeval, sacrificial urges.

7. Jay Winter, 'Under Cover of War: The Armenian Genocide in the Context of Total War', in *America*, 43.

8. Immanuel Geiss, 'Reflections on Total War in the 20th Century', in John Bourne, Peter Liddle, and Ian Whitehead, eds., *The Great World War 1914–1945: Lightning Strikes Twice* (London: HarperCollins, 2000), vol. 1, 459.

9. Winter, 'Under Cover', 43.

10. John Keegan, *The First World War* (London: Hutchinson, 1998), 8. See Sanborn, 'Unsettling', 293, for a robust refutation. For a complete overturning of the Keegan 'civilisation' argument, see Kramer, *Dynamic of Destruction*.

11. Winter, 'Under Cover', 47.

12. See Geoffrey Best, *Humanity in Warfare* (New York: Columbia University Press, 1980), chs 3 and 4.

13. Bernd Weisbrod, 'Military Violence and Male Fundamentalism: Ernst Jünger's Contribution to the Conservative Revolution', *History Workshop Journal*, 49 (2000), 69–94; Kramer, *Dynamic of Destruction*, 230–7. See also Bernd Hüppauf, ed., *War, Violence and the Modern Condition* (Berlin: Walter de Gruyter, 1997).

14. Quoted in John Horne and Alan Kramer, *German Atrocities, 1914: A History of Denial* (New Haven, CT, and London: Yale University Press, 2001), 423.

15. For Norman Angell's *The Great Illusion* (1910) and its context, see Paul Crook, *Darwinism, War and History: The Debate over the Biology of War from the 'Origin of Species' to the First World War* (Cambridge: Cambridge University Press, 1994), ch. 4, 'The Natural Decline of Warfare, Anti-war Evolutionism Prior to 1914'.

16. Wolfgang J. Mommsen, 'The Topos of Inevitable War in Germany in the Decade before 1914', in Volker R. Berghahn and Martin Kitchen, eds., *Germany in the Age of Total War* (London: Croom Helm, 1981), 25.

17. Hew Strachan, *The First World War*, vol. 1: *To Arms* (Oxford: Oxford University Press, 2001), 101.

18. Ronald Aronson, *Dialectics of Disaster: A Preface to Hope* (London: Verso, 1983).

19. Ivan Stanislavovich Bloch, *The Future of War in its Technical, Economic and Political Relations: Is War now Impossible?* trans. R. C. Long (London: Doubleday and McClure, 1899). See Horne and Kramer, *German Atrocities*, 118–19; Crook, *Darwinism*, 98–101, for commentary. Also Kramer, *Dynamic of Destruction*, 34–5, for the scale of the initial August–September bloodletting and the fact that this was actually far in excess of anything later, including Verdun or the final 1918 paroxysm.

20. See Strachan, *To Arms*, 'Society and the International', 111–33, for a full discussion.

21. Strachan, *To Arms*, 'Society and the International', 103–10.

22. Strachan, *To Arms*, 'Society and the International', 117. We might, at this point, reach out for a third countervailing force—feminism. But in spite of the fact, for instance, that in Britain there were radical anti-war suffragettes (such as Christabel Pankhurst), the women's movement here as elsewhere largely mobilised *for* patriotic war, not against it.

23. See George L. Mosse, 'War and the Appropriation of Nature', in Berghahn and Kitchen, *Germany*, 102–3.

24. Morrow, *Great War*, 165; Kramer, *Dynamic of Destruction*, 151–5.

25. Strachan, *To Arms*, 1138.

26. Gerald J. de Groot, *The First World War* (Basingstoke: Palgrave, 2001), 6.

27. Andreas Kappeler, *The Russian Empire: A Multiethnic History*, trans. Alfred Clayton (Harlow: Longman, 2001), 2, 84–5.

28. Peter Holquist, quoted in Pavel Polian, *Against their Will: The History and Geography of Forced Migrations in the USSR* (Budapest and New York: Central European University Press, 2004), 23.

29. Quoted in Holquist, 'To Count', 115.

30. See Moshe Gammer, *Muslim Resistance to the Czar: Shamil and the Conquest of Chechnia and Daghestan* (London: Frank Cass, 1994); Anna Zelinka, *In Quest for God and Freedom: The Sufi Response to the Russian Advance in the North Caucasus* (London: Hurst, 2000), for key studies.

31. Polian, *Against their Will*, 23.

32. For discussion of Heinrich Rauchenberg, *Der nationale Besitzstand in Böhmen* (1905) see Zeman, *The Making*, 28–36.

33. See Ronald Zweig, *The Gold Train: The Destruction of the Jews and the Second World War's Most Terrible Robbery* (London: Penguin, 2003), 7. As 5.9 per cent of Magyar Jews identified themselves as Magyar-speaking, this facilitated the 1910 census return of a 54.4 per cent Magyar majority.

34. Carnegie Inquiry, *Other Balkan Wars*, 26–7.

35. See Palmer, *Lands Between*, 103. Also Duncan M. Perry, *The Politics of Terror: The Macedonian Liberation Movements 1893–1903* (Durham, NC, and London: Duke University Press, 1988), 19, where, referring to the J. Larmeroux 1918 findings, the Macedonian population, depending on whom one reads, was made up of anything between 120,000 and 1.2 million Bulgarians; 210,000 and 900,000 Serbs; 50,000 and 1 million Greeks; not to mention 24,000 and 1,200,000 Vlachs—all this in a total three-vilayet population estimated at between 350,000 to 2,911,700(!)

36. See Carnegie Inquiry, *Other Balkan Wars*, 36.

37. Henry R. Wilkinson, *Maps and Politics: A Review of the Ethnographic Cartography of Macedonia* (Liverpool: Liverpool University Press 1951), 103; also Noel Malcolm, *Kosovo: A Short History* (London and Basingstoke: Palgrave Macmillan, 1998).

38. Wilkinson, *Maps*, 28.

39. See Weindling, *Epidemics*, esp. chs 3 and 4, for German obsessions with lice, border containment, and the dangers from displaced or dirty populations, very often a short-hand for eastern Jews.

40. See Luilevicius, *War Land*, esp. ch. 5, 'The Mindscape of the East'.

41. Luilevicius, *War Land*. 73–4, for labour battalion deaths from overwork, hypothermia, malnutrition, and related causes.

42. Palmer, *Lands Between*, 122.

43. See Fritz Fischer, *Germany's Aims in the First World War* (London: Chatto & Windus, 1967), 237–8; Zbynek A. B. Zeman, *A Diplomatic History of the First World War* (London: Weidenfeld & Nicolson, 1971), 93. Looking further afield, see also Elie Kedourie, *In the Anglo-Arab Labyrinth: The MacMahon–Husayn Correspondence and its Interpretations, 1914–1939* (Cambridge: Cambridge University Press, 1976), and Michael A. Reynolds, 'The Ottoman–Russian Struggle for Eastern Anatolia and the Caucasus, 1908–1918: Identity, Ideology and the Geopolitics of World Order', unpublished doctoral thesis, Princeton University, 2003, 207–8, 256, for further pointers as to these various efforts. Reynolds' thesis has, more recently, been published as *Shattering Empires: The Clash and Collapse of the Ottoman and Russian Empires, 1908–1918*

(Cambridge: Cambridge University Press, 2011), but it is reference to the original thesis that is utilized herein.

44. Fischer, *Germany's Aims*, 237–8.

45. The term comes from Mark von Hagen, 'The Great War and the Mobilisation of Ethnicity in the Russian Empire', in Barnett G. Rubin and Jack Snyder, eds., *Post-Soviet Political Order* (London and New York: Routledge, 1998), 34–57.

46. See Aviel Roshwald, *Ethnic Nationalism and the Fall of Empires: Central Europe, Russia and the Middle East, 1914–1923* (London and New York: Routledge, 2001), for sober assessment.

47. Prusin, *Lands Between*, 59. See Reynolds, 'Ottoman–Russian Struggle', 237–8, specifically on the Georgian Legion. Also Martin Watts, *The Jewish Legion and the First World War* (London and New York: Palgrave Macmillan, 2005).

48. Quoted in George Katkov, 'German Political Intervention in Russia during World War 1', in Richard Pipes, ed., *Revolutionary Russia* (London and Cambridge, MA: Harvard and Oxford University Presses, 1968), 65.

49. Pipes, *Revolutionary Russia*, 88–96, for the heated debate between Katkov, Alexander Dallin, and others.

50. Robert Geraci, 'Russian Orientalism at an Impasse: Tsarist Education Policy and the 1910 Conference on Islam', in Daniel R. Brower and Edward J. Lazzerini, eds., *Russia's Orient: Imperial Borderlands and Peoples, 1700–1917* (Bloomington, IN, and Indianapolis: Indiana University Press, 1997), 142–3, 151.

51. Reynolds, 'Ottoman–Russian Struggle', 261–2. Also Richard G. Hovannisian, *Armenia, On the Road to Independence, 1918* (Berkeley and Los Angeles: University of California Press, 1967), 47–8, for the population collapse in the Coruh valley.

52. Eric Lohr, *Nationalising the Russian Empire: The Campaign against Enemy Aliens during World War One* (Cambridge, MA, and London: Harvard University Press, 2003), 152.

53. Lohr, *Nationalising the Russian Empire*, 151, 160, 111.

54. See Strachan, *To Arms*, 722.

55. See Alexander Victor Prusin, *Nationalising a Borderland: War, Ethnicity, and Anti-Jewish Violence in East Galicia, 1914–1920* (Tuscaloosa: University of Alabama Press, 2005), 19.

56. Von Hagen, 'Great War', 44.

57. Prusin, *Nationalising a Borderland*, 32–3.

58. Lemkin, *Axis Rule*, 79.

59. Prusin, *Nationalising a Borderland*, 36.

60. Lohr, *Nationalising the Russian Empire*, 134, 18–21.

61. Prusin, *Nationalising a Borderland*, 20.

62. Lohr, *Nationalising the Russian Empire*, 20.

63. Lohr, *Nationalising the Russian Empire*, 125, 127.

64. Ann Sheehy and Bohdan Nahalyo, *The Crimean Tatars, Volga Germans and Meshke-tians: Soviet Treatment of Some National Minorities* (London: Minority Rights Group, 3rd edn, 1981), 18; Polian, *Against their Will*, 24; Peter Gatrell, *A Whole Empire Walking: Refugees in Russia during World War 1* (Bloomington, IN, and Indianapolis: Indiana University Press, 1999), 23–5.

65. Lohr, *Nationalising the Russian Empire*, 124; Prusin, *Nationalising a Borderland*, 20.

66. Sheehy and Nahalyo, *Crimean Tatars*, 18.

67. Lohr, *Nationalising the Russian Empire*, 88. See also Adam Giesinger, *From Catherine to Khrushchev: The Story of Russia's Germans* (Battleford, SK: Marian Press, 1974), for a more general overview.

68. See Hosking, *Russia*, 379, commenting on the influential role of the journalist Mikhail Katkov.

69. Polian, *Against their Will*, 50, n. 22.

70. See Peter Holquist, 'State Violence as Technique: The Logic of Violence in Soviet Totalitarianism', in David L. Hoffman, ed., *Stalinism: The Essential Readings* (Oxford: Blackwell, 2003), 137.

71. Lohr, *Nationalising the Russian Empire*, 155.

72. Lohr, *Nationalising the Russian Empire*, 137.

73. Lohr, *Nationalising the Russian Empire*, 137.

74. Lohr, *Nationalising the Russian Empire*, ch. 4, 'Nationalising the Land', esp. 98.

75. Polian, *Against their Will*, 50, n. 22

76. Sheehy and Nahalyo, *Crimean Tatars*, 18.

77. See Norman Stone, *The Eastern Front, 1914–1917* (London: Macmillan, 1975), 165–93, for details.

78. Prusin, *Lands Between*, 59.

79. John D. Klier, 'Cossacks and Pogroms: What was Different about "Military" Pogroms?', in O. V. Budnitsky, O. V. Belova, V. E. Kel'ner, and V. V. Mochalova, eds., *Mirovoi krizis 1914–1920 godov i sud'ba vostochnoevropeiskogo evreistva* (Moscow: Rosspen, 2005), 47–70. With thanks to the late John Klier for providing an (unpaginated) English version. See also Eric Lohr, 'The Russian Army and Jews: Mass Deportation, Hostages, and Violence during World War 1', *Russian Review*, 60:3 (2001), 404–19.

80. See Calvin Goldscheider and Alan S. Zuckerman, *The Transformation of the Jews* (Chicago and London: Chicago University Press, 1984); Paul R. Mendes-Flohr and Jehuda Reinharz, eds., *The Jew in the Modern World: Documentary History* (New York: Oxford University Press, 1980), Appendix, 'The Demography of Modern Jewish History', for brief Ashkenazi-centric introductions to the Jewish world.

81. See Slezkine, *Jewish Century*.

82. Sanborn, 'Unsettling', 307; Gatrell, *A Whole Empire*, 15, cites figures of 600,000 displaced Jews even before the spring 1915 crisis.

83. See Chimen Abramsky, *War, Revolution and the Jewish Dilemma* (London: Lewis, 1975), 9–11; Heinz-Dietrich Löwe, *The Tsars and the Jews: Reform, Reaction and Anti-Semitism in Imperial Russia, 1772–1917* (Chur, Switzerland, and Langhorne, PA: Harwood Academic Publishers, 1993), 323.

84. See Egmont Zechlin, *Die deutsche Politik und die Juden im Ersten Weltkrieg* (Göttingen: Vandenhoeck & Ruprecht, 1969), 116–25; Fischer, *Germany's Aims*, 141–3. The committee rapidly changed its name to the Kommittee für den Osten.

85. Gatrell, *A Whole Empire*, 16, cites the 18 February 1915 comment of General Evert to Iaunushkevich, as confirmation: 'The complete hostility of the Jewish population towards the Russian army is well established'.

86. Prusin, *Nationalising a Borderland*, 49; 'The Eastern War Zone: Ill-treatment of the Jews' (Conjoint Foreign Committee) report, cited in Mark Levene, *War, Jews and the New Europe: The Diplomacy of Lucien Wolf, 1914–1919* (Oxford: Littman Library of Jewish Civilisation and Oxford University Press, 1992), 49.

87. Prusin, *Nationalising a Borderland*, 52.

88. Sanborn, 'Unsettling', 310.

89. Prusin, *Nationalising a Borderland*, 52–3.

90. Marsha L. Rozenblit, *Reconstructing a National Identity: The Jews of Habsburg Austria during World War 1* (New York: Oxford University Press, 2001), 66; Frank Golczewski,

Polnisch-jüdische Beziehungen, 1881–1922: eine Studie zur Geschichte des Antisemitis-mus in Osteuropa (Wiesbaden: Steiner, 1981), 121–4.

91. See John D. Klier and Shlomo Lambroza, eds., *Pogroms, Anti-Jewish Violence in Modern Russian History* (Cambridge: Cambridge University Press, 1991).

92. See Prusin, *Nationalising a Borderland*, 53, 55, for examples.

93. Klier, 'Cossacks'.

94. Prusin, *Nationalising a Borderland*, 30–2.

95. See Mark Levene, 'Frontiers of Genocide: Jews in the Eastern War Zones, 1914 to 1920 and 1941', in Panikos Panayi, ed., *Minorities in Wartime: National and Racial Groupings in Europe, North America and Australia during the Two World Wars* (Oxford: Berg, 1993), 101–2.

96. See Levene, *Meaning*, 139–40, for broader discussion of this theme.

97. Prusin, *Nationalising a Borderland*, 31–2.

98. Prusin, *Nationalising a Borderland*, 31–2.

99. It was the American Jewish Committee which gave the half million estimate. See its *The Jews in the Eastern War Zone* (New York: American Jewish Committee, 1916), as quoted in Levene, *War*, 50. However, more cautious, recent estimates such as, for instance, Mordechai Altshuler, 'Russia and her Jews: The Impact of the 1914 War', *Wiener Library Bulletin*, 27 (1973–4), 14, offer a range of 5–600,000 Jews deported for the *whole* war.

100. Löwe, *The Tsars*, 325; Gatrell, *A Whole Empire*, 22.

101. Polian, *Against their Will*, 26.

102. See Michael Cherniavsky, ed., *Prologue to Revolution: Notes of I.A. Iakhantov on Secret Meetings of Council of Ministers, 1915* (Englewood Cliffs, NJ: Prentice Hall, 1967), 39, meeting of 30 June 1915.

103. See American Jewish Committee, *The Jews*. Also, 'The Eastern War Zone: Ill-treatment of the Jews' (Conjoint Foreign Committee) report, as above n. 86.

104. See Sanborn, 'Unsettling', 311–12; Gatrell, *A Whole Empire*, 54. Unfortunately, there was no registration, so the evidence we have is in the eyewitness reports of the enormous quantities of rotting bodies by roadsides.

105. Gatrell, *A Whole Empire*, Appendix, 211–15. The official figures repeatedly downplay the Jewish displaced element as 'very modest'.

106. See Justin McCarthy, *Death and Exile: The Ethnic Cleansing of Ottoman Muslims, 1821–1922* (Princeton: Darwin Press, 1995) for the key study, though with the unfortunate corollary that McCarthy radically downplays the specifically Armenian catastrophe. See also Yashar Kemal, *Salman the Solitary*, trans. Thilda Kemal (London: Harvill Press, 1998), for one vivid literary narrative of mass flight from the war zone, on this occasion from a Kurdish perspective.

107. Luilevicius, *War Land*, 20.

108. Cherniavsky, *Prologue*, 57.

109. Prusin, *Nationalising a Borderland*, 54.

110. Sanborn, 'Unsettling', 310.

111. Lohr, *Nationalising the Russian Empire*, 144; Prusin, *Nationalising a Borderland*, 58.

112. National Archives, London (hereafter NA) FO 800/74 (Grey Papers), Buchanan to Grey, 10 March 1915, cited in Levene, *War*, 51. Also see p. 54, for a range of British endorsements of the Russian view.

113. Prusin, *Nationalising a Borderland*, ix.

114. Prusin, *Nationalising a Borderland*, 56.

115. Prusin, *Nationalising a Borderland*, 39–41, here on civil appointees in occupied eastern Galicia.

116. Prusin, *Nationalising a Borderland*, 56; Lohr, *Nationalising the Russian Empire*, 140–1. See Gatrell, *A Whole Empire*, 21, for some of the critical rimland and near-rimland cities in the vortex of the crisis.

117. Prusin, *Nationalising a Borderland*, 56.

118. See *Crisis of Genocide*, vol. 2, ch. 3.

119. See Polian, *Against their Will*, 26, for the opposition of the Kurland governor, P. G. Kurlov, to the deportations.

120. See Levene, 'Frontiers', in Panayi, *Minorities*, 97.

121. Cherniavsky, *Prologue*, 60–72. Hans Rogger, *Jewish Policies and Right-Wing Politics in Imperial Russia* (London: Macmillan, 1985), 101–5, for further commentary on these meetings.

122. Cherniavsky, *Prologue*, 57–9.

123. Sanborn, 'Unsettling', 295.

124. Mahir Saul and Patrick Royer, *West African Challenge to Empire, Culture and History in the Volta-Bani Anticolonial War* (Athens, OH, and Oxford: Ohio University Press and James Currey, 2001), 2.

125. Saul and Royer, *West African Challenge*, 309–10.

126. Saul and Royer, *West African Challenge*, 25.

127. Saul and Royer, *West African Challenge*, 312–13.

128. See Kappeler, *Russian Empire*, 352. Also Holquist, as cited in Polian, *Against their Will*, 49–50, n.18.

129. Edward Dennis Sokol, *The Revolt of 1916 in Russian Central Asia* (Baltimore: John Hopkins Press, 1953), 158; Toynbee, *Western Question*, 342.

130. See Saul and Royer, *West African Challenge*, 202, for the notable events on the capture of La.

131. Sokol, *The Revolt*, 158.

132. Holquist, 'To Count', 121.

133. Toynbee, *Western Question*, 342.

134. Daniel R. Brower, 'Islam and Ethnicity: Russian Colonial Policy in Turkestan', in Brower and Lazzerini, *Russia's Orient*, 132.

135. Daniel Brower, 'Kyrgyz Nomads and Russian Pioneers, Colonisation and Ethnic Conflict in the Turkestan Revolt of 1916', *Jahrbücher fur Geschichte Osteuropas*, 44:1 (1996), 47–8. See also Sokol, *The Revolt*, esp. 41, 73, on the conflicting ethnic population 'aggregates'.

136. Holquist, 'To Count', 121; Sokol, *The Revolt*, 115.

137. See Kappeler, *Russian Empire*, 168–71, for the background. By some peculiar anomaly of Russian chop-logic, Jews were also classed as *inorodtsy* but without the military exemptions.

138. Morrow, *Great War*, 96–7.

139. Strachan, *To Arms*, 702–4.

140. See Isaiah Friedman, *The Question of Palestine, 1914–1918* (London: Routledge and Kegan Paul, 1973), 71. See also Elie Kedourie, *The Chatham House Version and Other Middle Eastern Studies* (London: Weidenfeld & Nicolson, 1970), 14–17.

141. Saul and Royer, *West African Challenge*, 91–8.

142. Brower, 'Kyrgyz Nomads', 51–2.

143. Levene, *Rise of the West*, 249–50.

144. Sokol, *The Revolt*, 126–7.

145. Sokol, *The Revolt*, 100.

146. Sokol, *The Revolt*, 116, 127. Holquist, 'To Count', 121.

147. See Holquist, 'To Count', 122; Sokol, *The Revolt*, 154–5.

440   Notes to Chapter 1

148. Sokol, *The Revolt*, 135. Also Michael Khodarkovsky, *Where Two Worlds Met: The Russian State and the Kalmyk Nomads 1600–1771* (Ithaca, NY: Cornell University Press, 1992), 232–4, on the 1771 events.

149. See Saul and Royer, *West African Challenge*, esp. 6–8, 13–14.

150. Saul and Royer, *West African Challenge*, 230.

151. Morrow, *Great War*, 83, 127–8.

152. Morrow, *Great War*, 274, 220–1.

153. Panayi, *Enemy*, 175–7.

154. Alyson Pendlebury, *Portraying 'the Jew' in First World War Britain* (London: Frank Cass, 2005), 65.

155. See Horne and Kramer, *German Atrocities*, 136.

156. Panayi, *Enemy*, 183.

157. Panayi, *Enemy*, 234.

158. Strachan, *To Arms*, 106–7.

159. See David French, 'Spy Fever in Britain, 1900–1915', *Historical Journal*, 21:2 (1978), 350–70; especially for the novels of William Le Queux. Also Panayi, *Enemy*, ch. 6, 'Anti-German Sentiment: Spy Fever, Anti-Alienism and the Hidden Hand'.

160. Morrow, *Great War*, 172, 227–8.

161. Peter Holquist, '"Information is the Alpha and Omega of Our Work": Bolshevik Surveillance in its Pan-European Context', *Journal of Modern History*, 69:3 (1997), 415–50, 426–32, 440–50; John Torpey, *The Invention of the Passport: Surveillance, Citizenship and the State* (Cambridge: Cambridge University Press, 2000), 111.

162. Gerhard Fischer, *Enemy Aliens: Internment and the Homefront Experience in Australia, 1914–1920* (St Lucia: University of Queensland Press, 1989). Also Raymond Evans, '"Pigmentia": Racial Fears and White Australia', in Moses, *Genocide and Settler Society*, 111.

163. Horne and Kramer, *German Atrocities*.

164. Arthur Ponsonby, *Falsehood in Wartime* (London: Allen & Unwin, 1928).

165. Horne and Kramer, *German Atrocities*, 94–113. Also, Levene, *Meaning*, 139–40, for the Vendée comparison.

166. Horne and Kramer, *German Atrocities*, 18, 164–5.

167. Horne and Kramer, *German Atrocities*, chs 1 and 2, 'German Invasion parts 1 and 2'; 24–53, more specifically for the Dinant events. Also Kramer, *Dynamic of Destruction*, ch. 1, 'The Burning of Louvain'.

168. Horne and Kramer, *German Atrocities*, 419.

169. Fernand van Langenhove, *Comment naît un cycle de légendes. Franc-tireurs et atrocités en Belgique* (Lausanne: Payot, 1916).

170. Horne and Kramer, *German Atrocities*, 90.

171. Levene, *Meaning*, 196–201.

172. See Christopher Clark, *Iron Kingdom: The Rise and Downfall of Prussia, 1600–1947* (London: Penguin, 2006).

173. Horne and Kramer, *German Atrocities*, 161.

174. Strachan, *To Arms*, 1136; for a broader discussion, 1128–39.

175. Horne and Kramer, *German Atrocities*, 426–7, for an assessment of the degree to which the myth was broadly believed.

176. NA FO 371/2767/938, Sykes to Nicolson, 18 March 1916.

177. Taken from the 1928 Jacob Lestschinsky demographic survey in Mendes-Flohr and Reinharz, *The Jew*, 528, table IV.

178. My emphasis. NA FO 371/2767/938, Sykes to Nicolson, 18 March 1916.

179. Roger Adelson, *Mark Sykes: Portrait of an Amateur* (London: Cape, 1975), 204–7, for Sykes' views of Jews. For further assessment see Mark Levene, 'The Balfour Declaration: A Case of Mistaken Identity', *English Historical Review*, 107 (1992), 54–77; Elie Kedourie, 'Sir Mark Sykes and Palestine, 1915–1916', *Middle Eastern Studies*, 6 (1970), 340–5; and, most recently, James Renton, *The Zionist Masquerade: The Birth of the Anglo-Zionist Alliance,1914–1918* (Basingstoke and New York: Palgrave Macmillan, 2007), esp. 24–6. One might add that the term 'philosemitism' is deployed here with some caution, not least as it is, more often that not, simply the flip side of 'anti-Semitism'.

180. Poliakov, *History*, vol. 4, viii.

181. Hosking, *Russia*, 392–3. More generally, Löwe, *The Tsars*, ch. 4, 'From Pogroms to Counter-Reforms'.

182. Norman Cohn, *Warrant for Genocide: The Myth of the Jewish World-Conspiracy and the Protocols of the Elders of Zion* (London: Penguin, 1967), 114.

183. See Count Lamsdorff, 'The Proposed Anti-Semitic Triple Alliance', in Lucien Wolf, *Notes on the Diplomatic History of the Jewish Question* (London: Spottiswoode, Ballantyne & Co., 1919), 57–62.

184. Quoted in Hosking, *Russia*, 396.

185. Lamsdorff, 'The Proposed Anti-Semitic Triple Alliance', 60.

186. Pierre Birnbaum and Ira Katznelson, eds., *Paths of Emancipation: Jews, States and Citizenship* (Princeton: Princeton University Press, 1995), 4–5. Levene, *War*, 109–10, 163–4.

187. See Carol Iancu, *Les juifs en Roumanie (1866–1919): De l'exclusion à l'émancipation* (Aix-en-Provence: Éditions de l'Université de Provence, 1978), for Rumania; Bernard Gainer, *The Alien Invasion: The Origins of the Aliens Act of 1905* (London: Heinemann, 1972), for Britain.

188. Sander L. Gilman, *The Jew's Body* (New York and London: Routledge, 1991); Bryan Cheyette, *Constructions of 'the Jew' in English Literature and Society: Racial Representations 1875–1945* (Cambridge: Cambridge University Press, 1993), for classic studies.

189. See Melson, *Revolution*, 119. More generally, Richard S. Levy, *The Downfall of the Anti-Semitic Parties in Imperial Germany* (New Haven, CT: Yale University Press, 1975).

190. Strachan, *To Arms*, 1138.

191. See Gavin Langmuir, *Towards a Definition of Antisemitism* (Berkeley and Los Angeles: University of California Press, 1990); Mark R. Cohen, *Under Crescent and Cross: The Jews in the Middle Ages* (Princeton: Princeton University Press, 1994), for the medieval background.

192. See Hillel J. Kieval, *Language of Community: The Jewish Experience in the Czech Lands* (Berkeley, Los Angeles, and London: University of California Press, 2000). Also Hillel J. Kieval, 'Representation and Knowledge of in Medieval and Modern Accounts of Jewish Ritual Murder', *Jewish Social Studies: History, Culture, Society*, 1 (1994–5), 52–72.

193. Löwe, *Tsars*, 326.

194. *The Times*, 30 July 1914, cited in Pendlebury, *Portraying 'the Jew'*, 140.

195. Mosse, 'War', 102–3. For the wider, including gendered, implications of going to war, see Michael C. C. Adams, *The Great Adventure: Male Desire and the Coming of World War One* (Bloomington, IN, and Indianapolis: Indiana University Press, 1990).

196. See Pendlebury, *Portraying 'the Jew'*, ch. 6, 'The Imagery of Crucifixion in Relation to the War', for cogent development of some of these themes.

197. See Sander L. Gilman, *Franz Kafka: The Jewish Patient* (New York and London: Routledge, 1995), esp. ch. 3, 'Males on Trial', for a notable example.

198. Löwe, *The Tsars*, 326.

199. Bartov, *Mirrors*, 96. See also Tim Grady, *The German Jewish Soldiers of the First World War in History and Memory* (Liverpool: Liverpool University Press, 2011), for a broader context and consequences.

200. For thoughtful discussion as to recrudescence of a '*mentalité collective*', see Albert S. Lindemann, *Esau's Tears: Modern Anti-Semitism and the Rise of the Jews* (Cambridge and New York: Cambridge University Press, 1997), 398–405.

201. Panayi, *Enemy*, 30–3, 163–4; Levene, *War*, 25–9.

202. Henry Wickham Steed, *Through Thirty Years: A Personal Narrative* (London: Heinemann, 1924), vol. 2, 390. See also André Liebich, 'The Antisemitism of Henry Wickham Steed', *Patterns of Prejudice*, 46:2 (2012), 180–208, for interpretation of this particular brand of 'Germanophobic' anti-Semitism.

203. Stephen Lucius Gwynn, ed., *The Letters and Friendships of Sir Cecil Spring-Rice: A Record* (Boston: Houghton Mifflin, 1929), vol. 2, 242–6, for full text of letter to Chirol and Grey, 13 November 1914.

204. NA FO 800/198 Cecil Papers, War Cabinet Secretariat memo., 14 April 1917, quoted in Levene, *War*, 137.

205. *The Times*, 23 November 1917, quoted in Carole Fink, *Defending the Rights of Others: The Great Powers, the Jews, and International Minority Protection, 1878–1938* (New York: Cambridge University Press, 2004), 89. See also Pendlebury, *Portraying 'the Jew'*, 151–3, 192, for Marsden and Wilton.

206. Cohn, *Warrant*, 166–70.

207. Nigel Nicolson and Joanne Trautmann, eds., *The Question of Things Happening: The Letters of Virginia Woolf, 1912–1922* (London: Chatto & Windus, 1976), doc. 1023, letter from Woolf to Vanessa Bell, 24 February 1919, 334–5. Equally revealing is Woolf's account of the endorsement of Lady Cromer's assertion by her companion at this South Kensington tea party, the well-known journalist, writer, and diplomat, Sir Valentine Chirol: 'They're ('the people') strung up, they're unreasonable, they want higher wages and, as Lady Cromer says, there are the Jews, the Russian Jews. There are Jews in every town—colonies of them. They will supply the motive power—and once the shooting begins—well, I'm a fatalist too, like Lady Cromer'.

208. Winston Churchill, 'Zionism versus Bolshevism: A Struggle for the Soul of the Jewish People', *Illustrated Sunday Herald*, 8 February 1920.

209. Churchill, 'Zionism versus Bolshevism'. See Sharman Kadish, *Bolsheviks and British Jews: The Anglo-Jewish Community, Britain, and the Russian Revolution* (London: Frank Cass 1992), 135–41, for full interpretation.

210. *Russia, No.1: A Collection of Reports on Bolshevism in Russia-Abridged Edition of Parliamentary Paper* (London: His Majesty's Stationery Office, 1919), nos 32/53.

211. Pendlebury, *Portraying 'the Jew'*, 195; Cohn, *Warrant*, 164–5.

212. 'The Unseen Hand', *National Review*, February 1917, quoted in Panayi, *Enemy*, 172.

213. Colin Holmes, *Anti-Semitism in British Society, 1876–1939* (London: Arnold, 1979), 127–37; Colin Holmes, 'The Myth of Fairness: Racial Violence in Britain, 1911–19', *History Today*, 35:10 (1985), 44–5.

214. See Susanne Terwey, 'Stereotypical Bedfellows: The Combination of Anti-Semitism with Germanophobia in Great Britain, 1914–1918', in Jenny Macleod and Pierre Pursleigh, eds., *Uncovered Fields: Perspectives in First World War Studies* (Leiden: Brill, 2004), 125–41.

215. Panayi, *Enemy*, 64–9, for anti-German legislation.

216. See Kadish, *Bolsheviks*, 120–34, for instance, for the infamous April 1919 'Letter of the Ten'.

217. Joseph Lee, quoted in Stephen Howe, *Ireland and Empire: Colonial Legacies in Irish History and Culture* (Oxford: Oxford University Press, 2000), 236.

218. Lindemann, *Esau's Tears*, 401–2.

219. *Der Bayerischer Wald*, 3 December 1918, cited in Robert Gerwarth, 'The Central European Counter-Revolution: Paramilitary Violence in Germany, Austria and Hungary after the Great War', *Past & Present*, 200 (2008), 199–200.

220. NA FO 608/196/602.2/1, Crowe, memorandum, 1 August 1919.

221. Leonard Shapiro, 'The Role of the Jews in the Russian Revolutionary Movement', *East European and Slavic Review*, 40 (1961–2), 148–67.

222. See, for corroboration, David Cesarani's review of Robert Service's *Trotsky* biography (2009), *Jewish Chronicle*, 26 November 2009.

223. William O. McCagg Jr, 'Jews in Revolutions: The Hungarian Experience', *Journal of Social History*, 6:1 (1972), 78–105.

224. See Robert J. Brym, *The Jewish Intelligentsia and Russian Marxism: A Sociological Study of Intellectual Radicalism and Ideological Divergence* (New York: Schocken Books, 1978); Robert S. Wistrich, *Revolutionary Jews from Marx to Trotsky* (New York: Barnes & Noble, 1976); Erich Haberer, *Jews and Revolution in Nineteenth-Century Russia* (Cambridge: Cambridge University Press, 1995), for notable analyses.

225. See, for example, the Rosa Luxemburg extract, 'No Room in My Heart for Jewish Suffering' (February 1916), in Mendes-Flohr and Reinharz, *The Jew*, 225–6.

226. Isaac Deutscher, *The Non-Jewish Jew and Other Essays* (London: Oxford University Press, 1968); George L. Mosse, *German Jews beyond Judaism* (Bloomington, IN, and Indianapolis: Indiana University Press, 1985). Also André Gerrits, *The Myth of Jewish Communism: A Historical Interpretation* (Brussels: P.I.E. Peter Lang, 2009), ch. 2, 'The Myth', for further commentary and analysis.

227. Lindemann, *Esau's Tears*, 445–6.

228. Quoted in Bernard K. Johnpoll, *The Politics of Futility: The General Jewish Workers Bund of Poland, 1917–41* (New York: Cornell University Press, 1967), 61.

229. Levene, *War*, 133–7, for the David Mowschowitch reports eschewed by the FO.

230. Slezkine, *Jewish Century*, 40.

231. NA FO 371/3053/87897, Sykes to Graham, 28 April 1917.

232. Renton, *Zionist Masquerade*, for a fuller development of this theme.

233. See Ram Marom, 'The Bolsheviks and the Balfour Declaration, 1917–1920', *Wiener Library Bulletin*, 29 (1976), 21; Levene, *War*, 143.

234. See Friedman, *The Question*; Mayir Verete, 'The Balfour Declaration and its Makers', *Middle Eastern Studies*, 6:1 (1970), 48–76; Ronald Saunders, *The High Walls of Jerusalem: A History of the Balfour Declaration and the Birth of the British Mandate in Palestine* (New York: Holt, Rhinehart and Winston, 1983), for key examples.

235. See Z. A. B. Zeman and W. B. Scharlau, *The Merchant of Revolution: The Life of Alexander Israel Helfhand 'Parvus', 1867–1924* (London and New York: Oxford University Press, 1965), ch. 10, 'Revolution in Russia'.

236. Slezkine, *Jewish Century*, 157.
237. See Richard B. Day and Daniel Gaido, eds., *Witnesses to Permanent Revolution, The Documentary Record* (Leiden and Boston: Brill, 2009), ch. 16, 'Our Tasks' (Parvus tract, 13 November 1905). Also Zeman and Scharlau, *The Merchant*, 130–5, for Parvus' early Great War efforts to foment Central Power insurrection in the Ukraine and Caucasus.
238. Quoted in Pendlebury, *Portraying 'the Jew'*, 153.
239. Holger Herwig, 'Tunes of Glory at the Twilight Stage: The Bad Homberg Crown Council and the Evolution of German Statecraft, 1917/1918', *German Studies Review*, 6 (1983), 477–8.
240. See Sir John Wheeler-Bennett, *Brest-Litovsk, The Forgotten Peace: March 1918* (London: Macmillan, 1939), esp. ch. 6, 'No War, No Peace'.
241. Richard Pipes, *The Russian Revolution* (New York: Knopf, 1990), 585.
242. See Chalmers Johnson, *Blowback: The Costs and Consequences of American Empire* (New York: Henry Holt and Company, 2001).
243. See Ervand Abrahamian, 'The US Media, Huntington and September 11th', *Third World Quarterly*, 3 (2003), 529–44, for one significant early analysis.
244. NA FO 371/3904/529, Wyndham to FO, 5 July 1919; Bevan to FO, 1 September 1919. Also FO 371/3903/529, Harmsworth memo., 5 September 1919, referring to views of Herbert Hoover, then head of the USA–European relief effort.
245. Quoted in Tom Segev, *One Palestine Complete: Jews and Arabs under the British Mandate*, trans. Haim Watzman (London: Little, Brown and Company, 2000), 119.
246. See NA FO 371/3414/183583, Bagley (British consul-general New York) to Drummond, 19 October 1918.
247. See Martin Kitchen, *The Silent Dictatorship: The Politics of the German High Command under Hindenburg and Ludendorff, 1916–1918* (London: Croom Helm, 1976), 16, for assessment.
248. Quoted in Steinberg, *All or Nothing*, 237.
249. Quoted in Steinberg, *All or Nothing*, 237.
250. Quoted in Braham, *Politics*, vol. 1, 165.
251. Quoted in Bartov, *Mirrors*, 250, n. 9.
252. Steinberg, *All or Nothing*, 236.
253. Quoted in Steinberg, *All or Nothing*, 238.
254. Hitler speech, 20 February 1920, as quoted in Werner Maser, *Hitler's Letters and Notes*, trans. Arnold Pomerans (London: Heinemann, 1974), 245. See also 218–77, for Hitler's accompanying notes and commentary.

CHAPTER 2

1. Quoted in Henry Morgenthau, *Ambassador Morgenthau's Story* (Garden City, NY: Doubleday, Page, 1918), 229.
2. Quoted in Raymond Kévorkian, *The Armenian Genocide: A Complete History* (London and New York: I.B.Tauris, 2011), 187.
3. See, notably, Ronald Grigor Suny, Fatma Müge Göçek, and Norman N. Naimark, eds., *A Question of Genocide: Armenians and Turks at the End of the Ottoman Empire* (Oxford: Oxford and New York University Press, 2011).
4. Donald Bloxham, *The Great Game of Genocide: Imperialism, Nationalism and the Destruction of the Ottoman Armenians* (Oxford: Oxford University Press, 2005), 69.

5. Kévorkian, *Armenian Genocide*, 1.
6. See Carnegie Inquiry, *Other Balkan Wars*, 95–9.
7. William Gladstone, *The Bulgarian Horrors and the Question of the East* (London: John Murray, 1876).
8. H. N. Brailsford, *Macedonia: Its Races and Their Future* (London: Methuen, 1906).
9. Carnegie Inquiry, *Other Balkan Wars*, 148.
10. Carnegie Inquiry, *Other Balkan Wars*, 309, quoting Panaghis Beglikis, 15 July 1913.
11. Carnegie Inquiry, *Other Balkan Wars*, 95, 62. Whatever the Carnegie report's failings, a more recent assessment is extremely positive. Alan Kramer, *Dynamic of Destruction*, 138: 'This remarkably well-documented and impartial investigation, cooly sceptical of exaggerated claims, reached conclusions that not have been improved upon to this day'.
12. Lucien Wolf, 'The New Bondage in the Balkans', *The Graphic*, 7 March 1914.
13. Quoted in Stefanović, 'Seeing the Albanians', 476.
14. See Levene, *Rise of the West*, 332.
15. Indeed, according to the Carnegie report, while IMRO issued a general appeal for humanity and against violence, exodus, and burnings, Athens, Sofia, and Belgrade were all conspicuous by their silence on this score. The report also suggested that the Bulgarians consciously relocated Macedonian volunteers to the Thracian front in the first war to avoid a real liberation of Macedonia by Macedonians on their own terms. Carnegie Inquiry, *Other Balkan Wars*, 73, 59.
16. Mark Mazower, *The Balkans* (London: Weidenfeld & Nicolson, 2000), 106.
17. Carnegie Inquiry, *Other Balkan Wars*, 199.
18. Carnegie Inquiry, *Other Balkan Wars*, 170–1; Palmer, *Lands Between*, 103.
19. McCarthy, *Death and Exile*, 152–3; Carnegie Inquiry, *Other Balkan Wars*, 77–8, 154–8.
20. Malcolm, *Kosovo*, 254–5.
21. See Carnegie Inquiry, *Other Balkan Wars*, 159–62, including text of Serb government 'Decree on Public Security', September 1913.
22. Malcolm, *Kosovo*, xxx.
23. Carnegie Inquiry, *Other Balkan Wars*, 67.
24. Reginald Rankin, *The Inner History of the Balkan War* (London: Constable & Co., 1914), 304.
25. McCarthy, *Death and Exile*, 139.
26. McCarthy, *Death and Exile*, 164.
27. Carnegie Inquiry, *Other Balkan Wars*, 72.
28. Rankin, *Inner History*, 303.
29. Soner Çağaptay, 'Crafting the Turkish Nation: Kemalism and Turkish Nationalism in the 1930s', unpublished doctoral thesis, Yale University, 2003, 454–5.
30. Stefanović, 'Seeing the Albanians', 476.
31. Carnegie Inquiry, *Other Balkan Wars*, 99–106.
32. Carnegie Inquiry, *Other Balkan Wars*, 204–6.
33. Carnegie Inquiry, *Other Balkan Wars*, 154.
34. Mark Levene, '"Ni grec, ni bulgare, ni turc": Salonika Jewry and the Balkan Wars, 1912–13', *Jahrbuch des Simon-Dubnow Instituts*, 2 (2003), 65–97.
35. Edith Durham, *High Albania* (London: Beacon Press, [1909] 1987), 263.
36. See Branimir Anzulović, *Heavenly Serbia: From Myth to Genocide* (New York: New York University Press, 1999), esp. ch. 5, 'A Vicious Circle of Lies and Fears'.

37. Stefanović, 'Seeing the Albanians', 470; Malcolm, *Kosovo*, 196–7, on the Arnautas thesis.
38. Stefanović, 'Seeing the Albanians', 472.
39. See John Kolsti, 'Albanian Gypsies: The Silent Survivors', in David Crowe and John Kolsti, eds., *The Gypsies of Eastern Europe* (New York and London: M Armonk/ M.E. Sharpe Inc., 1991), 52. Thanks also to Beryl Nicholson for a copy of her unpublished paper, 'New States, New Problems: The Resettlement in Albania of Refugees from Yugoslavia after 1919', presented to the 'Refugees and the End of Empire' conference, De Montfort University, Leicester, 29–30 June 2007.
40. Malcolm, *Kosovo*, 197.
41. Beryl Nicholson, 'New States', unpaginated.
42. Quoted in Malcolm, *Kosovo*, 253.
43. Malcolm, *Kosovo*, 253; Carnegie Inquiry, *Other Balkan Wars*, 151; Tim Judah, *Kosovo, War and Revenge* (New Haven, CT, and London: Yale University Press, 2000), 18–19.
44. Malcolm, *Kosovo*, 254.
45. Malcolm, *Kosovo*, 241–3.
46. Carnegie Inquiry, *Other Balkan Wars*, 149–51, 181–2.
47. Carnegie Inquiry, *Other Balkan Wars*, 149.
48. Carnegie Inquiry, *Other Balkan Wars*, 182.
49. Carnegie Inquiry, *Other Balkan Wars*, 130, 148.
50. Carnegie Inquiry, *Other Balkan Wars*, 133; 124–35 for the entire Malgara sequence.
51. Carnegie Inquiry, *Other Balkan Wars*, esp, 127–8, 135.
52. Mann, *Dark Side*, 143.
53. Aron Rodrigue, 'The Mass Destruction of Armenians and Jews in the 20th Century in Historical Perspective', in Hans-Lukas Kieser and Dominik Schaller, eds., *Der Völkermord an den Armeniern und die Shoah* (Zurich: Chronos Publishing, 2002), 308.
54. Michael Llewellyn Smith, *Ionian Vision, Greece in Asia Minor 1919–1922* (London: Hurst & Co., [1973] 1998), 212.
55. See Lieberman, *Terrible Fate*, ch. 1, 'Bag and Baggage: Ethnic Cleansing Begins'.
56. Taner Akçam, *From Empire to Republic: Turkish Nationalism and the Armenian Genocide* (London and New York: Zed Books, 2004), 83.
57. See Levene, *Rise of the West*, 306.
58. McCarthy, *Death and Exile*, 144, 148. McCarthy quotes figures of 20–30,000 dead out of 40–50,000 POWs incarcerated on the island. By contrast, Carnegie Inquiry, *Other Balkan Wars*, 111–13, offers no such definitive figures.
59. See Philip Mansel, *Constantinople: City of the World's Desire, 1453–1924* (London: Penguin, 1997), 364–6; Toynbee, *Western Question*, 138.
60. Carnegie Inquiry, *Other Balkan Wars*, 129, 134.
61. Dmitri Pentzopoulos, *The Balkan Exchange of Minorities and its Impact on Greece* (London: Hurst & Co., [1962] 2002), 54–5; John Mourelos, 'The 1914 Persecutions of Greeks in the Ottoman Empire and the First Attempt at an Exchange of Minorities between Greece and Turkey', in Tessa Hofmann, Matthias Bjørnlund, and Vasileois Meichanetsidis, eds., *The Genocide of the Ottoman Greeks* (New York and Athens: Aristide D. Caratzas, 2011), 118–20.
62. Hans-Lukas Kieser, 'Dr Mehmed Reshid (1873–1919): A Political Doctor', in Kieser and Schaller, *Der Völkermord*, 258. On the systematic nature of the ethnic cleaning, see Toynbee, *Western Question*, 140.

63. Tessa Hofmann, 'The Massacres and Deportations of the Greek Population of the Ottoman Empire (1912–1923)', in Hofmann, Bjørnlund, and Meichanetsidis, *Geno-cide*, 51–5; Matthias Bjornlund, 'The 1914 Cleansing of Aegean Greeks as a Case of Violent Turkification', *Journal of Genocide Research* (hereafter *JGR*), 10:1 (2008), 41–57. See also the US consular reports on these events as referred to in Robert Paul Adalian, 'Comparative Policy and Differential Practice in the Treatment of Minorities in Wartime: The United States Archival Evidence on the Armenians and Greeks in the Ottoman Empire', paper presented at 'Conference on Greeks and Armenians', Aristotle University, 1994, esp. 7–15.

64. Andrew Mango, *Atatürk* (London: John Murray, 1999), 109.

65. Feroz Ahmad, 'Unionist Relations with Greek, Armenian and Jewish Communities of the Ottoman Empire 1908–1914', in Benjamin Braude and Bernard Lewis, eds., *Christians and Jews in the Ottoman Empire: The Functioning of a Plural Society* (New York and London: Holmes & Meier, 1982), vol. 1, 407.

66. Mourelos, '1914 Persecutions', 116, 122–4.

67. Hofmann, 'The Massacres', 59.

68. Hofmann, 'The Massacres', 59–65; 101–2, for more explicit details.

69. Fuat Dündar, 'The Settlement Policy of the Committee of Union and Progress, 1913–1918', in Hans-Lukas Kieser, ed., *Turkey beyond Nationalism: Towards Post-Nationalist Identities* (London and New York: I.B. Tauris, 2006), 38.

70. Akçam, *From Empire*, 92–6; Üngör, *The Making*, 44–7, for further examples.

71. See Feroz Ahmad, *The Young Turks: The CUP in Turkish Politics, 1908–1914* (Oxford: Oxford University Press, 1969), biographical index, 166–81.

72. Akçam, *From Empire*, 94.

73. See M. Naim Turfan, *Rise of the Young Turks: Politics, The Military and Ottoman Collapse* (London and New York: I.B. Tauris, 2000), 201, 204–5; Mango, *Atatürk*, 109.

74. Quoted in Harold Temperley and Lillian Pearson, *Foundations of British Foreign Policy: 1792–1902, from Pitt to Salisbury* (London: Frank Cass, 1966), 366.

75. Akçam, *From Empire*, 77.

76. Turfan, *Rise*, 336; Ibn Khaldun, *The Muqaddimah: An Introduction to History*, trans. Franz Rosenthal (Princeton: Princeton University Press, 1969), for the great Arab fourteenth-century study of empire.

77. Akçam, *From Empire*, esp. 67–78; Levene, *Meaning*, 186–7.

78. See Stanford J. Shaw and Ezel Kural Shaw, *History of the Ottoman Empire and Modern Turkey*, vol. 2: *The Rise of Modern Turkey 1808–1975* (Cambridge: Cambridge University Press, 1977), 296; M. Şükrü Hanioğlu, *Preparations for a Revolution: The Young Turks, 1902–1908* (New York: Oxford University Press, 2001), 250; Ahmad, *Young Turks*, 161, for various passing comments on Itilaf.

79. M. Şükrü Hanioğlu, 'The Young Turks and the Arabs before the Revolution of 1908', in Rashid Khalidi, Lisa Anderson, Muhammad Muslih, and Reeva Simon, eds., *The Origins of Arab Nationalism* (New York and London: Columbia University Press, 1991), 31–49, and Ahmad, *Young Turks*, for notably different positions on CUP *Turkish* nationalism. See also, for a more Arab-orientated perspective on this debate, Rashid Khalidi, 'Ottomanism and Arabism Before 1914: A Reassessment', 54, and C. Ernest Dawn, 'The Origins of Arab Nationalism', 18–20, both in Khalidi, et al., *Origins*: the latter for a notably vociferous rejection of the CUP as nationalizers.

80. David Kushner, *The Rise of Turkish Nationalism 1876–1908* (London: Frank Cass, 1977), 22.

81. Ernest E. Ramsaur Jr, *The Young Turks* (Princeton: Princeton University Press, 1957), 17–18. The group began as the Ottoman Union Society.

82. See George W. Gawrych, 'The Culture and Politics of Violence in Turkish Society 1903–13', *Middle Eastern Studies*, 22:3 (1985), 307–30.

83. James J. Reid, 'Total War: The Annihilation Ethic and the Armenian Genocide 1870–1918', in Hovannisian, *Armenian Genocide: History*, 21–52; Vakahn N. Dadrian, 'The Role of Turkish Physicians in the World War One Genocide of Ottoman Armenians', *Holocaust and Genocide Studies* (hereafter *HGS*), 1:2 (1986), 169–92, for additional background information on the emergence of a European-trained professional (including medical) officer class and their key leadership roles in the CUP.

84. Ahmad, *Young Turks*, 21.

85. See Halil İncalik and Donald Quataert, *An Economic and Social History of the Ottoman Empire, 1300–1914* (Cambridge: Cambridge University Press, 1994), 782. Also Ryan Gingeras, *Sorrowful Shores: Violence, Ethnicity, and the End of the Ottoman Empire, 1912–1923* (Oxford: Oxford University Press, 2009), 8–9, 12–18, for telling commentary.

86. M. Şükrü Hanioğlu, 'Turkism and the Young Turks, 1889–1908', in Kieser, *Turkey*, 7–9, 16.

87. Kushner, *The Rise*, 79, 93, 29–38.

88. Kushner, *The Rise*, 9–10, for the influence of Arminius Vámbéry and Léon Cahun.

89. See, for example, François Georgeon, *Aux origines du nationalisme turc: Yusuf Akçura 1876–1935* (Paris: Editions ADPF, 1980), 23–30; Shaw and Shaw, *History*, vol. 2, 260–3.

90. Vahakn N. Dadrian, *The History of the Armenian Genocide: Ethnic Conflict from the Balkans to Anatolia to the Caucasus* (Providence, RI, and Oxford: Berghahn Books, 1995), 196.

91. Kushner, *The Rise*, 22–4.

92. Uriel Heyd, *Foundations of Turkish Nationalism: The Life and Teachings of Ziya Gökalp* (London: Luzac, 1950), vii. Also R. Hrair Dekmejian, 'Determinants of Genocide: Armenians and Jews as Case Studies', in Richard G. Hovannisian, ed., *The Armenian Genocide in Perspective* (New Brunswick, NJ, and London: Transaction Publishers, 1986), for the hypothesis of social and ethnic marginality and its relationship to acute national identity, 85–96, esp. 92–3.

93. Heyd, *Foundations*, 79, 150.

94. Heyd, *Foundations*, 147–52.

95. Shaw and Shaw, *History*, vol. 2, 301–4; Heyd, *Foundations*, 132.

96. Akçam, *From Empire*, 129. CUP targeting was not only of national groupings: the labour movement and European companies were equally seen as threats to the CUP's monopoly of power.

97. See, for instance, Kévorkian, *Armenian Genocide*, 173, for the September 1913 Armenian Hnchak 7th General Congress at Constanza, whose concluding remarks stated that the CUP 'had no basic principles beyond that of safeguarding the Turkish bureaucracy...and [had] plainly set out not only to assimilate the constituent nations but to annihilate them, to massacre them'. Also, for a more immediate view of Jewish disenchantment with CUP rule, see Leon Sciaky, *Farewell to Salonika: Portrait of an Era* (London: Hodder & Stoughton, 1946), 178–82.

98. Akçam, *From Empire*, 131.

99. Akçam, *From Empire*, 131. See also Vahakn N. Dadrian, *Warrant for Genocide: Key Elements of the Turko-Armenian Conflict* (New Brunswick, NJ, and London: Transaction Publishers, 1999), 96–7.

100. Dadrian, *Warrant*, ch. 9, 'The Outlines of a Genocidal Scheme'.
101. Dadrian, *Warrant*, 178. See also Jacob M. Landau, *Tekinalp: Turkish Patriot, 1883–1961* (Leiden: Nederlands Historisch-Archaeologisch Instituut te Istanbul, 1984).
102. See Taner Akçam, 'The Ottoman Documents and the Genocidal Policies of the Committee for Union and Progress (Ittihat ve Terakki) towards the Armenians in 1915', *GSP*, 1:2 (2006), 132–3. Also Üngör, *The Making*, 50–4.
103. Rudi Paul Lindner, *Nomads and Ottomans in Medieval Anatolia* (Bloomington, IN: Research Institute for Inner Asian Studies, 1981). For the more recent Hamidian situation, see Selim Deringil, '"They Live in a State of Nomadism and Savagery": The Late Ottoman Empire and the Post-Colonial Debate', *Comparative Studies in Society and History*, 45:2 (2003), 311–42.
104. Matthew Frank, 'Fantasies of Ethnic Unmixing: "Population Transfer" and the End of Empire in Europe', in Panikos Panayi and Pippa Virdee, eds. *Refugees and the End of Empire: Imperial Collapse and Forced Migration during the Twentieth Century* (Basingstoke: Palgrave Macmillan, 2011), 84–9.
105. Dadrian, *Warrant*, 98.
106. See Mehrdad R. Izady, *The Kurds: A Concise Handbook* (Washington, DC: Taylor & Francis, 1992), 101–8.
107. Akçam, 'Ottoman Documents', 133.
108. Akçam, 'Ottoman Documents', 133. Also Taner Akçam, 'Deportations and Massacres in the Cipher Telegrams of the Interior Ministry in the Prime Ministerial Archive (Basbanlik Arsivi)', *GSP*, 1:3 (2006), 308–9.
109. Dündar, 'Settlement Policy', 39–41.
110. Mango, *Atatürk*, 109; Dominic Lieven, *Empire: The Russian Empire and its Rivals* (London: John Murray, 2000), 135.
111. Kemal H. Karput, 'Historical Continuity and Identity Change', in Kemal H. Karput, ed., *Ottoman Past and Today's Turkey* (Leiden: Brill, 2000), 22; Çağaptay, 'Crafting the Turkish Nation', 10.
112. Akçam, *From Empire*, 137–40; Turfan, *Rise*, 302–5.
113. Dündar, 'Settlement Policy', 38–9.
114. Akçam, *From Empire*, 141.
115. Reynolds, 'Ottoman–Russian Struggle', 149–50.
116. See Levene, *Rise of the West*, 313–14, for this and the earlier 1878 scheme; Kévorkian, *Armenian Genocide*, 155, for the main points of the plan.
117. Roderic H. Davison, 'The Armenian Crisis, 1912–1914', *American Historical Review*, 53:3 (1948), 486.
118. Davison, 'Armenian Crisis', 486.
119. Elie Kedourie, *England and the Middle East: The Destruction of the Ottoman Empire, 1914–1921* (London: Bowes and Bowes, 1956), 23.
120. Jeremy Salt, *Imperialism, Evangelism and the Ottoman Armenians, 1878–1896* (London: Frank Cass, 1993), 57.
121. Certainly the view of Manoug J. Somakian, *Empires in Conflict: Armenia and the Great Powers, 1895–1920* (London: I.B. Tauris, 1995), 55. Sykes-Picot envisaged Russian annexation of Erzurum, Van, Bitlis, and Trabzon—in addition to Constantinople. See Bloxham, *Great Game*, 135.
122. Bloxham, *Great Game*, 84; Shaw and Shaw, *History*, vol. 2, 315.
123. Reynolds, 'Ottoman–Russian Struggle', 279; Lohr, *Nationalising the Russian Empire*, 97.
124. Reynolds, 'Ottoman–Russian Struggle', 375, n. 43.

125. Lohr, *Nationalising the Russian Empire*, 97; Somakian, *Empires*, 111. See also Peter Holquist, 'The Politics and Practice of the Russian Occupation of Armenia, 1915–February 1917', in Suny, Goçek, and Naimark, *A Question*, 167, for Gadzhemukov's notably anti-Armenian animus.

126. See Reynolds, 'Ottoman–Russian Struggle', 275–6; Salahi Sonyel, *The Great War and the Tragedy of Anatolia* (Ankara: Turkish Historical Printing House, 2000), 136; Somakian, *Empires*, 280–1.

127. See Gerard J. Libaridian, *Modern Armenia: People, Nation, State* (New Brunswick, NJ, and London: Transaction Publishers, 2005), chs 4 and 5, for valuable analysis. Also Gerard J. Libaridian, 'What was Revolutionary about Armenian Revolutionary Parties in the Ottoman Empire', in Suny, Goçek, and Naimark, *A Question*, 82–112. For the most recent critical study of the ARF in its pre-war years, see Dikran M. Kaligian, *Armenian Organization and Ideology under Ottoman Rule 1908–1914* (New Brunswick, NJ: Transaction Publishers, 2009).

128. Louise Nalbandian, *The Armenian Revolutionary Movement: The Development of Armenian Political Parties through the Nineteenth Century* (Berkeley and Los Angeles: University of California Press, 1963), 28–9.

129. See Christopher J. Walker, *Armenia: The Survival of a Nation* (London: Croom Helm, 1980), 102–3.

130. See Libaridian, *Modern Armenia*, ch. 2, 'Nation and Fatherland in 19th century Armenian Political Thought'. Also Richard G. Hovannisian, ed., *Armenian People from Ancient to Modern Times*, vol. 1: *The Dynastic Periods: From Antiquity to the Fourteenth Century* (London and New York: Palgrave Macmillan and St Martin's Press, 2004), for measured assessments of past Armenian glories.

131. See Sonyel, *Great War*, 26.

132. Reynolds, 'Ottoman–Russian Struggle', 266–7, including n. 30 on this score.

133. Tessa Hofmann and Gerayer Koutcharian, 'The History of Armenian–Kurdish Relations in the Ottoman Empire', *Armenian Review*, 39:4 (1986), 7–10; Hilmar Kaiser, 'Genocide at the Twilight of the Ottoman Empire', in Donald Bloxham and A. Dirk Moses, eds., *The Oxford Handbook of Genocide Studies* (Oxford: Oxford University Press, 2010), 367–9.

134. Justin McCarthy, *Muslims and Minorities: The Population of Ottoman Anatolia at the End of Empire* (New York and London: New York University Press, 1983), 2.

135. Gingeras, *Sorrowful Shores*, 24–6, for background. Also Hovannisian, *Armenia, On the Road*, 35.

136. See Stephan H. Astourian, 'The Silence of the Land: Agrarian Relations, Ethnicity and Power', in Suny, Goçek, and Naimark, *A Question*, 65–7, 80.

137. Hofmann and Koutcharian, 'History', 31.

138. Hofmann and Koutcharian, 'History', 33–4.

139. The question of the statistical data remains, to this day, an issue of much contested interpretation. For different views see McCarthy, *Muslim*, 50–1; Kévorkian, *Armenian Genocide*, 265–78; Dadrian, *Warrant*, Appendix, 'The Questionable Features of the Ottoman Calculus of the Demography of the Armenians'.

140. Hovannisian, *Armenia, On the Road*, 33.

141. Ahmad, 'Unionist Relations', 424; Ahmad, *Young Turks*, 144.

142. Martin van Bruinessen, *Agha, Shaikh and State: The Social and Political Structure of Kurdistan* (London: Zed Books, 1990), esp. ch. 4, 'Shaikhs: Mystics, Saints and Politicians'.

143. See David McDowall, *A Modern History of the Kurds* (London: I.B. Tauris, 1997), 87–96; van Bruinessen, *Agha*, 75–6; Kamal Madhar Ahmad, *Kurdistan during the First World War* (London: Saqi Books, 1994), 60–2; Kendal, 'The Kurds under the Ottoman Empire', in Gérard Chaliand, ed., *People without a Country: The Kurds and Kurdistan* (London: Zed Books, 1980), 34–7.

144. Quoted in Hamit Bozarslan, 'L'extermination des Arméniens et des juifs, Quelques éléments de comparaison', in Kieser and Schaller, *Der Völkermord*, 321. See Hilmar Kaiser, *Imperialism, Racism, and Development Theories: The Construction of a Dominant Paradigm on Ottoman Armenians* (Ann Arbor, MI: Gomidas Institute, 1997), for a robust repudiation of the comprador attribution.

145. Davison, 'Armenian Crisis', 484. See also Ahmad, 'Unionist Relations', 418, for organisational comparison of the two groups.

146. Ramsaur, *Young Turks*, 129; Kévorkian, *Armenian Genocide*, 73, 117.

147. Hosking, *Russia*, 386–8.

148. Libaridian, *Modern Armenia*, 20–1; Reynolds, 'Ottoman–Russian Struggle', 172.

149. Libaridian, *Modern Armenia*, 145; Kaligian, *Armenian Organization*, 53–9.

150. Even Dadrian, who would prefer to locate responsibility solely with the CUP, acknowledges local drivers founded on rumour and counter-rumour. See Vahakn N. Dadrian, 'The Circumstances Surrounding the 1909 Adana Holocaust', *Armenian Review*, 41:16 (1988), esp. 9–10.

151. Astourian, 'The Silence', 77–81.

152. See Mann, *Dark Side*, 127–8; Luigi Villari, *Fire and Sword in the Caucasus* (London: T.F. Unwin, 1906), for the Baku comparison. Also Hans Rogger, 'Conclusion and Overview', in Klier and Lambroza, *Pogroms*, 341–3, for a comparative pogrom analysis.

153. Bloxham, *Great Game*, 62.

154. Compare Sonyel, *Great War*, 52–71, with Kévorkian, *Armenian Genocide*, 71–117.

155. Kévorkian, *Armenian Genocide*, 93–4, for close analysis.

156. Libaridian, *Modern Armenia*, 147–9; Reynolds, 'Ottoman–Russian Struggle', 172.

157. Ahmad, *Kurdistan*, 62; Reynolds, 'Ottoman–Russian Struggle', 126.

158. Reynolds, 'Ottoman–Russian Struggle', 133–4.

159. Reynolds, 'Ottoman–Russian Struggle', 131, 113.

160. Sonyel, *Great War*, 82.

161. Mann, *Dark Side*, 136; Bloxham, *Great Game*, 73.

162. See Roshwald, *Ethnic Nationalism*, 128–9; Z. A. B. Zeman, *The Break-up of the Habsburg Empire, 1914–1918: A Study in National and Social Revolution* (London: Octagon, 1977), 50–2, 55–7.

163. Levene, *Rise of the West*, 318–21.

164. David Gaunt, *Massacres, Resistance, Protectors: Muslim-Christian Relations in Eastern Anatolia during World War 1* (Piscataway, NJ: Gorgias Press, 2006), 22, and also 2–5, for the diverse Syriac churches and nomenclature.

165. Gaunt, *Massacres*, 28, 22. Also see R. S. Stafford, *The Tragedy of the Assyrians* (London: Allen & Unwin, 1935); John Joseph, *The Nestorians and their Muslim Neighbours: A Study of Western Influences on their Relations* (Princeton: Princeton University Press, 1961); Mark Levene, 'A Moving Target, The Usual Suspects and (Maybe) a Smoking Gun: the Problem of Pinning Blame in Modern Genocide', *Patterns of Prejudice*, 33:4 (1999), 3–24.

166. Gaunt, *Massacres*, 7.

167. Reynolds, 'Ottoman–Russian Struggle', 201–2, 141–2.

168. Reynolds, 'Ottoman–Russian Struggle', 202.
169. Gaunt, *Massacres*, 128–9, 310.
170. Gaunt, *Massacres*, 138–44.
171. Gaunt, *Massacres*, 146–7; Joseph, *Nestorians*, 135. See also, for a contemporary description, the Paul Shimmon testimony, November 1915, in Bryce and Toynbee, *The Treatment*, 198.
172. Feroz Ahmad, *The Making of Modern Turkey* (London: Routledge, 1993), 6.
173. See Leonard Stein, *The Balfour Declaration* (London and Jerusalem: Magnes Press and Jewish Chronicle Publications, [1961] 1983), 103.
174. Taner Akçam, 'Another History on Sèvres and Lausanne', in Kieser and Schaller, *Der Völkermord*, 284. See also Asli Çirakman, *From the 'Terror of the World' to the 'Sick Man of Europe': European Images of Ottoman Empire and Society from the Sixteenth Century to the Nineteenth* (New York and Oxford: Oxford University Press, 2002), esp. chs 3 and 4.
175. Bloxham, *Great Game*, 136–7.
176. Bloxham, *Great Game*, 85–6.
177. See David Fromkin, *A Peace to End Peace: Creating the Modern Middle East 1914–1922* (London: Penguin, 1991), 69–73.
178. Strachan, *To Arms*, 676; Ulrich Trumpener, *Germany and the Ottoman Empire 1914–1918* (Princeton: Princeton University Press, 1968), 11–12.
179. Strachan, *To Arms*, 651–80, for detailed analysis.
180. Trumpener, *Germany*, 13.
181. See Vakahn N. Dadrian, *German Responsibility in the Armenian Genocide: A Review of the Historical Evidence of German Complicity* (Cambridge, MA: Blue Crane Books, 1997) for detailed portraits of and/or commentary on the German officers.
182. See Edward Mead Earle, *Turkey, the Great Powers and the Bagdad Railway* (New York: Russell & Russell, [1923] 1966).
183. Strachan, *To Arms*, 694–8, especially on Max von Oppenheim.
184. Thomas C. Leonard, 'When News is Not Enough: American Media and Armenian Deaths', in Winter, *America*, 304–5, for some earthy American renditions of Christian versus Muslim 'moral drama', as in *Mohammedan Fanatics* (1896). More classically, and controversially, see Edward W. Said, *Orientalism* (New York: Vintage Books, 1979), for a critique of the broad sweep of Orientalist discourse.
185. E. E. Evans-Pritchard, *The Sanusi of Cyrenaica* (London: Oxford University Press, 1949).
186. Gaunt, *Massacres*, ch. 4, 'Playing with Fire: Occupied Urmia'. Also Tadeusz Swietochowski, *Russian Azerbaijan, 1905–1920: The Shaping of a National Identity in a Muslim Community* (Cambridge: Cambridge University Press, 1985), ch. 2, for religion as a factor in the shaping of Muslim border community consciousness.
187. Bloxham, *Great Game*, 75–6; Vahakn N. Dadrian, 'The Role of the Special Organisation in the Armenian Genocide during the First World War', in Panayi, *Minorities*, 62–3; Gaunt, *Massacres*, 103–5, for different perspectives on the border war.
188. Samuel P. Huntington, *The Clash of Civilisations and the Remaking of World Order* (London: Touchstone Books, 1998).
189. Gaunt, *Massacres*, 84.
190. See Ulrich Herbert, ed., *National Socialist Extermination Policies: Contemporary German Perspectives and Controversies* (New York and Oxford: Berghahn Books, 2000), for the key exemplar of this type of approach.

191. The name came from his 1916 defeat of the British at Kut al Amara in Mesopotamia.
192. Gaunt, *Massacres*, 108–10, corroborated in Rafael de Nogales, *Four Years beneath the Crescent*, trans. Muna Lee (London: Charles Scribner's Sons, 1924), 134, and in Sargis testimony, Bryce and Toynbee, *The Treatment*, 190.
193. See Rushdouni testimony, in Bryce and Toynbee, *The Treatment*, 95; Gaunt, *Massacres*, 107–8. For Cevdet's predecessor, Tahsin Pasha, and his supposed pro-Armenianism—or at least efforts to stop anti-Armenian assaults—see Morgenthau, *Ambassador's Story*, 195; Kaligian, *Armenian Organization*, 214.
194. Gaunt, *Massacres*, 57.
195. Kévorkian, *Armenian Genocide*, 319–21.
196. Roupen testimony, Rushdouni testimony, in Bryce and Toynbee, *The Treatment*, 116, 95. See Hovannisian, *Armenia, On the Road*, 41–2; Gaunt, *Massacres*, 56; Kévorkian, *Armenian Genocide*, 177; Mann, *Dark Side*, 134–5, for various commentaries on these developments.
197. Vakahn N. Dadrian, 'The Secret Young-Turk Ittihadist Conference and the Decision for the World War I Genocide of the Armenians', *HGS*, 7:2 (1993), 188.
198. Morgenthau, *Ambassador's Story*, 196.
199. Hovhannes Katchaznouni testimony, 1923, quoted in Sonyel, *Great War*, 84. Kaligian, *Armenian Organization*, 220–2, working from Dashnak archival sources, offers no corroboration of the Katchaznouni testimony. However, he does confirm that a bureau of nine party leaders continued to confer after the Congress, and that they split over the issue of whether volunteer units should be mobilized to defend Ottoman Armenians in the event of Russo-Ottoman hostilities.
200. Reynolds, 'Ottoman–Russian Struggle', 204–5.
201. In this sense, I take an overtly cautious view of any implicit intentionality as expressed in Dadrian, 'Special Organisation', and his many other studies of the Armenian genocide. See, however, Kévorkian, *Armenian Genocide*, 180–7, which posits the existence of two potentially competing Special Organizations, one under the auspices of Enver and the War Ministry, the second one associated with Shakir and Nâzim and more closely aligned to CUP central committee goals.
202. Morgenthau, *Ambassador's Story*, 215–16, ventures a nebulous range between 200,000 and 1 million deportees. In late 1917, Frank W. Jackson, chairman of the US Relief Committee for Greeks in Asia Minor, offered 'reliable' figures of between seven and eight hundred thousand. Quoted in Hofman, 'The Massacres', 63. See Üngör, *The Making*, 108–22, for close, contemporary analysis, more specifically 117, for the 700,000 Kurdish figure.
203. Roupen testimony, Bryce and Toynbee, *The Treatment*, 116; Gaunt, *Massacres*, 57.
204. Dadrian, 'Special Organisation', 66.
205. W. E. D. Allen and Paul Muratoff, *Caucasian Battlefields* (Cambridge: Cambridge University Press, 1953), 283–4; Strachan, *To Arms*, 728.
206. Hilmar Kaiser, '"A Scene from the Inferno", The Armenians of Erzerum and the Genocide, 1915–1916', in Kieser and Schaller, *Der Völkermord*, 131.
207. Vahakn N. Dadrian, 'The Armenian Genocide: An Interpretation', in Winter, *America*, 65–6; Üngör, *The Making*, 59.
208. Gaunt, *Massacres*, 66; Mann, *Dark Side*, 145.
209. See Erik Jan Zürcher, 'Ottoman Labour Battalions in World War 1', in Kieser and Schaller, *Der Völkermord*, 187–96, esp. 192; Ioannis K. Hassiotis, 'The Armenian

Genocide and the Greeks; Response and Records 1915–1923', in Hovannisian, *Armenian Genocide: History*, 136–7.

210. Gaunt, *Massacres*, 66–7, 109.
211. See Akçam, *From Empire*, 159–64, for more on these developments. The 30,000 figure is that cited by Dadrian, 'Special Organisation', 28, including n. 28.
212. Akçam, *From Empire*, 164–6.
213. Dadrian, 'Secret Young-Turk Ittihadist Conference'.
214. See Vahakn N. Dadrian, 'The Naim-Andonian Documents on the World War I Destruction of Ottoman Armenians: The Anatomy of a Genocide', *International Journal of Middle Eastern Studies*, 18:3 (1986), 311–60, for another key set of actually very 'dodgy' documents upon which Dadrian closely relies. See Erik-Jan Zürcher, *Turkey: A Modern History* (London: I.B. Tauris, 2004), 221, and Hilmar Kaiser, 'The Baghdad Railway and the Armenian Genocide, 1915–1916', in Richard G. Hovannisian, *Remembrance and Denial: The Case of the Armenian Genocide* (Detroit, MI: Wayne State University Press, 1999), 108, for more sceptical views. These are repeated in Mann, *Dark Side*, 140–1, n. 2, and 144, with regard to this and other evidence. See also, however, Kévorkian's *Armenian Genocide*, 243, where he argues with regard to 'The Ten Commandments' that 'the forger probably fabricated an "authentic fake" that summed up the [CUP] measures for liquidating the Armenian population actually decided upon'.
215. Dadrian, 'Naim-Andonian Documents', 329, 349–50, n. 45. However, by way of comparison see also the letter to Ahmet Emin Yalman in Akçam, 'Ottoman Documents', 136.
216. See Suzanne Elizabeth Moranian, 'Bearing Witness: The Missionary Archives as Evidence of the Armenian Genocide', in Winter, *America*, 191; Dadrian, 'Naim-Andonian Documents', 341.
217. Morgenthau, *Ambassador's Story*, 221, 233.
218. See Mann, *Dark Side*, 141, for his functionalist explanation of a descent into genocide by way of a series of aborted plans (A-D). Our 'politicide' argument as to what constituted Plan B is different from Mann's partial deportation hypothesis but, in general terms, concurs with the Mann explication.
219. Dadrian, 'Special Organisation', 75–6.
220. Dadrian, 'Naim-Andonian Documents', 328.
221. Dadrian, 'Armenian Genocide', 98. Also Vakahn N. Dadrian, 'The Role of the Turkish Military in the Destruction of Ottoman Armenians: A Study in Historical Continuities', *Journal of Political and Military Sociology*, 20:2 (1992), 276–7.
222. Mann, *Dark Side*, 158–9, 144. Dadrian's argument for genocide rests, in large part, on the notion of a conspiracy perpetrated within the inner, supposedly monolithic, circle of the CUP. On Cemal's variance from the main CUP line see Hilmar Kaiser, 'Regional Resistance to Central Government Policies: Ahmed Djemal Pasha, the Governors of Aleppo, and Armenian Deportees in the Spring and Summer of 1915', *JGR*, 12:3–4 (2010), 173–218.
223. Morgenthau, *Ambassador's Story*, 151, 155.
224. Uğur U. Üngör, 'When Persecution Bleeds into Mass Murder: The Processive Nature of Genocide', *GSP*, 1:2 (2006), 180.
225. Fuat Dündar, 'Pouring a People into the Desert: The "Definitive Solution" of Unionists to the Armenian Question', in Suny, Goçek, and Naimark, *A Question*, 281.
226. See Aram Arkun, 'Zeytun and the Commencement of the Armenian Genocide', in Suny, Goçek, and Naimark, *A Question*, 221–43, for a full assessment.

227. See Bloxham, *Great Game*, 72, 79–81. Also Sonyel, *Great War*, 105–7, for the various diaspora committees; Fromkin, *Peace*, 176–80, for the confabulated Arab army associated with the al-Faruqi episode.

228. Kaiser, 'Regional Resistance', 176–82; Dündar, 'Pouring a People', 281; Bloxham, *Great Game*, 81–3; Mann, *Dark Side*, 146–7.

229. Kaiser, 'Regional Resistance', 207–11.

230. Vahakn N. Dadrian, 'Ottoman Archives and Denial of the Armenian Genocide', in Hovannisian, *Armenian Genocide: History*, 298.

231. Morgenthau, *Ambassador's Story*, 231.

232. Talât memoirs, quoted in Dadrian, 'Secret Young-Turk Ittihadist Conference', 192.

233. Yusuf Sarınay, 'What Happened on 24 April 1915? The Circular of 24 April 1915, and the Arrest of the Armenian Committee Members in Istanbul', *International Journal of Turkish Studies*, 14:1–2 (2008), 75–101.

234. See Donald Bloxham, 'Cumulative Radicalisation: The Development of the Genocide', in Donald Bloxham, *Genocide, the World Wars and the Unweaving of Europe* (London and Portland, OR: Vallentine Mitchell, 2008), 52.

235. Mann, *Dark Side*, 148.

236. Bloxham, *Great Game*, 83; Zürcher, 'Ottoman Labour Battalions', 193.

237. Edward J. Erickson, *Ordered to Die: A History of the Ottoman Army in the First World War* (Westport, CT: Greenwood Press, 2001), 100–2; Sonyel, *Great War*, 113.

238. Gaunt, *Massacres*, 67.

239. Bloxham, *Great Game*, 84–5; Kaiser, 'Regional Resistance', 195–200, for growing CUP realisation of a lack of bureaucratic capacity to deal with deportations in an 'orderly' fashion.

240. See Ara Sarafian, ed., *United States Official Documents on the Armenian Genocide* (Watertown, MA: Armenian Review Books, 1994), vol. 1, 170–1, 172–6, for the texts. Sonyel, *Great War*, 112–22, significantly, reads these directives as evidence of Ottoman good intentions, putting down Armenian loss of life (which he states as 300–400,000) to general insecurity in a military war zone, guerrilla activity, brigandage, and Kurdish blood feuds.

241. See Dadrian, 'Naim-Andonian Documents', for attempted corroboration of the dossier of cipher orders by way of independent reports from German and other non-Turkish sources. But also see Kaiser, 'Scene', 151, which charts Talât's various directives seeking information on Armenians who had converted to Islam, or photographic evidence of Armenian uprisings, etc.

242. Dadrian, 'Naim-Andonian Documents', 338–43, for the 'two-track' system of CUP communication; Akçam, 'Ottoman Documents', 140–3, on the key role of the *Katib-i Mesuller*.

243. Somakian, *Empires*, 81–2; Christopher R. Browning (with Jürgen Matthaus), *The Origins of the Final Solution: The Evolution of Nazi Jewish Policy, September 1939–March 1942* (London: William Heinemann, 2004), esp. 309–14.

244. Bloxham, *Great Game*, 85–6, for the 'intense agitation in CUP ranks at the Entente announcement'.

245. Akçam, 'Ottoman Documents', 140; Kévorkian, *Armenian Genocide*, 289–336, for close analysis of the unfolding of violence in Erzurum and Van.

246. See Gerlach, *Extremely Violent Societies*, 96–106, for extensive analysis. Also Kaiser, 'Scene', 151, for the Erzurum case.

247. See, on this score, Niyazi Berkes, *The Development of Secularism in Turkey* (London: Hurst & Co., 1998), esp. 367–428.

248. See Rouben Paul Adalian, 'American Diplomatic Correspondence in the Age of Mass Murder: The Armenian Genocide in the US Archives', in Winter, *America*, 165–8, for acute analysis on this issue. More broadly, Çağlar Keyder, *State and Class in Turkey: A Study in Capitalist Development* (New York: Verso, 1987), 49–90.

249. See Hilmar Kaiser, 'The Ottoman Government and the End of the Ottoman Social Formation, 1915–1917', paper presented at Der Völkermord an den Armeniern und der Shoah, Zurich, November 2001 <http://www.hist.net/kieser/aghet/Essays/EssayKaiser.html>; Gerlach, *Extremely Violent Societies*, 103–5, on the wider Ottoman state wartime economic crisis.

250. Gerlach, *Extremely Violent Societies*, 93.

251. Somakian, *Empires*, 96.

252. See Panayi, *Enemy*, ch. 5, 'Measures against German Business Interests'. By way of comparison see Lohr, *Nationalising the Russian Empire*, ch. 3, 'Nationalising the Commercial and Industrial Economy', and ch. 4, 'Nationalising the Land'.

253. See Stephan Astourian, 'Genocidal Process: Reflections on the Armeno-Turkish Polarization', in Hovannisian, *Armenian Genocide: History*, 71–2. Also Kévorkian, *Armenian Genocide*, 200–6, for further commentary. Also Gerlach, *Extremely Violent Societies*, 114–15, for the resulting gulf between a corrupt rich and a starving poor in post-*Aghet* Ottoman society.

254. Morgenthau, *Ambassador's Story*, 225. See also Arthur Beylerian, ed., *Les grandes Puissances: l'Empire ottoman et les Arméniens dans les archives françaises (1914–1918)*, (Paris: Publications de la Sorbonne, 1983), 175–6, for an example of one such official request.

255. Kieser, 'Dr Mehmed Reshid', 260.

256. Uğur Ümit Üngör, '"A Reign of Terror": CUP Rule in Diyarbekir Province, 1913–1918', unpublished Master's thesis, University of Amsterdam, 2005, 62. With thanks to Dr Üngör for a copy.

257. Gerlach, *Extremely Violent Societies*, ch. 3, 'Participating and Profiteering: The Destruction of the Armenians, 1915–23', covers the whole range of robbery and venality at Armenian expense from the very top to the very bottom of Ottoman society. See Dadrian, 'Armenian Genocide', 84–5, for this scene at a local—Trabzon—level.

258. Kaiser, 'Scene', 172; Mann, *Dark Side*, 140–5, 177–9.

259. Matthias Bjørnlund, 'When the Cannons Talk, the Diplomats Must be Silent', *GSP*, 1:2 (2006), 197–224, for a notably astute effort to synthesize the two approaches.

260. Kaiser, 'Scene', 137–8.

261. Kaiser, 'Scene', esp. 131–53, for more on the intriguing role of Scheubner-Richter.

262. See Ara Sarafian, 'Introduction', to Bryce and Toynbee, *The Treatment*, vii–xviii, for origins and formulation of the report. See also Ara Sarafian, *United States Official Documents*, 3 vols. (1994, 1995), for the complete collection of US consular reports.

263. Kévorkian, *Armenian Genocide*, part IV.

264. Gorrini testimony, in Bryce and Toynbee, *The Treatment*, 316–18; Levene, *Rise of the West*, 106–7, for the *noyades*. Also Kévorkian, *Armenian Genocide*, 467–93.

265. Roupen testimony, in Bryce and Toynbee, *The Treatment*, 119–23. See de Nogales, *Four Years*, 116–17, and, more particularly Kévorkian, *Armenian Genocide*, 337–53, for corroboration.

266. Dadrian, 'Armenian Genocide', 65.

267. Gaunt, *Massacres*, 304.

268. Gaunt, *Massacres*, 304.
269. Üngör, 'Reign of Terror', 75–6. Also Gaunt, *Massacres*, 226–30, 241–4, for detailed, and in parts slightly differing, accounts of these events.
270. Üngör, 'Reign of Terror', 63.
271. By contrast with Dadrian, *German Responsibility*, which takes an unequivocally negative view, see some more recent nuanced readings, notably in Bloxham, *Great Game*, ch. 3, 'Imperial Germany: A Case of Mistaken Identity'; and Eric D. Weitz, 'Germany and the Young Turks: Revolutionaries into Statesmen' and Margaret Lavinia Anderson, 'Who Still Talked about the Extermination of the Armenians, German Talk and German Silences', both in Suny, Goçek, and Naimark, *A Question*, 175–98 and 199–217, respectively.
272. Üngör, *The Making*, 92–9; Gaunt, *Massacres*, 73–5.
273. Gaunt, *Massacres*, 76–7, 176.
274. Bryce and Toynbee, *The Treatment*, 635.
275. Bryce and Toynbee, *The Treatment*, 644.
276. Bloxham, *Great Game*, 79; Kévorkian, *Armenian Genocide*, 187.
277. Ian Kershaw, 'Working towards the Führer: Reflections on the Nature of the Hitler Dictatorship', in Christian Leitz, ed., *The Third Reich: The Essential Readings* (Oxford: Blackwell, 1999), 231–52, for the key Kershavian concept deployed here.
278. See Ügur Ümit Üngör, 'Fresh Understanding of the Armenian Genocide: Mapping New Terrain with Old Questions', in Adam Jones, ed., *New Directions in Genocide Research* (New York and London: Routledge, 2012), 207–9, for Feyzi and family connections; Gaunt, *Massacres*, 228–9, 246.
279. Üngör, *The Making*, 61–6.
280. Quoted in Gaunt, *Massacres*, 179; Kieser, 'Dr Mehmed Reshid', 261–3; Üngör, 'Reign of Terror', 41, for Reshid's 'apocalyptic' mindset.
281. Gaunt, *Massacres*, 305.
282. Gaunt, *Massacres*, 159.
283. Gaunt, *Massacres*, 305.
284. Üngör, *The Making*, 46–7, dates this sequence of massacres as occurring in mid-May; Gaunt, *Massacres*, 230–1, 245–6, by contrast, suggests a longer time period, beginning in mid-April and culminating in a final extermination of Kabiye's surviving women and children in September.
285. See, for instance, Donald E. Miller and Lorna Touryan Miller, *Survivors: An Oral History of the Armenian Genocide* (Berkeley and Los Angeles: University of California Press, 1993), for the repeated testimony to this effect.
286. See Ahmad, *Kurdistan*, 65–8, for the major wartime Kurdish revolt sequence. Also van Bruinessen, *Agha*, 277.
287. Gaunt, *Massacres*, 73–4.
288. See Sonyel, *Great War*, 122, for a less overtly propagandist version of this narrative. Also Guenter Lewy, *The Armenian Massacres in Ottoman Turkey: A Disputed Genocide* (Salt Lake City: University of Utah Press, 2005), esp. 250–6, for a recent apologia along these lines.
289. Leslie A. Davis, *The Slaughterhouse Province: An American Diplomat's Report on the Armenian Genocide, 1915–1917*, ed. Susan K. Blair (New Rochelle, NY: A.D. Caratzas, 1989), 51–2.
290. Davis, *Slaughterhouse Province*, 54–5.
291. See Miller and Miller, *Survivors*, ch. 5, 'The Experience of Women and Children'.

292. Katherine Derderian, 'Common Fate, Different Experience: Gender-Specific Aspects of the Armenian Genocide 1915–1917', *HGS*, 19:1 (2005), 1–25; Davis, *Slaughterhouse Province* 76; Nogales, *Four Years*, 130–1, for notable eyewitness accounts.

293. On the broader implications of this line of enquiry, see, among the growing literature, Adam Jones, *Genocide: A Comprehensive Introduction* (London and New York: Routledge, 2nd edn, 2011), ch. 13, 'Gendering Genocide'; Roger W. Smith, 'Women and Genocide: Notes on an Unwritten History', *HGS*, 8:3 (1994), 315–34; Alexandra Stiglmayer, ed., *Mass Rape: The War against Women in Bosnia-Herzegovina* (Lincoln, NE, and London: University of Nebraska Press, 1994).

294. See Ephraim K. Jernazian, *Judgement under Truth: Witnessing the Armenian Genocide* (New Brunswick, NJ, and London: Transaction Publishers, 1990), 94–5, for one Urfa example of officials pilfering.

295. Davis, *Slaughterhouse Province*, 31, 82–6. For further commentary see Mark Levene, 'The Experience of Genocide: Armenia 1915–16, Romania, 1941–42', in Kieser and Schaller, *Der Völkermord*, 435–6. It is notable that Atkinson seems to have been utterly traumatized by the experience and died soon after. His report was transcribed by his widow.

296. Miller and Miller, *Survivors*, 103–4, interestingly offer more modern-sounding explanations for these mass suicides, thereby avoiding a reading based on communal moral and cultural underpinnings. See Kaiser, 'Genocide at the Twilight', 377, for a more cogent reading, not least of the dowry issue.

297. There is a brief but vivid description of such a mart in Malatya in Kaiser, 'Scene', 162–3. Significantly, little scholarly attention has been paid to the social and political complexities of these people 'sales'. For one exception see Ara Sarafian, 'The Absorption of Armenian Women and Children into Muslim Households as a Structural Component of the Armenian Genocide', in Omer Bartov and Phyllis Mack, eds., *In God's Name: Genocide and Religion in the Twentieth Century* (New York: Berghahn, 2001), 209–21. See also Gerlach, *Extremely Violent Societies*, 110–11.

298. Bloxham, *Great Game*, 87. By contrast, see Steven T. Katz, 'The Holocaust and Comparative History', *Leo Baeck Memorial Lecture, 37* (New York: Leo Baeck, 1993), esp. 14–17, for an example of (flawed) analysis which seeks to undermine a case for genocide by the same route.

299. See Levene, *Meaning*, 35.

300. Raymond H. Kévorkian, 'Ahmed Djemal pacha et le sort des deportés arméniens de Syrie-Palestine', in Kieser and Schaller, *Der Völkermord*, 197.

301. Sarafian, *United States Official Documents*, vol. 1, 108: Jackson report, 16 October 1915. See also 142–58: Jackson's longer report, 'Armenian Atrocities', 4 March 1918.

302. Hilmar Kaiser, *At the Crossroads of Der Zor: Death, Survival and Humanitarian Resistance in Aleppo, 1915–1917* (Princeton: Gomidas Institute, 2001), 10–13; Kévorkian, *Armenian Genocide*, 625–7, 640–6.

303. See Sarafian, *United States Official Documents*, vol. 1, 129–35: Bernau to Jackson, 10 September 1916; Walker, *Armenia*, 227–9; Kaiser, 'Regional Resistance', 202–4, 208; Kévorkian, 'Ahmed Djemal', 199–203. However, also see Kévorkian, *Armenian Genocide*, 681–5, for his further exploration of Cemal's 'peculiar' role as bound up with his covert, but ultimately unsuccessful, negotiations with the Entente.

304. Gaunt, *Massacres*, 305.

305. Safrastian account in Bryce and Toynbee, *The Treatment*, 269–70. See also Kaiser, 'Scene', 160–4, for further eyewitness testimony and the role of Balaban and Reshvan tribesmen in Erzindjan area massacres.

306. G. S. Graber, *Caravans to Oblivion: The Armenian Genocide, 1915* (New York: J. Wiley, 1996), 104.

307. De Nogales, *Four Years*, 179–80.

308. See Sarafian, *United States Official Documents*, vol. 1, 129–35, for the important Bernau eyewitness account. One might note that normal resistance against typhus diminishes from middle age onwards.

309. Bloxham, *Great Game*, 88, referring to an unpublished Taner Akçam article, 'Rethinking the Ottoman Archival Material, Debunking Existing Myths'.

310. Dadrian, 'Naim-Andonian Documents', 354–5.

311. See Robert Fisk, 'Armenia's Holocaust', *The Independent Magazine*, 4 April 1992, 2–30, for the Shedadi and other similar, recently uncovered sites of mass killings.

312. Kévorkian, *Armenian Genocide*, 651, 655–70. Dadrian, 'Naim-Andonian Documents', 354. See also Sarafian, *United States Official Documents*, vol. 1, esp. 148–9, for Jackson's 1918 report.

313. Kévorkian, *Armenian Genocide*, 670–1; Gaunt, *Massacres*, 248–9.

314. Kévorkian, *Armenian Genocide*, 654.

315. Bryce and Toynbee, *The Treatment*, 647.

316. See Kévorkian, 'Ahmed Djemal', 206–7.

317. Bryce and Toynbee, *The Treatment*, 645. Also Kaiser, 'Genocide at the Twilight', 382–3, for a more recent analysis. Kaiser draws, in part, on an originally Talât-ordered confidential report, published by the Turkish journalist Murat Bardakçi in 2008, which provides a comprehensive province-by-province summary of the Armenian population in 1917 as set against official 1914 figures. See Ara Sarafian, ed., *Talaat Pasha's Report on the Armenian Genocide, 1917* (London: Gomidas Institute, 2011). The report's conclusion was that 1,150,000 Ottoman Armenians (or 77 per cent) had 'disappeared' in that three-year period.

318. Gaunt, *Massacres*, 300.

319. Joseph, *The Nestorians*, 135, estimates that perhaps one-third of the Ottoman Hakkâri population of Nestorians was killed or died during their flight or in subsequent war-time vicissitudes. See also Gabrielle Yonan, *Ein vergessener Holocaust: Die Vernichtung der christlicher Assyrer in der Türkei* (Göttingen: Gesellschaft für bedrohte Völker, 1989).

320. Gaunt, *Massacres*, 310–12. See also Üngör, *The Making*, 85, for a different set of later statistics which extrapolated even higher death tolls, especially of the Jacobites.

321. Trumpener, *Germany*, 232–3, more generally ch. 7, 'The Armenian Persecutions'; Hilmar Kaiser, 'Baghdad Railway'; Hovannisian, *Remembrance*, 76–7. See Bloxham, *Great Game*, 123–6, for sound assessment of the German diplomatic efforts.

322. Trumpener, *Germany*, 244.

323. Kaiser, 'Baghdad Railway', 87–92; Kévorkian, *Armenian Genocide*, 686–90.

324. Kaiser, *At the Crossroads*, esp. 37–57.

325. See Franz Werfel, *The Forty Days of Musa Dagh* (New York: Viking Press, 1934).

326. See Gaunt, *Massacres*, ch. 9, 'The Battle for Azakh', also 202–5, 223, 269–70.

327. On traditional Alevi and other sectarian group assistance to Armenians in times of persecution see Hans-Lukas Kieser, *Der verpasste Friede: Mission, Ethnie und Staat in den Ostprovinzen der Türkei 1839–1938* (Zurich: Chronos, 2000), 396–7, 430–1; Hofmann and Koutcharian, 'History', 6–7, 24–5; Yves Ternon, 'The Impossible

Rescue of the Armenians of Mardin: The Sinjar Safe Haven', in Jacques Semelin, Claire Andrieu, and Sarah Gensburger, eds., *Resisting Genocide: The Multiple Forms of Rescue*, trans. Emma Bentley and Cynthia Schoch (London: Hurst, 2010), 383–94; Gerlach, *Extremely Violent Societies*, 111.

328. Kaiser, *At the Crossroads*, 29–37, 52–7; Moranian, 'Bearing Witness', 185–213; Kévorkian, *Armenian Genocide*, 758–9.

329. McCarthy, *Death and Exile*, 230.

330. Sarafian, *Talaat Pasha's Report*.

331. Quoted in Dadrian, 'Armenian Genocide', 63.

332. Levene, *Meaning*, 147–9.

333. Libaridian, *Modern Armenia*, ch. 8, 'The Ultimate Repression', esp. 144–59; Kévorkian, *Armenian Genocide*, 52–70, 131–5, for a more sober assessment.

334. See Erik Jan Zürcher, *The Unionist Factor: The Role of the Committee of Union and Progress in the Turkish National Movement, 1905–1926* (Leiden: E.J. Brill, 1984), 172.

335. Mann, *Dark Side*, 158–60.

336. Vahakn N. Dadrian, 'The Determinants of the Armenian Genocide', *JGR*, 1:1 (1999), 74.

337. See Dadrian, 'Armenian Genocide', 68–83.

338. See Mann, *Dark Side*, 140–5, 177–9, for emphasis on default plans; Bloxham, 'The Beginning of the Armenian Catastrophe: Comparative and Contextual Considerations', in Kieser and Schaller, *Der Völkermord*, 101–28, and Bloxham, 'Cumulative Radicalisation', for explication around the Mommsen thesis.

339. See Kieser, 'Dr Mehmed Reshid', 253. See also Kaiser, 'Regional Resistance', 208, on the Aleppo governor, Bekir Sami.

340. Mann, *Dark Side*, 144. See also the revealingly adulatory portrait of Shakir penned by the veteran journalist, Hüseyin Cahit Yalçın, as quoted at length in Erik Jan Zürcher, 'Renewal and Silence: Postwar Unionist and Kemalist Rhetoric on the Armenian Genocide', in Suny, Goçek, and Naimark, *A Question*, 315.

341. See Roger Adelson, *London and the Invention of the Modern Middle East: Money, Power and War, 1902–1922* (New Haven, CT, and London: Yale University Press, 1995). Also James Renton, 'Changing Languages of Empire and the Orient: Britain and the Invention of the Middle East', *Historical Journal*, 50:3 (2007), 645–67.

342. Heyd, *Foundations*, 79.

343. Akçam, *From Empire*, 88.

344. Hans Kohn, *Nationalism and Imperialism in the Hither East* (New York: Harcourt Brace, 1932), 68.

345. See Gerlach, *Extremely Violent Societies*, 112–15.

346. Richard G. Hovannisian, 'Historical Dimensions of the Armenian Question, 1878–1923', in Hovannisian, *Armenian Genocide in Perspective*, 37.

347. See Fatma Ulgen, 'Reading Mustafa Kemal Atatürk on the Armenian Genocide of 1915', *Patterns of Prejudice*, 44:4 (2010), 369–91.

348. Lewis V. Thomas in Lewis V. Thomas and Richard N. Frye, *The United States and Turkey and Iran* (Cambridge, MA: Harvard University Press, 1951), 61.

CHAPTER 3

1. Quoted in Naimark, *Fires*, 521.

2. Quoted in Pearson, *National Minorities*, 230.

3. See discussions in Dadrian, *History*, 304–5; Akçam, 'Another History', 285–6.

4. See Fink, *Defending the Rights*, 151–60.
5. See Weindling, *Epidemics*, 111–18, for cogent examination of the epidemiological realities on the ground.
6. See Mark Cornwall, 'Austria-Hungary', in Hugh Cecil and Peter H. Liddle, eds., *At the Eleventh Hour: Reflections, Hopes and Anxieties at the Closing of the Great War, 1918* (Barnsley: Leo Cooper, 1998), ch. 19.
7. See Arno J. Mayer, *Politics and Diplomacy of Peacemaking: Containment and Counter-revolution at Versailles, 1918–1919* (New York: Knopf, 1967), for the most forceful rendition of this line of reasoning.
8. Palmer, *Lands Between*, 152.
9. Levene, *War*, 312–15, for text of the model Polish Minorities Treaty.
10. Zara Steiner, *The Lights that Failed: European International History, 1919–1933* (Oxford: Oxford University Press, 2004), 9.
11. See Mayer, *Politics*, 296–7.
12. Levene, *War*, 181. Also Alan Sharp, '"The Genie that Would Not Go Back into the Bottle": National Self-determination and the Legacy of the First World War and the Peace Settlement', in Seamus Dunn and T. G. Fraser, eds., *Europe and Ethnicity: The First World War and Contemporary Ethnic Conflict* (London and New York: Routledge, 1996), 18–19, for more general corroboration of Western diplomatic uncertainty as to the New Europe.
13. See Kenneth J. Calder, *Britain and the Origins of the New Europe, 1914–1918* (Cambridge: Cambridge University Press, 1976), 92–8, 113–19.
14. Harry Hanak, *Great Britain and Austria-Hungary during the First World War: A Study in the Formation of Public Opinion* (Oxford: Oxford University Press, 1962), 139–40.
15. Roshwald, *Ethnic Nationalism*, 219.
16. See Alan Fisher, *The Crimean Tatars* (Stanford, CA: Hoover Institute Press, 1978), 117.
17. Roshwald, *Ethnic Nationalism*, 219.
18. See Piotr Stefan Wandycz, *France and her Eastern Allies, 1919–25: French-Czechoslovak-Polish Relations from the Paris Peace Conference to Locarno* (Minneapolis: University of Minnesota Press, 1962), 75–91.
19. Mayer, *Politics*, 296–308, 338–43; John Bradley, *Allied Intervention in Russia* (London: Weidenfeld & Nicolson, 1968), 144.
20. Malcolm, *Kosovo*, 273; Roshwald, *Ethnic Nationalism*, 87–8.
21. Mayer, *Politics*, 602–3, 734–5.
22. Fink, *Defending the Rights*, 146; Mayer, *Politics*, 603.
23. See Fischer, *Germany's Aims*, ch. 20, 'The Elaboration of the Ostraum: The Ukraine, The Crimea, The Don Caucasus'; Herwig, 'Tunes of Glory', 486.
24. See Chapter 1, 47–8.
25. Levene, *War*, 196–7.
26. Joseph Rothschild, *Return to Diversity: A Political History of East Central Europe since World War II* (New York and Oxford: Oxford University Press, 1990), 3.
27. See Barbara Jelavich, *History of the Balkans* (Cambridge: Cambridge University Press, 1983), 35–6, for this insight.
28. Weindling, *Epidemics*, 111; Raymond Pearson, 'Hungary: A State Truncated, a Nation Dismembered', in Dunn and Fraser, *Europe*, 99.
29. Sir John Hope Simpson, 'Refugee Problem' (1938) preliminary report, quoted in Tony Kushner and Katharine Knox, *Refugees in an Age of Genocide* (London: Frank Cass, 1999), 9.

30. Sir John Hope Simpson, *The Refugee Problem: Report of a Survey* (London: Oxford University Press, 1939); Michael Marrus, *The Unwanted: European Refugees in the Twentieth Century* (New York and Oxford: Oxford University Press, 1985), esp. 68–74.

31. Pearson, *National Minorities*, 136.

32. See Alan Sharp, 'Britain and the Protection of Minorities at the Paris Peace Conference 1919', in A. C. Hepburn, ed., *Minorities in History* (London: Edward Arnold, 1978), 180–4.

33. S. Poliakov, quoted in Levene, *War*, 185.

34. See Brian Porter, *When Nationalism Begins to Hate: Imagining Modern Politics in Nineteenth-Century Poland* (Oxford and New York: Oxford University Press, 2000), esp. 176–82, 227–32; T. David Curp, 'Roman Dmowski Understood: Ethnic Cleansing as Permanent Revolution', *European Historical Quarterly*, 35:3 (2005), 405–27.

35. Porter, *When Nationalism*, 229–31, for Dmowski's seminal 1902 essay on the subject.

36. See Levene, *War*, 201–3.

37. The official figure, according to the 1921 census, was 7.8 per cent in the new Poland but it has been suggested that it should be adjusted up to 10 per cent, as the lower figure only referred to those who had given their 'nationality' as Jews (i.e. not their religion or background). See Joseph Marcus, *Social and Political History of the Jews in Poland, 1919–1939* (Berlin: Mouton, 1983), 16–17.

38. Levene, *War*, 202, for Wolf memorandum on the Polish Jewish question, 3 October 1918.

39. Zeman, *Diplomatic History*, 340–3.

40. See Sherman David Spector, *Rumania and the Paris Peace Conference: A Study of the Diplomacy of Ioan I.C. Bratianu* (New York: Bookman Associates, 1962), 228.

41. Levene, *War*, 250–1.

42. See Oscar I. Janowsky, *The Jews and Minority Rights (1898–1919)* (New York: Columbia University Press, 1933), 273; Levene, *War*, 217–18.

43. Levene, *War*, 210–11.

44. Levene, *War*, 212.

45. Jozef Lewandowski, 'History and Myth: Pinsk, April 1919', *Polin*, 2 (1987), 5–36; Fink, *Defending the Rights*, 173–86, for close analysis of these events.

46. See Norman Davies, 'Great Britain and the Polish Jews, 1918–1920', *Journal of Contemporary History*, 8:2 (1973), 132, 139; Cyrus Adler and Aaron A. Margalith, *With Firmness in the Right: American Diplomatic Action Affecting Jews, 1840–1945* (New York: American Jewish Committee, 1946), 150–61. Also *Report of Sir Stuart Samuel on his Mission to Poland, Presented to Parliament by Command of His Majesty*, CMD 674 (London: His Majesty's Stationery Office, 1920).

47. Quoted in Levene, *War*, 294.

48. Levene, *War*, 212.

59. Davies, 'Great Britain', 129, 141.

50. See Levene, *War*, 239–40.

51. Fink, *Defending the Rights*, 232–5.

52. Agnes Headlam-Morley, Russell Bryant, and Anna Cienciala, eds., *Sir James Headlam-Morley: A Memoir of the Paris Peace Conference, 1919–20* (London: Methuen & Co., 1972), 112–13: diary extract, *c.*18 May 1919.

53. Headlam-Morley, et al., *Sir James Headlam-Morley*, 113.

54. See Levene, *War*, 312, for Polish Minority Treaty Article 2.

55. Fink, *Defending the Rights*, 260; Steiner, *The Lights*, 86.

56. Sharp, 'Britain', 182.

57. See H. W. V. Temperley, *A History of the Paris Peace Conference* (London: Hodder & Stoughton, 1921), vol. 5, 137.

58. Quoted in Fink, *Defending the Rights*, 297.

69. Geoff Eley, 'Remapping the Nation: War, Revolutionary Upheaval and State Formation in Eastern Europe, 1914–23', in Howard Aster and Peter J. Potichnyi, eds., *Ukrainian–Jewish Relations in Historical Perspective* (Edmonton: Canadian Institute of Ukrainian Studies, 2nd edn, 1990), 290.

60. *Report of Sir Stuart Samuel*, 6.

61. Arno J. Mayer, *The Furies: Violence and Terror in the French and Russian Revolutions* (Princeton: Princeton University Press, 2000), 525.

62. Quoted in Levene, 'Frontiers', in Panayi, *Minorities*, 103.

63. Prusin, *Nationalising a Borderland*, 86.

64. Levene, 'Frontiers', in Panayi, *Minorities*, 102.

65. See Prusin, *Nationalising a Borderland*, 84–91, for details. See also, however, Leszek Tomaszewski, 'Pinsk, Saturday 5 April 1919', *Polin*, 1 (1986), 227–51, who puts the figure at 'some fifty' dead.

66. Prusin, *Nationalising a Borderland*, 85–6, 91.

67. See Šarūnas Liekis, *A State within a State? Jewish Autonomy in Lithuania, 1918–1925* (Vilna: Versus Aureus, 2003); Henry Abramson, *A Prayer for the Government: Ukrainians and Jews in Revolutionary Times, 1917–1920* (Cambridge, MA: Harvard University Press, 1999), 34–40.

68. See Arnold Margolin, *From a Political Diary: Russia, The Ukraine and America, 1905–1945* (New York: Columbia University Press 1946), esp. 46–7, for something of the flavour of these efforts.

69. See Katz, *Holocaust in Historical Context*, 162–5, for a demographic assessment of this disaster.

70. Quoted in Anna Reid, *Borderland: A Journey through the History of Ukraine* (London: Weidenfeld & Nicolson, 1997), 101.

71. For the intense debate about Petliura and his responsibility or otherwise for the Ukrainian pogroms see Taras Hunczak, 'A Reappraisal of Symon Petliura and Ukrainian–Jewish Relations, 1917–21', and Zosa Szajkowski, 'A Rebuttal', *Jewish Social Studies*, 31 (1969), 163–83 and 184–213, respectively. Also Abramson, *A Prayer*, 136–8.

72. Mayer, *Furies*, 381; Lieberman, *Terrible Fate*, 142.

73. Quoted in Poliakov, *History*, vol. 4, 175.

74. Quoted in Elias Heifetz, *The Slaughter of the Jews in the Ukraine in 1919* (New York: Thomas Seltzer, 1921), 244; also Poliakov, *History*, vol. 4, 183.

75. Quoted in Poliakov, *History*, vol. 4, 183–4.

76. Greg King and Penny Wilson, *The Fate of the Romanovs* (Hoboken, NJ: John Wiley & Sons, 2003), 352–3; Poliakov, *History*, vol. 4, 182.

77. For more on Knox and the other officers involved, see Richard M. Ullman, *Britain and the Russian Civil War, November 1918–February 1920* (Princeton: Princeton University Press, 1968), 30, 113–14; Levene, *War*, 54, 243–5; *Russia, No.1*, nos. 38, 45.

78. Heifetz, *The Slaughter*, 121. Levene, 'Frontiers', in Panayi, *Minorities*, 105.

79. Fink, *Defending the Rights*, 226–30, for the scope of Haller's excesses.

80. Prusin, *Nationalising a Borderland*, 107.

81. Quoted in Antony Polonsky and Michael Riff, 'Poles, Czechoslovaks and the "Jewish Question" 1914–1921: A Comparative Study', in Berghahn and Kitchen, *Germany*, 79.

82. Prusin, *Nationalising a Borderland*, 117.

83. Norman Davies, *White Eagle, Red Star: The Polish–Soviet War, 1919–20* (London: MacDonald, 1972), 162–3; Polonsky and Riff, 'Poles', 80–1.

84. See, for instance, Šarūnas Leikis, Lidia Miliakova, and Antony Polonsky, 'Three Documents on Anti-Jewish Violence in the Eastern Kresy during the Polish–Soviet Conflict', *Polin*, 14 (2001), 116–49.

85. Polonsky and Riff, 'Poles', 75; Levene, 'Frontiers', in Panayi, *Minorities*, 102.

86. See Reeva S. Simon, 'The Education of an Iraqi Ottoman Officer', in Khalidi, et al., *Origins*, 179–81.

87. According to Josef Halmi in 1922, as cited in Gerwarth, 'Central European Counter-Revolution', 199.

88. Gerwarth, 'Central European Counter-Revolution', 187–91, 203–6.

89. Gerwarth, 'Central European Counter-Revolution', 198–203.

90. Gerwarth, 'Central European Counter-Revolution', 203.

91. Gerwarth, 'Central European Counter-Revolution', 176–8, for further details. Significantly, Gerwarth, in his original MS, described this as an attempt to create a 'White International'.

92. Palmer, *Lands Between*, 163.

93. Gerwarth, 'Central European Counter-Revolution', 16.

94. See John W. Thompson, *Russia, Bolshevism and the Versailles Peace* (Princeton: Princeton University Press, 1966), 348.

95. See Chapter 1, 64–5.

96. See Hans Rogger, 'The Formation of the Russian Right, 1900–1906', *California Slavic Studies*, 3 (1964), 66–94.

97. See Poliakov, *History*, vol. 4, 82, 185–6.

98. Kiev Pogrom Relief Committee, 1920, quoted in Levene, 'Frontiers', in Panayi, *Minorities*, 104.

99. See Abramson, *A Prayer*, 122, 126–31; Heifetz, *The Slaughter*, 45–7.

100. Mayer, *Furies*, 517.

101. Heifetz, *The Slaughter*, 46.

102. Heifetz, *The Slaughter*, 243–5; Mayer, *Furies*, 518.

103. 'Kievan Echo', quoted in Bruce W. Lincoln, *Red Victory: A History of the Russian Civil War* (New York: Simon & Schuster, 1989), 323.

104. Mayer, *Furies*, 522; Lieberman, *Terrible Fate*, 145.

105. Peter Kenez, 'Pogroms and White Ideology in the Russian Civil War', in Klier and Lambroza, *Pogroms*, 307–8; Poliakov, *History*, vol. 4, 186. One is reminded here of the CUP 'twin-track' orders for the 1915 Armenian dispatch.

106. Mayer, *Furies*, 525.

107. Mayer, *Furies*, 524.

108. Zvi Y. Gitelman, *Jewish Nationality and Soviet Politics: The Jewish Sections of the CPSU 1917–1930* (Princeton: Princeton University Press, 1972), 114–19, 163–8.

109. Quoted in Mayer, *Furies*, 253.

110. Quoted in Robert Conquest, *Harvest of Sorrow: Soviet Collectivisation and the Terror-Famine* (London: Hutchinson, 1985), 24.

111. Conquest, *Harvest of Sorrow*, 53–4; Robert W. Thurston, *Life and Terror in Stalin's Russia 1934–1941* (New Haven, CT, and London: Yale University Press 1996), 1–2; Robert Bidelux, *Communism and Development* (London and New York: Methuen, 1985), 81, for slightly different assessments on this score.

112. Moshe Lewin, *The Making of the Soviet System: Essays on the Social History of Interwar Russia* (London and New York: Methuen, 1985), 210.

113. Prusin, *Nationalising a Borderland*, 20–1; Peter Holquist, *Making War, Forging Revolution: Russia's Continuum of Crisis, 1914–1921* (Cambridge, MA: Harvard University Press, 2002), 24.

114. Reignol'd, 6 July 1919, quoted in Holquist, *Making War*, 166.

115. Holquist, *Making War*, 203.

116. Holquist, *Making War*, 187, n. 81. Also Peter Holquist, '"Conduct Merciless, Mass Terror": Decossackisation in the Don, 1919', *Cahiers du monde russe*, 38:1–2 (1997), 128. See also Walter Laqueur, *Black Hundred: The Rise of the Extreme Right in Russia* (New York: Harper Perennial, 1993), 195–6.

117. See Schapiro, 'The Role of the Jews.

118. George Katkov, *Russia, 1917: The February Revolution* (London: Harper & Row, 1967), 61.

119. V. I. Lenin, *Selected Works* (Moscow: Progress Publishers, 1977), vol. 1, 44.

120. Lynn T. White III, *Policies of Chaos: The Organizational Causes of Violence in China's Cultural Revolution* (Princeton: Princeton University Press, 1989), 312.

121. See Alec Nove, *An Economic History of the USSR* (London: Penguin, 1969), 45.

122. Isaac Deutscher, *The Prophet Armed: Trotsky, 1879–1921* (New York and London: Oxford, University Press, 1954), 508–9.

123. See Mayer, *Furies*, for an example of the former; Richard Pipes, notably his *Russia under the Bolshevik Regime 1919–1924* (London: Harvill, 1994), and the oeuvre of Robert Conquest as examples of the latter.

124. Holquist, 'State Violence', 156.

125. Amir Weiner, *Making Sense of War: The Second World War and the Fate of the Bolshevik Revolution* (Princeton and Oxford: Princeton University Press, 2001), 365.

126. Zygmunt Bauman, 'The Camps: Eastern, Western, Modern', in Frankel, *Fate*, 32–3.

127. The terminology of Ron Aronson. See discussion in Levene, *Meaning*, 185–6.

128. Mayer, *Furies*, 376.

129. See John Ellis, *Armies in Revolution* (London: Croom Helm, 1973), ch. 7, 'The Russian Civil War, 1917–20'.

130. See E. H. Carr, 'The Origins and Status of the Cheka', *Soviet Studies*, 10:1 (1958), 1–11; George Leggett, *The Cheka: Lenin's Political Police, the All-Russian Extraordinary Commission for Combating Counterrevolution and Sabotage (December 1917 to February, 1922)* (Oxford: Clarendon Press, 1981).

131. See E. H. Carr, *The Bolshevik Revolution 1917–1923* (London: Macmillan, 1950), vol. 1, ch. 7, 'Consolidating the Dictatorship'.

132. See Mayer, *Furies*, 135.

133. Mayer, *Furies*, 272–4, 279–80.

134. Holquist, 'State Violence', 131.

135. Quoted in Nikolai Tolstoy, *Stalin's Secret War* (London: Pan Books, 1982), 25. Also Weitz, *A Century*, 61.

136. Anne Applebaum, *Gulag: A History of the Soviet Camps* (London: Penguin, 2003), 29.

137. Alexander M. Yakovlev, *A Century of Violence in Soviet Russia*, trans. Anthony Austin (New Haven, CT, and London: Yale University Press, 2002), 34.

138. As quoted in Holquist, 'Conduct Merciless, Mass Terror', 134. See also Holquist, *Making War*, 180, for full text.

139. Holquist, *Making War*, 180.

140. Holquist, 'Conduct Merciless, Mass Terror', 147.

141. Holquist, 'Conduct Merciless, Mass Terror', 132.

142. See Albert Seaton, *The Horsemen of the Steppes: The Story of the Cossacks* (London: The Bodley Head, 1985); Philip Longworth, *The Cossacks* (London: Constable, 1969); Robert H. McNeal, *Tsar and Cossack 1855–1914* (Basingstoke: Palgrave Macmillan, 1987).
143. Peter Holquist, 'A Russian Vendée: The Practice of Revolutionary Politics in the Don Countryside', unpublished PhD dissertation, Columbia University, 1995, 418–19.
144. Holquist, *Making War*, 7–10; Holquist, 'Conduct Merciless, Mass Terror', 133.
145. Hosking, *Russia*, 12; see also Holquist, *Making War*, 70.
146. Holquist, 'Russian Vendée', 105.
147. Holquist, 'Russian Vendée', 126, n. 42; 327.
148. Holquist, *Making War*, 115.
149. Holquist, 'Russian Vendée', 110.
150. Laqueur, *Black Hundred*, 195.
151. Holquist, 'Conduct Merciless, Mass Terror', 128.
152. Holquist, 'Russian Vendée', 215, 224.
153. Holquist, 'Russian Vendée', 499–500.
154. Holquist, *Making War*, 190–1.
155. Holquist, *Making War*, 197.
156. Holquist, *Making War*, 189.
157. Holquist, *Making War*, 184.
158. Holquist, *Making War*, 184–5; Yakovlev, *Century*, 101.
159. Polian, *Against their Will*, 59–60.
160. Quoted in Yakovlev, *Century*, 89.
161. Quoted in Weitz, *A Century*, 69.
162. See Levene, *Rise of the West*, 154; Holquist, *Making War*, 254–6.
163. The terminology is that of Claude Mazauric, pointing to the spectre of a genuinely people–peasant war. See Mayer, *Furies*, 7, 18, n. 21.
164. See Lewin, *Making*, ch. 5, 'Who was the Soviet Kulak?' for Bolshevik categorization of the peasantry.
165. Oliver H. Radkey, *The Unknown Civil War in Soviet Russia: A Study of the Green Movement in the Tambov Region 1920–21* (Stanford, CA: Hoover Institute Press, 1976), 197.
166. Radkey, *Unknown Civil War*, 406.
167. Radkey, *Unknown Civil War*, 319–21.
168. Radkey, *Unknown Civil War*, 190–1. Also Delano Dugarm, 'Peasant Wars in Tambov Province', in Vladimir N. Brovkin, ed., *The Bolsheviks in Russian Society: The Revolution and the Civil Wars* (New Haven, CT, and London: Yale University Press 1997), 186–7, for the independence of the 'Union of Toiling Peasantry' grouping.
169. Radkey, *Unknown Civil War*, 319–24, for details.
170. See Holquist, *Making War*, 273–5, for further discussion. Also Levene, *Rise of the West*, 159–60 for the French Vendée comparison.
171. Cited in Vladimir N. Brovkin, *Behind the Front Lines of the Civil War: Political Parties and Social Movements in Russia, 1918–1922* (Princeton: Princeton University Press, 1994), 384.
172. Radkey, *Unknown Civil War*, 301, 79.
173. Radkey, *Unknown Civil War*, 216.
174. Holquist, 'To Count', 131. Also see citation in Taisa Osipova, 'Peasant Rebellions: Origin, Scope, Dynamic and Consequences', in Brovkin, *The Bolsheviks*, 172.
175. Radkey, *Unknown Civil War*, 236–7, 263.

176. See Holquist, 'To Count'; Mayer, *Furies*, 395. Dugarm, 'Peasant Wars', 192, posits that the poison gas proved technically difficult to properly deploy.
177. Holquist, 'State Violence', 140–1; Radkey, *Unknown Civil War*, 232, 265–6.
178. Holquist, *Making War*, 277; Radkey, *Unknown Civil War*, 225–6.
179. Holquist, *Making War*, 277.
180. Radkey, *Unknown Civil War*, 271; Dugarm, 'Peasant Wars', 190–1.
181. Radkey, *Unknown Civil War*, 324; Yakovlev, *Century*, 90; Mayer, *Furies*, 394–5.
182. Radkey, *Unknown Civil War*, 329–31, 347. See also Alexander Statiev, *The Soviet Counter-Insurgency in the Western Borderlands* (Cambridge: Cambridge University Press, 2010), 19, for one particular egregious instance of hostage massacre of both men and women in the village of Parevka.
183. Radkey, *Unknown Civil War*, 268.
184. See Holquist, 'To Count', 130.
185. See Mayer, *Furies*, 307; Brovkin, *Behind the Front Lines*, 346.
186. Mayer, *Furies*, 310, for assessment of the fatality figures.
187. Mayer, *Furies*, 254.
188. Holquist, 'To Count', 129.
189. Reynolds, 'Ottoman–Russian Struggle', 258–9.
190. Bloxham, *Great Game*, 141.
191. For general background see Kedourie, *England and the Middle East*; Christopher M. Andrew and A. S. Kanya-Forstner, *The Climax of French Imperial Expansion 1914–1924* (Stanford, CA: Stanford University Press, 1981).
192. See John Fisher, *Curzon and British Imperialism in the Middle East 1916–1919* (London and Portland, OR: Frank Cass, 1999).
193. Mango, *Atatürk*, 213; Fromkin, *Peace*, 355–6.
194. Gingeras, *Sorrowful Shores*, 94–106, 118–38, on growing Circassian restiveness versus Turkish national intentions.
195. Reynolds, 'Ottoman–Russian Struggle', 361, 582.
196. Quoted in Ahmad, *Kurdistan*, 192.
197. Quoted in Richard G. Hovannisian, 'The Armenian Genocide and US Post-war Commissions', in Winter, *America*, 261.
198. Quoted in M. E. Yapp, *The Making of the Modern Near East, 1792–1923* (London and New York: Longman, 1987), 93. See also Joseph, *The Nestorians*, 149.
199. Arnold J. Toynbee, *Survey of International Affairs, 1920–1923* (London: Oxford, University Press, 1925), 373–4.
200. Van Bruinessen, *Agha*, 269.
201. Hovannisian, *Armenia, On the Road*, 194.
202. Reynolds, 'Ottoman–Russian Struggle', 377; McCarthy, *Death and Exile*, 198–200; Sonyel, *Great War*, 161–3.
203. McCarthy, *Death and Exile*, 210; Sonyel, *Great War*, 164.
204. Hovannisian, *Armenia, On the Road*, 194, 197.
205. Quoted in Lieberman, *Terrible Fate*, 136. See also McCarthy, *Death and Exile*, 224–5.
206. Bloxham, *Great Game*, 152–4.
207. Moranian, 'Bearing Witness', esp. 198–9. See also Harry J. Psomiades, 'The American Near East Relief (NER) and the *Megale Katastrophe* in 1922', in Hofmann, Bjørnlund, and Meichanetsidis, *Genocide*, 265–76.
208. Hovannisian, 'The Armenian Genocide and US Post-war Commissions', 265–70.
209. Akçam, 'Another History', 284, 289, for these ongoing tendencies.

210. Sonyel, *Great War*, 166; Reynolds, 'Ottoman–Russian Struggle', 475; Hovannisian, *Armenia, On the Road*, 227.

211. See Zürcher, *Unionist Factor*, 168.

212. Mango, *Atatürk*, 214–5.

213. Mango, *Atatürk*, 211.

214. Quoted in Üngör, 'Reign of Terror', 102.

215. Quoted in Hofmann and Koutcharian, 'History', 38.

216. Quoted in Walker, *Armenia*, 305. See also Shaw and Shaw, *History*, vol. 2, 346, for more on Harbord.

217. Cited in Dadrian, 'Role of Turkish Military', 282.

218. Llewellyn Smith, *Ionian Vision*, 67–8.

219. Mango, *Atatürk*, 212.

220. Llewellyn Smith, *Ionian Vision*, 46–7.

221. Toynbee, *Western Question*, 70; Llewellyn Smith, *Ionian Vision*, 71–2.

221. Llewellyn Smith, *Ionian Vision*, 74–80.

223. Cited in Llewellyn Smith, *Ionian Vision*, 81.

224. Toynbee, *Western Question*, 271–3; Llewellyn Smith, *Ionian Vision*, 88–91.

225. Toynbee, *Western Question*, 273; Llewellyn Smith, *Ionian Vision*, 208.

226. Mango, *Atatürk*, 210–13.

227. Mango, *Atatürk*, 212, 282–3, 301–2. See Gingeras, *Sorrowful Shores*, 138–48, however, for a more complex reading of Circassian grievances against the *kuva-yi milliye*.

228. See Llewellyn Smith, *Ionian Vision*, 123–8.

229. Quoted in Bloxham, *Great Game*, 155.

230. See Toynbee, *Western Question*, 275–6, 289–92; Renée Hirschon, '"Unmixing Peoples" in the Aegean Region', in Renée Hirschon, ed., *Crossing the Aegean: An Appraisal of the 1923 Compulsory Population Exchange between Greece and Turkey*, Studies in Forced Migration, vol. 12 (New York and Oxford: Berghahn, 2003), 5; McCarthy, *Death and Exile*, 287–8.

231. McCarthy, *Death and Exile*, 326, n. 138. McCarthy's estimates, as a general rule, emphasize Muslim fatalities as against Christian ones.

232. Toynbee, *Western Question*, 291.

233. See Llewellyn Smith, *Ionian Vision*, 91–101, for a portrait and assessment of Stergiadis' rule.

234. Mango, *Atatürk*, 329. See also McCarthy, *Death and Exile*, 278.

235. Toynbee, *Western Question*, 284–5; Gingeras, *Sorrowful Shores*, 111–13, for corroboration.

236. Toynbee, *Western Question*, 308–9, 299–311, for a full account.

237. Llewellyn Smith, *Ionian Vision*, 168.

238. Llewellyn Smith, *Ionian Vision*, 205.

239. Llewellyn Smith, *Ionian Vision*, 205; Toynbee, *Western Question*, 100.

240. Llewellyn Smith, *Ionian Vision*, 128–9.

241. Llewellyn Smith, *Ionian Vision*, 112.

242. Toynbee, *Western Question*, 61.

243. Walker, *Armenia*, 301–2; Marjorie Housepian, *Smyrna 1922: The Destruction of a City* (London: Faber, 1972), 87–9.

244. See Robert Farrer Zeidner, 'The Tricolor over the Taurus: The French in Cilicia and Vicinity, 1918–1922', unpublished PhD dissertation, University of Utah, 1991.

245. Llewellyn Smith, *Ionian Vision*, 163–4.

246. Llewellyn Smith, *Ionian Vision*, 215.

247. Walker, *Armenia*, 301–2; Housepian, *Smyrna*, 224–6. More generally, William Stivers, *Supremacy and Oil: Iraq, Turkey and the Anglo-American World Order, 1918–1930* (Ithaca, NY, and London: Cornell University Press, 1982).

248. Lloyd E. Ambrosius, 'Wilsonian Diplomacy and Armenia: The Limits of Power and Ideology', in Winter, *America*, 142.

249. Dadrian, 'Naim-Andonian Documents', 336; Bloxham, *Great Game*, 163. A larger group seems to have been mysteriously allowed to escape. The move would lead ultimately to a 'Declaration of Amnesty in the Treaty of Lausanne encompassing all offences committed between 1 August 1914 and 20 November 1922'. William A. Schabas, *Genocide in International Law: The Crime of Crimes* (Cambridge: Cambridge University Press, 2000), 22.

250. Mango, *Atatürk*, 294.

251. Mango, *Atatürk*, 294–5.

252. Toynbee, *Western Question*, 62.

253. See Llewellyn Smith, *Ionian Vision*, 209; Toynbee, *Western Question*, 276.

254. See Naimark, *Fires*, 46–7.

255. Naimark, *Fires*, 47–53, for eyewitness accounts. Llewellyn Smith, *Ionian Vision*, ch. 13, 'Catastrophe'. Also Housepian, *Smyrna*, chs 8–20.

256. Quoted in Naimark *Fires*, 51. See also Lieberman, *Terrible Fate*, 130.

257. Llewellyn Smith, *Ionian Vision*, 306–7.

258. Llewellyn Smith, *Ionian Vision*, 307–8.

259. Quoted in Llewellyn Smith, *Ionian Vision*, 310. See also Nikolaos Hlamides, 'The Smyrna Holocaust: The Final Phase of the Greek Genocide', in Hofman, Bjørnlund, and Meichanetsidis, *Genocide*, 195–244, for an extensive range of eyewitness accounts and photographic evidence.

260. See Naimark, *Fires*, 52.

261. Quoted in Llewellyn Smith, *Ionian Vision*, 115. See also Toynbee, *Western Question*, 69–70.

262. See Brubaker, *Nationalism Reframed*, 152.

263. Justin McCarthy, *The Ottoman Peoples and the End of Empire* (London: Hodder Headline Group, 2001), 146–7.

264. Elisabeth Kontogiorgi, 'Economic Consequences following Refugee Settlement in Greek Macedonia, 1923–1932', in Hirschon, *Crossing the Aegean*, 63.

265. McCarthy, *Death and Exile*, 304.

266. See Shaw and Shaw, *History*, vol. 2, 377; Mango, *Atatürk*, 387–8, for positive commentary.

267. Hirschon, 'Appendix', *Crossing the Aegean*, for text.

268. See Michael Barutciski, 'Lausanne Revisited: Population Exchanges in International Law and Policy', in Hirschon, *Crossing the Aegean*, 28–9, for commentary and analysis.

269. As quoted in Matthew Frank, 'Fantasies of Ethnic Unmixing: "Population Transfer" and the End of Empire', 7, unpublished paper presented at 'Conference on Refugees and the End of Empire', De Montfort University, 29 June 2007. With thanks to Dr Frank for providing a copy.

270. A. Dirk Moses, 'Partitions, Population "Transfer" and the Question of Human Rights and Genocide in the 1930s and 1940's', unpublished conference paper, significantly elaborates on this theme. With thanks to Dr Moses for a copy.

271. Thanos Veremis, '1922: Political Continuations and Realignments in the Greek State', in Hirschon, *Crossing the Aegean*, 57.

272. Ayhan Aktar, 'Homogenising the Nation, Turkifying the Economy: The Turkish Experience of Population Exchange Reconsidered', in Hirschon, *Crossing the Aegean*, 93–4.

Also Alexis Alexandris, 'Religion or Ethnicity: The Identity Issue of the Minorities in Greece and Turkey', in Hirschon, *Crossing the Aegean*, 124.

273. Aktar, 'Homogenising the Nation', 88; Hirschon, 'Preface', *Crossing the Aegean*, xii.
274. Veremis, '1922: Political Continuations', 61.
275. Bernard Lewis, *The Emergence of Modern Turkey* (London: Oxford University Press, 2nd edn, 1968), 355, also notes the 'nonsensicalness' of the groups exchanged.
276. Çağaptay, 'Crafting the Turkish Nation', 48–9.
277. Çağaptay, 'Crafting the Turkish Nation', 459.
278. See Bruce Clark, *Twice a Stranger: How Mass Expulsion Forged Modern Greece and Turkey* (London: Granta Books, 2006), 163–4.
279. See Marc David Baer, *The Dönme: Jewish Converts, Muslim Revolutionaries and Secular Turks* (Stanford, CA: Stanford University Press, 2010), ch. 6, 'Losing a Homeland, 1923–24'.
280. Çağaptay, 'Crafting the Turkish Nation', 172. Also Gingeras, *Sorrowful Shores*, 47–51, 148–65, for ongoing Turkish distrust and anxieties about Albanians in general.
281. Aktar, 'Homogenising the Nation', 88.
282. See Naimark, *Fires*, 54–5.
283. Quoted in Barutciski, 'Lausanne Revisited', 29.
284. Marrus, *Unwanted*, 86–91, 101–6, for Nansen's critical role.
285. Barutciski, 'Lausanne Revisited', 28, for exact numbers.
286. See Pentzopoulos, *The Balkan Exchange*, 257–63, for the Convention text.
287. See Penny Sinanoglou, 'The Peel Commission and Partition, 1936–1938', in Rory Miller, ed., *Britain, Palestine and Empire: The Mandate Years* (Aldershot: Ashgate 2010), 119–40, for a recent assessment.
288. Polian, *Against their Will*, 27.
289. Barutciski, 'Lausanne Revisited', 28.
290. Barutciski, 'Lausanne Revisited', 26.
291. Veremis, '1922: Political Continuations', 57.
292. Frank, 'Fantasies', in Panayi and Virdee, *Refugees*, 89–92, for further commentary on George Montandon's *Frontières nationales* (1916).
293. See Hovannisian, 'The Armenian Genocide and US Post-war Commissions', 264.
294. See Thomas Turner, *The Congo Wars: Conflict, Myth and Reality* (New York and London: Zed Books, 2007), 81, for discussion.
295. See Levene, *Rise of the West*, esp. 293–302, 313–14.
296. Bloxham, *Great Game*, 159–60.
297. Mark Mazower, *Dark Continent: Europe's Twentieth Century* (London: Penguin Press, 1998), 53.
298. See McCarthy, *The Ottoman Peoples*, 156–7; C. A. Macartney, *National States and National Minorities* (Oxford: Oxford University Press, 1934), 444.
299. Renée Hirschon, 'Consequences of the Lausanne Convention: An Overview', in Hirschon, *Crossing the Aegean*, 14–15; McCarthy, *Death and Exile*, 302.
300. Llewellyn Smith, *Ionian Vision*, 280–1.

CHAPTER 4

1. Quoted in Moses, 'Holocaust and Genocide', 536.
2. See Daniel Marc Segesser and Myriam Gessler, 'Raphael Lemkin and the International Debate on the Punishment of War Crimes (1919–1948)', *JGR*, 7:4 (2005), 457–8; Schabas, *Genocide*, 26.
3. Vladimir Zeev Jabotinsky, '"The Iron Wall": 4 November 1923', in Itamar Rabinovich and Jehuda Reinharz, eds., *Israel in the Middle East: Documents and Readings on Society,*

Politics, and Foreign Relations, Pre-1948 to the Present (Waltham, MA: Brandeis University Press, 2008), 41–3.

4. Levene, 'Moving Target', 4, for both Assyrian articulation of this aspiration and Zionist knock-on effects.

5. See Levene, *Rise of the West*, 174–6.

6. Moses, 'Holocaust and Genocide', 536.

7. Quoted in Christopher Sykes, *Crossroads to Israel* (London: Collins, 1965), 202.

8. Daniele Conversi, '"We are all equals!": Militarism, Homogenization and Egalitarianism in National State Building (1789–1945)', *Ethnic and Racial Studies*, 31:7 (2008), 1300.

9. See Leo Kuper, *Genocide: Its Political Use in the Twentieth Century* (New Haven, CT, and London: Yale University Press, 1982), title of ch. 10.

10. Italian fascism in its broader colonial behaviour would necessarily include discussion of genocide. But this would put it more accurately in the company of other 'liberal' Western powers in their imperial pursuits. See Levene, *Rise of the West*, 275–6.

11. Misha Glenny, *The Balkans 1804–1999: Nationalism, War and the Great Powers* (London: Granta Books, 1999), 396.

12. See discussion in Conversi, 'We are all equals', 1295–9.

13. Irina Livezeanu, *Cultural Politics in Greater Romania: Regionalism, Nation Building and Ethnic Struggle, 1918–1930* (Ithaca, NY, and London: Cornell University Press, 1995), 'Conclusion'.

14. Quoted in Mann, *Dark Side*, 63.

15. See Ivo Banac and Katherine Vedery, eds., *National Character and National Ideology in Interwar Europe* (New Haven, CT: Yale Center for International and Area Studies, 1995), 81, for more on this theme.

16. Derek H. Aldcroft and Steven Morewood, *Economic Change in Eastern Europe since 1918* (Aldershot and Brookfield, VT: E. Elgar, 1995), 53, for more on this theme.

17. See Katherine Vedery, *National Ideology under Socialism: Identity and Cultural Politics in Ceauşescu's Romania* (Berkeley: University of California Press, 1991), 57, for this terminology.

18. Raoul Giradet, *La Société militaire dans la France contemporaine, 1815–1939* (Paris: Librarie Plon, 1953), 169. See, more generally, Eugen Weber, *Peasants into Frenchmen: The Modernization of Rural France 1870–1914* (Stanford, CA: Stanford University Press, 1976).

19. Anderson, *Imagined Communities*, for more on this line of approach.

20. Anthony W. Marx, *Faith in Nation: The Exclusionary Origins of Nationalism* (Oxford and New York: Oxford University Press, 2003).

21. Mazower, *Dark Continent*, 58.

22. Kushner and Knox, *Refugees*, 82–3. Population pressure as a cause of war, and hence the movement of refugees outside Europe, continued to be advocated by the likes of Albert Thomas. See Marrus, *Unwanted*, 114–15.

23. Donald Bloxham and Tony Kushner, *The Holocaust: Critical Historical Approaches* (Manchester and New York: Manchester University Press, 2005), 62.

24. See, for instance, Gregory Michaelidis, 'Salvation Abroad: Macedonian Migration to North America and the Making of Modern Macedonia, 1870–1970', upublished dissertation, University of Maryland, 2005 <http://hdl.handle.net/1903/2407>

25. Brubaker, *Nationalism Reframed*, 100; Brown, *Biography*, 39; Jerzy Kochanowski, 'Gathering Poles into Poland: Forced Migration from Poland's Former Eastern Territories', in Phillip Ther and Ana Siljak, eds., *Redrawing Nations: Ethnic Cleansing in East-Central Europe 1944–1948* (Oxford and Lanham, MD: Rowman & Littlefield, 2001), 136.

26. Brailsford, *Macedonia*, quoted in Perry, *Terror*, frontispiece.
27. Albert Hirschman, *Exit, Voice and Loyalty* (Cambridge, MA: Harvard University Press, 1970), for the terminology.
28. Snyder, *Reconstruction*, 139.
29. Snyder, *Reconstruction*, 42, 52–3.
30. E. P. Thompson, *The Making of the English Working Class* (London: Pelican Books, 1968), 13. See also, by way of counterpoint, Robert W. Olson, *The Emergence of Kurdish Nationalism and the Sheikh Said Rebellion, 1880–1925* (Austin: University of Texas Press, 1989), xv, for the notion of people 'denied history'.
31. Paschalis Kitromilides, '"Imagined Communities" and the Origins of the National Question in the Balkans', *European History Quarterly*, 19:2 (1989), 149–92.
32. Noel Malcolm, *Bosnia: A Short History* (London and Basingstoke: Palgrave Macmillan, 1994). 159, 162–3.
33. Livezeanu, *Cultural Politics*, 56, and also 49 for the diverse ethnic composition of the Bukovina region.
34. Livezeanu, *Cultural Politics*, 59.
35. See, for instance, Mann, *Dark Side*, 223–8.
36. Andrew Rossos, 'Macedonianism and Macedonian Nationalism on the Left', in Banac and Vedery, *National Character*, 236.
37. R. J. Crampton, *Eastern Europe in the Twentieth Century* (London and New York: Routledge, 1994), 109.
38. See Livezeanu, *Cultural Politics*, ch. 7, 'The Generation of 1922'. See also Constantin Iordachi, *Charisma, Politics and Violence: The Legion of the 'Archangel Michael' in Inter-War Romania* (Trondheim: Trondheim Studies on East European Cultures and Societies, 2004); Rebecca Haynes, 'Corneliu Zelea Codreanu: The Romanian "New Man"', in Rebecca Haynes, ed., *In the Shadow of Hitler: Personalities of the Right in Central and Eastern Europe* (London: I.B. Tauris, 2011), 169–87.
39. See Stanley G. Payne, *A History of Fascism, 1914–45* (London: UCL Press, 1995), 136–7, for more on Codreanu. Also Gregor von Rezzori, *Memoirs of an Anti-Semite*, trans. Joachim Neugroschel and Gregor von Rezzori (New York: Viking Press, 1981), for further insights into the obsessive nature of Gentile attraction and repulsion towards Jews.
40. Payne, *History*, 271.
41. Conversi, 'We are all equals', 1303.
42. Reynolds, 'Ottoman–Russian Struggle', 517–20, for details.
43. Reynolds, 'Ottoman–Russian Struggle', 530–2.
44. Reynolds, 'Ottoman–Russian Struggle', 536–7.
45. Palmer, *Lands Between*, 178.
46. Toynbee, *Western Question*, 46.
47. Roshwald, *Ethnic Nationalism*, 87–8.
48. Palmer, *Lands Between*, 189–90.
49. See Crampton, *Eastern Europe*, 119–24; Payne, *History*, 133–4; Palmer, *Lands Between*, 180.
50. See Glenny, *Balkans*, 401.
51. Roshwald, *Ethnic Nationalism*, 52. See also 43–5, for further insight on Masaryk.
52. Roshwald, *Ethnic Nationalism*, 52.
53. Roshwald, *Ethnic Nationalism*, 133–8. Ivo Banac, *The National Question in Yugoslavia: Origins, History, Politics* (Ithaca, NY, and London: Cornell University Press, 1984), for the complex process of Yugoslav state formation.

54. Roshwald, *Ethnic Nationalism*, 36.
55. Snyder, *Reconstruction*, 58.
56. Snyder, *Reconstruction*, 68, also 64–5.
57. Snyder, *Reconstruction*, 64–5, 59.
58. Marcus, *Social and Political History*, 16–17, for the ethnic percentages under the 1921 census. A supposed 69.2 per cent 'Polish' majority was held in check by four main other communities, the Ukrainians uppermost with 14.3 per cent of the total.
59. Snyder, *Reconstruction*, 68–70.
60. Crampton, *Eastern Europe*, 43.
61. See Glenny, *Balkans*, 408–12, for vivid details of these events. Also Mark Biondich, *Stjepan Radić, The Croat Peasant Party and the Politics of Mass Mobilization* (Toronto: University of Toronto Press, 2000).
62. See Jill A. Irvine, *The Croat Question: Partisan Politics in the Formation of the Yugoslav Socialist State* (Boulder, CO: Westview Press, 1993), 45.
63. Malcolm, *Kosovo*, 268.
64. Malcolm, *Kosovo*, 279.
65. Stefanović, 'Seeing the Albanians', 478.
66. See Malcolm, *Kosovo*, 278, for some of the estimates, though only through to 1921.
67. Palmer, *Lands Between*, 189–90; Yves Ternon, *L'État criminel: les génocides au XXe siècle* (Paris: Éditions du Seuil, 1995), 380.
68. Greek attitudes, past and largely present, are summed up in the following chapter title by Anastasia Karakasidou, 'Cultural Illegitimacy in Greece: The Slavo-Macedonian "Non-minority"', in Richard Clogg, ed., *Minorities in Greece: Aspects of a Plural Society* (London: Hurst & Co., 2002), 122–64.
69. Roshwald, *Ethnic Nationalism*, 169; Livezeanu, *Cultural Politics*, 7–8.
70. Quoted in Brubaker, *Nationalism Reframed*, 90, n. 22.
71. Brubaker, *Nationalism Reframed*, 103.
72. Snyder, *Reconstruction*, 144–9, for more on this theme.
73. Brubaker, *Nationalism Reframed*, 103.
74. Tomasz D. I. Kamusella, 'Ethnic Cleansing in Silesia 1950–89 and the Ennationalising Policies of Poland and Germany', *Patterns of Prejudice*, 33:2 (1999), 54–7, for the background.
75. Roshwald, *Ethnic Nationalism*, 162–3.
76. Malcolm, *Kosovo*, 10, for this terminology.
77. Palmer, *Lands Between*, 161.
78. Morrow, *Great War*, 264.
79. See István Deák, 'A Fatal Compromise? The Debate over Collaboration and Resistance in Hungary', in István Deák, Jan T. Gross, and Tony Judt, eds., *The Politics of Retribution in Europe: World War II and its Aftermath* (Princeton: Princeton University Press, 2000), 47, 42–3, for commentary.
80. Charles Trevelyan, *From Liberal to Labour* (1921), quoted in Michael Howard, *War and the Liberal Conscience* (London: Temple Smith, 1978), 84.
81. Palmer, *Lands Between*, 154, for the cases of Radić, Hlinka, and the Sudeten Germans.
82. See Victor S. Mamety, 'The Development of Czechoslovak Democracy, 1920–1930', in Victor S. Mamety and Radomir Luza, *A History of the Czech Republic, 1918–1948* (Princeton: Princeton University Press, 1973), 99–166, for an essentially upbeat reading.
83. Ezra Mendelsohn, 'A Note on Jewish Assimilation in the Polish Lands', in Bela Vago, ed., *Jewish Assimilation in Modern Times* (Boulder, CO: Westview, 1981), 145.

84. Jan Tomasz Gross, *Revolution from Abroad: The Soviet Conquest of Poland's Western Ukraine and Western Belorussia* (Princeton: Princeton University Press, [1988] 2002), 6–7.

85. Snyder, *Reconstruction*, ch. 7, 'Galicia and Volhynia at the Margin (1914–1939)'.

86. See Ephraim Nimni, ed., *National–Cultural Autonomy and its Contemporary Critics* (London and New York: Routledge, 2005), for English translation and analysis of Karl Renner, *Der Kampf der österreichischen Nationen um den Staat* (1902).

87. See Uri Ra'anan, Marie Mesner, Keith Ames, and Kate Martin, eds., *State and Nation in Multi-Ethnic Societies: The Breakup of Multinational States* (Manchester: Manchester University Press, 1991), notably Theodor Hanf, 'Reducing Conflict through Cultural Sutonomy: Karl Renner's Contribution', 33–52. Also Tom Bottomore and Patrick Goode, eds., *Austro-Marxism* (Oxford: Clarendon Press, 1978).

88. Roshwald, *Ethnic Nationalism*, 55; Hosking, *Russia*, 386.

89. Roshwald, *Ethnic Nationalism*, 93. Also Levene, *War*, 188–9, 193–4, on the 1917 Lednicki proposals.

90. Mark Levene, 'The Limits of Tolerance: Nation-State Building and What it Means for Minority Groups', *Patterns of Prejudice*, 34:2 (2000), 40.

91. See Johnpoll, *Politics of Futility*.

92. See Donald L. Niewyk, *The Jews in Weimar Germany* (Manchester: Manchester University Press, 1980), esp. 26–38; also Walter Laqueur, *Weimar: A Cultural History, 1918–1933* (London: Weidenfeld & Nicolson, 1974).

93. Fink, *Defending the Rights*, 300.

94. Quoted in Brubaker, *Nationalism Reframed*, 129.

95. Fink, *Defending the Rights*, 278, 282.

96. Brubaker, *Nationalism Reframed*, 90.

97. Fink, *Defending the Rights*, 308. More generally see ch. 10, 'Berlin'.

98. Fink, *Defending the Rights*, 338–40.

99. David Vital, *A People Apart: A Political History of the Jews in Europe, 1789–1939* (Oxford: Oxford University Press, 1999), 800–2.

100. See Brubaker, *Nationalism Reframed*, 129–30.

101. Von Hagen, 'Great War', 34–5.

102. Robert Seely, *Russo-Chechen Conflict, 1800–2000: A Deadly Embrace* (London and Portland, OR: Frank Cass, 2001), 73–4.

103. Martin, 'The Origins', 827.

104. Martin, 'The Origins', 828; Abdurahman Avtorkhanov, 'The Chechens and Ingush during the Soviet Period and its Antecedents', in Marie Beningsen Broxup, ed., *The North Caucasus Barrier: The Russian Advance towards the Muslim World* (London: Hurst & Co., 1992), 154.

105. Sheehy and Nahalyo, *Crimean Tatars*, 18; Eric J. Schmaltz and Samuel D. Sinner, '"You will die under ruins and snow": The Soviet Repression of Russian Germans as a Case Study of Successful Genocide', *JGR*, 4:3 (2002), 328.

106. Martin, 'The Origins', 833. Also Terry Martin, 'An Affirmative Action Empire: The Soviet Union as the Highest Form of Imperialism', in Suny and Martin, *State of Nations*, 71.

107. Avtorkhanov, 'The Chechens', 154; Roshwald, *Ethnic Nationalism*, 179.

108. Fisher, *Crimean Tatars*, 133–4.

109. See Robert Service, *Stalin: A Biography* (Cambridge, MA: Belknap Press, 2005), 96–9.

110. Isaac Deutscher, *Stalin: A Political Biography* (London: Oxford University Press, [1949] 1961), 229.

111. Service, *Stalin*, 201–2.

112. Martin, 'Affirmative Action Empire', 73–4, for fuller development.

113. Martin, 'The Origins', 816. See also Francine Hirsch, *Empire of Nations: Ethnographic Knowledge and the Making of the Soviet Union* (Ithaca, NY, and London: Cornell University Press, 2005); Brown, *Biography*, 40.

114. Martin, 'Affirmative Action Empire', 71–2.

115. See Gitelman, *Jewish Nationality*; Robert Weinberg, 'Jews into Peasants? Solving the Jewish Question in Birobidzhan', in Yaacov Ro'i, ed., *Jews and Jewish Life in Russia and the Soviet Union* (Ilford, Essex, and Portland, OR: Frank Cass, 1995), 87–102.

116. Brubaker, *Nationalism Reframed*, 18.

117. Martin, 'The Origins', 816 (my emphasis).

118. Sheehy and Nahaylo, *Crimean Tatars*, 7.

119. Curtis Richardson, 'Stalinist Terror and the Kalmyks' National Revival: A Cultural and Historical Perspective', *JGR*, 4:3 (2002), 442–3.

120. Deutscher, *Stalin*, 229.

121. Sir Alfred Eckhard Zimmern, *Nationality and Government, with Other War-Time Essays* (London: Chatto & Windus, 1919), 53.

122. Brubaker, *Nationalism Reframed*, 18.

123. Fisher, *Crimean Tatars*, 139.

124. Percy T. Etherton, *In the Heart of Asia* (London: Constable & Co., 1925), 151. Alf Harald Brun, *Troublous Times: Experiences in Bolshevik Russia and Turkestan* (Constable & Co., 1931), for eyewitness accounts of some of these events. On the Armenian detachments see Andrea Graziosi, *The Great Soviet Peasant War: Bolsheviks and Peasants 1917–1933* (Cambridge, MA: Harvard University Press, 1996), 15.

125. Holquist, 'To Count', 111.

126. Stefanonvić, 'Seeing the Albanians', 479.

127. Quoted in McDowall, *Modern History*, 200. See also Üngör, *The Making*, 139, for full text as conveyed by Britain's ambassador in Ankara to London.

128. Welat Zeydanlioglu, 'The Kurds, the Turkish State and the Making of the Turkish Nation', unpublished paper presented at 'Conference on Refugees and the End of Empire', De Montfort University, 29 June 2007, 1. Thanks to Dr Zeydanlioglu for providing a copy.

129. Livezeanu, *Cultural Politics*, 58, 139.

130. See Avtorkhanov, 'The Chechens'.

131. Olson, *Emergence*, 161. In fact, considering the thirteen major incidents reported by Army Staff HQ between May 1925 (after Shaikh Said) and November 1930, the concentration in the Ararat area is even more marked. See Çağaptay, 'Crafting the Turkish Nation', 9.

132. Donald Bloxham, 'Changing Perceptions of State Violence: The Turkish Case', in Bloxham, *Genocide, the World Wars*, 201. Also Mark Levene, 'Creating a Modern "Zone of Genocide": The Impact of Nation and State Formation on Eastern Anatolia, 1878–1923', *HGS*, 12 (1998), 409, for a similar commentary.

133. See Mango, *Atatürk*, chs 20–2; Patrick Kinross, *Atatürk: The Rebirth of a Nation* (London: Phoenix Giant, [1964] 1993), 384–7, 411–17.

134. Reynolds, 'Ottoman–Russian Struggle', 605; Lewis, *Emergence*, 103, citing Kemal speech, September 1925.

135. See Mango, *Atatürk*, 438. For an altogether more critical reading see Hamit Bozarslan, 'Kemalism, Westernisation and Anti-liberalism', in Kieser, *Turkey*, 31.

136. See Peter J. Beck, '"A Tedious and Perilous Controversy": Britain and the Settlement of the Mosul Dispute 1918–1926', *Middle Eastern Studies*, 17:2 (1981), 256–76.

137. See Akçam, *From Empire*, 21–5, for explication.
138. Shaw and Shaw, *History*, vol. 2, 376.
139. See Bloxham, 'Changing Perceptions', 193. See also Council on Turkish–American Relations, *The Treaty with Turkey: Why it Should be Ratified* (1926). Quoted in Rouben Paul Adalian, ed., *Guide to the Armenian Genocide in the U.S. Archives 1915–1918* (Alexandria, VA: Chadwyck-Healey, 1994), 262.
140. Lewis, *Emergence*, 262.
141. Kinross, *Atatürk*, 397.
142. Huntington, *Clash*, esp. 144–9, 178–9.
143. Payne, *History*, 144–5.
144. Mann, *Dark Side*, 175, 179.
145. Çağaptay, 'Crafting the Turkish Nation', 200.
146. See Mango, *Atatürk*, chs 21–3, for full details.
147. See Zürcher, *Unionist Factor*, 140–1.
148. Çağaptay, 'Crafting the Turkish Nation', 25.
149. Çağaptay, 'Crafting the Turkish Nation', ch. 4, 'The Ideology of High Kemalist Nationalism in the 1930s'. For more on this theme see Foss, 'The Turkish View', 250–79.
150. Çağlar Keyder, 'The Consequences of the Exchange of Populations for Turkey', in Hirschon, *Crossing the Aegean*, 49–50.
151. Çağaptay, 'Crafting the Turkish Nation', 298, 172; Gingeras, *Sorrowful Shores*, esp. 124–7, for the Association for the Strengthening of Near Eastern Circassian Rights and the full text of their 24 November 1921 'General Statement'.
152. Çağaptay, 'Crafting the Turkish Nation', 166; Gingeras, *Sorrowful Shores*, 161–5. An estimated 800,000 post-Ottoman Muslim immigrants arrived in the period 1923–38, mostly from Yugoslavia, Bulgaria, and Rumania.
153. Çağaptay, 'Crafting the Turkish Nation', 197.
154. Quoted in Zeydanlioglu, 'The Kurds', 3.
155. Çağaptay, 'Crafting the Turkish Nation', 50–1.
156. Çağaptay, 'Crafting the Turkish Nation', 48, 259.
157. Çağaptay, 'Crafting the Turkish Nation', 50.
158. Çağaptay, 'Crafting the Turkish Nation', 41, 48, 259.
159. Izady, *The Kurds*, 61; Aktar, 'Homogenising the Nation', 93.
160. Kendal, 'Kurdistan in Turkey', in Chaliand, *People*, 60.
161. M. H. Yuvuz, 'Five Stages of the Construction of Kurdish Nationalism in Turkey', *Nationalism and Ethnic Politics*, 7:3 (2001), 8.
162. Zeydanlioglu, 'The Kurds', 5.
163. Zeydanlioglu, 'The Kurds', 6; Çağaptay, 'Crafting the Turkish Nation', 177; Kendal, 'Kurdistan in Turkey', 66.
164. See Welat Zeydanlioglu, '"The White Turkish Man's Burden": Orientalism, Kemalism and the Kurds in Turkey', in Guido Rings and Anne Ife, eds., *Neo-Colonial Mentalities in Contemporary Europe? Language and Discourse in the Construction of Identities* (Newcastle upon Tyne: Cambridge Scholars Publishing, 2008), 155–74.
165. Ahmad, *Kurdistan*, 174; Hofman and Koutcharian, 'History', 38, for the Armeno-Kurdish agreement between Boghos Nubar Pasha and Sherif Pasha.
166. McDowall, *Modern History*, 124; Kendal, 'Kurdistan in Turkey', 59; van Bruinessen, *Agha*, 277–9; Shaw and Shaw, *History*, vol. 2, 340–4; Zürcher, *Unionist Factor*, 68–105; Olson, *Emergence*, 30: all confirm various aspects of these tendencies.
167. Van Bruinessen, *Agha*, 269.

168. See Çağaptay, 'Crafting the Turkish Nation', 22. The Kurdish population in the southeast was put at 1,184,446, according to the 1927 census. With 13.58 per cent of this population said to be non-Turkish speaking, this was a considerable and probably quite intentional underestimate. Compare this, too, with a September 1925 internal regime report, which estimated that of the region's 1,360,000 inhabitants, the Kurds constituted 993,000: the rest mostly made up of Turks and Arabs. See Üngör, *The Making*, 134.

169. Olson, *Emergence*, 34.

170. McDowall, *Modern History*, 200.

171. See Olson, *Emergence*, 21–2, 52–3, not least for the pivotal role of Captain Noel, the British 'man on the spot' during 1919–20.

172. Üngör, *The Making*, 122–3, referring to the work of Hamit Bozarslan.

173. Yuvuz, 'Five Stages', 7.

174. Üngör, *The Making*, ch. 5, 'The Calm after the Storm: The Politics of Memory', for a wider reach of enquiry on these themes.

175. Izady, *The Kurds*, 1.

176. See Olson, *Emergence*, ch. 3, 'The Second Time Around: British Policy towards the Kurds from Mudros to Lausanne'.

177. See van Bruinessen, *Agha*, 278; Olson *Emergence*, 30–6.

178. Mango, *Atatürk*, 350.

179. See Olson, *Emergence*, 43–5, for details.

180. Van Bruinessen, *Agha*, 281.

181. Van Bruinessen, *Agha*, 279–81.

182. Olson, *Emergence*, 48–9, for the Diyarbekir Congress.

183. Van Bruinessen, *Agha*, 293.

184. Üngör, *The Making*, 131.

185. Van Bruinessen, *Agha*, 290.

186. Üngör, *The Making*, 127–9. Note also the symbolic significance of the 1978 founding of the Kuridstan Workers Party (PKK), committed to armed struggle against Turkey, in Fis—one of the massacred Lice villages, see 169.

187. Olson, *Emergence*, 120.

188. Olson, *Emergence*, 125.

189. Üngör, *The Making*, 148.

190. Çağaptay, 'Crafting the Turkish Nation', 32–3; Kendal, 'Kurdistan in Turkey', 65; Üngör, *The Making*, 135.

191. Üngör, *The Making*, 151.

192. Olson, *Emergence*, 39–41.

193. See Levene, *Rise of the West*, 58–9.

194. See Üngör, *The Making*, 168, for discussion.

195. Quoted in Olson, *Emergence*, 125.

196. Van Bruinessen, *Agha*, 283–5.

197. Van Bruinessen, *Agha*, 291.

198. Üngör, *The Making*, 162.

199. Kendal, 'Kurdistan in Turkey', 67.

200. See Régis Debray, *Revolution in the Revolution* (London: Penguin, 1967).

201. Kendal, 'Kurdistan in Turkey', 64–5; McDowall, *Modern History*, 202–7.

202. The terminology employed by minister of justice Mahmut Esat Bozkurt in September 1930. Bozkurt made the point very clear: 'Those who are not of pure Turkish stock can only have one right in this country, the right to be servants and slaves'. Quoted in Kendal, 'Kurdistan in Turkey', 65–6.

203. Omissi, *Air Power*. Omissi does not clearly refer to the Turkish campaign. But enough can be gleaned from his ch. 9, 'Comparisons', where Omissi cross-references British practice and 'technique' in Iraq in particular, with the French in Syria, and Italians and Spanish in north Africa, to surmise that the Turkish military were paying close attention.
204. Quoted in Zeydanlioglu, 'The Kurds', 6.
205. Quoted in Kendal, 'Kurdistan in Turkey', 65.
206. Üngör, *The Making*, esp. 169, 260.
207. Kendal, 'Kurdistan in Turkey', 66.
208. See Olson, *Emergence*, 56–7, 161.
209. Curzon is the senior figure one associates most with this position. But this was always a rather tenuous connection, not least as he argued for the return of the most heavily Kurdish parts of Mosul to the Turks. See McDowall, *Modern History*, 142–3. Ironically, Curzon was the major shareholder in Turkish Petroleum, the company with a monopoly of the Mosul oilfield. See Kendal, 'Kurdistan in Turkey', 59.
210. McDowall, *Modern History*, 195; Kendal, 'Kurdistan in Turkey', 62.
211. Kendal, 'Kurdistan in Turkey', 65.
212. See McDowall, *Modern History*, 330–40 for the full background.
213. Stafford, *The Tragedy*, 168–77, for details; revisited in Levene, 'Moving Target', 3–4.
214. Stafford, *The Tragedy*, 168. See, however, Khaldun S. Husri, 'The Assyrian Affair of 1933', *International Journal of Middle East Studies*, 5 (1974), 346–7, for an exculpatory argument that the decision came from a junior officer lower down the chain of command.
215. Stafford, *The Tragedy*, 201.
216. Stafford, *The Tragedy*, 199. See also Husri, 'Assyrian Affair', 353.
217. Husri, 'Assyrian Affair', 352. This slogan appeared on banners in the Baghdad victory parade.
218. See Reeva S. Simon, *Iraq between the Two World Wars: The Creation and Implementation of a Nationalist Ideology* (New York: Columbia University Press, 1986), 57.
219. See David Omissi, 'Britain, the Assyrians and the Iraqi Levies 1919–1932', *Journal of Imperial and Commonwealth History*, 17:3 (1989), 301–22; Olson, *Emergence*, 22, 56. An additional footnote to this story is the ephemeral consideration the British in Iraq gave to raising a cavalry security force from among the Circassians who had sided with the Greeks in the Turkish War of Independence. See Gingeras, *Sorrowful Shores*, 140–1.
220. Stafford, *The Tragedy*, 46–7; Joseph, *Nestorians*, 155.
221. Stafford, *The Tragedy*, 67–8; Omissi, 'Britain', 308–9, for different estimates of the dead, and consequent interpretations. British leniency was undoubtedly linked to the wider role of levies in the region, not least as political assassins on the British account. See C. J. Edmonds, *Kurds, Turks and Arabs: Politics, Travel and Research in North-Eastern Iraq 1919–1925* (London and New York: Oxford University Press, 1957), 420.
222. See Paul P. J. Hemphill, 'The Formation of the Iraqi Army, 1921–1933', in Abbas Kelidar, ed., *The Integration of Modern Iraq* (New York: St. Martin's Press, 1979), 91–2. Also Simon, *Iraq*, 56, and table, 179–81, listing the educational background of key members of the Iraqi political elite. Nine of fourteen premiers between 1922 and 1932 were ex-Ottoman officers, and thirty-two of fifty-six possible Cabinet ministers. See also Simon, 'The Education', 151–66.

223. See Ismet Sherrif Vanly, 'Kurdistan in Iraq', in Chaliand, *People*, 58–63; Olson, *Emergence*, 145–50. A League of Nations commission investigating the status of Mosul province in 1925 argued that, in ethnic terms, a Kurdish majority would assume the creation of an independent Kurdish state. Van Bruinessen, *Agha*, 274–5.

224. Joseph, *Nestorians*, 192.

225. Joseph, *Nestorians*, 180–4.

226. Stafford, *The Tragedy*, 117. Cross-reference here the Assyrian national pact with the Circassian national statement in Gingeras, *Sorrowful Shores*, 124–7 (see also note 151).

227. Hemphill, 'Formation', 94–8.

228. Hemphill, 'Formation', 94–8.

229. See Samir al-Khalil, *Republic of Fear: The Inside Story of Saddam's Iraq* (London: Hutchinson Radius, 1989), 171.

230. Quoted in Stafford, *The Tragedy*, 195. See also Husri, 'Assyrian Affair', 173.

231. Husri, 'Assyrian Affair', 358.

232. Stafford, *The Tragedy*, 211. Another potential destination was Brazil.

233. Stafford, *The Tragedy*, as quoted, 159.

CHAPTER 5

1. Stalin speech, 4 February 1931, quoted in I. V. Stalin, *Problems of Leninism* (Moscow: Foreign Languages Publishing House, 1945), 355–6. Service, *Stalin*, 272–3, for further discussion.

2. See discussion in Levene, *Meaning*, 181.

3. See Snyder, *Bloodlands*, for the most recent enunciation of the comparison. His chs 1–3, covering the period 1933–9, confirm Stalin's initial vast excess over Hitler in terms of death toll.

4. See, for examples, Zygmunt Bauman, *Modernity and the Holocaust* (Oxford: Blackwell, 1989); Holquist, 'State Violence'; Amir Weiner, 'Nature, Nurture and Memory in a Socialist Utopia: Delineating the Soviet Socio-Ethnic Body in the Age of Socialism', *American Historical Review*, 104:4 (1999), 1114–55. Also James C. Scott, *Seeing Like a State, How Certain Schemes to Improve the Human Condition Have Failed* (New Haven, CT, and London: Yale University Press, 1998), esp. 4–5, for more on the concept of high modernism.

5. Robert Conquest, *The Great Terror: A Reassessment* (New York and Oxford: Oxford University Press, 1990), and Conquest, *Harvest of Sorrow*; R. J. Rummel, *Lethal Politics, Soviet Genocide and Mass Murder since 1917* (New Brunswick, NJ, and London: Transaction Press, 1991).

6. See J. Arch Getty, *Origins of the Great Purges: The Soviet Party Reconsidered, 1933–1938* (Cambridge: Cambridge University Press, 1985), and J. Arch Getty and Roberta T. Manning, eds., *Stalinist Terror: New Perspectives* (Cambridge: Cambridge University Press, 1993), for key examples.

7. Michael Ellman, 'The Political Economy of Stalinism in the Light of the Archival Revolution', *Journal of Institutional Economics*, 4:1 (2008), 115.

8. N. A. Ivnitskii, cited in Polian, *Against their Will*, 87.

9. See Michael Ellman, 'The Role of Leadership Perceptions and of Intent in the Soviet Famine of 1931–1934', *Europe–Asia Studies*, 57:6 (2005), 823–41, for discussion.

10. Nicholas Werth, 'Stalin's System during the 1930s', in Rousso, *Stalinism*, 90.

11. See Lynne Viola, 'The Second Coming: Class Enemies in the Soviet Countryside, 1927–1935', in Getty and Manning, *Stalinist Terror*, 66, 79–80; Lewin, *Making*, 224; Barry McLoughlin, 'Mass Operations of the NKVD: A Survey', in Barry McLoughlin and Kevin McDermott, *Stalin's Terror: High Politics and Mass Repression in the Soviet Union* (Basingstoke: Palgrave, 2003), 140.

12. See Valery Bronstein, 'Stalin and Trotsky's Relatives in Russia', in Terry Brotherstone and Paul Dukes, eds., *The Trotsky Reappraisal* (Edinburgh: Edinburgh University Press, 1992), 8–15; Service, *Stalin*, 547; Weitz, *A Century*, 94.

13. Lynne Viola, *The Unknown Gulag: The Lost World of Stalin's Special Settlements* (New York: Oxford University Press, 2007), 155; Yakovlev, *Century*, 33.

14. See Yakovlev, *Century*, 29–32, more generally the chapter 'Socially Dangerous Children'.

15. Gross, *Revolution from Abroad*, 165–6.

16. Viola, *Unknown Gulag*, 155–9.

17. Nikita Petrov and Arsenii Roginskii, 'The "Polish Operation" of the NKVD, 1937–8', in McLoughlin and McDermott, *Stalin's Terror*, 158.

18. See, for example, Oleg Khlevniuk, 'Party and NKVD: Power Relations in the Years of the Great Terror', in McLoughlin and McDermott, *Stalin's Terror*, 21–33.

19. R. J. Rummel, 'Democide in Totalitarian States: Mortacracies and Megamurders', in Israel W. Charny, ed., *Genocide, A Critical Bibliographical Review*, vol. 3: *The Widening Circle of Genocide* (New Brunswick, NJ, and London: Transaction Publishers, 1994), 3.

20. See Levene, *Meaning*, 189–96.

21. Service, *Stalin*, 601.

22. Quoted in Mayer, *Furies*, 664.

23. See Weiner, *Making Sense*, 365, 32.

24. Deutscher, *Prophet Armed*, 508–9.

25. Edward A. Shils, *The Torment of Secrecy: The Background and Consequences of American Security Policies* (London: William Heinemann, 1956), 71.

26. Mikhail Bulgakov, *A Dog's Heart: An Appalling Story*, ed. Andrew Broomfield (London: Penguin, [1968] 2007); James Meek, 'The Hound of Hell', *The Guardian*, 18 August 2007.

27. Service, *Stalin*, 208–9.

28. Service, *Stalin*, 10. For a further grand, new analysis in which the psychopathology of Stalin himself is made the key to understanding the extreme Soviet violence of the 1930s, see Jörg Baberowski, *Verbrannte Erde, Stalins Herrshaft der Gewalt* (Munich: C.H. Beck, 2012).

29. Lewin, *Making*, 203.

30. V. V. Adamov, quoted in Lewin, *Making*, 295.

31. See Bidelux, *Communism*, as one obvious starting point.

32. See Terry Martin, *The Affirmative Action Empire: Nations and Nationalism in the Soviet Union, 1923–1939* (Ithaca, NY, and London: Cornell University Press, 2001), 269–72, for a fuller discussion.

33. Deutscher, *Stalin*, 352.

34. David Brandenberger, *National Bolshevism: Stalinist Mass Culture and the Formation of Modern Russian National Identity, 1931–1956* (Cambridge, MA: Harvard University Press, 2002). Also Maureen Perrie, *The Cult of Ivan the Terrible in Stalin's Russia* (London: Longman, 2003), esp. ch. 7, 'S.M. Eisenstein's Film'.

35. Tibor Szamuely, *The Russian Tradition*, ed. Robert Conquest (London: Fontana Press, [1974] 1988), quoting the Russian-born historian George Vernadsky, 25; Yakovlev, *Century*, xi.

36. Werth, 'Stalin's System', 39.
37. Szamuely, *Russian Tradition*, 77.
38. See Aronson, *Dialectics*, ch. 3, 'Why? Towards a Theory'.
39. Quoted in Aronson, *Dialectics*, 128.
40. See Graziosi, *Great Soviet Peasant War*, 35. See also Anna Geifman, *Death Orders: The Vanguard of Modern Terrorism in Revolutionary Russia* (Santa Barbara, CA: Praeger Security International, 2010), for the revolutionary *mentalité*.
41. Çağaptay, 'Crafting the Turkish Nation', 254.
42. See Philip Hoare, *Wilde's Last Stand: Decadence, Conspiracy and the First World War* (London: Duckworth, 1997).
43. See David Brion Davis, ed., *The Fear of Conspiracy: Images of Un-American Subversion from the Revolution to the Present* (Ithaca, NY, and London: Cornell University Press, 1971), 307.
44. Quoted in Conquest, *Harvest of Sorrow*, 112.
45. See Getty, *Origins*, for the ongoing problem of incompetence at lower levels.
46. Deutscher, *Prophet Armed*, 139.
47. Conquest, *Great Terror*, 26.
48. Conquest, *Great Terror*, 23.
49. Graziosi, *Great Soviet Peasant War*, 1. According to the 1926 census, out of 125 million people the rural population accounted for 102,700,000. See Yuzuru Taniuchi, *The Village Gathering in Russia in the Mid-1920*s (Birmingham: University of Birmingham Press, 1968), 1; Lewin, *Making*, 213, puts the peasant (as compared with nomad) element at 77 per cent.
50. R. W. Davies, *The Socialist Offensive: The Collectivisation of Soviet Agriculture 1929–30* (London: Macmillan 1980), 382.
51. Graziosi, *Great Soviet Peasant War*, 2.
52. Quoted in Mayer, *Furies*, 611.
53. Taniuchi, *Village Gathering*, 12.
54. Taniuchi, *Village Gathering*, 78.
55. Theda Skocpol, *States and Social Revolutions: A Comparative Analysis of France, Russia and China* (Cambridge: Cambridge University Press, 1979), 221.
56. Lewin, *Making*, 18, 43.
57. Weiner, *Making Sense*, 12.
58. See James W. Heinzen, *Inventing a Soviet Countryside: State Power and the Transformation of Rural Russia, 1917–1929* (Pittsburgh: Pittsburgh University Press 2004).
59. See Graziosi, *Great Soviet Peasant War*, 6–7, for insistence on this point.
60. See Service, *Stalin*, 255–6.
61. Nove, *Economic History*, 144–5.
62. Nove, *Economic History*, 148.
63. Martin, 'The Origins', 30.
64. Lewin, *Making*, ch. 4, 'The Immediate Background of Soviet Collectivization'. Davies, *Socialist Offensive*, 41–51, for a detailed background to the procurement crisis.
65. Quoted in Viola, *Unknown Gulag*, 35.
66. Viola, *Unknown Gulag*, 68.
67. Conquest, *Harvest of Sorrow*, 115.
68. Lewin, *Making*, 129. Also Taniuchi, *Village Gathering*, 42–8, for a more detailed commentary.
69. Moshe Lewin, *Russian Peasants and Soviet Power: A Study of Collectivization*, trans. Irene Nove (London: Allen & Unwin, 1968), 26–7, 85–93.

482 Notes to Chapter 5

70. See Viola, *Unknown Gulag*, 61–5.
71. See Lynne Viola, V. P. Danilov, N. A. Ivnitskii, and Denis Kozlov, eds., *The War Against the Peasantry, 1927–1930: The Tragedy of the Soviet Countryside*, trans. Steven Shabad (New Haven, CT: Yale University Press, 2005), doc. 19, 97–102, for full text of Stalin's speech at the 9–10 July 1928 plenum.
72. Nove, *Economic History*, 165.
73. Palmer, *Lands Between*, 107.
74. See Graziosi, *Great Soviet Peasant War*, 44–5.
75. See Radkey, *Unknown Civil War*, 399, 409, for further discussion.
76. Ellman, 'Role', 824.
77. See Yakovlev, *Century*, section 'The Clergy', esp. 157–62.
78. Viola, *Unknown Gulag*, 13–14. Perhaps Iagoda had a point, though, not so much about 'the clergy' but rather about religion, especially the sectarian, mystical counter-cultural variety, as focus of a genuinely 'apocalyptic' rural resistance to Soviet rule. See Lynne Viola, *Peasant Rebels under Stalin: Collectivization and the Culture of Peasant Resistance* (New York and Oxford: Oxford University Press, 1996), ch. 2, 'The Mark of Anti-Christ: Rumours and the Ideology of Peasant Resistance'; Brown, *Biography*, 58–74.
79. Viola, et al., *War against the Peasantry*, doc. 54, 218–20, for full text of Iagoda memo., 11 January 1930.
80. Lewin, *Making*, 129.
81. Quoted in Conquest, *Great Terror*, 17.
82. Quoted in William G. Rosenberg and Marilyn B. Young, *Transforming Russia and China: Revolutionary Struggle in the Twentieth Century* (Oxford and New York: Oxford University Press, 1982), 150.
83. Lewin, *Making*, 100.
84. Nove, *Economic History*, 126.
85. Lewin, *Making*, 19–20.
86. Viola, *Unknown Gulag*, 18–19.
87. Rosenberg and Young, *Transforming Russia*, 153.
88. Conquest, *Harvest of Sorrow*, 112, for more on Strumilin.
89. Browning, *Origins*, 315–23, for the 'euphoria' thesis as trigger to the Nazi mass murder of the Jews.
90. Nove, *Economic History*, 160.
91. Viola, *Unknown Gulag*, 24–6.
92. Polian, *Against their Will*, 70; Nicholas Werth, 'The Mechanism of a Mass Crime: The Great Terror in the Soviet Union 1937–38', in Kiernan and Gellately, *Spectre of Genocide*, 227; Christian Gerlach and Nicolas Werth, 'State Violence—Violent Societies', in Geyer and Fitzpatrick, *Beyond Totalitarianism*, 178; Viola, *Unknown Gulag*, 25.
93. Rosenberg and Young, *Transforming Russia*, 155.
94. Viola, *Unknown Gulag*, 26.
95. Viola, *Unknown Gulag*, 28.
96. See, for example, Lev Kopelev, *The Education of a True Believer*, trans. Gary Kern (London: Wildwood House, 1981).
97. Viola, *Peasant Rebels*, 30–2.
98. Graziosi, *Great Soviet Peasant War*, 50. The figure would rise to 2.25 million if one includes smaller deportations in the succeeding two years.
99. See Mendes-Flohr and Reinharz, *The Jew*, 506, for the key Wannsee text.

100. See R. W. Davies, 'Forced Labour under Stalin: The Archive Revelations', *New Left Review*, 214 (1995), 62–80; Viola, *Unknown Gulag*, 30–1.

101. Viola, *Unknown Gulag*, 110.

102. Viola, *Unknown Gulag*, ch. 5, 'The Penal-Economic Utopia, "Reforging through Labour"'.

103. Quoted in Yakovlev, *Century*, 35.

104. Viola, *Unknown Gulag*, 87, 46, 101.

105. Graziosi, *Great Soviet Peasant War*, 50.

106. Nicholas Werth, 'Strategies of Violence in the Stalinist USSR', in Rousso, *Stalinism*, 77–8.

107. Quoted in Viola, *Unknown Gulag*, 47–8.

108. Quoted in Yakovlev, *Century*, 36–7.

109. Werth, 'Strategies', 78.

110. Quoted in Yakovlev, *Century*, 37–8.

111. See Graziosi, *Soviet Peasant War*, 17–18.

112. Quoted in Viola, *Peasant Rebels*, 96.

113. Graziosi, *Great Soviet Peasant War*, 52. See Nicholas Werth, 'Forms of Autonomy in "Socialist" Society', in Rousso, *Stalinism*, 117–18, for further details. Also Viola, *Peasant Rebels*, chs 4 and 5, which include tables of OGPU statistics on the range, size, chronology, causes, and types of peasant resistance.

114. Viola, *Peasant Rebels*, 187–9.

115. Werth, 'Forms', 117–18; Viola, *Peasant Rebels*, chs 4 and 5.

116. Conquest, *Harvest of Sorrows*, 160; Viola, et al., *War against the Peasantry*, doc. 71, 276–9, for 'Dizzy with Success' text.

117. Viola, *Unknown Gulag*, 30.

118. Viola, *Peasant Rebels*, 34; Nove, *Economic History*, 168, 170.

119. Viola, *Unknown Gulag*, 30–1.

120. See Viola, *Peasant Rebels*, ch. 3, '"We Have No Kulaks Here": Peasant Luddism, Evasion and Self-Help', esp. 69–79. For wider comparisons, see, most notably, James C. Scott, *Weapons of the Weak: Everyday Forms of Peasant Resistance* (New Haven, CT: Yale University Press, 1986) and, of course, Thompson, *Making*, esp. 598–659, for the key Luddite parallels.

121. Martin, 'The Origins', 837.

122. Weiner, *Making Sense*, 140, quoting A. N. Ivnitskii. His figures propose that out of an initial total of 381,000 families, Ukrainians constituted the largest cohort (63,700 families), West Siberia offered the second largest element, and North Caucasia the third, with 38,400 families.

123. Martin, 'The Origins', 837.

124. See Martin, *Affirmative Action*, 293–4; Viola, *Peasant Rebels*, table 5–3, 138–9; Graziosi, *Great Soviet Peasant War*, 53, for fuller details.

125. Martin, 'The Origins', 839; Timothy Snyder, *Sketches from a Secret War: A Polish Artist's Mission to Liberate Soviet Ukraine* (New Haven, CT: Yale University Press, 2005), 102; Brown, *Biography*, 106–7.

126. Snyder, *Sketches*, 86, 89.

127. Stephen Oleskiw, *The Agony of a Nation: The Great Man Made Famine in Ukraine 1932–1933* (London: National Committee to Commemorate the Fiftieth Anniversary of the Artificial Fame in Ukraine, [1932–3] 1983), 50.

128. Martin, *Affirmative Action*, 253.

129. James E. Mace, 'Why did the Famine Happen?', *The Ukrainian Review*, 30:1 (1982), 47.

130. Martin, *Affirmative Action*, 285–91.

131. See W. G. Glaskow, 'The Cossacks as a Group', in Nikolai K. Deker and Andrei Lebed, eds., *Genocide in the USSR: Studies in Group Destruction* (New York: Scarecrow Press, 1958), 246–7.
132. Martin, *Affirmative Action*, 294–5; Viola, *Peasant Rebels*, 159–60. Also Avtorkhanov, 'The Chechens', 159, on the wider military operations.
133. Glaskow, 'Cossacks', 246–7.
134. Quoted in Martin, 'The Origins', 847.
135. Martin, 'The Origins', 846; also Martin, *Affirmative Action*, 301–2.
136. See, most obviously, R. W. Davies and Stephen Wheatcroft, *The Years of Hunger: Soviet Agriculture, 1931–1933* (Basingstoke: Palgrave, 2004); Mark B. Tauger, 'The 1932 Harvest and the Famine of 1933', *Slavic Review*, 50:1 (1991), 70–89. For close analysis of the historiographical debate, especially with regard to the Ukraine, see David R. Marples, *Heroes and Villains: Creating National History in Contemporary Ukraine* (Budapest: Central European University Press, 2007), ch. 2, 'The Famine of 1932–33'.
137. In addition to Marples, *Heroes and Villains*, see also Johan Dietsch, *Making Sense of Suffering: Holocaust and Holodomor in Ukrainian Historical Culture* (Lund: Lund University Press, 2006); Catherine Wanner, *Burden of Dreams: History and Identity in Post-Soviet Ukraine* (University Park, PA: Pennsylvania State University Press, 1998), for assessment of the role of *Holodomor* in the formation of contemporary Ukrainian national self-identity.
138. See 'Holodomor' <http://en.wikipedia.org/wiki/Holodomor>, section: 'death toll'.
139. See Stephen G. Wheatcroft, 'More Light on the Scale of Repression and Excess Mortality in the Soviet Union in the 1930s', in Getty and Manning, *Stalinist Terror*, 280. By contrast, see Conquest, *Harvest of Sorrow*, 296–7, operating on the basis of the analysis by 'dissident' Soviet demographer M. Maksudov.
140. Quoted in Polian, *Against their Will*, 87.
141. Polian, *Against their Will*, 87.
142. Conquest, *Harvest of Sorrow*, 197.
143. Conquest, *Harvest of Sorrow*, ch. 9, 'Central Asia and the Kazakh Tragedy'. Also Alec Nove, 'Victims of Stalinism? How Many?', in Getty and Manning, *Stalinist Terror*, 265.
144. Brown, *Biography*, 176–84, for a notable exception to the general rule in her intermeshing of forced Polish, Ukrainian, and other rimlands deportations *and* the Kazakh catastrophe. Also see Snyder, *Bloodlands*, 129–30, for further acknowledgement of the connection.
145. John Pilger, *The New Rulers of the World* (London: Verso, 2002), chapter 'Paying the Price', for perhaps the most high-profile advocacy of the charge.
146. See Eric Herring, 'Power, Propaganda and Indifference: An Explanation of the Continued Imposition of Economic Sanctions on Iraq despite their Human Cost', in Tareq Y. Ismael and William W. Haddad, eds., *Iraq: The Human Costs of History* (London: Pluto, 2003), 34–55, and Eric Herring, 'Between Iraq and a Hard Place: A Critique of the British Government's Case for UN Economic Sanctions', *Review of International Studies*, 28:1 (2002), 40–1.
147. Lewin, *Making*, ch. 6, ' "Taking Grain": Soviet Policies of Agricultural Procurements before the War'.
148. Lewin, *Making*, 155; Davies and Wheatcroft, *Years of Hunger*, 174.
149. See Martin, *Affirmative Action*, 298–9; Graziosi, *Great Soviet Peasant War*, 63.
150. See Oleskiw, *The Agony*, 24–40, for details.
151. Martin, *Affirmative Action*, 302, 306.

152. Martin, *Affirmative Action*, 24.

153. Seely, *Russo-Chechen Conflict*, 78.

154. Conquest, *Harvest of Sorrow*, 212. Also Alexander Y. Yurchenko, 'The Ukrainians', in Deker and Lebed, *Genocide*, 142; Oleskiw, *The Agony*, 50, for more on these events.

155. Reid, *Borderland*, 155.

156. Quoted in Martin, *Affirmative Action*, 297–8 (Stalin's underscoring of 'fortress'). Also Marples, *Heroes and Villains*, 54, 56–7, on the significance of Stalin's 11 August letter in the eyes of those, such as Mace, who read it as proof of an intentional, centrally organized, 'famine-as-terror' campaign.

157. Martin, *Affirmative Action*, 306.

158. Martin, *Affirmative Action*, 303.

159. Reid, *Borderland*, 120–1; Martin, *Affirmative Action*, 346–7.

160. Snyder, *Bloodlands*, 49–52; Marples, *Heroes and Villains*, 46–8, for some of the gruesome eyewitness testimonies to cannibalism.

161. Graziosi, *Great Soviet Peasant War*, 66, n. 155.

162. Martin, *Affirmative Action*, 306.

163. Conquest, *Harvest of Sorrow*, 237.

164. Conquest, *Harvest of Sorrow*, 291. The practice of depositing people on geographically isolated riverine sites as a method of disposal needs further investigation. Gerlach and Werth, 'State Violence', 141, report an almost parallel case in April 1933, when 4,000 out of 6,000 deported 'socially harmful elements' from Moscow and Leningrad died within weeks of having been dumped on a deserted island situated at the junction of the Ob and Nazina rivers near Tomsk. One might ask whether the result was incompetence, overstretch, or conscious mass murder.

165. Conquest, *Harvest of Sorrow*, 296–7.

166. Oleskiw, *The Agony*, 25.

167. Ellman, 'Role', esp. 824–7, 831.

168. See Levene, *Rise of the West*, 259.

169. Conquest, *Harvest of Sorrow*, 126, here quoting S. Swianiewicz, *Forced Labour and Economic Development* (1965).

170. Ellman, 'Role', 831.

171. See Graziosi, *Great Soviet Peasant War*, 68. For comparable special settlers' regimes, see Viola, *Unknown Gulag*, 99. See also Paul Hagenloh, *Stalin's Police: Public Order and Mass Repression in the USSR, 1926–1941* (Baltimore and Washington, DC: John Hopkins University Press and Woodrow Wilson Center Press, 2009), and David R. Shearer, *Policing Stalin's Socialism: Repression and Social Order in the Soviet Union, 1924–1953* (New Haven, CT, and Stanford, CA: Yale University Press and Hoover Institute, 2009), both of whom emphasize the introduction of the passport system as the key to Soviet internal policing, surveillance, and control of criminal, delinquent, and 'marginal' populations, most especially those who sought refuge in urban areas.

172. Quoted in Conquest, *Harvest of Sorrow*, 261.

173. Conquest, *Harvest of Sorrow*, as quoted, 197.

174. See Polian, *Against their Will*, 88–9.

175. William Henry Chamberlin, *Russia's Iron Age* (London: Duckworth, 1935), 76–7.

176. Sheehy and Nahalyo, *Crimean Tatars*, 7; Murat Tachmurat and Aman Berdimut, 'The Turkestanis', in Deker and Lebed, *Genocide*, 129.

177. Quoted in Ellman, 'Role', 832.

178. Graziosi, *Great Soviet Peasant War*, 35.

179. Graziosi, *Great Soviet Peasant War*, 69.

180. Quoted in Ellman, 'Role', 832.

181. See Karel C. Berkhoff, *Harvest of Despair: Life and Death in Ukraine under Nazi Rule* (Cambridge, MA, and London: Harvard University Press, 2004), ch. 7, 'Famine in Kiev'.

182. Thurston, *Life and Terror*, 2.

183. See Service, *Stalin*, 321–2, for details. More specifically, Viola, *Unknown Gulag*, 155–9, for kulak 'rehabilitation'.

184. See Applebaum, *Gulag*, 96–101. Also, more generally, Robert Conquest, *Kolyma: The Arctic Death Camps* (Oxford and New York: Oxford University Press, 1979), esp. 36–50.

185. Tolstoy, *Stalin's Secret War*, 28.

186. See Conquest, *Great Terror*, esp. ch. 2, 'The Kirov Murder'. While Conquest may have over-egged the 'all roads lead back to Stalin' smoking-gun argument, this is the finest account in English of the unravelling of the affair.

187. See Getty, *Origins*, for development and interpretation of the pre-Great Terror *chistki*.

188. Getty, *Origins*, 179.

189. Conquest, *Great Terror*, 164.

190. Getty, *Origins*, 133–4.

191. Avtorkhanov, 'The Chechens', 176.

192. Martin, *Affirmative Action*, 314.

193. Martin, *Affirmative Action*, 330–3. Also Michael Gelb, 'The Western Finnic Minorities and the Origins of Stalinist Nationalities Deportations', *Nationalities Papers*, 24:2 (1996), 242–4.

194. Martin, *Affirmative Action*, 357.

195. See Gelb, 'Western Finnic Minorities'; also Michael Gelb, '"Karelian Fever": The Finnish Immigrant Community during Stalin's Purges', *Europe-Asia Studies*, 43:9 (1993), 1091–116.

196. Martin, *Affirmative Action*, 336, 357.

197. Roy A. Medvedev, *Let History Judge: The Origins and Consequences of Stalinism* (New York: Knopf, 1972), 308.

198. Khlevniuk, 'Party and NKVD', 32.

199. See Thurston, *Life and Terror*, esp. 89–91.

200. Sheila Fitzpatrick, 'Introduction to Part 4', in Sheila Fitzpatrick, ed., *Stalinism: New Directions* (London and New York: Routledge, 2000), 258. See also commentary in Werth, 'The Mechanism', 219.

201. Thurston, *Life and Terror*, 62, 63 (table).

202. See Gabor Tamas Rittersporn, 'The Omnipresent Conspiracy: On Soviet Imagery and Politics of Social Relations in the 1930s', in Getty and Manning, *Stalinist Terror*, 99–115.

203. See Boris A. Starkov, 'Narkom Ezhov', in Getty and Manning, *Stalinist Terror*, 21–39; Conquest, *Great Terror*, 14–15.

204. Lewin, *Making*, 309–10.

205. See David Shearer, 'Social Disorder, Mass Repression and the NKVD during the 1930s', in McLoughlin and McDermott, *Stalin's Terror*, 87–9.

206. Conquest, *Great Terror*, for full details of the plenum transcripts.

207. McLoughlin, 'Mass Operations', 121.

208. Conquest, *Great Terror*, 438, referring to Khrushchev's 1956 'secret speech'.

209. Robert Conquest, *The Nation Killers: The Soviet Deportation of Nationalities* (London: Macmillan, 1970), 97; Glaskow, 'Cossacks', 249–50.
210. Conquest, *Great Terror*, 232–3; Kappeler, *Russian Empire*, 378.
211. Conquest, *Great Terror*, 215.
212. See Werth, 'The Mechanism', 222–3, for a development of this theme.
213. See Getty, *Origins*, 141; Conquest, *Great Terror*, 179.
214. Deutscher, *Stalin*, 348–9.
215. Getty, *Origins*, 119–22; Thurston, *Life and Terror*, 25.
216. Deutscher, *Stalin*, 310.
217. Deutscher, *Stalin*, 379.
218. See Viktor Alexandrov, *The Tukhachevsky Affair*, trans. John Hewish (London: Macdonald, 1965).
219. J. Arch Getty and William Chase, 'Patterns of Repression among the Soviet Elite in the Late 1930s', in Getty and Manning, *Stalinist Terror*, 326–8, argue that 69 per cent of senior military (compared with 62 per cent of 1917 revolutionary elite and 61 per cent of economic elite) were killed. See also Thurston, *Life and Terror*, 123, 200, for varying figures for military fatalities; Conquest, *Great Terror*, ch. 7, 'Assault on the Army', for details of the events themselves.
220. McLoughlin, 'Mass Operations', 105; Snyder, *Bloodlands*, 80.
221. Cited in Service, *Stalin*, 340; Snyder, *Bloodlands*, 72.
222. Albert Resis, ed., *Molotov Remembers: Inside Kremlin Politics, Conversations with Felix Chuev* (Chicago: Ivan R. Dee, 1993), 254.
223. John Maynard, *The Russian Peasant and Other Studies* (London: Victor Gollancz, 1942), 252.
224. McLoughlin, 'Mass Operations', 105; Viola, *Unknown Gulag*, 162.
225. Viola, *Unknown Gulag*, 126–7.
226. Viola, *Unknown Gulag*, 163.
227. Shearer, 'Social Disorder', 104.
228. McLoughlin, 'Mass Operations', 120.
229. See Applebaum, *Gulag*, 114–16; Conquest, *Great Terror*, 321. Some of Conquest's information is clearly at second or third hand, but this does not, in itself, negate its reliability.
230. Thurston, *Life and Terror*, 101.
231. McLoughlin, 'Mass Operations', 130.
232. Quoted in Werth, 'The Mechanism', 220. For a view which runs with the notion that the *Ezhovshchina* was a logical culmination to a growing police assault on a whole range of 'potentially dangerous populations', see Hagenloh, *Stalin's Police*, ch. 6, 'Nikolai Ezhov and the Mass Operations, 1937–1938'.
233. See Viola, *Unknown Gulag*, 159–66.
234. Werth, 'The Mechanism', 220.
235. Viola, *Unknown Gulag*, 160, but also see more revealingly, n. 73, for consideration of recent archival evidence.
236. Werth, 'The Mechanism', 235.
237. See Oleg Khlevniuk, 'The Objectives of the Great Terror, 1937–1938', in Hoffmann, *Stalinism*, 90–2. Petrov and Roginskii, 'Polish Operation', 160–2; Werth, 'The Mechanism', 235–6, for more on these aspects.
238. McLoughlin, 'Mass Operations', 129–30.
239. Quoted in Conquest, *Great Terror*, 287.

240. Werth, 'The Mechanism', 225.
241. McLoughlin, 'Mass Operations', 132.
242. McLoughlin, 'Mass Operations', 132. See also Khlevniuk, 'The Objectives', 93, for the problem of interpreting the January 1938 events.
243. Quoted in Thurston, *Life and Terror*, 145. More generally see ch. 5, 'Fear and Belief in the Terror, Response to Arrest'.
244. See Werth, 'The Mechanism', 231–2.
245. Petrov and Roginskii, 'Polish Operation', 154–5. The origins of the NKVD allegation of a POV 'conspiracy', involving the running of great numbers of Soviet Polish agents, and alleged links to the German and Ukrainian Military Organisation (UVO) underground, however, can be traced back at least to 1933. See Brown, *Biography*, 120–2.
246. Brown, *Biography*, 158–9.
247. McLoughlin, 'Mass Operations', 123.
248. Petrov and Roginskii, 'Polish Operation', 165–7.
249. Petrov and Roginskii, 'Polish Operation', esp. 154–5, 164–66; Martin, 'The Origins', 856, n. 266. It was, of course, ironic that nobody non-Polish who knew the way the wind was blowing after 1934—when the Polish Marchlevsk autonomous region was already being investigated by the security apparatus for alleged POV infiltration—would have gone out of their way to send their child to a 'failing' Polish school. See Brown, *Biography*, 124–5.
250. Werth, 'The Mechanism', 237.
251. Werth, 'The Mechanism', 236–7.
252. Martin, *Affirmative Action*, 343.
253. Weiner, *Making Sense*, 147.
254. Polian, *Against their Will*, 99.
255. Eric Markusen and David Kopf, *The Holocaust and Strategic Bombing: Genocide and Total War in the 20th Century* (Boulder, CO, San Francisco, and Oxford: Westview Press, 1995), 190–1.
256. J. Otto Pohl, 'Stalin's Genocide against the "Repressed Peoples"', *JGR*, 2:2 (2000), 278–9.
257. Yakovlev, *Century*, 184; Polian, *Against their Will*, 98; Martin, *Affirmative Action*, 335.
258. Martin, *Affirmative Action*, 424–5; Khlevniuk, 'The Objectives', 96–7.
259. See Service, *Stalin*, 352.
260. Suny and Martin, 'Introduction', in Suny and Martin, *State of Nations*, 14, and Martin, more generally, in *Affirmative Action*, describe these and the other targeted border populations in question as 'diaspora' nationalities. I find this nomenclature inappropriate. 'Diaspora' might suggest that they were not genuinely indigenous, which, by extension, could lead to an implication (not, of course, Martin or Suny's intention) that they had no business being where they were. The fact that ethnic groups found themselves on different sides of borders and, in the context of the 'New Europe', within different sovereign entities was simply a primary—and disastrous—consequence of imperial collapse in the rimlands arena.
261. See, for instance, Robert C. Tucker, 'Stalinism and Stalin: Sources and Outcomes', in Manfred Hildermeier and Elisabeth Müller-Luckner, *Stalinismus vor dem Zweiten Weltkrieg: neue Wege der Forschung* (Munich: Oldenbourg, 1998), 1–16.
262. See, for instance, Oleg Khlevniuk, 'The Reasons for the "Great Terror": The Foreign Political Aspect', in Silvio Pons and Andrea Romano, eds., *Russia in the Age of Wars, 1914–1945* (Milan: Feltrinelli, 2000), 163–8. For Spanish consequences see Georges

Vereeken, *The GPU in the Trotskyist Movement* (London: New Park Publications, 1976); and George Orwell, *Homage to Catalonia* (London: Penguin, [1938] 2003) for arresting personal testimony.

263. Martin, 'The Origins', 856.
264. Martin, 'The Origins', 855.
265. See Matthew Kott, 'Stalin's Great Terror (1937–38) as Antecedent and Other Aspects of the Recent Historiography of Soviet Genocide', *Yearbook of the Museum of the Occupation of Latvia* (Riga: Occupation Museum Foundation, 2007), 42–54. With thanks to Dr Kott for a copy of the original MS.
266. See Applebaum, *Gulag*, 149–52; Avtorkhanov, 'The Chechens', 175.
267. Avtorkhanov, 'The Chechens', 175.
268. 'Editorial: How We Murdered the Poles', *The Observer*, 6 October 1991, extract from Vladimir Tokaryev's confession.
269. Conquest, *Great Terror*, 269, 288.
270. William Millinship, 'Peace at Last for Stalin's Victims', *The Observer*, 14 October 1990. Also Snyder, *Bloodlands*, 99; Conquest, *Great Terror*, 288.
271. Service, *Stalin*, 355.
272. Conquest, *Great Terror*, 287.
273. McLoughlin, 'Mass Operations', 128.
274. See Werth, 'The Mechanism', 236–7; Martin, 'The Origins', 856, referring to the original Russian studies of Petrov and Roginskii. Snyder, *Bloodlands*, 104, concludes that *not less* than 85,000 Soviet ethnic Poles were directly executed in 1937–8. He adds that, though only 0.4 per cent of the population, they 'were about forty times more likely to die during the Great Terror than Soviet citizens generally'. Or, put another way, of the 681,692 direct victims of the Great Terror Poles were one in every eight.
275. McLoughlin, 'Mass Operations', 128.
276. See James Morris, 'Polish Terror: Spy Mania and Ethnic Cleansing in the Great Terror', *Europe–Asia Studies*, 56:5 (2004), 751–66. For confirmation of militant Polonophobia and Finnophobia in this period see Kopelev, *Education*, 123.
277. McLoughlin, 'Mass Operations', 135.
278. Kott, 'Stalin's Great Terror', 12 (original MS).
279. McLoughlin, 'Mass Operations', 139.
280. See Sergei Zhuravlev, 'Terror against Foreign Workers in the Moscow Elektrozavod Plant, 1937–8', in McLoughlin and McDermott, *Stalin's Terror*, 225–40, for a microcosm of this wider scene.
281. See Levene, *Rise of the West*, 156–7.
282. Martin, *Affirmative Action*, 320.
283. Martin, 'The Origins', 258.
284. Martin, *Affirmative Action*, 410–11.
285. McLoughlin, 'Mass Operations', 140.

CHAPTER 6

1. Quoted in Max Weinreich, *Hitler's Professors: The Part of Scholarship in Germany's Crimes against the Jewish People* (New Haven, CT, and London: Yale University Press, 1999), 27.
2. See Levene, *Rise of the West*, part 3, 'Empires in Advance: Empires in Retreat'.
3. David Norman Smith, '"Uncivil Society": Race and Murder in Nazi Germany', *Patterns of Prejudice*, 29:2/3 (1995), 124–5.

4. Quoted in Steven T. Katz, 'The Holocaust: A Very Particular Racism', in Michael Berenbaum and Abraham J. Peck, eds., *The Holocaust and History: The Known, The Unknown, The Disputed and The Reexamined* (Bloomington, IN, and Indianapolis: Indiana University Press, 1998), 60.

5. Slezkine, *Jewish Century*, 102.

6. Hitler, *Mein Kampf*, as here quoted in Cohn, *Warrant*, 206.

7. Katz, 'The Holocaust: A Very Particular Racism', 60–1.

8. Phillippe Burrin, *Hitler and the Jews: The Genesis of the Holocaust*, trans. Patsy Southgate (London: Edward Arnold, 1994), 27.

9. Cohn, *Warrant*, 209.

10. Quoted in Browning, *Origins*, 408.

11. See Christian Gerlach, 'Wannsee Conference: The Fate of German Jews, and Hitler's Decision in Principle to "Exterminate all European Jews"', in Omer Bartov, ed., *The Holocaust: Origins, Implementations, Aftermath* (London and New York: Routledge, 2000), 108–61.

12. Quoted in Browning, *Origins*, 404.

13. See Roger Chickering, *We Men Who Feel Most German: A Cultural Study of the Pan-German League 1886–1914* (Boston: Allen & Unwin, 1984); Woodruff D. Smith, *The Ideological Origins of Nazi Imperialism* (New York and Oxford: Oxford University Press, 1986), 102–11, 153.

14. Oded Heilbronner, 'German or Nazi Antisemitism?', in Stone, *Historiography*, 10–11. On the Vaterland party see Heinz Hagenlücke, *Deutsche Vaterlandspartei, Die nationale Rechte am Ende des Kaiserreiches* (Düsseldorf: Droste, 1997).

15. Robert G. L. Waite, *The Vanguard of Nazism: The Free Corps Movement in Germany, 1918–1923* (Cambridge, MA: Harvard University Press, 1952), 206.

16. Eley, 'What are the Contexts', 122–5.

17. See Jacques Kornberg, 'The Paranoid Style: Analysis of a Holocaust-denial Text', *Patterns of Prejudice*, 29:2/3 (1995), 33–44.

18. See Uwe Lohalm, *Völkischer Radikalismus: Die Geschichte des Deutschvölkischen Schutz- und Trutz-Bundes, 1919–1923* (Hamburg: Leibnitz-Verlag, 1970).

19. Michael Burleigh, *The Third Reich: A New History* (Basingstoke and Oxford: Pan Books, 2000), 51–2.

20. See Gunter W. Remmling, 'Discrimination, Persecution, Theft and Murder under the Colour of Law: The Totalitarian Corruption of the German Legal System 1933–1945', in Isidor Wallimann and Michael Dobkowski, eds., *Genocide and the Modern Age* (Westport, CT: Greenwood Press, 1987), 187. George L. Mosse, *Toward the Final Solution: A History of European Racism* (New York: Howard Fetig, 2nd edn, 1985), 183, cites a figure of 376 political murders in this period.

21. See Neil Gregor, *How to Read Hitler* (London: Granta, 2005), for background.

22. Stephen A. Schuker, *The End of French Predominance in Europe: The Financial Crisis of 1924 and the Adoption of the Dawes Plan* (Chapel Hill: University of North Carolina Press, 1976).

23. See William L. Patch Jr, *Heinrich Brüning and the Dissolution of the Weimar Republic* (Cambridge and New York: Cambridge University Press, 1998), for a recent assessment.

24. See Palmer, *Lands Between*, 207–8; Iago Gil Aguardo, 'The Credit Crisis of 1931 and the Fate of the Austro-German Customs Union', *Historical Journal*, 44:1 (2001), 199 221.

25. See Erich Fromm, *The Fear of Freedom* (London: Routledge and Kegan Paul, [1942] 1960); Klaus Theweleit, *Male Fantasies*, 2 vols (Cambridge: Polity Press, 1989), for

two classic explorations of these themes from different generations of scholars. Also Robert Gerwarth, *Hitler's Hangman: The Life of Heydrich* (New Haven, CT, and London: Yale University Press, 2011), xix.

26. Richard Bessel, *Germany after the First World War* (Oxford: Oxford University Press, 1993), 262.

27. Steven E. Aschheim, *The Nietzsche Legacy in Germany, 1880–1990* (Berkeley: University of California Press, 1992); Weisbrod, 'Military Violence'; Ulrich Herbert, *Best: Biographische Studien uber Radikalismus, Weltanschauung und Venunft* (Bonn: Dientz, 1996), for examples of the now very extensive literature on this theme.

28. See Slezkine, *Jewish Century*, 48.

29. Quoted in Guenter Lewy, *The Nazi Persecution of the Gypsies* (Oxford and New York: Oxford University Press, 2000), 29.

30. Quoted in Cohn, *Warrant*, 161.

31. Cohn, *Warrant*, 187.

32. Klaus P. Fischer, *The History of an Obsession: German Judeophobia and the Holocaust* (New York and London: Continuum, 2001), 144–6; Gilman, *The Jew's Body*, for broader analysis.

33. George L. Mosse, *The Crisis of German Ideology: Intellectual Origins of the Third Reich* (London: Weidenfeld & Nicolson, 1964), 140–2; Fischer, *History*, 141–2. See also Hannah Ewence, 'Blurring the Boundaries of Difference: *Dracula*, the Empire, and "the Jew"', in Tony Kushner and Hannah Ewence, eds., *Whatever Happened to British Jewish Studies?* (London and Portland, OR: Vallentine Mitchell, 2012), 221–30, for the wider prevalence of the Jew as vampire trope.

34. Mosse, *Crisis*, 228–9; Fischer, *History*, 116.

35. Eley, 'What are the Contexts', 122–4. Also Mosse, *Crisis*, 112, 141–2, for more on Fritsch.

36. Cohn, *Warrant*, 152; Mosse, *Crisis*, 112.

37. Quoted in Cohn, *Warrant*, 151.

38. Cohn, *Warrant*, 151, 160–1.

39. Mosse, *Crisis*, 143.

40. By autumn 1920, there were an estimated 560,000 Whites in Germany (including Balts), at least 70,000 of whom were congregated in Berlin. See Hans-Erich Volkmann, *Die russische Emigration in Deutschland, 1919–1929* (Würzburg: Holzner, 1966).

41. See Cohn, *Warrant*, 214–17. Michael Kellogg, *The Russian Roots of Nazism: White Émigrés and the Making of National Socialism, 1917–1945* (Cambridge: Cambridge University Press, 2005), 41–3, for Rosenberg's background and others of similar ilk, including Scheubner-Richter.

42. See Mann, *Dark Side*, 223–8, for further, interesting analysis.

43. Laqueur, *Weimar*, 72.

44. Niewyk, *The Jews*, 40.

45. See Hagit Lavsky, *Before Catastrophe: The Distinctive Path of German Zionism* (Detroit and Jerusalem: Wayne State University Press, Magnes Press, Leo Baeck Institute, 1996).

46. Karl Schleunes, *The Twisted Road to Auschwitz: Nazi Policy towards the Jews 1933–1939* (Urbana: University of Illinois Press, 1970), 38.

47. Quoted in Lucy Dawidowicz, *The War against the Jews, 1933–45* (London: Penguin 1975), 220.

48. Quoted in Paula Hyman, 'The History of European Jewry: Recent Trends in the Literature', *Journal of Modern History*, 54:2 (1982), 309, with reference to Adolph Asch and the National League of Jewish Frontline Veterans. Also Fischer, *History*, 193, for the case of Hans-Joachim Schoeps.

49. Levene, *Rise of the West*, 179, 199–200.
50. See Fischer, *History*, 181–9, for a valuable overview. More authoritatively, see Peter Gay, *Freud, Jews and Other Germans: Masters and Victims in Modernist Culture* (Oxford: Oxford University Press, 1978), and Peter Gay, *Weimar Culture: The Outsider as Insider* (London: Penguin, 1974).
51. Mazower, *Dark Continent*, 70–1; Walter Zwi Bacharach, 'Antisemitism and Racism in Nazi Ideology', in Berenbaum and Peck, *The Holocaust and History*, 68.
52. See Victor Klemperer, *The Language of the Third Reich: LTI—Lingua Tertii Imperii, A Philologist's Notebook*, trans. Martin Brady (London: The Athlone Press, 2000), 47.
53. See Fischer, *History*, 237–9.
54. Fischer, *History*, 127; Gunter Hartung, 'Pre-Planners of the Holocaust: The Case of Theodor Fritsch', in John Milfull, ed., *Why Germany?: National Socialist Anti-Semitism and the European Context* (Providence, RI, and Oxford: Berg, 1993), 31.
55. Hans Mommsen, 'The Realization of the Unthinkable: The "Final Solution" of the Jewish Question in the Third Reich', in Hans Mommsen, *From Weimar to Auschwitz*, trans. Philip O'Connor (Princeton: Princeton University Press, 1991), 237.
56. Hitler, *Mein Kampf*, cited here in Cohn, *Warrant*, 208.
57. Hartung, 'Pre-Planners', 31.
58. Burleigh, *Third Reich*, 106.
59. See Ulrich Herbert, 'Extermination Policy: New Answers and Questions', in Herbert, *National Socialist Extermination Policies*, 24–6.
60. Herbert, 'Extermination Policy', 20–1.
61. Herbert, 'Extermination Policy', 22.
62. Quoted in Gerald Fleming, *Hitler and the Final Solution* (Oxford: Oxford University Press, 1986), 17.
63. Oscar Wilde, *The Picture of Dorian Gray* (London: Penguin, [1891] 1949).
64. Among the many works, see Robert G. L. Waite, *The Psychopathic God: Adolf Hitler* (New York: Basic Books, 1977); the more determinist Rudolph Binion, *Hitler among the Germans* (New York: Elsevier, 1976); Joachim C. Fest, *The Face of the Third Reich* (London: Penguin, 1970), part 1: 'Adolph Hitler's Path from Men's Hostel to Reich Chancellery'; Joachim C. Fest, *Hitler*, trans. Richard and Clara Winston (London: Penguin 1974); Maser, *Hitler's Letters*, esp. ch. 1, 'Schoolboy, Art Student and Conscientious Objector'; and Ian Kershaw, *Hitler, 1889–1936: Hubris* (London: Penguin, 1998), for the latest, arguably magisterial, study.
65. See Hartung, 'Pre-Planners', 38; Evans, 'Pigmentia', 116.
66. Hartung, 'Pre-Planners', 39; Maser, *Hitler's Letters*, 245.
67. Mosse, *Crisis*, 296–7; Fischer, *History*, 134–5.
68. Mark Roseman, *The Villa, The Lake, the Meeting: Wannsee and the Final Solution* (London: Penguin, 2002), 36, 9.
69. Anna von der Goltz, *Hindenburg: Power, Myth, and the Rise of the Nazis* (New York and London: Oxford University Press, 2009), 168.
70. Sarah Gordon, *Hitler, Germans and the Jewish Question* (Princeton: Princeton University Press, 1984).
71. See Ian Kershaw, *Popular Opinion and Political Dissent: Bavaria, 1933–1945* (Oxford: Clarendon Press, 1983), 240–6.
72. Quoted in Jurgen Matthaus, 'Historiography and the Perpetrators of the Holocaust', in Stone, *Historiography*, 200–1, also n. 11.
73. By reference to figures in Ronnie S. Landau, *The Nazi Holocaust* (London and New York: I.B. Tauris, 1992), 100.

74. Landau, *Nazi Holocaust*, 102.
75. Klemperer, *Language*, 117, 110.
76. Klemperer, *Language*, 114–15.
77. Klemperer, *Language*, 105.
78. See Eugene Victor Walter, *Terror and Resistance: A Study of Political Violence, with Case Studies of Some Primitive African Communities* (London, Oxford, and New York: Oxford University Press, 1969), 74–86.
79. Fischer, *History*, 141.
80. Josh Cohen, 'Post-Holocaust Philosophy', in Stone, *Historiography*, 478–9, referring to Levinas, 'Reflections on the Philosophy of Hitlerism'.
81. See Klemperer, *Language*, 60–1.
82. Eric Johnson, *The Nazi Terror: Gestapo, Jews and Ordinary Germans* (London: John Murray, 1999), 223.
83. Bartov, *Mirrors*, 25, 18, for Hitler not only as the embodiment of the German unknown soldier but one who had come back from the dead.
84. Fest, *Face*, 84.
85. Martin Chalmers, ed., *I Shall Bear Witness: The Diaries of Victor Klemperer, 1933–1941*, trans. Martin Chalmers (London: Phoenix, 1999), 91.
86. See Burleigh, *Third Reich*, 75.
87. Burleigh, *Third Reich*, 63; Christopher R. Browning, *The Final Solution and the German Foreign Office: A Study of Referat DIII of Abteilung Deutschland, 1940–43* (New York and London: Holmes & Meier, 1978), 3.
88. See Gabriella Slomp, *Carl Schmitt and the Politics of Hostility, Violence and Terror* (Basingstoke: Palgrave, 2009).
89. Burleigh, *Third Reich*, 143, for Schleicher's advocacy of a 'Third Way' between Marxism and liberal capitalism, resting on a 'diagonal formula' of political support.
90. Fest, *Face*, 67–8.
91. Henry Ashby Turner, *German Big Business and the Rise of Hitler* (New York: Oxford University Press, 1985), for more on this theme.
92. This is, of course, much contested terrain. See Sally Marks, 'The Myths of Reparations', *Central European History*, 11:3 (1978), 231–55, for critical unravelling.
93. Burleigh, *Third Reich*, 151–5, for details.
94. See Michael Kater, 'Everyday Antisemitism in Pre-War Nazi Germany: The Popular Bases', *Yad Vashem Studies*, 16 (1984), 138.
95. Klemperer, *I Shall Bear Witness*, see entries esp. for March–May 1933.
96. The charge of 'statelessness' as a systematic critique of Nazism goes back to Franz Neumann's classic Marxist study, *Behemoth: The Structure and Practice of National Socialism* (London: Gollancz, 1942).
97. See Fischer, *History*, 202, for the 'Boxheim' documents.
98. Mommsen, 'The Realisation', 233.
99. Klemperer, *I Shall Bear Witness*, 10–11: 27 March 1933 entry.
100. See Helmut Krausnick and Martin Broszat, *Anatomy of the SS State*, trans. Dorothy Long and Marian Jackson (London: Paladin 1970), 44, for details.
101. Remmling, 'Discrimination', 190–5, for the development of the *Judengesetzgebung*.
102. See Yehuda Bauer, *Jews for Sale? Nazi–Jewish Negotiations 1933–1945* (New Haven, CT, and London: Yale University Press, 1995); David Yisraeli, 'The Third Reich and the Transfer Agreement', *Journal of Contemporary History*, 6:2 (1971), 129–48, for the origins and development of the scheme.
103. Burleigh, *Third Reich*, 297–8.

104. Avraham Barkai, *From Boycott to Annihilation: The Economic Struggle of German Jews 1933–1943*, trans. William Templar (Hanover, NH: Brandeis Press and University Press of New England, 1989), for more on this subject.

105. Burleigh, *Third Reich*, 305; Fischer, *History*, 258. See also Klemperer, *I Shall Bear Witness*, 158–9: 11 August 1935 entry.

106. Robert Gellately, *The Gestapo and German Society: Enforcing Racial Policy 1933–1945* (Oxford: Clarendon Press, 1990). Also Eric Johnson, *Nazi Terror*, esp. part 2, 'Nazi Terror and the Jews, 1933–1939'.

107. Krausnick and Broszat, *Anatomy*, 49–51, for details. Mommsen, 'The Realization', 231, for medieval antecedents.

108. Schleunes, *Twisted Road*, for the earlier revisionist position. Compare and contrast with Gerwarth, *Hitler's Hangman*, 98; Peter Longerich, *Holocaust, The Nazi Persecution and Murder of the Jews* (Oxford: Oxford University Press, 2010), 57–60.

109. See Klemperer, *I Shall Bear Witness*, 162: 17 September 1935 entry.

110. Ternon, *L'État criminel*, 145.

111. See Esriel Hildesheimer, *Jüdische Selbstverwaltung unter dem NS-Regime: der Existenzkampf der Reichsvertretung und Reichvereinigung der Juden in Deutschland* (Tübingen: Mohr, 1994).

112. Raul Hilberg, *The Destruction of the European Jews* (New York: Holmes & Meier, student edn, 1985), 29–32; Roseman, *Villa*, 80.

113. Fischer, *History*, 263–4.

114. Fischer, *History*, 267.

115. See David Cesarani, *Eichmann: His Life and Crimes* (London: Vintage, 2004), 42, 50.

116. Payne, *History*, 176.

117. Robert P. Ericksen and Sussanah Heschel, 'The German Churches and the Holocaust', in Stone, *Historiography*, 299–306; Christian Weise, 'An "Indelible Stain": The Churches between Silence, Ideological Involvement and Political Complicity', in Christian Wiese and Paul Betts, eds., *Years of Persecution, Years of Extermination: Saul Friedländer and the Future of Holocaust Studies* (London and New York: Continuum, 2010), 157–93, for overviews.

118. Johnson, *Nazi Terror*, 195.

119. See Burleigh, *Third Reich*, 153–4.

120. See Georges Passeleq and Bernard Suchecky, *The Hidden Encyclical of Pius XI*, trans. Steven Rendall (New York: Harcourt Brace, 1997); Frank L. Coppa, 'Between Anti-Judaism and Anti-Semitism: Pius XI's Response to Nazi Persecution of the Jews: Precursor to Pius XII's Silence?', *Journal of Church and State*, 47 (2005), 63–89.

121. Christine King, 'Jehovah's Witnesses under Nazism', in Michael Berenbaum, ed., *A Mosaic of Victims: Non-Jews Persecuted and Murdered by the Nazis* (London and New York: I.B. Tauris, 1990), 188–93.

122. King, 'Jehovah's Witnesses', 188–93.

123. Burleigh, *Third Reich*, 173.

124. Johnson, *Nazi Terror*, 238–9.

125. Johnson, *Nazi Terror*, 242–4.

126. Johnson, *Nazi Terror*, 239.

127. See Detlev Garbe, *Zwischen Widerstand und Martyrium: Die Zeugen Jehovas im 'Dritten Reich'* (Munich: R. Oldenbourg Verlag, 1994), 105.

128. Milton, 'Non-Jewish Children', 155.

129. Garbe, *Zwischen Widerstand*, 457–8. See also Peter Longerich, *Heinrich Himmler*, trans. Jeremy Noakes and Lesley Sharpe (Oxford and New York: Oxford University Press, 2012), 267.

130. See Martin Broszat and Elke Fröhlich, *Altag under Widerstand: Bayern im National-sozialismus* (Munich: Pier, 1987), for the seminal study.

131. Quoted in Detlev K. Peukert, *Inside Nazi Germany: Conformity, Opposition and Racism in Everyday Life*, trans. Richard Deveson (London: Penguin, 1989), 211.

132. Peukert, *Inside Nazi Germany*, 198–9, for further valuable development of this theme.

133. Quoted in Weinreich, *Hitler's Professors*, 34.

134. See, for instance, Elazar Barkan, *The Retreat of Scientific Racism: Changing Concepts of Race in Britain and the United States between the World Wars* (Cambridge and New York: Cambridge University Press, 1992); Tony Kushner, 'H.J. Fleure: A Paradigm for Inter-war Race Thinking in Britain', *Patterns of Prejudice*, 42:2 (2008), 151–66.

135. See Levene, *Rise of the West*, 195–7.

136. Benno Müller-Hill, 'Human Genetics and the Mass Murder of Jews, Gypsies, and Others', in Berenbaum and Peck, *The Holocaust and History*, 106.

137. See Stefan Kühl, *The Nazi Connection: Eugenics, American Racialism and German National Socialism* (Oxford: Oxford University Press, 1994).

138. Desmond King, *In the Name of Liberalism: Illiberal Social Policy in the United States and Britain* (Oxford: Oxford University Press, 2000), ch. 3, '"Cutting of the Worst": Voluntary Sterilisation in Britain in the 1930s'.

139. Quoted in Angus Fraser, *The Gypsies* (Oxford: Blackwell, 1992), 260.

140. See Weindling, *Epidemics*, 246–59, for the activities of the Hygiene Unit.

141. Phillippe Burrin, 'Charisma and Radicalism in the Nazi Regime', in Rousso, *Stalinism*, 146.

142. Herbert, 'Extermination Policy', 12.

143. See Levene, *Rise of the West*, 198.

144. Quoted in Weinreich, *Hitler's Professors*, 30.

145. See Ehmann, 'From Colonial Racism', 125.

146. Hilberg, *Destruction*, 30–1; John A. S. Grenville, 'Neglected Holocaust Victims: The *Mischlinge*, The *Jüdischversippte*, and the Gypsies', in Berenbaum and Peck, *The Holocaust and History*, 319.

147. Hilberg, *Destruction*, 30.

148. Hilberg, *Destruction*, 31–3; Johnson, *Nazi Terror*, 414–15.

149. See Wim Willems, *In Search of the True Gypsy: From Enlightenment to Final Solution* (London: Frank Cass, 1997), 229–30, 238.

150. Lewy, *Nazi Persecution*, 136; see Longerich, *Himmler*, 275–86, for some of the wider range of weird and fanciful Himmler notions that Ahnenerbe was tasked to research.

151. See Henry R. Huttenbach, 'The Romani Porajmos: The Nazi Genocide of Gypsies in Germany and Eastern Europe', in Crowe and Kolsti, *Gypsies*, 33; Anton Weiss-Wendt, 'Extermination of the Gypsies in Estonia during World War II: Popular Images and Official Policies', *HGS*, 17:1 (2003), 36, puts the figure as low as .04 per cent of the population.

152. Fraser, *Gypsies*, 8, 259.

153. For valuable additional studies on these aspects see Jean-Pierre Liégeois, *Gypsies: An Illustrated History*, trans. Tony Berrett (London: Al Saqi Nooks, 1986); Isabel Fonseca, *Bury Me Standing: The Gypsies and their Journey* (London: Chatto & Windus, 1995); Ian Hancock, *The Pariah Syndrome: An Account of Gypsy Slavery and Persecution* (Ann Arbor, MI: Karoma Publishers, 1987); Robbie McVeigh, 'Theorising Sedentarism', in Thomas Acton, ed., *Gypsy Politics and Traveller Identity* (Hatfield: University of Hertfordshire Press, 1997); Saul and Tebbutt, *The Role of the Romanies*.

154. Josef Kalvoda, 'The Gypsies of Czechoslovakia' and Ian Hancock, 'Introduction', in Crowe and Kolsti, *Gypsies*, 93 and 4, respectively.

155. See David Crowe, 'The Gypsy Historical Experience in Romania', in Crowe and Kolsti, *Gypsies*, 73. Also Willems, *In Search*, 30–4, for the new Habsburg policy and its wider intellectual impact; Levene, *Rise of the West*, 41, for the Tasmanian comparisons.

156. Crowe, 'Gypsy Historical Experience', 73.

157. See Gabrielle Tyrnauer, 'The Fate of the Gypsies in the Holocaust', in Charny, ed., *Genocide*, vol. 3: *The Widening Circle*, 224; Crowe, 'Gypsy Historical Experience', 67; Fraser, *The Gypsies*, 168–71, for these examples.

158. See Willems, *In Search*, 25–7, for details.

159. Ian Hancock, 'Chronology', in Crowe and Kolsti, *Gypsies*, 15; Kalvoda, 'Gypsies', 95.

160. Donald Kenrick and Grattan Puxon, *The Destiny of Europe's Gypsies* (New York: Basic Books, 1973), 46. Also see Tyrnauer, 'The Fate', 224.

161. Colin Clark, '"Severity has often enraged but never subdued a gypsy": The History and Making of European Romani Stereotypes', in Saul and Tebbutt, *The Role of the Romanies*, 240.

162. Weiss-Wendt, 'Extermination', 35–6; Gerlach and Werth, 'State Violence', 141.

163. Jiri Lipa, 'The Fate of Gypsies in Czechoslovakia under Nazi Domination', in Berenbaum, *Mosaic*, 208.

164. See Hancock 'Chronology', 15; Lewy, *Nazi Persecution*, 52–5, for terms of the decree.

165. Willems, *In Search*, 247.

166. Tyrnauer, 'The Fate', 226.

167. Lewy, *Nazi Persecution*, 38.

168. Quoted in Michael Zimmerman, 'The National Socialist "Solution of the Gypsy Question": Central Decisions, Local Initiative and their Interrelation', *HGS*, 15:3 (2001), 415–16.

169. Michael Zimmerman, 'The National Socialist "Solution of the Gypsy Question"', in Herbert, *National Socialist Extermination Policies*, 196.

170. Fraser, *Gypsies*, 261. The parallel terrorization, property sequestration, and complete eruction of the long-established 3,800-strong Jewish community of the Burgenland might also be noted here. See Gerwarth, *Hitler's Hangman*, 124.

171. See Zimmerman, 'National Socialist Solution', *HGS*, 413; Milton, 'Antechamber to Birkenau: The *Zigeunerlager* after 1933', in Berenbaum and Peck, *The Holocaust and History*, 390–1; Eve Rosenhaft 'A Photographer and his "Victims" 1934–1964: Reconstructing a Shared Experience of the Romani Holocaust', in Saul and Tebbutt, *The Role of the Romanies*, 186–7, for specific examples associated with the Magdeburg camp.

172. See Willems, *In Search*, ch. 5, 'Robert Ritter (1901–51): Eugenist and Criminological Biologist', for extensive analysis.

173. Thomas Acton, 'Modernity, Culture and "Gypsies": Is There a Meta-scientific Method for Understanding the Representation of "Gypsies"? And Do the Dutch Really Exist?', in Saul and Tebbutt, *The Role of the Romanies*, 105.

174. Willems, *In Search*, 252, 254.

175. Fonesca, *Bury Me*, 258.

176. Zimmerman, 'National Socialist Solution', in Herbert, *National Socialist Extermination Policies*, 192.

177. Zimmerman, 'National Socialist Solution', 192.

178. Milton, 'Antechamber', 392.

179. See Robert Manne, 'Aboriginal Child Removal and the Question of Genocide, 1900–1940', in Moses, *Genocide and Settler Society*, 217–43.

180. Carmel Finnan, 'From Survival to Subversion: Strategies of Self-Representation in Selected Works by Mariella Mehr', in Saul and Tebbutt, *The Role of the Romanies*, 146–7.

181. Huttenbach, 'Romani Porajmos', 31–3.

182. See Lewy, *Nazi Persecution*, 47–8, 209–10; Willems, *In Search*, 209.

183. Lewy, *Nazi Persecution*, 40–1.

184. See Weitz, *A Century*, 118–19. See also Burleigh and Wipperman, *Racial State*, 182, for the Reich Ministry Interior 1940 circular on 'asocials'.

185. Michael Burleigh, *Death and Deliverance: 'Euthanasia' in Germany, 1900–1945* (Cambridge: Cambridge University Press, 1994), esp. 5–20.

186. See H. M. Hanauske-Abel, 'Not a Slippery Slope or Sudden Subversion: German Medicine and National Socialism in 1933', *British Medical Journal*, 131 (1996), 1457.

187. Burleigh, *Third Reich*, 354; Fischer, *History*, 214.

188. Willems, *In Search*, 217–18.

189. Robert Proctor, *Racial Hygiene: Medicine under the Nazis* (Cambridge, MA: Harvard University Press, 1988), 89.

190. See Reiner Pommerin, *Sterilisierung der Rheinlandbastarde: Das Schicksal einer farbigen deutschen Minderheit 1918–1937* (Düsseldorf: Droste, 1979); Annegret Ehmann, 'From Colonial Racism to Nazi Population Policy: The Role of the So-Called *Mischlinge*', 124–5, and Robert Kesting, 'The Black Experience during the Holocaust', 360, both in Berenbaum and Peck, *The Holocaust and History*.

191. Karin Orth, 'The Concentration Camp SS as a Functional Elite', in Herbert, *National Socialist Extermination Policies*, 312; Huttenbach, 'Romani Porajmos', 36; Willems, *In Search*, 250.

192. Weindling, *Epidemics*, 7.

193. Burleigh, *Third Reich*, 166.

194. Goldhagen, *Hitler's Willing Executioners*, 33–4.

195. Outside the immediate scope of this discussion is the degree to which a private or 'separate' female sphere of domesticity was a factor helping to mobilize women in support of Nazism, or a fundamental aspect of Nazi victimhood. For strikingly contrasting assessments see Claudia Koonz, *Mothers in the Fatherland: Women, the Family and Nazi Politics* (New York: St. Martin's Press, 1987) and Gisela Bock, 'Racism and Sexism in Nazi Germany: Motherhood, Compulsory Sterlisation, and the State', *Signs*, 8:3 (1983), 400–21. For a direct challenge to the notion of a separate women's sphere, however, see also Adelheid von Saldern, 'Victims or Perpetrators? Controversies about the Role of Women in the Nazi State', in David F. Crew, ed., *Nazism and German Society, 1933–1945* (London and New York: Routledge, 1994), 141–65.

196. See George L. Mosse, *Nazi Culture: Intellectual, Cultural and Social Life in the Third Reich* (New York: Grosset & Dunlap, 1966), 66.

197. James J. Sheehan, 'National Socialism and German Society: Reflections on Recent Research', *Theory and Society*, 13:6 (1984), 866–7.

198. Grenville, 'Neglected Holocaust Victims', 316–17; also Levene, *Rise of the West*, 130, on *limpieza de sangre*.

199. Fest, *Face*, 155–7; Waite, *Psychopathic God*, 150–1; Gerwarth, *Hitler's Hangman*, 26–7, 36–7, for the repeated 'insinuations' that Heydrich's father was of Jewish origin.

200. Hilberg, *Destruction*, 36–7.

201. See Proctor, *Racial Hygiene*, ch. 4, 'The Progeny Law', for an extensive treatment of the subject.

202. Burleigh, *Third Reich*, 355.

203. Müller-Hill, 'Human Genetics', 107.

204. Burleigh, *Death*, 60–2; Proctor, *Racial Hygiene*, 111–12.

205. Burleigh, *Death*, 64–6.

206. Burleigh, *Third Reich*, 354.

207. Müller-Hill, 'Human Genetics', 106–7.

208. Götz Aly, *Final Solution: Nazi Population Policy and the Murder of the European Jews* (London: Arnold, 1999), 246–7.

209. Burleigh, *Death*, for a magisterial study. See also Henry Friedlander, *The Origins of Nazi Genocide: From Euthanasia to Final Solution* (Chapel Hill: University of North Carolina Press, 1995).

210. Burleigh, *Death*, 164.

211. Burleigh, *Death*, 160, 255.

212. See Rüdiger Lautmann, 'Homosexuals as "Enemies of the State"', in Berenbaum and Peck, *The Holocaust and History*, 348.

213. See Harry Oosterhuis, 'Medicine, Male Bonding, and Homosexuality in Nazi Germany', *Journal of Contemporary History*, 32:2 (1997), 189.

214. Oosterhuis, 'Medicine', 191. See also Longerich, *Himmler*, 232–40, for Himmler's intense homophobia, on the one hand, and *relative* wartime leniency with supposedly entrapped offenders, on the other.

215. Johnson, *Nazi Terror*, 287–9.

216. Quoted in Weitz, *A Century*, 119. See also Peukert, *Inside*, ch. 11, 'Order and Terror', for a probing commentary on the way Himmler's personal obsessions translated into the potential for policy change. The point is strongly corroborated throughout in Longerich, *Himmler*.

217. See Jürgen Förster, 'Complicity or Entanglement? Wehrmacht, War and Holocaust', in Berenbaum and Peck, *The Holocaust and History*, 272.

218. Quoted in Fest, *Face*, 83.

219. Quoted in Fest, *Face*, 83.

220. J. Noakes and G. Pridham, eds., *Nazism 1919–1945*, vol. 3: *Foreign Policy War and Racial Extermination: A Documentary Reader* (Exeter: University of Exeter Press, 1988), 679–87, for Hossbach's transcript of the 9 November 1937 conference.

221. Quoted in Fest, *Face*, 31.

222. Fischer, *History*, 271; Burleigh, *Third Reich*, 318.

223. See Bruce F. Pauley, *From Prejudice to Persecution: A History of Austrian Antisemitism* (Chapel Hill: University of North Carolina Press, 1989), esp. 277–93.

224. See Frank Bajohr, 'Expropriation and Expulsion', in Stone, *Historiography*, 58; Cesarani, *Eichmann*, 64.

225. See 'Hermann Goering—Number Two', in Fest, *Face*, 113–29.

226. Burleigh, *Third Reich*, 310.

227. Fischer, *History*, 273–4.

228. See Hans Safrian, 'Expediting Expropriation and Expulsion: The Impact of the "Vienna Model" on Anti-Jewish Policies in Nazi Germany', 1938, *HGS*, 14:3 (2000), 390–414.

229. Peter Hayes, 'State Policy and Corporate Involvement', in Berenbaum and Peck, *The Holocaust and History*, 203. See Burleigh, *Third Reich*, 312–14, for details of the Nacher affair.

230. Peter Hayes, 'The Deutsche Bank and the Holocaust', in Peter Hayes, ed., *Lessons and Legacies*, vol. 3: *Memory, Memorialisation and Denial* (Evanston, IL: Northwestern University Press, 1999), 71–92.

231. See Frank Bajohr, *'Aryanisation' in Hamburg: The Economic Exclusion of Jews and the Confiscation of their Property in Nazi Germany* (Oxford: Berghahn Books, 2001), for the seminal micro-study.

232. Hayes, 'State Policy', 208. For a more circumspect view on these 'returns' to the Nazi state, see Adam Tooze, *The Wages of Destruction: The Making and Breaking of the Nazi Economy* (London: Allen Lane, 2006), 279–80.

233. Hilberg, *Destruction*, 160.

234. Cesarani, *Eichmann*, 47–60, for Eichmann's early SD career.

235. Hannah Arendt, *Eichmann in Jerusalem: A Report on the Banality of Evil* (London: Penguin, 1965), 45–6.

236. See Cesarani, *Eichmann*, 64–9; Hans Safrian, 'Expediting Expropriation and Expulsion: The Impact of the "Vienna Model" on Anti-Jewish Policies in Nazi Germany, 1938', *HGS*, 14:3 (2000), 390–414; Hans Safrian, *Eichmann's Men*, trans. Ute Stargardt (Cambridge and New York: Cambridge University Press, 2010), 390–9, for more on Eichmann's Vienna operation.

237. Burleigh, *Third Reich*, 322.

238. Burleigh, *Third Reich*, 322; Cesarani, *Eichmann*, 73.

239. See Tony Kushner, *The Holocaust and the Liberal Imagination: A Social and Cultural History* (Oxford: Blackwell, 1994), 51–3.

240. See Götz Aly and Susanne Heim, 'Forced Emigration War, Deportation and Holocaust', in Frankel, *Fate*, 59–60.

241. Trude Maurer, 'The Background for Kristallnacht, The Expulsion of Polish Jews', in Walter H. Pehle, ed., *November 1938: From 'Reichskristallnacht' to Genocide*, trans. William Templar (Oxford: Berg, 1991), 52–3. More generally, see Joanna Michlic-Coren, 'Anti-Jewish Violence in Poland 1918–1939 and 1945–1947', *Polin*, 13 (2000), 37.

242. See Maurer, 'The Background', 44–5, 61–12, for eyewitness testimonies.

243. Aly and Heim, 'Forced Emigration', 60.

244. See, for instance, Klemperer, *I Shall Bear Witness*, 318–21: 12 and 27 July 1938 diary entries.

245. Schleunes, *Twisted Road*, 236.

246. Tooze, *Wages*, 280. Tooze's assessment is corroborated in Alan E. Steinweis, *Kristallnacht 1938* (Cambridge, MA, and London: Belknap Press, 2009), which emphasizes the popular, cathartic, and complicit nature of grass-roots participation in the pogrom.

247. Wolfgang Benz, 'The Relapse into Barbarism', in Pehle, ed., *November 1938*, 1–43, for further assessment of *Kristallnacht* and its aftermath. For a detailed case study of the localized effect see Michael Gehler, 'Murder on Command: The Anti-Jewish Pogrom in Innsbruck', *Leo Baeck Institute Year Book*, xxxviii (1993), 119–53.

248. Klemperer, *Language*, 101.

249. Pauley, *From Prejudice*, 287.

250. Richard Breitman, *The Architect of Genocide: Himmler and the Final Solution* (London: The Bodley Head, 1991), 53.

251. See Peukert, *Inside*, 58–60, for details. Also Kershaw, *Popular Opinion*, 264–71. In fairness, Kershaw does offer some examples of overt German support and succour to Jewish neighbours though this does not undermine his overall 'dismal' conclusion.

252. Burleigh, *Third Reich*, 354–5.

253. Broszat, *Anatomy*, 58.

254. See J. Noakes and G. Pridham, eds., *Nazism 1919–1945*, vol. 2: *State, Economy and Society: A Documentary Reader* (Exeter: University of Exeter Press, 1984), 558–60, for transcript extract of the 12 November meeting.

255. Noakes and Pridham, eds., *Nazism 1919–1945*, vol. 2: *State*, 259.

256. Burleigh, *Third Reich*, 354; Fischer, *History*, 284.

257. Broszat, *Anatomy*, 65–6.

258. Quoted in Burleigh, *Third Reich*, 316.

Select Bibliography

This bibliography lists the principal works that supported this study. For fuller references see the endnotes.

Abrahamian, Ervand, 'The US Media, Huntington and September 11th', *Third World Quarterly*, 3 (2003), 529–44.

Abramsky, Chimen, *War, Revolution and the Jewish Dilemma* (London: Lewis, 1975).

Abramson, Henry, *A Prayer for the Government: Ukrainians and Jews in Revolutionary Times 1917–1920* (Cambridge, MA: Ukrainian Research Institute and Center for Jewish Studies, Harvard University, Harvard University Press, 1999).

Acton, Thomas, ed., *Gypsy Politics and Traveller Identity* (Hatfield: University of Hertfordshire Press, 1997).

Adalian, Robert Paul, 'Comparative Policy and Differential Practice in the Treatment of Minorities in Wartime: The United States Archival Evidence on the Armenians and Greeks in the Ottoman Empire', *Journal of Genocide Research*, 3:1 (2001), 31–48.

Adalian, Robert Paul, ed., *Guide to the Armenian Genocide in the U.S. Archives 1915–1918* (Alexandria, VA: Chadwyck-Healey, 1994).

Adams, Michael C. C., *The Great Adventure: Male Desire and the Coming of World War One* (Bloomington, IN, and Indianapolis: Indiana University Press, 1990).

Adelson, Roger, *Mark Sykes: Portrait of an Amateur* (London: Cape, 1975).

Adelson, Roger, *London and the Invention of the Modern Middle East: Money, Power and War 1902–1922* (New Haven, CT, and London: Yale University Press, 1995).

Adler, Cyrus and Aaron A. Margalith, *With Firmness in the Right: American Diplomatic Action Affecting Jews 1840–1945* (New York: American Jewish Committee, 1946).

Aguardo, Iago Gil, 'The Credit Crisis of 1931 and the Fate of the Austro-German Customs Union', *Historical Journal*, 44:1 (2001), 199–221.

Ahmad, Feroz, *The Young Turks: The CUP in Turkish Politics 1908–1914* (Oxford: Oxford University Press, 1969).

Ahmad, Feroz, *The Making of Modern Turkey* (London: Routledge, 1993).

Ahmad, Kamal Madhar, *Kurdistan during the First World War* (London: Saqi Books, 1994).

Akçam, Taner, *From Empire to Republic: Turkish Nationalism and the Armenian Genocide* (London and New York: Zed Books, 2004).

Akçam, Taner, 'The Ottoman Documents and the Genocidal Policies of the Committee for Union and Progress (İttihat ve Terakki) towards the Armenians in 1915', *Genocide Studies and Prevention*, 1:2 (2006), 127–48.

Akçam, Taner, 'Deportations and Massacres in the Cipher Telegrams of the Interior Ministry in the Prime Ministerial Archive (Başbanlik Arşivi)', *Genocide Studies and Prevention*, 1:3 (2006), 305–25.

Aldcroft, Derek H. and Steven Morewood, *Economic Change in Eastern Europe since 1918* (Aldershot and Brookfield, VT: E. Elgar, 1995).

Alexandrov, Viktor, *The Tukhachevsky Affair*, trans. John Hewish (London: Macdonald, 1965).

Allen, W. E. D. and Paul Muratoff, *Caucasian Battlefields* (Cambridge: Cambridge University Press, 1953).

Altshuler, Mordechai, 'Russia and Her Jews: The Impact of the 1914 War', *Wiener Library Bulletin*, 27 (1973–4), 12–16.

Aly, Götz, *Final Solution: Nazi Population Policy and the Murder of the European Jews* (London: Arnold, 1999).

American Jewish Committee, *The Jews in the Eastern War Zone* (New York: American Jewish Committee, 1916).

Anderson, Benedict, *Imagined Communities: Reflections on the Origins and Spread of Nationalism* (London: Verso, 2nd ed., 1991).

Andrew, Christopher M. and A. S. Kanya-Forstner, *The Climax of French Imperial Expansion 1914–1924* (Stanford, CA: Stanford University Press, 1981).

Anzulović, Branimir, *Heavenly Serbia: From Myth to Genocide* (New York: New York University Press, 1999).

Applebaum, Anne, *Gulag: A History of the Soviet Camps* (London: Penguin, 2003).

Arendt, Hannah, *The Origins of Totalitarianism* (New York: Meridian, 1958).

Arendt, Hannah, *Eichmann in Jerusalem: A Report on the Banality of Evil* (London: Penguin, 1965).

Aronson, Ronald, *Dialectics of Disaster: A Preface to Hope* (London: Verso, 1983).

Aschheim, Steven E., *The Nietzsche Legacy in Germany 1880–1990* (Berkeley, CA: University of California Press, 1992).

Aster, Howard Aster and Peter J. Potichnyi, eds., *Ukrainian–Jewish Relations in Historical Perspective* (Edmonton: Canadian Institute of Ukrainian Studies, 2nd ed., 1990).

Baberowski, Jörg, *Verbrannte Erde: Stalins Herrshaft der Gewalt* (Munich: C.H. Beck, 2012).

Baer, Marc David, *The Dönme: Jewish Converts, Muslim Revolutionaries and Secular Turks* (Stanford, CA: Stanford University Press, 2010).

Bajohr, Frank, *'Aryanisation' in Hamburg: The Economic Exclusion of Jews and the Confiscation of their Property in Nazi Germany* (Oxford: Berghahn, 2001).

Balakian, Peter, *The Burning Tigris: The Armenian Genocide and America's Response* (New York: HarperCollins, 2003).

Banac, Ivo, *The National Question in Yugoslavia: Origins, History, Politics* (Ithaca, NY, and London: Cornell University Press, 1984).

Banac, Ivo, and Katherine Vedery, eds., *National Character and National: Ideology in Interwar Europe* (New Haven, CT: Yale Center for International and Area Studies, 1995).

Barkai, Avraham, *From Boycott to Annihilation: The Economic Struggle of German Jews 1933–1943*, trans. William Templar (Hanover, NH: Brandeis Press and University Press of New England, 1989).

Barkan, Elazar, *The Retreat of Scientific Racism: Changing Concepts of Race in Britain and the United States between the World Wars* (Cambridge and New York: Cambridge University Press, 1992).

Barker, A. J., *Rape of Ethiopia 1936* (New York: Ballantine Books, 1971).

Bartov, Omer, *Mirrors of Destruction: War, Genocide and Modern Identity* (New York and Oxford: Oxford University Press, 2000).

Bartov, Omer, ed., *The Holocaust: Origins, Implementations, Aftermath* (London and New York: Routledge, 2000), 108–61.

Bartov, Omer, and Phyllis Mack, eds., *In God's Name: Genocide and Religion in the Twentieth Century* (New York: Berghahn, 2001).

Bauer, Yehuda, *Jews for Sale? Nazi–Jewish Negotiations 1933–1945* (New Haven, CT, and London: Yale University Press, 1995).

Bauman, Zygmunt, *Modernity and the Holocaust* (Oxford: Blackwell, 1989).

Bauman, Zygmunt, *Postmodernity and its Discontents* (London: Polity, 1997).

Beck, Peter J., '"A Tedious and Perilous Controversy": Britain and the Settlement of the Mosul Dispute 1918–1926', *Middle Eastern Studies*, 17:2 (1981), 256–76.

Berenbaum, Michael, ed., *A Mosaic of Victims: Non-Jews Persecuted and Murdered by the Nazis* (London and New York: I.B. Tauris, 1990).

Berenbaum, Michael, and Abraham J. Peck, eds., *The Holocaust and History: The Known, The Unknown, The Disputed and The Reexamined* (Bloomington, IN, and Indianapolis: Indiana University Press, 1998).

Berghahn, Volker R. and Martin Kitchen, eds., *Germany in the Age of Total War* (London: Croom Helm, 1981).

Berkes, Niyazi, *The Development of Secularism in Turkey* (London: Hurst & Co., 1998).

Berkhoff, Karel C., *Harvest of Despair: Life and Death in Ukraine under Nazi Rule* (Cambridge, MA, and London: Harvard University Press, 2004).

Bessel, Richard, *Germany after the First World War* (Oxford: Oxford University Press, 1993).

Best, Geoffrey, *Humanity in Warfare* (New York: Columbia University Press, 1980).

Beylerian, Arthur, ed., *Les grandes Puissances, l'Empire ottoman et les Arméniens dans les archives françaises (1914–1918)*, (Paris: Publications de la Sorbonne, 1983).

Bidelux, Robert, *A History of Eastern Europe: Crisis and Change* (London: Routledge, 1998).

Bidelux, Robert, and Ian Jeffries, *Communism and Development* (London and New York: Methuen, 1985).

Binion, Rudolph, *Hitler among the Germans* (New York: Elsevier, 1976).

Biondich, Mark, *Stjepan Radić: The Croat Peasant Party and the Politics of Mass Mobilization* (Toronto: University of Toronto Press, 2000).

Biondich, Mark, *The Balkans: Revolution, War, and Political Violence since 1878* (Oxford: Oxford University Press, 2011).

Birnbaum, Pierre and Ira Katznelson, eds., *Paths of Emancipation: Jews, States and Citizenship* (Princeton: Princeton University Press, 1995).

Bjørnlund, Matthias, 'When the Cannons Talk, the Diplomats Must be Silent', *Genocide Studies and Prevention*, 1:2 (2006), 197–224.

Bjørnlund, Matthias, 'The 1914 Cleansing of Aegean Greeks as a Case of Violent Turkification', *Journal of Genocide Research*, 10:1 (2008), 41–57.

Bloch, Ivan Stanislavovich, *The Future of War in its Technical, Economic and Political Relations: Is War Now Impossible?* trans. R. C. Long (London: Doubleday & McClure, 1899).

Blouet, Brian W., *Halford Mackinder: A Biography* (College Station, TX: Texas A&M University Press, 1987).

Blouet, Brian W., ed., *Global Geostrategy: Mackinder and the Defence of the West* (Abingdon and New York: Frank Cass, 2005).

Bloxham, Donald, *The Great Game of Genocide: Imperialism, Nationalism and the Destruction of the Ottoman Armenians* (Oxford: Oxford University Press, 2005).

Bloxham, Donald, *Genocide, the World Wars and the Unweaving of Europe* (London and Portland, OR: Vallentine Mitchell, 2008).

Bloxham, Donald, and Tony Kushner, *The Holocaust: Critical Historical Approaches* (Manchester and New York: Manchester University Press, 2005).

Bloxham, Donald, and A. Dirk Moses, eds., *The Oxford Handbook of Genocide Studies* (Oxford: Oxford University Press, 2010).

Bock, Gisela, 'Racism and Sexism in Nazi Germany: Motherhood, Compulsory Sterilization, and the State', *Signs*, 8:3 (1983), 400–21.

Bottomore, Tom and Patrick Goode, eds., *Austro-Marxism* (Oxford: Clarendon Press, 1978).

Bourke, Joanne, *An Intimate History of Killing: Face-to-Face Killing in Twentieth Century Warfare* (London: Granta Books, 2000).

Bourne, John, Peter Liddle, and Ian Whitehead, eds., *The Great World War 1914–1945: Lightning Strikes Twice*, 2 vols (London: HarperCollins, 2000).

Bradley, John, *Allied Intervention in Russia* (London: Weidenfeld & Nicolson, 1968).

Braham, Randolph L., *The Politics of Genocide: The Holocaust in Hungary*, 2 vols (New York: Columbia University Press, 1981).

Brailsford, H. N., *Macedonia: Its Races and their Future* (London: Methuen, 1906).

Brandenberger, David, *National Bolshevism: Stalinist Mass Culture and the Formation of Modern Russian National Identity 1931–1956* (Cambridge, MA: Harvard University Press, 2002).

Brandon, Ray and Wendy Lower, eds., *The Shoah in Ukraine: History, Testimony, Memorialization* (Bloomington, IN, and Indianapolis: Indiana University Press, 2008).

Braude, Benjamin and Bernard Lewis, eds., *Christians and Jews in the Ottoman Empire: The Functioning of a Plural Society* (New York and London: Holmes & Meier, 1982).

Breitman, Richard, *The Architect of Genocide: Himmler and the Final Solution* (London: The Bodley Head, 1991).

Broszat, Martin and Elke Fröhlich, *Altag under Widerstand: Bayern im Nationalsozialismus* (Munich: Pier, 1987).

Brotherstone, Terry and Paul Dukes, eds., *The Trotsky Reappraisal* (Edinburgh: Edinburgh University Press, 1992).

Brovkin, Vladimir N., *Behind the Front Lines of the Civil War: Political Parties and Social Movements in Russia 1918–1922* (Princeton: Princeton University Press, 1994).

Brovkin, Vladimir N., ed., *The Bolsheviks in Russian Society: The Revolution and the Civil Wars* (New Haven, CT, and London: Yale University Press, 1997).

Brower, Daniel R., 'Kyrgyz Nomads and Russian Pioneers: Colonisation and Ethnic Conflict in the Turkestan Revolt of 1916', *Jahrbücher für Geschichte Osteuropas*, 44:1 (1996), 41–53.

Brower, Daniel R., and Edward J. Lazzerini, eds., *Russia's Orient: Imperial Borderlands and Peoples 1700–1917* (Bloomington, IN, and Indianapolis: Indiana University Press, 1997).

Brown, Kate, *A Biography of No Place: From Ethnic Borderland to Soviet Heartland* (Boston: Harvard University Press, 2005).

Browning, Christopher R., *The Final Solution and the German Foreign Office: A Study of Referat DIII of Abteilung Deutschland 1940–43* (New York and London: Holmes & Meier, 1978).

Browning, Christopher R. (with Jürgen Mätthaus), *The Origins of the Final Solution: The Evolution of Nazi Jewish Policy September 1939–March 1942* (London: William Heinemann, 2004).

Broxup, Marie Beningsen, ed., *The North Caucasus Barrier: The Russian Advance towards the Muslim World* (London: Hurst & Co., 1992).

Brubaker, Rogers, *Nationalism Reframed: Nationhood and the National Question in the New Europe* (Cambridge: Cambridge University Press, 1996).

Bruinessen, Martin van, *Agha, Shaikh and State: The Social and Political Structure of Kurdistan* (London: Zed Books, 1990).

Brun, Alf Harald, *Troublous Times: Experiences in Bolshevik Russia and Turkestan* (London: Constable & Co., 1931).

Bryce, James and Arnold J. Toynbee, eds., *The Treatment of Armenians in the Ottoman Empire 1915–16: Documents Presented to Viscount Grey of Falloden* (Princeton and London: Gomidas Institute, [1916] 2nd ed., 2005).

Brym, Robert J., *The Jewish Intelligentsia and Russian Marxism: A Sociological Study of Intellectual Radicalism and Ideological Divergence* (New York: Schocken Books, 1978).

Bulgakov, Mikhail, *A Dog's Heart: An Appalling Story*, ed. and trans. Andrew Bromfield (London: Penguin, [1968] 2007).

Burleigh, Michael, *Death and Deliverance: 'Euthanasia' in Germany 1900–1945* (Cambridge: Cambridge University Press, 1994).

Burleigh, Michael, *The Third Reich: A New History* (Basingstoke and Oxford: Pan Books, 2000).

Burleigh, Michael, and Wolfgang Wipperman, *The Racial State: Germany 1933–1945* (Cambridge: Cambridge University Press, 1991).

Burrin, Phillippe, *Hitler and the Jews: The Genesis of the Holocaust*, trans. Patsy Southgate (London: Edward Arnold, 1994).

Çağaptay, Soner, 'Crafting the Turkish Nation: Kemalism and Turkish Nationalism in the 1930s', unpublished PhD dissertation, Yale University, 2003.

Calder, Kenneth J., *Britain and the Origins of the New Europe 1914–1918* (Cambridge: Cambridge University Press, 1976).

Carr, E. H., 'The Origins and Status of the Cheka', *Soviet Studies*, 10:1 (1958), 1–11.

Cecil, Hugh and Peter H. Liddle, *At the Eleventh Hour: Reflections, Hopes and Anxieties at the Closing of the Great War* (Barnsley: Leo Cooper, 1998).

Cesarani, David, *Eichmann: His Life and Crimes* (London: Vintage, 2004).

Chaliand, Gérard, ed., *People without a Country: The Kurds and Kurdistan* (London: Zed Books, 1980).

Chamberlin, William Henry, *Russia's Iron Age* (London: Duckworth, 1935).

Charny, Israel W., ed., *Genocide: A Critical Bibliographical Review*, vol. 3: *The Widening Circle of Genocide* (New Brunswick, NJ, and London: Transaction Publishers, 1994).

Cherniavsky, Michael, ed., *Prologue to Revolution: Notes of I. A. Iakhantov on Secret Meetings of Council of Ministers 1915* (Englewood Cliffs, NJ: Prentice Hall, 1967).

Cheyette, Bryan, *Constructions of 'the Jew' in English Literature and Society: Racial Representations 1875–1945* (Cambridge: Cambridge University Press, 1993).

Chickering, Roger, *'We Men Who Feel Most German': A Cultural Study of the Pan-German League 1886–1914* (Boston: Allen & Unwin, 1984).

Çirakman, Asli, *From the 'Terror of the World' to the 'Sick Man of Europe': European Images of Ottoman Empire and Society from the Sixteenth Century to the Nineteenth* (New York and Oxford: Oxford University Press, 2002).

Clark, Bruce, *Twice a Stranger: How Mass Expulsion Forged Modern Greece and Turkey* (London: Granta Books, 2006).

Clark, Christopher, *Iron Kingdom: The Rise and Downfall of Prussia 1600–1947* (London: Penguin, 2006).

Clogg, Richard, ed., *Minorities in Greece: Aspects of a Plural Society* (London: Hurst & Co., 2002).

Cohen, Mark R., *Under Crescent and Cross: The Jews in the Middle Ages* (Princeton: Princeton University Press, 1994).

Cohn, Norman, *Warrant for Genocide: The Myth of the Jewish World-Conspiracy and the Protocols of the Elders of Zion* (London: Penguin, 1967).

Conquest, Robert, *The Nation Killers: The Soviet Deportation of Nationalities* (London: Macmillan, 1970).

Conquest, Robert, *Kolyma: The Arctic Death Camps* (Oxford and New York: Oxford University Press 1979).

Conquest, Robert, *Harvest of Sorrow: Soviet Collectivisation and the Terror-Famine* (London: Hutchinson, 1985).

Conquest, Robert, *The Great Terror: A Reassessment* (New York and Oxford: Oxford University Press, 1990).

Conversi, Daniele, '"We are all equals!": Militarism, Homogenization and Egalitarianism in National State Building (1789–1945)', *Ethnic and Racial Studies*, 31:7 (2008), 1286–314.

Coppa, Frank L., 'Between Anti-Judaism and Anti-Semitism: Pius XI's Response to Nazi Persecution of the Jews: Precursor to Pius XII's Silence?', *Journal of Church and State*, 47 (2005), 63–89.

Crampton, R. J., *Eastern Europe in the Twentieth Century* (London and New York: Routledge, 1994).

Crew, David F., ed., *Nazism and German Society 1933–1945* (London and New York: Routledge, 1994).

Crook, Paul, *Darwinism, War and History: The Debate over the Biology of War from the 'Origin of Species' to the First World War* (Cambridge: Cambridge University Press, 1994).

Crosby, Alfred W., *Ecological Imperialism: the Biological Expansion of Europe 900–1900* (Cambridge: Cambridge University Press, 2004).

Crowe, David and John Kolsti, eds., *The Gypsies of Eastern Europe* (New York and London: M. Armonk/M.E. Sharpe Inc., 1991).

Curp, T. David, 'Roman Dmowski Understood: Ethnic Cleansing as Permanent Revolution', *European Historical Quarterly*, 35:3 (2005), 405–27.

Dadrian, Vakahn N., 'The Naim-Andonian Documents on the World War I Destruction of Ottoman Armenians: The Anatomy of a Genocide', *International Journal of Middle Eastern Studies*, 18:3 (1986), 311–60.

Dadrian, Vakahn N., 'The Role of Turkish Physicians in the World War One Genocide of Ottoman Armenians', *Holocaust and Genocide Studies*, 1:2 (1986), 169–92.

Dadrian, Vakahn N., 'The Circumstances Surrounding the 1909 Adana Holocaust', *Armenian Review*, 41 (1988), 1–16.

Dadrian, Vakahn N., 'The Role of the Turkish Military in the Destruction of Ottoman Armenians: A Study in Historical Continuities', *Journal of Political and Military Sociology*, 20:2 (1992), 257–86.

Dadrian, Vakahn N., 'The Secret Young-Turk Ittihadist Conference and the Decision for the World War 1 Genocide of the Armenians', *Holocaust and Genocide Studies*, 7:2 (1993), 173–201.

Dadrian, Vakahn N., *The History of the Armenian Genocide: Ethnic Conflict from the Balkans to Anatolia to the Caucasus* (Providence, RI, and Oxford: Berghahn, 1995).

Dadrian, Vakahn N., *German Responsibility in the Armenian Genocide: A Review of the Historical Evidence of German Complicity* (Cambridge, MA: Blue Crane Books, 1997).

Dadrian, Vakahn N., *Warrant for Genocide: Key Elements of the Turko-Armenian Conflict* (New Brunswick, NJ, and London: Transaction Publishers, 1999).

Davies, Norman, *White Eagle, Red Star: The Polish–Soviet War 1919–20* (London: MacDonald, 1972).

Davies, Norman, 'Great Britain and the Polish Jews 1918–1920', *Journal of Contemporary History*, 8:2 (1973), 119–42.

Davies, R. W., *The Socialist Offensive: The Collectivisation of Soviet Agriculture 1929–30* (London: Macmillan 1980).

Davies, R. W., and Stephen Wheatcroft, *The Years of Hunger: Soviet Agriculture 1931–1933* (Basingstoke: Palgrave, 2004).

Davis, David Brion, ed., *The Fear of Conspiracy: Images of Un-American Subversion from the Revolution to the Present* (Ithaca, NY, and London: Cornell University Press, 1971).

Davis, Leslie A., *The Slaughterhouse Province: An American Diplomat's Report on the Armenian Genocide 1915–1917*, ed. Susan X. Bleair (New Rochelle, NY: A.D. Caratzas, 1989).

Davison, Roderic H., 'The Armenian Crisis, 1912–1914', *American Historical Review*, 53:3 (1948), 481–505.

Dawidowicz, Lucy, *The War against the Jews, 1933–45* (London: Penguin 1975).

Day, Richard B. and Daniel Gaido, eds., *Witnesses to Permanent Revolution: The Documentary Record* (Leiden and Boston: Brill, 2009).

Deák, István, Jan T. Gross and Tony Judt, eds., *The Politics of Retribution in Europe: World War II and its Aftermath* (Princeton: Princeton University Press, 2000).

Debray, Régis, *Revolution in the Revolution* (London: Penguin, 1967).

Deker, Nikolai K. and Andrei Lebed, eds., *Genocide in the USSR: Studies in Group Destruction* (New York: Scarecrow Press, 1958).

Derderian, Katherine, 'Common Fate, Different Experience: Gender-Specific Aspects of the Armenian Genocide 1915–1917', *Holocaust and Genocide Studies*, 19:1 (2005), 1–25.

Deringil, Selim, '"They Live in a State of Nomadism and Savagery": The Late Ottoman Empire and the Post-Colonial Debate', *Comparative Studies in Society and History*, 45:2 (2003), 311–42.

Deutscher, Isaac, *The Prophet Armed: Trotsky 1879–1921* (New York and London: Oxford University Press, 1954).

Deutscher, Isaac, *Stalin: A Political Biography* (London: Oxford University Press, [1949] 1961).

Deutscher, Isaac, *The Non-Jewish Jew and Other Essays* (London: Oxford University Press, 1968).

Dietsch, Johan, *Making Sense of Suffering: Holocaust and Holodomor in Ukrainian Historical Culture* (Lund: Lund University Press, 2006).

Dunn, Seamus and T. G. Fraser, *Europe and Ethnicity: The First World War and Contemporary Ethnic Conflict* (London and New York: Routledge, 1996).

Durham, Edith, *High Albania* (London: Beacon Press, [1909] 1987).

Earle, Edward Mead, *Turkey, the Great Powers and the Bagdad Railway* (New York: Russell & Russell, [1923] 1966).

Edmonds, C. J., *Kurds, Turks and Arabs: Politics Travel and Research in North-Eastern Iraq 1919–1925* (London and New York: Oxford University Press, 1957).

Ehrenreich, Barbara, *Blood Rites: Origins and History of the Passions of War* (London: Virago, 1997).

Ellis, John, *Armies in Revolution* (London: Croom Helm, 1973).

Ellman, Michael, 'The Role of Leadership Perceptions and of Intent in the Soviet Famine of 1931–1934', *Europe–Asia Studies*, 57:6 (2005), 823–41.

Ellman, Michael, 'The Political Economy of Stalinism in the Light of the Archival Revolution', *Journal of Institutional Economics*, 4:1 (2008), 99–125.

Erickson, Edward J., *Ordered to Die: A History of the Ottoman Army in the First World War* (Westport, CT: Greenwood Press, 2001).

Etherton, Percy T., *In the Heart of Asia* (London: Constable & Co., 1925).

Evans-Pritchard, E. E., *The Sanusi of Cyrenaica* (London: Oxford University Press, 1949).

Fernández, Silvio Castro, *La masacre de los independientes de color en 1912* (Havana: Editorial de Ciencias Sociales, 2002).

Fest, Joachim C., *The Face of the Third Reich* (London: Penguin, 1970).

Fest, Joachim C., *Hitler*, trans. Richard and Clara Winston (London: Penguin 1974).

Fink, Carole, *Defending the Rights of Others: The Great Powers, the Jews, and International Minority Protection 1878–1938* (New York: Cambridge University Press, 2004).

Fischer, Fritz, *Germany's Aims in the First World War* (London: Chatto & Windus, 1967).

Fischer, Gerhard, *Enemy Aliens: Internment and the Homefront Experience in Australia 1914–1920* (St Lucia: University of Queensland Press, 1989).

Fischer, Klaus P., *The History of an Obsession: German Judeophobia and the Holocaust* (New York and London: Continuum, 2001).

Fisher, Alan, *The Crimean Tatars* (Stanford, CA: Hoover Institute Press, 1978).

Fisher, John, *Curzon and British Imperialism in the Middle East 1916–1919* (London and Portland, OR: Frank Cass, 1999).

Fitzpatrick, Sheila, ed., *Stalinism: New Directions* (London and New York: Routledge, 2000).

Fleming, Gerald, *Hitler and the Final Solution* (Oxford: Oxford University Press, 1986).

Fonseca, Isabel, *Bury Me Standing: The Gypsies and their Journey* (London: Chatto & Windus, 1995).

Frankel, Jonathan, ed., *The Fate of the European Jews 1939–1945: Continuity or Contingency?* (Studies in Contemporary Jewry XIII) (New York and London: Oxford University Press, 1997).

Fraser, Angus, *The Gypsies* (Oxford: Blackwell, 1992).

French, David, 'Spy Fever in Britain 1900–1915', *Historical Journal*, 21:2 (1978), 350–70.

Friedlander, Henry, *The Origins of Nazi Genocide: From Euthanasia to Final Solution* (Chapel Hill: University of North Carolina Press, 1995).

Friedländer, Saul, *Nazi Germany and the Jews: The Years of Persecution 1933–1939* (New York: HarperCollins, 1997).

Friedländer, Saul, *The Years of Extermination: Nazi Germany and the Jews 1939–1945* (New York: HarperCollins, 2007).

Friedman, Isaiah, *The Question of Palestine 1914–1918* (London: Routledge and Kegan Paul, 1973).

Fromkin, David, *A Peace to End Peace: Creating the Modern Middle East 1914–1922* (London: Penguin, 1991).

Fromm, Erich, *The Fear of Freedom* (London: Routledge and Kegan Paul, [1942] 1960).

Gainer, Bernard, *The Alien Invasion: The Origins of the Aliens Act of 1905* (London: Heinemann, 1972).

Gammer, Moshe, *Muslim Resistance to the Czar: Shamil and the Conquest of Chechnia and Daghestan* (London: Frank Cass, 1994).

Garbe, Detlev, *Zwischen Widerstand und Martyrium: Die Zeugen Jehovahs im 'Dritten Reich'* (Munich: R. Oldenbourg Verlag, 1994).

Gatrell, Peter, *A Whole Empire Walking: Refugees in Russia during World War I* (Bloomington, IN, and Indianapolis: Indiana University Press, 1999).

Gaunt, David, *Massacres, Resistance, Protectors: Muslim–Christian Relations in Eastern Anatolia during World War I* (Piscataway, NJ: Gorgias Press, 2006).

Gawrych, George W., 'The Culture and Politics of Violence in Turkish Society 1903–13', *Middle Eastern Studies*, 22:3 (1985), 307–30.

Gay, Peter, *Weimar Culture: The Outsider as Insider* (London: Penguin, 1974).

Gay, Peter, *Freud, Jews and other Germans: Masters and Victims in Modernist Culture* (Oxford: Oxford University Press, 1978).

Geifman Anna, *Death Orders: The Vanguard of Modern Terrorism in Revolutionary Russia* (Santa Barbara, CA: Praeger Security International, 2010).

Gelb, Michael, '"Karelian Fever": The Finnish Immigrant Community during Stalin's Purges', *Europe–Asia Studies* 43:9 (1993), 237–68.

Gelb, Michael, 'The Western Finnic Minorities and the Origins of Stalinist Nationalities Deportations', *Nationalities Papers* 24:2 (1996), 237–68.

Gellately, Robert, *The Gestapo and German Society: Enforcing Racial Policy 1933–1945* (Oxford: Clarendon Press, 1990).

Georgeon, François, *Aux origines du nationalisme turc: Yusuf Akçura 1876–1935* (Paris: Éditions ADPF, 1980).

Gerlach, Christian, *Extremely Violent Societies: Mass Violence in the Twentieth-Century World* (Cambridge and New York: Cambridge University Press, 2010).

Gerrits, André, *The Myth of Jewish Communism: A Historical Interpretation* (Brussels: P.I.E. Peter Lang, 2009).

Gerwarth, Robert, 'The Central European Counter-Revolution: Paramilitary Violence in Germany, Austria and Hungary after the Great War', *Past & Present*, 200 (2008), 175–210.

Gerwarth, Robert, *Hitler's Hangman: The Life of Heydrich* (New Haven, CT, and London: Yale University Press, 2011).

Getty, J. Arch, *Origins of the Great Purges: The Soviet Party Reconsidered 1933–1938* (Cambridge: Cambridge University Press, 1985).

Getty, J. Arch, and Roberta T. Manning, eds., *Stalinist Terror: New Perspectives* (Cambridge: Cambridge University Press, 1993).

Geyer, Michael and Sheila Fitzpatrick, eds., *Beyond Totalitarianism: Stalinism and Nazism Compared* (Cambridge: Cambridge University Press, 2009).

Giesinger, Adam, *From Catherine to Khrushchev: The Story of Russia's Germans* (Battleford, SK: Marian Press, 1974).

Gilman, Sander L., *The Jew's Body* (New York and London: Routledge, 1991).

Gilman, Sander L., *Franz Kafka: The Jewish Patient* (New York and London: Routledge, 1995).

Gingeras, Ryan, *Sorrowful Shores: Violence, Ethnicity, and the End of the Ottoman Empire 1912–1923* (Oxford: Oxford University Press, 2009).

Giradet, Raoul, *La Société militaire dans la France contemporaine 1815–1939* (Paris: Librarie Plon, 1953).

Gitelman, Zvi Y., *Jewish Nationality and Soviet Politics: The Jewish Sections of the CPSU 1917–1930* (Princeton: Princeton University Press, 1972).

Gladstone, William, *The Bulgarian Horrors and the Question of the East* (London: John Murray, 1876).

Golczewski, Frank, *Polnisch-jüdische Beziehungen 1881–1922: eine Studie zur Geschichte des Antisemitismus in Osteuropa* (Wiesbaden: Steiner, 1981).

Goldhagen, Daniel Jonah, *Hitler's Willing Executioners: Ordinary Germans and the Holocaust* (London: Little, Brown and Company, 1996).

Goldscheider, Calvin and Alan S. Zuckerman, *The Transformation of the Jews* (Chicago and London: Chicago University Press, 1984).

Goltz, Anna von der, *Hindenburg: Power, Myth, and the Rise of the Nazis* (New York and London: Oxford University Press, 2009).

Gordon, Sarah, *Hitler, Germans and the Jewish Question* (Princeton: Princeton University Press, 1984).

Graber, G. S., *Caravans to Oblivion: The Armenian Genocide 1915* (New York: J. Wiley, 1996).

Grady, Tim, *The German Jewish Soldiers of the First World War in History and Memory* (Liverpool: Liverpool University Press, 2011).

Graziosi, Andrea, *The Great Soviet Peasant War: Bolsheviks and Peasants 1917–1933* (Cambridge, MA: Harvard University Press, 1996).

Gregor, Neil, *How to Read Hitler* (London: Granta, 2005).

Groot, Gerald J. de, *The First World War* (Basingstoke: Palgrave, 2001).

Gross, Jan Tomasz, *Revolution from Abroad: The Soviet Conquest of Poland's Western Ukraine and Western Belorussia* (Princeton: Princeton University Press, [1988] 2002).

Gwynn, Stephen Lucius, ed., *The Letters and Friendships of Sir Cecil Spring-Rice: A Record* (Boston: Houghton Mifflin, 1929).

Haberer, Erich, *Jews and Revolution in Nineteenth-Century Russia* (Cambridge: Cambridge University Press, 1995).

Hagenloh, Paul, *Stalin's Police: Public Order and Mass Repression in the USSR 1926–1941* (Baltimore and Washington, DC: John Hopkins University Press and Woodrow Wilson Center Press, 2009).

Hagenlücke, Heinz, *Deutsche Vaterlandspartei: Die nationale Rechte am Ende des Kaiserreiches* (Düsseldorf: Droste, 1997).

Hanak, Harry, *Great Britain and Austria-Hungary during the First World War: A Study in the Formation of Public Opinion* (Oxford: Oxford University Press, 1962).

Hanauske-Abel, H. M., 'Not a Slippery Slope or Sudden Subversion: German Medicine and National Socialism in 1933', *British Medical Journal*, 131 (1996), 1453.

Hancock, Ian, *The Pariah Syndrome: An Account of Gypsy Slavery and Persecution* (Ann Arbor, MI: Karoma Publishers, 1987).

Hanioğlu, M. Şükrü, *Preparations for a Revolution: The Young Turks 1902–1908* (New York: Oxford University Press, 2001).

Hayes, Peter, ed., *Lessons and Legacies III: Memory, Memorialization and Denial* (Evanston, IL: Northwestern University Press, 1999).

Haynes, Rebecca, ed., *In the Shadow of Hitler: Personalities of the Right in Central and Eastern Europe* (London: I.B. Tauris, 2011).

Headlam-Morley, Agnes, Russell Bryant, and Anna Cienciala, eds., *Sir James Headlam-Morley: A Memoir of the Paris Peace Conference 1919–20* (London: Methuen & Co., 1972).

Heifetz, Elias, *The Slaughter of the Jews in the Ukraine in 1919* (New York: Thomas Seltzer, 1921).

Heinzen, James W., *Inventing a Soviet Countryside: State Power and the Transformation of Rural Russia 1917–1929* (Pittsburgh: Pittsburgh University Press, 2004).

Hepburn, A. C., ed., *Minorities in History* (London: Edward Arnold, 1978).

Herbert, Ulrich, ed., *Best: Biographische Studien über Radikalismus, Weltanschauung und Venunft* (Bonn: Dientz, 1996).

Herbert, Ulrich, ed., *National Socialist Extermination Policies: Contemporary German Perspectives and Controversies* (New York and Oxford: Berghahn Books, 2000).

Herf, Jeffrey, *The Jewish Enemy: Nazi Propaganda during World War II and the Holocaust* (Cambridge, MA: Harvard University Press, 2006).

Herring, Eric, 'Between Iraq and a Hard Place: A Critique of the British Government's Case for UN Economic Sanctions', *Review of International Studies*, 28:1 (2002), 39–56.

Herwig, Holger, 'Tunes of Glory at the Twilight Stage: The Bad Homberg Crown Council and the Evolution of German Statecraft 1917/1918', *German Studies Review*, 6 (1983), 475–94.

Heyd, Uriel, *Foundations of Turkish Nationalism: The Life and Teachings of Ziya Gökalp* (London: Luzac, 1950).

Hilberg, Raul, *The Destruction of the European Jews* (New York: Holmes & Meier, 1985).

Hildermeier, Manfred and Elisabeth Müller-Luckner, *Stalinismus vor dem Zweiten Weltkrieg: neue Wege der Forschung* (Munich: Oldenbourg, 1998).

Hildesheimer, Esriel, *Jüdische Selbstverwaltung unter dem NS-Regime: der Existenzkampf der Reichsvertretung und Reichsvereinigung der Juden in Deutschland* (Tübingen: Mohr, 1994).

Hirsch, Francine, *Empire of Nations: Ethnographic Knowledge and the Making of the Soviet Union* (Ithaca, NY, and London: Cornell University Press, 2005).

Hirschman, Albert, *Exit, Voice and Loyalty* (Cambridge, MA: Harvard University Press, 1970).

Hirschon, Renée, ed., *Crossing the Aegean: An Appraisal of the 1923 Compulsory Population Exchange between Greece and Turkey* (New York and Oxford: Berghahn, 2003).

Hoare, Philip, *Wilde's Last Stand: Decadence, Conspiracy and the First World War* (London: Duckworth, 1997).

Hoffman, David L., ed., *Stalinism: The Essential Readings* (Oxford: Blackwell, 2003).

Hofmann, Tessa and Gerayer Koutcharian, 'The History of Armenian–Kurdish Relations in the Ottoman Empire', *Armenian Review*, 39:4 (1986), 1–45.

Hofmann, Tessa, Matthias Bjørnlund and Vasileios Meichanetsidis, eds., *The Genocide of the Ottoman Greeks* (New York and Athens: Aristide D. Caratzas, 2011).

Holmes, Colin, *Anti-Semitism in British Society 1876–1939* (London: Arnold, 1979).

Holmes, Colin, 'The Myth of Fairness: Racial Violence in Britain 1911–19', *History Today*, 35:10 (1985), 41–5.

Holquist, Peter, 'A Russian Vendée: The Practice of Revolutionary Politics in the Don Countryside', unpublished PhD dissertation, Columbia University, 1995.

Holquist, Peter, ' "Conduct Merciless, Mass Terror": Decossakisation in the Don, 1919', *Cahiers du monde russe*, 38:1–2 (1997), 127–62.

Holquist, Peter, ' "Information is the Alpha and Omega of Our Work": Bolshevik Surveillance in its Pan-European Context', *Journal of Modern History*, 69:3 (1997), 415–50.

Holquist, Peter, *Making War, Forging Revolution: Russia's Continuum of Crisis 1914–1921* (Cambridge, MA: Harvard University Press, 2002).

Horne, John and Alan Kramer, *German Atrocities 1914: A History of Denial* (New Haven, CT, and London: Yale University Press, 2001).

Hosking, Geoffrey, *Russia, People and Empire 1552–1917* (London: HarperCollins, 1997).

Hovannisian, Richard G., *Armenia: On the Road to Independence 1918* (Berkeley, CA, and Los Angeles: University of California Press, 1967).

Hovannisian, Richard G., *Armenian Genocide: History, Politics, Ethics* (New York: St. Martin's Press, 1992).

Hovannisian, Richard G., *Remembrance and Denial: The Case of the Armenian Genocide* (Detroit, MI: Wayne State University Press, 1999).

Hovannisian, Richard G., ed., *The Armenian Genocide in Perspective* (New Brunswick, NJ, and London: Transaction Publishers, 1986).

Hovannisian, Richard G., ed., *Armenian People from Ancient to Modern Times*, vol. 1: *The Dynastic Periods: From Antiquity to the Fourteenth Century* (London and New York: Palgrave Macmillan and St. Martin's Press, 2004).

Howard, Michael, *War and the Liberal Conscience* (London: Temple Smith, 1978).

Howe, Stephen, *Ireland and Empire: Colonial Legacies in Irish History and Culture* (Oxford: Oxford University Press, 2000).

Hunczak, Taras, 'A Reappraisal of Symon Petliura and Ukrainian–Jewish Relations 1917–21', *Jewish Social Studies*, 31 (1969), 163–83.

Huntington, Samuel P., *The Clash of Civilisations and the Remaking of World Order* (London: Touchstone Books, 1998).

Hüppauf, Bernd, ed., *War, Violence and the Modern Condition* (Berlin: Walter de Gruyter, 1997).

Husri, Khaldun S., 'The Assyrian Affair of 1933', *International Journal of Middle East Studies*, 5 (1974), 161–76, 344–60.

Hyman, Paula, 'The History of European Jewry: Recent Trends in the Literature', *Journal of Modern History*, 54:2 (1982), 303–19.

Iancu, Carol, *Les juifs en Roumanie (1866–1919): De l'exclusion à l'émancipation* (Aix-en-Provence: Éditions de l'Université de Provence, 1978).

İnalcik, Halil and Donald Quataert, *An Economic and Social History of the Ottoman Empire 1300–1914* (Cambridge: Cambridge University Press, 1994).

Iordachi, Constantin, *Charisma, Politics and Violence: The Legion of the 'Archangel Michael' in Inter-War Romania* (Trondheim: Trondheim Studies on East European Cultures and Societies, 2004).

Irvine, Jill A., *The Croat Question: Partisan Politics in the Formation of the Yugoslav Socialist State* (Boulder, CO: Westview Press, 1993).

Ismael, Tareq Y. and William W. Haddad, eds., *Iraq: The Human Costs of History* (London: Pluto, 2003).

Izady, Mehrdad R., *The Kurds: A Concise Handbook* (Washington, DC: Taylor & Francis, 1992).

Janowsky, Oscar I., *The Jews and Minority Rights (1898–1919)* (New York: Columbia University Press, 1933).

Jelavich, Barbara, *History of the Balkans* (Cambridge: Cambridge University Press, 1983).

Jensen, Uffa, Habbo Knoch, Daniel Morat, and Miriam Rürup, eds., *Gewalt und Gesellschaft: Klassiker modernen Denkens neu gelesen* (Göttingen: Wallstein Verlag, 2011).

Jernazian, Ephraim K., *Judgement under Truth: Witnessing the Armenian Genocide* (New Brunswick, NJ, and London: Transaction Publishers, 1990).

Johnpoll, Bernard K., *The Politics of Futility: The General Jewish Workers Bund of Poland, 1917–41* (New York: Cornell University Press, 1967).

Johnson, Chalmers, *Blowback: The Costs and Consequences of American Empire* (New York: Henry Holt and Company, 2001).

Johnson, Eric, *The Nazi Terror: Gestapo, Jews and Ordinary Germans* (London: John Murray, 1999).

Jones, Adam, *Genocide: A Comprehensive Introduction* (London and New York: Routledge, 2nd ed., 2011).

Jones, Adam, *New Directions in Genocide Research* (New York and London: Routledge, 2012).

Joseph, John, *The Nestorians and their Muslim Neighbours: A Study of Western Influences on their Relations* (Princeton: Princeton University Press, 1961).

Judah, Tim, *Kosovo: War and Revenge* (New Haven, CT, and London: Yale University Press, 2000).

Kadish, Sharman, *Bolsheviks and British Jews: The Anglo-Jewish Community, Britain, and the Russian Revolution* (London: Frank Cass, 1992).

Kaiser, Hilmar, *Imperialism, Racism, and Development Theories: The Construction of a Dominant Paradigm on Ottoman Armenians* (Ann Arbor, MI: Gomidas Institute, 1997).

Kaiser, Hilmar, *At the Crossroads of Der Zor: Death, Survival and Humanitarian Resistance in Aleppo 1915–1917* (Princeton: Gomidas Institute, 2001).

Kaiser, Hilmar, 'The Ottoman Government and the End of the Ottoman Social Formation, 1915–1917', paper presented at 'Der Völkermord an den Armeniern und die Shoah', Zurich, November 2001.

Kaiser, Hilmar, 'Regional Resistance to Central Government Policies: Ahmed Djemal Pasha, the Governors of Aleppo, and Armenian Deportees in the Spring and Summer of 1915', *Journal of Genocide Research*, 12:3/4 (2010), 173–218.

Kaligian, Dikran M., *Armenian Organization and Ideology under Ottoman Rule 1908–1914* (New Brunswick, NJ: Transaction Publishers, 2009).

Kamusella, Tomasz D. I., 'Ethnic Cleansing in Silesia 1950–89 and the Ennationalizing Policies of Poland and Germany', *Patterns of Prejudice*, 33:2 (1999), 51–73.

Kappeler, Andreas, *The Russian Empire: A Multiethnic History*, trans. Alfred Clayton (Harlow: Longman, 2001).

Karput, Kemal H., ed., *Ottoman Past and Today's Turkey* (Leiden: Brill, 2000).

Kater, Michael, 'Everyday Antisemitism in Pre-War Nazi Germany: The Popular Bases', *Yad Vashem Studies*, 16 (1984), 129–59.

Katkov, George, *Russia, 1917: The February Revolution* (London: Harper & Row, 1967).

Katz, Steven T., 'The Holocaust and Comparative History', *Leo Baeck Memorial Lecture* 37 (New York: Leo Baeck, 1993).

Katz, Steven T., *The Holocaust in Historical Context*, vol. 1: *The Holocaust and Mass Death before the Modern Age* (New York and Oxford: Oxford University Press, 1994).

Kedourie, Elie, *England and the Middle East: The Destruction of the Ottoman Empire 1914–1921* (London: Bowes & Bowes, 1956).

Kedourie, Elie, *The Chatham House Version and Other Middle Eastern Studies* (London: Weidenfeld & Nicolson, 1970).

Kedourie, Elie, 'Sir Mark Sykes and Palestine 1915–1916', *Middle Eastern Studies*, 6 (1970), 340–5.

Kedourie, Elie, *In the Anglo-Arab Labyrinth: The MacMahon–Husayn Correspondence and its Interpretations 1914–1939* (Cambridge: Cambridge University Press, 1976).

Keegan, John, *The First World War* (London: Hutchinson, 1998).

Kelidar, Abbas, ed., *The Integration of Modern Iraq* (New York: St. Martin's Press, 1979).

Kellogg, Michael, *The Russian Roots of Nazism: White Émigrés and the Making of National Socialism 1917–1945* (Cambridge: Cambridge University Press, 2005).

Kemal, Yashar, *Salman the Solitary*, trans. Thilda Kemal (London: The Harvill Press, 1998).

Kennan, George F., *The Other Balkan Wars: A 1913 Carnegie Endowment Inquiry in Retrospect with a New Introduction and Reflections on the Present Conflict* (Washington, DC: Carnegie Endowment for International Peace, [1914] 1993).

Kenrick, Donald and Grattan Puxon, *The Destiny of Europe's Gypsies* (New York: Basic Books, 1973).

Kershaw, Ian, *Popular Opinion and Political Dissent: Bavaria 1933–1945* (Oxford: Clarendon Press, 1983).

Kershaw, Ian, *Hitler 1889–1936: Hubris* (London: Penguin, 1998).

Kévorkian, Raymond, *The Armenian Genocide : A Complete History* (London and New York: I.B. Tauris, 2011).

Keyder, Çaglar, *State and Class in Turkey: A Study in Capitalist Development* (New York: Verso, 1987).

Khaldun, Ibn, *The Muqaddimah: An Introduction to History*, trans. Franz Rosenthal (Princeton: Princeton University Press, 1969).

Khalidi, Rashid, Lisa Anderson, Muhammad Muslih, and Reeva Simon, eds., *The Origins of Arab Nationalism* (New York and London: Columbia University Press, 1991).

Khalil, Samir al-, *Republic of Fear: The Inside Story of Saddam's Iraq* (London: Hutchinson Radius, 1989).

Khodarkovsky, Michael, *Where Two Worlds Met: The Russian State and the Kalmyk Nomads 1600–1771* (Ithaca, NY: Cornell University Press, 1992).

Kiernan, Ben and Robert Gellately, eds., *The Spectre of Genocide: Mass Murder in Historical Perspective* (Cambridge and New York: Cambridge University Press, 2003).

Kieser, Hans-Lukas, *Der verpasste Friede: Mission, Ethnie und Staat in den Ostprovinzen der Türkei 1839–1938* (Zurich: Chronos, 2000).

Kieser, Hans-Lukas, ed., *Turkey beyond Nationalism: Towards Post-Nationalist Identities* (London and New York: I.B. Tauris, 2006).

Kieser, Hans-Lukas and Dominik J. Schaller, eds., *Der Völkermord an den Armeniern und die Shoah* (Zurich: Chronos Publishing, 2002).

Kieval, Hillel J., 'Representation and Knowledge in Medieval and Modern Accounts of Jewish Ritual Murder', *Jewish Social Studies: History, Culture, Society*, 1 (1994–5), 52–72.

Kieval, Hillel J., *Language of Community: The Jewish Experience in the Czech Lands* (Berkeley, CA, Los Angeles, and London: University of California Press, 2000).

King, Desmond, *In the Name of Liberalism: Illiberal Social Policy in the United States and Britain* (Oxford: Oxford University Press, 2000).

King, Greg and Penny Wilson, *The Fate of the Romanovs* (Hoboken, NJ: John Wiley & Sons, 2003).

Kinross, Patrick, *Atatürk: The Rebirth of a Nation* (London: Phoenix Giant, [1964] 1993).

Kitchen, Martin, *The Silent Dictatorship: The Politics of the German High Command under Hindenburg and Ludendorff 1916–1918* (London: Croom Helm, 1976).

Kitromilides, Paschalis, '"Imagined Communities" and the Origins of the National Question in the Balkans', *European History Quarterly*, 19:2 (1989), 149–92.

Klemperer, Victor, *I Shall Bear Witness: The Diaries of Victor Klemperer, 1933–1941*, ed. and trans. Martin Chalmers (London: Phoenix, 1999).

Klemperer, Victor, *The Language of the Third Reich: LTI—Lingua Tertii Imperii: A Philologist's Notebook*, trans. Martin Brady (London: The Athlone Press, 2000).

Klier, John D., 'Cossacks and Pogroms: What was Different about "Military" Pogroms?', in O. V. Budnitsky, O. V. Belova, V. E. Kel'ner, and V. V. Mochalova, eds., *Mirovoi krizis 1914–1920 godov i sud'ba vostochnoevropeiskogo evreistva* (Moscow: Rosspen, 2005), 47–70.

Klier, John D., and Shlomo Lambroza, eds., *Pogroms: Anti-Jewish Violence in Modern Russian History* (Cambridge: Cambridge University Press, 1991).

Kohn, Hans, *Nationalism and Imperialism in the Hither East* (New York: Harcourt Brace, 1932).

Koonz, Claudia, *Mothers in the Fatherland: Women, the Family and Nazi Politics* (New York: St. Martin's Press, 1987).

Kopelev, Lev, *The Education of a True Believer*, trans. Gary Kern (London: Wildwood House, 1981).

Kornberg, Jacques, 'The Paranoid Style: Analysis of a Holocaust-Denial Text', *Patterns of Prejudice*, 29:2/3 (1995), 33–44.

Kott, Matthew, 'Stalin's Great Terror (1937–38) as Antecedent and Other Aspects of the Recent Historiography of Soviet Genocide', in *Yearbook of the Museum of the Occupation of Latvia* (Riga: Occupation Museum Foundation, 2007), 42–54.

Kramer, Alan, *Dynamic of Destruction: Culture and Mass Killing in the First World War* (Oxford: Oxford University Press, 2007).

Krausnick, Helmut and Martin Broszat, *Anatomy of the SS State*, trans. Dorothy Long and Marian Jackson (London: Paladin, 1970).

Kühl, Stefan, *The Nazi Connection: Eugenics, American Racialism and German National Socialism* (Oxford: Oxford University Press, 1994).

Kuper, Leo, *Genocide: Its Political Use in the Twentieth Century* (New Haven, CT, and London: Yale University Press, 1982).

Kushner, David, *The Rise of Turkish Nationalism 1876–1908* (London: Frank Cass, 1977).

Kushner, Tony, *The Holocaust and Liberal Imagination: A Social and Cultural History* (Oxford: Blackwell, 1994).

Kushner, Tony, 'H.J. Fleure: A Paradigm for Inter-War Race Thinking in Britain', *Patterns of Prejudice*, 42:2 (2008), 151–66.

Kushner, Tony, and Katharine Knox, *Refugees in an Age of Genocide* (London: Frank Cass, 1999).

Kushner, Tony, and Hannah Ewence, eds., *Whatever Happened to British Jewish Studies?* (London and Portland, OR: Vallentine Mitchell, 2012).

Landau, Jacob M., *Tekinalp: Turkish Patriot 1883–1961* (Leiden: Nederlands Historisch-Archaeologisch Instituut te Istanbul, 1984).

Landau, Ronnie S., *The Nazi Holocaust* (London and New York: I.B. Tauris, 1992).

Langenhove, Fernand van, *Comment naît un cycle de légendes: Franc-tireurs et atrocités en Belgique* (Lausanne: Payot, 1916).

Langmuir, Gavin, *Towards a Definition of Antisemitism* (Berkeley, CA, and Los Angeles: University of California Press, 1990).

Laqueur, Walter, *Weimar: A Cultural History 1918–1933* (London: Weidenfeld & Nicolson, 1974).

Laqueur, Walter, *Black Hundred: The Rise of the Extreme Right in Russia* (New York: Harper Perennial, 1993).

Lavsky, Hagit, *Before Catastrophe: The Distinctive Path of German Zionism* (Detroit and Jerusalem: Wayne State University Press, Magnes Press, Leo Baeck Institute, 1996).

Leggett, George, *The Cheka: Lenin's Political Police. The All-Russian Extraordinary Commission for Combating Counterrevolution and Sabotage (December 1917 to February 1922)* (Oxford: Clarendon Press, 1981).

Leitz, Christian, ed., *The Third Reich: The Essential Readings* (Oxford: Blackwell, 1999).

Lemkin, Raphael, *Axis Rule in Occupied Europe* (Washington, DC: Carnegie Endowment for International Peace, 1944).

Lenin, V. I., *Selected Works*, vol. 1 (Moscow: Progress Publishers, 1977).

Levene, Mark, 'The Balfour Declaration: A Case of Mistaken Identity', *English Historical Review*, 107 (1992), 54–77.

Levene, Mark, *War, Jews and the New Europe: The Diplomacy of Lucien Wolf 1914–1919* (Oxford: Littman Library of Jewish Civilisation and Oxford University Press, 1992).

Levene, Mark, 'Creating a Modern "Zone of Genocide": The Impact of Nation and State Formation on Eastern Anatolia, 1878–1923', *Holocaust and Genocide Studies*, 12 (1998), 393–433.

Levene, Mark, 'A Moving Target, the Usual Suspects and (Maybe) a Smoking Gun: The Problem of Pinning Blame in Modern Genocide', *Patterns of Prejudice*, 33:4 (1999), 3–24.

Levene, Mark, 'The Limits of Tolerance: Nation-State Building and What it Means for Minority Groups', *Patterns of Prejudice*, 34:2 (2000), 19–40.

Levene, Mark, '"Ni grec, ni bulgare, ni turc": Salonika Jewry and the Balkan Wars, 1912–13', *Jahrbuch des Simon-Dubnow Instituts*, 2 (2003), 65–97.

Levy, Richard S., *The Downfall of the Anti-Semitic Parties in Imperial Germany* (New Haven, CT: Yale University Press, 1975).

Lewandowski, Jozef, 'History and Myth: Pinsk, April 1919', *Polin*, 2 (1987), 5–36.

Lewin, Moshe, *Russian Peasants and Soviet Power: A Study of Collectivisation*, trans. Irene Nove (London: Allen & Unwin, 1968).

Lewin, Moshe, *The Making of the Soviet System: Essays on the Social History of Interwar Russia* (London and New York: Methuen, 1985).

Lewis, Bernard, *The Emergence of Modern Turkey* (Oxford, University Press, 2nd ed., 1968).

Lewy, Guenter, *The Nazi Persecution of the Gypsies* (Oxford and New York: Oxford University Press, 2000).

Lewy, Guenter, *The Armenian Massacres in Ottoman Turkey: A Disputed Genocide* (Salt Lake City: University of Utah Press, 2005).

Libaridian, Gerard J., *Modern Armenia: People, Nation, State* (New Brunswick, NJ, and London: Transaction Publishers, 2005).

Lieberman, Benjamin, *Terrible Fate: Ethnic Cleansing in the Making of Modern Europe* (Chicago: Ivan R. Dee, 2006).

Liebich, André, 'The Antisemitism of Henry Wickham Steed', *Patterns of Prejudice*, 46:2 (2012), 180–208.

Liégeois, Jean-Pierre, *Gypsies: An Illustrated History*, trans. Tony Berrett (London: Al Saqi Books, 1986).

Liekis, Šarūnas, *A State within a State?: Jewish Autonomy in Lithuania 1918–1925* (Vilna: Versus Aureus, 2003).

Liekis, Šarūnas, Lidia Miliakova, and Antony Polonsky, 'Three Documents on Anti-Jewish Violence in the Eastern Kresy during the Polish–Soviet Conflict', *Polin*, 14 (2001), 116–49.

Lieven, Dominic, *Empire: The Russian Empire and its Rivals* (London: John Murray, 2000).

Lincoln, Bruce W., *Red Victory: A History of the Russian Civil War* (New York: Simon & Schuster, 1989).

Lindemann, Albert S., *Esau's Tears: Modern Anti-Semitism and the Rise of the Jews* (Cambridge and New York: Cambridge University Press, 1997).

Lindner, Rudi Paul, *Nomads and Ottomans in Medieval Anatolia* (Bloomington, IN: Research Institute for Inner Asian Studies, 1981).

Liulevicius, Vejas Gabriel, *War Land on the Eastern Front: Culture, National Identity and German Occupation in World War I* (Cambridge and New York: Cambridge University Press, 2000).

Livezeanu, Irina, *Cultural Politics in Greater Romania: Regionalism, Nation Building and Ethnic Struggle 1918–1930* (Ithaca, NY, and London: Cornell University Press, 1995).

Lohalm, Uwe, *Völkischer Radikalismus: Die Geschichte des Deutschvölkischen Schutz- und Trutz-Bundes 1919–1923* (Hamburg: Leibnitz-Verlag, 1970).

Lohr, Eric, 'The Russian Army and Jews: Mass Deportation, Hostages, and Violence during World War I', *Russian Review*, 60:3 (2001), 404–19.

Lohr, Eric, *Nationalizing the Russian Empire: The Campaign against Enemy Aliens during World War One* (Cambridge, MA, and London: Harvard University Press, 2003).

Longerich, Peter, *Holocaust: The Nazi Persecution and Murder of the Jews* (Oxford: Oxford University Press, 2010).

Longerich, Peter, *Heinrich Himmler*, trans. Jeremy Noakes and Lesley Sharpe (Oxford and New York: Oxford University Press, 2012).

Longworth, Philip, *The Cossacks* (London: Constable, 1969).

Löwe, Heinz-Dietrich, *The Tsars and the Jews: Reform, Reaction and Anti-Semitism in Imperial Russia 1772–1917* (Chur, Switzerland and Langhorne, PA: Harwood Academic Publishers, 1993).

Lower, Wendy, *Nazi Empire-Building and the Holocaust in Ukraine* (Chapel Hill: University of North Carolina Press, 2005).

Macartney, C. A., *National States and National Minorities* (Oxford: Oxford University Press, 1934).

McCagg William O. Jr, 'Jews in Revolutions: The Hungarian Experience', *Journal of Social History*, 6:1 (1972), 78–105.

McCarthy, Justin, *Muslims and Minorities: The Population of Ottoman Anatolia at the End of Empire* (New York and London: New York University Press, 1983).

McCarthy, Justin, *Death and Exile: The Ethnic Cleansing of Ottoman Muslims 1821–1922* (Princeton: Darwin Press, 1995).

McCarthy, Justin, *The Ottoman Peoples and the End of Empire* (London: Hodder Headline Group, 2001).

McDowall, David, *A Modern History of the Kurds* (London: I.B. Tauris, 1997).

Mackinder, Sir Halford J., *Democratic Ideals and Reality: A Study in the Politics of Reconstruction* (London: Constable & Co., 1919).

Mackinder, Sir Halford J., *The Geographical Pivot of History* (London: John Murray, 1951).

Macleod, Jenny and Pierre Pursleigh, eds., *Uncovered Fields: Perspectives in First World War Studies* (Leiden: Brill, 2004).

McLouglin, Barry and Kevin McDermott, *Stalin's Terror: High Politics and Mass Repression in the Soviet Union* (Basingstoke: Palgrave, 2003).

McNeal, Robert H., *Tsar and Cossack 1855–1914* (Basingstoke: Macmillan, 1987).

McNeill, William H., *Arnold J. Toynbee: A Life* (New York and Oxford: Oxford University Press, 1989).

Malcolm, Noel, *Bosnia: A Short History* (London and Basingstoke: Macmillan, 1994).

Malcolm, Noel, *Kosovo: A Short History* (London and Basingstoke: Macmillan, 1998).

Mamety, Victor S. and Radomir Luza, *A History of the Czech Republic 1918–1948* (Princeton: Princeton University Press, 1973).

Mango, Andrew, *Atatürk* (London: John Murray, 1999).

Mann, Michael, *Sources of Social Power* (Cambridge: Cambridge University Press, 1993).

Mann, Michael, *The Dark Side of Democracy: Explaining Ethnic Cleansing* (Cambridge and New York: Cambridge University Press, 2005).

Mansel, Philip, *Constantinople: City of the World's Desire 1453–1924* (London: Penguin, 1997).

Marcus, Joseph, *Social and Political History of the Jews in Poland 1919–1939* (Berlin: Mouton, 1983).

Margolin, Arnold, *From a Political Diary: Russia, the Ukraine and America 1905–1945* (New York: Columbia University Press, 1946).

Marks, Sally, 'The Myths of Reparations', *Central European History*, 11:3 (1978), 231–55.

Markusen, Eric and David Kopf, *The Holocaust and Strategic Bombing: Genocide and Total War in the 20th Century* (Boulder, CO, San Francisco, and Oxford: Westview Press, 1995).

Marom, Ram, 'The Bolsheviks and the Balfour Declaration, 1917–1920', *Wiener Library Bulletin*, 29 (1976), 20–9.

Marples, David R., *Heroes and Villains: Creating National History in Contemporary Ukraine* (Budapest: Central European University Press, 2007).

Marrus, Michael, *The Unwanted: European Refugees in the Twentieth Century* (New York and Oxford: Oxford University Press, 1985).

Marshalian, Levon, *Politics and Demography: Armenians, Turks and Kurds in the Ottoman Empire* (Cambridge, MA: Zoryan Institute, 1991).

Martin, Terry, 'The Origins of Soviet Ethnic Cleansing', *Journal of Modern History*, 70:4 (1998), 813–61.

Martin, Terry, *The Affirmative Action Empire: Nations and Nationalism in the Soviet Union 1923–1939* (Ithaca, NY, and London: Cornell University Press, 2001).

Marx, Anthony W., *Faith in Nation: The Exclusionary Origins of Nationalism* (Oxford and New York: Oxford University Press, 2003).

Maser, Werner, *Hitler's Letters and Notes*, trans. Arnold Pomerans (London: Heinemann, 1974).

Mayer, Arno J., *Politics and Diplomacy of Peacemaking: Containment and Counterrevolution at Versailles 1918–1919* (New York: Knopf, 1967).

Mayer, Arno J., *The Furies: Violence and Terror in the French and Russian Revolutions* (Princeton: Princeton University Press, 2000).

Maynard, John, *The Russian Peasant and Other Studies* (London: Victor Gollancz, 1942).

Mazower, Mark, *Dark Continent: Europe's Twentieth Century* (London: Penguin Press, 1998).

Mazower, Mark, *The Balkans* (London: Weidenfeld & Nicolson, 2000).

Mazower, Mark, *Hitler's Empire: Nazi Rule in Occupied Europe* (London: Penguin, 2009).

Medvedev, Roy A., *Let History Judge: The Origins and Consequences of Stalinism* (New York: Knopf, 1972).

Melson, Robert F., *Revolution and Genocide: On the Origins of the Armenian Genocide and the Holocaust* (Chicago: Chicago University Press, 1992).

Mendes-Flohr, Paul R. and Jehuda Reinharz, eds., *The Jew in the Modern World: A Documentary History* (New York: Oxford University Press, 1980).

Michaelidis, Gregory, 'Salvation Abroad: Macedonian Migration to North America and the Making of Modern Macedonia 1870–1970', unpublished PhD dissertation, University of Maryland, 2005.

Michlic-Coren, Joanna, 'Anti-Jewish Violence in Poland, 1918–1939 and 1945–1947', *Polin*, 13 (2000), 34–61.

Milfull, John, ed., *Why Germany?: National Socialist Anti-Semitism and the European Context* (Providence, RI, and Oxford: Berg, 1993).

Miller, Donald E. and Lorna Touryan Miller, *Survivors: An Oral History of the Armenian Genocide* (Berkeley, CA, and Los Angeles: University of California Press, 1993).

Miller, Rory, ed., *Britain, Palestine and Empire: The Mandate Years* (Aldershot: Ashgate, 2010).

Mommsen, Hans, *From Weimar to Auschwitz*, trans. Philip O'Connor (Princeton: Princeton University Press, 1991).

Morgenthau, Henry, *Ambassador Morgenthau's Story* (Garden City, NY: Doubleday, Page, 1918).

Morris, James, 'The Polish Terror: Spy Mania and Ethnic Cleansing in the Great Terror', *Europe–Asia Studies*, 56:5 (2004), 751–66.

Morrow, John. H. Jr, *The Great War: An Imperial History* (London and New York: Routledge, 2004).

Moses, A. Dirk, ed., *Genocide and Settler Society: Frontier Violence and Stolen Indigenous Children in Australian History* (New York and Oxford: Berghahn, 2001).

Moses, A. Dirk, ed., 'Paranoia and Partisanship: Genocide Studies, Holocaust Historiography and the "Apocalyptic Conjuncture"', *The History Journal*, 54:2 (2011), 553–83.

Mosse, George L., *The Crisis of German Ideology: Intellectual Origins of the Third Reich* (London: Weidenfeld & Nicolson, 1964).

Mosse, George L., *Nazi Culture: Intellectual, Cultural and Social Life in the Third Reich* (New York: Grosset & Dunlap, 1966).

Mosse, George L., *German Jews beyond Judaism* (Bloomington, IN, and Indianapolis: Indiana University Press, 1985).

Mosse, George L., *Toward the Final Solution: A History of European Racism* (New York: Howard Fetig, 2nd ed., 1985).

Naimark, Norman M., *Fires of Hatred: Ethnic Cleansing in Twentieth-Century Europe* (Cambridge, MA, and London: Harvard University Press, 2001).

Nalbandian, Louise, *The Armenian Revolutionary Movement: The Development of Armenian Political Parties through the Nineteenth Century* (Berkeley, CA, and Los Angeles: University of California Press, 1963).

Neumann, Franz, *Behemoth: The Structure and Practice of National Socialism* (London: Gollancz, 1942).

Newman, Leonard S. and Ralph Erber, eds., *Understanding Genocide: The Social Psychology of the Holocaust* (New York and Oxford: Oxford University Press, 2002).

Nicholson, Beryl, 'New States, New Problems: The Resettlement in Albania of Refugees from Yugoslavia after 1919', unpublished paper presented at 'Refugees and the End of Empire Conference', De Montfort University, Leicester, 29–30 June 2007.

Nicolson, Nigel and Joanne Trautmann, eds., *The Question of Things Happening: The Letters of Virginia Woolf, Vol. 2: 1912–1922* (London: Chatto & Windus, 1976).

Niewyk, Donald L., *The Jews in Weimar Germany* (Manchester: Manchester University Press, 1980).

Nimni, Ephraim, ed., *National-Cultural Autonomy and its Contemporary Critics* (London and New York: Routledge, 2005).

Noakes, J. and G. Pridham, eds., *State, Economy and Society: A Documentary Reader*, vol. 2: *Nazism 1919–1945* (Exeter: University of Exeter Press, 1984).

Noakes, J. and G. Pridham, eds., *Foreign Policy War and Racial Extermination: A Documentary Reader*, vol. 3: *Nazism 1919–1945* (Exeter: University of Exeter Press, 1988).

Nogales, Rafael de, *Four Years beneath the Crescent*, trans. Muna Lee (London: Charles Scribner's Sons, 1924).

Nove, Alec, *An Economic History of the USSR* (London: Penguin, 1969).

Oleskiw, Stephen, *The Agony of a Nation: The Great Man-Made Famine in Ukraine 1932–1933* (London: National Committee to Commemorate the 50th Anniversary of the Artificial Famine in Ukraine 1932–33, 1983).

Olson, Robert W., *The Emergence of Kurdish Nationalism and the Sheikh Said Rebellion 1880–1925* (Austin: University of Texas Press, 1989).

Omissi, David E., 'Britain, the Assyrians and the Iraqi Levies 1919–1932', *Journal of Imperial and Commonwealth History*, 17:3 (1989), 301–22.

Omissi, David E., *Air Power and Colonial Control: The Royal Air Force 1919–1939* (Manchester: Manchester University Press, 1990).

Oosterhuis, Harry, 'Medicine, Male Bonding, and Homosexuality in Nazi Germany', *Journal of Contemporary History*, 32:2 (1997), 187–205.

Orwell, George, *Homage to Catalonia* (London: Penguin, [1938] 2003).

Palmer, Alan, *The Lands Between: A History of East-Central Europe since the Congress of Vienna* (London: Weidenfeld & Nicolson, 1970).

Panayi, Panikos, *The Enemy in Our Midst: Germans in Britain during the First World War* (London and New York: Berg, 1991).

Panayi, Panikos, *Minorities in Wartime: National and Racial Groupings in Europe, North America and Australia during the Two World Wars* (Oxford: Berg, 1993).

Panayi, Panikos, and Pippa Virdee, eds., *Refugees and the End of Empire: Imperial Collapse and Forced Migration during the Twentieth Century* (Basingstoke: Palgrave Macmillan, 2011).

Passeleq, Georges and Bernard Suchecky, *The Hidden Encyclical of Pius XI*, trans. Steven Rendall (New York: Harcourt Brace, 1997).

Patch, William L. Jr, *Heinrich Brüning and the Dissolution of the Weimar Republic* (Cambridge and New York: Cambridge University Press, 1998).

Pauley, Bruce F., *From Prejudice to Persecution: A History of Austrian Antisemitism* (Chapel Hill: University of North Carolina Press, 1989).

Payne, Stanley G., *A History of Fascism 1914–45* (London: UCL Press, 1995).

Pearson, Raymond, *National Minorities in Eastern Europe 1848–1945* (London and Basingstoke: Macmillan, 1983).

Pehle, Walter H., ed., *November 1938: From 'Reichskristallnacht' to Genocide*, trans. William Templar (Oxford: Berg, 1991).

Pendlebury, Alyson, *Portraying 'the Jew' in First World War Britain* (London: Frank Cass, 2005).

Pentzopoulos, Dmitri, *The Balkan Exchange of Minorities and its Impact on Greece* (London: Hurst & Co., [1962] 2002).

Perrie, Maureen, *The Cult of Ivan the Terrible in Stalin's Russia* (London: Longman, 2003).

Perry, Duncan M., *The Politics of Terror: The Macedonian Liberation Movements 1893–1903* (Durham, NC, and London: Duke University Press, 1988).

Petersen, Roger D., *Understanding Ethnic Violence: Fear, Hatred and Resentment in Twentieth-Century Eastern Europe* (Cambridge and New York: Cambridge University Press, 2002).

Peukert, Detlev K., *Inside Nazi Germany: Conformity, Opposition and Racism in Everyday Life*, trans. Richard Deveson (London: Penguin, 1989).

Pilger, John, *The New Rulers of the World* (London: Verso, 2002).

Pipes, Richard, *The Russian Revolution* (New York: Knopf, 1990).

Pipes, Richard, *Russia under the Bolshevik Regime 1919–1924* (London: Harvill, 1994).

Pipes, Richard, ed., *Revolutionary Russia* (London and Cambridge, MA: Harvard and Oxford University Presses, 1968).

Pohl, J. Otto, 'Stalin's Genocide Against the "Repressed Peoples"', *Journal of Genocide Research*, 2:2 (2000), 267–93.

Poliakov, Léon, *History of Anti-Semitism*, vol. 4: *Suicidal Europe 1870–1933*, trans. George Klin (Oxford: Littman Library and Oxford University Press, 1985).

Polian, Pavel, *Against Their Will: The History and Geography of Forced Migrations in the USSR* (Budapest and New York: Central European University Press, 2004).

Pommerin, Reiner, *Sterilisierung der Rheinlandbastarde: Das Schicksal einer farbigen deutschen Minderheit 1918–1937* (Düsseldorf: Droste, 1979).

Pons, Silvio and Andrea Romano, eds., *Russia in the Age of Wars 1914–1945* (Milan: Feltrinelli, 2000).

Porter, Brian, *When Nationalism Begins to Hate: Imagining Modern Politics in Nineteenth-Century Poland* (Oxford and New York: Oxford University Press, 2000).

Powell, Christopher, *Barbaric Civilization: A Critical Sociology of Genocide* (Montreal and Kingston: McGill-Queen's University Press, 2011).

Preston, Paul, *The Spanish Holocaust: Inquisition and Extermination in Twentieth-Century Spain* (London: W.W. Norton & Co., 2012).

Proctor, Robert, *Racial Hygiene: Medicine under the Nazis* (Cambridge, MA: Harvard University Press, 1988).

Prusin, Alexander V., *Nationalizing a Borderland: War, Ethnicity, and Anti-Jewish Violence in East Galicia 1914–1920* (Tuscaloosa, AL: University of Alabama Press, 2005).

Prusin, Alexander V., *The Lands Between: The East European Frontiers in Wars, Revolutions and Nationality Conflicts 1900–1992* (Oxford: Oxford University Press, 2010).

Ra'anan, Uri, Marie Mesner, Keith Ames, and Kate Martin, eds., *State and Nation in Multi-Ethnic Societies: The Breakup of Multinational States* (Manchester: Manchester University Press, 1991).

Rabinovich, Itamar and Jehuda Reinharz, eds., *Israel in the Middle East: Documents and Readings on Society, Politics, and Foreign Relations, pre-1948 to the Present* (Waltham, MA: Brandeis University Press, 2008).

Radkey, Oliver H., *The Unknown Civil War in Soviet Russia: A Study of the Green Movement in the Tambov Region 1920–21* (Stanford, CA: Hoover Institute Press, 1976).

Ramsaur, Ernest E. Jr, *The Young Turks* (Princeton: Princeton University Press, 1957).

Rankin, Reginald, *The Inner History of the Balkan War* (London: Constable & Co., 1914).

Redlich, Shimon, *Together and Apart in Brzezany: Poles, Jews, and Ukrainians 1919–1945* (Bloomington, IN, and Indianapolis: Indiana University Press, 2002).

Reid, Anna, *Borderland: A Journey through the History of Ukraine* (London: Weidenfeld & Nicolson, 1997).

Renton, James, 'Changing Languages of Empire and the Orient: Britain and the Invention of the Middle East', *Historical Journal*, 50:3 (2007), 645–67.

Renton, James, *The Zionist Masquerade: The Birth of the Anglo-Zionist Alliance 1914–1918* (Basingstoke and New York: Palgrave Macmillan, 2007).

Resis, Albert, ed., *Molotov Remembers: Inside Kremlin Politics, Conversations with Felix Chuev* (Chicago: Ivan R. Dee, 1993).

Reynolds, Michael A., 'The Ottoman–Russian Struggle for Eastern Anatolia and the Caucasus 1908–1918: Identity, Ideology and the Geopolitics of World Order', unpublished PhD dissertation, Princeton University, 2003.

Rezzori, Gregor von, *Memoirs of an Anti-Semite*, trans. Joachim Neugroschel and Gregor von Rezzori (New York: Viking Press, 1981).

Richardson, Curtis, 'Stalinist Terror and the Kalmyks' National Revival: A Cultural and Historical Perspective', *Journal of Genocide Research*, 4:3 (2002), 441–51.

Rings, Guido and Anne Ife, eds., *Neo-Colonial Mentalities in Contemporary Europe?: Language and Discourse in the Construction of Identities* (Newcastle upon Tyne: Cambridge Scholars Publishing, 2008).

Ro'i, Yaacov, ed., *Jews and Jewish Life in Russia and the Soviet Union* (Ilford, Essex, and Portland, OR: Frank Cass, 1995).

Rodogno, Davide, *Fascism's European Empire: Italian Occupation during the Second World War* (Cambridge: Cambridge University Press, 2006).

Rogger, Hans, 'The Formation of the Russian Right 1900–1906', *California Slavic Studies*, 3 (1964), 66–94.

Rogger, Hans, *Jewish Policies and Right-Wing Politics in Imperial Russia* (London: Macmillan, 1985).

Roseman, Mark, *The Villa, The Lake, the Meeting: Wannsee and the Final Solution* (London: Penguin, 2002).

Rosenberg, William G. and Marilyn B. Young, *Transforming Russia and China: Revolutionary Struggle in the Twentieth Century* (Oxford and New York: Oxford University Press, 1982).

Roshwald, Aviel, *Ethnic Nationalism and the Fall of Empires: Central Europe, Russia and the Middle East 1914–1923* (London and New York: Routledge, 2001).

Rothschild, Joseph, *Return to Diversity: A Political History of East Central Europe since World War II* (New York and Oxford: Oxford University Press, 1990).

Rousso, Henry, ed., *Stalinism and Nazism: History and Memory Compared*, trans. Lucy B. Golsan, Thomas C. Hilde, and Peter S. Rogers (Lincoln and London: University of Nebraska Press, 2004).

Rozenblit, Marsha L., *Reconstructing a National Identity: The Jews of Habsburg Austria during World War 1* (New York: Oxford University Press, 2001).

Rubin, Barnett G. and Jack Snyder, eds., *Post-Soviet Political Order* (London and New York: Routledge, 1998).

Rummel, R. J., *Lethal Politics: Soviet Genocide and Mass Murder since 1917* (New Brunswick, NJ, and London: Transaction Press, 1991).

Safrian, Hans, 'Expediting Expropriation and Expulsion: The Impact of the "Vienna Model" on Anti-Jewish Policies in Nazi Germany 1938', *Holocaust and Genocide Studies*, 14: 3 (2000), 390–414.

Safrian, Hans, *Eichmann's Men*, trans. Ute Stargardt (Cambridge and New York: Cambridge University Press, 2010).

Said, Edward W., *Orientalism* (New York: Vintage Books, 1979).

Salt, Jeremy, *Imperialism, Evangelism and the Ottoman Armenians 1878–1896* (London: Frank Cass, 1993).

Sanborn, Joshua A., 'Unsettling the Empire: Violent Migrations and Social Disaster in Russia during World War I', *Journal of Modern History*, 77:2 (2005), 290–325.

Sarafian, Ara, ed., *United States Official Documents on the Armenian Genocide*, 3 vols (Watertown, MA: Armenian Review Books, 1994).

Sarafian, Ara, ed., *Talaat Pasha's Report on the Armenian Genocide 1917* (London: Gomidas Institute, 2011).

Sarınay, Yusuf, 'What Happened on April 24, 1915? The Circular of April 24 1915, and the Arrest of the Armenian Committee Members in Istanbul', *International Journal of Turkish Studies*, 14:1–2 (2008), 75–101.

Saul, Mahir and Royer, Patrick, *West African Challenge to Empire: Culture and History in the Volta-Bani Anticolonial War* (Athens, OH, and Oxford: Ohio University Press and James Currey, 2001).

Saul, Nicholas and Susan Tebbutt, eds., *The Role of the Romanies: Images and Counter-Images of 'Gypsies'/Romanies in European Cultures* (Liverpool: Liverpool University Press, 2004).

Saunders, Ronald, *The High Walls of Jerusalem: A History of the Balfour Declaration and the Birth of the British Mandate in Palestine* (New York: Holt, Rhinehart and Winston, 1983).

Schabas, William A., *Genocide in International Law: The Crime of Crimes* (Cambridge: Cambridge University Press, 2000).

Schaller, Dominik J., 'From Lemkin to Clooney: The Development and State of Genocide Studies', *Genocide Studies and Prevention*, 6:3 (2011), 245–56.

Schapiro, Leonard, 'The Role of the Jews in the Russian Revolutionary Movement', *East European and Slavic Review*, 40 (1961–2), 148–67.

Schleunes, Karl, *The Twisted Road to Auschwitz: Nazi Policy towards the Jews 1933–1939* (Urbana, IL: University of Illinois Press, 1970).

Schmaltz, Eric J. and Sinner, Samuel D., '"You will die under ruins and snow": The Soviet Repression of Russian Germans as a Case Study of Successful Genocide', *Journal of Genocide Research*, 4:3 (2002), 327–56.

Schuker, Stephen A., *The End of French Predominance in Europe: The Financial Crisis of 1924 and the Adoption of the Dawes Plan* (Chapel Hill: University of North Carolina Press, 1976).

Sciaky, Leon, *Farewell to Salonika: Portrait of an Era* (London: Hodder & Stoughton, 1946).

Scott, James C., *Weapons of the Weak: Everyday Forms of Peasant Resistance* (New Haven, CT: Yale University Press, 1986).

Scott, James C., *Seeing Like a State: How Certain Schemes to Improve the Human Condition Have Failed* (New Haven, CT, and London: Yale University Press, 1998).

Seaton, Albert, *The Horsemen of the Steppes: The Story of the Cossacks* (London: The Bodley Head, 1985).

Seely, Robert, *Russo–Chechen Conflict 1800–2000: A Deadly Embrace* (London and Portland, OR: Frank Cass, 2001).

Segesser, Daniel Marc and Myriam Gessler, 'Raphael Lemkin and the International Debate on the Punishment of War Crimes (1919–1948)', *Journal of Genocide Research*, 7:4 (2005), 453–68.

Segev, Tom, *One Palestine Complete: Jews and Arabs under the British Mandate*, trans. Haim Watzman (London: Little, Brown and Company, 2000).

Semelin, Jacques, Claire Andrieu, and Sarah Gensburger, eds., *Resisting Genocide: The Multiple Forms of Rescue*, trans. Emma Bentley and Cynthia Schoch (London: Hurst, 2010).

Service, Robert, *Stalin: A Biography* (Cambridge, MA: Belknap Press, 2005).

Shaw, Stanford J. and Ezel Kural Shaw, *History of the Ottoman Empire and Modern Turkey*, vol. 2: *The Rise of Modern Turkey 1808–1975* (Cambridge: Cambridge University Press, 1977).

Shearer, David R., *Policing Stalin's Socialism: Repression and Social Order in the Soviet Union 1924–1953* (New Haven, CT, and Stanford, CA: Yale University Press and Hoover Institute, 2009).

Sheehan, James J., 'National Socialism and German Society: Reflections on Recent Research', *Theory and Society*, 13:6 (1984), 851–67.

Sheehy, Ann and Bohdan Nahalyo, *The Crimean Tatars, Volga Germans and Meshketians: Soviet Treatment of Some National Minorities* (London: Minority Rights Group, 3rd ed., 1981).

Shils, Edward A., *The Torment of Secrecy: The Background and Consequences of American Security Policies* (London: William Heinemann, 1956).

Simon, Reeva S., *Iraq between the Two World Wars: The Creation and Implementation of a Nationalist Ideology* (New York: Columbia University Press, 1986).

Simpson, Sir John Hope, *The Refugee Problem: Report of a Survey* (London: Oxford University Press, 1939).

Skocpol, Theda, *States and Social Revolutions: A Comparative Analysis of France, Russia and China* (Cambridge: Cambridge University Press, 1979).

Slezkine, Yuri, *The Jewish Century* (Princeton and Oxford: Princeton University Press, 2004).

Slomp, Gabriella, *Carl Schmitt and the Politics of Hostility, Violence and Terror* (Basingstoke: Palgrave, 2009).

Smith, David Norman, 'Uncivil Society: "Race" and Murder in Nazi Germany', *Patterns of Prejudice*, 29:2/3 (1995), 123–6.

Smith, Michael Llewellyn, *Ionian Vision: Greece in Asia Minor 1919–1922* (London: Hurst & Co., [1973] 1998).

Smith, Roger W., 'Women and Genocide: Notes on an Unwritten History', *Holocaust and Genocide Studies*, 8:3 (1994), 315–34.

Smith, Roger W., ed., *Genocide: Essays toward Understanding, Early Warning and Prevention*, (Williamsburg, VA: Association of Genocide Scholars, 1999).

Smith, Woodruff D., *The Ideological Origins of Nazi Imperialism* (New York and Oxford: Oxford University Press, 1986).

Snyder, Timothy, *The Reconstruction of Nations: Poland, Ukraine, Lithuania, Belarus 1569–1999* (New York and London: Yale University Press, 2003).

Snyder, Timothy, *Sketches from a Secret War: A Polish Artist's Mission to Liberate Soviet Ukraine* (New Haven, CT: Yale University Press, 2005).

Snyder, Timothy, *Bloodlands: Europe between Hitler and Stalin* (London: The Bodley Head, 2010).

Sokol, Edward Dennis, *The Revolt of 1916 in Russian Central Asia* (Baltimore: The John Hopkins Press, 1953).

Somakian, Manoug J., *Empires in Conflict: Armenia and the Great Powers 1895–1920* (London: I.B. Tauris, 1995).

Sonyel, Salahi, *The Great War and the Tragedy of Anatolia* (Ankara: Turkish Historical Printing House, 2000).

Spector, Sherman David, *Rumania and the Paris Peace Conference: A Study of the Diplomacy of Ioan I.C. Bratianu* (New York: Bookman Associates, 1962).

Stafford, R. S., *The Tragedy of the Assyrians* (London: Allen & Unwin, 1935).

Stalin, I. V., *Problems of Leninism* (Moscow: Foreign Languages Publishing House, 1945).

Statiev, Alexander, *The Soviet Counter-Insurgency in the Western Borderlands* (Cambridge: Cambridge University Press, 2010).

Steed, Henry Wickham, *Through Thirty Years: A Personal Narrative* (London: Heinemann, 1924).

Stefanović, Đorđe, 'Seeing the Albanians through Serbian Eyes: The Inventors of the Tradition of Intolerance and their Critics, 1804–1939', *European History Quarterly*, 35:3 (2005), 465–92.

Steinberg, Jonathan, *All or Nothing: The Axis and the Holocaust 1941–43* (London and New York: Routledge, 1990).

Steiner, Zara, *The Lights that Failed: European International History 1919–1933* (Oxford: Oxford University Press, 2004).

Steinweis, Alan E., *Kristallnacht 1938* (Cambridge, MA, and London: Belknap Press, 2009).

Stiglmayer, Alexandra, ed., *Mass Rape: The War against Women in Bosnia-Herzegovina* (Lincoln, NE, and London: University of Nebraska Press, 1994).

Stivers, William, *Supremacy and Oil: Iraq, Turkey and the Anglo-American World Order 1918–1930* (Ithaca, NY, and London: Cornell University Press, 1982).

Stone, Dan, ed., *The Historiography of the Holocaust* (Basingstoke and New York: Palgrave, 2004).

Stone, Norman, *The Eastern Front 1914–1917* (London: Macmillan, 1975).

Strachan, Hew, *The First World War*, vol. 1: *To Arms* (Oxford: Oxford University Press, 2001).

Suny, Ronald Grigor and Terry Martin, eds., *A State of Nations: Empire and Nation-Making in the Age of Lenin and Stalin* (Oxford: Oxford University Press, 2001).

Suny, Ronald Grigor, Fatma Müge Göçek, and Norman N. Naimark, eds., *A Question of Genocide: Armenians and Turks at the End of the Ottoman Empire* (Oxford: Oxford and New York University Press, 2011).

Swietochowski, Tadeusz, *Russian Azerbaijan 1905–1920: The Shaping of a National Identity in a Muslim Community* (Cambridge: Cambridge University Press, 1985).

Szajkowski, Zosa, 'A Rebuttal', *Jewish Social Studies*, 31 (1969), 184–213.

Szamuely, Tibor, *The Russian Tradition*, ed. Robert Conquest (London: Fontana Press, [1974] 1988).

Taniuchi, Yuzuru, *The Village Gathering in Russia in the Mid-1920s* (Birmingham: University of Birmingham Press, 1968).

Tauger, Mark B., 'The 1932 Harvest and the Famine of 1933', *Slavic Review*, 50:1 (1991), 70–89.

Temperley, Harold, *A History of the Paris Peace Conference*, vol. 5 (London: Hodder and Stoughton, 1921).

Temperley, Harold, and Lillian Pearson, *Foundations of British Foreign Policy 1792–1902: From Pitt to Salisbury* (London: Frank Cass, 1966).

Ternon, Yves, *L'État criminel: Les génocides au XXe siècle* (Paris: Éditions du Seuil, 1995).

Ther, Phillip and Ana Siljak, eds., *Redrawing Nations: Ethnic Cleansing in East-Central Europe 1944–1948* (Oxford and Lanham, NY: Rowman & Littlefield, 2001).

Theweleit, Klaus, *Male Fantasies*, 2 vols (Cambridge: Polity Press, 1989).

Thomas, Lewis V. and Richard N. Frye, *The United States and Turkey and Iran* (Cambridge, MA: Harvard University Press, 1951).

Thompson, E. P., *The Making of the English Working Class* (London: Pelican Books, 1968).

Thompson, John W., *Russia, Bolshevism and the Versailles Peace* (Princeton: Princeton University Press, 1966).

Thurston, Robert W., *Life and Terror in Stalin's Russia 1934–1941* (New Haven, CT, and London: Yale University Press, 1996).

Todorova, Maria, *Imagining the Balkans* (New York and Oxford: Oxford University Press, 1997).

Tolstoy, Nikolai, *Stalin's Secret War* (London: Pan Books, 1982).

Tomaszewski, Leszek, 'Pinsk, Saturday 5 April, 1919', *Polin*, 1 (1986), 227–51.

Tooze, Adam, *The Wages of Destruction: The Making and Breaking of the Nazi Economy* (London: Allen Lane, 2006).

Torpey, John, *The Invention of the Passport: Surveillance, Citizenship and the State* (Cambridge: Cambridge University Press, 2000).

Toynbee, Arnold J., *The Western Question in Greece and Turkey: A Study in the Contact of Civilisations* (London: Constable & Co., 1923).

Toynbee, Arnold J., *Survey of International Affairs 1920–1923* (London: Oxford University Press, 1925).

Toynbee, Arnold J., *Mankind and Mother Earth: A Narrative History of the World* (Oxford: Oxford University Press, 1976).

Trumpener, Ulrich, *Germany and the Ottoman Empire 1914–1918* (Princeton: Princeton University Press, 1968).

Turfan, M. Naim, *Rise of the Young Turks: Politics, the Military and Ottoman Collapse* (London and New York: I.B. Tauris, 2000).

Turner, Henry Ashby, *German Big Business and the Rise of Hitler* (New York: Oxford University Press, 1985).

Turner, Thomas, *The Congo Wars: Conflict, Myth and Reality* (New York and London: Zed Books, 2007).

Ulgen, Fatma, 'Reading Mustafa Kemal Atatürk on the Armenian Genocide of 1915', *Patterns of Prejudice*, 44:4 (2010), 369–91.

Ullman, Richard M., *Britain and the Russian Civil War: November 1918–February 1920* (Princeton: Princeton University Press, 1968).

Üngör, Uğur Ümit, '"A Reign of Terror": CUP Rule in Diyarbekir Province 1913–1918', unpublished MA thesis, University of Amsterdam, 2005.

Üngör, Uğur Ümit, 'When Persecution Bleeds into Mass Murder: The Processive Nature of Genocide', *Genocide Studies and Prevention*, 1:2 (2006), 173–95.

Üngör, Uğur Ümit, *The Making of Modern Turkey: Nation and State in Eastern Anatolia 1913–1950* (Oxford: Oxford University Press, 2011).

Vago, Béla, ed., *Jewish Assimilation in Modern Times* (Boulder, CO: Westview, 1981).

Vedery, Katherine, *National Ideology under Socialism: Identity and Cultural Politics in Ceausescu's Romania* (Berkeley: University of California Press, 1991).

Vereeken, Georges, *The GPU in the Trotskyist Movement* (London: New Park Publications, 1976).

Verete, Mayir, 'The Balfour Declaration and its Makers', *Middle Eastern Studies*, 6:1 (1970), 48–76.

Villari, Luigi, *Fire and Sword in the Caucasus* (London: T. F. Unwin, 1906).

Viola, Lynne, *Peasant Rebels under Stalin: Collectivization and the Culture of Peasant Resistance* (New York and Oxford: Oxford University Press, 1996).

Viola, Lynne, *The Unknown Gulag: The Lost World of Stalin's Special Settlements* (New York: Oxford University Press, 2007).

Viola, Lynne, V. P. Danilov, N. A. Ivnitskii, and Denis Kozlov, eds., *The War Against the Peasantry 1927–1930: The Tragedy of the Soviet Countryside*, trans. Steven Shabad (New Haven, CT: Yale University Press, 2005).

Vital, David, *A People Apart: A Political History of the Jews in Europe 1789–1939* (Oxford: Oxford University Press, 1999).

Volkmann, Hans-Erich, *Die russische Emigration in Deutschland 1919–1929* (Würzburg: Holzner, 1966).

Waite, Robert G. L., *The Vanguard of Nazism: The Free Corps Movement in Germany 1918–1923* (Cambridge, MA: Harvard University Press, 1952).

Waite, Robert G. L., *The Psychopathic God: Adolph Hitler* (New York: Basic Books, 1977).

Walker, Christopher J., *Armenia: The Survival of a Nation* (London: Croom Helm, 1980).

Wallerstein, Immanuel, *The Modern World System*, 3 vols (San Diego and New York: Academic Press Inc., 1974–89).

Wallimann, Isidor and Michael Dobkowski, eds., *Genocide and the Modern Age* (Westport, CT: Greenwood Press, 1987).

Walter, Eugene Victor, *Terror and Resistance: A Study of Political Violence, with Case Studies of Some Primitive African Communities* (London, Oxford, and New York: Oxford University Press, 1969).

Wandycz, Piotr Stefan, *France and Her Eastern Allies 1919–25: French-Czechoslovak-Polish Relations from the Paris Peace Conference to Locarno* (Minneapolis: University of Minnesota Press, 1962).

Wanner, Catherine, *Burden of Dreams: History and Identity in Post-Soviet Ukraine* (University Park, PA: Pennsylvania State University Press, 1998).

Watts, Martin, *The Jewish Legion and the First World War* (London and New York: Palgrave Macmillan, 2005).

Weber, Eugen, *Peasants into Frenchmen: The Modernization of Rural France 1870–1914* (Stanford, CA: Stanford University Press, 1976).

Weindling, Paul, *Epidemics and Genocide in Eastern Europe 1890–1945* (Oxford: Oxford University Press, 2000).

Weiner, Amir, 'Nature, Nurture and Memory in a Socialist Utopia: Delineating the Soviet Socio-Ethnic Body in the Age of Socialism', *American Historical Review*, 104:4 (1999), 1114–55.

Weiner, Amir, *Making Sense of War: The Second World War and the Fate of the Bolshevik Revolution* (Princeton and Oxford: Princeton University Press, 2001).

Weiner, Amir, ed., *Landscaping the Garden: Twentieth-Century Population Management in a Comparative Framework* (Stanford, CA: Stanford University Press, 2003).

Weinreich, Max, *Hitler's Professors: The Part of Scholarship in Germany's Crimes against the Jewish People* (New Haven, CT, and London: Yale University Press, 1999).

Weisbrod, Bernd, 'Military violence and Male Fundamentalism: Ernst Jünger's Contribution to the Conservative Revolution', *History Workshop Journal*, 49 (2000), 69–94.

Weiss-Wendt, Anton, 'Extermination of the Gypsies in Estonia during World War II: Popular Images and Official Policies', *Holocaust and Genocide Studies*, 17:1 (2003), 31–61.

Weitz, Eric D., *A Century of Genocide: Utopias of Race and Nation* (Princeton and Oxford: Princeton University Press, 2003).

Werfel, Franz, *The Forty Days of Musa Dagh* (New York: Viking Press, 1934).

Wheeler-Bennett, Sir John, *Brest-Litovsk: The Forgotten Peace, March 1918* (London: Macmillan, 1939).

White, Lynn T., *Policies of Chaos: The Organizational Causes of Violence in China's Cultural Revolution* (Princeton: Princeton University Press, 1989).

Wiese, Christian and Paul Betts, eds., *Years of Persecution, Years of Extermination: Saul Friedländer and the Future of Holocaust Studies* (London and New York: Continuum, 2010).

Wilde, Oscar, *The Picture of Dorian Gray* (London: Penguin, [1891] 1949).

Wilkinson, Henry R., *Maps and Politics: A Review of the Ethnographic Cartography of Macedonia* (Liverpool: Liverpool University Press, 1951).

Willems, Wim, *In Search of the True Gypsy: From Enlightenment to Final Solution* (London: Frank Cass, 1997).

Williams, Lewis, Rose Roberts, and Alastair Macintosh, eds., *Radical Human Ecology: Intercultural and Indigenous Approaches* (Farnham and Burlington, VT: Ashgate, 2012).

Winter, Jay, ed., *America and the Armenian Genocide of 1915* (Cambridge: Cambridge University Press, 2003).

Wistrich, Robert S., *Revolutionary Jews from Marx to Trotsky* (New York: Barnes & Noble, 1976).

Wolf, Lucien, *Notes on the Diplomatic History of the Jewish Question* (London: Spottiswoode, Ballantyne & Co., 1919).

Yakovlev, Alexander M., *A Century of Violence in Soviet Russia*, trans. Anthony Austin (New Haven, CT, and London: Yale University Press, 2002).

Yapp, M. E., *The Making of the Modern Near East 1792–1923* (London and New York: Longman, 1987).

Yisraeli, David, 'The Third Reich and the Transfer Agreement', *Journal of Contemporary History*, 6:2 (1971), 129–48.

Yonan, Gabrielle, *Ein vergessener Holocaust: Die Vernichtung der christlicher Assyrer in der Türkei* (Göttingen: Gesellschaft für bedrohte Völker, 1989).

Yuvuz, M. Hakan, 'Five Stages of the Construction of Kurdish Nationalism in Turkey', *Nationalism and Ethnic Politics*, 7:3 (2001), 1–24.

Zechlin, Egmont, *Die deutsche Politik und die Juden im Ersten Weltkrieg* (Göttingen: Vandenhoeck & Ruprecht, 1969).

Zeidner, Robert Farrer, 'The Tricolor over the Taurus: The French in Cilicia and Vicinity 1918–1922', unpublished PhD dissertation, University of Utah, 1991.

Zelinka, Anna, *In Quest for God and Freedom: The Sufi Response to the Russian Advance in the North Caucasus* (London: Hurst, 2000).

Zeman, Zbynek A. B., *A Diplomatic History of the First World War* (London: Weidenfeld & Nicolson, 1971).

Zeman, Zbynek A. B., *The Break-up of the Habsburg Empire 1914–1918: A Study in National and Social Revolution* (London: Octagon, 1977).

Zeman, Zbynek A. B., *The Making and Breaking of Communist Europe* (Oxford and New York: Basil Blackwell, 1991).

Zeman, Zbynek A. B., and W. B Scharlau, *The Merchant of Revolution: The Life of Alexander Israel Helfhand 'Parvus' 1867–1924* (London and New York: Oxford University Press, 1965).

Zeydanlioglu, Welat, 'The Kurds, the Turkish State and the Making of the Turkish Nation', unpublished paper presented at 'Conference on Refugees and the End of Empire', De Montfort University, Leicester, 29 June 2007.

Zimmerer, Jürgen, *Deutsche Herrschaft über Afrikaner: Staatlicher Machtanspruch und Wirklicheit im kolonialen Namibia* (Münster, Hamburg, and London: Lit Verlag, 2nd ed., 2002).

Zimmerman, Michael, 'The National Socialist "Solution of the Gypsy Question": Central Decisions, Local Initiative and their Interrelation', *Holocaust and Genocide Studies*, 15:3 (2001), 412–27.

Zimmern, Sir Alfred Eckhard, *Nationality and Government, with Other War-time Essays* (London: Chatto & Windus, 1919).

Zürcher, Erik-Jan, *The Unionist Factor: The Role of the Committee of Union and Progress in the Turkish National Movement 1905–1926* (Leiden: E. J. Brill, 1984).

Zürcher, Erik-Jan, *Turkey: A Modern History* (London: I.B. Tauris, 2004).

Zweig, Ronald, *The Gold Train: The Destruction of the Jews and the Second World War's Most Terrible Robbery* (London: Penguin, 2003).

Index

Note: Page numbers in *italics* indicates figures. The suffix 'n' indicates an endnote, the number following 'n' indicates the endnote number.

Printed and bound by CPI Group (UK) Ltd, Croydon, CR0 4YY